# Moscow

## THE ROUGH GUIDE

There are more than sixty Rough Guide titles covering
destinations from Amsterdam to Zimbabwe

**Forthcoming titles include**
Bali • Costa Rica • Goa • Hawaii • Majorca • Rhodes
Singapore • Vietnam

**Rough Guide Reference Series**
Classical Music • World Music

**Rough Guide Phrasebooks**
Czech • French • German • Greek • Italian • Spanish

**Rough Guide Credits**

| | |
|---|---|
| Editor: | Lemisse Al-Hafidh |
| Series Editor: | Mark Ellingham |
| Editorial: | Martin Dunford, Jonathan Buckley, Graham Parker, Samantha Cook, Jo Mead, Alison Cowan, Amanda Tomlin, Annie Shaw, Catherine McHale |
| Production: | Susanne Hillen, Andy Hilliard, Alan Spicer, Judy Pang, Link Hall, Nicola Williamson |
| Cartography | Melissa Flack |
| Finance: | John Fisher, Celia Crowley, Simon Carloss |
| Marketing and Publicity: | Richard Trillo (UK), Jean-Marie Kelly (US) |
| Administration: | Tania Hummel |

**Acknowledgements**

Bottomless thanks to friends **in Moscow** whose help and hospitality made all the difference: Lena, Kostya, Shura, Kyril, Anna, Olga, Anton, Serge, Anna, Stefan, Lena and Roger, John and Lucy, and Galina Mikhailovna. Thanks also to EV Shakurova at the Kremlin Armoury, and LA Krapachova at the Shchusev Museum of Architecture. Thanks **in England** to everyone at the Rough Guides, especially Lemisse Al-Hafidh, Alan Spicer, Melissa Flack, Martin Dunford, and Catherine McHale for editing and production, and Kate Berens for proofreading. To Anna for tolerating all the absences and a joyous welcome to Sonia, after all these months.

This first edition published 1995 by Rough Guides Ltd, 1 Mercer Street, London WC2H 9QJ.

Distributed by the Penguin Group:

Penguin Books Ltd, 27 Wrights Lane, London W8 5TZ

Penguin Books USA Inc., 375 Hudson Street, New York NY10014, USA

Penguin Books Australia Ltd, 487 Maroondah Highway, PO Box 257, Ringwood, Victoria 3134, Australia

Penguin Books Canada Ltd, 10 Alcorn Avenue, Toronto, Ontario, Canada M4V 1E4

Penguin Books (NZ) Ltd, 182–190 Wairau Road, Auckland 10, New Zealand

Rough Guides were formerly published as Real Guides in the United States and Canada.

Printed in the United Kingdom by Cox & Wyman Ltd (Reading).

Typography and original design by Jonathan Dear and The Crowd Roars.

Illustrations throughout by Edward Briant.

# Moscow

## THE ROUGH GUIDE

Written and researched by
Dan Richardson

with contributions by
Anna Parizhskaya, Paul Gould
and Robert Farish

THE ROUGH GUIDES

# The Contents

# Maps

## MAP SYMBOLS

| | | | |
|---|---|---|---|
| Railway | | Forest | |
| Road | | Beach | |
| Path | | Gorge | |
| Road with steps | | Airport | |
| Wall | | Synagogue | |
| Chapter division boundary | | Tourist Office | |
| Building | | Post Office | |
| Church | | Underground station | |
| Cemetery | | Riverboat station | |
| Park | | Gate | |

# Introduction

**M**oscow is all things to all people. In Siberia, they call it "the West", with a note of scorn for the bureaucrats and politicians who promulgate and posture in the capital. For Westerners, the city may look European, but its unruly spirit seems closer to Central Asia. To Muscovites, however, Moscow is both a "Mother City" and a "big village" (*bolshaya derevnya*), a tumultuous community which possesses an underlying collective instinct that shows itself in times of trouble. Nowhere else reflects the contradictions and ambiguities of the Russian people as Moscow does – nor the stresses of a country undergoing meltdown and renewal.

The city is huge, surreal and apocalyptic. After a few weeks here, the bizarre becomes normal, and you realize that life is – as Russians say – *bespredel* (without limits). Traditionally, Moscow has been a place for strangers to throw themselves into debauchery, leaving poorer and wiser. Its puritan stance in Soviet times was seldom heartfelt, and with the fall of Communism it has reverted to the lusty, violent ways that foreigners have noted with amazement over the centuries, and Gilyarovskiy chronicled in his book, *Moscow and the Muscovites*.

As the home of one in fifteen Russians, Moscow exemplifies the best and worst of Russia. Its beauty and ugliness are inseparable, its sentimentality the obverse of a brutality rooted in centuries of despotism and fear of anarchy. Private and cultural life are as passionate as business and politics are cynical. The irony and resilience honed by decades of propaganda and shortages now help Muscovites to cope with the "Wild Capitalism" that intoxicates the city. Yet, for all its assertiveness, Moscow's essence is moody and elusive, and uncovering it is like opening an endless series of *Matryoshka* dolls, or peeling an onion down to its core.

Both images are apposite, for Moscow's concentric geography mirrors its historical development. At its heart is the Kremlin, whose foundation by Prince Dolgoruky in 1147 marked the birth of the city. Surrounding this are rings corresponding to the feudal settle-

△ Sergiev Posad

MOSCOW RING ROAD (MKHAD)

Losniy Ostrov

YAROSLAVSKOE SHOSSE

Izmaylovo
Park

SHOSSE ENTUZIASTOV

Art Market

5 km

0

MOSCOW RING ROAD (MKHAD)

ALTUFEVSKOE SHOSSE

Yauza River

Sokolniki
Park

Leningrad Station

Kazan Station

PROSPEKT MIRA

Kursk
Station

VDNKh &
Botanical
Gardens

Riga Station

Belarus
Station

Yaroslavl Station

BOULEVARD RING

Kremlin

△ Sheremetevo airport

DIMITROVSKOE SHOSSE

GARDEN RING

Pushkin
Museum
of Fine Art

White House
(Beliy dom)

Air Terminal

LENINGRADSKIY PROSPEKT

Kiev Station

Mostva River

LENINGRADSKOE SHOSSE

Northern River
Terminal

VOLOKOLAMSKOE SHOSSE

Serebryaniy Bor

Krylatskoe

MOSCOW RING ROAD (MKHAD)

▽ Arkhangelskoe

CENTRAL MOSCOW

MOSCOW

ments of medieval times, rebuilt along more European lines after the great fire of 1812, and ruthlessly modernized in accordance with Stalin's vision of Moscow as the Mecca of Communism. Further out lie the fortified monasteries that once guarded the outskirts, and the former country estates of Tsars and nobles, now well within the urban sprawl encircled by the Moscow Ring Road.

Moscow's identity has been imbued with a sense of its own destiny since the fourteenth century, when the principality of Muscovy took the lead in the struggle against the Mongols and Tatars who had reduced the Kievan state to ruins. Under Ivan the Great and Ivan the Terrible – the "Gatherers of the Russian Lands" – its realm came to encompass everything from the White Sea to the Caspian, while after the fall of Constantinople to the Turks, Moscow assumed Byzantium's suzerainty over the Orthodox world. Despite the changes wrought by Peter the Great – not least the transfer of the capital to St Petersburg, which Slavophiles have always abhorred – Moscow kept its mystique and bided its time until the Bolsheviks made it the fountainhead of a new creed. Long accustomed to being at the centre of an empire, and being misled that their society was the envy of the world, Muscovites have inevitably felt the disillusionments of *perestroika* and recent years more keenly than most Russians.

All this is writ large in Moscow's **architecture** and **streetlife**. The Kremlin's cathedrals are Byzantine, like its politics. Ministries and hotels the size of city blocks reach their apotheosis in the "Seven Sisters" – Stalin-Gothic skyscrapers that brood over the city like vampires. The streets and metros resemble bazaars, with kiosks and hawkers on every corner. BMWs cruise past *babushki* whose monthly pensions wouldn't cover the cost of admission to a nightclub (the city has more casinos than any capital in the world). Fascists and Communists march together, bankers live in fear of bombs and policemen wear bulletproof vests. From all this, Muscovites seek solace in backstreet churches and shady courtyards; in the steamy conviviality of the bathhouse, and over tea or vodka. Discovering the private, hidden side of Moscow is as rewarding as visiting the usual tourist sights.

## When to go and what to bring

Moscow lies on about the same latitude as Edinburgh in Scotland, but its **climate** is closer to that of Edmonton in Canada (a bit further south), due to its location far from the sea, on a great conti-

| Average daily temperatures and rainfall in Moscow | | | | | | | | | | | |
| --- | --- | --- | --- | --- | --- | --- | --- | --- | --- | --- | --- |
| | Jan | Feb | Mar | Apr | May | Jun | Jul | Aug | Sep | Oct | Nov | Dec |
| Max °C | -7 | -5 | 0 | 8 | 15 | 20 | 21 | 20 | 15 | 9 | 2 | -3 |
| Min °C | -13 | -12 | -8 | 0 | 6 | 11 | 13 | 13 | 9 | 4 | -2 | -8 |
| mm | 35 | 30 | 31 | 36 | 45 | 50 | 72 | 78 | 64 | 76 | 46 | 40 |

nental landmass. Summers are hot, and winters cold by Western European standards, although the dry, often sunny weather makes them tolerable, if not always pleasurable.

As most foreigners have an exaggerated fear of the cold in Russia, the most popular time to go is **summer**, lasting from the beginning of June to mid-September. Days and nights are warm and sultry, with heatwaves likely during August, when Muscovites leave in droves for their *dachas* in the countryside. Culturally, things are rather slack during this period, with the Bolshoy Ballet away from June till early September and many other theatres closed for the duration. Conversely, politics often hot up in August, sometimes boiling over a month or so later. By mid-September, **autumn** is underway, with cloudy skies and falling temperatures, but you can still look forward to a week or two of *Babe leto* ("Granny's Summer"), when Moscow is an Impressionist's vision of autumnal hues, in the final glow of warmth.

Sub-zero temperatures and snow can set in up to two months before **winter** officially begins in December. Blanketed in fresh snow, Moscow is magically hushed and cleansed, and Muscovites revel in the crispness of the air. Days are often gloriously sunny, and the temperature only a few degrees below zero, so skiing and sledging are popular pursuits. The secular New Year and Orthodox Christmas in early January are occasions for shopping and merry-making, much as in the West – so if you have friends here, it's a great time to come. At some point, however, a cold snap will send the temperature down to -20°C or lower, while traffic and thaws turn the snow into mounds and lakes of black ice or brown slush, which linger on until late March.

By this time, everyone is longing for **spring**, whose arrival is unpredictable, with trees starting to bud weeks before the slush disappears in mid-April. Mid- to late spring is perhaps the best time for festivals, with the Orthodox Easter celebrations followed by the "Moscow Stars" festival, May Day, and the Victory Day celebrations on May 9. On the downside, however, cold snaps can happen at any time until the end of the month, and thundery showers may occur well into the summer.

It's wise to give some thought as to **what to bring** – and worth packing that bit more to stave off problems later. Expect occasional showers almost any time of the year, and bring a waterproof jacket or compact umbrella. Mosquitoes can also be a pest, so some form of barrier/treatment cream is advisable. For travel in winter (or late autumn or early spring), take as many layers as you can pack. Gloves, a hat and scarf, and thick socks are mandatory; thermal underwear saves you from cold legs; and a pair of boots with non-slip soles are recommended for the snow and ice. Indoors, you'll have nothing to worry about, as apartment buildings and hotels are well (if not over-) heated.

## A note on the calendar

In 1700, Peter the Great forced the Russians to adopt the Julian calendar which was then in use in Western Europe, in place of the old system dictated by the Orthodox church. Ironically, Western Europe changed to the Gregorian calendar not long afterwards, but this time the Russians refused to follow suit. The Julian calendar was less accurate and by the twentieth century lagged behind the Gregorian by almost two weeks. The Soviet regime introduced the Gregorian calendar in February 1918 – January 31 ran straight onto February 14. This explains why the Soviets always celebrated the Great October Revolution on November 7. In this book we have kept the old style calendar before February 1918, and the new style only after it was introduced.

## Changes in the new Russia

The speed of change in Russian society inevitably means that certain sections of this book are going to be out of date by the time you read them. Rampant inflation means that ruble prices rise weekly, or even daily (though costs reckoned in hard currency are more stable). Laws and regulations frequently change without warn-

---

### Cyrillic script, street names and abbreviations

Throughout the text, we've transliterated the names of all the streets and squares, and translated those of the sights, which means that no Cyrillic appears in the main text. To help you find your way around the city, however, we've included a list of the main streets, squares and museums in the original Cyrillic in *Contexts*, pp.372–376. For details of the transliteration system we've used from the Cyrillic to the Latin alphabet, see p.363.

Many streets have officially reverted to their former (mostly pre-revolutionary) titles, though some people still use the old Soviet names. In the following chapters, streets are referred to by their "correct" name at the time of writing, but as some further changes are likely, don't be surprised at the occasional difference between the names given in this book and those on the ground. The main abbreviations used throughout are: ul. (for *ulitsa*, street); nab. (for *naberezhnaya*, embankment); pr. (for *prospekt*, avenue); per. (for *pereulok*, lane); and pl. (for *ploshchad*, square). Other terms include *most* (bridge), *bulvar* (boulevard), *shosse* (highway), *alleya* (alley) and *sad* (garden).

ing. Restaurants, clubs and services come and go. Above all, there is the continuing **political uncertainty**, which makes for universally gloomy news reports about Russia. That said, Muscovites are resilient and the city is big enough to absorb a lot of trouble – so don't be deterred by run-of-the-mill reports of Mafia killings, epidemics, and so on.

---

**Help us update**

We've gone to a lot of effort to ensure that this first edition of the Rough Guide to Moscow is completely up-to-date and accurate. However, things do change: hotels and restaurants come and go, opening hours are notoriously fickle, and prices are extremely volatile. We'd appreciate any suggestions, amendments or contributions for future editions of the guide. We'll credit all letters and send a copy of the next edition (or any other Rough Guide) for the best.

Please mark all letters "Rough Guides Moscow Update" and send to:
Rough Guides, 1 Mercer Street, London WC2H 9QJ
or
Rough Guides, 375 Hudson Street, 3rd Floor, New York NY10014.

---

# The Basics

# Getting There from Britain

By far the most convenient way to reach Moscow is by plane. Scheduled flights from London take just three hours (compared to over 48 hours by train), and there are direct services every day on *Aeroflot* or *British Airways*. If you have more time to devote to the journey itself, then the train becomes a more attractive proposition, since you can travel via Berlin, Prague or the Baltic States. Note that the air fares quoted below do not include airport departure tax. Note also that travelling independently won't always save much money and your visa arrangements may be more complicated – and time-consuming.

## By plane

The Russian airline *Aeroflot* and *British Airways* (*BA*) between them operate sixteen **scheduled flights** a week **from London** to Moscow. *Aeroflot* flies daily from Heathrow, and is usually the cheapest, with standard APEX returns currently around £310, and non-APEX tickets (valid for one year) costing £400. You can only pay for the ticket with cash, money orders or building society cheques. *BA* flies daily on weekdays and twice a day at weekends from Heathrow, and once daily on weekdays from Gatwick. Unless there's a special offer going, APEX returns will set you back £430 for a weekday flight, or £442 at weekends. *Lufthansa* offers daily flights from Heathrow to Frankfurt and onward connections to Moscow for

the same prices as *BA*, as does *SAS*, via Copenhagen, which also flies from Manchester (for £542). With all APEX tickets reservations must be made at least fourteen days in advance; you must spend one Saturday abroad; the date of the return flight is fixed; and the ticket is valid for up to three months. Non-APEX tickets are normally valid for up to a year, and can have open return dates.

Happily, you can usually get **discounted deals** that cost much less than the fares quoted above. Some are only valid for those under 26, others for any age group. For example, *Farnley Travel* often does a youth/student deal on *BA* flights to Moscow, from about £265, while *Scott's Tours* offer a transaero from Gatwick via Riga for £255, and *Travel Power* charges £256 for an *Austrian Airlines* flight via Vienna, or £277 via Zurich on *Swissair* – irrespective of your age. Also check with the youth/student specialists *Campus Travel* or *STA* (see box overleaf for all these addresses), and adverts in London's *Time Out* and the *Evening Standard*, or the quality Sunday papers.

If you have more time, it might be worth considering flying to somewhere in central Europe like Berlin or Prague and taking the train the rest of the way. Return fares can be as little as £100 for Berlin, though of course you'll have to add on the cost (and time) of travel overland to Moscow; see "By train", below.

## Package tours

Given the price of flights and hotels in Moscow, there's a strong incentive to look for a **package tour** – an easy way of cutting the cost and trouble of organizing a trip. There are all kinds, from city breaks to Trans-Siberian tours, luxury cruises and ecotourism. Unless stated otherwise, all prices below are for a single person, twin share;

| Airlines | |
|---|---|
| Aeroflot | ☎ 0171/355 2233 |
| British Airways | ☎ 0181/897 4000 |
| Lufthansa | ☎ 0181/750 3500 |
| SAS | ☎ 0171/734 4020 |

where two prices are given, these refer to low- and high-season rates.

The biggest operator is *Intourist*, which offers three- (£299–365) or seven- (£389–525) night **city breaks** to Moscow or St Petersburg; two-centre tours of five (£352–472), seven (£379–535) or fourteen (£615–725) nights, including an overnight train journey between **Moscow and St Petersburg**; a five- (£489) or seven- (£529) night Christmas trip that features both cities, plus a gala dinner and a performance at the Bolshoy or Mariinskiy theatre; and a similar tour over New Year (£529). These prices compare favourably with the two-centre tours available from *Multitours* (from around £600) and *Room with the Russians* (about £500). All are inclusive of flights and transfers; *Intourist* uses *BA*, the others fly *Aeroflot*.

Ranging further afield, *Intourist* combines Moscow and St Petersburg with a coach tour of the "**Golden Ring**" towns of Suzdal, Rostov,

Yaroslavl, Kostroma and Sergiev Posad, lasting nine nights in all (£690–750); or with two days in **Kiev** (£625–661). During summer, a more luxurious option is to **cruise** from St Petersburg to Moscow via the fabulous wooden churches of Kizhi, Lake Onega, Yaroslavl, Kostroma and Uglich. *Intourist* does a fifteen-day tour for £1045–1075; *Voyages Jules Verne* seven days for £1120, and *Noble Caledonia* ten days for £1195.

**Trans-Siberian journeys** (see p.13) are increasingly popular. *Progressive Tours* offers the widest choice, from a cheap, no-frills Moscow–Beijing trip (£285–325) with just one night's accommodation in Moscow, to itineraries featuring Irkutsk and Vladivostok or Mongolia, starting from £375–390 (these prices don't include flights to Russia or home from China). *Intourist* does a fifteen-night Moscow–Beijing package (£799–845) including flights, meals, accommodation and tours, plus excursions to Lake Baikal, the Great Wall and the Ming Tombs.

---

### Discount ticket agents

**Campus Travel**

52 Grosvenor Gardens
London SW1     ☎ 0171/730 3402

541 Bristol Rd, Selly Oak
Birmingham     ☎ 0121/414 1848

39 Queen's Rd, Clifton
Bristol     ☎ 0117/929 2494

5 Emmanuel St
Cambridge     ☎ 01223/324 283

Forest Rd
Edinburgh     ☎ 0131/668 3303

166 Deansgate
Manchester     ☎ 0161/273 1721

13 High St
Oxford     ☎ 01865/242067

*Student/youth travel specialists, with branches also in YHA shops and on university campuses.*

**Council Travel**

28a Poland St
London W1     ☎ 0171/437 7767

*Discounted flights.*

**Farnley Travel**

Diamond House
37–38 Hatton Garden
London EC1 N8DX     ☎ 0171/404 6822

*Specialist discounts on Russian and Baltic flights.*

**North South Travel**

Moulsham Mill Centre
Parkway
Chelmsford CM2 7PX     ☎ 0245/492882

*Contributes profits to projects in the developing world.*

**Scott's Tours**

159 Whitfield St
London W1P 5RY     ☎ 0171/383 5353

**STA Travel**

74 Old Brompton Rd
London W7     ☎ 0171/937 9962

25 Queen's Rd
Bristol     ☎ 0117/929 3399

38 Sidney St
Cambridge     ☎ 01223/66966

75 Deansgate
Manchester     ☎ 0161/834 0668

Personal callers only at the following addresses:

117 Euston Rd
London NW1

28 Vicar Lane
Leeds

36 George St
Oxford

and offices at the universities of Birmingham, London, Kent and Loughborough.

*Independent travel specialists offering discount fares, with good deals for students and young people.*

## Tour operators & specialist agents

**East–West Travel**

15 Kensington High St
London W8 5NP                ☎0171/938 3211

In Moscow:

ul. Bolshaya Lubyanka 24/15   ☎095/924-0629;
                              fax: 095/925-0460.

*Visa services, flights and hotel accommodation
throughout the CIS.*

**China Travel Service**

7 CTS House, Upper St Martin's Lane
London WC2H 9DL              ☎0171/836 9911

*Sells one-way tickets for flights to Moscow or
Beijing, and travel in either direction on the
Trans-Siberian.*

**Ecologia**

The Park, Forres
Moray, IV36 0TZ             ☎01309/690995;
    fax: 01309/ 690933, attn. Liza Hollingshead

*Individual and group tours focused on ecology
or New Age mysticism.*

**Goodwill Holidays**

Manor Chambers, School Lane
Welwyn, Herts AL6 9EB       ☎01438/716421

*Hotels and B&B accommodation in Moscow
and St Petersburg.*

**Intourist**

219 Marsh Walk, London E14   ☎0171/538 8600
*The former state tourist agency, offering
various good-value packages.*

**Interchange**

Interchange House, 27 Stafford Rd
Croydon CRO 4NG             ☎0181/681 3612
*Flights, hotel and B&B accommodation in
Moscow.*

**Multitours**

7 Denbigh St, London SW1    ☎0171/262 1676
*Individual tours and Moscow–St Petersburg
packages.*

**Noble Caledonia Ltd.**

11 Charles St, London W1    ☎0171/491 4752
*All-inclusive St Petersburg–Moscow cruises.*

**ProgressiveTours**

12 Porchester Place
London W2                   ☎0171/262 1676
*Trans-Siberian packages; hotel and B&B
accommodation.*

**Room with the Russians**

1–7 Station Chambers, High St North
London E6 1JE               ☎0181/472 2694
*Week and weekend B&B packages in Moscow.*

**Voyages Jules Verne**

21 Dorset Square
London NW1                  ☎0171/723 5066
*All-inclusive St Petersburg–Moscow cruises.*

Other operators offer **homestays** with Russian families, or tours tailored to specific interests. The Quaker firm *Goodwill Holidays* can arrange bed and breakfast (B&B) in Moscow from £28 a night – and flights, transfers and other services if required. *Ecologia*, affiliated with the Scotland-based Findhorn Foundation, runs **spiritual heritage** tours of Moscow, St Petersburg and Valaam Island (£850), summer **ecology** camps in the Urals (£735), and **wilderness survival** courses in Karelia (£650). They can also supply details of the annual New Age **Rainbow Gathering**, at a camp to the south of St Petersburg on the Yaschera River (two days' travel from Moscow).

## By train

Travelling by train **from London to Moscow** takes two days and two nights, and costs easily as much as flying there, so the only incentive to travel by rail is the chance to stop and savour the countries en route.

A regular second-class **return ticket** from London (bookable through some high-street travel agents or at London's Victoria Station) will currently set you back £298, plus a surcharge for the **couchette** (£36) or **sleeper** (£60) that only covers the outward journey; you must pay the same again in Moscow for the trip back. On the Ostend–Moscow train, only sleepers are available, whereas travelling via the Hook of Holland, you won't be able to book a couchette until you reach Berlin (don't leave it until Warsaw).

One way of saving money is to buy a discounted ticket from *Wasteels* (see below for address). People under 26 qualify for a **BIJ ticket**, costing £231, which is valid for two months and allows unlimited stopovers along a pre-specified route (which can be different going out and coming back). For those over 26, there's a deal that includes one night's hostel accommodation in Belgium or Holland (depending on your route), for around £250. In both cases, there's a sleeper or couchette supplement.

A more flexible option is the **InterRail pass** (currently £249 for under-26s and £269 for those over 26), which is valid for one month's unlimited travel through much of Europe and gives half-price discounts in Britain and on some Channel ferries. Neither *InterRail* pass is valid in Russia, Belarus, Ukraine or the Baltic States, but the cost of travelling there by train from, say, Poland is quite low. The over-26 pass isn't valid in France or Belgium either, which effectively limits you to the Harwich–Hook of Holland ferry. *InterRail* passes are available from major train stations or travel agents; to qualify for one you must have been resident in Europe for at least six months.

### Routes

There are no direct train services from London to Moscow, but there are daily through trains from Ostend. To make the connection you must set off early from London Victoria and take the boat train via the **Dover/Ostend** ferry crossing. An alternative route, which takes you via the **Harwich/Hook of Holland** ferry crossing, takes significantly longer, requires a change of trains in Berlin, and is no cheaper once you've added the obligatory night-crossing supplement.

At Ostend, you'll step into a **Russian wagon** that's visibly shabbier than the other carriages in the train. Its staff and (few) other passengers will all be Russian, providing a chance to familiarize yourself with the language and habits of the natives. Whichever route you take, bring **food** and drink for the whole journey, since there's nothing available in the wagon except hot water from the *samovar*, and the odd can of beer.

The route will take you **through Germany, Poland and Belarus**. The most stringent **customs check** comes at Brest on the Polish–Belarus border, where trains are jacked-up in order to change their wheel-bogies to fit the Russian tracks, whose wide gauge was designed to make it difficult for invaders to use the network.

Since Russian visas are not issued at border crossings, you must get one in advance from a consulate (addresses on p.18).

## By car

It doesn't make a lot of sense to travel from Britain to Moscow **by car**, especially since Western vehicles are so vulnerable to unwelcome attention inside Russia, but if you're intent on doing so, it's just about possible to make the journey in under three days. However, since this allows little time for stopping and sleeping, it is sensible to spread the journey out over a longer period and take in a few places en route.

The most convenient way of taking your car to the continent is to drive down to the Channel Tunnel, load your car onto the train shuttle, and be whisked under the Channel in 35 minutes. The **Channel Tunnel** entrance is off the M20 at Junction 11A, just outside Folkestone. *Le Shuttle* has 21 services daily, including one every hour or so throughout the night. Because of the frequency of the service, you don't have to buy a ticket in advance; just arrive and wait to board – there's a promised loading time of just ten minutes. While you're inside the carriages, you can get out of your car to stretch your legs.

Tickets are available through *Le Shuttle Customer Service Centre* (☎01303/271100) or from your local travel agent, and fares are – per carload – £110–155 one-way, £220–310 return.

Once across the Channel, the most direct route is **through Germany, Poland and Belarus**, broadly sticking to the following itinerary: Ostend–Berlin–Warsaw–Brest–Minsk–Smolensk–Moscow. You're unlikely to need a Polish visa, but will certainly have to have a transit visa for Belarus (see above). Driving **licence and insurance** requirements in Russia are covered on p.28.

## Hitching

If anyone is reckless enough to consider **hitching** from Britain to Moscow, the route to follow is basically the one outlined above.

Don't bank on reaching Moscow in under four days. Once you enter what used to be the USSR, anything can happen; unless you're extremely familiar with post-Communist conditions you'd be foolhardy to attempt it.

## Approaches from Central Europe and the Baltic

Travellers roaming Europe by train or flying in from North America to a city on the continent can consider various **approaches to Moscow from Central Europe or the Baltic** countries. As your train pass won't cover all of the journey to Moscow, wherever you start, it's worth noting that fares from the Baltic States are lowest. All the **prices** below are for second-class return tickets; one-way fares are half the sum.

Starting **from Berlin or Prague** is a popular approach. In both cases, the cost of the journey as far as Poland is covered by rail passes, while *InterRail* extends to the Belarus border, so that the price could be equal to, or less than the fare from Warsaw (see below). You need to book tickets in advance, as the demand can be heavy. The journey from Berlin to Moscow (via Warsaw and Minsk) takes 29hr; from Prague 38–40hr (depending on the route). Starting **from Warsaw** is also feasible, but the queues of homebound Russians can make buying tickets a nightmare. About 6 trains a day make the 22-hour journey to Moscow, some of them originating in Ostend, Berlin or Prague. The best Polish train is the *Polonez*; a regular berth costs £78/$110, but it can be worth paying for a first-class compartment (£100/$160).

There are also plenty of connections from the **Baltic States**. From Lithuania to Moscow takes 18hr by train, although the significantly lower fare is offset by the cost of the visa you need to cross Belarus. There are two services daily **from Vilnius** (£44/$66). Advance tickets can be bought at an office near the *Hotel Lietuva*, or at Sopeno g.3, down the road from the train station (where tickets for trains leaving in under 24hr are sold at windows #1–6). Failing that, you can travel directly to Russia from Latvia, **from Riga** (17hr). The *Latvijas Ekspresis* boasts videos, newspapers and hot meals in your compartment; tickets (£23/$38) are sold from the advance sales windows of the long-distance booking section of Riga station. Tickets for the other, less flashy train (£15/$24) are sold at the international ticket office in the station. There's a daily express to Moscow **from Tallinn in Estonia**, which takes 19hr, and a slower train via Tartu. Tickets (£33/$50) are sold at windows #7–12, in the small hall of Tallinn's train station. Note that you can buy a **round-trip** Tallinn–Moscow–Tallinn ticket in Tallinn, but not a Moscow–Tallinn–Moscow ticket in Moscow.

## Visas and embassies

Since **Russian visas** are not issued at border crossings, you must get one in advance from a consulate (addresses on p.18).

All foreign nationals travelling **through Belarus** require a transit visa, *except* for those on trains routed from Warsaw to Moscow who already hold a Russian visa. If required, Belarus visas must be obtained from one of their embassies (£20/$32). For transit **through Lithuania**, British, Australian and US passport holders don't need a visa. Most other nationals, however, do require a visa, best obtained beforehand from a Lithuanian embassy for £21/$34 for a multiple-entry visa. British nationals do not require visas to travel **through Latvia**. Most other nationals require a transit visa, obtained beforehand from a Latvian embassy. These are available to US passport holders free of charge, though there's a $13 processing charge levied. Neither British, US, Canadian, Australian or New Zealand passport holders require a visa to travel through, or visit, **Estonia**.

| **Belarus Embassy** | | **Latvian Embassy** | |
|---|---|---|---|
| 1 St Stephen's Crescent | | 45 Nottingham Place | |
| London W2 5QT | ☎0171/221 3941 | London W1M 3FE | ☎0171/312 0040 |
| 1619 New Hampshire Ave NW | | 4325 17th Street NW | |
| Washington DC 20009 | ☎202/986-1604 | Washington DC 20011 | ☎202/726-8213 |
| **Estonian Embassy** | | **Lithuanian Embassy** | |
| 16 Hyde Park Gate | | 17 Essex Villas | |
| London SW7 5DG | ☎0171/589 3428 | London W8 | ☎0171/938 2481 |
| 1030 15th Street NW, Suite 1000 | | 2622 16th Street NW | |
| Washington DC | ☎202/789-0320 | Washington DC 20009 | ☎202/234-5860 |

# Getting There from Ireland

*Aeroflot* flies direct to Moscow **from Dublin** every Monday and Friday, and **from Shannon**, County Clare, every day; flights take about three and a half hours. Return fares cost IR£345 for a ticket valid for 45 days, or IR£410 for one valid for a year. Lower priced youth/student deals may be available from *USIT*, in Dublin or Belfast (see box).

It's worth checking also to see if you're better off flying to London in the first instance and picking up a connecting flight or package from there. There are numerous daily flights **from Dublin to London**, operated by *Ryanair*, *Aer Lingus* and *British Midland*; the cheapest is *Ryanair*, which costs from around IR£150 for a return to Luton or Stansted, though the cost of the bus and underground journeys across London may make the total cost greater than *Aer Lingus* or *British Midland*'s IR£175 fares to Heathrow. **From Belfast**, there are *BA* and *British Midland* flights to Heathrow, but the cheapest service is with *Britannia Airways* to Luton, at around IR£70 return.

From Dublin, you can slightly undercut the plane's price by getting a *Eurotrain* ticket to London, but from Belfast you'll save nothing by taking the train and ferry.

Alternatively, you could opt for a **package tour** with the likes of *Group & Educational Travel*, who offer an eight-day trip to Moscow and St Petersburg for around IR£459.

Finally, Irish citizens may be gratified to know of the high-profile Irish presence in Moscow, what with the *Irish House* supermarket on the New Arbat, *Rosie O'Grady's* pub near the Kremlin, and *AirRianta* running the duty-free shops at Moscow's international airport.

---

### Airlines & travel agents in Ireland

#### AIRLINES

**Aer Lingus**

| | |
|---|---|
| Dublin | ☎ 01/705 6565 |
| Belfast | ☎ 01232/245151 |
| 2 Academy St, Cork | (no telephone calls) |

**Aeroflot**

| | |
|---|---|
| Dublin | ☎ 01/679 1453 |

**British Airways**

| | |
|---|---|
| Belfast | ☎ 0345/222111 |
| in Dublin contact *Aer Lingus* | |

**British Midland**

| | |
|---|---|
| Dublin | ☎ 01/283 8833 |
| Belfast | ☎ 0345/554554 |

**Britannia Airways**

No reservations office in Ireland: bookings from Luton Airport, Luton, Beds ☎ 01582/424155

**Ryan Air**

| | |
|---|---|
| Dublin | ☎ 01/6774422 |

#### TRAVEL AGENTS AND TOUR OPERATORS

**USIT**

19–21 Aston Quay
O'Connell Bridge

| | |
|---|---|
| Dublin 2 | ☎ 01/6798833 |

Fountain Centre
College St

| | |
|---|---|
| Belfast BT1 | ☎ 01849/324073 |

**Group & Educational Travel**

11 South Anne St

| | |
|---|---|
| Dublin 2 | ☎ 01/671 3422 |

**Thomas Cook**

118 Grafton St

| | |
|---|---|
| Dublin | ☎ 01/677 1721 |

# Getting There from the USA and Canada

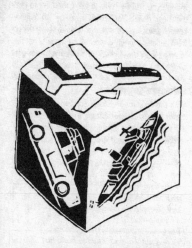

All flight fares quoted below are exclusive of taxes. Unless stated otherwise, the tickets must be purchased at least 21 days in advance, and are valid for a maximum of one month's stay.

**Prices** with *Aeroflot* start at $699 from New York in low season, $755 in shoulder season and $830 in high season. From Miami and Washington prices start at $749 (low), $808 (shoulder) and $888 (high). Fares from Chicago can be as low as $625, but are more often around $749. From Los Angeles, low-season fares start at $999 and rise to $1078 in high season. Generally, low season is from November to March and the first two weeks of September; shoulder season is April and May, and high season is June to August. Bear in mind, also, that *Aeroflot* doesn't operate every day: this changes depending on winter or summer months.

In the low season you may get a better deal with *Finnair*, which flies from New York to Helsinki and then on to Moscow for $616; though the price for a midweek flight rises to $1048 in the summer, and weekend flights cost $50 more. Also look out for promotional deals offered by the Czechoslovak airline, *CSA*, which can only be purchased two weeks prior to departure. Their flight from New York stops in Prague before heading on to Moscow. The low-season price is $668; expect to pay around $1028 in high season.

Other **European carriers** are pricier, but offer a wider choice of departures. *Air France* flies out of Chicago, Houston, Miami, Los Angeles, New York JFK, Newark, San Francisco and Washington Dulles, with daily connections on from Paris to Moscow. The low/high season midweek fare from New York is $768/1008; from Los Angeles $968/1188. Weekend flights cost $25 extra. *British Airways* (*BA*) flies from Atlanta, Baltimore, Boston, Charlotte, Chicago, Dallas, Detroit,

It's relatively easy to fly direct to Moscow from the US or Canada. *Aeroflot* flies from several gateways two to five times a week, while European carriers offer daily flights from a wider range of cities to their homebase airport, mostly with an onward connection to Moscow (see box for airlines and flight frequencies). Alternatively, you could fly direct to a European city and then proceed overland by train or bus. The nearest (and cheapest) jumping-off point for Moscow is the Latvian capital, Riga. See "Getting There from Britain", for a rundown of the trans-European options.

## Flights from the USA

*Aeroflot* flies **directly to Moscow** from New York, Miami, Washington DC, Chicago, Los Angeles, San Francisco, Seattle and Anchorage. The New York and West Coast flights are non-stop; planes from Miami and Washington refuel at Shannon, in Ireland, while the Anchorage flight usually requires an overnight stay in the Siberian city of Khabarovsk. If you're coming from Alaska, therefore, it might be best to fly to Seattle or San Francisco, from where there are direct flights to Moscow.

Houston, LA, Miami, New York JFK, Newark, Orlando, Philadelphia, San Francisco, Seattle and Washington (plus 53 other cities in tandem with *US Air*), with a daily onward flight from London to Moscow. The low/high season midweek fare from New York to Moscow is $768/968; the low/high season weekend fares are $818/1008. From Los Angeles the low/high season fares are $968/1188. *Lufthansa* flies to Frankfurt from Chicago, Los Angeles and New York. Its New York and LA fares are comparable to most other European carriers: Chicago–Moscow low/high season costs $838/1118, with a $50/60 surcharge at weekends.

Before running out to book with a major airline, however, check with a reputable **discount travel agent**, like *STA, Council Travel, Nouvelles Frontières*, or others listed in the box opposite. These firms have special deals on non-direct flights with the major carriers, some of which are

just for students or younger travellers, while others have no age restrictions.

Another option is to contact a **discount travel club** – organizations that specialize in selling off the unsold seats of travel agents for bargain rates, often at up to half the original price, though you usually have to be a member to get the best deals. You could also try an airline **consolidator**, which sell the unsold seats direct from airlines, though discounts are usually not as large as with travel clubs, and you might not get exactly the flight that you had in mind.

## Package tours

With the situation in Russia still very changeable, **travel agencies specializing in Russia**, such as *Pioneer East/West Initiative* (see box overleaf for addresses), are excellent sources of up-to-date advice, as well as being the best way to find out about any available cheap flight deals.

---

### Airlines

**Air Canada**
US ☎ 800/776-3000; Canada ☎ 800/555-1212
*Daily flights from all their gateways to Paris, London or Frankurt, with onward connections to Moscow or St Petersburg on another carrier.*

**Air France**
US ☎ 800/237-2747; Canada ☎ 800/667-2747
*Daily flights from New York JFK and Newark, Washington Dulles, Miami, Houston, Chicago, Los Angeles and San Francisco, with connections from Paris to Moscow or St Petersburg.*

**Aeroflot**
US ☎ 800/995-5555 or 212/265-1185; Canada ☎ 514-288-2125
*Flies to Moscow 5 times a week from New York (9hr); 4 times a week from Miami; twice a week from Chicago (11hr), LA (13hr), Washington DC, Anchorage and Montréal; and once a week from Seattle and San Francisco.*

**British Airways**
US ☎ 800/247-9297; Canada ☎ 800/668-1059
*Daily flights from all their gateways, with connections from London to Moscow and St Petersburg.*

**CSA Airlines**
US ☎ 800/223-2365; no Canada office
*Flies twice a week from New York; also from Montréal and Toronto in winter, and once a week from Toronto in summer. You'll have to stay overnight in Prague before flying on to Moscow.*

**Delta Airlines**
US ☎ freephone international 800/241-4141; no Canada office
*Flies to Moscow directly from New York JFK 4–5 times a week, and via Frankfurt from Washington Dulles 6–7 times a week.*

**Finnair**
US ☎ 800/950-5000; no Canada office
*Flies daily except Sunday from New York, with connections from Helsinki to Moscow or St Petersburg.*

**KLM**
US ☎ 800/374-7747; Canada ☎ 514/939-4040 (Montréal), ☎ 800-361-5330 (Toronto)
*Daily flights from all their gateways, and connections from Amsterdam.*

**Lufthansa**
US ☎ 800/645-3880; Canada ☎ 800/563-5954
*Daily flights from all their gateways, and connections from Frankfurt.*

**Northwest Airlines**
US ☎ freephone international 800/447-4747; no Canada office
*Daily flights from Chicago, Boston, Detroit, Minneapolis and San Francisco to Amsterdam, and connections on to Moscow.*

**SAS**
US ☎ 800/221-2350; no Canada office
*Daily flights to Stockholm, and on to Moscow and St Petersburg.*

**Swissair**
US ☎ 800/221-4750; Canada ☎ 800/267-9477

---

## Discount flight agents, travel clubs, consolidators

**Council Travel**
☎ 800/226-8624
*Student travel organization with branches in many US cities.*

**Encore Travel Club**
☎ 800/444-9800
*Discount travel club*

**Interworld Travel**
☎ 305/443-4929
*Southeastern US consolidator.*

**Moment's Notice**
☎ 212/486-0500
*Travel club that's good for last-minute deals.*

**Nouvelles Frontières**
US ☎ 800/366-6387
Canada ☎ 514/526-8444
*French discount travel outfit, with branches in New York, Montréal, LA, San Francisco and Québec City.*

**STA Travel**
☎ 800/777-0112
*Worldwide specialist in independent and student travel, with branches in New York, San Francisco, LA and Boston.*

**TFI Tours International**
☎ 800/745-800
*The very best East Coast deals, especially worth looking into for one-way flights.*

**Travac**
☎ 800/872-8800
*Good US consolidator and charter broker.*

**Travel Avenue**
☎ 800/333-3335
*Discount travel agent.*

**Travel Charter**
☎ 800/521-5267
*Reliable charter agency, based in Michigan.*

**Travel Cuts**
Canada ☎ 416/979-2406
*Canadian student travel organization based in Toronto, with branches all over the country.*

**Travelers Advantage**
☎ 800/548-1116
*Reliable discount travel club.*

**UniTravel**
☎ 800/325-2222
*Reliable consolidator.*

**Worldwide Discount Travel Club**
☎ 305/534-2082.
*Discount travel club based in Miami Beach, Florida.*

---

**Package tours** are still dominated by the former Soviet tourist agency, *Intourist*, which offers nine-day Moscow–St Petersburg trips for $1395 and ten-day Kiev–Moscow–St Petersburg packages for $1595. Prices include *Aeroflot* flights, transfers, excursions, museum tickets, accommodation and three meals a day. Two other firms offering **Moscow/St Petersburg tours** are *American Express Vacations*, whose eight-day "Best Buy Russia" package costs from $899 (low season) or $1799 (high season), and *Delta Dream Vacations Eastern Europe*, whose identically priced tour lasts six days. Both packages include flights, all meals, accommodation and transport.

## Flights from Canada

Depending on the carrier, you can fly directly from Montréal to Moscow, or from a wider range of gateway cities to a European airport, and then on to Moscow with the same airline. Note that flights at the weekend may cost $60 more than the midweek fares given below.

*Aeroflot* flies twice a week from Montréal to Moscow, with fares from CDN$890 (low season),

and upwards of CDN$1000 (high season). Other European carriers offer a wider choice of gateway cities and flights, with daily connections to Moscow from their homebase airport. *BA*, for example, flies daily from Montréal and Toronto and five times a week from Vancouver, via London. Low-season fares from Montréal and Toronto start at CDN$1285 and rise to CDN$1626 during the summer; fares from Vancouver range from CDN$1635 to CDN$1976, according to the season. *KLM*, *Air France* and *Lufthansa* all fly daily from Toronto and Montréal via their home bases and offer similar fares to those of *BA*. *Air Canada* has no direct flights to Moscow, but can fly you from a wide range of gateways to Paris, London or Frankfurt, where you can pick up another carrier to Moscow. It's also worth checking with the student/youth travel agency *Travel Cuts* for their latest flight deals (they have some flights for non-students, too).

## Travelling by train

If you're interested in seeing more of Europe en route to Moscow, travelling by train from Britain or the Continent may appeal. However, as *Eurail*

## Specialist operators

### Abercrombie & Kent
1520 Kensington Rd, Oak Brook, IL 60521; ☎708/954-2944 or 800/323-7308.
*All-inclusive deluxe tours of Moscow and St Petersburg.*

### American Express Vacations
300 Pinnacle Way, Norcross, GA 30093; ☎800/241-1700.
*Does a 9-day, all-inclusive Moscow/St Petersburg tour.*

### Delta Dream Vacations Eastern Europe
139 Main St, Cambridge, MA 02142; ☎800/872-7786.
*Offers a 6-day Moscow/St Petersburg package with an overnight train journey between the two cities.*

### Home & Host International
2445 Park Ave, Minneapolis, MN 55404; ☎612/871-0596; fax: 612/871-8853.
*Arranges visa support and B&B in several Russian cities.*

### Host Families Association (HOFA), in US
☎202/333-9343.
*Agents for a St Petersburg-based firm offering private rooms and various services in Moscow and other cities.*

### IBV Bed and Breakfast Systems
13113 Ideal Drive, Silver Spring, MD 20906; ☎301/942-3770; fax: 301/933-0024.
*Arranges B&B and visa support in Russia.*

### Intourist USA, Inc.
630 Fifth Ave, Suite 868, New York, NY 101111; ☎800/982-8416 or 212/459-0031.
*Privatized offshoot of the old state tourist company, running a 9-day Moscow/St Petersburg tour and a 10-day trip that also includes Kiev.*

### Pioneer East/West Initiatives
88 Brook Ave, Arlington, MA 02174; ☎617/648-2020; fax: 617/648-7304.
*Tailor-made packages for groups and individuals, and B&B arrangements.*

### Russia House
1800 Connecticut Ave NW, Washington DC 20009, attn. Chris Poor; ☎202/986-6010; fax: 202/667-4244. In Moscow: Leningradskiy pr. 17; ☎250-0143; fax: 250-2503.
*Arranges visas, registration, tickets and accommodation in Russia.*

### Russian Travel Service
PO Box 311, Fitzwilliam, NH 03447, attn. Helen Gates; fax & ☎603/585-6534. In Moscow ☎095/193-2514 or 457-3508; fax: 095/152-7493.
*Arranges visas, B&B and other tourist services in Moscow.*

### Russian Youth Hostels
409 N Pacific Coast Highway, Building 106, Suite 390, Redondo Beach, CA 90277; ☎310/379-4136; E-mail 71573.2010@compuserve.com); fax: 310/379-8420. Also has agents in Britain, Finland, Germany and Estonia.
*Arranges visas and hostel accommodation in St Petersburg.*

---

passes are **not valid** in Russia, Belarus, Poland, Ukraine or the Baltic States, it's only worth getting one if you plan to travel fairly extensively around Europe by train, in addition to visiting Moscow.

If you're under 26, a range of youth fares are available, including a **Eurail Youthpass**, which gives unlimited travel in 17 countries (including France, Germany and Finland) and costs $578 for one month or $768 for two. It must be bought before leaving home (outlets are given above), as

must the other kinds of *Eurailpass*. For those over 26 there's the standard **Eurailpass**, giving 15 days' first-class travel for $498, 21 days' for $648, a month's for $1098, or three months' for $1398. Alternatively, there's the **Eurail Flexipass**, which entitles you to a number of days' first-class travel with a two-month period: 5 days for $348, 10 days for $560, 15 days for $740; the under-26 version of this card, the **Eurail Youth Flexipass**, costs $225, $398 and $540 respectively.

# Getting There from Australia and New Zealand

You can fly directly from Sydney to Moscow on *Aeroflot*, or use one of the many carriers that travel there via their home base in Europe or Asia (see box for airlines and flight frequencies). Moscow can be a stopover on round-the-world flights, and lies at the end of a 6000-mile train journey from Beijing via Mongolia or Manchuria.

## Flights

*Aeroflot* flies directly from Sydney to Moscow once a week; from elsewhere in Australia, you travel on *Qantas* to Singapore, and transfer to *Aeroflot*. The low/high season price is $1650/1850 in both cases. *Japan Airlines* (*JAL*) has a weekly service from the east coast to Tokyo, with a flight on to Moscow next day; the price ($1660/2110) includes accommodation in Tokyo. Other Asian carriers with next-day flights to Moscow are *Korean Airlines*, flying weekly via Seoul ($1750 year-round), and *Air India*, which flies from Perth to Moscow only, via Delhi/Bombay (from $1620, plus $499 for Sydney–Perth return). There are also combination deals using *British Airways* (*BA*) to reach an Asian hub city, and thence to Moscow with another airline, via Europe. For example, *Finnair* flies via Bangkok/Singapore and Helsinki ($1720/2050 low/high season), and *LOT* via Bangkok/Singapore and Warsaw (from $2000).

More expensive carriers, offering daily connections to Moscow from their homebase, include *KLM*, flying twice a week via Amsterdam ($1900/2500); *Lufthansa*, via Singapore and Frankfurt, flies three times a week ($1940/2565) *BA* flies daily from around the country to London ($2200/2700); and *Singapore Airlines* three times a week ($2250/3750). For the same price you can get a **round-the-world ticket** with Moscow as a stopover. The *Global Explorer* allows six stopovers anywhere on the *Qantas*, *BA* or *US Air* network except South America, for as little as $2250.

The only direct option **from New Zealand** to Moscow is *JAL*, which flies weekly from Auckland, with an overnight stopover in Tokyo; the price (NZ$2035/2699) includes accommodation there. The alternatives use combinations of airlines across Asia or the US to Europe, and then on to Russia. For example, *Qantas/Air New Zealand* flies from Auckland to Singapore or Los Angeles, and thence to Moscow either with *KLM* via Amsterdam (NZ$2399/2799), or *Alitalia* via Rome (NZ$2299/2699). For the same price you can use either option as a **round-the-world fare**, travelling through Asia on the outward leg and returning through the US. Alternatively, *Global Explorer* fares (see above) start at NZ$2840.

## From China by train

Many people are drawn by the idea of travelling **overland from China to Russia** by the Trans-Siberian Railway. The trip can be arranged by various firms in Australia, which offer packages based around the Trans-Siberian routes (see below), or – less expensively – by simply booking a ticket in Hong Kong or Beijing, through *Moonsky Star Ltd* or *Global Union Express*. All of them can obtain Russian **visas** (and transit visas for Mongolia, if required), but need advance notification. See the box below for addresses.

There are two services from Beijing to Moscow. The Chinese **Trans-Mongolian Express**

## Airlines

### Aeroflot

Australia ☎02/233 7911, ☎02/9233 7911 from July 1996; No New Zealand office.
*Direct from Sydney to Moscow twice a week.*

### Air France

Australia ☎02/321 1030, ☎02/9321 1030 from July 1996; New Zealand ☎09/303 1229.
*Flights from Sydney to Paris once a week, with daily connections to Moscow.*

### Air New Zealand

Australia ☎02/223 4666, ☎02/9223 4666 from July 1996; New Zealand ☎09/366 2424.
*Flights from Auckland to Frankfurt via Los Angeles three times a week; an onward connection with another airline is required.*

### British Airways

Australia ☎02/258 3300, ☎02/9258 3300 from July 1996; New Zealand ☎09/367 7500.
*Daily flights from Sydney or Melbourne to London, and daily connections on to Moscow.*

### Japanese Airlines (JAL)

Australia ☎02/233 4500, ☎02/9233 4500 from July 1996; New Zealand ☎09/379 9906.
*Weekly flights from Sydney and Auckland to Moscow, with a stopover in Tokyo; one night's accommodation is included in the price.*

### KLM

Australia ☎02/231 6333; No New Zealand office.
*Twice weekly from Sydney to Amsterdam via Singapore, with onward connections to Moscow.*

### Korean Airlines

Australia ☎02/267 6000; No New Zealand office.

### LOT

Australia ☎02/232 8340 or 232 8642; No New Zealand office.
*Twice weekly from Sydney to Warsaw, via Singapore and Bangkok. You have to stay overnight in Warsaw before flying on to Moscow.*

### Lufthansa

Australia ☎02/367 3800; New Zealand ☎09/303 1529.
*Flights from Sydney to Frankfurt via Bangkok three times a week, with a daily connection to Moscow.*

### Qantas

Australia ☎02/957 0111 or 236 3636, ☎02/9236 3636 from July 1996; New Zealand ☎09/303 2506.
*Regular flights from Sydney to Frankfurt; an onward connection to Moscow with another airline is required.*

## Discount travel agents

### Accent on Travel

545 Queen St, Brisbane; ☎07/832 1777.

### The Adventure Specialists

1st floor, 69 Liverpool St, Sydney; ☎02/261 2927.
*Agents for Sundowners Adventure Travel (see below).*

### Adventure World

73 Walker St, North Sydney ☎1800/221 931; 101 Great South Rd, Remuera, PO Box 74008, Auckland ☎09/524 5118; also has offices in Melbourne, Brisbane, Adelaide and Perth.

### Anywhere Travel

345 Anzac Parade, Kingsford, Sydney ☎02/663 0411.

### Bay Travel

Level 1, 20–26 Cross St, Sydney; ☎02/327 8266.

### Brisbane Discount Travel

360 Queen Street, Brisbane ☎07/3229 9211.

### Budget Travel

PO Box 505, Auckland ☎09/309 4313.

### Flight Centres

Circular Quay, Sydney ☎02/241 2422, ☎02/9241 2422 from July 1996; National Bank Towers, 202–225 Queen St, Auckland ☎09/309 6171; branches all over New Zealand and Australia.

### Harvey World Travel

247 Pitt St, Sydney; ☎02/261 2800; has other branches across Australia.

### Passport Travel

320b Glenferrie Rd, Malvern, Melbourne ☎03/824 7183, ☎03/9824 7183 from July 1996.
*Agents for Red Bear Tours (see below).*

### STA Travel

732 Harris St, Sydney ☎02/212 1255 or 281 9866, ☎02/9212 1255 from July 1996 ; 256 Flinders St, Melbourne ☎03/347 4711; other offices in Townsville, Cairns and state capitals.

### Topdeck Travel

45 Grenfell St, Adelaide ☎08/410 1110, ☎08/9410 1110 from Aug 1996.

### Traveller's Centre

10 High St, Auckland ☎09/309 9995; 233 Cuba St, Wellington ☎04/385 0561; 223 High St, Christchurch ☎03/379 9098; has other offices in Dunedin, Palmerston North and Hamilton.

### Tymtro Travel

Suite G12, Wallaceway Shopping Centre, Chatswood, Sydney ☎02/413 1219.

### Specialist tour operators & agents

**Allways Travel**
70–70a Castlereagh St, Sydney; ☎ 02/235 1022.
*Offers a variety of packages including Moscow and St Petersburg.*

**Eastern European Travel Bureau**
75 King St, Sydney; ☎ 02/262 1144, ☎ 02/9262 1144 from July 1996. Also has offices in Melbourne, Brisbane, Adelaide and Perth.
*Bejing-St Petersburg via Mongolia, Lake Baikal and Moscow, or Moscow twinned with St Petersburg. Can also arrange B&B.*

**Global Union Express (H.K.) Ltd**
Room 22–23 New Henry House, 10 Ice House Street, Central, Hong Kong; ☎ 868-3221; fax: 845-5078.
*Agents for the Travellers Guest House in Moscow (p.291), which can arrange trips on the Trans-Siberian or the historic Silk Road, visa support, registration and accommodation in Moscow.*

**Host Families Association (HOFA)** in Australia; ☎ 03/725 8555.
*Agents for a St Petersburg-based firm offering private accommodation and other services in several Russian cities. Can provide visa support.*

**Moonsky Star Ltd**
Chung King Mansion, Nathan Rd 36–44, E block, 4th floor, flat 6, Kowloon, Hong Kong; ☎ 852/723-1376; fax: 852/723-6656; E-mail 100267.2570@compuserve.com). In Beijing: *Qiao Yuan Hotel*, room 716, Dongbinhe Rd, Youanmenwei, Beijing; fax & ☎ 1/301-2444 ext. 716; fax ext. 444.
*Arranges train tickets from Beijing to Moscow, and Russian visas.*

**Red Bear Tours**
320b Glenferrie Rd, Malvern, Melbourne; ☎ 008/33 70 31; fax: 822 3956.
*Does various tours of Siberia, China and Mongolia, based on the Trans-Siberian, -Mongolian and -Manchurian railways.*

**Russia and Beyond**
100 Clarence St, Sydney; ☎ 02/290 3856.
*Specialists in trips to western Russia and the Baltic States. Packages include two nights in Moscow; Moscow/St Petersburg; and a Volga cruise.*

**Russian Specialists**
Shop 6, Royal Arcade, 175 Oxford St, Bondi Junction, 2022 NSW; ☎ 02/387 1333.
*Good for self-tailored packages. Their Beijing-Moscow trip can be extended to St Petersburg. Arranges B&B.*

**Sundowners Adventure Travel**
151 Dorcas St, South Melbourne; ☎ 03/690 2499.
*Major agent for Trans-Siberian packages. One includes a one-way flight from London to St Petersburg, and travel by rail on to Vladivostok (from $2160).*

---

(train #4) departs every Monday, travelling via the Mongolian capital, Ulan Bator, to arrive in Moscow five and a half days (and 7885km) later. Travellers on this route require a Mongolian transit visa ($30), in addition to a Russian visa. Alternatively, there's the Russian **Trans-Manchurian Express** (train #20), leaving on Saturday, which takes a longer (9001km) route through Harbin and Zaibaikalsk, reaching Moscow six and a half days later. First class isn't as plush as on the Chinese train, but second class is pretty much the same. No Mongolian visa is needed.

For much of the way, both trains follow the **Trans-Siberian Railway** that runs from Moscow to Vladivostok ("Ruler of the East") on the Pacific Coast. This feat of Tsarist engineering also carries the **Rossiya Express**, which takes six and a half days to travel the 9296km from Vladivostok, and slower trains which take nine days. All terminate in Moscow at **Yaroslavl Station** (see p.267).

If you're planning to travel **towards China** tickets can be obtained in Moscow at the Central Ticket Agency or the *Travellers Guest House* (see p.291). The Chinese consulate will only issue a tourist visa if you can show them your ticket to China and an onward ticket from there, while the Mongolians insist on you getting a Chinese visa before they will issue a transit visa the same day. For consular details in Moscow, see p.18.

Whichever train you're on, bring fruit, bread, juice and bottled water to last three or four days, and a lot more **food** than that if you're vegetarian, as the restaurant car meals usually involve meat. Instant soup, tea or coffee can be topped up with hot water from the *samovar* in each carriage.

## Package tours

**Package tours** available in Australia do *not* include flights to Russia (or China), as it's assumed that you'll be making your own way there – though most agencies can arrange them if required. The main reason to take a tour is to avoid the hassle of booking train tickets between Moscow, St Petersburg and/or Beijing, and finding somewhere to stay there. All the prices cited below are for a single person, at twin share rates.

The most popular tours link **Beijing, Moscow and St Petersburg** with a journey on the Trans-Siberian (see above). The *Eastern European Travel Bureau*'s includes stopovers at Ulan Bator and Lake Baikal, five nights in Moscow and the same in St Petersburg (from $2050). *Sundowners Adventure Travel* does a seven-day tour for $940; an 18-day tour via Manchuria ($1860) and a 19-day trip via Mongolia ($2165). Cheaper is the *Russian Specialists*' "Beijing–Moscow Express" ($788), with two nights' accommodation at each end, and an overnight train journey to St Petersburg as an optional extra ($80). This also features in **Moscow–St Petersburg** packages such as the *Eastern European Travel Bureau*'s

eight-day tour ($625), and *Russia and Beyond*'s eight-day "Grand Russia" package ($1150), including a visit to the Moscow Circus. From May to September, the latter also offers eleven to twelve day **Volga cruises** ($1480), with two nights in Moscow and three in St Petersburg. All these deals are fully inclusive (except for flights).

If you just want accommodation, you can arrange **bed and Breakfast** (B&B) in Moscow with the *Eastern European Travel Bureau* ($46 a night) or *Russian Specialists* ($65 a night), or **hotel** rooms through *Russia and Beyond* (two nights from $260) or *Sundowners Adventure Travel*. The last's three-night deal includes transport to and from your Moscow points of arrival and departure; prices depend on whether you stay at the *Moskva* ($410), *Intourist* ($490) or *Metropol* ($1340).

# Red Tape and Visas

Bureaucracy has been the bane of visitors to Russia since the Middle Ages, and despite the collapse of the USSR, little has changed in this respect. All foreign nationals visiting Russia require a full passport and a visa, which must be obtained in advance from a Russian embassy or consulate abroad. Each embassy sets its own visa prices according to the speed of delivery (see below). Although the cheapest method is to apply yourself a month in

advance, this involves lots of hassle, so it's worth spending another £20–30 to have the entire business done through a visa agency or tour operator. If you foresee having to register yourself or extend your visa in Moscow, be sure that the agency has a bona fide address there.

## Visas

There are several types of **visa** available, so it's important to know which one you want. The most common one is a straight **tourist visa**, valid for a precise number of days up to a maximum of thirty. To get this, you must have proof of prebooked accommodation in Moscow. If you're going on a package tour, all the formalities can be sorted out for you by the travel agency, though they may charge extra for this. If you're travelling independently, the *Travellers Guest House* in Moscow (see p.291) can arrange the necessary visa support.

A **business visa** is more flexible in that it is valid for up to sixty days (occasionally longer), and doesn't require that you prebook accommodation. You don't actually have to be involved in any business in order to get one; you simply need to provide the embassy/consulate with a stamped letter of invitation (or fax) from a registered business organization in Russia. This can be arranged by firms like *East-West Travel* in Britain (see p.5), *Russia House* in America (p.12), or *Russian Specialists* in Australia (p.15). The cost may depend on whether or not you also book a tour and/or accommodation with them.

If you don't have a business visa, and wish to stay with Russian friends, you'll need a **private individual visa**, which is the most difficult kind to obtain. This requires a personal invitation from your Russian host – cleared through *OVIR* (see below) – guaranteeing to look after you for the duration of your stay. The whole process can take up to three or four months to complete.

If you are only planning to pass through Russia en route to another country, you must apply for a **transit visa**, valid for a 24-hour stopover in one city (usually Moscow). Although the authorities now claim to issue them at Sheremetevo-2 Airport, the cost exceeds $150, and it's by no means a sure thing that they'll grant you one. Travellers without a visa are confined in the so-called *Transit Hotel* – a lock-up for illegal aliens – until their flight leaves Moscow.

Those anticipating a long stay and subsequent visits to Russia should get a business visa, and then have it converted into a **multiple-entry visa** valid for a year (which can't be obtained outside Russia). The process takes about a week, costs $50–120, and requires three to six photos; several agencies in Moscow can handle this. See under "Registration and OVIR", below, for more on changing your visa status, or obtaining a visa extension.

With all these visas, what you get is a document to slip into your passport. With the single-entry visas, one half (the entry visa) is collected on arrival, the other half (the exit visa) on departure. Multiple-entry visas are stamped, as is your passport, on arrival and departure. **Lost visas** must be reported to the main *OVIR* office in Moscow, which should eventually issue you with a replacement.

**Note** that if you intend to leave Russia and enter any other republics of the former Soviet Union, you not only need a separate visa for each independent state, but also a multiple-entry visa to get back into Russia. Foreigners wishing to stay in Russia for longer than three months must obtain a doctor's letter certifying that they are not HIV-positive.

## How to app...

It really is worth th... agency to obtain yo... you are determined to ... is as follows. First you ... **form** from your Russian e... (addresses given below); an... tions, writing "not applicable" ra... any of the answers blank. The "ob... should be given as "tourism", "b... "study". You should then send the ... form, plus **three passport-sized photographs** with your name printed on the back of each, reference or confirmation numbers from the hotels where you'll be staying, and a photocopy of the computerized last page of your passport (in the case of US or new-style EC passports), or the first six pages (of the old-style British ones) to the Russian Embassy – together with a stamped addressed envelope and a cheque payable to the Russian Embassy. If you're staying as a guest of a Russian, your host must get a signed letter from the Russian authorities as proof of your arrangements, which he/she will send to you.

Submitting your application **in person** is not advised, as visitors have to wait outside for hours, while visa-service couriers breeze in and out. If you can muster the nerve, march straight up to the security phone and say firmly: *Zdrástye, mogú ya poluchít srochnúyu vísu?* (Hello, can I get an urgent visa?). You'll probably be buzzed in at once. This is a basic lesson about how things work in Russia. Consular working hours are Mon, Tues, Thurs & Fri 10am–12.30pm; they close on Wed, on Russian national holidays, and those of the host nation.

The speed at which your application is processed and the **cost** of the visa are directly related. In Britain, the cheapest option is the 14-day service, which costs £10. It is possible to get your visa quicker, for £60, but the minimum amount of time is three days. In the US, the two-week service costs $20, the one-week service $30, and the three-day service $60. In Australia, they normally charge $60, or $90 for urgent issue.

## Registration and OVIR

By law, all foreigners are supposed to register within three days of arrival at *OVIR*, the *Visa and Foreign Citizen's Registration Department*, and obtain a stamp on their exit visa to that effect. In practice, **registration** isn't as bad as it sounds, since anyone coming on a tour or staying at a

## Embassies and consulates
...ad

### Australia
Embassy: 76 Canberra Ave, Griffith
Canberra, ACT 2603 ☎06/295 9033
Consulate: 7–9 Fullerton St, Woollahra
NSW 2000 ☎02/326 1188

### Britain
Embassy: 5 Kensington Palace Gardens
London W8 ☎0171/229 8027

### Canada
Embassy: 52 Range Rd, Ottawa
Ontario K1N 8G5 ☎613/594 8488
Consulate: 3655 Ave du Musée
Môntréal, Québec H3G 2E1 ☎514/843 5901

### Finland
Embassy: Vuorimiehenkatu 6
00140 Helsinki ☎90/661 876

### Germany
Embassy: Waldstrasse 42
W-5300, Bonn 2 ☎0228/31 20 89

### Ireland
Embassy: 186 Orwell Rd, Rathgar,
Dublin ☎01/492 3492

### Netherlands
Embassy: Laan van Meerdervoort 1
2517-AA, The Hague ☎070/346 79 40

### New Zealand
Embassy: 57 Messines Rd, Karori
Wellington ☎04/476 6113

### Poland
Embassy: ul. Belwederska 49
Warsaw ☎022/213 453

### USA
Embassy: 1825 Phelps Place NW
Washington, DC 20008 ☎202/298 5700
Consulate: 9E 91st St ☎212/348 0926 or
New York, NY 10128 ☎ 348 0779 (visa hotline)

## Foreign embassies and consulates in Moscow

### Australia
Kropotkinskiy per. 13 ☎956-6070
*Mon–Fri 9am–12.30pm & 1.30–5pm.*

### Belarus
ul. Maroseyka 17/6 ☎924-7095

### Britain
Sofiyskaya nab. 14 ☎230-6333
*Mon–Fri 9am–5pm.*

### Canada
Starokonyushenniy per. 23 ☎241-5882
*Mon, Tues, Thurs & Fri 9am–noon.*

### China
ul. Druzhby 6 ☎145-1543
*Mon, Wed & Fri 9am–noon. You have to show an onward ticket from China to get a tourist visa.*

### Ireland
Grokholskiy per. 5 ☎288-4101

### Latvia
ul. Chaplygina 3 ☎921-1422

### Lithuania
Borisoglebskiy per. 10 ☎291-7586

### Mongolia
Spasopesovskiy per. 7 ☎244-7867
*Visa applications Mon–Fri 9am–1.30pm; collection 4.30–5pm. Same-day delivery $30; one-week $15. You must already have a Chinese visa.*

### New Zealand
Povarskaya ul. 44 ☎956-3579
*Mon–Fri 8.30am–12.30pm & 1.30–5.30pm.*

### United States
Novinskiy bulvar 19/23 ☎252-2451 through
*Mon–Fri 9am–6pm.* ☎252-2459

*Other embassies are listed in several publications available in Moscow (see p.31).*

## Visa services in Moscow

### East-West Travel
Bolshaya Lubyanka ul. 24/15
☎924-0629; fax: 925-0460.
*The Moscow end of a London-based travel firm that can arrange visas, hotels and tickets for all the CIS states.*

### Russia House
Leningradskiy pr. 17
☎250-0143; fax: 250-2503.
*US travel firm, offering similar services to the above.*

### Russian Travel Service
☎193-2514 or 457-3508; fax: 152-7493.
*Visa support for its B&B clients.*

### Travellers Guest House
Bolshaya Pereyaslavskaya ul. 50, 10th floor
☎971-4059; fax: 280-7686
*Full Russian visa support, train tickets and tours.*

### Tourservice International
bulvar Yana Raynisa 5
☎493-2330; fax: 493-9212
*Visas and other tourist services related to Ukraine.*

hotel will have this done for them automatically, so it only applies to those staying in some kind of "unofficial" accommodation. Then, the problem is that *OVIR* insists that whoever supplied or sponsored your visa becomes involved in your registration. If you got a visa through a firm abroad, with no office in Moscow, one solution is to check into a hotel for a few days (or bribe a receptionist to stamp your exit visa and date it for the period needed). Visitors who do *not* get a registration stamp may be fined $120 upon leaving Russia.

*OVIR* is also responsible for issuing visa extensions, residence permits, and passports for Russian citizens. Their **head office** in Moscow – called *UVIR* – is at ul. Pokrovka 42 (Mon, Tues & Thurs 10am–1pm & 3–6pm, Fri 10am–1pm & 3–5pm; ☎924-9349). Its bureaucrats are notoriously rude and lazy, guaranteeing hours of tedium and annoyance for anyone who comes into contact with them. Bring along a Russian friend to help out if possible.

To obtain a **visa extension**, you'll need a supporting letter from the firm that issued your visa, which must exactly correspond to the format specified by *OVIR*. Bring this, and your passport and visa, to room 1 on the second floor, where you fill out a form on the spot, and submit all the documents. You may have to make a payment of about £10/16 (in rubles) into *OVIR*'s account at the *Sberbank* savings bank, across the road. However, if your original visa was issued by *Intourist*, their main office on Manezhnaya pl. (see p.31) can have it extended with less hassle, for £20/30. Extensions are deemed to start from the day of application, rather than the expiry date of the original visa. A supporting letter from your visa sponsor is also needed **to change a single-entry visa into a multi-entry one**. It is impossible to get a multi-entry visa if you are changing visa sponsors at the same time.

## Customs and allowances

Over the last couple of years, **border controls** have relaxed considerably. Bags are no longer searched for "subversive" literature, but simply passed through an X-ray machine. However, you must declare all foreign currency that you bring in to the country, and you will be asked to do the same when you leave (see p.35 for details).

**Export controls** are now the biggest problem that you'll face. Officially, you can take out goods worth up to fifty times the minimum wage, which currently gives you around $400-worth tax-free; on anything over this amount, you'll have to pay sixty percent tax. You can expect to encounter serious problems if you try to take any of the following items out of the country: icons (fake or otherwise), any artwork, military souvenirs, antique *samovars* or electrical goods, as well as anything else that the customs officials decide to object to at the time.

Permission to export **contemporary art and antiques** (anything pre-1960, in effect) must be applied for at the *Cultural Assessment Committee*, ul. Neglinnaya 8 (☎921-3258; Mon & Tues 10am–2pm), but you would be well advised to ask the seller to do the paperwork for you. If the export is approved, you can be liable for tax of up to 100 percent of the object's value. **Pre-1960 books** must be approved by the Russian State Library's *Committee on the Export of Publications Abroad*, which requires details of the edition, publisher, print run, number of pages, and the price paid for the book.

**Duty-free allowances from Russia** into EU countries are currently 250 cigarettes, 2 litres of wine/champagne and 1 litre of spirits; into the US and Australia, allowances are 200 cigarettes, 1 litre of wine or spirits, and goods up to the value of $400. These allowances may change in the future, so check with customs before you leave the country.

# Insurance

On production of a passport, most foreign nationals can technically get free emergency medical care in public hospitals, with a nominal charge for certain medicines. However, if you don't want to go to a Russian hospital, then the only option is a private clinic charging US rates, which means that it's vital to take out some sort of travel insurance policy, preferably one which covers you for medical evacuation, before you leave home. Without insurance, an accident such as breaking a leg could cost you up to $10,000.

Travel insurance will enable you to claim back the cost of any treatment and drugs as well as covering your baggage and tickets in case of theft. Before you purchase any insurance, however, check what you have already. North Americans, in particular, may find themselves covered for medical expenses, and possibly loss of or damage to valuables while abroad, as part of a family or student policy. Some credit cards, too, now offer insurance benefits if you use them to pay for your holiday tickets.

Ask about policies at any bank or travel agency. It's worth shopping around to see what's on offer since premiums vary considerably. Again

this applies particularly to North Americans, who if transiting via Britain might consider buying a policy from a British travel agent. British policies tend to be cheaper than American ones, and routinely cover thefts – often excluded from the more health-based American policies.

**In Britain**, as well as those policies offered by travel agents, consider using a specialist, low-priced firm like *Endsleigh* (Cranfield House, 97–107 Southampton Row, London WC1; ☎0171/436 4451), which offers two weeks' basic cover for £17.40, or *Columbus Travel Insurance* (17 Devonshire Square, London EC2; ☎0171/375 0011), whose two-week policy costs £24. For medical treatment and drugs, you should keep all the bills and claim the money back later. If you have anything stolen (including money), register the loss immediately with the local police – without their report you won't be able to claim.

**In the US**, the best deals are usually through student/youth travel agencies – *ISIS* policies (sold by *STA Travel*, 48 E 11th St, New York, NY 10003; ☎800/777-0112), for example, cost $48–69 for fifteen days (depending on coverage), $80–105 for a month, $149–207 for two months, right up to $510–700 for a year. Other policies worth considering are those from *Access America* (PO Box 90310, Richmond, VA 23230; ☎800/284-8300); *Carefree Travel Insurance* (PO Box 310, 120 Mineola Blvd, Mineola, NY 11501; ☎800/323-3149); *Travel Assistance International* (1133 15th St NW, Suite 400, Washington, DC 20005; ☎800/821-2828); *Travel Guard* (1145 Clark St, Stevens Point, WI 54481; ☎800/826-1300); and *Travel Insurance Services* (2930 Camino Diablo, Suite 300, Walnut Creek, CA 94596; ☎800/937-1387).

> For details of hospitals, pharmacies and private clinics, see "Health Matters" on p.38.

# Disabled Travellers

In the past, very little attention has been paid to the needs of the disabled anywhere in Russia. Attitudes are slowly changing, but there is a long way to go, and the chronic shortage of funds for almost everything does not help matters.

Wheelchair access to most of the top international **hotels** is possible with some assistance, but only the *Metropol* and *Radisson Slavyanskaya* are fully wheelchair-accessible. **Transport** is a big problem, since buses, trams and trolleybuses are impossible to get on with a wheelchair, and the metro and suburban train systems only slightly better. Though major **sights** like Red Square, the Kremlin, the Novodevichiy Convent and the VDNKh are accessible, churches and museums often require you to negotiate steps.

Disabled people may visit many **museums** at a reduced price (or free of charge), and are usually permitted to jump the queues in **shops**.

---

## Contacts for Disabled Travellers

### UK

**Holiday Care Service**, 2 Old Bank Chambers, Station Rd, Horley, Surrey RH6 9HW; ☎01293/774535. *Provides information on all aspects of travel.*

**Mobility International**, 228 Borough High St, London SE1 1JX; ☎0171/403 5688. *Has a quarterly newsletter that keeps up to date with developments in disabled travel; also has information, access guides and organizes tours and exchange programmes for disabled people.*

**RADAR**, 25 Mortimer St, London W1; ☎0171/637 5400. *A good source of advice on holidays and travel abroad for disabled drivers.*

### US and Canada

**Directions Unlimited**, 720 N Bedford Rd, Bedford Hills, NY 10507; ☎800/533-5343). *Tour operator specializing in custom tours for people with disabilities.*

**Information Center for People with Disabilities**, Fort Point Place, 27–43 Wormwood St, Boston, MA 02210; ☎617/727-5540 or 345-9743. *Clearing house for information, including travel, primarily in Massachusetts.*

**Jewish Rehabilitation Hospital**, 3205 Place Alton Goldbloom, Montréal, PQ H7V 1R2; ☎514/688-9550, ext 226. *Guide books and travel information.*

**Kéroul**, 4545 Ave. Pierre de Coubertin, CP 1000, Station M, Montréal, PQ H1V 3R2; ☎514/252-3104. *Organization promoting and facilitating travel for mobility-impaired people, primarily in Québec. Annual membership $10.*

**Mobility International USA**, PO Box 10767, Eugene, OR 97440; ☎503/343-1284. *Information and referral services, access guides, tours and exchange programmes. Annual membership $20 (includes quarterly newsletter).*

**Society for the Advancement of Travel for the Handicapped** (SATH), 347 5th Ave, New York, NY 10016; ☎212/447-7284. *Non-profit travel-industry referral service that passes queries on to its members as appropriate; allow plenty of time for a response.*

**Travel Information Service**, Moss Rehabilitation Hospital, 1200 West Tabor Rd, Philadelphia, PA 19141; ☎215/456-9600. *Telephone information and referral service.*

**Twin Peaks Press**, Box 129, Vancouver, WA 98666; ☎206/694-2462 or 800/637-2256. *Publisher of the* Directory of Travel Agencies for the Disabled *($19.95), listing more than 370 agencies worldwide;* Travel for the Disabled *($14.95); the* Directory of Accessible Van Rentals *and* Wheelchair Vagabond *($9.95), which is loaded with personal tips.*

### Australia and New Zealand

**ACROD**, PO Box 60, Curtain, ACT 2605; ☎06/682 4333.

**Barrier Free Travel**, 36 Wheatley St, North Bellingen, NSW 2454; ☎066/551733.

**Disabled Persons Assembly**, PO Box 10–138, The Terrace, Wellington; ☎04/472 2626.

---

# Points of Arrival

Most visitors arrive by air and enter the city by the Leningrad highway, passing a monument in the form of giant anti-tank "hedgehogs" that marks the nearest that the Nazis got in 1941. If you're not being met at the airport, finding a bus or haggling for a taxi will be your first taste of the uncertainties of life in Moscow. Arriving by train at one of the city's mainline stations, you'll be pitched straight into streetlife at its rawest, and the Moscow metro. Few people arrive by bus or boat.

## Airports

Moscow's main **international airport**, Sheremetevo-2, is 28km northwest of the city centre. Built by German contractors for the 1980 Olympics, it is still inadequate – with too few passport control kiosks and baggage carousels. The concourse contains a hard-currency duty-free shop, car rental and hotel reservation desks, an exchange bureau and a 24-hour cash dispenser.

If you know that you'll be **arriving** after dark or with a lot of baggage, it's worth arranging to be met at the airport. The *Travellers Guest House* and most top hotels offer this service; the fee ($40–60) is similar to what private taxis charge, without any haggling or worries about whether the driver is a crook. **Taxis** charge whatever they can get away with, which can mean $100 after the last bus has left. The normal going rate is about $35–40, but they'll open the bidding at $60–70. Taxis leaving from the departures terminal may charge significantly less, as they don't belong to the "taxi mafia" that operates at the arrivals section.

The alternative is to get into town by **public transport**, which involves a two-stage journey by bus and metro, and costs the ruble equivalent of about $2–3. This is not feasible after 10 or 11pm, depending on the airport. There are two express **buses** into town from outside the terminal. One runs to Rechnoy Vokzal bus station, near the metro of the same name (every 30min till 8.30pm); the other to the Air Terminal, 600–700m from Aeroport or Dinamo station, further in on the same metro line (every 90 minutes till 10pm).

| Airport enquiries | |
|---|---|
| Sheremetevo-2 | ☎ 578-5633, 578-5614 |
| Sheremetevo-1 | ☎ 578-5791 |
| Bykovo | ☎ 155-0922 |
| Domodedovo | ☎ 234-8656, 234-8655 |
| Vnukovo | ☎ 234-8656, 234-8655 |

If you're flying in **from St Petersburg** you'll arrive at the older Sheremetevo-1 airport, across the runway, which is likewise connected by express buses to Rechnoy Vokzal and the Air Terminal (hourly until 10pm). Moscow's three **other airports** handle flights from Central Asia, Siberia or southern Russia, and have fewer facilities. *Bykovo*, to the west of the city, is linked by suburban train to Kazan Station, while Domodedovo and Vnukovo, south of Moscow, are connected by buses #511 and #5113 to Yugo-Zapadnaya metro, thirty minutes' ride from the centre. All three stations are also connected to the Air Terminal by express **buses**, running from Bykovo every one and a half hours until 6pm; from Domodedovo every half-hour till 11pm; and from Vnukovo hourly until 10pm. **Taxi fares** are comparable to (or higher than) those from Sheremetevo-2.

### Leaving Moscow

When **leaving Moscow**, allow plenty of time to get to the airport. The options are as outlined above, though it's worth noting that the trip to the airport by taxi or prearranged transfer often costs less than the journey in. By public transport, the obvious starting point is the **Air Terminal** (*Aerovokzal*) on Leningradskiy prospekt, behind two sea-green towerblocks midway between Dinamo and Aeroport metro stations. Express buses leave from outside; you buy tickets from the driver, in rubles. The frequencies of buses to the airports and length of journeys are as follows: Sheremetevo-2 (8.30am–10pm; 35min), Sheremetevo-1 (6.25am–11.30pm; 45min), Bykovo (6.30am–6.30pm; 1hr 30min), Vnukovo (6.30am–11pm; 1hr) and Domodedovo (5.30am–midnight; 1hr 30min). However, to spare yourself a long walk from the metro station, it's easier to travel to **Rechnoy Vokzal**, whose bus depot is near the metro; take the exit at the front of the train, then bear right beyond the kiosks beyond to find the stop for red-lettered express services to Sheremetevo-1 and -2 (every 30min 7am–9pm).

The **Departures** terminal at Sheremetevo-2 is even gloomier than Arrivals – especially at night – and you should guard your baggage. Check-in opens ninety minutes before take-off for Western airlines and two hours before for *Aeroflot* flights. The **customs** officer will expect to see your original currency declaration (see p.35) and a duplicate form detailing what you're taking out of the country (forms are available in the hall). Your baggage will be X-rayed before you can pass through to the check-in desk – be careful, though, as Russian film-safe X-rays do not always live up to their name. Another official will then check your passport and remove your exit visa before you're allowed into the departure lounge, with its *Irish House* **bar** and **duty-free shop**, which only accept hard currency.

## Train stations

Most of Moscow's eight mainline **train stations** are on the Circle line of the metro, and relatively central. Don't hang around, as they're full of beggars, thieves and drunks, and have nothing useful aside from left-luggage facilities and sometimes an exchange bureau.

Arriving by train **from London, Berlin or Warsaw**, you'll end up at **Belarus Station** (*Belorusskiy vokzal*), about 1km northwest of the Garden Ring, which is served by Belorusskaya metro. Most trains **from the Baltic States** arrive at **Riga Station** (*Rizhskiy vokzal*), 2km north of the Garden Ring (Rizhskaya metro), while services **from Prague, Budapest or Kiev** terminate at **Kiev Station** (*Kievskiy vokzal*), south of the Moskva River (Kievskaya metro).

Trans-Siberian trains **from China or Mongolia** pull into **Yaroslav Station** (*Yaroslavskiy vokzal*) on Komsomolskaya ploshchad, while services **from St Petersburg** and some trains from Finland and Estonia arrive at the neighbouring **Leningrad Station** (*Leningradskiy vokzal*), and trains **from Central Asia** and western Siberia terminate at **Kazan Station** (*Kazanskiy vokzal*), across the square. All three stations are linked to Komsomolskaya metro.

Trains **from Crimea and the Caucasus** arrive at **Kursk Station** (*Kurskiy vokzal*), on the southeastern arc of the Garden Ring (Kurskaya metro), while services **from central southern Russia** wind up at **Pavelets Station** (*Paveletskiy vokzal*), further round the Ring to the south of the river (Paveletskaya metro).

## Bus terminals

Arriving by *Mostransavto* **bus from Helsinki**, you'll be dropped outside their office on Tsvetnoy bulvar, next to the metro station of the same name, in the centre of town. Only in the unlikely event of you arriving by bus from elsewhere in Russia will you arrive at the **Central Bus Station** (*Tsentralniy Avtovokzal*) near Shcholkovskaya metro, which is actually in the northeastern suburbs, about 25 minutes' ride from Kurskaya metro, on the Circle line.

---

### Airline offices in Moscow

**Aeroflot**, ul. Koroviy val 7; ☎158-8019 (Sheremetevo-2 ☎578-9101). Mon–Fri 9am–1pm & 2–5pm.

**Air France**, ul. Koroviy val 7; ☎237-2325 (Sheremetevo-2 ☎578-2757). Mon–Fri 9am–1pm & 2–6pm.

**Austrian Airlines**, Krasnopresnenskaya nab. 12, 18th floor, room #1805. Mon–Fri 9am–5.30pm, Sat 9am–1pm.

**British Airways**, Krasnopresnenskaya nab. 12, 19th floor, room #1905; ☎253-2492. Mon–Fri 9am–5.30pm. (Sheremetevo-2 ☎578-2923; daily 10.30am–7pm).

**CSA**, 2-aya Brestskaya ul. 21/27; ☎250-4571. Mon–Fri 9am–1pm, Sat 9am–noon.

**Delta**, Krasnopresnenskaya nab. 12, 11th floor, room #1102A; ☎253-2658. Mon–Fri 9am–5.30pm.

**Finnair**, Kamergerskiy per. 6; ☎292-8788 (Sheremetevo-2 ☎578-2718). Mon–Fri 9am–5pm.

**Lufthansa**, *Olympic Penta Hotel*, Olimpiyskiy pr. 18/1; ☎975-2501. Mon–Fri 9am–5.30pm, Sat & Sun 9am–5pm. (Sheremetevo-2 ☎578-3151; daily 11am–7.30pm & 9pm–7am).

**Malév**, Kamergerskiy per. 6; ☎292-1434. Mon–Thurs 9am–1pm & 2–5.30pm, Fri 9am–1pm & 2–5pm.

**SAS**, Krasnopresnenskaya nab. 12, 20th floor, room #2003; ☎253-8988 (Sheremetevo-2 ☎578-2740). Mon–Fri 8.30am–noon & 1–5.30pm, Sat 9am–2pm.

---

## River terminals

Passengers arriving by boat **from St Petersburg or Nizhniy Novgorod** dock at one of Moscow's river terminals, miles from the centre. The **Northern River Terminal** (*Severniy rechnoy vokzal*) is fifteen minutes' walk from Rechnoy

Vokzal metro on the (green) Zamoskvoretskaya line, while the **Southern River Terminal** (*Yuzhniy rechnoy vokzal*) lies a similar distance from Kolomenskaya metro, at the other end of the same line. In both cases, the route to the metro station is signposted at the terminal.

# Getting Around

Although central Moscow is best explored on foot, the city is so big that you're bound to rely on its famous metro system to get around. As almost everywhere that you're likely to want to visit is within fifteen minutes' walk of a metro stop, there's little need to take buses, trolleybuses or trams – which aren't as efficient. Unless you speak good Russian and know the score, taxis will charge a fortune.

## City public transport

Tickets (*talony*) for buses, trams and trolleybuses are available from some street kiosks and vendors, or from the driver of the vehicle, who sells them in batches of ten. You must use a separate *talon* each time you board, punching it in one of the archaic gadgets mounted inside the vehicle. In rush hour, when it may be difficult to reach one, fellow passengers will oblige. Roaming plain-clothes inspectors will issue on-the-spot fines to anyone caught without a ticket.

A different system applies on the metro, where passengers buy plastic **tokens** (*zhetony*) to slip into the seemingly barrierless turnstiles. If you don't insert a token, or try to walk through before the light turns green, automatic barriers slam shut, with painful force. Providing you don't leave the metro you can travel any distance and change lines as many times as you like using a single token. The current ruble price of a *zheton* is posted on the window of the *kassa* that sells the tokens.

To avoid queuing and to save money, most Russians buy a **monthly pass** (*yediniy bilet*), which goes on sale in metro stations and kiosks towards the end of the calendar month, for a few days only. This covers all forms of transport, although it is possible to buy a pass just for the metro or for overland transport. To use the pass on the metro, flash it as you walk by the barrier at the end of the line of turnstiles. On buses, trams and trolleybuses, you only need to produce it at the request of an inspector.

Although the price of tickets, tokens and passes increases regularly in line with inflation, public transport is still affordable for the locals and very good value for foreigners. At the time of writing, a metro ride costs about 2 pence and a month's pass is £3/$5.

### The metro

The Moscow **metro** was one of the proudest achievements of the Soviet era – its efficiency and splendour once seemed a foretaste of the Communist utopia that supposedly lay ahead. Inaugurated in 1935, the system had four lines by the time of Stalin's death, and has since grown into a network of 9 **lines** and over 150

# A Sightseer's Guide to the Moscow metro

When **sightseeing on the metro**, try to avoid rush hour and forgo photography or blatant gawping. Stations are apt to be less crowded during August, when many Muscovites leave the city. Bear in mind that some stations have two or even three levels whose decor varies with their vintage; get the wrong level and you'll miss the real attraction.

Our alphabetical list of top ten stations includes all the obvious classics. Many can be seen by riding the Circle line in a clockwise direction, between Park Kultury and Komsomolskaya stations.

**Arbatskaya** (Filyovskaya & Arbatsko-Pokrovskaya lines). The platforms on the Arbatsko-Pokrovskaya line, opened in 1953, share a vestibule whose arches rise from red marble seat-plinths to vaults dripping with ceramic flowers and hanging bronze lamps. At the top of the escalator to street level is an arched wall that originally bore a mural of Stalin smoking a pipe, which periodically emerges from coats of whitewash.

**Belorusskaya** (Circle & Zamoskvaretskaya lines). The lower Circle line station, opened in 1952, has a stuccoed, coffered hall with a tesselated floor in a Belarus rug pattern, and mosaic panels of flower-bedecked citizens in national dress enjoying a peaceful life won by the sacrifices of the muscular partisan figures in the transit hall between the two levels.

**Kievskaya** (Filyovskaya, Arbatsko-Pokrovskaya & Circle lines). Its Circle line station was completed shortly after Belorusskaya, and likewise has an ethnic slant. Mosaic vignettes from the history of Russo-Ukrainian amnity, in stucco frames imitating lace, unfold under the benign gaze of Lenin. The Arbatskovo-Pokrovskaya line station features variations on the same.

**Komsomolskaya** (Sokolnicheskaya & Circle lines). Dedicated to the Communist Youth activists whose work on the first line in 1935 is depicted on majolica panels in the rose marble columned hall on the upper level. A ceiling awash with gold-encrusted mosaics ennobles the Circle line station, opened in 1952. The mosaic of the parade in Red Square was retouched as the Soviet leadership changed, with Beria and Stalin being effaced in the mid-1950s, and Khrushchev in 1964.

**Kropotkinskaya** (Sokolnicheskaya line). Built in 1935, when metro stations were classical in their perfection, Kropotkinskaya has an open-plan platform of dazzling simplicity, its vault upheld by a row of lotus-bud columns. Sadly, however, there is no sign of its namesake, the Anarchist Prince Kropotkin.

**Mayakovskaya** (Zamoskvaretskaya line). Part of the second line, completed in 1938; its magnificent design – by Alexei Dushkin – won the Grand Prix at the World Fair that year. The station is spacious, rhythmic and stylish, with ribbed steel, red and black marble columns, lit by 36 oval cupolas decorated with mosaic panels on the theme of sports and aviation. Stalin spoke here during the dark days of 1941 (see p.151).

**Novokuznetskaya** (Zamoskvaretskaya line). Built and opened during wartime, this station's pale marble hall (designed by Vladimir Gelfreykh and Igor Rozhin) is decorated with a bas-relief frieze of military heroes, and mosaic ceiling panels showing athletic youths garlanded in flowers. The artist responsible, Frolov, died during the siege of Leningrad; his designs were airlifted out of the city as a vital contribution to the war effort.

**Park Kultury** (Sokolnicheskaya & Circle lines). Originally the end station of the Sokolnicheskaya line, its barrel-vaulted main hall (by Rozhin) is clad in marble to head-height, with niches displaying bas-relief medallions portraying workers skating, dancing, playing chess and reading poetry (by Sergei Ryabushkin).

**Ploshchad Revolyutsii** (Arbatsko-Pokrovskaya line). Opened as part of the third line, which employed the most renowned Soviet architects of the late 1930s. Dushkin designed the red marble central hall, flanked by 36 lifesize crouching bronze statues personifying the defence of Soviet power and its achievements (by Matvei Manizer), interspersed with Art Nouveau sheaves of corn and circular lamps.

**Taganskaya** (Circle & Tagansko-Krasno-presnenskaya lines). Its Circle line station is themed on the Great Patriotic War, with marble archways bearing pale blue and white ceramic cameos of partisans, pilots, tank-drivers and munitions workers, in tulip-shaped frames.

stations (see colour map insert). Though the pace of expansion has abated in the past decade, a new station still opens every year and a whole new line is currently underway (and another is projected). In 1994, its Soviet **title**, "The Moscow Metro in the name of Lenin", was quietly replaced by the plain "Moscow Metro" (*Moskóvskiy Metropolitan*).

As everyone knows, the **decor** in many of the stations is palatial, with marble, mosaics, stained-glass, lifesize statues, elaborate stucco and bronze fittings. With practice, you can distinguish the styles associated with each phase of construction, from the neo-Classical pre-war stations to the High Stalinist opulence of the Circle line, or the lavatorial utility of 1970s stations. See the box for more about **sightseeing** on the metro, which is one of Moscow's major tourist attractions.

Although the stations are starting to look a bit shabby and accidents are no longer unheard of, the metro still works remarkably well. Trains run daily from 6am until 1am (entrance doors and underground walkways linking interchange stations close at 12.30am), with **services** every 1–2 minutes during peak periods (8–10am and 5–7pm) and every 3–5 minutes at other times. On major holidays like New Year and the Russian Orthodox Christmas and Easter, they run until 2am. On normal days, passengers are unceremoniously turfed off the last train at the stroke of 1am, no matter where it's standing.

**Stations** are marked with a large "M" and have separate doors for incoming and outgoing passengers. Many have two or three **exits**, located 500–700m apart at street level, which can be disorienting if you pick the wrong one. Though each exit is signposted with the appropriate street names (and even bus routes) at platform level, this is of no help if you can't read Cyrillic. Where directions in the text advise that you use the exit near the front (or rear) of the train, it's assumed that you're travelling out from the centre.

It's a peculiarity of Russian metros that where two or three lines meet, the **interchange stations** often have different names for each line. In a quirk of its own, the Moscow metro also has two sets of stations called "Arbatskaya" and "Smolenskaya", on different lines (the Filyovskaya and Arbatsko-Povarskaya). Also note that the southern end of the Zamoskvaretskaya line forks, with trains terminating at Kakhovskaya or Krasnogvardeyskaya, as signposted on the front.

All **signs** and **maps** are in Russian only, so you'll have to learn to recognize the Cyrillic form of the words for "entrance" (vkhód), "exit" (výkhod) and "passage to another line" (perekhód). If the station names seem incomprehensible, concentrate on recognizing the first three letters only (our map shows both the English and Cyrillic versions).

Since the platforms carry few signs indicating which station you're in, it's advisable to pay attention to tannoy **announcements** in the carriages (in Russian only). As the train pulls into each station, you'll hear its name, immediately followed by the words Sléduyushchaya stántsiya – and then the name of the next station. Most importantly, be sure to heed the words Ostorózhno, dvéry zakryváyutsa – "Caution, doors closing" – they slam shut with great force.

Due to Moscow's swampy subsoil – and the prospect of war – many of the lines were built extremely deep underground, with vertiginous **escalators** that almost nobody walks up, although the left-hand side is designated for that purpose. Interchange stations are often on several levels, with intermediary passages and transit halls where **beggars** and **vendors** have staked out their patch. Muggings are fairly rare, but obvious foreigners may be targeted by **pickpockets**, and could be in danger of assault if travelling alone late at night. Try to look like a Russian, and avoid speaking unless necessary.

Generally, however, the main problem is being jostled by **crowds** – during rush hour, you can well believe that nine million people travel on the metro each day. Beware of **trolleys** that can bruise your ankles. The problem is worst on the **Circle line**, which connects seven mainline stations; their respective metros are choked by passengers in transit with vast amounts of luggage.

## Buses, trams and trolleybuses

In theory, Moscow has a fully integrated network of buses, trams and trolleybuses, covering almost every part of the city. The reality is an overstretched and dilapidated system that battles on somehow, but is hardly user-friendly. Aside from the antiquated and clapped-out vehicles, the **overcrowding** on some routes is such that you may find it physically impossible to get on board. Many visitors are also discouraged by the pushing and shoving, but Russians rarely take this personally, and once inside the vehicle will cheerfully help each other to punch tickets or buy them from the driver. Should anyone ask if you are getting off at the next stop – Vy vykhodíe? – it means that they are, and need to squeeze past.

The other big problem is that **routes** are often altered due to roadworks, so even the most recent transport maps can't be relied on. As a rule, buses and trolleybuses are supposed to operate from 6am to 1am, and trams from 5.30am to 1.30am, although cutbacks may see these **hours** reduced on some lines after 9pm. Owing to a shortage of vehicles, you may find buses or trolleybuses covering a tram route, with the driver announcing "This is a tram". Such hybrid services are nicknamed "Mutants" (*Mutánty*). The most useful route for sightseeing is bus #6, which circles the Garden Ring. Trams mostly take roundabout routes, and don't run in the centre at all.

**Stops** are relatively few and far between, so getting off at the wrong one can mean a lengthy walk. Bus stops are marked with an "A" (for *avtobus*); trolleybus stops with what resembles a squared-off "m", but is in fact a handwritten Cyrillic "t" (for *trolleybus*). Both are usually attached to walls, and therefore somewhat inconspicuous, whereas the signs for tram stops (bearing a 'T' for *tramvay*), are suspended from the overhead cables above the road.

In addition to the services outlined above, there are special **express buses** (*ekspress*) on certain routes. These are not to be confused with **minibuses**, which Russians confusingly call *marshrutnoe taksi*. These tend to leave from metro or mainline stations and serve outlying destinations, like the airports. On both, you pay the driver instead of using a *talon*, and the fares are a lot higher than on regular buses.

## Walking

The old centre within the Boulevard and Garden Rings is best explored by **walking**, starting from a convenient metro station. Off the Stalinist squares and avenues that were imposed in the 1930s and 50s, you find a mellower Moscow of courtyards and lanes in every hue of crumbling brick and stucco, with gaunt trees that burst into greenery as the slush of winter recedes. Moscow is a city of hidden charms, and whenever you least expect it, localities are enlivened by a fairytale church, or some glimpse into a private world.

Less metaphysically, there are several **minor hazards** to bear in mind. Traffic is unpredictable, and you can't take the surface underfoot for granted. Watch out for potholes, crevices, open storm drains and protruberant bits of metal. In winter, everything is covered with snow or ice, causing hundreds of Muscovites to slip and break their legs every week. With the spring thaw, beware of roofs shedding their layers of snow; where roof-clearing is in progress, the pavement below is "marked" as a danger zone by a plank laid across a pair of benches, or something similar.

Organized walking tours of Moscow are covered on p.32.

## Taxis

**Taxis** come in all shapes and sizes. The old **official taxis** are pale blue or yellow Volgas, with a checkered logo on the doors and a dome light on the roof, or a green light in the window, either of which will be lit up when the taxi is unoccupied. Official taxis are theoretically metered and accept payment in rubles, but meters are rarely used in practice, and foreigners are often asked to pay in dollars. It's best to negotiate the fare before getting in, to avoid unpleasant surprises. A useful phrase is *Kakáya u vas táksa?* (How much per unit?); you must then ascertain whether the "unit" means the charge per kilometre or per hour. See the box for details of taxi firms.

Nowadays, official vehicles are being squeezed out by **private taxis**. Generally Ladas or Fords, these are unmetered and their drivers will charge whatever they think they can get away with. As a foreigner, you will probably be expected to pay in hard currency; usually no less than $10, and often more. Rates are especially high at airports (see "Points of Arrival") and isolated hotels like the *Mezhdunarodnaya* (see box below), where business is monopolized by a taxi "mafia".

---

### Taxi companies

**Mariano** ☎ 927-0000 or 927-2108
*State-run firm open 24 hours. Small booking fee and fixed rate per kilometre. Only Russian spoken.*

**Metropol Hotel** ☎ 927-6972 (8am–11pm) or ☎ 927-6974 (11pm–8am)
*Has a 24-hour taxi service for guests and non-residents; the hourly rate depends on the model of car.*

**Mezhdunarodnaya Hotel**
*Go to the 24-hour taxi kiosk in the lobby (offering fixed rates) rather than approach the taxis waiting outside.*

**Pride** ☎ 451-0858
*Private agency with (supposedly) fixed rates, open 24 hours. You can ask for English-, French- or German-speaking drivers.*

Most Russians ignore both types of taxi in favour of **hitching rides in other vehicles**, especially after the public transport system closes down; you'll see people flagging down anything that moves, even ambulances or trucks. If the driver finds the destination acceptable, he'll state a price, which may or may not be negotiable; if not, wait for another car to come along. Sometimes no price is quoted and you just pay the driver the going rate on arrival. To give you an idea, Russians pay the equivalent of $3–5 to ride several kilometres, even late at night. Foreigners, however, are likely to be charged considerably more, unless their Russian is impeccable. If hitching with Russian friends, it's best not to speak until the deal has been concluded.

## Driving and car rental

**Traffic** in Moscow is heavy and many Russian drivers act like rally drivers, swerving at high speed to avoid potholes and tramlines, with a reckless disregard for pedestrians and other cars. Bear in mind also that many young men are likely to have purchased their licence rather than passed a test. **Driving**, therefore, requires a fair degree of skill and nerve.

To drive a car in Russia you are required to carry all the following **documents**: your home driving licence and an international driving permit (available from motoring organizations) with a Russian-language insert; an insurance certificate from your home insurer, and one from a Russian insurance company, such as *Ingosstrakh* (Pyatnitskaya ul. 12; ☎231-1677) or *Rosgosstrakh* (ul. Neglinnaya 23; ☎200-2995); your passport and visa; the vehicle registration certificate; and a customs document asserting that you'll take the car back home when you leave (unless, of course, you rented it in Moscow).

If you don't have an international permit and you're staying here a while, it's possible to get a **Russian driving licence** (which you must do as a resident) by taking your valid home licence plus two photos to *GlavUPDK* (Kievskaya ul. 8; ☎240-2092). Besides a road test, you will probably have to pass a written test and a simulation using model cars. Good luck.

### Rules of the road – and the GAI

Despite drivers' cavalier attitude to the *kírpich* (the red-slashed sign meaning "no entry") and an utter disregard for keeping in lane, other **rules of**

**the road** are generally observed. Traffic coming from the right has right of way – something that's particularly important to remember at roundabouts – while left-turns are (theoretically) only allowed in areas indicated by a broken centre line in the road and an overhead sign. If you are turning into a side street, pedestrians have right of way crossing the road. **Trams** have right of way at all times, and you are not allowed to overtake them when passengers are getting on and off, unless there is a safety island.

Unless otherwise specified, **speed limits** are 60km (37 miles) per hour in the city and 80km (50 miles) per hour on highways. It is illegal to drive after having consumed *any* **alcohol**; the rule is stringently enforced, with heavy fines for offenders. Safety-belt use is mandatory (though many Russians only drape the belt across their lap), and crash helmets are obligatory for motorcyclists.

Rules are enforced by the Citizens Automobile Inspectorate, or *GAI*, whose uniformed officers are empowered to stop vehicles and impose on-the-spot **fines** for real or imaginary violations. The *GAI* regards cars driven by foreigners as a

---

**Car repairs and parts**

**ABC Opel**, ul. Sergeya Eyzenshteyna 2; ☎181-0407.

**Autoshop Toyota**, pr. Marshala Zhukova 49/1; ☎199-5977.

**Avtodom**, ul. Zorge 17; ☎943-1001. *BMW and Michelin.*

**Bosch Auto Parts Store**, *Petrovskiy Passazh*, ul. Petrovka 10; Mon–Sat 9am–8pm.

**Diplomat Auto Service**, Kievskaya ul. 8; ☎249-9197. *US and German cars.*

**Express Motors**, Alyabana ul. 12; ☎198-0034. *American cars.*

**Nefto Agip**, Bolshoy Cherkasskiy per. 7, korpus D; ☎930-7973.

**Rosartson**, 2-ya Baumanskaya ul. 9/23, korpus 18; ☎265-7094. *Audi, VW, Porsche.*

**Service-Resource**, Aviamotornaya ul. 44; ☎273-1733. *Volvo.*

**Sovinteravtoservice**, Institutskiy per. 2/1; ☎299-7773, 299-5900. *The first number is for emergency breakdowns.*

**Spetzavtotsentr**, Kievskaya ul. 8; ☎240-2092, 240-4330.

**UVL Plus**, ul. Svobody 79; ☎496-5163. *Goodyear and Monarch tyres.*

prime source of income, so unless your Russian is fluent it's better not to argue, but simply concentrate on negotiating a lower fine. Officers may try to extract hard currency, but will probably settle for rubles in the end. Insisting on a receipt may persuade them to reduce their demand, on the tacit understanding that you then drop the matter.

Note that **driving in winter conditions** (between October and March) demands extra caution. To avoid spinning the wheels when there's snow on the ground, accelerate and decelerate smoothly. Changes in direction should not be made suddenly and you should always keep a good distance between your car and the one on front. If you hit a patch of ice, the braking distance is up to ten times longer than usual and steering is almost useless. In this situation, letting off the throttle and pumping the brakes on and off should slow you down. On no account ignore a **summons** to pull over (indicated by a wave of a baton), as Moscow's *GAI* have been known to shoot at motorists "trying to escape".

Although cars involved in **accidents** are legally obliged to wait until the *GAI* arrive, where minor damage has occurred drivers may agree to settle in cash on the spot, and scram before the cops appear. Unless you get a *správka* from the police or *GAI*, you'll lose the right to claim **insurance**. Russian insurers won't pay compensation if you are found to be driving under the influence of alcohol. An average of ninety **car thefts** a day occur in Moscow.

### Fuel and breakdowns

**Petrol** (*benzín*) is fairly easy to come by, but the decent stuff – 95 octane (3-star) or 98 octane (4-star) – is nearly as expensive as in the West. If you're driving a Russian car it's safe to use 93 or 92 octane, but 76 invites trouble (and will ruin Western cars). Selling watered-down fuel is a common scam, so to be sure of purity go to a filling station owned by a foreign company, and never buy from street tankers unless absolutely necessary. One of the few filling stations where you can be sure of getting **lead-free petrol** and high-octane fuel suitable for cars fitted with catalytic converters is *Nefto Agip* at Leningradskoe shosse 63 (☎457-2013), on the way to Sheremetevo Airport, which accepts credit cards. Poor-quality **diesel** is widely available.

If you **break down**, emergency help is difficult to get hold of. Your only hope is to call *Sovinteravto Service* on ☎299-7773, or phone ☎267-0113; the latter is a 24-hour tow-away service. Though some Western dealers now have branches in Moscow, **parts** and labour both cost more than you'd pay back home. However, low-priced Lada spares are universally available, and the charge for repairs is usually modest. See the box for addresses.

### Car rental

A growing number of car rental agencies offer Western models, with or without a driver. Hiring a **driver** actually deserves serious consideration; it could spare you a lot of anxiety, and may not cost a lot more than straightforward car rental. Most **rental agencies** prefer payment by credit card and require the full range of documentation for self-drive rental. Although it's worth comparing prices and conditions, most places tend to ask about $100 a day after you take all the hidden charges into account, so you might as well go for a well-known firm rather than an obscure one. Addresses are given in the box.

---

**Car rental**

**AVIS**, Sheremetevo-2 Airport; ☎280-3600.

**Budget Rent-a-Car**, Novoryazanskaya ul. 28; ☎262-2876.

**Europcar**, Novaya pl. 14; ☎923-9749. At Sheremetevo-2 ☎578-3878. Also at *Mezhdunarodnaya* (☎253-1369), *Novotel* (☎578-9407), *Olympic Penta* (☎971-6101) and *Pullman Iris* (☎488-8000) hotels.

**Hertz**, Leninskiy pr. 152; ☎434-5332. At Sheremetevo-2 ☎578-7532.

**InNis**, ul. Bolshaya Ordynka 32; ☎238-3077. *Nissan cars.*

**Intourist Car Rental**, *Kosmos Hotel*; ☎215-6191.

**Intourservice Car Rental**, *Rossiya Hotel*; ☎298-5853.

---

## Out from Moscow

The main reason for travelling **out from Moscow** is to visit outlying sights such as the Trinity Monastery of St Sergei or the Abramtsevo artists' colony, which are described in Chapter 10. Roughly half of them are accessible **by suburban train** (*prigorodniy poezda*, or *elektrichka*) from one of Moscow's mainline stations. Most of the stations have a separate ticket office (*prigorodniy kassa*) for suburban trains, which may depart from an annexe to the main building. To make it easier to buy tickets and check timetables, get someone to write out the name of your destination in Cyrillic. Fares are extremely cheap, as foreigners pay the same price as Russians do – unlike on long-distance and international trains. A few sites that are not accessible by train can be reached **by suburban bus** (*prigorodniy marshruty*) from an outlying depot near the end of a metro line. Fares are also low, but the bus is likely to be standing-room only for much of the way. Specific routes are detailed in Chapter 10.

Many tourists plan to travel **to St Petersburg by overnight train** (8hr). Of the dozen trains leaving Leningrad Station within an hour or so of midnight, five are fast and comfortable, namely trains #2, #4, #6, #10 and #36. The last is a commercial train, run by a private firm, which is notorious for **robberies** (particularly on the route back to Moscow). Even on the other trains, it's wise to insert a wedge into the flip-lock in the upper left corner of the door, and sleep with your valuables underneath you. Shortly after leaving Moscow, the sleeping-car attendant will come around dispensing sheets (for a surcharge), and offering tea to passengers in first class. After that, there's no legitimate reason to be disturbed, so thieves masquerading as officials can be ignored unless they're armed (you may also see genuine *OMON* guards, riding shotgun on the train).

The other popular journey is **to China**, on the Trans-Mongolian or Trans-Manchurian express from Yaroslavl Station. The former, Chinese-run train (#4) departs every Tuesday at 11.50pm; the latter, Russian train (#20) leaves on Friday at 8.25pm, with an additional service at the same time on Saturday from June to September. As the demand for seats can be heavy, and visas take time to arrange, it's wise to start the ball rolling as soon as possible. See p.13 for more about both routes, and tips for the journey.

## Buying tickets

**Buying tickets** for long-distance or international trains is rarely easy. Aside from being unsure which outlet currently handles bookings for their destination, **foreigners** are also subject to ever-changing rules, and charged twice as much for tickets as the natives are. All this makes it extremely tempting to use the *Travellers Guest*

*House* booking facility (see box), which frequently offers **discounts** on tickets to St Petersburg, China or Europe, and levies only a modest fee.

If you're determined to handle things yourself, the best place is generally the **Central Railway Agency**, *Intourtrans*, at ul. Griboedova 6/4, near Turgenevskaya and Chistye Prudy metro (Mon–Fri 9am–8pm, Sat & Sun 9am–7pm). The right-hand building handles **advance bookings** (up to ten days) for the Baltic States and all points within the CIS; go to windows #1 and #2 in the room to the right of the entrance. International sales are handled in the left-hand building, or by another *Intourtrans* branch at ul. Petrovka 15/13, near the Bolshoy Theatre – but you may find that both have few tickets to offer. The other source is the station from which the train departs, where you can book up to one month in advance. For tickets to Warsaw, visit window #9 of the office on Leningradskiy pr., just past Belarus Station; for Mongolia and China, windows #5–8 on the first floor of Krasnoprudnaya ul. 1, next to Yaroslav Station; both are open daily 8am–1pm & 2–7pm. For Helsinki, you need to go to window #35 (daily 8am–1pm & 2–4pm) on the first floor of Leningrad Station, while tickets for St Petersburg and Tallinn are sold at windows #19–21 of the *Intourist* section, on the floor above. All these offices also sell **same-day tickets**. Always bring your passport along when buying tickets.

---

**Ticket agencies**

**Intourtrans**
ul. Petrovka 15/13, 1st floor, ☎927-1181; and ul. Griboedova 6/4.
*The first handles international train tickets and domestic Aeroflot bookings, the second train tickets for travel inside Russia.*

**Mostransavto**
Tsvetnoy bulvar 21, 2nd floor, room 11; ☎200-6060.
*Tickets for twice-weekly buses to Helsinki, leaving from outside. Ten percent discount for students.*

**Travellers Guest House**
Bolshaya Pereyaslavskaya ul. 50, 10th floor; ☎971-4059.
*Tickets for St Petersburg, Europe and the Trans-Siberian routes, often at a discount.*

---

# Information, Maps and Addresses

The collapse of the old state tourist monopoly, *Intourist*, has resulted in a fragmentation of tourist services in Russia and abroad, which is good news in some respects, but hasn't made it any easier to ask questions on the spot. However, you can now obtain a mass of publications that supply much of the information tourists might need.

## Information and tours

Amazingly, Moscow has no centralized **tourist information centre** where you can walk in and get a map, or an answer to any question. The main *Intourist* office at Mokhovaya ul. 13, near the corner of Tverskaya ul., seems better at hiding from tourists than helping them (daily 9am–8am; ☎292-2365, 292-1278; fax: 200-143). Enter the door on the left behind the faded signboard and turn right inside. When you reach the seated guard turn left and head on to the far end, through another door with a brochure stuck to it. Inside are desks for car rental, currency exchange, theatre bookings and other services (including guides for $15 an hour). However, nobody seems able to supply information about anything else, or a map of Moscow.

Instead, most travellers use the information/service desks at downtown **hotels** like the *Intourist* or *Metropol*, which are usually willing to help out even if you're not staying there, though they're not so good on more unusual requests such as where to get a vegetarian meal. If you decide to use any of their booking services, however, you can expect to pay handsomely for the privilege.

The best source for details of what's on in Moscow are the local **English-language free newspapers**, the *Moscow Times* and the *Moscow Tribune* (see p.42). Other publications aimed at tourists are the colour *Moscow Guide* ($5), published quarterly (or less often) by the *Moscow Times*; the glossier bimonthly *Moscow Magazine* ($5); a poorly edited but quaint Russian-produced colour monthly, *Time Out in Moscow* ($2, but usually given away); and the free *What & Where in Moscow*, which simply lists upmarket shops and restaurants.

Don't confuse this last publication with *Where In Moscow* ($13.50), an annually updated cross between an *A–Z* and *Yellow Pages* that's ideal for long-term residents but less use to tourists – except for its city map, which is easier to handle than the fold-out version (see below). Most of the information in the book is available for free in the *Moscow Business Telephone Guide*, a tabloid **directory** that's widely distributed and updated every month – an important consideration given the pace of change in Moscow.

However, the best source of information and help is **Russian friends** and acquaintances, who are usually generous with both. Most Muscovites know their city well, and the grapevine is highly efficient.

## Guided tours

If you don't speak Russian and you find Moscow a bit daunting, **guided tours** can make things a lot easier. As in Soviet times, *Intourist* runs daily sightseeing tours of the city ($10), the Kremlin and the Armoury Museum ($20) or the State Diamond Fund ($25) every day except Thursday;

and tours of the Pushkin Museum of Fine Arts or the Tretyakov Gallery once or twice a week ($10) – all museum tickets are included in the prices. Their tours are well-run but rather impersonal, with large groups and prosaic commentary.

A wider, more offbeat programme is offered by the US–Russian firm **Patriarchi Dom** (☎255-4515), which organizes walking tours of the Kitay-gorod; "orientation" trips to markets; visits to monasteries, literary shrines and even the *McDonald's* factory; cookery lessons and other activities. You'll find leaflets detailing their current schedule in the *Garden Ring Supermarket* near Mayakovskaya metro. As each tour occurs only once or twice a month, people on a short visit to Moscow may be disappointed. Phone to verify the departure point (often Bolshoy Devyatinskiy per., along the south side of the US Embassy) and register. Tours cost $8-12 per person, excluding admission tickets.

*Patriarchi Dom* also runs **out-of-town excursions** ($15-20) to the Trinity Monastery of St Sergei, Tchaikovsky's home and other places

covered in Chapter 10 of this book – plus longer day trips to the "Golden Ring" towns of Vladimir and Suzdal ($40). Although *Intourist*'s excursions to the Trinity Monastery (Fri) and Vladimir and Suzdal (Sun) cost $20 more, they have the advantage of running every week.

If you *can* understand Russian, there's a large choice of **Russian-language tours** for rubles, ranging from a whiz around the Kremlin for the equivalent of $1 (offered by touts on Red Square) to serious literary, historical and architectural walking tours ($3-8) run by the **Moscow Excursion Bureau**, at ul. Rozhdestvenka 5, behind *Detskiy Mir* (daily 10am–2pm & 3–6pm; ☎923-8953), which also has reasonably priced day excursions to Vladimir and Suzdal. A smaller branch of the bureau is located in the *Intourist Hotel*.

Other agencies offer **personal tours and excursions** for large sums of hard currency. The **Intourservice Central Excursion Bureau** at ul. Belinskovo 4a, around the corner from the *Intourist Hotel* (daily 9am–6pm; ☎203-8016,

---

## UK, North American & Australian map outlets

### UK

*Daunt Books*, 83 Marylebone High St, London W1; ☎0171/224 2295.

*National Map Centre*, 22–24 Caxton St, London SW1; ☎0171/222 4945.

*Stanfords*, 12–14 Long Acre, London WC2; ☎0171/836 1321; mail or phone order also available.

*The Travel Bookshop*, 13–15 Blenheim Crescent, London W11 2EE; ☎0171/229 5260.

*The Travellers' Bookshop*, 25 Cecil Court, London WC2; ☎0171/836 9132.

*Thomas Nelson and Sons Ltd*, 51 York Place, Edinburgh EH1 3JD; ☎0131/557 3011.

*John Smith and Sons*, 57–61 St Vincent St, Glasgow; ☎0141/221 7472.

### US

*The Complete Traveler Bookstore*, 199 Madison Ave, New York, NY 10016; ☎212/685-9007.

*Rand McNally*, 150 East 52nd St, New York, NY 10022; ☎212/758-7488. Has branches all over the US; call ☎800/333-0136 (ext. 2111) for the address of your nearest store or for mail order maps.

*Traveler's Bookstore*, 22 W 52nd St, New York, NY 10019; ☎212/664-0995.

*The Complete Traveler Bookstore*, 3207 Filmore St, San Francisco, CA 92123; ☎415/923-1511.

*Pacific Traveler Supply*, 529 State St, Santa Barbara, CA 93101; ☎ 805/963-4438 (phone orders: ☎805/965-4402).

*Elliot Bay Book Company*, 101 S Main St, Seattle, WA 98104; ☎206/624-6600.

### Canada

*Open Air Books and Maps*, 25 Toronto St, Toronto M5R 2C1; ☎416/363-0719.

*World Wide Books and Maps*, 736A Granville St, Vancouver V6Z 1G3; ☎604/687-3320.

### Australia

*The Map Shop*, 16a Peel St, Adelaide, SA 5000; ☎08/231 2033.

*Hema*, 239 George St, Brisbane, QLD 4000; ☎07/221 4330.

*Bowyangs*, 372 Little Bourke St, Melbourne, VIC 3000; ☎03/670 4383.

*Travel Bookshop*, 20 Bridge St, Sydney, NSW 2000; ☎02/241 3554.

*Perth Map Centre*, 891 Hay St, Perth, WA 6000; ☎09/322 5733.

203-8271; fax: 200-1243), can arrange virtually anything – including a visit to the former KGB Museum (see p.135). Other firms include *Moscow Tours Limited*, Bolshoy Stariy Danilovskiy per. 5, #535a (☎954-0431), and *Novoye Vremya*, Avtozavodskaya ul. 17, korpus 1 (☎274-4694).

## Maps

The **maps** in this book should be fine for most purposes, but it's worthwhile investing in a detailed street plan of Moscow, especially if you're staying outside the centre. The most commonly found map in the West is a fold-out 1:15,000 plan by *Geocenter International*, which is clearly drawn and fairly up to date, but stops short of the Sparrow Hills and the VDNKh, and uses a weird transliteration system. Its main rival is the *New Moscow City Map and Guide*, which comes in fold-out or laminated wall-chart form, and appears in *Where in Moscow* (see above). This covers a larger area than the *Geocenter* map and marks restaurants, airlines and shops as well.

In Moscow, both maps are available for about $7 at Sheremetevo-2 airport, the *Travellers Guest House* (p.30) and *Zwemmer's* bookshop (p.326), while a variety of locally produced maps are sold in the underpass leading from Okhotniy Ryad metro to Red Square, and along Tverskaya ul. and the Arbat. The ones in Cyrillic are usually cheaper, the transliterated ones dearer and more up to date. Any map printed before 1992 will feature numerous street names that have since been changed (see "Addresses", below).

At the time of writing, there is no reliable map covering **transport routes**, although you may well see old editions of the Cyrillic *Moskva Skhema Passazhirskovo Transporta*, which comes in a folder with a poster-sized map and a booklet detailing all the routes. Although the most recent edition (published in 1985) is still accurate in many respects, there's no way of knowing when it's not. In any case, it's seldom that you'll need to use any other form of transport than the metro, for which our map should be more than adequate; there are also maps posted in stations and sold on the streets.

## Addresses

The street name is always written before the number in **addresses**. When addressing letters, Russians start with the country, followed by a six-digit postal code, then the street, house and apartment number, and finally the addressee's name; the sender's details are usually written on the bottom of the envelope. The number of the house, block or complex may be preceded by *dom*, abbreviated to *d*. Two numbers separated by an oblique dash (for example, 16/21) usually indicates a corner, the second number being the address on the smaller side street. However, buildings encompassing more than one number are also written like this (for example, 4/6); you can tell when this is the case as the numbers will be close to each other and both even or both odd. *Korpus* or *k*. indicates a building within a complex; *podezd* (abbreviated to *pod*.) an entrance number, *etazh* (*et*.) the floor and *kvartira* (*kv*.) the apartment.

**Floors** are numbered in the American or continental fashion: the ground floor is known as the first floor (*etazh 1*) – a usage followed in this book to avoid confusion. In residential buildings, the **lift** may be located on a landing up the stairs from the entrance, and the outer door may be locked by a device that requires you to punch in a code. **Door codes** usually have three digits; you have to push all three buttons simultaneously to make it work.

The main **abbreviations** used in Moscow (and in this book) are: ul. (for *ulitsa*, street); nab. (for *naberezhnaya*, embankment); pr. (for *prospekt*, avenue); per. (for *pereulok*, lane) and pl. (for *ploshchad*, square). Other **terms** include *most* (bridge), *bulvar* (boulevard), *shosse* (highway), *alleya* (alley) and *sad* (garden).

Since mid-1992 many **street names** have officially reverted to their former (mostly pre-Revolutionary) titles, though you'll still hear the

| Cyrillic address terms | |
|---|---|
| alleya | аллея |
| bulvar | бульвар |
| dom | дом |
| etazh | Этаж |
| kvartira | квартира |
| most | мост |
| naberezhnaya | набережная |
| pereulok | переулок |
| ploshchad | площадь |
| prospekt | проспект |
| sad | сад |
| shosse | шоссе |
| ulitsa | улица |

old Soviet names used in everyday speech. In this book, streets are referred to by their "correct" name at the time of going to press, but further changes are likely. Don't be surprised by the occasional difference between the names in this book and those you see.

One final oddity is that some names are preceded by an **ordinal number**, for example: 2-y Kadashevskiy per. 1-ya or 1-y (pronounced *pérvaya* or *pérviy*) mean "1st"; 2-ya or 2-y (*vtóraya* or *vtóriy*) "2nd", and so on. This usually applies to a series of parallel lanes or side streets.

# Costs, Money and Banks

Since early 1992, the Russian ruble has been in freefall; the end of 1994 saw it lose forty percent of its value in two weeks. This has intensified the dual economy that was a feature of Soviet life, dividing the population into those with access to hard currency (*valyúta*) that provides a hedge against inflation, and those stuck with rubles. As Moscow is flooded with imported goods that cost as much or more than in the West, there's obviously a lot of wealth here, as well as poverty.

Indeed, foreigners are often shocked to find themselves priced out of the market: a recent business survey rated Moscow as the third most expensive city in the world, after Tokyo and Paris. Of course, it needn't be so costly if you adopt a lifestyle nearer to that of ordinary Russians, but even then it's hard to avoid the two-tier pricing system that exists for museum entrance charges, whereby foreigners are charged up to ten times what locals pay.

Because of soaring inflation, most of the **prices** in this book have been given in US$, as a

fairly stable measure of **costs** in real terms – but in practice they're usually charged and paid in rubles. You'll find more details about the cost of accommodation, eating out and nightlife in the relevant sections of this book: see Chapter 11, "Accommodation", Chapter 12, "Eating and Drinking", Chapter 13, "Nightlife", and Chapter 14, "The Arts". However, it is possible to make some general comments here about how much you're likely to spend.

**Package tourists** with pre-paid accommodation including full- or half-board really only need money for tickets to museums or clubs, buying drinks and grabbing the odd snack. Unless you go overboard in expensive places, $36/£20 a day should suffice. **Independent travellers** can easily spend a lot more than this, since hotels charge between $40 and 70 (£25–45) a night, even at the budget end of the market. However, there is an excellent cheap hostel, and relatively inexpensive private accommodation is available, too.

If you stay in a hotel, though, and frequent only upmarket bars and restaurants, you'll be lucky to get by on less than you would spend in a major European or American city, say $110/£60 a day or more. Alternatively, if you stay with a family and do what the Russians do, you could spend less than $50/£30 a day on the whole works – lodging, food and drink.

## Money

The official **currency** in Russia is the **ruble**. There's a bewildering variety of denominations in circulation: 1, 5, 10, 50 and 100 ruble **coins** (stamped with the Russian eagle) and **notes** to the value of 100, 200, 500, 1000, 5000, 10,000 and 50,000 rubles. Higher denominations may be introduced in the future. Beware that any notes printed before 1993 and bearing Lenin's head are worthless, except in the breakaway People's Republic of Transdneistria, formerly part of the Soviet Republic of Moldavia and a long way from Moscow.

**Counterfeiting** is a major problem in Russia, where the value of fake notes in circulation has been estimated at $200 million. Shops and currency exchanges therefore err on the side of caution, which makes it hard to change foreign banknotes that are worn or scribbled upon. **Pre-1989 dollar bills** are widely rejected in Moscow, so be sure to get recent notes if you buy dollars before leaving home, and avoid being palmed off with dubious ones in Russia. Another, bizarre hazard of Moscow's money world is **radioactive rubles**. A minority of 10,000 and 50,000 ruble notes are marked with radioactive isotopes that can cause skin irritations if you carry them around for a few days.

In January 1994, it was decreed that all **cash transactions** in Russia must be carried out in rubles, and the use of foreign money was banned. At the many stores and agencies that still price their goods or services in dollars (or Deutschmarks), you have to pay in rubles at a rate of exchange set by the management, usually to the customer's disadvantage. If it's way out of line with the bank rate, and they accept credit cards, you'll save money by paying **by credit card** instead. But as many places still don't take plastic, you must either go armed with large sums of rubles or be sure that you have access to an exchange point (which isn't so easy after 6pm).

If you've got an ear for the language and enjoy haggling, using Russian **slang** can help. In markets, a single item is often referred to as a *shtúka* (thing), which is also the slang term for 1000 rubles – so shoppers can protest: *Shtúka za shtúku? Vy s umá soshlí?* ("A thousand apiece? Are you crazy?"). Larger sums are likened to fruit – a *millión* rubles is a *limon* (lemon), and a billion (or *miliárd*) an *árbus* (watermelon) – while dollars are called *báksy* or *báksov* (from "bucks").

### The exchange rate

As the **exchange rate** (*kúrs*) is now set by market forces and the black market offers nothing but risks, there's no reason to change money anywhere other than in an official bank or **currency exchange** (*obmén valyúty* in Russian). These are to be found all over town, including inside shops and restaurants (they usually stay open the same hours as the shop or restaurant). Most **banks** charge a maximum of a few hundred rubles commission, if anything at all. Exchange rates vary slightly, but with a rate of roughly 4000 rubles to the dollar at the time of writing, twenty rubles a dollar difference is negligible, unless you're changing thousands of dollars.

**Surplus rubles** can be converted back into hard currency at most banks, for which you'll need your passport and currency declaration. Better, though, to spend your rubles before you go, or give them away to elderly or crippled beggars.

### Currency declaration

All foreigners entering Russia must fill in a **currency declaration** form stating exactly how much money they are bringing into the country. Forms are often handed out on the plane shortly before landing, and can be obtained at Sheremetevo-2 airport or any border crossing. You'll also need to list valuables such as personal stereos, gold jewellery, video cameras or laptop computers. The form will be stamped at customs.

When **leaving the country**, you must fill in a duplicate form stating how much currency you are taking out of Russia, the aim being to prevent you taking more out than you brought in. This is a hangover from the old days, but since you can now take out up to $500 without a declaration, if you happen to lose your incoming declaration you can usually get away with it.

## Travellers' cheques and credit cards

Although you'll find it useful to bring one or two hundred dollars in cash (low-denomination bills are best), it's safest to carry the bulk of your funds in **travellers' cheques** (TCs), preferably in a money-belt. US dollar cheques are universally acceptable, and you should encounter few problems with Deutschmarks or sterling. That said, the only brand of TCs that can be replaced if lost or stolen in Moscow is **American Express**, whose office (☎956-9000) on the Garden Ring is ten minutes' walk from Mayakovskaya metro. If you can't get through during office hours, call their 24-hour international refund hotline for holders

## Banks and exchange

### American Express

Sadovaya-Kudrinskaya ul. 21a; ☎956-9000; fax: 253-9372. Mon–Fri 9am–5pm, Sat 9am–1pm.

*Charges 1 percent on the sale of TCs; 5–10 percent to cash TCs into any hard currency; and 4 percent on cash advances on Amex cards. Will hold mail for users of Amex cards or TCs.*

### Consantrade

ul. Nemirovicha-Danchenka 3, office #310 (☎292-9930), and Bolshoy Savvinskiy per. 5 (☎248-1901).

*Exchanges worn or spoilt hard currency for 20 percent commission.*

### Credobank

In the *Mezhdunarodnaya Hotel* (24hr; ☎252-6481) and the Manège (daily 9.30am–7pm; ☎202-4836, 202-8556).

*Accepts TCs and international money orders in all major currencies, and gives cash advances on Visa cards for 4 percent commission.*

### DialogBank

In the *Radisson Slavyanskaya Hotel*; ☎941-8434, 941-8020. Daily 8am–1pm & 2–8pm.

*Charges 5 percent on TCs, Eurocheques and Mastercard, and 3 percent on Amex cash advances (backed by a cheque) or wire transfers.*

### Inkombank

Sadovaya-Triumfalnaya ul. 14/12 (daily 9am–4pm); Telegrafniy per. 12/8 (daily 9am–4pm; ☎923-3810); and in the *Belgrad* (daily 10am–7pm; ☎248-1628), *Olympic Penta* (daily 9am–8pm; ☎235-9003 ext. 2660) and *Pullman-Iris* (☎488-8102) hotels.

*Charges 2 percent on Visa, Amex and Thomas Cook TCs, and 5 percent on Visa cash advances.*

### Sberbank

Branches all over Moscow.

*Cashes Visa, Amex and Thomas Cook TCs, and all hard currencies.*

### Stolichniy Bank

In *GUM*, on the first floor of the 2nd gallery (line)(Mon–Sat 8am–7pm).

*Accepts most hard currencies.*

### Western Union

Branches in *Inkombank* at Sadovaya-Triumfalnaya ul. 14/12 and Telegrafniy per. 12/8; *Vostok Bank* at ul. Marksa–Engelsa 5, and other locations (☎119-8250 for details). Mon–Fri 9am–4pm.

*Accepts wire transfers from WU outlets worldwide.*

of *Amex* TCs (☎8 10 44/800 521313) or credit cards (☎8 10 44/1273 696933). Replacing either will take up to a week.

*Amex* will cash TCs into dollars, DM or sterling, but it's worth changing them into rubles somewhere else, as they offer a lousy rate of exchange. You can also use your *Amex* card to obtain cash advances of up to $500 (backed by a personal cheque), or use it to draw smaller amounts from the ATM machine in the lobby, if you have registered a PIN for your card. There is another *Amex* cash dispenser in the lobby of the *Mezhdunarodnaya Hotel*, which functions 24 hours.

Travellers' cheques are accepted by most hotels but few exchange bureaux, so it's best to cash them at a bank, although you may find that not all banks will do this. The pamphlet *Moscow Express Directory*, available free from most big hotels and updated fortnightly, gives the addresses of those that do, as well as places that sell TCs.

**Credit cards** are now more widely accepted in restaurants and shops, but unless you're certain they are taken it's wise to carry enough rubles. Many places take only one or two types of card – mostly *Visa*, *Mastercard/Access* or *Amex* (in that order). You will usually need to show your passport or some other form of identification when paying by credit card. Always make sure that the transaction is properly recorded, keep the receipt and verify that the carbons are destroyed. Aside from *Amex* (see above), the local emergency numbers for reporting **lost or stolen** cards are: *Diner's Club* ☎284-4873; *Mastercard/Access* ☎284-4794; *Visa* ☎284-4802.

Holder of *Visa* or *Amex* cards can obtain **cash advances** (in dollars or rubles) at several venues, notably *DialogBank* and *Credobank* (see box above). Alternatively, you can use the ATM machines that now exist on Tverskaya ul. (opposite the *Intourist Hotel*), in the 24-hour supermarket at ul. Noviy Arbat 48, and in Sheremetevo-2 Airport. These accept *Eurocard*, *Mastercard* and bankcards on the Cirrus network, and pay out in dollars or rubles.

The quickest method of **transferring money from abroad** is by wire transfer from a **Western**

Union (WU) office outside Russia (most American and major European cities have one). The money should be available within minutes at whichever WU branch in Moscow has been specified. (For a current list, phone ☎119-8250.) There's no limit on the amount that can be transferred, but the commission at the sending end decreases proportionally the more you send. Another way is through **DialogBank**, which won't, however, transfer amounts less than $1000. The money is wired to *DialogBank*'s New York account, with details of the recipient's full name and passport number; the cash can be picked up in Moscow two to three working days after the wire arrives in New York.

| | |
|---|---|
| currency exchange | обмен валюта |
| convertible currency | СКВ |
| buying rate | передажа |
| selling rate | перекупка |
| exchange rate | курс |

## Changing money

When **changing money** in Russia, it's wise to exercise caution. You will need wads of rubles if you're going to eat out, although taxi drivers may accept dollars. However, changing money is now so easy that it is perfectly feasible to do it every day, thus avoiding the necessity of carrying around huge bundles of notes. You'll need your passport if you're changing travellers' cheques or getting a cash advance on your credit card, but not for changing notes.

In addition to the banks detailed in the box and the hundreds of exchange bureaux dotted around the city, most hotels have a currency exchange point, as do all large shops and a number of restaurants. So, if you change as much as you think you need each morning, be aware that there will be no problem changing later in the day if you need a top-up. The only time you should ever change unofficially is with friends, having first checked the rate in a bank and making sure that you are both happy with the deal. Otherwise stick to official changing points.

# Health Matters

Following recent health scares, visitors to Moscow and other cities in western Russia are advised to get booster-shots for diphtheria, tetanus and polio, but it's unnecessary to be inoculated against typhoid and hepatitis A unless you're planning to visit remote rural areas. Though fears of malaria in Moscow have proved groundless, it's a good idea to pack some mosquito repellent anyway. However, the most likely hazard is an upset stomach, caused by the food or water. To play safe, wash fresh fruit and vegetables in boiled water; be suspicious of dairy products in summer; and watch out for bootleg liquor (see p.303).

## Specific problems: pollution, dirt and stress

Moscow's **water** supply is obtained from four reservoirs outside the city rather than the polluted Moskva River, but even so few Muscovites will drink tap water unless it has been boiled first. It is regarded with particular suspicion in the spring, when the melting snow cover is believed to cause manure and other pollutants to enter the reservoirs. To play safe, use only bottled water for drinking and cleaning your teeth, or tap water that has been boiled for fifteen minutes and then allowed to stand overnight.

While the authorities maintain that the concentrations of heavy metals, nitrates, phenol, ammonia and other chemicals in the water

## Ambulances

Public ambulances (☎03) leave much to be desired. Two reliable **fee-paying services** are *Ambulance Ltd* (☎924-6472) and *VYEK* (☎350-0131, 200-5851).

*For tracing people in public hospitals, phone ☎928-9572 or 208-9157.*

## Contact lenses and sundries

**Optic Moscow**, ul. Arbat 30, korpus 2; ☎241-1577. *Mon–Sat 10am–7pm.*

**Optika**, ul. Kuztnetskiy most 4; ☎292-0573. *Mon–Sat 9am–7pm.*

## Medical and dental care

**Adventist Health Centre**, pr. 60-Letiya Oktyabrya; ☎126-7906. *Physiotherapy. Mon–Thurs 9am–5.30pm, Fri 9am–1pm.*

**American Medical Center (AMC)**, Shmitovskiy proezd 3; ☎256-8212, 256-3366; fax: 973-2142. *Almost Western-style care at very high prices; OK if you're insured. Annual/monthly membership $250/50 (10 percent less for students). Pharmacy. Mon–Fri 8am–8pm, Sat 9am–4pm, Sun 9am–1pm. 24-hour emergency access for members.*

**Athens Medical Center**, Michurinskiy pr. 6; ☎143-2387, 143-2503. *Private clinic with a 24-hour emergency service and a well-equipped ambulance. As expensive as the AMC.*

**Beiker Dental Clinic**, ul. Kuznetskiy most 9/10; ☎923-5322. *Russo-German joint venture. Mon–Fri 8am–6pm.*

**British Embassy Doctor**, Sofiyskaya nab. 14; ☎231-8511.

**Diplomatic Policlinic**, 4-y Dobryninskiy pe. 4; ☎237-8338. *Once exclusive clinic that now admits anyone who can afford it. Also has a pharmacy.*

**Delta Consulting Medical**, Berezhkovskaya nab. 12; ☎245-9999. *24-hour medical evacuation service.*

**Euromedical Emergency Service**; ☎432-1616. *Another 24-hour medivac service.*

**European Medical Centre**, Gruzinskiy per. 3, korpus 2; ☎253-0703, 229-6536; near Belorusskaya metro. *French joint-venture offering walk-in medical care. Consultation $80 (students $64); injection $10. Pharmacy. Mon–Fri 9.30am–6.30pm.*

**French Embassy Doctor**, ul. Bolshaya Yakimanka 45; ☎237-4655.

**Intermedservice**, *Intourist Hotel* rooms 2030–2031, Tverskaya ul. 3/5; ☎203-8631. *Russo-Swiss medical and dental clinic. Mon–Fri 9am–8pm.*

**Moscow International Medical Center**, ul. Obukha 14; ☎297-1848.

**Mosta Clinic**, Bolshoy Cherkasskiy per. 15, 2nd floor; ☎927-0765. *Dental care. Mon–Fri 10am–5pm.*

**SANA**, Nizhnaya Pervomayskaya ul. 65; ☎464-1254. *Russo-French clinic with a pharmacy, offering inpatient care at the nearby Republican Hospital. Tues–Sat 10am–9pm, Sun 10am–5pm.*

**Tourist's Clinic**, Gruzinskiy proezd 2; ☎254-4396. *Medical and dental care.*

**The Dental Clinic**, *Pullman Iris Hotel*, Korvinskoe shosse 10; ☎488-8279. *Daily 10am–5pm.*

**US Embassy Medical Clinic**, Novinskiy bulvar 19/23; ☎252-2451.

## Pharmacies

*Besides the following, there are pharmacies in the American and European Medical Centres, the Diplomatic Policlinic, and the SANA (see above).*

**Apteka**, *Detskiy Mir* 4th floor, Lubyanskaya pl. *Daily 8.30am–8pm.*

**Eczacibasi Drug Store**, ul. Maroseyka 2/15; ☎928-9189. *Mon–Sat 9am–7pm.*

**Interoko Drug Store**, *Petrovskiy Passazh* 2nd floor, ul. Petrovka 10; ☎292-3451. *Mon–Sat 9am–8pm.*

**Pharmacon**, ul. Tverskaya 2/4; ☎292-0843. *There's also a 24-hour dispensing outlet next door.*

**Pharmacy Rossiskaya**, ul. Noviy Arbat 31; ☎205-2135. *Mon–Fri 8am–8pm, Sat 10am–6pm.*

**Stariy Arbat**, ul. Arbat 25; ☎291-7101. *Mon–Sat 10am–8pm.*

**The Medicine Man**, ul. Chernyakhovskovo 4; ☎155-7080, 155-8788.

**VITA**, Poklonnaya ul. 6; ☎249-7818. *Open 24 hours.*

supply are well below the limits set by the World Health Organization, **air pollution** is acknowledged as a serious problem. In many areas of Moscow, the level is thirty to fifty times above WHO limits – or even higher. Though brief exposure shouldn't do you any harm, visitors may feel inexplicably tired after a day or two, while long-term residents can suffer from apathy and skin complaints as a result.

The commonest visitor's ailment is **diarrhoea**, caused by spoilt food or poor hygiene. While restaurants and cafés are generally safe, street food and cheap self-service canteens are best avoided. On the streets, however, it's hard to escape from **dirt**, as practically every surface is covered with dust, mud or grime, according to the season. Always wash your hands before eating or preparing food, and don't use the reusable towels in restaurants or public toilets.

Anyone staying in Moscow for several months or longer should beware of **other, subtler malaises**. As winter lasts up to six months, you can easily get run-down owing to a lack of vitamins, and depressed by the darkness and ice. According to a survey of Moscow's expat community, the chief problems are alcoholism, nervous breakdowns and sexually transmitted diseases. A lot of this stems from the **stress** of living in an exhilarating, brutal and bewildering city, where foreigners can take little for granted. If you're going to be here a while, pace yourself and adapt to the rhythms of Russian life. Because Moscow is, as Russians say, "without limits", you must determine your own in order to stay sane here.

## Pharmacies, doctors and hospitals

For minor complaints, it's easiest to go to a high-street **pharmacy** (*aptéka*), many of which now have a fair selection of Western drugs; the outlets with the widest range are listed in the box opposite. It goes without saying, however, that if you are on any prescribed medication, you should bring enough supplies for your stay. This is particularly true for diabetics, who should ensure that they have enough needles.

The standard of **doctors** varies enormously, so seek recommendations before consulting one. Many Russians distrust doctors in general, preferring to treat themselves with herbal or vodka-based remedies, often taken in conjunction with a visit to the *banya* or bathhouse. If neither can help, or your condition is serious, public **hospitals** will provide free emergency treatment to foreigners on production of a passport (but may charge for medication). However, standards of hygiene and expertise are low by Western standards and horror stories abound.

Aside from routine shortages of anaesthetics and drugs, nurses are usually indifferent to their patients unless bribed to care for them properly. Anyone found to be **HIV-positive** or carrying an **infectious disease** like hepatitis risks being confined in a locked isolation ward and treated like a subhuman. If you suspect such a condition and need to see a doctor, go to your embassy instead – or leave Russia at once.

Consequently, foreigners tend to rely on **special private clinics** with imported drugs and equipment, which charge American rates – a powerful reason to take out insurance. Alternatively, you could try contacting your **embassy**, which will have a staff doctor; it's essential to make an appointment during office hours, and the treatment isn't cheap, either. Expect to pay $100 at the very least.

# Post, Phones and the Media

Communications in Moscow have greatly improved in recent years, but still can't be taken for granted. Likewise, the media is freer than it ever was in Soviet or Tsarist times, but can't afford to be complacent in the face of constant attempts to reimpose state control by stealth.

## Post

The Russian postal system is notoriously inefficient. Incoming **international mail** takes up to three weeks to arrive, while the outbound service is even less reliable. As a result, most Russians entrust letters with someone travelling to the West, for safer postage there, or employ an international courier firm, or resort to using a fax (see below).

Assuming you decide to risk the postal system, all district post offices have **post restante** (*do vostrébovania*) sections, while *American Express* at Sadovaya-Kudrinskaya ul. 21a, 103001, will hold mail for *Amex* card or travellers' cheque holders for up to two months.

Owing to its convenient location only a few blocks from the Kremlin, many visitors use the *poste restante* (Mon–Fri 8am–2pm & 3–9pm, Sat 8am–2pm & 3–7pm, Sun 9am–2pm & 3–7pm) in the **Central Telegraph Office** (*tsentrálniy telegráf*) at Tverskaya ul. 7, 103009 (☎924-9004; fax: 292-6511), or the **Intourist Hotel Post Office** (Mon–Fri 9am–1pm & 2–5pm, Sat 9am–1pm &

2–4pm) just down the road at Tverskaya ul. 3/5, rather than the **Main Post Office** (*glávniy póchtamt*) at Myasnitskaya ul. 26/2, 101000 (Mon–Fri 8am–8pm, Sat 8am–7pm, Sun 9am–7pm; ☎928-6311; fax: 924 7503), near Chistye Prudy metro. The **International Post Office** at Varshavskoe shosse 37 (☎114-4584) is even further out, so seldom used by visitors.

**Parcels** must be taken to one of these offices unwrapped; there they'll be inspected and wrapped for you, whereupon you can send them from any post office, or by a courier (see below). If you only want **stamps**, it's easier to go to the postal counters in hotels like the *Intourist* or *Moskva*, rather than queue in a post office, though there's a mark-up on the price. For a **fast delivery service**, you can use the **EMS Garantpost** in the Main Post Office or the House of Communications (see "Phones"). Though advertised to arrive within 72 hours, delivery is likelier to take four to seven days, and costs the ruble equivalent of $25 a letter.

If that seems pricey, wait until you hear the rates charged by international **courier services**. *DHL Worldwide Express*, at per. Chernyshevskovo 3 (Mon–Fri 8am–5pm; ☎956-1000; fax: 971 2219), has pick-up offices in the *Olympic Penta Hotel* (☎971-6101); the Press Centre in the *Radisson Slavyanskaya Hotel* (☎941-8621); and room 902 of *Mezhdunarodnaya Hotel* (☎253-1194). Other firms offer **subscribers** a twice-weekly courier service to London (*PX Post*, ul.

| Signs | |
|---|---|
| Communications centre | Переговорный пункт |
| Fax | Факс |
| Inter-city telephone | Междугородный телефон |
| International telephone | Международный телефон |
| Local telephone | Таксофон шк телефон |
| Post office | Почта |
| Poste restante | До Востребования |

Kusinena 9, room #26; ☎956-2230; fax: 956 2231) or New York (*Post International*, in the *Novoe Vremya* building on Pushkinskaya pl.; Mon–Fri 8am–8pm; ☎209-3118).

## Phones

Virtually all public **phones** (*taksofóny*) in Moscow now take brown plastic tokens (*zhetony*) – though you might still find the occasional old-style phone, taking 1-ruble coins (no longer legal tender, but still valued for making calls). The *zheton*, which are purchasable at most metro stations, must be placed in the slot before dialling; when your call connects, it will drop. A series of beeps indicates that the money is about to run out. The chances of getting a wrong number or being cut off are quite high. Ordinary public phones can only be used for **local calls**, and the few inter-city pay-phones (*mezhdugoródniy telefón*) that exist usually require special tokens that are impossible to find.

The various ways of making **inter-city** or **international calls** are covered here in ascending order of cost. If you are lucky enough to have access to a **private phone**, it is nowadays possible to call just about anywhere direct (see box for codes), and considerably cheaper than booking calls through the **international operator** (☎8-194 or 8-196 on a private phone; ☎333-4101 from a hotel). If you do go through the operator, specify *po anglískiy* when they answer and you should get someone who speaks English. The operator will ring you back with the call connected, usually within a couple of hours. Depending on the time of day, the cost of a one-minute call to Europe is about $1 in rubles; $2 per minute for the US, and $3–4 for Australia. It's cheapest to call between 10pm and 8am, or at weekends.

If you don't have access to a private phone, you can go to a communications centre (*peregovórniy punkt*) – there's one in every district. The main ones are the **Central Telegraph Office** (see "Post") and the **House of Communications** (*Dom Svyázi*) at ul. Noviy Arbat 22, both of which are open 24 hours. At the international calls desk, state your name, the number you're calling, plus the desired duration of your call. You will then be directed to the *kassa* to pay in advance (in rubles), and be given the number of a booth from which you can dial direct; it might take several attempts to get through. If you don't succeed, you'll have to

stand in line again at the same counter to reclaim your money.

One way of avoiding such hassles is to use a **phone card**. Holders of *AT&T USA Direct* (☎155-5042) or *Sprint Express* (☎155-6133) cards can dial the Moscow number given here to get an immediate connection to the US operator, while with an *MCI Call USA* card, you call Helsinki (☎8-10-358-9800-102-80) to get a US link-up. All three allow you to place **collect calls** (for which you don't need a card – the recipient is billed), or call other countries through the US operator.

However, as it's hard to obtain these cards in Moscow, you're more likely to use *Comstar* phones in the lobbies of major hotels, which take prepaid cards (sold on the spot) or *Amex, Visa* or *JCB* **credit cards**. These phones enable you to dial direct (but not call collect) at even steeper rates: $6 per minute for Western Europe, $12 for the US, and $18 for Australia. This can still work out cheaper than calling through a hotel switchboard or business centre, which may charge up to $25 a minute.

Always bear in mind the **time difference** when calling Russia from the West (3 hours ahead of GMT, 8 hours ahead of EST). Lines are at their busiest during UK or US office hours, but you'll have fewer problems getting through at, say, 7am in the UK – which is 10am in Moscow. Conversely, should you phone Moscow after 3pm UK time, everyone will have already left the office (it's acceptable to call people at home up to 11pm, local time).

## Fax, telex, telegrams and e-mail

Given the inadequacy of the postal system, a lot of international communications are carried out by fax, telex, telegram or electronic mail.

To send a **fax** you can either pay $5–10 per page at any business centre and have it sent immediately, or around $3–4 a page (in rubles) at the fax desk (daily 8am–8pm) of the Central Telegraph Office or the House of Communications. This entails filling in a form stating the country, city and fax number desired plus the date, number of pages, your telephone number and surname; and then paying at the same desk. The rates for "express" dispatch (the same day) are twice that for "normal" delivery (within 72 hours). For a fee, you can also arrange to receive faxes; each client is assigned a personal number and notified by phone whenever a fax arrives.

Telex is still widely used throughout Russia, and a service is available at the Central Telegraph Office. From there (queue at windows #7–9), or from any large post office or communications centre, you can also send telegrams, which are surprisingly reliable and inexpensive. Fill out the blank international form in Roman letters and pay at the counter. Russian-speakers can dictate them over the phone by dialling ☎927-2002.

Lastly, for those with personal computers, there is electronic mail, which allows customers to send faxes and telexes directly from their computers at a lower cost than normal transmissions. Short term e-mail accounts are available from Infocom, Teterenskiy per. 10 (☎915-5093); Sovam Teleport, Bryusov per. 2a (☎229-3466); and Sprint, Tverskaya ul. 7 (☎201-6890).

Moscow's numerous business centres offer all communication links, as well as photocopying and use of computers and printers. The main ones include the Americom Business Center in the Radisson Slavyanskaya Hotel, Berezhovskaya nab. 2 (☎941-84270); the Comstar Business Center in room 301 of the Petrovskiy Passazh, ul. Petrovka 10 (☎924-0892); the Metropol Business Center in the Metropol Hotel, Teatralniy proezd 1/4 (☎927-6090); and the Telesource Business Center at Sheremetevo-2 Airport (☎578-4848).

## Direct dialling codes

### To Moscow

| | |
|---|---|
| From Britain | ☎00 7 095 |
| From Ireland | ☎00 7 095 |
| From the US & Canada | ☎011 7 095 |
| From Australia & New Zealand | ☎0011 7 095 |

### From Moscow

| | |
|---|---|
| Australia | ☎8 (pause) 10 61 |
| Finland | ☎8 (pause) 10 358 |
| France | ☎8 (pause) 10 33 |
| Germany | ☎8 (pause) 10 49 |
| Ireland | ☎8 (pause) 10 353 |
| Netherlands | ☎8 (pause) 10 31 |
| New Zealand | ☎8 (pause) 10 64 |
| Poland | ☎8 (pause) 10 48 |
| UK | ☎8 (pause) 10 44 |
| US & Canada | ☎8 (pause) 10 1 |

# The media

For years, foreign newspapers were restricted to old copies of the British Communist Morning Star and its fraternal equivalents. Now you can find a wider range of Western papers (and even Playboy) at all major hotels and hard-currency supermarkets, but prices are usually heavily marked up, and the papers often up to a week old. See p.326 for details of the best outlets.

If you can understand the language, it's better to check out the Russian press, which holds some surprises for those who remember it from olden days. Izvestiya, formerly the turgid organ of the Soviet government, is now a critical, liberal paper, whereas the erstwhile Young Communists' daily, Komsomolskaya Pravda, has become a tabloid rag. Russian yuppies read Commersant (akin to Britain's The Independent), while die-hard Communists peruse Sovietskaya Rossiya (which published the notorious Andreeva letter in praise of Stalin) and nationalists go for Zavtra, which replaced Den after the latter was banned in the wake of the 1993 coup. The best-selling local papers are Moskovskiy Komsomolets, which covers international, national and local news, and has earned the hatred of corrupt bureaucrats and the far right for its fearless investigative journalism; and the evening paper, Verchernaya Moskva. For those who enjoy style features, nudes and scandal, there is a whole range of tabloids, including Russia's first home-grown "tasteful" porno mag, Andrey.

The two main local English-language papers are the Moscow Times and the Moscow Tribune, which appear every day except Monday and carry extensive listings of what's on in their Saturday editions. Both papers are free and stocked by hard-currency supermarkets. The Times has better feature articles and regards itself as the mouthpiece of the foreign community; the Tribune combines a similar selection of press agency reports and national news with facetious local coverage.

## TV and radio

Moscow is served by six main television stations. There are two national stations: Russian Public Television (Channel 1, better known by its old name, Ostankino), whose main news programme is at 9pm, and the Rossiya channel, showing news at 8 and 11pm. Many Muscovites prefer the commercial stations TV6, NTV and the Moscow channel, for their cartoons, pop shows and movies. Confusingly, *NTV* broadcasts on the same frequency as the *Educational Channel*, which it replaces at 6pm. Additionally, many television sets can also receive *TV Petersburg*, which offers similar fare plus an independent-minded news programme, *Inform TV* (7.30 & 11pm). There are also half a dozen local **cable TV stations** that deliver *MTV, CNN, BBC, Eurosport* or *Sky* to their subscribers.

It's not exactly thrilling stuff: the big hits are Mexican soaps, such as *Wild Rose* and *Simply Maria*, and the US soap *Santa Barbara*. There are no longer any of the exciting dramas or investigative programmes that made Russian TV so interesting in the late 1980s and early 90s. Besides game shows, adverts now predominate,

particularly those for privatization and investment companies. Among the **foreign news** bulletins are *BBC News* in English (7am) and *ITN News* in Russian (11.45am) on the *Moscow* channel, and *CNN World News* on *TV6* (7pm). A weekly **TV guide** appears in the Saturday editions of the *Moscow Times* and *Moscow Tribune*.

As far as **radio** goes, most cafés and bars tune into one of the many FM music stations. The most popular is *Europa Plus*, which dishes out "the best of the West" on 100.5 FM; *Radio Rox* (102.0 FM) is another. *Prestige Radio* (101.7 FM) caters to jazz, blues and soul fans. Should you have a short-wave radio, it is also possible to pick up the *BBC World Service* and the *Voice of America*.

# Opening Hours and Public Holidays

Shops in Moscow are generally open Monday to Saturday from 9am to 6 or 7pm, though many large stores remain open till 8pm. Most shops close for an hour or two for lunch between 1 and 4pm. Sunday opening hours are less predictable, but most bars and restaurants stay open. As for the street kiosks that litter the city, many are open daily, 24 hours.

## Museums, galleries and churches

Opening hours for **museums and galleries** tend to be from 9 or 10am to 5 or 6pm. You'll find that they are invariably closed at least one day a week (usually Monday) and, in addition, one further day in the month will be set aside as a *sanitarniy den* or "cleaning day". Full opening hours are given in detail in the text. Note that museum visitors are often required to put on *tapochki* (felt overshoes) to protect the parquet floors.

Opening hours for **churches** are unfortunately less easy to predict. During Soviet times, many places of worship were converted into workshops or simply left to fall into ruin. Though

the majority have now reverted to their original function, many are only open for **services**. The morning liturgy (*liturgia*) – which commemorates the Last Supper – begins at 7, 8 or 9am; there may also be an evening service (*vechernaya sluzhba*) at 5 or 6pm; both usually take around one and a half hours. Additional services may occur on saints' days (*Prestolniy prazdnik*), accompanied by processions.

Orthodox believers cross themselves with three fingers (first the head, then the stomach, followed by the right shoulder and then the left).

---

### Closed for repair

On any one day, anything up to a quarter of Moscow's museums, galleries, cafés, shops, and government buildings may be **"closed for repair"** (*na remont*) or **"for technical reasons"** (*po tekhnicheskim prichinam*). Notices are rarely more specific than that, and it's often impossible to predict what will be closed when. Given this fact, it's a good idea to have alternative plans when visiting galleries and museums.

---

Visitors are expected to **dress** modestly; women should wear headscarves, and men remove their hats in church.

## National holidays

Russia's official national holidays (*prazdnik*) have been in a state of flux for the past couple of years, since so many were associated with the former Soviet regime. Many of these have now been done away with and replaced by the traditional **religious holidays**, such as Christmas and Easter, which are reckoned according to the Orthodox calendar.

---

**Public holidays**

January 1

January 7 (Orthodox Christmas)

February 23 (Defenders of the Motherland Day)

March 8 (International Women's Day)

Good Friday

May 1 & 2

May 9 (Victory Day)

June 12 (Russian Independence Day)

August 21 (Anniversary of the 1991 *putsch*)

---

# Festivals and Celebrations

Moscow's annual festival calendar is fairly brief compared to most Western European capitals, with just a couple of major cultural events each year, plus the usual religious festivities and anniversary celebrations. Unfortunately, *Intourist* is unable to supply information on events further than a month ahead.

The main festive periods are the **Russian Winter** (December 25–January 5) and the **Moscow Stars** festival (in May), which feature classical and folk music at venues like the Moscow Conservatory and the Tchaikovsky

Concert Hall. During the winter festival, you can also enjoy folk dancing and *troyka* rides at the VDNKh exhibition park, and concerts of classical music in the Pushkin Museum of Fine Arts.

Other annual music and arts events are desperately short of funds at present, but may manage to stagger on with commercial sponsorship. In previous years there have been two "alternative" music festivals in April or May. The **Independent Music Festival** is akin to Britain's *WOMAD*, with foreign and native bands playing everything from Celtic rock to Tuvan throat-music – while the **Alternative Music Festival** offers a diet of modernist and avant-garde "classical" music.

Depending on the year in which you visit Russia, you might also catch the **Moscow International Film Festival**, which presents dozens of new movies over two weeks in May every odd-numbered year – or the **Tchaikovsky Competition**, the world's stiffest test of classical musicianship, held at the Conservatory every four years (next scheduled for 1998).

Although great parades on Red Square are now a thing of the past, diehard Communists still celebrate **May Day** and the **anniversary of the October Revolution** (November 9) by laying flowers at Lenin's Mausoleum, while Yeltsin's government associates itself with other anniversaries from Soviet times. **Victory Day** (May 9), commemorating the surrender of the Nazis in 1945, is still fervently marked by the older generation, with gatherings of bemedalled veterans in Victory Park and firework displays around the city. In 1995, the anniversary of the birth of the Red Army was resurrected as a holiday called **Defenders of the Motherland Day** (February 23), marked by wreath-laying ceremonies at the Tomb of the Unknown Soldier (in the Kremlin) and other war memorials.

During spring, the run up to the Orthodox Easter overshadows two other anniversaries that are not official holidays, but occasion parades nonetheless. On **St Patrick's Day** (March 17), Moscow's Irish community organizes a parade of floats along the New Arbat, while on the **Day of Slav Culture** (May 24), Orthodox priests bearing icons proceed from the Kremlin to the Cyril and Methodius statue on the edge of the Kitay-gorod.

1992 was the first year since the early 1920s that Muscovites were able to freely celebrate the **Russian Orthodox Christmas** (*Rózhestvo*) in a church. The service starts at midnight on January 6 and goes on until dawn the following day. The choir, the liturgy, the candles and the incense combine to produce a hypnotic sense of togetherness, which Russians call *sobornost*. Despite their emotional charge and Byzantine splendour, Orthodox services are come-and-go as you please, allowing non-believers to attend without embarrassment, though women should cover their heads and avoid wearing trousers. At midnight, worshippers circumambulate the church holding candles – an unforgettable sight. For both Easter and Christmas celebrations, local churches overflow with worshippers.

Less obviously, there are also the religious festivals of other faiths. The synagogue on ul. Arkhipova comes alive at *Rosh Hashana*, *Yom Kippur*, *Hannuka* and other **Jewish festivals**, while the mosque near the Olympic Sports Complex is the focus for **Ramadan** celebrations among the city's Muslim community.

Except among the expat community, the Western Christmas is passed over in the rush to prepare for **New Year** (*Noviy God*). Generally, this remains a family occasion until midnight, when a frenzied round of house-calling commences, people getting ever drunker and continuing until dawn. In recent years, however, a crowd has gathered on Red Square to pop bottles of champagne as the Saviour clocktower tolls the New Year. In residential areas, people dressed as *Dyed Moroz* ("Grandfather Frost", the Russian equivalent of Father Christmas) and his female sidekick, *Snegurochka* ("The Snow Maiden"), do the rounds wishing neighbours Happy New Year (*s Novim Godom*). To enjoy it all over again, many Russians also celebrate the Orthodox New Year or **Old New Year** on the night of January 13–14 – though this isn't an official holiday.

# Security, Police and the Mafia

It's a measure of the New Russia that tourists no longer worry about hidden microphones or KGB agents, but muggers and mobsters. Moscow, in particular, is often viewed as a city overrun by gangsters, with shootings on every corner. Although such dangers are exaggerated by the Western media, visitors should certainly observe obvious precautions like not flashing money or cameras around, or going off with strangers. Try to blend in whenever possible: the less you look like a tourist, the smaller the risk of being targeted.

Under "normal" circumstances in Moscow, personal **security** is generally in inverse proportion to personal wealth. The main targets of crime, both Mafia-related and petty, are rich Russian businessmen, compared to whom foreign tourists are considered small fry. Though innocent bystanders are occasionally killed on the streets in Mafia shoot-outs or car-bombings, there's a higher risk of violence in posh nightclubs or casinos. Of course, a different risk-assessment prevails during political crises like the battle between Yeltsin and parliament in 1993 – but even then, visitors aren't likely to be endangered providing they avoid obvious troublespots.

## The police and the OMON

In Soviet times, the **police** – still known as the **militia** (*Militsiya*) – were poor relations of the **KGB**, being a mere arm of the Ministry of the Interior (MVD), while the KGB, the "sword and shield of the state" enjoyed a seat on the Politburo. Today, the KGB, in its latest incarnation as the Federal Counter Intelligence Service, has been obliged to improve its image by vowing to concentrate on organized crime and ecological violations, but the regular police still bear the brunt of public scorn for failing to check the soaring crime rate.

The militia are easily recognized by their blue-grey uniforms with red lapels and cap bands. Some of them now drive Western cars, some drive police jeeps and, along with the traffic police, they may well be armed. It's indicative of Russia's present economic state that you may also encounter militia men in full uniform sitting just inside the entrance to clubs and restaurants, moonlighting as security guards.

To augment the police, the state relies on the **OMON**, or Special Purpose Militia Detachments of the Ministry of the Interior. Originally known as the "Black Berets" – and notorious for terrorizing the Baltic states before they gained independence – the OMON now patrols the home front. Dressed in paramilitary garb (trousers tucked into boots, a field cap and a stripy T-shirt), they are more pugnacious than the militia. The OMON patrol markets and stations and are deployed at demonstrations and soccer matches, armed with teargas and Kalashnikovs.

In addition, there are dozens of **private security firms**, staffed by army veterans or ex-KGB heavies, who tend to be extremely officious in their protection of banks, stores and nightclubs.

## The mafia

Like everywhere else in the former USSR, Moscow is pervaded by the **Mafia**. Its origins lie in the nexus between black marketeering and political power in Soviet times. The size of the old USSR and the vagaries of central planning promoted provincial corruption on a massive scale, leading to the establishment of regional and ethnic mafias like the Tambov and Chechen mobs. The transition to full-blown capitalism has meant even bigger opportunities for these gangs, who now have interests as far afield as Italy and America.

In Russia, the Mafia are believed to control some 40,000 private and state-run companies, utterly blurring the distinction between legitimate business and organized crime. In 1993, there were over 1300 murders in Moscow (just under half the number of New York), and car-bombs became so popular a way of disposing of rivals that mothers warned their children not to play near Mercedes 600s (the car of choice for rich businessmen and mobsters).

## Avoiding trouble

As a tourist, you are only likely to come into contact with the Mafia in their more respectable guise, spending cash in some of the city's better restaurants. Otherwise, the Mafia is less of a hazard than **petty crime**: mostly thefts from cars and hotel rooms. Sensible precautions include making photocopies of your passport and visa, leaving passports and tickets in the hotel safe, and noting down travellers' cheque and credit card numbers.

If you have a car, don't leave anything in view when you park it. Vehicles without an alarm are regularly stolen and luggage and valuables make a tempting target, particularly from easily recognizable foreign and rental cars. **Gypsies** should be avoided at all times. Don't take pity on the children or give in to hassle from groups of women – they often simply note where you keep your money and somebody else gets you further down the street. Gangs of ten- to twelve-year-olds often stalk tourists in the underpasses near Red Square and the Garden Ring, or the Kalininskiy Bridge that leads to the *Ukrainiya Hotel*. Their tactic is to rush in from all sides and pick your pockets while you're too shocked to resist – relying on their youth to inhibit any resistance, or escape prosecution if they're caught.

In the event of your stay in Moscow coinciding with some kind of **civil unrest**, it's obviously best to avoid focal points like the White House or the Kremlin, and demonstrations anywhere. Tune into foreign radio or TV for news; the Russian stations will be censored. Real trouble should be localized in a few areas, with life continuing as normal elsewhere. If the 1993 crisis is anything to go by, you can expect barricades around Barrikadnaya and Ulitsa 1905 Goda metros, tanks on the Garden Ring, spot checks by the *OMON*, and a curfew (*Komandántskiy chas*).

In theory, you're supposed to carry some form of **identification** at all times, and the militia can stop you in the street and demand it. In practice, they're rarely bothered if you're clearly a foreigner (unless you're driving) and tend to confine themselves to activities like traffic control and harassing Gypsies.

## What to do if you're robbed

There's much less risk of **being mugged** in Moscow than in, say, New York, but resisting an armed robbery is equally foolish: the possession of firearms has been partially legalized, following quickly after the legalization of gas pistols (hard to tell apart from the real thing when you're looking down the barrel). Thankfully, most crimes of this type are faced only by drunken tourists who follow prostitutes back to strange rooms or into a taxi late at night. You're far more likely to be at risk from **pickpockets** – particularly groups of Gypsies or street kids, who dance around you (or stick pins into you) while they rifle your pockets. If you've got the stomach for it, lash out immediately; hurt one or two and the others will run away.

If you are unlucky enough to have something stolen, you will need to **go to the police** to report it, not least because your insurance company will require a police report. It's unlikely that there'll be anyone who speaks English, and even less likely that your belongings will be retrieved, but at the very least you should get a statement detailing what you've lost for your insurance claim. Try the phrase *Menya obokrali* – "I have been robbed". There are militia departments in most hotels and metro stations.

# Women's Moscow

The "emancipation" of women under Communism always had a lot more to do with increasing the numbers of the available workforce than with promoting equality or encouraging women to pursue their own goals. Although equal wages, maternity benefits and subsidized crèches were all prescribed by law, their provision fell far short of the ideal, saddling women with a double burden of childcare and full-time work. As a result, "feminism" is something of a dirty word in Russia, and self-proclaimed feminists will get short shrift from both sexes here.

As a visitor to Moscow, you will find that Russian men veer between extreme gallantry and crude chauvinism. **Sexual harassment** is marginally less of a problem than in Western Europe – and nowhere near as bad as in Mediterranean countries – but without the familiar linguistic and cultural signs, it's easy to misinterpret situations. Attitudes in Moscow are much more liberal than in the countryside, where women travelling alone can still expect to encounter stares and comments. Single women should nonetheless avoid going to certain nightclubs and bars, where their presence may be misconstrued by the local pimps and prostitutes. Although you'll see plenty of Russian women flagging down cars as potential taxis, unaccompanied foreign women would be ill-advised to do likewise.

Should the worst occur, Moscow now has a **Rape Crisis Hotline** (☎141-7226), staffed by English-speaking volunteers on Saturday only.

# Directory

**BRING** A universal sink plug; toilet paper; warm clothing for winter (thermal leggings, scarf, hat, gloves, etc); a torch for dark stairwells.

**CHILDREN** While children (*détey*) and babies are doted on by Russians, you'll actually see very few in public places other than parks and shops, and public facilities for younger children are virtually nonexistent. Disposable nappies are now available in many supermarkets, which usually also stock baby food, but it's best to bring a small supply to tide you over. Note that breast-feeding in public is totally unacceptable. Children up to the age of seven ride free on all forms of public transport. See p.327 for a list of places and activities in Moscow that might appeal to children.

**CIGARETTES** Nearly all Western brands are available, though many of the packets sold from kiosks are made under licence (or counterfeited) in Russia or Turkey; Marlboro kiosks and hotel shops are likelier to stock the genuine article. Traditional Soviet brands like *Belomor* and *TU-144* are truly revolting. *Belomor* are what are called *papirosi*, with an inch of tobacco at the end of a long cardboard tube, that is twisted to make a crude filter. The brand name *Belomor* celebrates the White Sea Canal – a map of which decorates the packet. It is normal to be approached by strangers asking for a light (*Mozhno pokurit?*) or a cigarette. While museums

and public transport are no-smoking (*ne kurit*) zones, Russians puff away everywhere else, and see nothing wrong with it.

**COMPUTERS** If bringing a portable computer into the country, write it on your customs declaration and avoid putting it through the X-ray (insist on a hand examination). When using a computer in Russia, be wary of the fluctuations in the electricity current. Computer dealers in Moscow will only honour guarantees on machines purchased in Russia.

**CONTRACEPTIVES** Condoms (*prezervativiy*) are now available in most pharmacies, but neither the Russian ones (aptly nicknamed "galoshes") nor many of the imported brands are trustworthy, so it makes sense to bring your own, or buy only known brands in upmarket shops. The same goes for any other method of contraception that you might use.

**DRUGS** Grass and cannabis resin (*plastilin*) from the Altai Mountains are now commonplace on the club scene, where acid, heroin and Ecstasy also do the rounds. At some clubs, the merest whiff will draw the bouncers; at others, dope-smokers are stolidly ignored. While simple possession of dope may incur a caution, hard drugs – and smuggling – are still punishable, in theory at least, by the death penalty. Obviously, the safest policy is to avoid drugs entirely.

**ELECTRICITY** A standard continental 220 volts AC; most European appliances should work as long as you have an adapter for European-style two-pin round plugs. North Americans will need this plus a transformer.

**FILM AND PHOTOS** The number of outlets for Western colour film, one-hour development and more, has increased rapidly. Try *Fuji* (Stolesnikov per. 5/20 and ul. Noviy Arbat 25), *Kodak Express* (Tverskaya ul. 25 and the 4th floor of *Detskiy Mir*) or one of the dozen of other outlets around Moscow. When leaving the country by air, put films in your pocket, as Russian film-safe X-rays do not always live up to their name.

**GAY AND LESBIAN LIFE** This is emerging from the closet after decades of repression, but Russian society remains extremely homophobic. Male homosexuality is no longer a criminal offence and there are a number of self-declared homosexual singers and artists, although private individuals are unlikely to be open about their sexuality. Several gay and lesbian groups have been active over the past few years in Moscow, where the gay magazines *Tema*, *Risk* and *Malchisnik* are published. Information contacts include Kevin Gardner at the *International Gay and Lesbian Human Rights Commission*, ul. Bolshevistskaya 21/15 (☎252-3316), and Sergei Simonov at the *Rainbow Foundation*, Malomoskovskaya ul. 4 (☎489-2543 or 282-0540), where less English is spoken. See p.315 for a brief rundown on gay and lesbian life in Moscow.

**LANGUAGE COURSES** Russian-language tuition in Moscow can be arranged by local firms, like *Patriarchi Dom* (see p.32), or agencies abroad. In Britain, try companies such as *Kremlin 2000*, 7 Courtney Rd, Colliers Wood, London SW19 (☎0181/544 1718), or the South Manchester College, Wythenshawe Park Centre, Moor Rd, Manchester M23 9BQ (☎0161/957 1500). In America, *Volunteers for Peace*, 43 Tiffany Rd, Belmont, VT 05730 (☎802/946-1614), offers a variety of language programmes and workcamp placements across Russia. If you'd rather arrange private tuition in Moscow yourself, Galina Mikhailovna Kozadaevoy (☎209-0824) is an excellent teacher who lives just off Leningradskiy prospekt, near Belorusskaya metro.

**LAUNDRIES** Russians generally do their laundry at home in the bathtub, and few would risk their garments at one of Moscow's municipal laundries, which take a week to return clothing. If you don't want to do your own laundry, you can pay $3–4 to have it washed at the *Travellers Guest House* (ul. Bolshaya Pereyaslavskaya 50), or considerably more for a dry cleaning firm like *California Cleaners* (☎497-0005) or *MBTS Dry Cleaning* (☎335-6192). Washing powder is sold at most supermarkets.

**LEFT LUGGAGE** Most train stations have lockers and/or a 24-hour left luggage office, but you would be tempting fate to use them.

**LOST PROPERTY** For similar reasons, anything you might lose is unlikely to end up at the lost property depots (*Stol Nakhodok*) dealing with items lost on the metro (☎222-2085), or in other public transport or licensed taxis (☎923-8753). Only Russian is spoken.

**PATRONYMICS AND FIRST NAMES** Besides their fore- and surname, every Russian has a patronymic derived from their father's name (such as Kostantinovich, son of Konstantin, or Ivanova, daughter of Ivan), which is used in conjunction with their forename as a polite form of address. This is *de rigueur* among older Russians, who find American informality rather crass ("Hi, I'm Bob"). Once genuine intimacy has been established, people love to use affectionate diminutives like Sasha or Shura (for Alexander), Anya or Anichka (for Anna) – and may try coining one from your own name. If you happen to be called Hugh, it's best to invent another name, as to Russian ears, this suggests the word for "prick" or "cock".

**PROSTITUTION** Most hotels and nightclubs have their quota of prostitutes, run by whichever Mafia gang has struck a deal with the management. Business is fairly blatant and strictly in hard currency; the risks are the same as anywhere else in the world, if not higher. Less obviously, it also causes problems for Russian women *not* involved in prostitution, who fear to enter such places alone lest they be mistaken for a freelance prostitute and get beaten up by the mob. If you should arrange to meet with a Russian woman, respect any doubts she might express about the venue, and rendezvous outside so that you can go in together.

**RACISM** It is a sad fact that racism in Russia is a casual and common phenomenon. Mostly directed against other ethnic groups of the old Soviet Union, such as Gypsies, Azerbajanis and Central Asians, it also extends to Africans, Arabs, Vietnamese and Jews (the last being an old enmity, exploited by Tsars and Communists alike). Anyone dark-skinned can expect to arouse, at the very least, a certain amount of curiosity.

**SUPERSTITIONS** Russians consider it bad luck to kiss or shake hands across a threshold, or return home to pick up something that's been forgotten. If you step on someone's foot, they are duty-bound to do the same back to you. Before departing on a long journey, Russians gather all their luggage by the door and sit on it for a minute or two, to bring themselves luck for the journey. When bringing flowers for your hostess, make certain that there's an odd number of blooms, as even-numbered bouquets are for funerals.

**TAPOCHKI** Visiting a Russian home, you'll be invited to slip off your shoes and ease into *tapochki* (slippers), thus preventing dirt from being tracked into the flat, and drawing you into the cosy ambience of domestic life. Their institutional equivalent (such as museum visitors are obliged to wear) are felt overshoes with tapes to tie around the ankles, which are also called *tapochki*.

**TAMPONS** These are widely available all over town. Local chemists sell Ukrainian-made Tampax and imported brands can be found in large Western-run supermarkets.

**TIME** Moscow time is generally three hours ahead of Britain and eight hours ahead of EST, with the clocks going forward one hour on the last Saturday in March, and back again on the last Saturday of October. Confusingly, the Russian word for clock or watch – *chas* – also means hour.

**TIPPING** In taxis, the fare will be agreed in advance and is usually payable in dollars, so there's no need to tip. In restaurants it's considered proper to leave an extra ten percent or so, but it's not compulsory, so check that it hasn't already been included. It's also done to give a small tip to the cloakroom attendant if he helps you on with your coat.

**TOILETS** Public toilets (*tualét*) are few and far between; toilet paper (*tualétnaya búmaga*) is unlikely to be provided and standards of hygiene are often low. Assuming you can get past the bouncers, the toilets in restaurants or hotels are preferable; the cleanest, most accessible toilets are in *McDonald's*, at three locations in the centre of Moscow.

# The City

# Chapter 1

# Introducing the City

Discounting a couple of satellite towns beyond the outer ring road, **Moscow** covers an area of about 900 square kilometres, which makes mastering the public transport system (or at least the metro) a top priority. Yet, despite Moscow's size and the inhuman scale of many of its buildings and avenues, the general layout is easily grasped – a series of concentric circles and radial lines, emanating from the Kremlin – and the centre is compact enough to explore on foot.

**Red Square and the Kremlin** are the historic nucleus of the city (Chapter 2), a magnificent stage for political drama, signifying a great sweep of history that includes Ivan the Terrible, Peter the Great, Stalin and Gorbachev. Here you'll find Lenin's Mausoleum and St Basil's Cathedral, the famous GUM department store, and the Kremlin itself, whose splendid cathedrals and Armoury Museum head the list of attractions.

Immediately to the east of Red Square lies the **Kitay-gorod** (Chapter 3), traditionally the commercial district, and originally fortified like the Kremlin. Stretches of the ramparts remain behind the *Metropol* and *Rossiya* hotels, and the medieval churches of Zaryade and the shops along Nikolskaya ulitsa may tempt you further into the quarter, where you'll find the former headquarters of the Communist Party and the KGB.

The Kremlin and the Kitay-gorod are surrounded by two quarters defined by ring boulevards built over the original ramparts of medieval times, when Moscow's residential areas were divided into the "White Town" or **Beliy Gorod** (Chapter 4), and the humbler "Earth Town" or **Zemlyanoy Gorod** (Chapter 5). Today, both are an inviting maze where every style of architecture is represented. Situated within the Boulevard Ring that encloses the Beliy Gorod are such landmarks as the Bolshoy Theatre and the Lubyanka headquarters of the secret police, while the Zemlyanoy Gorod that extends to the Garden Ring is enlivened by the trendy Old and New Arbat streets, with three Stalin-era skyscrapers dominating the Ring itself.

**CHAPTER DIVISIONS**

CHAPTER 2
RED SQUARE AND
THE KREMLIN

CHAPTER 3
KITAY-GOROD

CHAPTER 4
BELIY GOROD

CHAPTER 5
ZEMLYANOY GOROD

CHAPTER 9
THE NORTHERN SUBURBS

MOSCOW RING ROAD (MKHAD)

Losniy Ostrov

Izmaylovo
Park

Yauza River

Sokolniki
Park

VDNKh &
Botanical
Gardens

Moskva River

YAROSLAVSKOE SHOSSE

ALTUFEVSKOE SHOSSE

DIMITROVSKOE SHOSSE

LENINGRADSKIY PROSPEKT

LENINGRADSKOE SHOSSE

VOLOKOLAMSKOE SHOSSE

MOSCOW RING ROAD (MKHAD)

MOSCOW RING ROAD (MKHAD)

PROSPEKT MIRA

CHAPTER 8
TAGANKA AND ZAVAUZE

CHAPTER 7
ZAMOSKVARECHE
AND THE
SOUTH

CHAPTER 6
KRASNAYA PRESNYA,
FILI AND THE
SOUTHWEST

Moskva River

5 km

0

RYAZANSKIY PROSPEKT

VOLGOGRADSKY PROSPEKT

MOSCOW RING ROAD (MKHAD)

KASHIRSKOE SHOSSE

VARSHOVSKOE SHOSSE

MOSCOW RING ROAD (MKHAD)

PROSOUZNAYA ULITSA

LENINSKY PROSPEKT

PROSPEKT VERNADSKOVO

GARDEN RING

MOZHAYSKOE SHOSSE

Beyond this historic core Moscow is too sprawling to explore on foot: you'll need to rely on the metro, which is why our division of the city is based mostly on transport connections and ease of access. **Krasnaya Presnya, Fili and the Southwest** (Chapter 6) describes a swathe which includes the Russian Parliament building (known as the White House); Tolstoy's house and the Novodevichiy Convent further south across the Moskva River; Victory Park, out beyond Fili; and Moscow State University, in the Sparrow Hills.

Across the river from the Kremlin, **Zamoskvareche and the South** (Chapter 7) are the home of the Tretyakov Gallery of Russian art and the well-known Gorky Park, and also of the Donskoy and Danilov monasteries that once stood guard against the Tatars, and the romantic ex-royal estates of Kolomenskoe and Tsaritsyno.

**Taganka and Zayauze** (Chapter 8), to the east of the centre, likewise harbour fortified monasteries – the Andronikov, Novospasskiy, and Simonov – and erstwhile noble estates (Kuskovo and Kuzminki) but the main lure for tourists is the Izmaylovo Art Market, near Izmaylovo Park. Other attractions include the Pet Market and the Old Believers' Commune, and a trail of Baroque churches culminating in the stupendous Stalin-Gothic Kotelnicheskaya Apartments.

The **Northern Suburbs** (Chapter 9) cover a vast area with a sprinkling of sights. Foremost is the VDNKh, a huge Stalinist exhibition park with amazing statues and pavilions, in the vicinity of Moscow's Botanical Gardens and TV Tower. Closer to the centre are a clutch of museums and the Durov Animal Theatre, while further east lies the verdant Sokolniki Park. In the opposite direction, stadiums and a racetrack flank Leningradskiy prospekt as it runs out towards Sheremetevo Airport, north of the lakeside summer resort of Serebryaniy Bor.

**Outside Moscow** (Chapter 10) there is scope for excursions to such diverse places as the Trinity Monastery of St Sergei, the Abramtsevo artists' colony, Tchaikovsky's house in Klin, Lenin's country retreat at Gorki Leninskie, and the battlefield of Borodino. Many of them can be visited on tours, sparing you the trouble of getting there by public transport.

# Practicalities

**Transport details** – bus, trolleybus and tram routes, as well as metro stations – are given throughout the following chapters, but for a full rundown of how to use the network you should turn to p.24. Also, see the colour insert for a plan of the metro. Most visitors arrange **accommodation** in advance, but if you need to find somewhere to stay, or want to know about a place beforehand, all the options are covered on pp.291–297. Despite scores of new **restaurants, cafés and bars**, decent, affordable ones are still relatively few and far between, so when planning your day out, it's best to consult the listings of places to eat and drink on pp.305–312. The "Listings" section also gives details of nightlife and cultural events, activities for children, sports and shopping.

---

**Transliteration**

The problem with transliterating Russian from the Cyrillic alphabet into the Roman alphabet is that there is no agreed way to do it. In addition to the German, French, and American systems, there are several English systems. In this book we've used the Revised English System, with a few minor modifications to help pronunciation and readability. All proper names appear as they are best known, not as they would be transliterated (for example Tchaikovsky not Chaykovskiy).

Place-names (streets and squares, metro stations, museums and land-marks) are listed on pp.372–376.

---

Chapter 2

# Red Square and the Kremlin

Every visitor to Moscow is irresistibly drawn to **RED SQUARE AND THE KREMLIN**, the historic and spiritual heart of the city, so loaded with associations and drama that they seem to embody all of Russia's triumphs and tragedies. Exalted by the poet Mayakovsky as the centre of the world, the vast square has a slight curvature that seems to follow that of the earth's surface. On one side, the **Lenin Mausoleum** squats beneath the ramparts and towers of the Kremlin, confronted by the long facade of **GUM**, while **St Basil's Cathedral** erupts in a profusion of onion domes and spires at the far end. For sheer theatricality, Red Square is only surpassed by the Kremlin itself, whose fortifications, palaces and cathedrals are an amalgam of European and Asiatic splendour, redolent of the Italian Renaissance and the court of Genghis Khan alike. While the treasures of its **Armoury Palace** and other **museums** are a must for visitors, it's the frisson of proximity to power and the sense that history is being made here that sets the Kremlin apart from other palatial citadels the world over.

This chapter begins with Red Square, as you can and should visit it at any time of the day or night, without worrying about **opening times and admission tickets**. The Kremlin is different, insofar as it's only open at set times, and each cathedral or museum requires a ticket. Moreover, the visitors' entrance is around the far side, in the Alexander Gardens, rather than on Red Square as you might expect. Otherwise, **access** is simple, with three metro stations (Ploshchad Revolyutsii, Okhotniy Ryad and Teatralnaya) within a few minutes' walk of Red Square, and two others (Aleksandrovskiy Sad and Biblioteka Imeni Lenina) equally near the entrance to the Kremlin.

Starting from Okhotniy Ryad or Teatralnaya metro, you'll probably approach Red Square via a long pedestrian underpass, crowded with souvenir sellers, buskers and beggars, which is a favourite spot for gangs of Gypsy kids to pounce on unwary tourists. The underpass brings you out near the City Duma, within sight of Lenin's

Mausoleum and St Basil's, just uphill. You may also notice faded no-smoking signs, from the days when smoking on Red Square was forbidden, as a sign of respect for the hallowed precincts of Lenin's tomb.

# Red Square

The name **Krasnaya ploshchad – Red Square** – has nothing to do with Communism, but derives from *krasniy*, the old Russian word for "beautiful", which probably came to mean "red" due to people's thirst for bright colour during the long, drab winter months. When the square came into being towards the end of the fifteenth century – after Ivan III ordered the clearance of the wooden houses and traders' stalls that huddled below the eastern wall of the Kremlin – it was called Trinity Square, after the Trinity Cathedral that stood on the future site of St Basil's; later known as the Square of Fires, its current name was only bestowed in the late seventeenth century.

For much of its **history**, the square was a muddy expanse thronged with peddlers, idlers and drunks – a potential mob that Vasily III (1505–1533) sought to distance from the Kremlin by digging a moat alongside its wall, spanned by bridges leading to the citadel's gates. The moat also acted as a firebreak against the conflagrations that frequently engulfed Moscow. Like the Forum in ancient Rome, the square was also used for public announcements and executions, particularly during the reigns of Ivan the Terrible and Peter the Great, and the anarchic Time of Troubles in the early seventeenth century. The square lost much of its political significance after the capital moved to St Petersburg in 1712, but remained an integral part of Moscow life as the site of religious processions and the Palm Sunday Fair, where vendors sold everything from icons and carpets to "penny whistles, trumpets and chenille monkeys".

It was the Bolsheviks who returned Red Square to the centre of events, as the Kremlin became the seat of power once again, and the square the setting for great **demonstrations and parades** on May 1 and November 7 (the anniversary of the Revolution). The most dramatic was the November 7 parade in 1941, when tanks rumbled directly from Red Square to the front line, only miles away; on June 24, 1945, they returned for a victory parade where captured Nazi regimental standards were flung down in front of the Lenin Mausoleum, to be trampled by Soviet Marshals riding white horses. In the Brezhnev years, these parades degenerated into an empty ritual, where pre-recorded hurrahs boomed from loudspeakers, and the marchers attended under duress. As if to puncture their pomposity, a young West German, Mathias Rust, landed a light aircraft on Red Square in May 1987, having evaded the much vaunted Soviet air-defences.

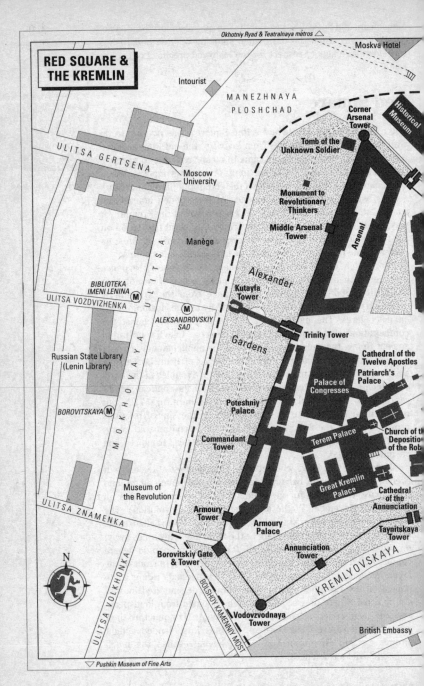

# RED SQUARE & THE KREMLIN

Okhotniy Ryad & Teatralnaya métros △

Moskva Hotel

Intourist

MANEZHNAYA
PLOSHCHAD

Historical Museum

Corner Arsenal Tower

ULITSA GERTSENA

Moscow University

Tomb of the Unknown Soldier

Monument to Revolutionary Thinkers

Middle Arsenal Tower

Arsenal

Manège

*BIBLIOTEKA IMENI LENINA* (M)

ULITSA VOZDVIZHENKA

Alexander

Kutayfa Tower

(M) *ALEKSANDROVSKIY SAD*

Gardens

Trinity Tower

Russian State Library (Lenin Library)

Cathedral of the Twelve Apostles

Patriarch's Palace

Palace of Congresses

*BOROVITSKAYA* (M)

Poteshniy Palace

Church of the Deposition of the Robe

Terem Palace

Commandant Tower

Museum of the Revolution

ULITSA ZNAMENKA

Great Kremlin Palace

Cathedral of the Annunciation

Armoury Tower

Armoury Palace

Taynitskaya Tower

Borovitskiy Gate & Tower

Annunciation Tower

KREMLYOVSKAYA

N

BOLSHOY KAMENNIY MOST

Vodovzvodnaya Tower

British Embassy

ULITSA VOLKHONKA

▽ Pushkin Museum of Fine Arts

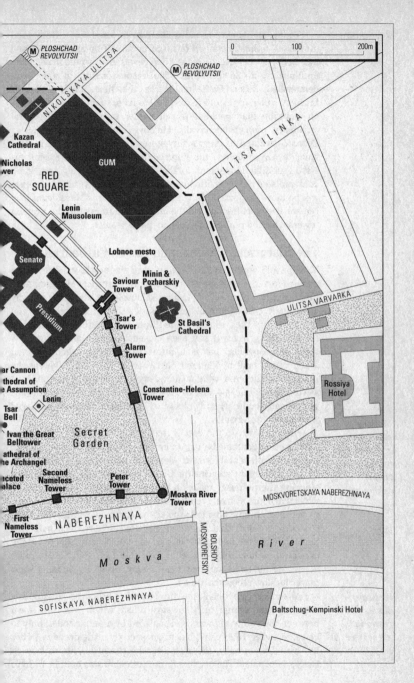

**Red Square**

Today, the square is more likely to be used for a Hollywood movie set, to host a concert or be cordoned off by barricades – and has become the site of **New Year** revels that would have been unthinkable in Soviet times. The reconstruction of the long-demolished Kazan Cathedral marks the first stage of Mayor Luzhkov's plan to restore Red Square to its pre-revolutionary state – an ambition that would be much harder to achieve had several "visionary" projects been realized in Soviet times, when the architect Leonidov wanted to erect a fifty-storey building in the shape of a giant factory chimney, the Futurist Tatlin dreamed of raising his 1300-foot-high Monument to the Third International, and Stalin contemplated the demolition of St Basil's. Hopefully, future changes will be more respectful of the past, so that Lenin's Mausoleum may remain an object lesson, and the magical red stars atop the Kremlin towers won't be replaced by pseudo-Tsarist eagles.

## The Historical Museum and Kazan Cathedral

Most people approach Red Square from the north, via one of the cobbled streets that slope uphill beside the Historical Museum, for a thrilling first glimpse of Lenin's Mausoleum standing proudly alongside the Kremlin wall, and St Basil's Cathedral looming at the far end of the square. The liver-red **Historical Museum** (*Istoricheskiy muzey*) has been closed for years and shows few signs of reopening, but is a prime example of Pseudo-Russian architecture, built by Vladimir Sherwood in 1875–81. Whereas the exterior is cluttered with medieval-style pinnacles, chevrons and sawtoothed cornices – as if to compete with St Basil's – the interior is rationally laid out, with plenty of light let in through the large windows in the airwells.

*See the "Glossary" (p.368) for an explanation of styles of Russian architecture.*

Across the way to the east is the Tsarist Provincial Government building that contained a prison known as "the Pit" (*Yama*), where the eighteenth-century writer Alexander Radishchev awaited exile for his critique of Catherine the Great's autocracy. Sadly, a jewellery store on the premises makes it difficult to get into the courtyard, which harbours a stately red-brick **Mint** founded by Peter the Great, as yet unrestored. Outside is the site of the medieval **Iberian Gate** (*Iverskiy vorota*) that once led into Red Square. The gate was demolished in the mid-1930s as part of Stalin's campaign to rid the capital of its holy relics and churches, and make Red Square more accessible for tanks and marchers. Today, desultory building work marks its slow reconstruction.

*Nikolskaya ulitsa is covered in the next chapter (see p.98).*

A similar fate befell the tiny **Kazan Cathedral** (*Kazanskiy sobor*) on the corner of Nikolskaya ulitsa, which was torn down between the two world wars and replaced by a public toilet, only to be recreated in 1993 using blueprints secretly made decades earlier by Pyotr Baranovskiy, the architect who risked his life to save St Basil's (see p.69). The original Kazan cathedral was built in 1636 to commemorate Tsar Mikhail Romanov's victory over the Poles, and dedicated to the Virgin of Kazan, whose icon was carried into battle by Prince Pozharskiy during the Time of Troubles. Its modern-day counterpart sports a tan-and-cream exterior replete with the elaborate window frames (*nalichniki*) and ogee-shaped gables (*kokoshniki*) characteristic of early Muscovite church architecture, crowned by a cluster of green and gold domes. Opened in 1993 on the feast day of the Icon of Kazan (November 4), the cathedral is unpatined by age, but already warm in spirit.

# GUM

Almost the entire eastern side of Red Square is taken up by **GUM** (pronounced "Goom": the initials stand for "State Department Store"), whose ornate Pseudo-Russian facade – drawing on motifs from the medieval churches of Borisoglebsk and Rostov Veliky – conceals an elegantly utilitarian interior, employing the same steel-frame and glass construction techniques as the great train stations of London and Paris. Executed by Alexander Pomerantsev in 1890–93, this three-storey, modern arcade replaced the old hall of the Upper Trading Rows that burned down in 1825, whose 1200 shops shared a common roof "so awkwardly constructed, that in the strongest sunshine people stumble in darkness, and after the slightest shower wade through mud".

Nationalized and renamed GUM after the 1917 Revolution, it continued to function as a shop until bureaucrats overseeing the First Five Year Plan took over the building. In 1932 it was used for the lying-in-state of Stalin's wife, Nadezhda, after her suicide; Stalin stayed there for days, silently noting who came to pay their respects. Here, too, the giant photographic portraits of Communist leaders that emblazoned Red Square were assembled, having been developed in swimming pools. Not until 1952 was GUM reopened as a great emporium famed throughout the world. Less well known was "Section 100", a special clothing store for the Party elite, tucked away on the top floor. With the advent of *perestroika*, GUM received an infusion of investments from Western firms keen to get a prestigious foothold on the Russian market, and a facelift in time to celebrate the store's centenary in 1993.

GUM is laid out in three parallel arcades or "lines" (designated *1-ya liniya, 2-ya liniya, 3-ya liniya*), which meet at a central fountain, overlooked by galleries. Glass canopy roofs flood the whole complex with light, or give a startling view of the stars on winter nights. While the bottom floor is now largely occupied by foreign stores like *Estée Lauder*, various old, Soviet-style shops survive on the floor above. You can enter GUM at either end of lines 1 and 3, or from the street behind the store, but not from Red Square itself. GUM is open from 8am to 8pm, Monday to Saturday, and sometimes on Sundays (as advertised).

# Lenin's Mausoleum

For nearly seventy years, the Soviet state venerated its founder by acts of homage at the **Lenin Mausoleum** (*Mavzoley V.I. Lenina*) – an image associated with Soviet Communism the world over. In post-Communist Russia, the Mausoleum tends to be regarded as either an awkward reminder or a cherished relic of the old days: hence the uncertainty surrounding the fate of Lenin's corpse and the future of the Mausoleum, whose inviolability was one of the last taboos of *glasnost* to go. Indeed, not until October 1993 – in the first flush of victory over the White House – did Boris Yeltsin feel bold enough to strip the Mausoleum of its guard of honour and pledge the removal of Lenin's body "within months". However, the parliamentary elections backfired and the whole idea was quietly dropped.

During **visiting hours** (Tues–Thurs & Sat 10am–1pm, Sun 10am–2pm) the northern end of Red Square is cordoned off, and the Mausoleum can only be approached by the lane to the west of the Historical Museum, where visitors must leave their bags in a special cloakroom. However, there are now plans afoot to close the Mausoleum by stealth, so don't be surprised to find it shut in the future.

## The Mausoleum

When Lenin died on January 21, 1924, his widow, Krupskaya, pleaded: "Do not let your sorrow for Ilyich find expression in outward veneration of his personality. Do not raise monuments to him, or palaces to his name, do not organize pompous ceremonies in his memory." Nonetheless, a crude wooden mausoleum was hastily erected on Red Square for mourners to pay their respects, and the Party leadership decided to preserve his body for posterity. The embalming was carried out by Professors Vorobyov and Zbarskiy, and by August 1924 the body was fit to be viewed in a newly built wooden mausoleum, which was replaced by a permanent stone one in 1930, once it became clear that the embalming process had been successful.

Designed by Alexei Shchusev, the **Mausoleum** itself is basically a step-pyramid of cubes, a form revered by Russian avant-gardists. Faced with red granite and black labradorite, it bears the simple inscription *Lenin* above its bronze doors, which were traditionally flanked by a **guard of honour** (changed every hour, as the Saviour Tower clock chimed). After Stalin's death in 1953, he, too, was displayed in what became the Lenin-Stalin Mausoleum, but in 1961 it reverted to its old title after Stalin's body was spirited away and reburied by the Kremlin wall. For decades, the Politburo reviewed **anniversary parades** from its podium (with a supply of machine guns stashed behind them in the event of trouble), and diplomats noted who stood nearest the General Secretary as an indication of their influence. The septuagenarian Chernenko contracted fatal pneumonia from standing there on a chilly day*, and the swan song of such events occurred when Gorbachev was booed during the October Revolution parade in 1989, and on May Day the following year.

In the days when **visiting Lenin's tomb** was *de rigueur* for visitors to Moscow, the queue stretched right around the corner of the Kremlin into the Alexander Gardens, and guards made visitors line up in pairs, remove their hats and their hands from their pockets, and refrain from talking except in whispers – a regime that has only slightly relaxed today, when you're unlikely to have to wait in line more than ten minutes. Descending into the bowels of the Mausoleum, past motionless sentries and doors that emit the crackle of walkie-talkies, one enters the funerary chamber, faced in grey and black labradorite inset with carmine zigzags. Softly spotlit in a crystal casket, wearing a polka-dot tie and a dark suit-cum-shroud, Lenin looks shrunken and waxy, his beard wispy and his fingers discoloured. The chamber's layout ensures that it's impossible to linger, so that visitors emerge blinking into the daylight less than a minute later.

During the latter years of *glasnost*, it was revealed that Lenin's body was dabbed with embalming fluid twice a week and received a full bath and a new suit every eighteen months, under the supervision of Dr Debov (who denies rumours that the body was long ago replaced by a wax model). Debov's **laboratory** lies two floors below the funerary chamber, beneath another sub-level which contains a **bar-buffet** for distinguished visitors and a **gymnasium** where the guards exercise when off duty. While leaving Lenin's body *in situ* now seems grossly inappropriate (he actually wished to be buried beside his mother in St Petersburg's Volkov Cemetery), the Mausoleum really deserves to be preserved as a stylish piece of architecture and a bizarre, modern counterpart to the pyramids of ancient Egypt.

## The Kremlin wall and its towers

The Kremlin wall behind the Mausoleum constitutes a kind of **Soviet pantheon**, which is likely to change should Lenin ever go. Some predict wholesale evictions, or at the very least the removal of Stalin (whose home town of Gori has already asked for his remains). Visitors leaving the Mausoleum pass a mass grave of Bolsheviks who perished during the battle for Moscow in 1917, to reach an array of luminaries whose ashes are interred in the Kremlin wall. These include the American journalist John Reed; Lenin's wife Krupskaya, and his lover Inessa Armand; the writer Maxim Gorky;

---

*The deaths of three successive leaders between 1982 and 1985 gave rise to the joke about a loyal citizen hurrying to Red Square to watch Chernenko's funeral. When asked if he had a pass, he replied, "No, I have a season ticket".

various foreign Communist leaders; and the world's first astronaut, Yuri Gagarin. Beyond lies a select group of Soviet leaders, distinguished by idealized busts on plinths. The first to be encountered is Chernenko's (causing Russians to snigger), followed by an avuncular Andropov, a pompous Brezhnev and a benign-looking Stalin. Conspicuously absent from this roll-call of leaders is Khrushchev, who died in obscurity and was buried in the Novodevichiy Cemetery (see p.194).

The **Kremlin wall** is 19m high and 6.5m thick, topped with swallow-tailed crenellations and defended by eight towers mostly built by Italian architects in the 1490s. The distinctive jade-green spires were added in the seventeenth century, and the ruby-red stars (which revolve in the wind) in 1937. At the northern end is the round **Corner Arsenal Tower**, which takes its name from the adjacent Kremlin Arsenal. Further along is the triple-tiered **St Nicholas Tower**, built by Pietro Antonio Solari. The tower's massive red star (3.75m wide and 1.5 tons in weight) gives it a total height of 70.4m.

Beyond the **Senate Tower**, named after the green-domed building visible behind Lenin's Mausoleum, looms the Gothic-spired **Saviour Tower**. In Tsarist times, an icon of the Saviour was installed above its gate, and everyone who entered doffed their hats; when Napoleon rode in without doing so, his horse shied and his hat fell off, confirming the Russians' belief in its miraculous powers. On Lenin's orders, the chimes of the tower's clock were adjusted to play the *Internationale*; they have now been altered to play the new Russian national anthem. It was from the Saviour Gate that soldiers formerly goose-stepped to the Mausoleum to change the guard at what was known as Sentry Post No.1.

The small **Tsar's Tower**, erected in 1680, gets its name from an earlier wooden tower whence the young Ivan the Terrible used to hurl dogs to their deaths and watch executions on Red Square. Also opposite St Basil's is the **Alarm Tower**, whose bell warned of fires; Catherine the Great had the bell's tongue removed as a "punishment" after it was rung to summon a dangerous mob during the Plague Riot of 1771. In medieval times, the chunky **SS Constantine-Helena Tower** served as the Kremlin's torture chamber; the screams of victims were audible on Red Square. The circular **Moskva River Tower**, built by Marco Ruffo in 1487, protects the southeastern corner of the Kremlin wall, which was usually the first part of the fortress to be attacked by the Tatars.

## St Basil's Cathedral

No description can do justice to the inimitable and magnificent **St Basil's Cathedral** (*sobor Vasiliya Blazhennovo*), silhouetted against the skyline where Red Square slopes down towards the Moskva River. Foreigners have always seen it as a cryptic clue to the mysterious Russian soul. The French diplomat, the Marquis de Custine, thought its colours combined "the scales of a golden fish, the enamelled skin of a serpent, the changeful hues of the lizard, the glossy rose and azure of the pigeon's neck", and questioned whether "the men who go to worship God in this box of confectionery work" could be Christians.

St Basil's was commissioned by Ivan the Terrible to celebrate his capture of the Tatar stronghold of Kazan in 1552, on the feast day of the Intercession of the Virgin. Officially named the Cathedral of the Intercession of the Virgin by the Moat (after the moat that then ran beside the Kremlin), its popular title commemorates a "holy fool", St Basil the Blessed, who came to Ivan's notice in 1547 when he foretold the fire that swept Moscow that year, and was later buried in the Trinity Cathedral that then stood on this site. St Basil's was built in 1555–60, most likely by Postnik Yakovlev (nicknamed "Barma" – the Mumbler), who, legend has it, was afterwards blinded on the Tsar's orders so that he could never create anything to rival the cathedral. (In fact, he went on to build another cathedral in Vladimir.) In modern times, this unique masterpiece was almost destroyed by Stalin, who resented the fact that it prevented his soldiers from leaving Red Square en masse. Its survival is due to the architect Baranovskiy, whose threat to cut his own throat on the cathedral's steps in protest changed Stalin's mind, though he was punished by five years in prison.

Despite its apparent disorder, there is an underlying **symmetry** to the cathedral, which has eight domed chapels (four large and octagonal, the others smaller and squarish) symbolizing the eight assaults on Kazan, clustered around a central, lofty tent-roofed spire, whose cupola was compared by the poet Lermontov to "the cut-glass stopper of an antique carafe". In 1588, Tsar Fyodor added a ninth chapel on the northeastern side, to accommodate the remains of St Basil; its small yellow and green cupola is studded with orange pyramids. Rather than using the main arcaded staircase, visitors enter through an inconspicuous door near the ticket kiosk (Wed–Mon 9.30am–5.30pm; $2). Sadly, the **interior** is far plainer than the facade, with restorers' scaffolding making the small chapels even more claustrophobic. The floral designs covering the walls and vaults (painted in the seventeenth century), and the fact that the floor tiles have been so worn down that the grouting forms ridges underfoot, are the most notable features.

In the garden out in front stands an impressive bronze **statue of Minin and Pozharskiy** who rallied Russia during the Time of Troubles. They made a curious team, as Dmitry Pozharskiy was a prince, while Kuzma Minin was a butcher from Nizhniy Novgorod, whose patriotic citizens funded the volunteer army that drove out the invading Poles in 1612. Erected in 1818, by public subscription, the statue was Moscow's first monumental sculpture, and originally stood in front of what is now GUM.

# The Lobnoe mesto

En route to St Basil's, you'll see the circular stone platform known as the **Lobnoe mesto**, whose name (derived from *lob*, meaning "forehead") is usually translated as the "place of executions" or the "place of proclamations", since it served for both. Early in his reign, it was here that Ivan the Terrible begged for the people's forgiveness after Moscow was razed by a fire that the Patriarch pronounced to be God's punishment for his misdeeds. In 1570, however, Ivan staged a festival of torture on the square, where two hundred victims perished in a man-sized frying pan or on ropes stretched taut enough to saw bodies in half; on another occasion, he amused himself by letting loose wild bears into the crowd. In 1605, the False Dmitry proclaimed his accession here, a year later, his mutilated corpse was burned to ashes and fired from a cannon in the direction of Poland, from the same spot. Most famously, in 1698, Peter the Great carried out the mass execution of the mutinous *Streltsy* regiments on scaffolds erected nearby – personally wielding the axe on a score of necks (see box below).

*Confusingly, there were two False Dmitrys during the Time of Troubles: for more about them see p.340.*

# The Alexander Gardens

To visit the Kremlin or merely view it from another angle, leave Red Square and turn left around the corner into the **Alexander Gardens** (*Aleksandrovskiy sad*). The gardens were laid out in 1819–22, after the Neglina River that ran alongside the western wall of the Kremlin was channelled into an underground pipe. Just inside the gates is the **Tomb of the Unknown Soldier**, whose eternal flame was kindled from the Field of Mars in Leningrad when the memorial was unveiled in 1967. Beneath a granite plinth topped by a giant helmet and furled banner lie the remains of a nameless soldier disinterred from the mass grave of those who died halting the Nazi advance at Kilometre 41 on the Leningrad highway; the inscription reads: "Your name is unknown, your feat immortal". Nearby is a line

---

**The Streltsy**

In medieval times, Red Square and the suburbs across the river teemed with thousands of *Streltsy*, the shaggy pikemen and musketeers who guarded the Kremlin and were Russia's first professional soldiers. Garbed in caftans, fur-trimmed hats and yellow boots, their banners emblazoned with images of God smiting their foes, they made a fearsome host whenever they assembled at the Tsar's bidding – or in revolt. In 1682, when Peter was ten years old, they butchered several of his relatives on the Red Staircase in the Kremlin – an experience that crystallized his hatred for Old Muscovy and its ragtaggle army. It was to beat them that Peter later formed his own "toy" regiments drilled in European tactics by foreign officers, which routed the *Streltsy* when they revolted again in 1698. A famous painting by Surikov depicts the Tsar gazing pitilessly over the wives and children of the condemned, in the shadow of St Basil's.

---

of porphyry blocks containing earth from the "Hero Cities" of Leningrad, Kiev, Volgograd, Sevastapol, Minsk, Smolensk, Odessa, Novorossisk, Tula, Murmansk, Kerch and the Brest Fortress. Newly-weds and VIPs often come here to lay flowers beside the monument, and it is carpeted with floral tributes on Victory Day (May 9).

Further along near the **Middle Arsenal Tower** are a whimsical arched **Grotto** that really belongs in a country estate, and an obelisk erected to mark the 300th anniversary of the Romanov dynasty. Lenin ordered that the obelisk be converted into a **Monument to Revolutionary Thinkers**, inscribed with the names of Bakunin, Marx, Engels, Plekhanov, Hume and other personages deemed to be intellectual precursors of Marxism. In Bulgakov's famous novel, *The Master and Margarita*, it was on one of the nearby benches that the grieving heroine Margarita met the Devil's sidekick, Azazello, and accepted an invitation to Satan's Ball, which led to the release of her beloved from a mental asylum.

Midway along the ramparts, a brick ramp with swallow-tailed cren-ellations descends to the white **Kutafya Tower**, the last survivor of several outlying bastions that once protected the bridges leading to the Kremlin, whose decorative parapet was added in the seventeenth century. The bridge leads up to the eighty-metre-high **Trinity Tower**, the tallest of the Kremlin towers, whose gateway admits visitors to the citadel (see below). Further south, the **Commandant's Tower** and the **Armoury Tower** abut the Kremlin's Armoury Palace, while another rampway leads up to the multi-tiered **Borovitskiy Tower**, whose name derives from the pine-grove (*bor*) covered hillock on which the citadel was founded. In winter, when the steep hillside is covered with snow, kids zoom down on sledges and shoot across the path of unsuspecting tour groups heading for the Borovitskiy Gate.

# The Kremlin

*This curious conglomeration of palaces, towers, churches, monas-teries, chapels, barracks, arsenals and bastions . . . this complex functions as fortress, sanctuary, seraglio, harem, necropolis and prison, this violent contrast of the crudest materialism and the most lofty spirituality – are they not the whole history of Russia, the whole epic of the Russian nation, the whole inward drama of the Russian soul?*

Maurice Paléologue, *An Ambassador's Memoirs*

Brooding and glittering in the heart of Moscow, the **Kremlin** thrills and tantalizes whenever you see its towers stabbing the skyline, or its cathedrals and palaces arrayed above the Moskva River. Its name* is

---

*In Russia, *kreml* means fortress, and every medieval town had one. The origin of the word is obscure: some think it derives from the Greek *kremn* or *krimnos*, meaning a steep hill above a ravine; others from a Slav term for thick coniferous woods in a swampy place.

synonymous with Russia's government, and in modern times assumed connotations of a Mecca for believers, and the seat of the Antichrist for foes of Communism. Hostile foreign perceptions long predate the Soviet era, for as far back as 1839 the Marquis de Custine fulminated: "To inhabit a place like the Kremlin is not to reside, it is to protect oneself. Oppression creates revolt, revolt obliges precautions, precautions increase dangers, and this long series of actions and reactions engenders a monster." Unsurprisingly, Russians generally feel more respectful than paranoid, being inclined to agree with Lermontov, who rhapsodized: "What can compare to the Kremlin which, having ringed itself with crenellated walls and adorned itself with the golden domes of cathedrals, sits on a high hill like the crown of sovereignty on the brow of an awesome ruler."

## A brief history

According to **legend**, a band of *boyars* (nobles) hunting in the forest saw a giant two-headed bird swoop down on a boar and deposit its corpse on a hilltop overlooking two rivers. That night, they dreamt of a city of tent-roofed spires and golden domes, where people shuffled in chains towards a huge gallows – and waking next morning, they resolved to build upon the site. More prosaically, the **founding of the Kremlin** is attributed to Prince **Yuri Dolgorukiy**, who erected a wooden fort above the confluence of the Moskva and Neglina rivers in about 1147 – although the site may have been inhabited as long ago as 500 BC. Crammed with wooden houses, churches and stables, Dolgorukiy's Kremlin was razed to the ground by the Mongols in 1238, but, like the city that had grown up around it, soon arose from the ashes, bigger and stronger than before.

Between 1326 and 1339, the Kremlin was surrounded by oaken walls and the first stone cathedral appeared in its midst; some forty years later the original fortifications were replaced by stone walls, whose colour earned Moscow the sobriquet "the White City". Despite being sacked by the Tatars in 1382, its development proved unstoppable. During the reign of Grand Duke **Ivan III** (1462–1505) – dubbed "the Great" – the realm of Muscovy quadrupled in size and threw off the Tatar yoke, becoming pre-eminent among the Russian states. To confirm Moscow's stature, Ivan embarked on an ambitious building programme, using craftsmen from Pskov, Tver and Novgorod, supervised by Italian architects, who arrived in 1472.

It was the Italians who built most of the cathedrals and fortifications that exist today, which were subsequently embellished by Ivan III's grandson Ivan IV (1553–84) – better known as **Ivan the Terrible** (*Ivan Grozniy*) – who first assumed the title of "Tsar", and made the Kremlin notorious for murders and orgies. The demise of his son, Fyodor I, brought the Rurik dynasty to an end and the wily **Boris Godunov** to power in 1598. His unpopularity with the nobility encouraged a pretender, claiming to be the youngest son of Ivan the

Terrible, to invade Russia from Poland and proclaim himself Tsar following Godunov's death in 1605. This so-called **False Dmitry** soon alienated his supporters and was murdered by a mob; the ensuing **Time of Troubles** saw Russia ravaged by famine, civil wars and invasions. After the Kremlin was recaptured from the Poles by Minin and Pozharskiy in 1612 (see p.340), the nobility elected **Mikhail Romanov** as Tsar, inaugurating the dynasty that would rule Russia until 1917.

Under Mikhail and his successors, Alexei and Fyodor II, the Kremlin was rebuilt and order restored; the Terem and Patriarch's Palaces date from this era. The next Tsar, **Peter the Great** (1682–1725), changed everything by spurning Moscow and the Kremlin for the new city that he founded by the Gulf of Finland, and by enforcing reforms that struck at everything held dear by traditionalists. Henceforth, the Tsars and the government dwelt in St Petersburg, only visiting the Kremlin for coronations, weddings and major religious celebrations. Although **Catherine the Great** (1762–96) added the Senate building and commissioned a vast new palace that was never built, the Kremlin was otherwise neglected until the French invasion of 1812, when the great fire that destroyed Moscow and forced **Napoleon** to withdraw necessitated major repairs to the parts of the Kremlin that he had spitefully blown up.

During the reign of the arch-conservative **Nicholas I** (1825–55), the Russo-Byzantine-style Armoury and Great Kremlin Palaces were constructed, and the Terem Palace was refurbished in a recreation of early Romanov times. However, St Petersburg remained the capital and the focus of events until after the fall of the Romanov dynasty and the overthrow of the Provisional Government by the **Bolsheviks**, whose Moscow contingent took the Kremlin by storm on November 3, 1917.

In March 1918, **Lenin** moved the seat of government back to Moscow and into the Kremlin, as if anticipating how a party founded in the spirit of internationalism would later, under the rule of **Stalin** (1929–53), identify itself with Ivan the Terrible and other "great Russian patriots". Like "Genghis Khan with a telephone", Stalin habitually worked at night, obliging his ministers and their staffs to do likewise, giving rise to the pasty "Kremlin complexion". As purges decimated the Party, fear and secrecy pervaded the Kremlin, which remained closed to outsiders until 1955. Yet, despite the murderous decisions taken here, it saw little actual blood spilt, the most dramatic moment being the arrest of Lavrenty Beria, the dreaded chief of the secret police, following Stalin's demise.

Under later Soviet leaders, the Kremlin retained an aura of power and mystery, but gradually lost its terrible associations. Today – since the end of the Soviet Union and the emergence of a Russian parliament at loggerheads with the presidency – its occupants probably wield less power than at any time in the Kremlin's colourful history.

# Visiting the Kremlin

In general, visiting the Kremlin is surprisingly easy. The complex is **open** to the public from 10am to 5pm every day except Thursday, but may be closed without notice for state occasions or during political crises. One significant exception to this rule is the **Armoury Palace**, which can only be entered at set times on Kremlin open days (see p.88) – although pre-arranged package tours may continue when the rest of the Kremlin is closed without notice; such groups enter through the Borovitskiy Gate at the far end of the western wall, rather than via the Kutafya and Trinity gates, as other visitors do.

Assuming you're not with a group, the procedure is to deposit your bag at the cloakroom tucked away at the base of the Kutafya Tower's southern side, and buy **tickets** at one of the kiosks on either side of the tower. One ticket, for a nominal sum, admits you to the Kremlin, while four others (sold *en bloc* for the equivalent of $2) are required to enter its cathedrals, and a further one (costing about $1) is needed for the Patriarch's Palace. These can sometimes be individually purchased inside the relevant building, but it's better to play safe and buy them all at the outset.

There's no need to sign up for a tour unless you want to. The **tours** run by folks touting their services through megaphones on Red Square simply whisk you around the outside of the cathedrals, with a commentary in Russian. More expensive ones by *Intourist* or private companies like *Patriarchi Dom* (see p.32) take you into the buildings, escorted by an English-speaking guide, but don't necessarily provide any more enlightenment than a decent guidebook. Alternatively, you can engage a **personal guide** from the hopefuls that wait near the Kutafya Tower. Rates are negotiable and the quality is variable; accredited guides should wear a badge issued by *Intourist*. If you're seriously interested in icons or history, the English-speaking **consultants** on duty inside the Assumption and Annunciation cathedrals can answer most questions for free. **Photography** is not permitted inside any of the cathedrals or museums.

Visitors' **movements** within the Kremlin are strictly controlled, with white lines and whistle-tooting policemen marking the limits beyond which you can't stroll (or even cross the road) – the descriptions in this book are structured to take account of these restrictions. While it's possible to see almost everything in one visit, a couple of visits are better if you have the time: one to see the inside and outside of the cathedrals, and another for touring the Armoury Palace.

Those with the energy should also try viewing the Kremlin from **different vantage points**. The view from across the Moskva River Tower is the finest in Moscow, with a glorious panorama of palaces and cathedrals arrayed above the wall that stretches from the

Vodovzvodnaya (Water-Drawing) Tower to the Moskva River below Red Square. From high up on the Bolshoy Kamenniy bridge, you can even glimpse the Terem Palace, which is inaccessible to visitors. Lastly, you might consider walking right around the outside of the Kremlin walls, which total 2,235 metres in length.

## Restricted zones and the Palace of Congresses

Roughly two-thirds of the Kremlin is off-limits to tourists, namely the trio of buildings in the northern half of the citadel, and the wooded Secret Garden sloping down towards the river. Entering via the Trinity Gate, the "government zone" lies to your left, where cannons captured during the Napoleonic Wars are ranged alongside the **Arsenal**. Commissioned by Peter the Great, but virtually redundant by the time it was completed in 1736, this occupies the site of the medieval *boyars'* quarter, where the higher nobility resided until the fifteenth century.

Opposite the Arsenal stands the imposing **Senate** building, erected in 1776–87 by Matvei Kazakov, whose Classical design was cleverly adapted to the awkward triangular site. The edifice was commissioned by Catherine the Great for meetings of the Moscow branch of the Senate, an advisory body established in 1711; since 1991 it has been the official **residence of Russia's president** (though Yeltsin is known to prefer his suburban *dacha*). From Red Square you can see the green cupola of its grand hall, formerly used for meetings of the USSR Council of Ministers and the awarding of Lenin Prizes. During the recent modernization of the building, Yeltsin got rid of **Lenin's quarters**, which had been preserved as a hallowed shrine, only shown to VIPs.

To the southeast is another Classical structure, built in 1934 as a school for "Red Commanders", which subsequently housed the Presidium of the Supreme Soviet and now contains government offices; for want of a new title, it is still referred to as the **Presidium**. In June 1953, it was here that secret police chief Beria was arrested at gunpoint during a meeting. Some allege that he was shot on the premises, and the body smuggled out in a carpet for fear that his bodyguards would take revenge on the other ministers. Previously, in Tsarist times, the site was occupied by the Monastery of Miracles and the Convent of the Ascension, which many royal daughters were forced to enter as nuns, owing to a lack of suitably Orthodox foreign rulers whom they could marry. By the nineteenth century, the convent had become so disreputable that one visitor described it as a "complete bagnio", where "the favours of any particular nun may be had for the asking".

To the right of the Trinity Gate, a narrow lane runs parallel to the Kremlin wall; also out of bounds, this contains the former **Kavalerskiy Building** where Lenin and Krupskaya lived after they first moved into the Kremlin, before moving into a modest suite of rooms in the Senate. Across the way is the seventeenth-century **Poteshniy Palace**, where Stalin had his private apartments and his wife, Nadezhda, shot herself in 1932. The yellow palace is recognizable by its protruding bay-window; its name derives from the word for "amusements" (*potekhi*), as Tsar Alexei had a theatre here.

Further east stands the **Palace of Congresses** (*Dvorets sezdov*), a 120-metre-long glass and concrete box sunk 15m into the ground so as not to dwarf the other buildings in the Kremlin. Built in 1959–61 to host Party congresses, the stage of its 6000-seat auditorium was adorned by a giant bas-relief of Lenin's head, emanating gilded rays. The stage hosts performances by the Kremlin Ballet Company; for details, see p.319.

## The Patriarch's Palace and Cathedral of the Twelve Apostles

As far as tourists are concerned, the accessible part of the Kremlin begins around the corner from the Palace of Congresses, where the **Patriarch's Palace** (*Patriarshie palaty*) and the **Cathedral of the Twelve Apostles** (*sobor Dvenadtsati Apostolov*) hove into view. The two form one structure, painted flesh-pink, with an arched, covered balcony inset with polychrome tiles, and gilt frills on the three rounded gables and the balcony roof, surmounted by five small domes. Though the palace was begun in 1640, it is chiefly associated with **Patriarch Nikon**, who split the Russian Orthodox Church by his reforms during the years that he held the post (1652–58). While Nikon desired to restore the Church to the purity of its Byzantine origins, many Russians saw him as a heretic bent on imposing foreign ways. He also tried to assert the primacy of the Church over the state, thus angering Tsar Alexei, who refused to reinstate Nikon as Patriarch after he resigned in a fit of pique.

Today, the palace is a **Museum of Seventeenth-century Life and Applied Art**, displaying ecclesiastical regalia, period furniture and domestic utensils – an English-language guide tape can be rented inside. The palace's highlight is the vaulted **Cross Chamber** (*Krestovnaya palata*), measuring 19 by 13 metres, which was the first hall of such size to be built in Russia without a central supporting column. Its inauguration occasioned a day-long feast where guests placed their empty goblets on their heads between toasts, while monks chanted the *Life of the Saints*. Among the goblets in case 3 is one without a base, which can't stand up, given to guests who arrived late to drain in one go. Decades later, the chamber was used for the preparation of *miro*, or holy oil, which explains the huge stove.

Other **exhibits** worth noting include a box for wine bottles made in the shape of an evangelistary, and a wine ladle with a capacity of 100 litres, belonging to Peter the Great's "Drunken Synod", whose riotous parties mocked Church rituals. The exhibition concludes in the former Cathedral of the Twelve Apostles, which was built above the archway leading to Sobornaya ploshchad, as it was deemed sacrilegious to site an altar above rooms used for everyday life. The cathedral's Baroque iconostasis was moved here from the now-demolished Convent of the Ascension; on the wall to the left hangs the *Passion of the Apostles*, depicting a dozen martyrdoms in detail. Also notice the small window high up on the west wall, through which Nikon could observe services from his private chapel on the floor above. Like all the windows in the palace, this is glazed with mica instead of glass, imparting a frosty hue to views of the outside world.

## The Tsar Bell and Cannon

Before passing through the archway into Sobornaya ploshchad, you can make a brief detour to find two of the Kremlin's most famous sights. The **Tsar Cannon** (*Tsar-pushka*) is one of the largest cannons ever made; its bronze barrel (bearing a relief of Ivan the Terrible's son, Fyodor) is 5.34m long, weighs 40 tons and has a calibre of 890mm. Cast by Andrei Chokhov in 1586, it was intended to defend the Saviour Gate, but has never been fired. Its enormous chassis, decorated with a lion and a snake fighting on either side and a snarling lion's head beneath the barrel, was cast in 1835, like the cannonballs piled in front (which are purely ornamental, as the cannon was originally meant to fire stone case-shot).

Further along, behind the Ivan the Great Belltower, looms the earthbound **Tsar Bell** (*Tsar-kolokol*), the largest in the world, weighing 200 tons (almost fifteen times as much as London's Big Ben) and measuring 6.14m in height and 6.6m in diameter. Its bronze surface is emblazoned with portraits of Tsar Alexei and Empress Anna, who decreed the creation of the original and existing versions of the bell. The first, 130-ton version was cast in 1655, during Alexei's reign, but nineteen years elapsed before anyone could work out how to hoist it into the belfry, whence it fell to the ground and shattered in the fire of 1701. Thirty years later, Anna ordered the fragments to be used for a much larger bell, which lay in its casting pit for over a century, having cracked in 1737, when fire once again swept the Kremlin and water was poured on the red-hot bell. Finally, in 1836, the Tsar Bell was excavated and installed in its present location, accompanied by a chunk that broke off, itself weighing 11 tons.

The nineteenth-century dissident Pyotr Chaadayev mused that, "in Moscow every foreigner is taken to look at the great cannon and the great bell – the cannon which cannot be fired and the bell which fell down before it was rung. It is an amazing town in which the objects of interest are distinguished by their absurdity, or perhaps that great bell without a tongue is a hieroglyph symbolic of this huge, dumb land."

Also worthy of reflection is the **statue of Lenin** that still broods in the wooded garden across the road. Erected to mark the fiftieth anniversary of the Bolshevik Revolution, this provided Soviet guidebooks with an excuse to relate how Lenin participated in cleaning up the war-ravaged Kremlin during the first Communist *Subbotnik* (day of voluntary labour) on May 1, 1918. Among other deeds, he helped some workmen carry a log; in the years that followed, over a thousand people claimed to have shouldered the burden beside him.

## Sobornaya ploshchad and the Ivan the Great Belltower

Beyond the Patriarch's Palace lies the historic heart of the Kremlin, surrounded by a superb array of buildings that gives the square its name. **Sobornaya ploshchad** (Cathedral Square) was first laid out in the early fourteenth century, making it the oldest square in Moscow, although the buildings that you see today were erected later. Throughout Tsarist times, the square was used for Imperial coronations and weddings, and before the capital was transferred to St Petersburg it was also the setting for court life and political dramas. Every morning, the *boyars* and gentry converged here in carriages or sledges to assemble in order of rank; the *ploshchadniki* or "people of the square" being inferior to the *komnatniki* or "people of the apartments", who enjoyed access to the Tsar's palace. At other times, commoners were free to gather on the square – providing they prostrated themselves whenever the Tsar appeared.

Soaring above the square, the magnificent white **Ivan the Great Belltower** (*Kolokolnya Ivana Velikovo*) provides a focal point for the entire Kremlin, being the tallest structure within its walls. The main belltower was erected in 1505–08 by the Italian architect **Marco Bono** (known in Russia as Bon Fryazin), whose octagonal tower was increased to its present height of 81m during the reign of Boris Godunov, as proclaimed by the inscription in gold letters beneath its gilded onion dome. It remained the tallest structure in Russia until 1707, and dominated Moscow's skyline for long after that. Adjacent is the four-storey belfry (*Zvonitsa*) added in 1532–43 by the architect Petrok Maliy, which also has a gilded dome. The 64-ton Resurrection Bell, dating from the nineteenth century, is the largest of its 21 bells. On the ground floor of this section is a hall used for **temporary exhibitions**, for which a special ticket (sold on the spot) is required. The final, tent-roofed part of the building – known as the Filaret Annexe, after the Patriarch who commissioned it in 1624 – was badly damaged in 1812, when the French attempted (but failed) to blow up the entire belltower.

## The Cathedral of the Assumption

Across the square from the Ivan the Great Belltower stands the oldest and most important of the Kremlin churches, whose massive walls and gilded helmet-shaped domes have the stern serenity of a warrior monk. The **Cathedral of the Assumption** (*Uspenskiy sobor*) has symbolized Moscow's claim to be the protector of Russian Orthodoxy ever since the seat of the Church was transferred here from Vladimir in 1326, together with a revered icon that was installed in a small cathedral erected by Ivan I.

By the 1470s this cathedral had become so decrepit that Ivan III ordered a replacement worthy of Moscow's stature; unfortunately the first effort by native builders collapsed before completion, so Ivan hired the Bolognese architect **Alberti Fioravanti** – dubbed "Aristotle" – who arrived in 1475, bringing engineering techniques a century ahead of any in Russia. Having visited the ancient cities of Vladimir, Suzdal and Novgorod to study Russian architectural traditions, he took only four years to finish the cathedral, which so harmonized with native forms that Patriarch Nikon (see p.76) would later recommend it as a model for Russian architects. Fioravanti's reward was to be thrown in prison after he begged permission to return to Italy; he died there in 1486.

The cathedral's subsequent **history** reflects its role as Russia's premier church, used throughout Tsarist times for coronations and solemn acts of state. Here, Ivan III tore up the charter that bound

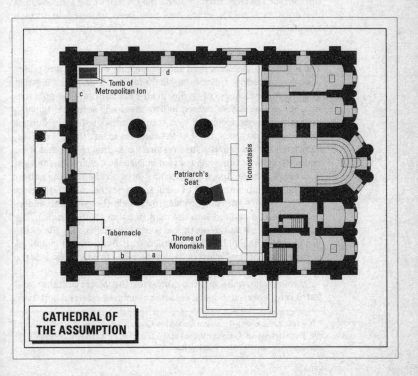

Tomb of
Metropolitan Ion

d

c

Iconostasis

Patriarch's
Seat

Tabernacle

Throne of
Monomakh

b     a

**CATHEDRAL OF
THE ASSUMPTION**

Russia's princes to pay tribute to the Tatar Khans; divine intercession was invoked during calamities; Te Deums were sung to celebrate victories; and the Patriarchs of the Orthodox Church were inaugurated and buried. In times of woe, the cathedral also suffered: Napoleon's cavalry stabled their horses here in 1812, while in 1917 it was shelled during fighting between the Bolsheviks and White troops. Following the Revolution, no services took place here for more than seven decades, until a special mass was permitted in honour of the tercentenary of the Russian Patriarchate in 1989. Though still a museum rather than a place of worship, the cathedral is likely to be used for religious services with increasing frequency in the future.

Given the cathedral's exalted status, its **exterior** is remarkably plain, like that of the Cathedral of the Assumption in Vladimir, which Fioravanti was ordered to emulate. Built of limestone with brick drums and vaulting, its rectangular form incorporates portals on three sides and barely protruberant apses on the eastern facade. The only decorative features are a horizontal belt of blind arcading punctuated by slit windows, a series of frescoes added in the 1660s beneath the gables on the east and west sides, and the ogee-shaped porches on the north and south facades. The current entrance is through the doorway sited opposite the Church of the Deposition of the Robe (see p.72), which has now been enclosed to form a vestibule.

### Frescoes, tombs and thrones

The **interior** is spacious, light and echoing, its walls, roof and pillars entirely covered by frescoes applied onto a gilt undercoating that gives them the richness of an illuminated manuscript – the predominant colours are amber, russet, indigo, green and scarlet. Originally, the cathedral was decorated by a team of artists led by the famous icon-painter Dionysius; most of the **frescoes** extant today, however, date from the cathedral's first restoration in the 1640s, and were restored in Soviet times. As is usual in Orthodox churches, the west wall bears a huge *Apocalypse*, with Christ flanked by the saintly host floating above a pair of scales. Notice the infernal serpent writhing in coils of iron, prodded by angels (below), and sinners being scourged and fed into the maw of Satan (bottom right). The upper three tiers on the north and south walls depict the life of the Virgin, while the pillars are adorned with five rows of paintings portraying saints and martyrs (which decrease in height towards the roof, so as to accentuate the loftiness of the cathedral).

Around the walls are the **tombs of the Metropolitans\* and Patriarchs**, encased in metal caskets resembling caterers' hotboxes,

---

*The title reflected the Russian Orthodox Church's nominal subordination to the Patriarchate of Constantinople until 1589, when it finally became fully autonomous, with its own Patriarch.

with the conspicuous exceptions of a bronze **Tabernacle** containing the remains of Patriarch Hermogenes, who perished in prison for opposing the Polish occupation in 1612 and was later canonized; and the **tomb of Metropolitan Ion** in the northwest corner, surmounted by a gold and silver arch. Aside from Patriarch Nikon, who lies in the New Jerusalem Monastery, the only absentees are Tikhon and Alexei I, two Patriarchs of Soviet times.

When not officiating during services, the head of the Church sat in the stone **Patriarch's Seat**, built into one of the cathedral's pillars. Nearby stands the **Throne of Monomakh**, covered by an elaborate tent-roofed canopy crowned with a double-headed eagle, made for Ivan the Terrible in 1551. The throne's name derives from its carvings, depicting the campaigns of Grand Prince Vladimir, who supposedly received the famous Crown of Monomakh from the Byzantine Emperor Constantine IX – a legend that Ivan used to support Moscow's claim to be the "Third Rome" and the heir to Byzantium.

*The Crown of Monomakh can be seen in the Armoury Palace.*

## Icons

The cathedral's lofty **iconostasis** dates from 1652, but its bottom row incorporates several older icons. On the far left is the enthronement of the Virgin known as *All Creatures Rejoice in Thee*, followed by a cutaway section revealing fragments of the cathedral's original frescoes, both of which were painted by Dionysius. A tent-roofed box to the left of the central Royal Door contains an early sixteenth-century copy of the revered *Virgin of Vladimir*, while to the right of the southern door is a blue-cloaked *St George the Victorious*, painted in Novgorod during the twelfth century. Between the two pillars nearest the iconostasis hangs the 46-branch **Harvest Chandelier**, presented to the cathedral by Cossacks after they recaptured much of the 5330 kilos of silver that had been looted from the premises by the French army in 1812.

Around the walls hang **other icons** of historic interest. Dionysius is supposed to have painted *The Life of Metropolitan Peter* [a], which honours the prelate who engineered the transfer of the Metropolitanate from Vladimir to Moscow; the foundation of the original Cathedral of the Assumption is depicted near its bottom left corner. Nearby hangs *The Apostles Peter and Paul*, painted by an unknown Greek master of the fourteenth or fifteenth century [b]. By the west wall, an early fifteenth-century *Crucifixion* is followed by another copy of the *Virgin of Vladimir* [c], which, like the copy in the iconostasis, was venerated almost as much as the original (now held by the Tretyakov Gallery), believed to have been painted by St Luke and to have saved Moscow from the army of Timerlane. The aptly named *Saviour with the Severe Eye*, painted in the 1340s, hangs nearby, while along the north wall are *St Nikolai and his Life*, by the school of Novgorod, and several icons from the Solovetskiy Monastery in the White Sea [d].

## The Church of the Deposition of the Robe

Almost hidden behind the Cathedral of the Assumption, the lowly white Church of the Deposition of the Robe (*tserkov Rizpolozheniya*) was built by craftsmen from Pskov in 1484–86, on the foundations of an older church erected to celebrate the prevention of a Tatar attack on Moscow some thirty years earlier. Its name refers to the festival of the deposition of the robe or veil of the Virgin Mary in Constantinople, which was believed to have saved the city from capture on several occasions; the miraculous relic was paraded around the city walls in times of danger, as was an icon of the same name in Moscow during medieval times.

Externally, the church is notable for the slender pilasters and intricate friezes that decorate its apses, and the ogee-shaped portal on its south side, reached by an open stairway. Nowadays visitors enter by a covered stairway facing the Cathedral of the Assumption, which leads up to an **exhibition of wooden figures**, which believers once imbued with almost as much holiness as icons. The effigies of Nikita Muchenik (wearing armour and hefting a flail) and Patriarch Nikola (carrying a model of a cathedral) are particularly striking.

Inside the chapel there's hardly room to swing a censer, but it's worth lingering over the **frescoes**, which were painted in 1644 by Sidor Osipov and Ivan Borisov, and restored in the 1950s. Above the door as you come in are Mary and Joseph in the wilderness and the *Adoration of the Magi*; on the other walls, the uppermost tiers depict scenes from the apocryphal life of the Virgin, while the bottom two rows illustrate the 25 stanzas of the *Hymn to the Virgin*. Christ, the Virgin and the prophets cover the ceiling, while the pillars bear portraits of Prince Vladimir, Alexander Nevsky and other heroes of Russian Christianity.

## The Cathedral of the Archangel

The last of the great churches to be erected on Sobornaya ploshchad, the **Cathedral of the Archangel** (*Arkhangelskiy sobor*) was built in 1505–08 as the burial place for the rulers of Muscovy, who claimed the Archangel Michael as their celestial guardian. Unlike the vernacular Cathedral of the Assumption, its debt to the Italian Renaissance is obvious, for the architect **Alevisio Novi** incorporated such features as Corinthian capitals and the Venetian-style shell scallops that form the gables. Another characteristic is its asymmetrical layout, with the east and west walls being divided into three sections, and the north and south walls into five. To compensate for this, the western pair of domes is larger than the eastern pair; both sets are clad in silvery iron, in contrast to the gilded central dome. The cathedral's plan was further complicated by the addition of chapels to the apses during the sixteenth century; buttresses along the south wall were added after it cracked in 1773; and an annexe or *palatka* was attached to the southwest corner in 1826.

You enter the cathedral through its west **portal**, whose archway is framed by carvings of plants and a faded fresco depicting Christ and the saints (above), and the mass baptism of the Russians during the reign of Prince Vladimir (at the bottom, on either side).

## The frescoes and iconostasis

Four heavy square pillars take up much of the dimly lit interior, which is covered in **frescoes** executed (1652–66) by a team of artists under Simon Ushakov and Stepan Rezanets, which replaced the originals by Dionysius. Ochre, pale blue, red, white and dark brown predominate, with *The Apocalypse* in its usual position on the west wall. Notice the angels summoning the dead from their graves [a], and Satan sitting on a fiery beast whose mouth emits a

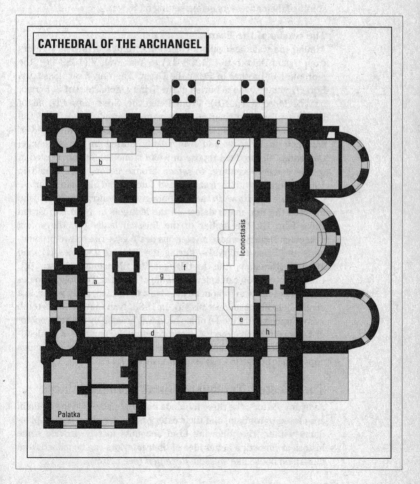

CATHEDRAL OF THE ARCHANGEL

serpent that drags sinners down into Hell [b]. *The Adoration of the Magi* and *The Annunciation* are depicted on the third and fourth tiers of the north wall [c], while the south wall portrays the deeds of the Archangel Michael. Stylized portraits of early Russian rulers, martyrs and saints cover the pillars, and a white-robed Christ surveys the iconostasis from inside the central cupola.

The four-tiered scarlet and gold iconostasis dates from 1813, replacing the original one that French troops chopped up for firewood. In the bottom row, however, the second icon to the right of the Royal Door is thought to date from the fourteenth century and may have been commissioned by the wife of Prince Dmitry Donskoy. It portrays the Archangel Michael wearing armour, as befits the patron saint of Russia's rulers, who used to pray here and commune with the spirits of their ancestors before setting off to war.

### The tombs of the Tsars

Around the walls and pillars cluster the tombs of Russia's rulers from Grand Duke Ivan I (1328–41) to Tsar Ivan V (1682–96), the moronic half-brother of Peter the Great. The only Tsar missing is Boris Godunov, who is buried at the Trinity Monastery of St Sergei, outside Moscow (p.276). From Peter the Great onwards, all of Russia's rulers and their consorts were interred in the Peter and Paul Cathedral in St Petersburg, except for Peter II, who died of smallpox in Moscow and was hastily buried in the Archangel Cathedral. All the dead repose in white stone sarcophagi carved in the seventeenth century, to which bronze covers were added in 1903, inscribed with their names and dates in Old Slavonic script.

Visitors are drawn to the sarcophagus of **Dmitry Donskoy**, who inflicted the first major defeat on the Mongols in 1380 [d]; Grand Duke **Ivan III**, the unifier of the Russian lands [e]; the young **Tsarevich Dmitry**, whose mysterious death gave rise to two pretenders – or "False Dmitrys" – during the Time of Troubles [f]; and **Mikhail Romanov**, the founder of the Romanov dynasty [g]. Unfortunately, you can't view the tomb of **Ivan the Terrible**, who lies beside his sons Ivan (whom he killed in a fit of rage) and Fyodor, in a chapel behind the iconostasis [h]. In 1963, Ivan the Terrible's tomb was exhumed and a model of his head was created by the anthropologist Gerasimov, an expert at reconstructing the features of unidentified corpses from their skulls, who makes a pseudonymous appearance in Martin Cruz Smith's novel *Gorky Park*.

## The Faceted, Terem and Great Kremlin palaces

Sadly for visitors, the three fabulous Imperial palaces in the Kremlin are closed to tourists, and their exteriors fall far short of the splendours within. The following brief accounts merely provide some historical context; a better idea of their interiors can be gained from illustrated books like *Moscow Revealed* (see p.359).

The white **Faceted Palace** (*Granovitaya palata*) that juts out between the cathedrals of the Assumption and the Annunciation is currently enclosed by a fence, but you can't miss the diamond-patterned facade that gives the palace its name. Built for Ivan III in 1487–91 by Marco Ruffo and Pietro Antonio Solario, its outstanding feature is the large chamber that forms its upper storey, whose vaults are supported by a single massive pillar. Painted and gilded, this served as a banqueting hall and audience chamber; it was here that Ivan the Terrible treated foreign ambassadors to roast swan and elks' brains, and Gorbachev held banquets for Mrs Thatcher and President Reagan. In medieval times, the tsars descended from the hall to Sobornaya ploshchad by the gilded **Red Staircase** (*Krasnaya lesnitsa*), whence several relatives of the ten-year-old Peter the Great were thrown down onto the pikes of the *Streltsy* during the revolt of 1682. Wantonly demolished in the 1930s, the staircase is now being rebuilt at vast expense.

Directly behind the Church of the Deposition of the Robe you can see the eleven gilded onion domes of the **Terem Palace** (*Teremnoy dvorets*), the oldest building in the Kremlin, which served as the Imperial residence until Peter the Great moved the capital to St Petersburg in 1712. The palace incorporates two medieval churches built one on top of the other and two levels of service quarters, above which is the royal suite created for Mikhail Romanov in 1635–36 – *terem* means "tower-chamber". All the rooms were connected by a corridor used for the *smotriny*, the selection of the Tsar's bride from a parade of eligible virgins – Ivan the Terrible indulged in this rite at least seven times. In 1837, the long-disused palace was refurbished in a recreation of the seventeenth-century style, with elaborately tiled stoves, gilded stucco and painted vaultings.

The aptly named **Great Kremlin Palace** (*Bolshoy Kremlevskiy dvorets*) stretches for 125m along the crest of the Kremlin hill. Commissioned in 1837 by Nicholas I, who preferred Moscow to St Petersburg and admired ancient Russia, its yellow-and-white facade employs old Russo-Byzantine motifs according to the rules of Classical harmony. Above the Imperial apartments on the ground floor are five splendid reception halls dedicated to the chivalric orders of the Empire. The white **St George's Hall** is used for the presentation of state awards, while international treaties are usually signed in the adjacent **St Vladimir's Hall**. Access to the Terem and Faceted palaces is through the **Holy Vestibule**, with its multiplicity of gilded doorways.

## The Cathedral of the Annunciation

To the south of the Faceted Palace glints the golden-domed **Cathedral of the Annunciation** (*Blagoveshchenskiy sobor*), which served as the private church of the Grand Dukes and Tsars. It

**The Kremlin** stands on the site of a church built by Dmitry Donskoy's son, Vasily I, the foundations and undercroft of which were incorporated into the existing structure, erected in 1448–49 by master stonemasons from Pskov at the behest of Ivan III. The cathedral was badly damaged in the conflagration that swept Moscow in 1547, shortly after the coronation of Ivan the Terrible, and it was restored in 1562–64. The Tsar had the cathedral's gallery enclosed, a domed chapel added to each corner, and two false domes erected, bringing the total to nine. The domes, roof and tops of the apses were then sheathed in gold (supposedly looted from Novgorod, after Ivan sacked the city), giving rise to the cathedral's nickname, "gold-topped" (*Zlatoverkhniy*). Its tiers of gables and *kokoshniki* reflect the influence of early Moscow architecture, while the intricately carved frieze below the domes is a typical feature of Pskov churches.

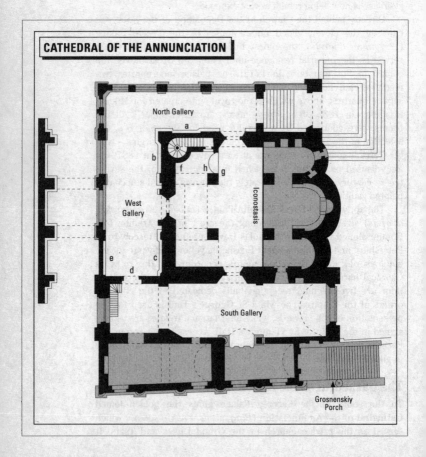

CATHEDRAL OF THE ANNUNCIATION

North Gallery

West Gallery

Iconostasis

South Gallery

Grosnenskiy Porch

Visitors enter via the steps at the northeast corner; the other, covered, porch was added in 1572, after Ivan the Terrible married for the fourth time, contrary to the rules of the Orthodox faith, which allow only three marriages. The Church Council dared not refuse him a special dispensation, but salved its conscience by stipulating that the Tsar henceforth attend services via a separate entrance, and observe them from behind a grille. Should the guard stationed nearby permit it, you can follow in his footsteps by climbing the steps of the **Groznenskiy Porch** (whose name derives from the sobriquet *Grozniy*, meaning "Awesome" or "Terrible") alongside the road leading to the Armoury Palace.

## The galleries

The royal chapel is enclosed by three **galleries**, two of which are richly decorated with **frescoes** painted in the 1560s. An elaborate but faded *Tree of Jesse*, symbolizing the continuity between the Old and New Testaments, covers the ceiling and merges into portraits of Muscovite princes and Greek philosophers on the vaults and pilasters. Just beyond the magnificent blue and gold **portal** carved with floral tracery, you'll see *Jonah and the Whale*, with two anatomically preposterous fish, one swallowing Jonah and the other disgorging him [a]. In the west gallery, another gilded portal is flanked by the hymn to the Virgin known as *In Thee Rejoiceth* [b] and *The Trinity* [c], around the corner from which, the *Feats of the Monastic Recluses* [d] shows their fasts and flagellations, and a brightly coloured *Annunciation* [e] was added in the nineteenth century. The third gallery, decorated at the same time, now exhibits diverse icons and ecclesiastical objects, including two crosses carved with miniature biblical scenes, which are best viewed after the royal chapel.

## The chapel and its iconostasis

Lofty and narrow, with much of the space occupied by the pillars supporting a gallery from which the female members of the royal family would have observed services, the interior seems far more "Russian" than the other cathedrals within the Kremlin. Its floor of irregularly shaped, brown jaspar flagstones enhances the impression of warmth and intimacy created by the soft-toned murals and lustrous iconostasis. The restored **frescoes** were originally painted in 1508 by a fraternity of icon-painters from the Iosifo-Volotskiy Monastery, headed by the monk Feodosius, son of the Dionysius who created the original murals in the Cathedral of the Archangel.

The *Last Judgement* in the northwest corner is populated by mythical creatures and huddled sinners, covetously regarded by Satan [f], while on the overhead gallery you can discern toppling buildings and beasts attacking men in *The Apocalypse* [g]. Portraits of Russian princes, including Dmitry Donskoy and Vasily I, adorn the nearby pillar [h]; the other one features the Byzantine Emperors and their families. Scenes from the lives of Christ and the Virgin cover the north and south walls, while angels, patriarchs and prophets cluster around *Christ Pantokrator* in the central dome.

The **iconostasis** – which dates from 1405 and survived the fire of 1547 – is regarded as the finest in Russia, containing as it does the work of three masters: Theophanes the Greek, Andrei Rublev and Prokhor of Gorodets. In the bottom row to the right of the Royal Door are *Christ Enthroned* and the *Ustyug Annunciation* (whose central panel is a copy of the twelfth-century original now in the Tretyakov Gallery). To the left of the Royal Door are icons of the *Hodegetria Virgin* and the *Virgin of Tikhvin* (far left), both dating from the sixteenth century. Theophanes created most of the icons in the third, Deesis Row, where Christ is flanked by John the Baptist and the Virgin, next to whom is an Archangel Michael attributed to Rublev, who collaborated with Prokhor on the Festival Row, above. This is surmounted by a row devoted to the prophets, topped by ogee-shaped finials containing small images of the patriarchs.

## The Armoury Palace

Situated between the Great Kremlin Palace and the Borovitskiy Gate, the **Armoury Palace** (*Oruzheynaya palata*) conceals a staggering array of treasures behind its Russo-Byzantine facade. Here are displayed the Tsars' coronation robes, carriages, jewellery, dinner services and armour – made by the finest craftsmen with an utter disregard for cost or restraint – whose splendour and curiosity value outweigh the trouble and expense involved in seeing them. As an institution, the Kremlin Armoury probably dates back to the fourteenth century, if not earlier, though the first recorded mention was in 1547. Initially, its purpose was utilitarian – one foreigner described it as being "so big and so richly stocked that twenty thousand cavalry men could be armed with its weapons" – but it soon became a storehouse for state treasures and, in 1813, a semi-public museum. The existing building was designed in 1851 in the same style as the Great Kremlin Palace, by Nicholas I's favourite architect, Konstantin Ton.

Unless you sign up for an *Intourist* tour, **visiting the Armoury** is far from easy. Admission is limited to four times a day (currently at 10am, noon, 2.30 & 4.30pm), and you can only remain inside for a single session of one hour and 45 minutes' duration. Visitors enter via the third door along from the Great Kremlin Palace, which is only identifiable by a small sign in Russian and a crush barrier outside. Tickets are sold inside for rubles only, though prices are equivalent to $10 ($5 for card-carrying students) at whatever rate is posted at the exchange desk. Most foreigners arrive in groups, with their own guide to smooth the way; if you just turn up, it may be hard to buy a ticket until they've gone in.

Hiring a **guide** is less of a problem, and not obligatory. Beyond the cloakroom is an information desk, followed by another desk purveying glossy art books. Stairs at the far end lead to a small foyer with two doors, one leading to the Armoury Museum, the other to the State Diamond Fund (see p.94). Having passed through a ticket check, you ascend to larger foyer with two staircases, the left-hand one leading to the lower floor of the Armoury, the other to the upper floor.

## The lower floor

The **lower floor** of the Armoury holds the most appeal, displaying the fabulous costumes, thrones, crowns and carriages of Russia's rulers, from medieval times onwards. Besides their sheer sumptuousness, one is struck by the abrupt stylistic change from Russo-Byzantine forms to the familiar fashions of Western European courts, introduced by Peter the Great in the early eighteenth century. The exhibits are labelled in Russian only, but the keyed plan below should help you to figure out what's what.

### Court dress and vestments

The first room is largely devoted to **court dress**. In the left-hand case are Peter the Great's Dutch-style frock coat, thigh-boots and walking stick [1]; the falconry outfit of Mikhail Romanov, with a Tsarist eagle on its breast [2]; typical long-sleeved, old-style caftans [3]; the gold brocade robes and jewellery worn by Peter at his coronation, and the house-caftans that he relaxed in [4]. The central display is fronted by an archaic gold caftan and sable hat worn by Nicholas II at a costume ball in 1903 [5]. Beyond the cerise coronation dress of Catherine I [6] are the frock coat and stockings of Peter II; the gold-embroidered coronation dresses of empresses Anna [7] and Elizabeth [8]; and the wasp-waisted wedding dress of Princess Catherine [9]. Finest of all are Catherine the Great's coronation dress [10] and ermine-trimmed cape [11], embroidered with Tsarist eagles. The coronation dresses of Alexandra Fyodorovna [12] and Maria Aleevna [13] are in the French Empire style of the 1820s and 30s.

Along the right wall are **ecclesiastical vestments and fabrics**, the oldest of which is the pale blue and silver satin *sakkos* (ceremonial robe) of Metropolitan Peter, made in 1322 [14]. Metropolitan Photius had two *sakkos* [15]: the Maliy, decorated with crucifixions, saints and

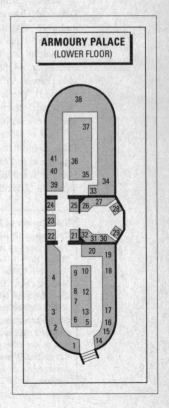

**ARMOURY PALACE**
(LOWER FLOOR)

royal portraits; and the Bolshoy, with similar designs outlined in pearls (a symbol of good luck in old Russia). Past a *sakkos* given by Ivan the Terrible to Metropolitan Dmitry [16] are the pearl-embroidered Venetian velvet robes, mantle, cuffs and crowns of Patriarch Nikon [17]. Imported European fabrics began to be used from the seventeenth century onwards, as evinced by the cloth-of-gold pearl-hemmed cape given by Mikhail Romanov to the Novospasskiy Monastery [18]; Patriarch Adrian's Italian robe, embroidered with Tsarist eagles [19]; and a French velvet cape criss crossed with pearl tracery and emblazoned with a huge diamond and emerald cross, given by Catherine the Great to Metropolitan Platon [20].

## Crowns and thrones

The corridor beyond showcases **crowns and thrones**. Ivan the Terrible's ivory throne, carved with battle and hunting scenes, stands beside a low golden throne studded with turquoises, given to Boris Godunov by the Shah of Persia [21]. Opposite are the throne of Mikhail Romanov, made in the Kremlin Armoury, and the Diamond Throne of his son Alexei, adorned with silver elephants and over eight hundred diamonds, a gift from Armenian merchants [22]. The huge silver double throne [23] was made for the dual coronation in 1682 of the young Peter the Great and his feeble-minded half-brother Ivan V, who were prompted by their elder sister Sofia from a secret nook behind the throne (now exposed). The hefty Empress Elizabeth sat on a wide Empire-style "armchair" throne, while the more runty Emperor Paul had a smaller one with a foot-tuffet [24].

Best of all are the **crowns and imperial regalia** in the last case [25]. Behind the famous Crown of Monomakh (see box) at the right-hand end of the lower shelf are the gold-leafed Kazan Crown of Ivan the Terrible, made to celebrate the capture of that city from the Tatars in 1552; the eighteenth-century European-style Silver Crown

---

**The Crown of Monomakh**

The Cap or **Crown of Monomakh** (*Shapka Monomakha*) symbolized the Tsars' claim to heritage of Byzantium and Moscow's boast of being the "Third Rome". Legend has it that the crown was presented to Prince Vladimir of Kiev (980–1015) by the Byzantine Emperor Constantine IX Monomachus, though experts believe that the existing crown actually dates from the late thirteenth or early fourteenth century. In any event, it visibly differs from other European crowns, consisting of eight gold-filigree triangles joined to form a cone, studded with rough-cut gems and trimmed with sable. It served for the coronation of every Tsar from the end of the fifteenth century to 1682; some years later Peter the Great introduced Western-style crowns, which were used thereafter. However, his successors retained Mikhail Romanov's original orb and sceptre, symbolizing the Tsar's dominion over the earth.

that belonged to Empress Anna, encrusted with 2500 diamonds; a cruder "second" Crown of Monomakh and the sable-trimmed Diamond Crowns of Peter the Great and Ivan V. On the lower shelf can be seen Ivan V's Siberian Crown, trimmed in silver sable, and Mikhail Romanov's emerald-topped Dress Crown and enamelled orb and sceptre.

## Saddlery and coaches

The adjacent octagonal room displays **equestrian regalia**, including Ivan the Terrible's saddle, covered in dark red velvet, turquoises and gold embroidery [26]. Beyond the saddles of Prince Pozharskiy and Boris Godunov (the latter embossed with lions' heads) is a saddle decorated with gems and a saddlecloth made from over four hundred parrotskins, given by the Persian Shah to Mikhail Romanov in 1635 [27]. The stuffed horse in ceremonial attire was one of a hundred such horses that used to precede the Imperial coach during processions. Catherine the Great received jewelled harnesses and saddles from sultans Abdul Hamid [28] and Selim III [29], as did Alexei and Mikhail Romanov from earlier Turkish rulers [30], and tsars Fyodor and Boris Godunov from the monarchs of Persia [31] and Poland [32] – the last is embroidered with hunting scenes in silver wire.

The oldest of the **carriages and coaches** in the end room is an English carriage presented to Boris Godunov by James I, decorated with hunting scenes on the sides and decapitated heads beneath the pillion [33]. Nearby stand an early seventeenth-century Russian coach with mica windows [34] and tiny summer and winter coaches made for the child Peter the Great, which had dwarves for coachmen and were drawn by ponies [35]. The French coach with paintings of cherubs by Boucher [36] was given to Empress Elizabeth by her lover Razumovskiy; she also owned a winter coach whose sleds were carved with dolphins [37], and several gilt travel coaches [38]. Catherine the Great received a gilded summer coach from her favourite Orlov [39] and used a bronze and silver one for state occasions [40], whereas Peter the Great contented himself with a single red and gold travel coach [41].

## The upper floor

From the same lobby, a grand staircase with brass balustrades ascends to the **upper floor**, whose landing is decorated with paintings of parades and processions outside the Kremlin, with the Soviet crest incongruously inset above a massive doorway. The rooms that follow are crammed with treasures and armour, which soon overwhelm visitors, and eventually pall. Either concentrate on the Russian gold and silver in the initial rooms, or return another day to view the rest with a fresher eye. Unlike on the lower floor, each case has an explanatory note in English, although individual pieces are only labelled in Russian.

# The Kremlin

## Russian gold and silver

The first room contains the **Russian gold and silver** collection ranging from the twelfth to the sixteenth centuries. Though many medieval treasures disappeared during the Mongol invasion, two buried troves of jewelled pectorals and necklaces were found at Ryazan and Tula in the nineteenth century [1]. Bibles and icons often used to be encased in gold covers like the foliage-engraved *okhlad* for the *Virgin of Vladimir* [2], while holy relics were kept in cathedral-shaped receptacles such as the Great and Small Sions [3]. The sixteenth century was the golden age of Russian jewellery [4]. Notice the Evangelistry studded with gems as big as grapes, which Ivan the Terrible gave to the Cathedral of the Annunciation, and the pearl-rimmed crucifix that he bestowed upon the Solovetskiy Monastery [5]. Ornate Byzantine crosses and icons [6] pale before the solid gold, gem-encrusted tomb covers that were made for Tsarevich Dmitry and the founder of the Arkhangelsk Monastery [7].

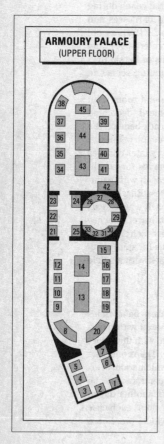

The dark green hall beyond exhibits more of the same, from the seventeenth century onwards. Near a squinting *Don Virgin* with a pearl choker is a gold cover for *The Trinity* icon, featuring three face-shaped ovals suspended in mid-frame [8]. At court, mead was drunk from a scoop-shaped *kovsh*, while guests toasted each other with a shared friendship cup, or *bratina* [9]. Moscow craftsmen specialized in the technique of *niello*, whereby etched grooves were filled with a powder that turned a soft black after firing, highlighting the designs that appeared on the surface [10]. At Solvychedosk, they excelled at enamelling, with tiny birds a favourite motif [11], whereas the Volga towns went in for minutely detailed silverwork [12]. The Kremlin workshops produced the enamelled chalice given by Boyarina Morozova to the Monastery of Miracles, and the gold goblet presented by Tsar Alexei to the Monastery of the Ascension [13].

The early eighteenth-century inlay and enamel work on display [14] is less striking, and the collection of French-Empire-style stuff [15, 16 & 18] is positively tedious. However, notice the Style Moderne cup, jug and sugar bowl [20] near the "modern masterpieces" [19], and the utterly kitsch Evangelistry commissioned by Catherine the Great, which glitters like a disco mirror-ball [17].

Among the **foreign weapons and armour** in the next room are arquebuses and plate armour from Germany [21]; a complete set for a horse and rider, presented to Tsar Fyodor by King Stephen Bathory of Poland [22]; and a miniature suit of armour made for Tsarevich Alexei in 1634 [23]. Across the way are jewelled maces and Egyptian sabres, rifles inlaid with ivory and mother-of-pearl, gilded helmets and arm-guards studded with turquoises and carnelians – all hailing from various parts of the Ottoman Empire [24]. Also notice the spiked helmets with sinister face-masks, and the gem-encrusted dagger presented by the Shah of Persia to Mikhail Romanov, in the showcase of Persian arms and armour [25].

The adjacent circular chamber – decorated by a frieze of royal portraits – displays **Russian weapons and armour**. To the left are the spiked helmets and chainmail armour of Boris Godunov and Prince Shuyskiy, and a teardrop-shaped helmet made for Ivan Ivanovich, the three-year-old son of Ivan the Terrible [26]. The *saadak* (weapons case) and quiver of Mikhail Romanov are made of gold and encrusted with jewels [27], while his gold-chased helmet appears beyond the mail-and-plate armour of his son, Alexei [28]. Russian cavalrymen customarily wore a mixture of Russian-made and Turkish or Persian armour, as on the lifesize model [29]. Beyond various products of the Kremlin Armoury [30] are a host of drums, trumpets and officer's throat guards, captured from the Swedes during the Northern War [31]. Brilliants glitter on the hilt and scabbard of Alexander I's sword, made in Tula [32], and a display of the Chivalric Orders of the Tsarist Empire concludes the exhibition [33].

## European gold and silver

The final hall is stuffed with **European gold and silver**, much of it presented as ambassadorial gifts. The Dutch gave Count Stroganov ewers, tankards and a leaf-shaped wall candelabra [34], while Tsar Alexei received a silver banqueting set from the Poles, which included a bird-figure that poured water on guests' hands [35]. In 1644, the Danes lavished similar gifts in the hope of marrying their Crown Prince to Tsarevna Irina, and the Hanseatic League sent huge goblets with gryphons on the lids [36]. Nuremburg goldsmiths devised receptacles moulded to fit pineapples [37] and a drinking vessel in the form of a cockerel [38], while Hamburg specialized in "smoking hills" that wafted aromatic fumes across the table [39]. From France came gold *toilette* sets for the Stroganovs and Trubetskoys [40], the *Tête-à-Tête* tea service [41], and the *Olympic* dessert service that Napoleon gave to Alexander I to commemorate the Treaty of Tilsit [42]. Among the Armoury's peerless collection of English Tudor silver are two leopard-shaped flagons and a pair of jugs with dragon spouts [43]. Finally, don't miss the triple-layer Swedish table fountain [44], nor the caseful of *objéts* fashioned from shells, bone and other unusual materials [45].

The Kremlin    **The State Diamond Fund**

The Armoury Palace also houses the **State Diamond Fund** (*Almazniy Fond*), a separate section under the auspices of the Ministry of Finance, which contains the most valuable gems in Russia. Access is strictly limited to groups, with twenty-minute guided **tours** running from 10am to 12.20pm and from 2.20 to 5.20pm. Though **tickets** are usually only available from *Intourist* for the equivalent of $22, and need to be booked two to three days in advance, they can occasionally be purchased at the Armoury counter for around $16, at shorter notice. There's an exchange office on the spot.

The exhibition features numerous *objéts* by the St Petersburg jewellers, Fabergé, including some of the 56 **Imperial Eggs** that were exchanged as Easter gifts by the Tsar and Tsarina every year from 1884 until the fall of the Romanov dynasty. Even finer is the **Grand Siberian Railway Egg**, produced to mark the completion of the line to Vladivostok. Its enamelled gold shell is engraved in silver with a map of the route, each station marked by a gem; inside is a tiny gold and platinum replica of the Trans-Siberian Express, which runs when the clockwork locomotive is wound up. Also on display is the diamond-encrusted crown made by J Pozier for Catherine the Great's coronation, and the 190-carat **Orlov Diamond** that was given to the Empress by Count Grigory Orlov, in an attempt to revive their relationship; she never wore it, but had it set into the **Imperial Sceptre**. Another notable gem is the 89-carat **Shah Diamond**, presented to Nicholas I by the Shah of Persia as compensation for the murder of the Russian diplomat and playwright Griboedov by a mob in Teheran. Besides this, there are dozens of jewelled necklaces and earrings, the world's largest sapphire (258.8 carats), and a gold nugget weighing 36 kilos.

# Chapter 3

# The Kitay-gorod

To the east of Red Square lies the old quarter of **KITAY-GOROD**, whose eclectic mix of churches and palaces, banks, workshops and offices reflects its 800-year-old history. Although Kitay-gorod means "China Town" in modern Russian, there is no evidence that Chinese merchants ever resided here, and most scholars believe that the name derives from *kita*, an old word meaning "wattle", after the palisades that reinforced the earthen wall erected around this early Kremlin suburb. In the fifteenth century, nobles began to settle here in preference to the Kremlin, displacing the original population of artisans and traders, but the nobility later moved further out to escape the risk of fires and plagues, leaving the quarter to rich merchants. Finally, the merchants too relocated to more salubrious areas, and the Kitay-gorod became what it still is today, predominantly commercial, with new banks and emporiums replacing the older shops and dwellings.

Aside from the busy **streetlife** on thoroughfares like Nikolskaya ulitsa, the main attractions are its churches, particularly the **Church of the Trinity** and the **Church of All Saints**; while the interior of the **Palace of the Romanov Boyars**, in the **Zaryade** area, should also not be missed. Two sections of the **fortified walls** that once ran for 2.6km around the Kitay-gorod attest to its embattled ancient history – with frequent attacks from the Poles, the Lithuanians and the Tatars. The former Lenin Museum and Communist Party headquarters are reminders of a Soviet era only recently concluded.

Being just off Red Square, **ploshchad Revolyutsii** is a good place to start, with access from Ploshchad Revolyutsii or Okhotniy Ryad metro stations; or you can approach the quarter from its periphery instead, starting from the Kitay-gorod or Lubyanka stations. As the Kitay-gorod is small and contained, you can walk around the whole quarter in an hour.

## Around ploshchad Revolyutsii

Just off Red Square, some kind of counter-revolution has triumphed on **ploshchad Revolyutsii** (Revolution Square), where kiosks

*Some Lenin
exhibits may
find a new
home in the
Museum of the
Revolution on
Tverskaya
ulitsa (p.149),
or the Gorki
Leninskie estate
outside
Moscow, where
Lenin died
(p.285).*

proliferate and crowds congregate outside the **former Lenin Museum**, a striking red-brick, Pseudo-Russian edifice that originally housed the pre-revolutionary City Duma, or municipal council. Its 22 halls contained the world's largest collection of Leninalia, including Lenin's Rolls-Royce Silver Ghost and a replica of his study in the Kremlin. After the 1991 *putsch*, the museum lost its state funding and was forced to shed 150 staff, but struggled on until October 1993, when Mayor Luzhkov decreed its eviction to make way for the newly elected **City Duma**, due to take up residence in the near future.

Meanwhile, Communists and neo-Nazis regularly gather outside to rant about Jews and treason, particularly on Lenin's birthday (April 22), when the crowd spills over onto Teatralnaya ploshchad. From the row of kiosks alongside (called *Krasniy ugol*, "Red Corner"), steps ascend to a lively vendor-packed passage leading to Nikolskaya ulitsa and GUM.

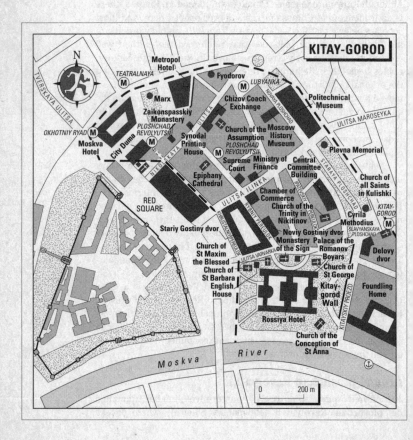

Across the road stands the leviathan grey **Moskva Hotel**, a building erected to accommodate delegates to Party congresses, and where the British defector Guy Burgess lived until his death in 1963. An amusing story explains its asymmetrical facade facing Manezhnaya ploshchad. In 1931, its architect, Alexei Shchusev, submitted two variations to Stalin, who casually approved both, not realizing that he was supposed to choose between them – but no one dared correct his mistake. Had the 1935 city reconstruction plan been fully realized, this facade would have faced the never-built Palace of Soviets (see p.128) down a wide avenue, intended as the focal point of the city.

The opposite side of the hotel faces the park-like **Teatralnaya ploshchad**, which is bisected by a main road. Near the roadside, a giant **statue of Karl Marx** looms out of a granite menhir flanked by slabs engraved with testimonials: "His name will endure through the ages, and so will his work" (Engels); "Marxist doctrine is omnipotent because it is true" (Lenin) – both now sprayed with graffiti.

On the far side of the square is the handsome Style Moderne (p.369) **Metropol Hotel**, built in 1899–1903 by the Odessa-born British architect, William Walcott. The north wall features a huge ceramic panel, *The Princess of Dreams*, designed by the Symbolist artist Mikhail Vrubel in his characteristic palette of indigo, violet and bottle green. Also notice the wrought-iron gateway facing Teatralnaya ploshchad, and the two plaques beside the main entrance, attesting to the hotel's role as the "Second House of Soviets" in the years after the Revolution. It was here that the Central Executive of the Soviets of Workers' and Peasants' Deputies met in 1918–19.

Until 1991, the ploshchad Revolyutsii was named after the Central Executive's boss, Yakov Sverdlov, a statue of whom stood nearby. The Bolshevik who ordered the execution of the Imperial family at Yekaterinburg, Sverdlov is especially hated by contemporary ultra-nationalists; these days only the shattered plinth of his statue remains. Behind it looms the best-preserved section of the sixteenth-century **Kitay-gorod wall**, whose zigzag around the back of the *Metropol* can be explained by a bend in the now-buried Neglina River. Behind the wall rise the Proofreading House and the belltower of the Zaikonspasskiy Monastery (see below), both of which can be reached by taking the stairway behind Sverdlov's plinth.

Another approach is to walk uphill past the *Metropol* and cut in through the tent-roofed **ornamental gateway** that fronts Tretyakovskiy proezd. This passage is named after the merchant, Sergei Tretyakov, who knocked it through the wall in 1871, for quicker access to the banks along Kuznetskiy most. Just uphill from the gateway is an appealing **statue of Ivan Fyodorov**, Russia's first printer (see below).

## Nikolskaya ulitsa

Running off from Red Square either side of GUM are the two main thoroughfares of the Kitay-gorod, Nikolskaya ulitsa and ulitsa Ilinka. Named after the St Nicholas Gate of the Kremlin, facing the Red Square end of the street, **Nikolskaya ulitsa** bustles with shoppers emerging from GUM or the passage leading from ploshchad Revolyutsii. As its shopfronts are gradually restored to their pre-revolutionary elegance, it's easy to imagine Nikolskaya ulitsa becoming a swanky pedestrian precinct – though it still has a long way to go.

On the left-hand side, the iron gateway of no. 9 leads into a courtyard harbouring the remains of the **Zaikonspasskiy Monastery**. Founded in 1600, the monastery supported itself by selling icons on the street outside – hence its name, "Behind the Icon of the Saviour". In 1687, its seminary was converted into Russia's first institution of higher education, the Slavo-Greco-Latin Academy. Now being restored, the monastery's cathedral has a red and white octagonal belltower crowned by a gilded finial, linked to the adjacent monks' quarters by an overhead arcade.

It's indicative of how many monasteries there were in Moscow that just up the road and around the corner, past the *Stariy Gorod* kiosk-row, is the Monastery of the Epiphany. Its hulking **Epiphany Cathedral** (*Bogoyavlenskiy sobor*) is decorated with crested *nalichniki* and an intricate cornice. Although the cathedral was constructed in the 1690s, the monastery itself was founded by Prince Daniil (p.337) in the thirteenth century, making it the second oldest in Moscow. Here the restoration process is advanced due to gift-shop funds, and so services are held in the cathedral. Its entrance is around the left-hand side, past the former monks' quarters at the back, which now serve as offices.

Returning to Nikolskaya ulitsa, you'll catch sight of the **Synodal Printing House**, a picturesque turquoise structure with Gothic pinnacles and lacey stucco-work, erected on the site of the sixteenth-century Royal Print Yard (*Pechatniy dvor*), where Ivan Fyodorov produced Russia's first printed book, *The Apostle*. Ivan the Terrible took a keen interest, visiting nearly every day until it was completed in 1564, whereupon superstitious Muscovites incensed by this "Satan's work" stormed the press, forcing Fyodorov to flee for his life. In 1703, however, Russia's first newspaper, *Vedomosti*, was produced here without any mishap. The heraldic lion and unicorn of the old print yard appear over the existing building's central arch. In the courtyard out back lurks the original **Proofreading House**, tiled blue and red, which can be reached by entering the door on the left and turning right down some stairs – although you may need to persuade them to let you in.

Further along on the other side stands the **Slavyanskiy bazaar** restaurant, which was the first eating place in Russia to employ professional waiters rather than household servants when it opened in 1870. Most of its clientele were merchants, who each ordered an average of 24 pancakes at one sitting. The Slavyanskiy bazaar was also famous for hosting an eighteen-hour discussion between Konstantin Stanislavsky and Vladimir Nemirovich-Danchenko, which led to the foundation of the Moscow Arts Theatre. The restaurant obligingly stayed open until they had finished at 2am, on June 22, 1897. Unfortunately, a fire gutted its ornate interior in 1994 so it's unlikely to be open for a while yet.

*For more about the Moscow Arts Theatre, see p.110; and for the Stanislavsky Museum p.117.*

Nikolskaya ulitsa's commercial life concludes with the century-old **Ferryn Pharmacy** at no. 21 (Mon–Sat 8am–8pm, Sun 10am–6pm), which is worth a look for its Empire-style facade and the gilded and pillared room upstairs. Since the demolition in the 1930s of the medieval gate-tower at the end of the street, there's been an uninterrupted view of the secret police headquarters on the far side of Lubyanskaya ploshchad (p.134). Assuming you don't cross the square for a closer look, a right turn will take you in the direction of the Politechnical and Moscow History museums, described on p.104.

# Ulitsa Ilinka

The parallel **ulitsa Ilinka** used to be the financial centre of the Kitay-gorod, and is gradually reverting to type. Its name derives from the former Church of St Elijah (*tserkov Ili*) – now a video shop and only recognizable by its belfry – across the road from the oval-shaped **Stariy Gostiniy dvor** that occupies the entire block between Khrustalniy (Crystal) and Ribniy (Fish) pereulok. The Russian equivalent of an Oriental caravanserai for visiting merchants and their wares, it was designed in the 1790s by Catherine the Great's court architect, Quarenghi, who embellished its yellow facade with colonnades of Corinthian pilasters. After much neglect, a motley array of bars, workshops and offices have brought some life to its ravaged interior.

On the other corner of Ribniy pereulok stands the former Stock Exchange that now serves as **Moscow's Chamber of Commerce**, its Ionic pillars and bas-relief gryphons confronting a small square flanked by buildings of equal probity. Across the way stand the **Supreme Court** – housed in another Pseudo-Russian pile – and the former **Ryabushinskiy Bank**, a cream-coloured, glazed brick building designed by the great Style Moderne architect, Fyodor Shekhtel. Pavel Ryabushinskiy, Chairman of the Stock Exchange, also commissioned Shekhtel to build him a house that is one of the glories of Moscow (p.155). Take a brief look down Ribniy pereulok, where the **Noviy Gostiniy dvor** bears a kitsch bas-relief of a merchant's ship sailing into the sunset.

Continuing along Ilinka, you'll pass a striking pair of buildings: to the right, an emerald facade upheld by writhing atlantes and caryatids, facing the austere grey tiers of the **Ministry of Finance**, across the road. Further on, gates bar access to the side streets leading to the complex previously occupied by the Communist Party's Central Committee – beyond which Ilinka emerges on to Novaya and Staraya squares (see the final section of this chapter).

# Zaryade

The most interesting part of the Kitay-gorod is the area known as **Zaryade**, situated due east of St Basil's. From the twelfth century onwards, the swampy slope above the Moskva River was settled by craftsmen and artisans, whose homes lay behind the rows (*za ryade*) of stalls that covered what is now Red Square. Though nobles and foreign merchants displaced them during the fifteenth and sixteenth centuries, the quarter gradually reverted to being the heart of popular Moscow, crammed with booths and huts, and smelling of "perfumed Russian leather, spiritous liquors, sour beer, cabbages, and grease of Cossacks' boots", and undrained cesspits that rendered it prone to epidemics. In *War and Peace*, Tolstoy wrote of peasants lying unconscious in the mud, and drunken soldiers staggering after prostitutes.

Today, Zaryade's main sights lie along or just off **ulitsa Varvarka** (St Barbara Street), which is the oldest street in Moscow, dating back to the fourteenth century. During Soviet times it was called ulitsa Razina, after the leader of the 1670 peasant revolt, Stenka Razin, who was led along it to his execution on Red Square. Seen from Red Square, Varvarka's vista of onion domes and gilded crosses is marred only by the towering **Rossiya Hotel**, a 1960s eyesore covering nearly ten acres, whose architects originally intended to demolish the churches and medieval residences lining the street's south side. The appeal of the churches owes less to their interiors than to the totality of their variegated facades, which appear taller on the hotel-facing side, being built against a steep bank.

First comes the compact salmon-pink and white **Church of St Barbara** (*tserkov Varvary*), built in 1796–1804, on the site of an earlier church by Alevisio Novi, the architect of the Archangel Cathedral in the Kremlin. Having suffered decades of neglect under the stewardship of the All-Russia Society for the Protection of Monuments of History and Culture, it has recently been returned to the Orthodox Church – but currently hosts a tacky "art" gallery, like most of the former churches along Varvarka.

Next door is a chunky building with a steep wooden roof and narrow windows seemingly distributed at random, known as the **English House** (*Angliskoe podvore*). In 1555, Ivan the Terrible requisitioned the house and gave it to the English merchants of the Muscovy Company as a kind of embassy. While the first two envoys were warmly received, the third incurred Ivan's wrath by prevaricating over his demand to marry Queen Elizabeth I, and was confined under house arrest for four months. The house is currently being restored, but the builders might let you clamber around its warren of vaulted chambers.

The nearby **Church of St Maxim the Blessed** (*tserkov Maksima Blazhennovo*) is a simple Novgorod-style church erected by merchants from Novgorod in 1690–99, as a repository for the mortal remains of the fifteenth-century "holy fool", St Maxim, venerated for his mortification and self-denial. Behind St Maxim's rises another, pointed belltower, belonging to the **Monastery of the Sign** (*Znamenskiy monastyr*), established on the estate of the Romanov family in 1634. Its red-brick **Cathedral**, founded on oak piles that became harder than stone when wet, is decorated with intricate *nalichniki* and *kokoshniki*, surmounted by four onion domes covered in green and red shingles, and a central, gilded dome. During Soviet times it was converted into a concert hall, which has now been closed pending the cathedral's restoration to the Church.

# The Palace of the Romanov Boyars

Varvarka's most interesting building – and the only one whose interior should not be missed – is the **Palace of the Romanov Boyars** (*Muzey Palaty v Zaryade*; Wed 11am–6pm; Thurs–Sun 10am–6pm; also closed the last Mon of each month). Built in the sixteenth century by Nikita Romanov, the brother-in-law of Ivan the Terrible, it once formed the nucleus of a vast complex of seven thousand households stretching down to the river, made almost entirely of wood, with the exception of the palace.

The Romanov family's menfolk used the first floor, built of stone, whose rooms are low and vaulted, with mica windows, tiled stoves and gilded, embossed leather "wallpaper", in contrast to the spacious, airy women's quarters upstairs, panelled in blonde wood. Here, married couples slept on benches against the walls, while unmarried daughters spent the daytime weaving in the adjacent *svetlitsa* or "light room", with its latticed windows overlooking the street. The residence was abandoned after Mikhail Romanov was elected Tsar in 1613, and the whole family and their retainers moved into the Kremlin. In 1859, it was restored on the orders of Nicholas I as a tribute to his ancestors, and opened as a public museum.

Beyond the palace rises the sky-blue belltower of the **Church of St George** (*tserkov Georgiya na Pskovskoy Gorke*), whose sea-green onion domes spangled with gold stars and sprouting intricate crosses add a final touch of colour to the street. Although dedicated to the patron saint of Moscow, it was erected by merchants from Pskov in 1657, the belfry being a nineteenth-century addition. From here you can cross the road and walk up Ipatevskiy pereulok to find the wonderful Church of the Trinity, or head downhill towards Slavyanskaya ploshchad.

## The Church of the Trinity on Nikitinov

By following Ipatevskiy pereulok uphill and turning right, you'll come upon the Church of the Trinity on Nikitinov pereulok (*tserkov Troitsy v Nikitinkakh*), whose exuberant colours and asymmetrical form are all the more striking for being hemmed in by the anonymous premises of the Moscow Regional Soviet and the former Central Committee of the Communist Party. The church defies its confinement with an explosion of decorative features: white ogee-shaped *nalichniki* and *kokoshniki*, columns and cornices contrasting with crimson walls, green roofs and domes. Its height and dynamism are accentuated by a tent-roofed stairway climbing above a deep arcaded undercroft, and an open pyramid-spired belfry that would have soared above the wooden houses of the medieval Kitay-gorod.

Erected in 1635–53 by the wealthy merchant Grigory Nikitinov, who stashed his valuables in its basement, the church was squatted by numerous families after the Revolution, before being turned into a museum (Mon & Fri–Sun 10am–6pm, Wed & Thurs noon–8pm) in 1967. If it's not shut for an unofficial lunch break, you'll be able to admire its beautiful **frescoes** by Simon Ushakov and other icon-painters from the Kremlin Armoury. The nave's right-hand wall depicts *The Passion*, while Christ calms the Disciples in a storm-tossed boat on the opposite wall. On this side of the lower tier of the iconostasis is a copy of Ushakov's *The Holy Virgin of Vladimir*; the original is in the Tretyakov Gallery. Best of all is the side chapel of St Nikita the Martyr, where members of Nikitinov's family are portrayed alongside various martyrdoms and a green seraphim.

*For more about Ushakov, icon-painters and Russian art history, see the account of the Tretyakov Gallery, p.209.*

## Down towards the river

Downhill from the Church of St George and around the corner to the right, another remnant of the **Kitay-gorod wall** runs alongside Kitayskiy proezd. Though its swallow-tailed crenellations resemble those of the Kremlin, the Kitay-gorod walls were constructed a century later, when Russian fortifications became lower and thicker owing to the advent of cannons in siege warfare, and they were originally wide enough for a carriage to drive along the top. The pedestrian subway exposes some fragments of the **Varvarka Gate** that once straddled this exit under the protection of a supposedly miraculous icon of the Virgin. During the plague of 1771, this was taken down and repeatedly kissed in frenzied services that spread contagion; when Archbishop Amvrosy realized this and tried to replace the icon above the gate, he was pursued by a mob to the Donskoy Monastery and torn to bits.

Visible through the trees across the road from the ramparts is the vast Classical edifice of the **Foundling Home** (*Vospitalniy dom*), established by Catherine the Great to discourage infanticide and teach orphans trades useful to the state. Over 13,000 children resided here; but in 1812 as the French army approached, although the older ones were evacuated, the toddlers and babies were left behind in the care of a general (and, amazingly, survived). It now houses the Dzerzhinskiy Artillery Academy and the grounds are off-limits.

Beside the embankment below the *Rossiya* stands the small grey **Church of the Conception of St Anna** (*tserkov Zachatiya Anny*), where Salomonia Saburova, Grand Duke Vasily III's barren wife, often prayed for a child. In 1526 she was confined to a convent so that he could marry Yelena Glinskaya, who gave birth to the future Ivan the Terrible four years later.

# From Slavyanskaya ploshchad to the Lubyanka

**Slavyanskaya ploshchad**, at the foot of ulitsa Varvarka, takes its name from an imposing **statue of Cyril and Methodius** (*Kiril i Metodi*), the "Apostles of the Slavs" who invented the Cyrillic alphabet in order to bring them Christianity and let them write in their own language. On May 24, an icon is borne in a procession from the Kremlin to the monument, in honour of their contribution to Slavic culture. Before the statue was erected in 1991, on the millennial anniversary of the Russian Orthodox Church, the square was named after the Stalinist *apparatchik* Viktor Nogin. During Tsarist times, it was the site of an outdoor "winter market", heaped with deep-frozen Crimean oxen, Caspian sheep, Siberian deer and fish from the White Sea, which purchasers stored in their ice cellars and thawed as needed. The Royal Salt Yard (*Solyaniy dvor*) that once stood here has left its name to ulitsa Solyanka, nearby.

With the Kitay-gorod's transformation into a modern financial centre early this century, the market was superseded by the **Delovy dvor** (Business House), on the corner of Kitayskiy proezd. During the "heroic phase" of Socialist construction during the 1930s, it housed the Commissariat for Heavy Industry, whose boss, Sergei Ordzhonikidze, also had a hand in building the first line of the metro system. Almost next door is the small but striking blood-red, gold-domed **Church of All Saints in Kulishki** (*tserkov Vsekh Svyatykh na Kulishkakh*), erected by Ivan III to replace a wooden church built in a forest clearing (*kulishki*) by Prince Dmitry Donskoy, whose army passed by en route to the battle of Kulikovo on the River Don (1380), where the Russians defeated the Mongols for the first time.

From
Slavyan-
skaya
ploshchad to
the
Lubyanka

Behind the statue of Cyril and Methodius, the steep slope called **Staraya ploshchad** (Old Square) falls away from an embankment crowned by a row of office blocks dating from the beginning of the century. On the corner stands the former premises of the Moscow Insurance Company, an early design by Shekhtel, distinguished by its sea-green tiles and sinuous balconies. In Soviet times, this became the headquarters of the Moscow Regional Party organization, while the adjacent building (no. 4) housed the **Central Committee of the Communist Party**, the nexus of power in the Soviet Union. The day after the failure of the 1991 *putsch*, its nervous *apparatchiki* frantically shredded compromising documents, afraid to burn them lest the smoke caused the angry crowd outside to storm the building. Now flying the Russian tricolour, the severe grey building may be cordoned off in times of crisis, as it still houses bureaucrats serving the Russian prime minister.

At the top end of the wooded **Ilinskiy Gardens** that run down the middle of the hill stands the **Plevna Memorial**, honouring the Russian Grenadiers who died in the 1878 siege of Plevna against the Turks. Financed by battle veterans, it was designed by Vladimir Sherwood, the architect of the Historical Museum on Red Square. The gardens are named after the former Ilinskiy Gate, which was demolished in the 1930s, like the other gates in the Kitay-gorod wall.

### The Moscow History and Politechnical museums

These two museums are on **Novaya ploshchad** (New Square), beyond the corner of ulitsa Ilinka. Sadly, the **Moscow History Museum** (*muzey Istorii Goroda Moskvy*; Tues, Thurs, Sat & Sun 10am–6pm, Wed & Fri noon–6pm) at no. 12 is far less interesting than it could be, its only highlights a series of drawings of medieval Moscow by the historical painter Apollinarius Vasnetsov, and wooden scale models of the Kremlin and *boyars'* compounds in Zaryade. The first floor also boasts a corner of a log house with wooden waterpipes from the same era. The building's porticoed facade and green cupola are a reminder that it used to be the Church of St John the Divine Under the Elm.

*More of Vasnetsov's scenes can be seen at his former apartment on Furmanniy pereulok (p.170).*

Across the road at Novaya ploshchad 3–4 stands the **Politechnical Museum** (*Politekhnicheskiy muzey*; Tues–Sun 10am–6pm; closed every Mon & the last Thurs of each month), a long, mustard-coloured edifice in the Pseudo-Russian style. Founded in the 1870s to promote science and technology, the museum hosted an ambitious experiment in telepathy in 1967, when Yuri Kamenskiy attempted to transmit messages to the psychic, Karl Nikolaev, at Leningrad University, with some success. Research was subsequently conducted in secret under the auspices of the KGB. Tickets are sold inside entrance 9, on the side facing the Lubyanka, but you enter via the main door opposite the Moscow History Museum. The first floor covers everything from the development of lamps and typewriters to mining and the petroleum industry, while the floor above deals with space travel, antique music boxes, clocks and computers. In an unusual touch, visitors can play with soft-porn computer games by prior arrangement.

Chapter 4

# The Beliy Gorod

T he **BELIY GOROD** or "White Town" is the historic name of the residential district that encircled the Kremlin and the Kitay-gorod – derived from the white stone ramparts erected around it at the end of the sixteenth century. It remains a useful designation for the area within the horseshoe-shaped **Boulevard Ring** (*Bulvarnoe koltso*), laid out on the rampart sites after the great fire of 1812. Despite widening and modernization, many of the boulevards are still divided by long parks with wrought-iron lampposts and fences, redolent of nineteenth-century Moscow, and many squares bear the names of the original gate-towers. Fortunately, the Futurist El Lissitskiy's vision of buildings suspended above the Ring on giant legs (trumpeted as "architecture for world revolution", to "raise human consciousness") was never implemented.

Besides cultural meccas like the **Bolshoy Theatre**, the **Pushkin Museum of Fine Arts** and the **Conservatory**, the Beliy Gorod displays every style of architecture. Along its main thoroughfare, **Tverskaya ulitsa**, gigantic Stalinist edifices with Italianate loggias obscure older backstreets that lead to narrower radial avenues like Petrovka and Rozhdestvenka, where medieval **monasteries** and **churches** and the **Sandunovskiy Baths** are secluded. Further east, beyond the infamous **Lubyanka** prison and headquarters of the secret police, lies the former **Ukrainian quarter**, another fascinating area to wander around.

The Beliy Gorod's web-like layout and hilly topography makes **orientation** fairly difficult. This account begins with the **central axis** of Tverskaya ulitsa, before covering the remainder of the Beliy Gorod in **wedge-shaped sections** – first the western and then the eastern sectors. Each itinerary starts from the point nearest the Kremlin or the Kitay-gorod and works outwards to the Boulevard Ring – a distance of between one and two kilometres. In practice, you'll probably zigzag across several "wedges" rather than follow a single one to the end. Your starting point here is Tverskaya ulitsa, on the far side of the huge square to the north of the Kremlin.

# Tverskaya ulitsa

As its name suggests, **Tverskaya ulitsa** originated as the road leading to the old town of Tver, continuing to Novgorod and (after 1713) on to St Petersburg. Inns and smithies soon grew up alongside, until they were displaced during the sixteenth century by the stone palaces of the *boyars* and merchants. The road was surfaced with logs and varied in width from eight to fifteen metres along its zigzag course. As Moscow's main thoroughfare from the seventeenth century onwards, it boasted two monasteries and four churches, past which the Tsars proceeded on arrival from St Petersburg; for victory parades, Tverskaya was bedecked with carpets, flowers and icons. During the nineteenth century it became more commercial, as the point of departure for stagecoaches to St Petersburg, and the site of six hotels: photographs from the turn of the century show it festooned with billboards and shop signs.

Its present form owes to a massive **reconstruction** programme during the mid-1930s, when Tverskaya was also renamed in honour of the writer Maxim Gorky (it reverted to its old name in 1990). To straighten and widen the street, rows of houses were demolished, while other buildings were moved back to create a new avenue forty to sixty metres wide, lined with gargantuan buildings. Despite their scale, the variety of ornamentation and the older, often charming side streets that are visible through their huge archways give the avenue a distinctive character. Its **sights** are best appreciated by walking up the eastern side as far as Pushkinskaya ploshchad, and then crossing over and backtracking a bit to check out a few side streets to the west.

Before heading up Tverskaya ulitsa, take a look at the buildings that flank its juncture with Manezhnaya ploshchad and Okhotniy ryad. On the left-hand corner stands the tarpaulin-swathed **National Hotel**, an eclectic-style construction that was Moscow's finest hotel before the Revolution. In 1918, Lenin lived in room 107 before moving into the Kremlin; as the "First House of Soviets", it subsequently accommodated Party officials and fellow travellers, such as John Reed (p.360). Somewhat neglected, it is now being refurbished by an Austrian firm. The ponderous columned building immediately next door represents a watershed in Soviet architecture, as its Palladian Renaissance features signified the end of Constructivism and a return to traditional forms in the mid-1930s. Having served as the US Embassy, it now contains the headquarters of **Intourist** and its reticent **tourist information office** (see p.31 for details).

*For more on Manezhnaya ploshchad see p.114.*

On the other side of the road, facing the *Moskva Hotel* (see p.97), looms a grey 1930s building erected for **Gosplan**, the agency that drafted the Five Year Plans and oversaw the Soviet economy for seven decades. Now reassigned to the fractious Lower House of the

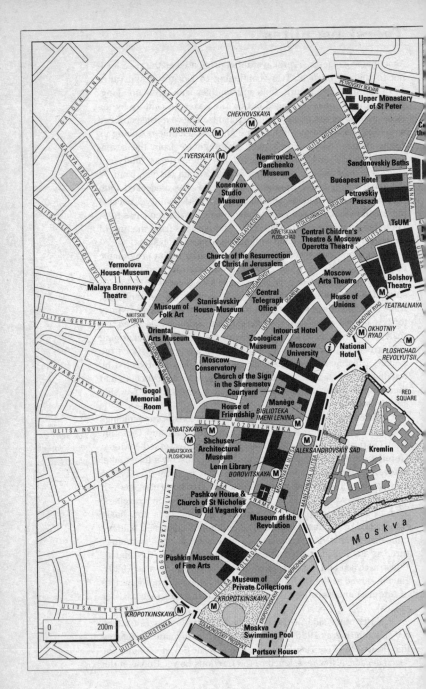

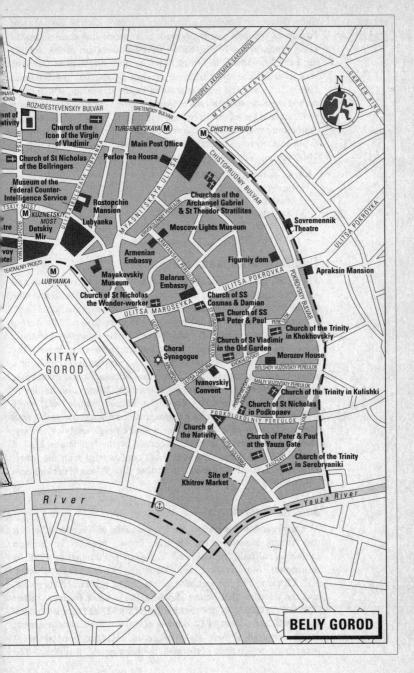

ROZHDESTEVENSKIY BULVAR
SRETENSKY BULVAR
PROSPEKT AKADEMIKA SAKHAROVA
MYASNITSKAYA ULITSA
N
GARDEN RIN

ent of ativity

Church of the Icon of the Virgin of Vladimir

TURGENEVSKAYA Ⓜ
Ⓜ CHISTYE PRUDY

Main Post Office

Perlov Tea House

CHISTOPRUDNY BULVAR

Church of St Nicholas of the Bellringers

Museum of the Federal Counter-Intelligence Service

Rostopchin Mansion

Churches of the Archangel Gabriel & St Theodor Stratilites

SKIY MOST
Ⓜ KUZNETSKIY MOST
Lubyanka

Moscow Lights Museum

Sovremennik Theatre

ULITSA POKROVKA

Detskiy Mir

voy tel

Ⓜ LUBYANKA

TEATRALNIY PROEZD

Armenian Embassy

ARMYANSKIY PEREULOK

Figurniy dom

Apraksin Mansion

Mayakovskiy Museum

Belarus Embassy

ULITSA POKROVKA

POKROVSKIY BULVAR

Church of St Nicholas the Wonder-worker

ULITSA MAROSEYKA

Church of SS Cosmas & Damian

Church of SS Peter & Paul

PERE LOK

Church of the Trinity in Khokhovskiy

KITAY-GOROD

Choral Synagogue

Church of St Vladimir in the Old Garden

Morozov House

BOLSHOY VUZOVSKIY PEREULOK

MALIY VUZOVSKIY PEREULOK

Church of the Trinity in Kulishki

Ivanovskiy Convent

Church of St Nicholas in Podkopaev

PODKOLOKOLNIY PEREULOK

Church of the Nativity

Church of Peter & Paul at the Yauza Gate

Church of the Trinity in Serebryaniki

Site of Khitrov Market

YAUZSKIY

River

Yauza River

BELIY GOROD

State Duma, or Russian parliament, it totally dwarfs the adjacent **House of Unions** (*dom Soyuzov*), a green-and-white Classical edifice built in the 1780s, which served as the Club of the Nobility until the Revolution. In Soviet times its glittering Hall of Columns was used for the show trials of veteran Bolsheviks like Bukharin (see p.351), and the lying in state of Lenin and Stalin, which occasioned mass demonstrations of genuine grief. The queue to bid farewell to Lenin lasted for three days and nights, despite arctic weather conditions; while nobody knows how many people were crushed to death in the crowd at Stalin's funeral – estimates range as high as 1500 victims. The poet Yevtushenko (who was there) later wrote:

> *Judgement was passed on the*
> *day of the funeral*
> *when the people came to Stalin*
> *over people*
> *for he taught them to*
> *walk over people.*

## Uphill to Sovetskaya ploshchad

The initial uphill stretch of Tverskaya boasts several landmarks and various curiosities tucked away off the street. On the left-hand side stands the 22-storey **Intourist Hotel**, aptly known as the "glass box", followed by the diminutive **Yermolova Theatre** (see p.117). Across the road, a huge archway leads through to Georgievskiy pereulok, where the fence behind the Gosplan building allows a glimpse of the modestly sized **Troyekurov Palace**, a rare surviving example of a seventeenth-century *boyar*'s townhouse. Sticking to the main road, you can't miss the dour **Central Telegraph Office**, with its illuminated globe. In Brezhnev times its ill-paid female staff were renowned for moonlighting as prostitutes, imbuing the globe with the significance of a red light in a seedy neighbourhood. Today, Muscovites are lured around the corner by the "golden arches" of *McDonald's* on ulitsa Ogareva. Don't confuse this with the other, larger branch of *McDonald's* further uphill, on Pushkinskaya ploshchad.

## Just off Tverskaya

At Kamergerskiy pereulok 3, on the east side of Tverskaya, stands the famous **Moscow Arts Theatre**, known here by its Russian initials as **MKhAT** (pronounced "Em-*Khat*"). Founded in 1898 by Konstantin Stanislavsky and Vladimir Nemirovich-Danchenko, MKhAT pioneered the methodical training of actors and directors, and the doctrine that acting should express inner feelings, rather than merely consist of gestures and vocal tricks. Its foundation coincided with the advent of Chekhov's plays, the first modern drama, which required a new style of acting. Having flopped in St Petersburg when first performed by hammy old thespians, *The*

*Seagull* became an overnight sensation thanks to MKhAT's production.

In Soviet times, MKhAT specialized in the plays of Gorky and grew increasingly conservative, but nevertheless produced outstanding directors like Meyerhold and brilliant actors such as the late Inokennty Smoktunovskiy, famous for his portrayal of Hamlet in particular. The theatre building itself was converted by Fyodor Shekhtel according to Stanislavsky's belief that nothing should distract audiences from the stage. Its foyer and auditorium are extremely simple, and the exterior decorations are limited to a stylized seagull on the pediment and a bas-relief wave above the doorway. (For more on MKhAT, see "The Arts", p.320.)

Returning to Tverskaya, check out the courtyard of no. 6, which harbours a spectacular Pseudo-Russian residential complex whose silver tent-roofed towers and pale green and lilac-tiled frontage contrast with the Stalinist gloom that now surrounds it. Built in 1905–7 as a speculative venture by the Orthodox Church, the **Savvinskoe podvore**'s huge apartments, turned into communal flats after the Revolution, are now being converted back into luxury residences and offices.

Opposite are two mammoth brownstone buildings (nos. 9–11) erected just after the war, united by a great arch made from granite intended for a Nazi victory memorial, captured in 1941. Further on from ultisa Nezhdanovoy stands the pretty pink and white **Church of the Resurrection of Christ in Jerusalem**, dating from 1629, one of the few Moscow churches that functioned throughout Soviet times.

## Sovetskaya ploshchad to the Boulevard Ring

Soon afterwards, Tverskaya levels out at **Sovetskaya ploshchad**, named after the former **Mossovet** (or Moscow City Council) building on the left-hand side, whose history is checkered. Originally the residence of Moscow's governor generals, it was "sold" sometime in the nineteenth century to an English lord by a gang of conmen, with the help of the notoriously gullible Governor Dolgorukov. Following the overthrow of Tsarism, it housed the Moscow Soviet of Workers' and Soldiers' Deputies and the

Military-Revolutionary Committee, which Lenin addressed on occasions now commemorated by sculpted plaques. Before *perestroika*, it was traditional to register him as deputy no. 1 whenever a newly elected council convened. In 1993, this bastion of the old guard was dissolved by Yeltsin and later replaced by a new City Duma, under the thumb of the powerful Mayor Luzhkov. While the Duma waits to move into the Lenin Museum, the mayor and his staff remain in their palatial offices. The building's appearance today bears little relation to Kazakov's original design of 1782. When Tverskaya was widened in Stalin's time, the building was moved back fourteen metres, its wings removed, and two storeys and a new entrance added.

Across the road prances an equestrian **statue of Yuri Dolgorukiy**, the founder of Moscow, belatedly unveiled seven years after the city's 800th anniversary in 1947. The large building on the right, with a fruity cornice, was once the *Dresden Hotel*, where Schumann, Chekhov and Turgenev stayed; it now houses the famous Georgian **Aragvi Restaurant**, whose patrons joke that Dolgorukiy had the sense to found his city near a good place to eat. Just beyond is the small seventeenth-century **Church of SS Cosmas and Damian** (*tserkov Kosmy i Damiana*), whose congregation includes many dissidents from the Brezhnev era, vindicated by the decline of the **Archives of the Institute of Marxism-Leninism** at the end of the square.

### Off to the east

Running downhill from the Church of SS Cosmas and Damian, the cobbled **Stoleshnikov pereulok** takes its name from the tablecloth weavers (*Stoleshniki*) who resided here in the sixteenth century. Towards the end of the last century, no. 9 was inhabited by Vladimir Gilyarovskiy, whose book *Moscow and the Muscovites* brilliantly portrayed the city's life before the Revolution. He is now recalled by a basement café tweely called *Uncle Gilly's*. Antique shops and a large old-fashioned state wine store may entice you to follow Stoleshnikov pereulok to the end, emerging onto ulitsa Petrovka near the Petrovskiy Passazh (p.132).

The next side street to the right of Tverskaya is named after Nemirovich-Danchenko, who co-founded MKhAT with Stanislavsky; their flats on opposite sides of Tverskaya were both within walking distance of the theatre. MKhAT fanatics can try to locate the **Nemirovich-Danchenko Museum** within the huge labyrinthine apartment block at no. 5–7: go through the heroic arch, head upstairs to the left and hope to encounter someone to provide directions beyond the lift shaft. Further downhill, Chekhov's widow, the actress Olga Knipper-Chekhova, lived in a similar apartment from 1938 until her death in 1959, as did other People's Artists recalled by plaques outside the building.

Near the corner with Tverskaya, a shabby entrance discourages
visitors to the **Tsentralniy Restaurant**, whose richly stuccoed ceiling and plump caryatids betray its origins as a fashionable coffee-
house opened in 1905 by the court baker, Filippov. Famously,
Filippov's bread was rushed to St Petersburg for the Tsar's breakfast; and the idea of raisinbread occurred to him after Moscow's
governor complained of a cockroach in his loaf – Filippov had to
prove it was a raisin, and he succeeded. By means not apparent
from the street, the restaurant connects with the seedy
**Tsentralnaya Hotel**, further up Tverskaya. Built in 1911 as the
*Luxe*, this served as a residential hostel for many of the Communist
International during the 1930s, when their ranks were decimated by
Stalin's purges. Victims were arrested at night and hustled out
through the kitchens into a waiting "bread" van*; their families were
then moved into worse rooms and shunned by everyone else in the
hostel.

## Yeliseyev's, the Wax Figure and Ostrovskiy museums

Nearer Pushkinskaya ploshchad, Tverskaya no. 14 houses a disparate trio of institutions. **Yeliseyev's** (Mon–Sat 8am–9pm, Sun 8am–
7pm) used to be Moscow's foremost delicatessen and still boasts the
finest interior of any shop in the city, replete with stained-glass
windows, floral chandeliers and mahogany counters, its lofty ceiling
upheld by voluptuous gilded pillars. The entrance hall displays a
bust of Pyotr Yeliseyev, the serf-gardener who won his freedom by
growing a perfect strawberry, and traded so successfully in St
Petersburg that in 1843 his sons were able to found the *Brothers
Yeliseyev*, opening branches in Moscow and Kiev.

Next door is the **Museum of Wax Figures** (Tues–Sun 11am–
7pm), which is full of surreal and didactic tableaux. In the "Triumph
of the State", Ivan the Terrible cradles Pushkin's corpse, as Stalin
tramples a skeleton; the "Time of Troubles" features Catherine the
Great with Rasputin, the rabble-rousing journalist Nevzorov and the
fascist hypnotist Kashpirovskiy. Others feature Yeltsin performing
open-heart surgery on Russia, and juxtapositions of Hitler, Lenin,
Peter the Great and Gorbachev, which shocked people when the
museum first opened in 1987, but now seem merely laughable. As
wax figures go, the most convincing is Zhirinovsky's, dressed in one
of his own suits; across the way, the figure of the rock star Viktor
Tsoy (see p.161) wears the clothes that he died in, donated by his
fans.

The floor above houses the **Nikolai Ostrovskiy Museum**
(Tues–Sun 11am–7pm) and a **Humanitarian Centre** in his name.
Ostrovskiy (1904–36) was a true believer who sacrificed everything

---

* To allay public unease over the scores of grey prison-vans shuttling around
Moscow during the purges, they were repainted to resemble the vans that
delivered bread and meat to the shops.

for Communism, becoming a Party activist at the age of thirteen, and contracting a wasting disease while laying a railway line after the Civil War. By the age of 25 he was blind and paralyzed; having contemplated suicide, he dictated his semi-autobiographical novel, *How the Steel was Tempered*, a classic of Stalinist literature. Ironically, much of it was censored because it dwelt on his love life, or mentioned persons later branded "enemies of the people". The museum preserves his study and bedroom, while the centre showcases the achievements of disabled people, for whom Ostrovskiy has been appointed a kind of exemplar.

There is also a section on the scintillating **salon of Zinaida Volkonskaya** that existed here in the 1820s. After her brother, Prince Volkonskiy, was exiled for life to Siberia for his part in the Decembrist revolt, his wife Maria set an example to other wives by joining him and enduring the same hardships for thirty years – she then ran off with another man, to everybody's dismay. The prince's second cousin, Tolstoy, possibly had this tale in mind when he invented Anna Karenina, a woman prepared to sacrifice all for love. In real life, another fate was sealed when Pushkin met his future wife, Natalya, at the salon in 1830 (for more about them, see p.162).

*Pushkinskaya ploshchad and the section of Tverskaya ulitsa beyond the Boulevard Ring are covered on p.145.*

## To Pushkinskaya ploshchad

Further on, Tverskaya crosses the heavily trafficked Tverskoy and Strastnoy sections of the Boulevard Ring at **Pushkinskaya ploshchad**. By negotiating your way through a maze of underpasses, you can emerge on the corner of Tverskoy bulvar, near the **Armeniya** shop – take a look at its Soviet Classicist interior. Next door is the **Konenkov Studio Museum** (Wed–Sun 11am–7pm; closed every Mon & Tues & the last Fri of each month), commemorating the sculptor Sergei Konenkov (1874–1971), who left Russia following the Revolution but returned from America in 1945, ensuring himself a warm welcome by bringing busts of the Politburo sculpted from photographs. The studio contrasts such orthodox works (which eventually won him a Stalin Prize) with playfully private creations using branches, roots and tree trunks.

# From Manezhnaya ploshchad to the Boulevard Ring

Beyond the Kremlin's Alexander Gardens stretches **Manezhnaya ploshchad**, a bleak expanse created by the demolition of shops and houses in the late 1920s. It was here that columns of tanks and marchers assembled prior to entering Red Square for the great parades of the Soviet era; in 1967, it was renamed the Fiftieth Anniversary of October Square. Having since reverted to its original name, there are now plans to redevelop the square by constructing a subterranean shopping arcade and concert hall, and to display the medieval foundations uncovered by an "archeological dig" using bulldozers. Meanwhile, the long **pedestrian subway** that leads from **Teatralnaya** and **Okhotniy Ryad** metro stations to the vicinity of Red Square is thronged with buskers, portrait-artists, souvenir vendors and beggars.

## The Manège

Manezhnaya ploshchad is named after the old **Manège** (*Manezh*), or military riding school, beside the Alexander Gardens. Built in only six months to the plans of the engineer General Betancourt, it was opened by Alexander I in 1817, on the fifth anniversary of Napoleon's defeat. Contemporaries marvelled at how its 45-metre-wide roof was unsupported by interior columns, allowing two cavalry regiments to manoeuvre indoors – but in the 1930s Soviet engineers had to prop up the sagging roof with steel columns, spoiling the effect. After the Revolution the Manège became the Kremlin's garage, reopening in 1957 as the **Central Exhibition Hall** (*Tsentralniy Vystavochniy zal*). In December 1962 it hosted the first modern art exhibition since early Soviet times, famous for a row between Khrushchev and the sculptor Ernst Neizvestniy, whose work Khrushchev lambasted as "dogshit". Nowadays, the Manège is just as likely to exhibit foreign cars as abstract art.

## Old Moscow University

Across the square are the canary-yellow edifices of **Moscow University** (*Moskovskiy universitet*), whose "old" building, completed in 1793, is reckoned among the finest works of Russian Classicism and Matvei Kazakov, who died soon after the fire of 1812 ravaged dozens of his buildings. The university was repaired and bas-reliefs and lions' heads added to its imposing facade. Behind the scenes is a warren of buildings whose "gloomy corridors, grimy walls, bad light and depressing stairs, coat-stands and benches have undoubtedly played an important role in the history of Russian pessimism" – or so wrote Chekhov of his own student days. Outside stand statues of Herzen and Ogaryov, two graduates who were among the founders of Russia's radical tradition in the nineteenth century.

On the other side of ulitsa Gertsena are the "new" buildings of the university, which date from 1836. The **rotunda** on the corner was originally a chapel dedicated to St Tatyana, the patron saint of students. Closed down after the Revolution, it later became a Students Theatre, noted mainly for its bold productions in the late Brezhnev years, and was only recently evicted so that the chapel can reopen. In front of the main college building is **a statue of Mikhail Lomonosov**, the "Russian Leonardo" who founded Moscow

From
Manezhnaya
ploshchad to
the
Boulevard
Ring

University in 1775. Amid the lesser buildings around the back rises the frilly belltower of the **Church of the Sign in the Sheremetev Courtyard** (*tserkov Znameniya na Sheremtevom dvore*), a lovely example of seventeenth-century Moscow Baroque with a filigreed spire. Earlier still, this was the site of Ivan the Terrible's **Oprichniy dvor**, a great fortified palace whence his infamous *Oprichniki* (police force) sallied forth to murder, rape and rob (see "A History of Moscow", p.339).

## Ulitsa Gertsena

*Most of the science faculties are in the University skyscraper in the Sparrow Hills, covered on p.196.*

One route to the Boulevard Ring is **ulitsa Gertsena**, a narrow street lined with university buildings in various shades of yellow, which looks fetchingly nineteenth-century when blanketed with snow. Pending the restoration of its traditional name, Bolshaya Nikitskaya, the street still bears its Soviet-era title honouring the radical journalist Alexander Herzen, who set Ogaryov's salon that once stood at no. 23 buzzing in the early 1820s. Today, the initial stretch is notable for the **Zoological Museum** (Tues–Sun 10am–5pm; closed the last Tues of each month), recognizable by its mural and stucco frieze of animals cavorting in flora. The collection includes a mammoth's skeleton from Yakuta, stuffed bison and bears, and a mongoose fighting two cobras at once.

### The Moscow Conservatory

Across the road further on is Russia's foremost music school, the **Moscow Conservatory** (*Moskovskaya Konservatoriya*). Founded in 1866 by Nikolai Rubenstein, the Conservatory occupies an eighteenth-century mansion fronted by a **statue of Tchaikovsky** waving his hands as if to conduct an orchestra – its railing is in the form of notes from six of his works, including *Swan Lake*. Tchaikovsky taught for twelve years at the Conservatory, which now bears his name. There is still a great deal of controversy over Tchaikovsky's death. According to some biographers, the Conservatory bears responsibility for his death, having supposedly pressed him to commit suicide to avoid a scandal concerning the composer's homosexual affair with the son of a high-ranking official, Vladimir – the official cause of death was cholera.

Try to attend a concert in the **Grand Hall** (*Bolshoy zal*), decorated with giant medallions of composers. It was here that one of Shostakovich's most virulent critics suffered a fatal heart attack during the premiere of a symphony that expressed the composer's torment at the years when his works were branded "formalist perversions". Every four years, it hosts the Tchaikovsky Competition, one of the most prestigious contests in the world of classical musicianship; almost always won by a Russian, the Irish pianist Barry Douglas was catapulted to worldwide fame after his win in 1990.

# Nikitskie vorota and Tverskoy bulvar

From Manezhnaya ploshchad to the Boulevard Ring

Just beyond the Conservatory, ulitsa Gertsena meets the Boulevard Ring, as a dozen roads converge on the site of the medieval St Nicholas Gate – still called **Nikitskie vorota**, although the gate was demolished in Stalin's time. There are several places of interest within five minutes' walk, but the junction itself has no appeal.

Bearing off to the right along this quiet street, it's not far to the **Stanislavsky House-Museum** at no. 6 (Thurs, Sat & Sun 11am–6pm; Wed–Fri 2–9pm; closed every Mon & Tues & the last Thurs of each month), which preserves the first-floor quarters allocated to the ailing director, after his own mansion on Karetniy ryad was requisitioned as a chauffeurs' club, until his death in 1938. The large hall was used for rehearsals during times when Stanislavsky was too ill to attend the Moscow Arts Theatre, while the original furniture with its traditional white dust-covers was donated by his daughters when the museum opened in 1948. The *babushkas* will proudly point out the vase given to Stanislavsky by the dancer Isadora Duncan. In the basement are preserved costumes from his productions of Shakespeare's *Othello* and Gogol's *The Government Inspector*.

*From Nikitskie vorota you can also head for the amazing Gorky House further east (p.155), or the Oriental Arts Museum 150m south along Suvorovskiy bulvar (p.119).*

Over the road, a small **Museum of Folk Art** (*muzey Narodnovo iskusstva*; Tues–Sun 11am–7pm; closed Mon), housed in a Pseudo-Russian building with arched windows and a church-like porch, mounts temporary exhibitions of ethnic crafts from across the former Soviet Union.

## Along Tverskoy bulvar

To slog the whole length of **Tverskoy bulvar** between Nikitskie vorota and Pushkinskaya ploshchad isn't recommended due to the heavy traffic either side of the wooded central strip, but it is worth a 250m walk to the **Yermolova House-Museum** at no. 11 (Mon 1–7pm, Wed, Thurs & Fri 1–8pm, Sat & Sun noon–7pm, closed the last Mon of each month). Its decrepit Empire frontage hides a charming period interior that conveys how affluent Russians lived before the Revolution. While her lawyer husband fled into exile, the Maliy Theatre actress Maria Yermolova remained here from 1880 till 1928, dying a People's Artist of the USSR. Her personality pervades the house upstairs, especially the study, filled with statues and biographies of Joan of Arc, her favourite role. There are two grand pianos, a palmy conservatory, and a covered balcony from which she greeted admirers. Head straight upstairs, leaving the exhibition on the ground floor till last, but don't miss seeing its clockwork puppet-stage nor the diorama of Teatralnaya ploshchad in the early nineteenth century.

Tverskoy bulvar's theatrical connections go way beyond this, what with the **Pushkin Drama Theatre** and the huge new **MKhAT Annexe** located towards the northern end of the boulevard, and the **Malaya Bronnaya Theatre** close to Nikitskie vorota.

# Towards the Arbat

Another route to the Boulevard Ring – and the Arbat beyond it – is to head along **ulitsa Vozdvizhenka**, which starts beside the gigantic Lenin Library (see p.120). Beyond the library are two monumental buildings currently clad in scaffolding, though their future remains uncertain. On the right-hand side at no. 10 is the **Military Department Store** or *Voyentorg*, an eclectic-style edifice, decorated with peacock and camel bas-reliefs and statues of medieval Slav warriors, that originally catered to officers of the Imperial Army and later to their Soviet counterparts. Higher up the pecking order, Central Committee staff enjoyed access to the euphemistically entitled **Bureau of Special Passes**, a deluxe food store tucked away around the corner at ulitsa Granovskovo 2, which was glaringly exposed during Yeltsin's stint as Moscow Party boss, when a film showing the chauffered cars waiting outside was broadcast on local television.

Across the road from *Voyentorg*, the eighteenth-century Talyzin mansion still nominally houses the **Shchusev Architectural Museum**, boasting a host of models and photos of buildings from medieval times to the Soviet era, when its namesake, Alexei Shchusev (1873–1949), designed such varied structures as the Lenin Mausoleum and the *Moskva Hotel*. At present, however, the museum has been reduced to a temporary **exhibition hall** (Tues–Sun 10am–6pm) in the converted Apothecary's Palace around the back, while the mansion is slowly being overhauled. The whitewashed palace once served the German apothecaries who laid out the Tsar's medicinal herb garden on Vagankov Hill (p.121).

## Tolstoy's grandfather and the House of Friendship

Slightly further along on the corner of pereulok Yanasheva stands a two-storey beige house with a floral cornice (no. 9) that once belonged to **Tolstoy's grandfather**. Though he died before Tolstoy's birth, in 1821, Prince Nicholas Volkonskiy was imaginatively resurrected in *War and Peace* as the irascible Prince Bolkonskiy, with his "gloomy house on the Vozdvizhenka". He should not be confused with Tolstoy's second cousin, the other real-life Prince Volkonskiy, who was exiled to Siberia for his part in the Decembrist revolt.

Immediately beyond appear the pale modular offices of the Armed Forces **General Staff** (*Generalniy Shtab*), familiarly known to Muscovites as the "Pentagon". Its concrete bowels contain the decorative 1930s **Arbatskaya metro** station on the Arbatsko-Pokrovskaya line, whose exit brings you out opposite the **House of Friendship** (*dom Druzhby*). This amazing mansion was built in 1898 for a dissipated heir, Arseny Morozov, who shot himself in the foot to see whether he could bear the pain and died of septicemia at the age of 24. Its lace-trimmed towers and sculpted seashells were inspired by the Casa de las Conchas in Salamanca, seen during Arseny's travels. After the Revolution it was briefly taken over by Anarchists before becoming the headquarters of *Proletcult*, an organization involving Mayakovsky and Meyerhold that aimed to turn workers and peasants into artists. Since the 1950s it has housed the Union of Friendship Societies, responsible during Soviet times for staging meetings between foreign visitors and approved artists. Try to bluff your way in to see its wildly opulent **interior** (Mon–Fri 10am–6pm).

## Arbatskaya ploshchad and along the Ring

Further up the road, **Arbatskaya ploshchad** (Arbat Square) bears the scars of several bouts of redevelopment. Most visibly, it has a 1950s **underpass** serving traffic on the Boulevard Ring, and another, multi-branched pedestrian subway whose steps are lined with people selling **puppies**, while thrash rockers busk in its depths till late at night. On the surface, you'll also notice the pavilion of **Arbatskaya metro** station on the Filyovskaya line, built in the shape of a five-pointed star (a favourite architectural conceit of the 1930s), and the custard-yellow **Praga Restaurant** across the square. Founded before the Revolution, the *Praga* was long regarded as Moscow's top restaurant, and regularly hosted diplomatic banquets in Soviet times. Now shabby and deeply unfashionable, it still boasts of a dozen highly ornate dining rooms.

*The Arbat district is covered on p.159.*

While visitors are usually drawn into the Arbat district beyond the *Praga*, a few sights beg a detour **along the Boulevard Ring** itself. At the head of Gogolevskiy bulvar, beside the square, stands what locals call the **Happy Gogol statue**, since it replaced a statue that the Soviet authorities deemed too gloomy for the late 1940s. The original, by the sculptor Andreev, was banished to the courtyard of no. 7 Suvorovskiy bulvar, just off the square, where the **Sad Gogol statue** huddles in a cape, eyes downcast; the plinth bears a jolly frieze of characters from *The Government Inspector* and *Taras Bulba*. In the public library on the right, devoted scholars have created the **Gogol Memorial Room** (Mon, Wed & Thurs 1–7pm; Sat & Sun noon–6pm) in what was Nikolai Gogol's study during his last years. Here he burned the second part of *Dead Souls* and lapsed into religious melancholia, eating only pickled cabbage. As a sufferer from cataleptic fits, he was mistakenly buried alive in 1852.

*Gogol's grave is in the Novodevichiy Cemetery (p.194).*

Across the road and 150m further north at no. 12A Suvorovskiy bulvar, a pale yellow, Corinthian-pilastered mansion contains the **Oriental Arts Museum** (Tues–Sun 11am–6pm). Its superb collection includes Caucasian rugs, Indonesian shadow-puppets, Vietnamese silver Buddhas, Samurai swords, lacquer, porcelain, Chinese screens and robes. As the museum is located south of Nikitskie vorota, it's also feasible to reach it from there.

# From the Lenin Library to the Pushkin Museum

The corner of Vozdvizhenka and Mokhovaya streets is dominated by the immense **Russian State Library** – better known by its former title, the **Lenin Library** (*Biblioteka imeni Lenina* ) – where some forty million books and periodicals repose on two hundred kilometres of shelving. Looming above a hillock behind a lanky arcade of black pillars, the library's main building was actually a reworking of a design for a hydroelectric power station, which became progressively more encrusted with reliefs and statues as its construction (1928–50) was influenced by the Palace of Soviets that was supposed to arise in the vicinity (see p.128).

Although you can't go beyond the cloakrooms without a reader's pass, have a look at the **grand staircase** (entrance #1) that ascends to the library's four main halls, decorated in the apogee of Soviet Classicism (Mon–Sat 9am–9pm, Sun 9am–8pm; closed the last Mon of each month). Keen bibliophiles can also visit the **Museum of Books** (Mon–Fri 10am–7pm, Sat 10am–5pm; closed Sun) on the third floor of the wing (entrance #3). Its collection includes a cuneiform tablet from ancient Mesopotamia; *The Gospel of the Archangel*, one of Russia's earliest handwritten books (1092); and the first book ever printed in Russia, Fyodorov's *The Apostle* (1564).

Sadly, since *perestroika* the library has fallen on hard times and now lacks the money to heat its rooms, let alone modernize its facilities and replenish its stocks. Its troubles date back to the opening of **Borovitskaya metro station** in 1985, which caused subsidence beneath the library's huge depository and the loss of some forty thousand books. Ensuring its structural integrity had to come before anything else, at a time of shrinking budgets.

## The Pashkov House and Mokhovaya ulitsa

Subsidence also badly affected the impressive **Pashkov House** (*dom Pashkova*) that overlooks the Kremlin's Borovitskiy Gate from a hilltop. Stripped of its stucco, the mansion is a ghost of its former magnificence, once enhanced by a garden running down to the Kremlin moat, where peacocks strutted. When built by Bazhenov in the 1780s it was the finest private house in Moscow, and constituted a bridge between Baroque and Neo-Classical architecture. Mortgaged away by the gambling-mad Count Pashkov, it was purchased by a book-loving Marshal and turned into the Rumyantsev Library, whose collection of one million volumes later formed the core of the Lenin Library, located on the premises until 1950. It was from the rooftop of this building that the Devil and his entourage surveyed the chaos they had sown across Moscow in Bulgakov's *The Master and Margarita*.

Despite its grand facade facing the Kremlin, the main entrance actually lies around the back on what is still signposted as ulitsa Marksa-Engelsa. Though the gateway's fine proportions have only just survived ruination, the adjacent walled **Church of St Nicholas in Old Vagankov** (*tserkov Nikolaya v Starom Vagankove*) is back in business after decades of neglect. Its newly restored compound sports a plaque boasting that Gogol was a regular worshipper in the 1840s. While the church's title recalls the village of Vagankov that existed here in the Middle Ages, the main road below the library, **Mokhovaya ulitsa**, is named after the moss (*mokh*) once sold for caulking the chinks in wooden houses, and later for inserting between the panes of double-glazed windows to prevent fogging from condensation. But whereas the church is redolent of its past, the road now only stinks of cars.

At no. 6, opposite the Pashkov House and Borovitskaya metro, a lowlier Empire mansion contains a small **Museum of the Revolution** (*Muzey Kevolyutsii*; Tues–Sat 10am–6pm, Sun 10am–5pm) that soberly documents the collapse of the USSR. Its exhibits include a huge globe from the Council of Ministers' office, the desk where Gorbachev sat at the last Party Congress, and the lectern from which Yeltsin declared Russia's independence from the Soviet Union. Also look out for temporary exhibitions on the floor above.

*The main Museum of the Revolution is on Tverskaya ulitsa (p.149).*

# The Pushkin Museum of Fine Arts

Like the larger Hermitage Museum in St Petersburg, Moscow's **Pushkin Museum of Fine Arts** (*muzey Izobrazitelnykh Iskusstv imeni A.S. Pushkina*) has a collection that ranges from Egyptian antiquities to Picasso, and is so vast that only a fraction can be displayed. Besides the constraints imposed by lack of space, politics have also played a part, as in the decades when abstract works were ideologically taboo. In recent years, the museum has also revealed much of the "Trophy Art" that was seized from the Nazis in 1945, including the treasure of King Priam of Troy and a host of European masterpieces, which are on display at the time of writing.

### Visiting the museum
The **museum** is at ulitsa Volkhonka 12 (Tues–Sun 10am–7pm; last tickets sold 6pm; $5), a few minutes' walk from Kropotkinskaya metro. Although not as dauntingly large as the Hermitage in St Petersburg, it's still wise to see what appeals first, lest you run out of steam midway through the rooms full of plaster casts.

A bigger problem is that the contents of certain sections are liable to change depending on the space allotted to **temporary exhibitions**, which can mean that all the Impressionists and Post-Impressionists are crammed into two rooms, with not enough space to show many of the works one expects to find.

Identifying the exhibits is less of a problem, as most are captioned in English, and **guide tapes** can be rented in the basement. **Photography** is not allowed. Since the rooms are numbered in a way that bears little relation to their **layout** in terms of access, the following account is loosely structured on a thematic basis, starting on the first (or ground) floor.

Since the 1980s the museum has also been the venue for annual concerts, known as the **December Evenings**.

## Antiquities and Byzantine art

Heading upstairs from the basement, visitors are supposed to begin by turning right into **Room 14**, which displays plaster casts of **ancient Greek monuments**, the most impressive being a corner of the Parthenon.

Alternatively, you can enter **Room 3**, which opens with a fine display of **Coptic textiles** and funerary masks (left), and the amazingly vivid **Fayoum portraits** (right), which were painted while their

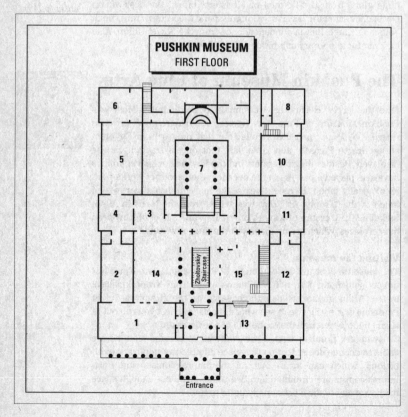

subjects were alive and then pasted onto their mummies – all from Egypt, between the first and sixth centuries AD. On the far wall are several glorious **Byzantine icons**, most notably a serene *Christ Pantokrator* from the ninth or tenth century AD.

From here, you can proceed through the Italian art in Room 4 (see below) to reach **Room 2**, devoted to magnificent limestone **Babylonian bas-reliefs** from the Palace of Ashurnaziral (885–860 BC), whose portal flanked by winged bulls forms the entrance to the hall. At the far end lies **Room 1**, decorated like an Egyptian temple and filled with **Pharaonic artefacts** collected by the orientalist Golenischev. Mostly dating from the New Kingdom (c.1567–1085 BC), they include funerary figures, Canopic chests, a mummified woman's head and the mummy of Hor-Ha.

The Antiquities are rounded off by an assortment of **Roman, Greek and Mycenaean statues** in **Room 7**, which can be visited later as you cross the lobby. Look out for the sarcophagus carved with orgiastic revels.

## Gothic and Renaissance art

Room 4 exhibits **Italian art** from the thirteenth to the fifteenth centuries, as it evolved from Byzantine to Gothic forms. On the wall as you enter is a splendid *Madonna and Child Enthroned* with a gem-studded halo, framed with scenes from Christ's life, by an anonymous Florentine artist (c.1280). Two exquisite altar triptychs from the second half of the fourteenth century hang at the left side of the partition, whose other side features a skeletal *Crucifixion* by Jacobello del Fiore. Notice the jealous expressions in Pietro di Giovanni Liapri's rose and yellow-hued triptych of the *Virgin and Child with Saints*, and the brilliantly coloured *Madonna Enthroned with Angels* by Giovanni di Bartolomeo Cristiani.

Room 5 features **Italian, German and Dutch art** of the fifteenth and sixteenth centuries. Left of the doorway hangs Vittore Crivelli's sumptuously decorative *Virgin and Child with Saints*, while on the right-hand wall are a sadistic *Flagellation of Christ* by Johann Koerbecke, and *St Michael* trampling a hairy demon, attributed to Pedro Espalargves. In the next section, Guilio Romano's *Woman at her Toilet* faces an exquisite *Annunciation* by **Sandro Botticelli** and a lovely *St Sebastian* by da Vinci's pupil and assistant, Giovanni Boltraffio; while across the way is a magnificently pain-wracked *Golgotha* by the mysteriously named Master of the Prodigal Son.

The following partition features two small works by **Lucas Cranach the Elder**, whose *The Results of Jealousy* hints at rape and murder. On the right-hand wall of the final section hangs a *Winter Landscape with Bird Trap* by **Pieter Brueghel the Younger** – actually a copy of a like-named painting by his father, Brueghel the Elder, in Brussels.

Italian art of the sixteenth century enjoys a final fling in **Room
6**, where a diminutive *Minerva* by **Paolo Veronese** is accompanied
by larger works of his school. In the far right corner is an over-the-
top *Solomon and the Queen of Sheba* by **Claus Vredman de Vries**,
where figures in Renaissance dress are posed against an oddly
metallic-looking palazzo.

## Rubens, Rembrandt and Baroque art

Crossing the lobby to reach the seventeenth-century **Flemish and
Spanish art** in **Room 11**, you'll be greeted by three gigantic still
lifes of dead fish and poultry by **Frans Snyders**, below which hangs
a portrait of the corpulent merchant Adriaen Stevens, by **Anthony
van Dyck**. Both Snyders and van Dyck worked as assistants at the
studio of **Peter Paul Rubens**, whose three works owned by the
Pushkin Museum include *Bacchanalia*, featuring an intoxicated
Bacchus supported by his slaves while a cloven-hoofed woman suck-
les a brood of baby satyrs. To the right of the door is a trio of paintings by the Spaniard **Bartolomé Murillo**, whose *Archangel
Raphael and Bishop Domonte* was commissioned to adorn the
bishop's own cathedral.

The far door leads into **Room 10**, devoted to **seventeenth-
century Dutch art**, where everyone makes a beeline for six works
by **Rembrandt**. His mastery of dark tones and free brushwork is
evinced by *Ahasuerus, Haman and Esther*, where the males are
almost lost in the shadows, while Esther's embroidered tunic is
rendered by merely scratching the paint's surface. On the other side
of the partition, two religious works – *Christ Cleansing the Temple*
and *The Incredulity of Thomas* – face a trio of portraits depicting
Rembrandt's mother (*An Old Woman*), brother (*An Old Man*) and
sister-in-law (*An Elderly Woman*), all painted in 1654, when the
artist was struggling to come to terms with bereavement and
poverty.

**Room 12**, reached by the door nearest the Murillos, contains
Italian art of the seventeenth and eighteenth centuries. On the right
as you enter are Salvatori Rossa's cruel *Old Coquette*, followed by
Domenico Gargiulo's action-packed *The Ark brought by King
David to Jerusalem*, which leads one towards the large *Betrothal
of the Doge and the Sea* at the far end – a sumptuous vista of gilded
barges and Venetian palazzi attributed to **Canaletto**.

**Room 13** covers **French art** of the same period, which was
much favoured by Catherine the Great. A misty-eyed
*Voluptuousness* is the most memorable of three works by **Jean-
Baptiste Greuze**, while portraits of the Prince and Princess Golitsyn
strike a Russian note. More interesting than the small genre paintings by **Jean-Honoré Fragonard** and two miniatures by **Jean-
Antoine Watteau** are the Classical scenes by **François Boucher**,
notably his explicitly erotic *Hercules and Omphale*. Along the main

wall hang five works by **Nicolas Poussin**, including a surreal *Landscape with Hercules and Cacus* and a frenzied *Battle of the Israelites and Amorites*. Also note the gilded **Rhinoceros Clock** near the window.

## Copies of masterpieces – and Rockwell Kent

The large hall designated as **Room 15** contains bronze and plaster **copies of Medieval and Renaissance masterpieces** such as the Golden Arch of Freiburg Cathedral, the Bishop's Seat of Ulm Cathedral, Michelangelo's *David*, and the famous *condottieri* statues from Padua and Venice.

Its stairway leads **upstairs** into a gallery used for **temporary exhibitions**, which often extend into the lobby of the main Zholtovskiy Staircase, flanked by Grecian friezes and red marble columns, whence an arrow directs you into **Room 16**, filled with plaster casts of ancient Greek sculptures and friezes. This marks the start of a series of rooms devoted to copies of statues by Michelangelo (**Room 29**); other Renaissance masterpieces, such as Ghiberti's "Doors of Paradise" from the Florentine Baptistry (**Room 28**); medieval cathedral art from France and Germany (**Room 26**); and Roman statuary (**Room 25**) – whose period decor complements the exhibits.

Depending on the current state of play, you may also find a room devoted to the American artist **Rockwell Kent** (1882–1971), who is little known in his homeland, but famous in Russia ever since he presented his *oeuvre* to the Soviet Union in 1961. His misty, icebound vistas of Greenland and Alaska definitely strike a chord in the Russian soul.

## Barbizon, Orientalist and Academic painters

**Room 23** exhibits a fraction of the museum's huge collection of **Barbizon painters**, which rivals the Louvre's. Though nowadays unfashionable, they paved the way for the Impressionists by abandoning the studio in favour of *plein air* painting. The emphasis on spontaneity and naturalism is particularly evident in landscapes by **Jean-Baptiste-Camille Corot**, such as *Stormy Weather* and *A Gust of Wind*.

In the same room you will also find picturesque **Orientalist** paintings like Jean Fromentin's *Awaiting the Boat to Cross the Nile*, and a small *View of the Mountains* by one of the greatest German Romantic painters, **Caspar David Friedrich**.

At the far end of the room is a host of works in the **Academic** style that Russian artists were obliged to ape during the eighteenth and nineteenth centuries, including a serene *Virgin with the Host* by **Ingres**, commissioned by Tsar Alexander II; an equestrian *Portrait of Prince Yusupov* by **Antoine-Jean Gros**; and *After the Shipwreck* by **Eugène Delacroix**.

# French Impressionism

In the early 1900s, the Moscow millionaires Sergei Shchukin and
Ivan Morozov bought scores of paintings by Picasso, Matisse and
the French Impressionists, which now form the core of the modern
European art collections of the Hermitage and the Pushkin Museum.
The latter generally devotes **Rooms 21 and 22** to its **French
Impressionists**, rotating them so as to show different works by vari-
ous artists.

Of several paintings by **Claude Monet**, you're likely to find
*Rouen Cathedral at Sunset* (one of a series that captured the
changing light on the cathedral's facade throughout the day), foggy
views of the River Thames, and his sun-dappled *Déjeuner sur
l'Herbe*. The most striking of those by **van Gogh** are *Prisoners at
Exercise* and the corruscating *Red Vineyard at Arles*. The latter
was the only painting he sold in his lifetime, about which he wrote:
"Oh, the beautiful sun of midsummer! It beats upon my head, and I
do not doubt that it makes one a little queer" – shortly before
cutting off his ear and leaving it in a brothel.

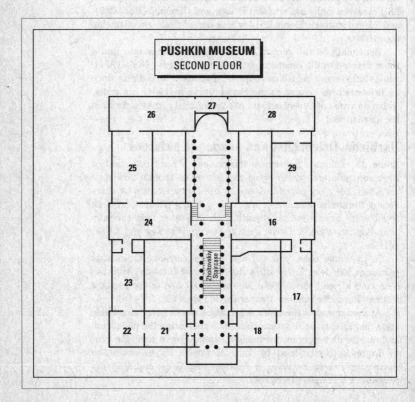

The museum also owns several landscapes and Parisian street scenes by **Camille Pissarro**; vivid pastels by **Edgar Degas**, such as *Ballet Rehearsal* and *Dancers in Blue*; and a *Portrait of Yvette Guilbert* by **Henri de Toulouse-Lautrec**, who often sketched this *chanteuse* at the Moulin Rouge. Its large collection of works by **Auguste Renoir** includes various portraits of actresses and a gorgeous plump nude known as "The Pearl", while versions of *The Burghers of Calais* and *The Kiss* are numbered among its sculptures by **Auguste Rodin**.

## Post-Impressionism and Modernism

Rooms 17 and 18 are usually reserved for **Post-Impressionist and Modernist** art, mostly originating from the collections of Morozov and Shchukin, both of whom bought more than fifty works apiece by Picasso and Matisse.

Those by **Picasso** range from a Cézanne-like *Cottage with Trees* and the Cubist *Queen Isabeau*, to paintings from his Blue, Rose and Spanish periods, such as *Young Acrobat on a Ball*, *Portrait of Sabartès*, *Old Jew with Boy* and *Spanish Woman from Majorca*. The paintings by **Henri Matisse** include a *Moroccan Triptych* in saturated blues, several still lifes with vases, and *The Goldfish*; the museum also owns his bronze sculpture, *Jaguar and Hare*.

The museum's collection of works by **Paul Cézanne** is equally rich, ranging from landscapes and self portraits to still lifes and pictures from his Pierrot and Harlequin series, such as *Mardi Gras*.

By the doorway into Room 18 hang two enormous canvases by **Pierre Bonnard**: *Autumn* and *Early Spring in the Country*. You will also find an amazing selection of Tahitian works by **Paul Gauguin**, including *Relax*, *The Great Buddha*, *Still Life with Parrots* and *Landscape with Peacocks*.

Complementing these are a host of diverse works by later artists, ranging from the pioneer of abstract art, **Vasily Kandinsky**, to the Surrealist **Giorgio de Chirico**. The gallery also features three colourful compositions by the card-carrying Communist **Fernand Léger** and a fantastic, dream-like *Nocturne* by the Russian-Jewish artist **Marc Chagall**. Also look out for the decadent Symbolist paintings of **Odilon Redon**, and drawings by the Russian Futurist **Natalya Goncharova**.

## The Museum of Private Collections

If the Pushkin Museum wasn't enough, there is also a brand new **Museum of Private Collections** right next door (*muzey Lichnykh Kollektsiy*; Wed–Sun noon–7pm). The brainchild of Ilya Zilbershtein, a collector himself, the museum displays antique and modern art that hasn't been seen in public for decades – if ever. It's amazing what people managed to acquire, even when "unofficial" art was taboo and private collections highly suspect.

The individual tastes and limited resources of a score of collectors makes for a well-rounded, quirky exhibition, augmented by loans from the Pushkin Museum and flattered by a stylishly refurbished interior. Although some rooms host temporary exhibitions, the rest shouldn't change much. It's too early for catalogues or guide tapes, but everything is clearly labelled in English.

## The exhibition

The permanent exhibition begins on the **second floor** with **Salvador Dalí's** pen and wash drawings from the series *Mythology* and *The Hippies*, and anthropophagic illustrations to *Faustus* and *The Songs of Maldoror*. Next door features drawings of vases and women by **Matisse**, and the artist's own palette. Look out for the portraits of Lydia Delektorskaya, Matisse's model and secretary

---

### A Tale of Two Buildings

Before the Revolution, the derelict site of the Moskva swimming pool, downhill from the museums, was occupied by the huge **Cathedral of Christ the Redeemer**, honouring Russia's victory over Napoleon, which took forty-three years to build and had room for ten thousand worshippers. In 1931, Stalin ordered it to be destroyed to make way for the centrepiece of his new Moscow – a gargantuan Palace of Soviets, envisaged as the most important building in the USSR. Demolition crews toiled in vain for a year, until the *Cheka* were called in to dynamite the cathedral in a blast heard for miles around. Legend has it that several monks who refused to leave were buried in the rubble. Unabashed, the Soviet government held an international competition to design the palace; Gropius and Le Corbusier were among those who submitted designs, only to be appalled when the winning entry was announced in 1934.

The **Palace of Soviets** conceived by Boris Iofan, Vladimir Gelfreykh and Vladimir Shchuko cloaked its rocket-like ascent to a height of 315 metres with a Classical facade, and was crowned by a one-hundred-metre-tall aluminium **statue of Lenin** that would make it higher than the Empire State Building and the Statue of Liberty combined. Legend has it that the statue was added at Stalin's bidding, and its eyes were intended to emit a bright red beam, like a beacon – though given Moscow's lugubrious climate, Lenin would have frequently been obscured by clouds. Work progressed as far as sinking the foundations, but the girders were ripped out to make anti-tank "hedgehogs" in 1941, and when construction resumed after the war, it was with less conviction. Ultimately the palace was never realized because the high water table made the ground unstable, so in 1959 the plan was dropped and the swimming pool was built instead. Pious Russians whispered that it was God's revenge that smote Stalin's Tower of Babel.

Incredibly, it has now been decided to **rebuild the cathedral** from scratch at an estimated cost of $150 million, which the city and the Orthodox Church are supposed to find somehow. The absurdity is all the more poignant when you see the old *babushki* soliciting for donations with a candle-lit box and a quavering blessing.

---

from 1928 until his death, who donated many of his works to Russian museums.

The **third floor** is more Russian in spirit, with nineteenth-century works by the Wanderers, such as **Ilya Repin**, whose lurid pink and gold *Duel* is counterposed by **Vasily Polonev's** gentle *Christ in the Wilderness*. You will also find set designs by **Boris Kustodiev** and **Alexander Benois** from the golden age of Russian ballet; views of St Petersburg and Kronstadt in the eighteenth century; and a score of **icons**. Of historical interest are the tiny **portraits of the Decembrists** exiled to Siberia in 1825, drawn by fellow prisoner Nikolai Bestuzhev, and a painting of Countess Maria Volkonskaya, who followed Tolstoy's second cousin into exile (see p.114).

The **fourth floor** offers a feast of twentieth-century art, to which the concert pianist Svatoslav Richter contributed his own paintings and grand piano, still lifes by **Robert Falk**, and a personally dedicated *Composition* by **Alexander Calder**. Look out for Moulin-Rougey oils by **Leonid Pasternak** (father of Boris) in a tiny side-chamber, and Kustodiev's *After the Storm with a Rainbow* in the room that unites *fin-de-siècle* artists into Parisian nightlife and rural Russia. Beyond a horde of whimsical Miróesque woodcarvings by **Alexander Tyshler** are two rooms devoted to **Alexander Rodchenko** and his wife **Varvara Stepanova** – arguably the museum's prime attraction. Rodchenko pioneered photocollage and unorthodox perspectives, and his photos, posters and Constructivist book jackets are now classics of the genre, while Stepanova's Cubist textile designs have equal retro appeal.

# East of Tverskaya – theatreland to Lubyanka

**East of Tverskaya** is a wedge of the Beliy Gorod that encompasses some of Moscow's oldest monasteries and most treasured cultural landmarks. The Bolshoy Theatre and the fashionable shops of ulitsa Kuznetskiy most and ulitsa Petrovka were the hub of Moscow's social life before the Revolution, and the whole area seethes with activity today. Although its hotdog vendors and renovation work might seem a far cry from Anna Karenina, rubbish and mud were a bigger problem in her day, as the Neglina River – channelled into an underground pipe – often flooded the whole area with putrid sludge.

Adding to the squalor was the **Okhotniy ryad** (Hunters' Row), a meat and pie market that sprawled from Teatralnaya ploshchad to Manezhnaya ploshchad, serving hot food and drinks all night – a convivial fixture of Moscow life that was swept away in the 1930s and is now recalled by a renamed metro station whose underpasses constitute a bazaar of sorts. However, the best place to start is Teatralnaya metro.

# The Bolshoy

*Bolshoy* means "big" or "grand", and the **Bolshoy Theatre** (*Bolshoy teatr*), dominating Teatralnaya ploshchad, is both – with a massive eight-columned portico, surmounted by Apollo's chariot. A net strung across the sugary pink and white frontage to catch falling stucco betrays the crisis afflicting the Bolshoy. In fact, the premises are in danger of falling apart, due to its position above the underground Neglina River.

In 1906 part of the 2000-seater auditorium suddenly sagged during a matinee, but nothing was done about it until 1921, and when subsidence returned in the late 1980s, the state was unable to afford repairs and told the Bolshoy to raise the funds itself. Despite all this, you feel uplifted by the theatre's vast **auditorium**, with its glittering chandeliers and tiers of gilded red-velvet boxes.

The Bolshoy's **history** goes back to 1776, when the English showman Michael Maddox founded a company that became established on the corner of ulitsa Petrovka as the first permanent theatre in Moscow. The company's ballet tradition was firmly established after it came under state control in 1806, while some of the first Russian operas were performed here in the 1890s. However, the Bolshoy played second fiddle to St Petersburg's Mariinskiy Theatre until the early 1900s and only became supreme following the return of the capital to Moscow in 1918. Its international reputation was gained in the 1950s to the 1970s by new works such as Khachaturian's *Spartacus* and star dancers like Maya Plisetskaya and Vladimir Vasiliev. It is also famous for defections in protest at the autocratic management and conservative choreography associated with Yuri Grigorovich, the artistic director for thirty years until his abrupt dismissal in 1995. Since *perestroika*, the Bolshoy has cashed in on its world fame with little regard for quality or the home audience, and several stars have resigned over contractual rows.

*See p.319 for
details of
performances
and how to
obtain tickets.*

Besides opera and ballet, the Bolshoy has been a stage for **political dramas**, the stormiest of which was the Fifth Party Congress of July 1918, which witnessed the final split between the Bolsheviks and the Left Socialist-Revolutionaries, whose leader Maria Spriridonova denounced Lenin for treating the peasantry like "dung" and called for war. The Left SR delegation were held prisoner in the Bolshoy while the *Cheka* put down an uprising by their followers; in the words of Bruce Lockhardt, "the revolution, which was conceived in a theatre, ended in the same place".

## Other theatres and TsUM

The long, low-slung **Maly Theatre** (*Maliy teatr*) on the eastern side of the square was originally built as a warehouse for Moscow's only honest army provisioner. After he was jailed on false charges, it was sold off and converted into a theatre in 1838. Its drama company traces its history back to the university theatre founded in 1757, but really came of age in tandem with the playwright Alexander Ostrovskiy (1823–86), who is honoured by a seated statue outside. The actress Maria Yermolova (1853–1928) spent five decades at the Maly, providing a continuity from the age of Ostrovskiy into the Soviet era, when she was the first person to be awarded the title of People's Artist (for more on Yermolova, see p.117). Across the square is a florid yellow Empire-style edifice occupied by the **Central Children's Theatre** (*Tsentralniy Detskiy teatr – TsDT*), founded in 1921. Opera buffs should also note the **Moscow Operetta Theatre** (*Moskovskiy teatr Operetty*), tucked away just off the square on the corner of Pushkinskaya ulitsa. In the 1890s, the composer Rachmaninov and the singer Chaliapin began their careers at what was then the avant-garde Private Opera of Savva Mamontov, which hired leading artists to design the costumes and sets.

*Some of the opera set designs are in the Museum of Private Collections (p.129). Mamontov's activities as a patron are described under "Abramtsevo" (p.278).*

There's also something theatrical about the TsUM (pronounced "tsoom") department store, sandwiched between the Maly Theatre and ulitsa Petrovka. Built as Moscow's first modern store in 1909 for the Scottish firm *Muir & Merilees*, its spiky Neo-Gothic exterior conceals the pioneering use of reinforced concrete and curtain walls. A metallic 1960s extension has been grafted onto the rear, where kiosks selling designer clothing herald the proximity of ulitsa Kuznetskiy most and the Petrovskiy Passazh (see below).

## Ulitsa Kuznetskiy most

As a connoisseur of bookshops, cafés and scandal, Mayakovsky wrote: "I love Kuznetskiy most . . . and then Petrovka" – two streets whose buzz isn't what it was, but is coming back. **Ulitsa Kuznetskiy most** is where the aristocracy used to take their afternoon promenade and browse in shops selling everything from Fabergé bracelets to English woollens. Tolstoy listened to an early phonograph in what used to be the music shop at no. 12, and wrote of Anna Karenina shopping in *Gautier's* at no. 20.

Today, the street still meanders picturesquely over hills and across thoroughfares, past arresting buildings like the crested Style Moderne structure on the corner of Neglinnaya ulitsa. The rich are pulled in by foreign **airlines** and home appliances, the **banks** are back and the **bookshops** have been augmented by a branch of the English chain *Zwemmers*, opposite the **Union of Artists Exhibition Hall** at no. 11. On the cobbled street itself you can buy leather coats, frozen chicken-legs and spoof KGB warrant cards.

## Ulitsa Petrovka

Long before the Bolshoy was built, **ulitsa Petrovka** was one of the most aristocratic streets in Moscow, as the *boyars* emulated Grand Duke Vasily III, who built a palace here with grounds extending between today's Boulevard and Garden Rings. It was also a major thoroughfare leading to the St Peter's Gate in the city's walls, which was protected by a medieval fortified monastery.

Gradually, the aristocracy moved out and merchants took over – a process culminating with the opening in 1903 of the **Petrovskiy Passazh** (Mon–Sat 9am–8pm), an elegant twin-arcaded mall along the lines of GUM. Restored by Turkish contractors some years ago, the Passazh is one of the slickest spots in Moscow, with a glossy Euro-ambience far removed from the mud and kiosks outside.

### The Upper Monastery of St Peter and beyond

From the Passazh, walk 600m uphill to the **Upper Monastery of St Peter** (*Vysoko-Petrovskiy monastyr*). Although you may have to slip in by the gates off Petrovskiy bulvar while restoration continues, it's certainly worth investigating this faintly sinister relic of family ambition. Enclosed by a high red-brick wall whose blank lower half contrasts with the ornately framed windows above, the fortified complex is a superb example of late Moscow Baroque architecture – a style promoted by the Naryshkin relatives of Peter the Great who financed its reconstruction in the 1680s.

To the left as you enter, the Naryshkin family vault lies beneath the **Church of the Icon of the Virgin of Bogolyubovo** (*tserkov Bogolyubskoy Bogomateri*), which commemorates three of Peter's uncles killed in the 1682 *Streltsy* revolt (see p.341). Behind this, his mother Natalya founded the single-domed **Church of Metropolitan Peter** (*tserkov Petra-Mitropolita*) to celebrate their defeat of the Regent Sofia in 1689. The ensemble is completed by a domed Baroque **belltower** above the old main entrance on ulitsa Petrovka, and a **Refectory Church** with five cupolas on tall drums (where services are held on Mon & Sat at 6pm), linked by a shadowy **arcade** to the monks' cells inside the outer walls.

Beyond the monastery, ulitsa Petrovka's traffic-choked intersection with Petrovskiy and Strastnoy boulevards marks the site of the long-demolished St Peter's Gate that lends its name to **ploshchad Petrovskiy vorota**. Nearby, in medieval times, there was a large market called the *Skorodom* (literally "quick house"), specializing in everything needed to assemble a house within two or three days. Business thrived thanks to the fires that regularly gutted whole districts of Moscow; citizens preferred their traditional wooden houses to European-style, stone dwellings, which were colder and damper in winter.

## The Neglinka and Rozhdestvenka ulitsa

**Neglinka** is the popular diminutive for the Neglina River that once flowed into the heart of Moscow, encircling the Kremlin and the Kitay-gorod; *neglina* means "without clay". In Catherine the Great's time the river was channelled into a pipe running underneath what is now Neglinnaya ulitsa, but continued to flood due to infrequent cleaning and the locals' habit of dumping rubbish – and victims of robberies – into the storm drains. Today, this hilly area is only hazardous for its icy slopes in winter, and otherwise invites a wander ending at the Convent of the Nativity near the Boulevard Ring.

## The Sandunovskiy Baths

Two blocks north of ulitsa Kuznetskiy most, at Neglinnaya ulitsa 14, the **Sandunovskiy Baths** (*Sandunovskie bani*; Mon & Wed–Sun 8am–10pm) flaunt a grandiose *Beaux Arts* facade built in 1895. Its great arch leads into a courtyard, modelled on the Moorish Alhambra Palace in Andalucía, that originally formed the main entrance. The baths occupy the crumbling red-brick building around the back, and are entered by an alleyway with separate doors for either sex, leading to foyers rich in crumbling majolica. While most punters opt for the "first class" *banya* on the floor above, wealthy Muscovites patronize the "luxe" ones on the top floor, with their vaulted pool and private rooms, stained-glass windows and mahogany benches.

*Bathing details appear on p.330.*

## Up ulitsa Rozhdestvenka to the Convent of the Nativity

Running parallel to Neglinnaya ulitsa along what was once a high riverbank, a steeper road, **ulitsa Rozhdestvenka,** ascends to the Convent of the Nativity. The lower end of the street is practically a cul-de-sac owing to building work and the exclusion zone around the ultra-ritzy **Savoy Hotel.** Built in 1912, its glorious Style Moderne interior has been immaculately restored, but doormen generally restrict entry to those who look like they can pay $500 a night.

You can cut onto Rozhdestvenka from Kuznetskiy most, or join it later on by walking uphill and then along 1-y Neglinniy pereulok, by the Sandunovskiy Baths. Further uphill stands the seventeenth-century **Church of St Nicholas of the Bellringers** (*tserkov Sveta Nikolay v Zvonaryakh*) – now a studio for students. Its name refers to the street's old settlement of bellringers from the Ivan the Great Belltower in the Kremlin. In medieval Russia, holy days were celebrated by ringing all the bells of Moscow's "forty times forty" churches in unison, until "the earth shook with their vibrations like thunder", as waves of sound passed over the city.

At the end of Rozhdestvenka a tall Baroque belltower proclaims the **Convent of the Nativity** (*Rozhdestvenskiy monastyr*), which otherwise retires behind a wall. Duck in through the arch to find a complex of nuns' cells surrounding the sixteenth-century **Cathedral of the Nativity** and the eighteenth-century **Church of St John Chrysostom.** Both are small and currently being repaired by black-cowled nuns and architectural students, with financial help from the far-right group *Pamyat*. Previously, the derelict convent was squatted by homeless people who formed a commune of sorts. The convent can also be entered via a stairway from Rozhdestvenskiy bulvar, where a corner turret and brick **ramparts** attest to its dual role as a perimeter fortress in medieval times.

# Lubyanka and around

The name Lubyanka resounds like a gunshot at the far end of a darkened corridor – the traditional method of killing prisoners in the **headquarters of the secret police** on Lubyanka Square. For Russians, the building represents a historically malevolent force, whereas foreigners can afford to be curious and genuinely blasé – in the old days it was almost a sport for foreigners to bait *Intourist* guides with awkward questions whenever KGB HQ hoved into sight at the top of the long rise from Okhotniy ryad. The secret police are still ensconced here – though nowadays called the FSK.

The building is named after its location on **Lubyanskaya plosh-chad**. Last century, this was the smelliest square in Moscow, surrounded by stables, fountains for watering horses and dens for the refreshment of the *izvoschiki* (coachmen). In the 1890s the newly rich insurance companies transformed the neighbourhood with residential and office buildings, which – expropriated after the Revolution – formed the nucleus of a 1930s redevelopment plan that included the demolition of the Kitay-gorod's Vladimir Gate.

Today, you're struck by the grotesque decision to construct Moscow's largest toyshop (1957) just across the square from the Lubyanka – supposedly as a tribute to the founder of the secret police, who also chaired a commission on children's welfare. Located on the site of the medieval cannon foundry where the giant Tsar Cannon in the Kremlin was cast, the **Detskiy Mir** (Children's World) still sells toys and kids' clothing, but now also contains a car showroom, a bar and boutiques (daily, 8am–8pm). Its numerous exits and escalators make the store a good place for budding James Bonds to shake off any tails.

## The Lubyanka

The Lubyanka rises in tiers of caramel- and toffee-coloured stucco from a stone-faced lower storey that discreetly flaunts the Soviet crest. Once the head office of the Rossiya Insurance Company, it was taken over by the Bolshevik *Cheka* in March 1918, only months before the repression of the Anarchists and Left SRs. In Stalin's time, generations entered its maw via the infamous Lubyanka "kennel", a whitewashed cellar used for body searches. Such was the volume of arrests that the versatile Shchusev was commissioned to design an extension that doubled its size by 1947. Even so, its bureaucracy engulfed neighbouring buildings as the secret service burgeoned through successive name changes, finally into the KGB (see box).

### Spying

Spying has played a big part in Russian history since the time of Ivan the Terrible; every Tsar had a Secret Office or Third Section to sniff out intrigues and spy on foreign powers. Its apotheosis came with Soviet rule, as the "organs" waxed all-powerful at home and seemingly omniscient abroad. When establishing the All-Russian Extraordinary Commission for the Struggle against Counter-Revolution, Speculation and Sabotage – or *Cheka* – in December 1917, Dzerzhinsky asserted that "every Chekist should have clean hands, a cool head and a warm heart". Such perverted idealism soon faded, but its myth helped sustain the organization through decades of bloodshed and fabricated conspiracies.

As the **NKVD** it controlled the slave empire of the Gulag and a large private army, making its boss, Beria, the prime contender for supremacy after Stalin's demise – a prospect that galvanized the rest of the Politburo into having him shot and pruning the ministry's powers. As a pillar of the establishment, the **KGB** proved more durable than the Communist Party, affecting cosmetic changes under Gorbachev and enduring several shake-ups by Yeltsin, from which it emerged as two agencies. The Lubyanka is now occupied by the **Federal Counter-Intelligence Service** (FSK) that monitors the home front, while the **Foreign Intelligence Service** is based in a modern block in the suburb of Yantsevo, near the Moscow Ring Road.

For several decades, a six-metre-tall **statue of "Iron Felix" Dzerzhinsky**, the *Cheka*'s founder, loomed from its massive pedestal on the grassy knoll out in front. The night after the collapse of the 1991 *putsch*, crowds cheered as the statue was toppled by a crane, the head in a wire noose, a symbol of the end of Soviet Communism; it's now in the "graveyard of fallen monuments" behind the Central House of Artists (p.215).

Equally discreetly, the spooks have reopened what is now called the **Museum of the Federal Counter-Intelligence Service** (Mon–Fri 9am–6pm; ☎224-1982), whose message is that Mother Russia has always been threatened by subversion and foreign foes; and spying in her defence is inevitable – and honourable. Much is made of master-spies Richard Sorge and Sterlitz, who provided advance warning of Hitler's invasion (which Stalin ignored) and penetrated his General Staff. The museum can be visited on **guided tours** only, at $50 a head, where the guide will rattle off his fanatical spiel like a machine-gun. Visitors should bring their passports, as the museum shares the building with the secret service **Officers Club**, at ulitsa Bolshaya Lubyanka 12.

## Behind the Lubyanka

On either side of the Officers Club on ulitsa Bolshaya Lubyanka are the **Central Gastronom** food store – an ageing Stalinist showpiece of cracked marble and chandeliers – and the royal-blue **Rostopchin mansion**, withdrawn behind a fence topped by urns. Long used by the secret service, it once belonged to Count Rostopchin, the

governor who ordered Moscow to be burned in 1812, and escaped
from a mob besieging his home by throwing them an alleged traitor.
During the first night of the French occupation, Rostopchin's agents
set fire to wine stalls in the Kitay-gorod and the carriage-workshops
on Karetniy ryad. By the next morning, a powerful wind had fanned
the flames and the fire had spread to engulf half of Moscow –
Lubyanka was one of the few quarters to survive, owing to vigorous
fire-fighting by its residents.

From the Rostopchin mansion, Bolshaya Lubyanka runs 500m
uphill to the Boulevard Ring, where the small white **Church of the
Icon of the Virgin of Vladimir** (daily 9am–6pm) is all that remains
of the fortified Sretenskiy Monastery, erected on the spot where
Muscovites had welcomed the arrival of a miraculous icon of the
Virgin in 1395 (see p.207).

The only inducement to walk along Sretenskiy bulvar is the
statue of **Nadezhda Krupskaya** (1869–1939), Lenin's wife. The
lithe, gamine figure bears little resemblance to the real dumpy, fish-
eyed Krupskaya – just like the hagiographies that failed to mention
Lenin's infidelity before the Revolution, or how Krupskaya was
browbeaten by Stalin after Lenin's death.

## The Mayakovsky Museum

Across the road to the east of the Lubyanka, a granite head gazing
from a portal at ulitsa Myatninskaya 3–6 betrays the **Mayakovsky
Museum** in the courtyard behind (Thurs 1–9pm; Fri–Tues 10am–
6pm; closed the last Fri of each month). **Vladimir Mayakovsky**
(1893–1930) was an enthusiastic supporter of the Bolsheviks from
an early age, who got into Futurism at the Moscow School for
Painting and Sculpture after meeting the Burlyuk brothers. Together
they published a manifesto called *A Slap in the Face for Public
Taste* and embarked on a publicity tour, Mayakovsky wearing
earrings and a waistcoat with radishes in the buttonholes. In 1917 he
threw himself into the October Revolution, founding the Left Front of
Art with Alexander Rodchenko and Osip Brik, and producing over six
hundred giant cartoon advertisements with pithy verse captions for
the Russia Telegraph Agency. Mayakovsky's suicide at the age of 37
has been variously ascribed to despair over his love for Osip's wife,
Lili; to disillusionment with Soviet life and its censors; or to hostile
reviews of his last exhibition. Thousands filed past his open coffin at
the Writers' Union, and Stalin would later decree that "Mayakovsky
was and remains the most talented poet of our Soviet epoch.
Indifference to his memory and to his work is a crime."

Opened in 1990, and run by the poet's granddaughter, the
Mayakovsky Museum is quite unlike other memorial museums in the
ex-residences of writers or artists, with their period decor and
display cases. Rather, it feels like walking around inside
Mayakovsky's head during a brainstorm. Melting chairs an

Constructivist vortices breathe life into editions of his poetry and
agitprop posters, mixed in with personal effects and symbolic *objéts*
– viewed as you descend a spiral ramp from the upper floor.
Although nothing remains of the original flat, it was here that
Mayakovsky lived from 1919 onwards, and ultimately committed
suicide with a stage-prop revolver, leaving an unfinished poem
beside him.

## Towards Chistye prudy

The section of the Boulevard Ring known as **Chistye prudy** is notable for several architectural curiosities, mostly within five minutes'
walk of Chistye Prudy or Turgenevskaya metro stations. Another
approach is to walk up **ulitsa Myatninskaya**, where at no. 19, on
the left, you'll recognize the **Perlov Tea House** (*Chayniy magazin*;
Mon–Sat 8am–1pm & 2–8pm) by its facade crawling with bronze
dragons and pagoda-like flourishes, matched inside by lacquered
columns and Chinese vases. Legend has it that the shop was decorated in this fashion by the wealthy tea merchant Perlov, who
desired to impress the young Emperor of China during his visit to
Russia in 1893. Sadly for Perlov, the emperor chose to visit a rival
tea merchant instead.

Next door, the former **Yushkov House** is currently swathed in
scaffolding that obscures the plaque testifying that the Moscow
School of Painting and Sculpture was established here in 1844. By
1872, when it hosted the first major exhibition of the Wanderers
movement (see p.211), the Moscow School had begun to outshine
the Academy of Arts in St Petersburg; four decades later, it was at
the forefront of the avant-garde. The teaching staff included Leonid
Pasternak, whose son Boris – the future author of *Doctor Zhivago* –
spent his childhood in a nearby annexe. In 1920, it was transformed
into the Higher Technical-Artistic Workshop or *VKhuTeMas*, the
short-lived Soviet equivalent of the Bauhaus, whose radical
Futurism dismayed Lenin.

Apart from the Tea House, the best sights are located along or
just off Chistoprudy bulvar, on the other side of the **main post office**
(*Glavpochtamt*). The boulevard and the locality are named after the
pond at the far end, which was used for the disposal of butchers'
waste until 1703, when it was mucked out on the orders of Prince
Menshikov and henceforth known as Chistye prudy (Clean Ponds).

## Menshikov's Tower and Double Knee-Bend Lane

In the early eighteenth century, this part of Moscow belonged to
**Prince Menshikov** (1673–1729), who rose from being a humble
pie-lad to fortune and power, owing to Peter the Great's apprecia-
tion of his ruthless ability and artful blend of "servility, familiarity
and impertinence". Menshikov understood Peter's impatience with
Muscovite conservatism and the Orthodox Church, and surpassed

...ar in ostentatious gestures. Accordingly, he commissioned ...Zarudniy to build (1705–07) an outstanding edifice that incorporated secular Western forms into Orthodox architecture – the Church of the Archangel Gabriel (*tserkov Arkhangela Gavriila*), right along Chistoprudy bulvar, 150m beyond the post office and directly behind the lower Classical Church of St Theodor Stratilites (*tserkov Fyodora Stratilita*).

Popularly known as **Menshikov's Tower** (*Menshikova bashnya*), this boasted a wooden-spired belfry holding fifty bells and crowned by a gilded statue of the Archangel, three metres higher than the Ivan the Great Belltower in the Kremlin – hitherto the tallest building in all Russia. His hubris was punished in 1723, when lightning set the spire ablaze. Since Menshikov was then living at Orianenbaum, and shortly had to fight for survival following Peter's death, no rebuilding took place until 1766–80, when the freemason Izmaylov devised a belfry with only two of the three original octagonal tiers and a gilded coronet instead of a spire. However, many features of Zarudniy's design remain, such as the bible-clutching seraphims that flit across the facade, and the massive buttresses scrolling upwards beside the door on the left-hand side. The interior looks more Catholic than Orthodox, its frescoes offset by swags and cherubs – but Izmaylov's Masonic symbols were removed after the Freemasons were banished from the Church in 1863. It now provides meals for the poor on Sundays.

By turning right after both churches, you'll find yourself in **Double Knee-Bend Lane** (Krivokolenniy pereulok), so-called because it has two sharp bends instead of one. Its cute name aside, this is a nice, quiet way into the Ukrainian quarter, coming out on Armyanskiy pereulok (p.140).

## Along the Ring to the Apraksin Mansion

Alternatively, you can return to the Boulevard Ring and carry on to the limpid pond that gives Chistye prudy its name. On the far side stands the **Sovremennik Theatre**, occupying a former cinema with an elegant, rounded portico flanked by bas-reliefs of Greek deities. Further along at no. 23 is a florid sky-blue apartment building where the film director Sergei Eisenstein lived from 1920 to 1934. On the near side of the boulevard, don't miss the **Figurniy dom** (Figured House) at no. 14, built by Sergei Vashkov at the beginning of this century, whose frontage crawls with a bestiary of supernatural creatures.

While in the area, try to get outside the Ring for a look at the former **Apraksin Mansion** near the corner of ulitsa Pokrovka. Erected in the 1760s, overlooking the Pokrovka Gate and the road leading to the royal palaces in the old foreigners' quarter, the mansion was Moscow's ultimate in decorative Baroque: a rambling mass of bay windows and scalloped niches, clusters of angels and Corinthian pilasters. Though its stucco is shot and its bold aquamarine paint grimy, the mansion still draws you into a court-yard that once backed on to gardens, through mews archways lined with plaques listing technical journals based at the premises – a legacy of the Industrial Academy for "Red managers" that existed here after the Revolution. Its students included Stalin's wife Nadezhda Allilueva, and Nikita Khrushchev, who was the school's Party secretary.

# The Ukrainian quarter

The erstwhile **Ukrainian quarter** to the east of the Kitay-gorod no longer has a distinct ethnic flavour, but its hilly winding lanes are a reminder of the time when Moscow's residential quarters consisted of "quiet lanes where wooden gates open into courtyards planted with lilacs, acacias and senna".

In late medieval times this area was prosperous and cosmopoli-tan, for scores of Westerners chose to settle here after Tsar Mikhail Romanov allowed non-Orthodox believers to live where they pleased. But as income for local Orthodox churches declined, protests impelled the Tsar to order the demolition of their chapels and a ban on further settlers; his successor, Alexei, later banished them to a colony beyond the city walls. Ukrainians began moving in after the Russo-Polish war of 1654–67 left Ukraine under Russian control, followed by other races as the empire grew. Today, embassies and diverse places of worship maintain something of this tradition, but the area's real charm lies in its meandering backstreets and odd juxtapositions of medieval, nineteenth-century and Soviet architec-ture. The nearest metro stations are Kitay-gorod and Chistye Prudy.

## Along Maroseyka

Running from the edge of the Kitay-gorod through the heart of the quarter, **ulitsa Maroseyka** takes its name from *Malorosseyka* or "Little Russia", the old Tsarist title for Ukraine, which came under the jurisdiction of the Little Russian Office. During Soviet times, the street was patronizingly named after Bogdan Khmelnitskiy, the Cossack Hetman who transferred control of Ukraine from Poland to Russia in 1653. Nowadays far too narrow for its heavy traffic, Maroseyka is shabby and congested, but redeems itself with some fine old buildings and picturesque lanes before becoming ulitsa Pokrovka, nearer the Boulevard Ring.

Starting from the vicinity of Staraya ploshchad, the first sight is the small white **Church of St Nicholas the Wonderworker** (*tserkov Nikolay Chudotvortsa*), characterized by chunky *nalichniki*, orange grilles and a dull brown onion dome, and entered from the rear. The church dates from 1687, its belltower from 1748. Further on at no. 17 stands a sky-blue and white mansion dripping with caryatids. Originally the Little Russian Office, it now contains the

**Belarus Embassy**, which maintains a hotel for visiting dignitaries around the corner. Across the main road is the sage-green **Church of SS Cosmas and Damian** (*tserkov Kosmy i Damiana*), built by Kazakov in 1791–1803, which is unique among Moscow churches for its central cylinder, topped by a gilt-knobbed cupola and abutted by several rounded chapels.

## Armenians' Lane

Around the corner from the embassy lies the original heart of the foreign quarter, **Armyanskiy pereulok** (Armenians' Lane), whose security was half-assured by the fact that Artamon Matveev, Tsar Alexei's foreign minister, lived here with his Scottish wife, Mary Hamilton, surrounded by mirrors, clocks and paintings that attested to his fascination with European ways. Although this didn't stop Alexei from evicting all the foreigners in 1652, it was here that he later met his second wife, **Natalya Naryshkina** – the upshot being a child that upset the dynastic ambitions of the **Miloslavskiy** *boyars*, whose intrigues against Matveev and Natalya led to the *Streltsy* revolt of 1682. The rival families lived directly opposite each other: Matveev where the Belarus Embassy stands today; the Miloslavskiys in a house that still exists (albeit much remodelled) around the corner. During the late nineteenth century this was inhabited by the Slavophile poet Fyodor Tyutchev, who famously wrote that you cannot understand Russia, only believe in her.

At the far end of the lane, the **Armenian Embassy** occupies a pale yellow mansion (no. 2) that retires behind an elegant portico and wrought-iron gates, which was formerly the Lazarev Institute for Oriental Languages, established by a wealthy Armenian family. Armenians have lived here since the time of the Miloslavskiys , who also owned a house across the road at no. 3. Unlike their other place, this looks more of its time, having low brick vaulted rooms at several levels, and is now given over to a **Moscow Lights Museum** (Tues–Thurs noon–4pm), covering the history of illuminating the city. If antique gas lamps don't get you going, there are switchboards from the metro and an album of photos showing Moscow ablaze with neon and fireworks at the victory celebrations in 1945.

## To the Ivanovskiy Convent

By turning off ulitsa Maroseyka beside SS Cosmas and Damian, you can follow **Starosadskiy pereulok** (Old Garden Lane) downhill to the **Church of St Vladimir in the Old Garden** (*tserkov Vladimira v Starykh sadakh*), recently restored as the only surviving example of the dozen or so stone parish churches erected under Grand Duke Vasily III. Built in 1514 by the Italian Alevisio Novi (creator of the Archangel Cathedral in the Kremlin), it was altered and truncated in the 1680s and thereafter nicknamed "domeless" (*bez glavy*). St Vladimir's feast day falls on July 28.

Across the slope looms the high-walled **Ivanovskiy Convent**
(*Ivanovskiy monastyr*), whose fanged belltowers and scabrous
cupolas reflect its sinister history. Founded in the sixteenth century,
it was used as a dumping-ground for unwanted wives and daughters
and as a prison for noblewomen guilty of heinous crimes or vaguely
defined political offences. Among those detained in the reign of
Catherine the Great were the notorious Countess Dariya Saltykova –
confined for murdering 139 of her serfs – and the tragic Princess
Trakhanova, who fell foul of the Empress. In Soviet times the
convent was disbanded and the complex turned into a police training school, onto which a modern block was grafted. It has now been
returned to the Church and is slowly being restored as a working
convent. Until this reopens, you must hope for a truck passing
through the iron gates to provide a glimpse of the interior.

*The story of
Princess
Trakhanova is
told on p.242.
Countess
Saltykova is
buried in the
Donskoy
Monastery
(p.221).*

While the convent is a dramatic highlight, various other
churches invite further rambling around the **backstreets**, back
towards the centre. Head down ulitsa Zabelina, the busiest road
running away from the convent, turning right up what may be signposted as ulitsa Arkhipova. At no. 10 on the left, a discreet brownstone facade cloaks the **Choral Synagogue**, Moscow's oldest and
largest Jewish place of worship, which has been under 24-hour
guard since another synagogue was suspiciously destroyed by fire in
1994. However, it's not worth causing any alarm by trying to enter
or taking photographs.

## To the Boulevard Ring and back

If you're still keen on exploring, try the lane running uphill to the
east of St Vladimir's Church, whose name, **Khokhlovskiy pereulok**,
comes from *khokhli*, an old Russian nickname for Ukrainians,
derived from their traditional hairdos (*khokhol* means "tuft" or
"crest").

At the triple fork beyond the first bend you'll see a terraced
garden, overlooked by a turquoise mansion whose ornamental
Pseudo-Russian archway invites a closer look. The **Morozov House**
once belonged to Maria Morozova, a fervent Old Believer who inherited her husband's textile empire and ran it regardless of her sons,
leaving them to patronize the arts. While Savva bankrolled the
Moscow Arts Theatre and resided elsewhere, Sergei lived here with
mother and her ban on baths and electricity. However, he did sponsor a museum, took up art himself and built a studio in the garden,
which he later gave as a sanctuary to the painter Isaak Levitan, who
would otherwise have been included in the expulsion of twenty thousand Jews from Moscow in 1891. After the Revolution the Morozovs
fled and the house was seized by Left SRs, who transformed it into a
fortress. During their abortive "Bolshoy coup" of July 6, 1918, they
held Dzerzhinsky a prisoner here until he was freed by Latvian
sharpshooters. It now serves as a playschool.

From the park below the house, a glimpse of the **Church of the Trinity in Khokhlovskiy** lane (*tserkov Troitsy v Khokhlovke*) might lure you further uphill past a seventeenth-century Ukrainian Baroque *boyar's* house converted into a business lunch-club. There are fine **views** of Moscow if you look back, and the prospect of an especially leafy stretch of the Boulevard Ring to draw you on.

To link up with the final itinerary, follow Pokrovskiy bulvar past the erstwhile **Pokrovskiy Barracks** – a long beige building with eight massive columns, now occupied by the National Bank of Credit – and turn right into Maliy Vuzovskiy pereulok. This brings you back into the Ukrainian quarter and to the former **Church of the Trinity in Kulishki** (*tserkov Trekh Svyatiteley na Kulishkakh*), whose deep undercroft supports a nest of chapels and shingled domes, their ogee-gables picked out in red against the whitewashed brickwork. Finished in 1674, this multi-level structure once contained an upper "summer" church, and a smaller, warmer one for winter worship, below – a functional division common in those times, which suits the offices ensconced there today.

## Down towards Solyanka and the Yauza River

The tail end of the Beliy Gorod lies around ulitsa Solyanka and the Yauza River embankment. There are several routes down from the Ukrainian quarter, all of which bring you out on **Podkolokolniy pereulok** (Under the Bells Lane). Starting from the Ivanovskiy Convent and walking down Maliy Ivanovskiy pereulok, you'll hit the road near its junction with Solyanka, which is dominated by the Baroque belfry of the eighteenth-century **Church of the Nativity** – now a cosmetics institute – and the **Academy of Medical Sciences**, in a flaking Classical pile built by Gilardi in 1826.

Alternatively, a left turn at the far end of the lane beyond the Church of the Trinity in Kulishki will lead you to the **Church of St Nicholas in Podkopaev** lane (*tserkov Nikoly v Podkopae*), built in 1750. This blithely defies the rules of Classical harmony by juxtaposing a tiny church painted lime green with emerald cupolas and a massive red belltower, yet impresses despite its decrepitude, now being remedied by repairs.

The first turning across the main road to the east of St Nicholas will lead you to another church, the **Church of Peter and Paul at the Yauza Gate** (*tserkov Petra i Pavla u Yauzkikh vorot*). Erected on a hill near one of the city gates in 1700, this once enjoyed a lovely view across the river to the churches of Zayauze, extending upstream as far as the Andronikov Monastery. Though its view has been curtailed by high-rise apartments, the church remains peacefully aloof from the city, its visual appeal enhanced by a salmon-pink paint job, against which its crested *nalichniki* stand proud.

One final church worth seeing rises just beyond the Boulevard Ring near ploshchad Yauzkikh vorota, where the gate once stood.

The Church of the Trinity in Serebryaniki (*tserkov Troitsy v Serebryanikakh*) takes its name from the quarter of silversmiths (*serebryanki*) that existed here when Karl Blank built the church in 1781. Its lofty freestanding belfry of three tiers buttressed by Corinthian pilasters and jutting pediments is a local landmark, painted a bright cerulean blue; the refectory and chapel (services 8am & 5pm) are secluded on Serebryanicheskiy pereulok, beneath the Boulevard Ring flyover. At this point, you might be drawn across the Yauza by the looming mass of the Stalin-Gothic Kotelnicheskaya Apartments, described on p.238.

---

### The Khitrov Market

No description of the Beliy Gorod quarter would be complete without a mention of the **Khitrov Market** (*Khitrovskiy rynok*) that existed on the corner of the Boulevard Ring from 1826 to 1923. Sited in a dell surrounded by flophouses and mudbanks astream with sewage, this so-called labour market constituted an underworld of ten thousand beggars, orphans, thieves and whores, which Stanislavsky took as a model when staging Gorky's play *The Lower Depths*. Its robbers and pimps drank in dives called "Siberia" and "Hard Labour", while local kids were raised to steal or sell their bodies by the age of ten. The whole area was unlit and shrouded in fog, so the police never ventured in after dark; outsiders who did were found stabbed to death and stripped naked the next morning. After the Civil War, this urban sore was cauterized by bulldozing away the slums and erecting a huge model apartment building entered by an arch flanked by **statues of an armed worker and peasant**, which can still be seen at the far end of Podkolokolniy pereulok.

---

Chapter 5

# The Zemlyanoy Gorod

I n medieval times, the white-walled Beliy Gorod was encircled by a humbler **ZEMLYANOY GOROD** or "Earth Town", ringed by an earthen rampart fifteen kilometres in diameter. Its wooden houses and muddy lanes proved impervious to change until its total destruction in the fire of 1812. Reconstruction presented an ideal opportunity for gentrification, as former artisans' quarters were colonized by the nobility and the old ramparts were levelled to form a ring of boulevards, where anyone building a house was obliged to plant trees – the origin of the **Garden Ring** (*Sadovoe koltso*) that marked the division between the bourgeois centre and the proletarian suburbs.

Although Moscow's growth eroded this distinction and the Revolution turned it inside out, the area's cachet endured. Its roll-call of famous residents includes Pushkin, Lermontov, Chekhov, Gorky and Bulgakov, all of whom are recalled by museums and associated with certain neighbourhoods – in particular, Bulgakov and the **Patriarch's Ponds**. Besides its **literary associations**, this is one of the best-looking parts of Moscow, with Classical and Art Nouveau **mansions** on every corner of the backstreets off the **Arbat**. This quarter has inspired poet-musicians like Bulat Okudzhava, giving rise to a vibrant **streetlife** that was unique in Moscow during the 1980s and is still more tourist-friendly than anything else currently on offer, though the future lies with the malls of the **New Arbat**.

The modern Garden Ring is a Stalinist creation whose name has been a misnomer since all the trees were felled when it was widened to an eight-lane motorway in the 1930s. Vast avenues, flanked by leviathan blocks and the **Stalin-Gothic skyscrapers** whose pinnacles and spires dominate Moscow's skyline, exude power and indifference. In 1944, hordes of German POWs were herded along the Ring en route to Siberia; some Muscovites jeered, others threw them bread. The Ring witnessed **barricades** and bloodshed during the crises of 1991 and 1993 and seems guaranteed a role in any future troubles.

**Approaches**

The size of the Zemlyanoy Gorod and its uneven distribution of sights calls for two **approaches**. Whereas the western half – particularly the Arbat district – repays exploration **on foot**, the rest is best tackled on a hit and run basis, making forays from the nearest **metro** station. Some Circle line stations coincide with the Garden Ring, but most are sited further out. Travelling overground is an experience in itself. Despite the Ring's heavy traffic and brutal functionalism, its sheer width and rollercoaster succession of underpasses and flyovers make for a dramatic ride by **car**, or a slow parade of skyscrapers aboard **trolleybus 6**, which takes about an hour to circle the Ring, stopping at all the main intersections.

Each section of the Ring is individually named (eg Bolshaya Sadovaya ulitsa, Sadovaya-Triumfalnaya ulitsa) and numbered in a clockwise direction with the odd numbers on the rim. Our account follows the pattern of the previous chapter by starting with Tverskaya ulitsa and dividing the rest into wedge-shaped sectors. Many of these tie in with points on the Boulevard Ring, mentioned in the previous chapter, although in other cases the starting point is the Garden Ring or a metro station.

*The lower end of Tverskaya ulitsa is covered on pp.107–114.*

# Tverskaya ulitsa

The long, flat stretch of **Tverskaya ulitsa** beyond the Boulevard Ring starts with an elongated slab of greenery underlaid by pedestrian subways and three metro stations (Pushkinskaya, Tverskaya and Chekhovskaya), one of which takes its name from the statue of the poet that gazes over **Pushkinskaya ploshchad** (Pushkin Square).

Alexander Opekushin's bronze **statue of Pushkin** is Moscow's best-loved monument. Paid for by public donations and unveiled in 1880 to eulogies by Ivan Turgenev and other writers, the statue was moved from its original location on the other side of Tverskaya ulitsa to its present site in 1950. Floral tributes always lie at the foot of its plinth, while on Pushkin's birthday (June 6), thousands of admirers gather to recite his poetry. In the 1970s and 80s, the statue was also a focal point for demonstrations, as Russians regard Pushkin as the embodiment of moral honesty, and the protestors hoped that the police would be too ashamed to wade in (they weren't).

Crazed nationalists detect a sinister plot in the placement of Pushkin with his back to Russia – or rather, to the **Rossiya Cinema**, whose glass facade and bronzed pediment loom further back into the park. The cinema was one of the first daringly modern buildings in post-war Moscow when it was erected in 1961 on the site of the demolished Strastnoy (Passion) Convent, recalled by the name of the boulevard nearby. Behind it are the offices of **Noviy Mir**, the

monthly literary journal that printed Solzhenitsyn's *One Day in the Life of Ivan Denisovich* during Khrushchev's "thaw" a generation ago, and Orwell's *Nineteen Eighty-Four* under *glasnost*.

Today, however, Muscovites are keener on **McDonald's**, across the square. The first *McDonald's* in the Soviet Union when it opened in 1990, this remains the second largest branch in the world after the one in Beijing, and serves 35,000–40,000 customers a day. All the food is prepared at an ultra-modern factory in the suburb of Solntsevo – nicknamed "McGulag" – which can be visited on tours organized by *Patriarchi Dom* (see p.32).

Pushkinskaya ploshchad is Moscow's main newspaper area. The northern side of the square is flanked by the offices of **Izvestiya** ("News"), once the organ of the Soviet government, and now an independent, liberal newspaper. Abutting its original Constructivist premises with asymmetrical balconies and circular upper windows is a 1970s extension, fronted by a plaza where mainly Central Asians and Arabs congregate. Next to this stands the **Sytin dom**, a Style Moderne edifice faced with grey and yellow tiles, where the Communist Party newspaper *Pravda* ("Truth") was printed in the 1920s. This gave rise to the old joke that "There is no news in *Pravda* and no truth in *Izvestiya*".

Around the corner of the Sytin dom lurks the concrete, Workerist building block of a third newspaper, *Trud* ("Labour"). This faces the **Ssudnaya kazna**, an impressive Pseudo-Russian pile with a faceted facade, which serves as a repository for billions of rubles held by the Central Bank of Russia. The Museum of the Revolution is visible from the corner of the main road (see below).

## A brief detour off Pushkinskaya

Before checking out the Museum of the Revolution, it's a good idea to take a look around the corner of the old wing of the *Izvestiya* building, where a delightful church stands at the beginning of **ulitsa Chekhova**. This street is named after Chekhov because he liked it so much that he lived in three separate houses here (nos. 11, 12 and 29) over the years.

Startlingly white, with azure onion domes, the **Church of the Nativity of Our Lady in Putinki** (*tserkov Rozhdestva Bogroditsy shto v Putinkakh*) was the last church to be built with tent-roofs before Patriarch Nikon banned them in 1652. Its complex form includes three steeples atop the church proper; a protruding chapel crowned with a tent-roof and a pyramid of ogival *kokoshniki*; an arched, open belfry; and a one-storey narthex and porch, the latter also decorated with a tent-roof and *kokoshniki*. Alas, the interior is as plain as the exterior is lavish, retaining only a portion of the original iconostasis.

Up the road at no. 6, the **Lenkom Theatre** occupies the former **Merchants' Club**, built in 1909. Its sedate facade hides a slick Style

### The Kuptsy

Before the Revolution, Russia's merchant-industrialists or *Kuptsy* were on the verge of supplanting the aristocracy as the most powerful class in the Empire. Many were former serfs who ended up owning their ex-masters' estates, and Old Believers who read only the bible but had their children educated abroad, producing a sophisticated second generation that endowed hospitals and patronized contemporary art. **Savva Mamontov** sponsored an artists' colony at Abramtsevo, **Pavel Tretyakov** founded the Tretyakov Gallery, while **Sergei Shchukin** and **Ivan Morozov** collected the French Impressionists, and the works of Matisse and Picasso now held by the Hermitage and Pushkin museums.

Others were chiefly known for their eccentricities. **Mikhail Khludov** walked a pet tiger on a leash and once gave his wife a crocodile as a birthday present. One of the **Lapin** brothers acquired his seed-money by agreeing to be half-castrated by a religious sect; once rich, he refused to have the operation completed. **Maria Morozova** regarded electricity as satanic, never bathed for fear of catching cold, and dressed her children in hand-me-downs, while the millionaire **Fersanov** was so miserly that he lived in a hut and lost sleep over the expenditure of three *kopecks*.

Moderne interior whose doorways are framed in marble and rare hardwoods, where Moscow's *Kuptsy* (see box above) gathered every Tuesday to feast on sturgeon, milk-fed lamb, sucking pigs and twelve-layer *bliny* (pancakes), accompanied by Russian, Magyar and Gypsy orchestras. Afterwards, they would gamble at the English Club or rent *troykas* (horse-drawn sledges) and drive singing and shouting to the *Yar* restaurant on Moscow's outskirts, returning to the club at dawn to start planning next week's binge. Following the Revolution, it was taken over by Anarchists, until they, too, were evicted from their luxurious base by the Bolshevik secret police.

## The Museum of the Revolution

With a crude sense of irony, the **Museum of the Revolution** (Tues–Sat 10am–6pm, Sun 10am–5pm) is housed in the former English Club, a pre-Revolutionary haunt of aristocrats and *bon viveurs*. Built by the poet Kheraskov in 1722, the orangey-red mansion was one of the few secular buildings to survive the fire of 1812 and is noted for the hyena-like stone lions on top of its gatehouses, mentioned in Pushkin's *Yevgeny Onegin*.

Originally used for Masonic meetings, in 1831 it became the **English Club** ("so-called because hardly any Englishman belongs to it"), virtually the only place where political discussions were tolerated during the reign of Tsar Nicholas I. Soon, the club turned into a "cathedral of idleness" where Tolstoy lost 1000 rubles and Mikhail Morozov blew over a million in one night, in the card-room called "Hell"; and in 1913 it hosted a costume ball in honour of the tricentenary of the Romanov dynasty that was the last truly grand social event before the Revolution.

The museum's **exhibits** reflect its uneasy transformation from a bastion of ideological rectitude to an "objective chronicle of modern Russian history", but everything may be rearranged if the contents of the Lenin Museum find a new home here; hopefully, they'll also add some captions in English. In the courtyard are an armoured car from the street battles of 1917 and a trolleybus that was used to barricade the White House during the 1991 *putsch*. Inside, highlights include a sledge-mounted machine-gun from the Civil War (1918–1921; hall 6); posters of rascally *kulaks* (see p.350) from the time of Collectivization (hall 7); masses of Stalin kitsch (hall 11); a *glasnost*-era admission of social problems (hall 12); and the final room displaying banners and weapons from the White House.

## On to Triumfalnaya ploshchad

The final stretch of Tverskaya ulitsa is fairly unremarkable, featuring the **Moscow Dramatic Theatre** (next to the Museum of the Revolution), a good stand-up **café** for Middle Eastern food (just up from the *Minsk Hotel*, across the road), and several pretentious **shops**. Notice the old-fashioned *Elysée Concorde*, on the left, whose Art Deco windows depict Parisian landmarks – worth a look inside for its coffered ceilings.

*For coverage of the other side of the Garden Ring, see p.165. Triumfalnaya ploshchad is also within walking distance of the Museum of Musical Culture (p.253) and the Tishkin flea market (p.176).*

Shortly afterwards, Tverskaya ulitsa meets the Garden Ring at **Triumfalnaya ploshchad**, named after the festive arches that were erected here to greet monarchs in the eighteenth century. As these were surmounted by a statue of a charioteer, Muscovites joked that there were only two coachmen in Moscow who weren't drunk: the one on the arch and the one on top of the Bolshoy Theatre.

The square is, in fact, better known by its former Soviet name – ploshchad Mayakovskovo – and for its craggy **statue of Mayakovsky**, unveiled in 1958. Its truculent pose and baggy trousers call to mind Mayakovsky's eulogy on the first Soviet passport, issued in the 1920s: "I take from the pocket of my wide trousers my red-skinned passport, the priceless object I carry. Read it and envy me! I am a citizen of the Soviet Union." Beyond the statue rises the **Pekin Hotel**, a yellow and white wedding-cake from the era of Sino-Soviet Friendship.

Above the main entrance to Mayakovskaya metro looms the massive square-pillared portico and diamond-patterned facade of the **Tchaikovsky Concert Hall**. Originally built as a theatre for the avant-garde director Meyerhold, who wished to design it "for the wonderful future a hundred years ahead", it was to have two circular stages – able to revolve, descend or rise as the director wished – and a "creative tower" on the corner of Tverskaya ulitsa, for artistic experiments. Then Meyerhold was arrested and tortured to death, and in 1938 the theatre was converted into a concert hall, now used by the State Symphony Orchestra.

That same year saw the completion of **Mayakovskaya metro** station, internationally acclaimed for its light and silvery ribbed hall. As one of the deepest stations on the metro, this hosted a dramatic wartime meeting on the eve of the anniversary of the Revolution in November 1941, when the Nazis were on the outskirts of Moscow, at which Stalin gave a sombre briefing to the assembled generals and Party activists.

Beside the concert hall are the **Satirical Theatre** and the **Aquarium Gardens**, containing the **Mossovet Theatre**. If you're heading in this direction you're on the right track for the next stage of the itinerary.

# Around the Patriarch's Ponds, Vosstaniya and Nikitskie vorota

The quarter to the southwest of Tverskaya is notable for its pretty, leafy backstreets and **literary associations**, which make the Patriarch's Ponds one of the priciest neighbourhoods in Moscow. Admirers of Bulgakov, Chekhov, Gorky, Pushkin or Alexei Tolstoy will find their former homes preserved as **museums**, while fans of **Style Moderne** and **Stalinist architecture** can revel in the Ryabushinskiy mansion near Nikitskie vorota or the Stalin-Gothic skyscraper on ploshchad Vosstaniya (visible from Triumfalnaya ploshchad, around the curve of the Ring).

## Bulgakov and the Patriarch's Ponds

Past a row of kiosks beyond the Aquarium Gardens, a plaque beside the archway of no. 10 Bolshaya Sadovaya ulitsa attests that **Mikhail Bulgakov** (see box below) lived here from 1921 to 1924. His satirical fantasy *The Master and Margarita* is indelibly associated with Moscow – and this area in particular – as Bulgakov transposed his own flat to "302A Sadovaya Street" and made it the setting for Satan's Ball and other events in the novel. During the 1980s, it grew into a place of pilgrimage, to the annoyance of residents, who grew sick of fans of the author gathering on the stairway and covering the walls with graffiti and images of the impish cat, Behemoth. The present owners vow that it will soon become a **Bulgakov Flat-Museum**. To pay a visit, go into the courtyard and look for entrance 6, on the left; the flat (no. 50) is at the very top of the stairs. Until opening hours are decided, you'll have to risk a rebuff by just turning up and hoping for the best.

The **Patriarch's Ponds** (*Patriarshiy prudy*) are actually one large pond, descended from three fishponds dug from the medieval Goat's Marsh. Surrounded by wrought-iron railings and mature trees, this beautiful pond forms the heart of a square flanked by tall apartment blocks, which before the Revolution were largely

Around the
Patriarch's
Ponds,
Vosstaniya
and Nikitskie
vorota

## Bulgakov and The Master and Margarita

Born in Kiev in 1891, **Mikhail Bulgakov** practised medicine and experienced the Civil War in the Ukraine and the Caucasus before he settled in Moscow in 1921 and became a full-time writer. His early success as a satirist and playwright aroused a backlash from RAPP (Russian Association of Proletarian Artists), which attacked his sympathetic portrayal of White characters in *The Days of the Turbins*, and his anti-Bolshevik allegory, *The Heart of the Dog*. Luckily for Bulgakov, *The Days of the Turbins* was Stalin's favourite play, so despite being blacklisted, his life was spared. Eventually, he asked Stalin's permission to emigrate; Stalin refused, but authorized the staging of his play *Molière*.

Bulgakov began **The Master and Margarita** in 1928, but knew from the outset that it wouldn't be published for political reasons. The book was completed just days before his death in 1940, and his widow was obliged to hide the manuscript, which wasn't published in Russia until 1966. Its huge popularity in the 1980s owed much to the Taganka Theatre's amazing production of the novel – but its enduring fame rests on its piquant absurdities, as the Devil and his gang sow chaos across Moscow. Tellingly, it contains many instances of behaviour and dialogue which ring as true in the New Russia as they did when Bulgakov satirized *Homo Sovieticus* in the 1920s and 30s.

inhabited by students, earning it the sobriquet of Moscow's "Latin Quarter". Today, its flats are rented out to foreigners at premium rates, and often owned by Mafiosi, which keeps the neighbourhood looking respectable, if not exactly safe.

Readers of *The Master and Margarita* will know the Ponds from its opening chapter as the place where two literary hacks meet the Devil in the guise of a stage magician. His prediction that one of them will die soon is borne out when the editor Berlioz slips on spilt sunflower oil just outside the park on the corner of Malaya Bronnaya and Yermolaevskiy streets, and falls under a tram. Since Bulgakov's day the trams have gone and Yermolaevskiy has been renamed Zholtovskovo, but the park salvages some literary credibility with its **monument to Ivan Krylov** (1769–1844), a pensive bronze figure surrounded by creatures from his popular fables.

To see more of the area, follow **Malaya Bronnaya ulitsa** off to the south. Like Bolshaya Bronnaya, it is named after the quarter of armourers (*bronoviki*) that existed here in medieval times – a name that suits the armed clientele of the *Aist* restaurant, 200 metres past the trendy *Café Margarita* on the corner of the square. The *Marco-Polo Presnya Hotel* is visible to the right, on Spiridonevskiy pereulok. Alternatively, you can head down **Vspolniy pereulok** and turn off into ulitsa Alekseea Tolstovo to reach the impressive Morozov and Ryabushinskiy houses, or follow the pereulok to the end to emerge near Beria's mansion and ploshchad Vosstaniya (see below).

# Around ploshchad Vosstaniya

Around the Patriarch's Ponds, Vosstaniya and Nikitskie vorota

Ploshchad Vosstaniya (Uprising Square) is a jumping-off point for several sights in the vicinity and one of the most distinctive junctions on the Garden Ring – but you'll probably think twice about getting there from Triumfalnaya ploshchad. It's a bit far to walk (1.2km) and you can wait ages for a trolleybus 6 around the Ring; while the metro journey involves changing at Belorusskaya station.

As you can see from afar, Vosstaniya is dominated by a 22-storey **Stalin skyscraper** laden with pinnacles. Built by Mikhail Posokhin and Ashot Mndoyants in 1950–54, it was the last of Moscow's skyscrapers (a term eschewed as capitalist; the Soviets called them *vysotnie zdaniya*, "tall buildings") and purely residential. Each entrance has an aged porter who tries to head visitors off before they reach the lift. By muttering "*bizness*", you should be able to get upstairs to see the stylish wainscotting and lighting. By Stalinist standards, the exterior is relatively free of reliefs and statuary, which is just as well, since what statues there are have begun to crumble and nets have been strung around the sides of the tower to catch falling masonry.

Shortly before Vosstaniya you'll glimpse the **Planetarium** set back on the right. Built by Barshch and Sinyavskiy in 1928, its aluminium and ferroconcrete structure was considered revolutionary, especially the silvery ovoid dome. (See under "Children's Moscow", p.327.)

*From Vosstaniya you can also head south to Chaliapin's house or back into the centre along Povarskaya ulitsa (see p.156), or westwards into Krasnaya Presnya (covered in Chapter 6).*

## Chekhov's house

Diagonally across the road at Sadovaya-Kudrinskaya ulitsa 6, a pink two-storey dwelling sandwiched between two taller buildings has been preserved as the **Chekhov House-Museum** (Tues, Thurs, Sat & Sun 11am–6pm, Wed & Fri 2–8pm; closed the last day of each month). Here, Anton Chekhov, his parents and his brother lived from 1866 to 1890, during which time he wrote *Ivanov*, three one-act farces and over 100 short stories, while practising as a doctor. He also found time for an active sex life, as evinced by letters that discuss the pros and cons of making love on the floor, in bed, or over a trunk – and what to do if the servants walked in.

Despite Chekhov's lifestyle, the house looks as prim as the "Doctor A.P. Chekhov" nameplate by its front door. The second room was Chekhov's **study** and consulting room; notice his doctor's bag. While Chekhov's **bedroom** and that of his student brother are small and spartan, the family **salon** upstairs is replete with gold-brocaded sofas and chairs. Next to the salon are his mother's room with her easel and sewing machine, and the **dining room**, now given over to exhibits of playbills and first editions of Chekhov's works. An old photograph of Chekhov with Tolstoy hangs by the window.

Around the
Patriarch's
Ponds,
Vosstaniya
and Nikitskie
vorota

**Beria's mansion**

One of several streets leading back towards the Beliy Gorod, **ulitsa Kachalova** may soon revert to its pre-Revolutionary name, Malaya Nikitskaya ulitsa. Not far from the Ring, the **Tunisian Embassy** at no. 28 was abashed to make news in 1993 when workmen found a dozen skeletons buried outside, reminding Muscovites that this was once **Beria's mansion**. The most odious and feared of Stalin's cohorts, **Lavrenty Beria** headed the secret police from 1938 onwards, and oversaw high-priority projects such as the construction of Moscow's skyscrapers and the development of the Soviet atomic bomb. Beria's son recently alleged that the US scientist Oppenheimer revealed atomic secrets in this very house, in 1939, but recalls nothing of Beria's countless rapes in the same building. After Stalin's death, his Politburo colleagues feared for their lives and had Beria arrested at a meeting in the Kremlin. It's unclear whether he was shot at once, or first tried *in camera* as a "foreign agent", but the outcome was the same. Since then, he has remained one of the few disgraced persons whom *nobody* has cared to rehabilitate.

## To Nikitskie vorota

There are several possible routes from the Patriarch's Ponds or the Garden Ring to Nikitskie vorota, not to mention approaching it from the Boulevard Ring (see p.117). Perhaps the most obvious – and nicest – is **ulitsa Alekseya Tolstovo**, a long, quiet, residential street that may return to its pre-Revolutionary name, ulitsa Spiridonovka. Its present title honours the Soviet author Alexei Tolstoy, who lived near the Nikitskie vorota end of the road.

Walking down from the Patriarch's Ponds, you'll pass the former **Savva Morozov mansion** at no. 17. The first of over a dozen mansions designed by the prolific Shekhtel, this creamy Neo-Gothic edifice with mock crenellations was built (1893–98) for a liberal scion of the Morozov textiles dynasty, who sponsored the Moscow Arts Theatre and funded Lenin's newspaper, *Iskra*. In 1905, with revolution raging in Russia and his own contradictions pulling him apart, Morozov committed suicide while on a visit to France. The mansion now belongs to the Ministry of Foreign Affairs, which holds press conferences in its Neo-Gothic grand hall.

Further along the street are several mid-rise blocks that look nothing special from outside, but are finished to a high standard within. When **Gorbachev** joined the Politburo as a candidate member in 1979, he and Raisa were allotted an apartment in one of these enclaves; after he became Soviet leader, they moved to the Lenin Hills. Soon afterwards, you'll reach a small park containing a **statue of Alexander Blok** (1880–1921) looking every inch the Symbolist poet that he was, in a flowing overcoat and cravat. Just beyond stands the house where Blok lived before World War I, which is scheduled to become a **Blok House-Museum**, along the lines of the nearby Tolstoy and Gorky museums.

## Alexei Tolstoy's flat

The **Alexei Tolstoy Flat-Museum** (Thurs, Sat & Sun 11am–6pm, Wed & Fri 1–6pm; closed the last day of each month) is tucked away around the back of the Gorky Museum (see below), much as its owner lived in the shadow of his illustrious distant relative, Lev Tolstoy. Count **Alexei Tolstoy** (1882–1945) was a White émigré who returned in 1923 to establish himself as a popular author and later as a Deputy of the Supreme Soviet, occupying this flat from 1941 until his death.

It is decorated in the *haut-bourgeois* style of the last century, making the copy of *Pravda* in the drawing room seem an anachronism. In his columned salon, Tolstoy entertained friends at the grand piano or Lombard table like an aristocrat, while his study was a cosy world of history books, Chinese tea urns and pipes, with a copy of Peter the Great's death mask for inspiration. Here he wrote *Peter I*, *Darkness Dawns* and half an epic about the time of Ivan the Terrible. In the hallway hangs a tapestry picture of Peter crowning Catherine I, and a portrait of the Tsar made of seeds.

## Gorky's house

Unlike Tolstoy's flat, the **Gorky House-Museum** (Thurs, Sat & Sun 10am–5pm, Wed & Fri noon–7pm; closed the last Thurs of each month) next door is worth seeing purely for its amazing decor, both inside and out. Still widely known as the **Ryabushinskiy mansion**, the house was built in 1900 for the art-collecting chairman of the Stock Exchange, Stepan Ryabushinskiy, who fled after the Revolution. If not unquestionably the finest Style Moderne creation

---

**Maxim Gorky**

Orphaned and sent out to work as a young boy, Alexei Peshkov achieved literary success in his thirties under the *nom de plume* of **Maxim Gorky**, and took a leading role in the 1905 revolution. After protests from Western writers, his subsequent prison sentence was commuted to exile abroad, where he raised funds for the Bolsheviks from his hideaway on Capri. Returning home in 1913, Gorky continued to support them until after the October Revolution, when he began attacking Lenin for his dictatorial methods.

Having left Russia in 1921 – ostensibly on the grounds of ill health – Gorky was wooed back home by Stalin in 1928 to become chairman of the new Union of Soviet Writers. His own novel *Mother* was advanced as a model for **Socialist Realism**, the literary genre promulgated by the Union in 1932, and he also collaborated on a paean to the White Sea Canal, built by slave labour. As a murky finale, his **death** in 1936 was used as a pretext for the arrest of Yagoda, the head of the NKVD, who was charged with killing Gorky by seating him in a draught until he caught pneumonia.

---

Around the
Patriarch's
Ponds,
Vosstaniya
and Nikitskie
vorota

of the architect Fyodor Shekhtel, it is certainly his most accessible, as the others are now embassies.

Its glazed-brick exterior has sinuous windows and a shocking-pink floral mosaic frieze, while inside there's hardly a right-angle to be seen, nor a square foot unadorned by mouldings or traceries. It seems ironic that this exotic residence was given to such an avowedly "proletarian" writer as Maxim Gorky (see box), who lived here from 1931 to 1936. The first room you encounter belonged to his NKVD-appointed secretary, who screened his visitors. In Gorky's own study, notice the thick coloured pencils that he used for making notes and revisions. His library is installed in Ryabushinskiy's salon, whose ceiling is decorated with stucco snails and flowers. Repeated wave-like motifs are a feature in both the parquet flooring and the ceiling of the dining room, while the crowning glory is a limestone staircase that drips and sags like molten wax, as if melted by the stalactite-lamp atop its newel post. Alas, you can't go upstairs.

### The Church of the Great Ascension and the embassy quarter

Across the road from Gorky's house stands the bronze-domed Church of the Great Ascension (*tserkov Bolshovo Vozneseniya*), where Pushkin married Natalya Goncharova on February 18, 1831. During the ceremony, someone dropped one of the rings and Pushkin turned pale, muttering in French: "All the omens are bad" – as indeed they were, for he was killed in a duel over his wife's honour six years later (see p.162). From here, you can orientate yourself *vis-à-vis* Nikitskie vorota and cross over to the south side, where any lane will take you into an embassy quarter full of Style Moderne and Neo-Gothic mansions, whence you should emerge somewhere along Povarskaya ulitsa.

# Povarskaya and the New Arbat

The area to the south of Vosstaniya and Nikitskie vorota bears the stamp of two distinct epochs: the twilight of the Romanov era and the apogee of the Soviet period.

Povarskaya ulitsa and its side streets reflect a time when the old aristocracy was being supplanted by a new class of merchants and financiers, whose preference for Style Moderne and Neo-Gothic was a rejection of the Classical aesthetic revered by the nobility. Picturesque and on a human scale, it is one of the nicest areas in Moscow to wander around.

By contrast, the New Arbat, south of Povarskaya, is a brutal 1960s slash of traffic lanes, mega-blocks and bloated stores, meant to prove that the Soviet capital was as racy, modern and consumerist as anywhere in the West, but only now realizing those Brezhnevite aspirations in the post-Soviet era. Though there's little to see as such, anyone staying a week in Moscow will probably go drinking or shopping here at some point.

## Chaliapin's house and the US Embassy

Before delving into the backstreets, it's worth mentioning two places just **south of ploshchad Vosstaniya**, on the same side of the Ring as the Stalin skyscraper, from which they're a few minutes' walk.

At Novinskiy bulvar 25, the **Chaliapin House-Museum** (Tues, Sat & Sun 10am–4pm, Wed & Thurs 11.30am–6pm) is recognizable by a bas-relief of the singer outside the yellow house where he lived from 1910 to 1922. Fyodor Chaliapin's family life was as remarkable as his career – from riverboat stevedore to the foremost opera singer of his age. In Moscow, he married a ballerina who gave up dancing to be a housewife, while in St Petersburg he had another family by a woman whom he bigamously wed in 1927. His first wife had to move upstairs after their house was turned into a *komunalka*, and their children emigrated to the West. It was they who financed the house's restoration and supplied the mementoes, leading to the opening of the museum in 1988; it also hosts **concerts** and lectures (☎205-6236 for details).

The house is richly decorated in a mixture of French Empire and Style Moderne. His **wife's room** is papered with silk and enshrines the candles from their wedding. After his operatic performances, Chaliapin loved to throw parties in the gilded white **ballroom**, but hated to be beaten in the **billiard room**. When he was feeling low, his wife would invite friends over who would deliberately lose. You can see his **costumes** from *Prince Igor*, *Faust* and *Judith*; his blue **study** hung with self-portraits of himself as Don Quixote; and a replica of his **green room**, awash with wigs, cosmetics and trunks. Upstairs is an exhibition of dull portraits by his son Boris, who worked as an illustrator for *Time* magazine in the 1950s.

Immediately beyond, the **US Embassy** occupies a massive block whose Soviet-crested pediment and custard- and bile-coloured paint job might have been designed to make its occupants feel nauseous. In fact, they had worse reasons for feeling so, as from the 1970s the embassy was subjected to a constant bombardment of microwaves from KGB listening posts in the vicinity. The Americans' discovery of this coincided with the fiasco over their new embassy annexe, which was found to be riddled with bugs from the outset (see p.176).

## Povarskaya ulitsa

**Povarskaya ulitsa** (Cooks' Street) once served the royal household, together with nearby settlements on Khlebniy (Bread), Stoloviy (Table) and Skaterniy (Table cloth) lanes. During the eighteenth century it became as fashionably aristocratic as the Old Equerries' quarter beyond the Arbat – and enjoyed the same complacent decline until revitalized by an influx of *Kuptsy* in the late nineteenth century. In 1918, a dozen local mansions were seized by Anarchists, who held wild orgies there until flushed out by the Bolshevik *Cheka*, leaving the interiors riddled with bullet holes and smeared with excrement. Under Soviet rule the mansions were refurbished and put to institutional uses; today many have privatized themselves, as their real estate value reverts to its pre-Revolutionary level.

### From the House of Writers to the New Arbat

Near the ploshchad Vosstaniya end of the street, the graceful Classical mansion with a horseshoe-shaped courtyard (no. 52) is thought to have been the model for the Rostov family house in Tolstoy's *War and Peace*. In 1932 it became the **House of Writers**, the headquarters of the Writers' Union that dispensed *dachas* and other perks to authors who toed the Party line. They also enjoyed a subsidized restaurant next door, which features in Bulgakov's *The Master and Margarita*. "Lovely to think of all that talent ripening under one roof," muses the Devil's henchman to the magical cat Behemoth, before their supper ends in mayhem, with the restaurant in flames.

Across the road stands an asymmetrical Constructivist building created (1931–34) by the Vsenin brothers for the Society of Former Political Prisoners. After the Society was dissolved a few years later it became the **Studio Theatre of Cinema Actors** (*Kinoakter*), which now seems to be giving ground to boutiques and a bar. Further along at no. 25, the pink and white Empire-style Gagarin mansion is notable for its stucco eagles and a statue of Gorky in peasant dress outside. Formerly the Gorky Institute of World Literature, it now contains the **Austrian Library**.

The corner of Povarskaya and the New Arbat juxtaposes a huge, striking 24-storey block and the small white **Church of St Simeon the Stylite** (*tserkov Simeon Stolpnika*). Built in the mid-seventeenth century on the model of the Church of the Trinity on Nikitinov (see *The Kitay-gorod*, p.102), the nave is capped by tiers of *kokoshniki* and green domes (services 6am & 5pm). It was here that Count Sheremetev secretly married the serf-actress Parasha Kovalyeva-Zhemchugova, and Gogol was a regular worshipper when he lived in the vicinity (see p.119).

*The Count's romance with Zhemchugova is related under Ostankino, in Chapter 9.*

Before emerging onto the New Arbat, consider a detour off to the right, where the **Lermontov House-Museum** at ulitsa Malaya Molchanovka 2 (Thurs, Sat & Sun 11am–6pm, Wed & Fri 2–8pm) preserves the wooden dwelling where Mikhail Lermontov lived from 1829 until 1832. Then enrolled at Moscow University, he spent so much time writing poems and dramas that he never sat his exams. Among these was an early version of *The Demon*, a theme that haunted Lermontov for years.

## The New Arbat

Among its many changes to the capital, the 1935 General Plan for Moscow envisaged an arterial avenue linking the Boulevard and Garden Rings to create a crosstown route between the Kremlin, Kiev Station and points west. By Khrushchev's time this had become imperative since the narrow Arbat could no longer cope with the volume of traffic. Between 1962 and 1967, a one-kilometre-long swathe was bulldozed through a neighbourhood of old wooden houses, and a wide avenue flanked by high-rise complexes was laid out. Though officially named prospekt Kalinina (after the Bolshevik Head of State, Kalinin) until 1991, Muscovites called it the **Noviy Arbat** – or **New Arbat** – from the outset.

Its inhuman scale and assertive functionalism won the architects a prize in 1966. Along the northern side are ranged five 24-storey apartment blocks awarded to People's Artists and other favoured citizens, which featured in 1970s Soviet films as symbols of *la dolce vita*. Moscow's largest bookshop, the **Dom knigi** (House of Books), is located between the first and second blocks, while the 3000-seat **Oktyabr Cinema** fills the gap between the penultimate and final blocks, its entire facade covered with a revolutionary mosaic. Trolleybus #2 runs the length of the Noviy Arbat.

The other side of the avenue is flanked by four 26-storey administrative blocks shaped like open books, which tower above an 850-metre-long glass-fronted gallery that embodies Moscow's new mall culture, spearheaded by the **Irish House** supermarket and the **Valdai Centre**. In recent years, the street has seen a colourful **St Patrick's Day Parade** (March 17) of bands and floats, organized by Moscow's small but enterprising Irish community. Further along are the **Cherry Casino** and the huge *Arbat* restaurant, topped by a globe showing Aeroflot's routes.

At the far end of the avenue, beyond the Garden Ring, the former SEV building presages the White House beside the river (see p.177).

# On and off the Arbat

*Oh Arbat, my Arbat, you are my destiny,*
*You are my happiness and my sorrow*

(Bulat Okudzhava)

Celebrated in song and verse, the **Arbat** once stood for Bohemian Moscow in the way that Carnaby Street represented swinging London. Narrow and cobbled, with a tramline down the middle, it was the heart of a quarter where writers, actors and scientists frequented the same shops and cafés. This cosy world of the Soviet intelligentsia drew strength from the neighbourhood's identity a century earlier, when the **Staraya Konyushennaya** or **Old**

**Equerries' quarter** between the Arbat and Prechistenka streets was
the home of the *ancien* nobility, later supplanted by *arriviste*
dynasties from St Petersburg, who still measured their wealth by the
number of "souls" (male serfs) that they owned (women didn't
count), and trained them to cook French pastries or play chamber
music so as to be able to boast that their estate provided every
refinement of life.

Divided into communal flats after the Revolution, each household felt Stalin's Terror, as recalled in Anatoly Rybakov's novel
*Children of the Arbat*, which wasn't published until *glasnost*. By
then, the Arbat was established as the hippest place in Moscow,
having been pedestrianized in the early 1980s (for the worse, many
thought). *Perestroika* made it a magnet for young Muscovites and
tourists in search of something happening, although the Arbat has
done less well from the real-estate boom of **recent years**, as the new
rich prefer living either right in the centre or outside the city – so
you'll see derelict buildings alongside the boutiques and cafés.

### Getting to the Arbat

*Places to eat
and drink in
the Arbat are
detailed under
"Cafés" (p.308)
and
"Restaurants"
(p.311).*

Most visitors approach the Arbat via the pedestrian underpass on
**Arbatskaya ploshchad** (p.119). If you're **coming by metro**, bear in
mind that there are two pairs of identically named stations on separate lines. On the dark blue line, Arbatskaya station exits opposite
the House of Friendship on ulitsa Vozdvizhenka, while Smolenskaya
brings you out behind *McDonald's* at the far end of the Arbat.
Arbatskaya station on the light blue line is also conveniently situated, but the other Smolenskaya is way off on the Garden Ring and
best avoided.

## Beyond the Peace Wall

The Arbat begins with an array of fast-food outlets and antique
shops, but barring a detour into the backstreets – harbouring the
**Arbat Blues Club** and two picturesque derelict churches – there's
nothing especially remarkable until you reach the **Peace Wall**. A
cute example of propaganda against Reagan's Star Wars, the wall
consists of scores of tiles painted by Soviet schoolchildren, express-
ing their hopes for peace and fears of war. The names of the side
streets beyond recall the era when the neighbourhood served the
Tsar's court: Serebryaniy (Silver) and Starokonyushenniy (Old
Stables) lanes. As you pass by the latter, notice the green **wooden
house** with carved eaves, dating from 1872, a model of which won a
prize at the Paris Exhibition as the epitome of the "Russian Style".

Thereafter, the Arbat gets busier with portrait artists, buskers,
and photographers offering a range of props from Gorby to Mickey
Mouse, while the buildings bloom with bright colours and quirky
details. Stuccoed ivy flourishes above the lilac Style Moderne edifice
at no. 27, while the next block consists of a Neo-Gothic apartment

complex guarded by statuesque knights and containing the **House of Actors**. Opposite stands the **Vakhtangov Theatre**, named after its founder, Yevgeny Vakhtangov (1883–1922), who split from MKhAT to pursue a fusion of Realism and the Meyerhold style. The post-war building is notable for its heavy Stalinist facade.

## Around the backstreets

While Vakhtangov himself lived on the Arbat, the neighbouring ulitsa Vakhtangova is more tangibly associated with the composer Alexander Scriabin (1872–1915), who spent his last years at no. 11. The **Scriabin House-Museum** (Thurs, Sat & Sun 10am–5pm, Wed & Fri noon–7pm; closed the last Fri of each month) preserves his personal effects and recordings of his music. Scriabin evolved his own musical language and some eccentric philosophical theories, which the curators are happy to explain if you're interested (and speak Russian).

The next lane on the right – Spasopeskovskiy pereulok – retains a seventeenth-century church with a tent-roofed belfry and an ornamental gate. Currently being restored after decades as a studio, the **Church of the Saviour in Peski** (*tserkov Spasa na Peskakh*) derives its name from the original sixteenth-century site (*peskiy* means "sandy") – though it still looked rural as late as the nineteenth century, as depicted by Vasily Polonev in his well-known painting, *A Moscow Courtyard*. At the far end is a guarded green dignified by the Neo-Classical residence of the US Ambassador, **Spaso House**.

More immediately grabbing is Krivoarbatskiy pereulok (Crooked Arbat Lane), around the far side of the House of Actors. The walls of the building are luridly covered in **graffiti about Viktor Tsoy**, the lead singer of the group Kino (Film), whose fatal car crash ensured his immortality as a cult-hero. Though fans constantly gather here to sing his songs and contemplate (or add to) the graffiti, nobody seems to know why this spot became a shrine in the first place.

### The Melnikov House

Around the corner past the Tsoy graffiti, the lane's Art Nouveau buildings are interrupted by the defiantly Constructivist **Melnikov House** (no. 10). Konstantin Melnikov (1890–1974) was one of the most original architects of the 1920s, who was granted a plot of land to build a house after winning the Gold Medal at the Paris World Fair in 1925. Though his career nosedived once the Party spurned Modernism, he was allowed to keep his home – the only privately built house in Moscow after the Revolution – but died in obscurity. Belatedly honoured owing to the efforts of his children, his unique house was declared a historic monument in 1987, since when it has been covered in scaffolding and has become the object of a bitter dispute between his heirs.

By walking around the back of the derelict building alongside, you can get a better view of the house. A Constructivist creation in the shape of three concrete cylinders, and decorated with scores of hexagonal windows, it predated (1929) the breakthroughs of Melnikov's contemporaries, Le Corbusier and Mies van der Rohe, with self-reinforcing floors that eliminated the need for internal load-bearing walls. The rooms are divided up by slim partitions and feature built-in furniture (as in peasant cottages), while the intersection of the cylinders creates a space for the staircase that spirals up through the core of the house. Despite its revolutionary design, the materials are simple and traditional: timber, brick and stucco.

### Pushkin on the Arbat

The sky-blue Empire-style house at no. 53 enshrines the fleeting domicile of Russia's most beloved writer as the **Pushkin on the Arbat Museum** (Wed–Sun 11am–6pm; closed the last Fri of every month). In the spring of 1831, it was here that Pushkin held his stag night and spent the first months of married life with Natalya Goncharova. Then they moved to St Petersburg, where Pushkin was later killed in a duel with a French officer whose advances to Natalya were the talk of the town. After Pushkin's death, their apartment was preserved as an evocative museum, which is worth seeing should you visit St Petersburg. The Arbat museum, however, is strictly for manuscript buffs, offering few insights into their lifestyle other than a taste for gilded chairs.

Given that Moscow fondly devotes two museums to him, it's ironic that Pushkin scorned the city as a "Tatar nonentity" where "nobody receives periodicals from France", and lamented being "condemned to live among these orangutans at the most interesting moment of our century". Worse for newlyweds, he wrote, "here you live, not as you wish but as aunties wish. My mother-in-law is just such an auntie. It's a quite different thing in Petersburg! I'll start living in clover, as a petty bourgeois, independently, and taking no thought of what Maria Alexeevna will say."

As the Symbolist poet Andrei Bely was born next door at no. 51 and stayed there during his last visit to Moscow in 1920, the complex also contains a small **Bely Memorial Room**. Tickets for both are sold at the *kassa*, reached by the door on the right as you enter the compound.

## Smolenskaya ploshchad and further south

Traditionally, **Smolenskaya ploshchad** was Moscow's haymarket, ankle-deep in straw and dung and thronged with ostlers and farriers. Today, it bears the stamp of Stalinist planning, dominated by 1940s monoliths and the Stalin-Gothic skyscraper of the **Ministry of Foreign Affairs**. Known by its initials as the MID, the central block is 172m high, with three portals surmounted by bas-reliefs of furled flags, fronted by granite propylae and lamps. Having been led by Molotov (known to Western diplomats as "Old Stony-face") and Gromyko ("Mr *Nyet*") during the Cold War, and at the forefront of *perestroika* with Sheverdnadze ("The Silver Fox"), the ministry is now trying to restore Russia's stature under Kozyrev (who has yet to acquire a nickname).

Across the square rise the twin blocks of the *Belgrad* and the *Zolotoe Koltso* hotels. In October 1993, hotel guests had a ringside view of days of pitched battles on Smolenskaya ploshchad, which ended with parliamentary supporters routing the OMON (riot police) and breaking through the police cordon around the White House – the prelude to the storming of the TV Centre that night.

### South towards Prechistenka

To explore the Old Equerries' quarter and link up with the next itinerary, you can follow almost any street running off the Arbat and emerge on ulitsa Prechistenka.

Although a bit of a detour, **pereulok Sivtsev Vrazhek** (Grey Mare's Gully) boasts an array of stuccoed wooden houses. The poet Maria Tsvetaeva lived at no. 19 this century, while no. 27 was once the residence of Alexander Herzen and his family. Thereafter, Herzen lived abroad, was expelled from France after the 1848 Revolution, moved to London and founded the radical newspaper *Kolokol* (The Bell), which, although published in London, had a great impact in Russia despite being banned; even the Tsar read it. A dull **Herzen House-Museum** (Tues, Thurs, Sat & Sun 11am–6pm, Wed & Fri 1–6pm; closed every Mon & the last day of each month; $2) records the family's odyssey around Europe (where Herzen died) – its best exhibit is a picture of a giant bell borne aloft over unenlightened Russia.

One direct route to ulitsa Prechistenka is **Denezhniy pereulok**, which turns off the Arbat just before the MID and brings you to a typical wooden house of the early nineteenth century (no. 9), painted turquoise and white. Halfway down the next block, the **Italian Embassy** (no. 5) occupies the former Berg mansion, a sandstone pile whose interior manifests every style from Baroque to Neo-Gothic. Confiscated from its owner after the Revolution, the mansion was given to Imperial Germany as an embassy just after the Bolsheviks signed the humiliating Peace of Brest-Litovsk. By following the road to the very end, across Lyovshinsky pereulok, you'll emerge on Prechistenka opposite the Serbskiy Institute.

# Along Prechistenka

**Ulitsa Prechistenka,** the road leading from the Kremlin to the Novodevichiy Convent, delineating the southern edge of the Old Equerries' quarter, has been one of Moscow's poshest avenues since the sixteenth century. Its array of mansions in the Russian Empire style – newly built after the fire of 1812 – can really only be appreciated by walking along Prechistenka. If you're not coming from the direction of the Arbat, the best starting point is **Kropotkinskaya metro**, whose stylish platform is itself an attraction. In Soviet times, the avenue was also named "Kropotkinskaya", after the Anarchist Prince Kropotkin, who was born nearby.

Prechistenka starts at the bottom of the hill with a **statue of Friedrich Engels**, erected in 1976. The idea was that this would be "united" with the statue of Marx on Teatralnaya ploshchad by prospekt Marksa, to form a kind of Communist ley-line. Behind the statue rises the **Golovin palace**, a simple red-brick structure with barred windows, built at the end of the seventeenth century by a family associated with Peter the Great.

## The Pushkin and Tolstoy museums

Further uphill and across the road at no. 12, the former Khrushchev mansion contains the **Pushkin Museum** (Fri, Sat & Sun 10am–6pm, Wed & Thurs 11am–7pm; closed the last Fri of each month), with ten rooms devoted to the life and works of the poet. If his sketches and first editions don't appeal, the mansion's interior is notable for its elegant fireplaces and ceiling frescoes. Built of wood covered in stucco, its exterior is colonnaded on two sides; the entrance is on Khruschevskiy pereulok, around the corner. On the next block is another impressive pile whose gatehouses are topped by lions, which now serves as the **House of Scientists** and is an occasional venue for classical concerts.

Directly opposite at no. 11, the former Lopukhin mansion has been turned into a **Tolstoy Literary Museum** (Tues–Sun 11am–6pm; closed the last Fri of each month), which, like the Pushkin Museum, exhaustively documents the man and his times. Though its engravings and photos are less interesting than Tolstoy's actual residence in the Khamovniki district (p.187), the ceiling decorated with sphinxes rates a look. Like the Khrushchev mansion, the house was built by Afanasy Grigoriev (1782–1868), one of the most prolific architects of the Russian Empire style.

## Other sights

The remainder of Prechistenka has several addresses associated with diverse personages. Until his death in 1898, the vodka magnate **Pyotr Smirnov** resided at no. 20. Several years ago, a descendant rented a backroom on the premises and set up a firm producing vodka according to the traditional family recipe, only to be sued by the multinational *Smirnoff* company for infringement of copyright – the legal battle continues. On the other side of the road, the house at no. 17 once belonged to **Denis Davydov** – the partisan leader of 1812 who inspired the character Denisov in *War and Peace* – while

**Prince Kropotkin**

The life of **Prince Pyotr Kropotkin** (1842–1921) spanned the most tumultuous years of Russian history, from the reign of Nicholas I to that of Lenin. Born into the old Moscow nobility and a graduate of the elite Corps des Pages, Kropotkin's service with a Cossack regiment in Siberia established his reputation as a geographer and opened his eyes to the injustices of Tsarism. In 1872, he joined the International Working Men's Association in Geneva and adopted **Anarchism** as his creed, expounding a pacifistic version that advanced such models of non-statist cooperation as the British Lifeboat Association. Upon returning home in 1874, Kropotkin was imprisoned in the Peter and Paul Fortress (where he spent a week tapping out the story of the Paris Commune to a prisoner in the next cell) and then exiled to Siberia. In 1896 he escaped and came to England, where he was elected to the Royal Geographical Society. After the Revolution he returned to Russia, but was too ill to play an active role and died in poverty. On Lenin's orders, Kropotkin was accorded a lying in state in the Hall of Columns as an honorary Marxist, and buried in the prestigious Novodevichiy Cemetery.

the old Dolgorukov mansion (no. 19) contains the **Academy of Arts**, whose gallery hosted Mayakovsky's last exhibition, *Twenty Years of Work*.

Beyond this stands the discreetly barred and euphemistically entitled **Serbskiy Institute for Forensic Medicine**, a psychiatric clinic that became notorious in the Brezhnev era for "treating" incarcerated dissidents with toxic drugs. In 1983, the USSR withdrew from the International Psychiatric Association to avoid expulsion for such abuses, which were widely practised in Soviet mental hospitals until the late 1980s.

If you're still in the mood for walking, check out the extremities of an attractive lane called Kropotkinskiy pereulok, which crosses Prechistenka. Off to the south at no. 13, the **Australian Embassy** occupies a Style Moderne masterpiece by Shekhtel – the former Derozhinskaya mansion, built for a textile manufacturer's daughter in 1901. Less florid than the Ryabushinskiy mansion (p.155), its superb woodwork is sadly hidden from view, though Australian citizens might stand a chance of admission. At the other end of the lane, north of Prechistenka, the house at no. 26 was the **birthplace of Prince Kropotkin** (see box).

# Between Triumfalnaya ploshchad and Tsvetnoy bulvar

Halfway around the Garden Ring to the east of Prechistenka, the flyover- and underpass-ridden stretch **between Triumfalnaya ploshchad and Tsvetnoy bulvar** musters a few low-key sights along its outer edge, but you're more likely to be tempted in by the leafy streets adjacent to the Boulevard Ring – Karetniy ryad or Tsvetnoy bulvar itself.

## Along the Garden Ring

There's nothing along the initial stretch – called Sadovaya-Triumfalnaya and Sadovaya-Karetnaya – so you should take trolleybus 6 directly to the **Museum of Applied, Decorative and Folk Art**, on the corner of Delegatskaya ulitsa (Mon, Wed, Sat & Sun 10am–6pm, Tues & Thurs 12.30–8pm; closed the last Thurs each month; $2). Its diverse collection occupies the main wing of the eighteenth-century Osterman mansion, and an annexe off to the right of the courtyard – wherever you begin, keep your ticket for the other bit. The star attraction (in the annexe, upstairs) is **classic Soviet porcelain** of the 1920s and 1930s, decorated with Futurist designs or metro-building motifs; among the figurines, notice the Uzbek family rejoicing over the Stalin Constitution. Downstairs are scores of Palekh boxes painted with fairytale scenes; nineteenth-century folk costumes and contemporary tapestries.

Thereafter, the Ring is designated as Sadovaya-Samotyochnaya ulitsa and known to all motorists for the **headquarters of the GAI**, the traffic police. The next city block (no. 3) contains the **Central Puppet Theatre**, founded by Sergei Obraztsov, whose concrete facade is enlivened by a decorative clock consisting of twelve little houses. Every hour, one of them opens to reveal an animal puppet; at noon all the figures dance to a Russian folk song. Before *glasnost*, dissidents and Western reporters often arranged to meet here to clandestinely hand over news stories or *samizdat* literature.

The spot was convenient for the journalists since many of them lived nearby on the other side of the Ring, where a spacious post-war block (no. 12) still houses Reuters, CBS, the BBC, the *Daily Telegraph* and the *New York Times*. A 677-metre-long flyover carries the Ring across the old valley of the Neglina River at Samotyochnaya ploshchad, with Tsvetnoy bulvar on the right (see below), and the wonderful Viktor Vasnetsov house in the other direction.

*The Vasnetsov house is described on p.256.*

## Karetniy ryad

The wide **Karetniy ryad** (Coach Row) gets its name from the carriage- and coach-making workshops that lined the road during the nineteenth century, whose artisans burned their vehicles rather than let them be stolen by the French in 1812. Turned into state garages after the Revolution, they are still recognizable behind the arched houses along the eastern side. No. 4 was the family mansion of the director Stanislavsky until it was requisitioned as a chauffeurs' club in 1918.

Ironically, Stanislavsky first achieved professional success in the **Hermitage Gardens**, opposite, where his Moscow Arts Theatre premiered *The Seagull* in 1898. The Hermitage pleasure-garden was founded by Yakov Shchukin, an ex-manservant who ensured that it remained respectable by spreading rumours that he threw drunks into the pond; he later invited the Lumière brothers to screen the first film in Moscow there. Today, the gardens have gone to pot, constituting an obstacle course for ravers stumbling through the darkness towards the *Hermitage* club behind one of the derelict theatre buildings.

The southern end of the avenue is designated as a continuation of ulitsa Petrovka (p.131) and dominated by the vast beige **headquarters of the Militia** and the Criminal Investigations Department. "**Petrovka 38**" is as famous in Russia as Scotland Yard is in Britain, having been acclaimed in Soviet pulp fiction and TV dramas since the 1970s, and more recently reviled by the press and public for its impotence in the face of organized crime.

Around the corner on 2-y Kolobovskiy pereulok moulders a derelict relic of law enforcement from the years before Peter the Great. The multi-domed **Church of the Sign** was erected by a company of *Streltsy* in the late seventeenth century, when several companies were settled in this quarter to defend the ramparts and keep order in the Earth Town.

## Tsvetnoy bulvar

**Tsvetnoy bulvar** is the prettiest radial avenue along this stretch of the Ring, having a wooded park with wrought-iron railings running up the middle from Trubnaya ploshchad. From 1851, when flowers (*tsvety*) began to be sold on Trubnaya ploshchad, the boulevard became Moscow's flower market, and its red-light district. The side streets to the east harboured dozens of **brothels** coyly referred to in the 1875 *Murray's Handbook* as "several *guinguettes* where the male traveller may study "life"". There, Chekhov wrote from personal experience: "No one hurried, no one hid his face in his coat, no one shook his head reproachfully. This unconcern, that medley of pianos and fiddles, the bright windows, wide open doors – it all struck a garish, impudent, dashing, devil-may-care note."

Today, the boulevard takes its tone from a trio of places near Tsvetnoy Bulvar metro station, where a few disconsolate vendors linger outside the padlocked **Central Market** (*Tsentralniy rynok*). Formerly a pungent Aladdin's cave of produce, where shoppers were tempted with morsels of sturgeon and caviar, melons and dried fruits from Central Asia, the market has now been closed for much-needed modernization, which Muscovites fear will result in a glossy mall that excludes small traders.

Next door stands the famous **Moscow Circus**, which celebrated its centenary in 1986 by rebuilding what is now known as the "Old Circus" (there is a "New Circus" in the Sparrow Hills). This was recently embroiled in controversy after the contract killing of its deputy director led to the souring of a joint venture with an

American catering firm. Passions got so heated that the famous ex-clown Yuliy Nikulin remarked: "When the history of the third world war is written, it will be remembered that America's capture of Russia began from the Moscow Circus."

# To Krasnye vorota

The eastern half of the Garden Ring – from Tsvetnoy bulvar to Krasnye vorota, and on to Kursk Station – is the least appealing part of the Zemlyanoy Gorod, unless you're mad about **Constructivist and Stalinist architecture**, in which case it merits a trolleybus 6 ride around the Ring as far as Krasnye vorota. A seat on the left of the vehicle affords the best view.

Otherwise, the quarter's attractions boil down to the archaic Yusupov mansion, a flat-museum devoted to the historical painter Apollinarius Vastnetsov, and a couple of churches – all best reached on foot from Krasnye Vorota or Chistye Prudy metro stations. You can also walk there from the Boulevard Ring in about ten minutes.

## Sukharevskaya ploshchad and Sadovaya-Spasskaya ulitsa

If you opt for a trolleybus ride, the first notable junction is **Sukharevskaya ploshchad**, which – like the local metro station – is named after the bygone **Sukharev Tower** (*Sukhareva bashnya*). Erected in honour of Colonel Sukharev – whose soldiers had escorted the young Peter the Great and his mother to safety during the *Streltsy* mutiny of 1682 – this was designed in the form of a ship, with the tower representing a mast and its surrounding galleries a quarterdeck. Reputedly, Peter's private Masonic lodge held rituals in the tower, which was thereafter regarded as unlucky. In 1829, it was converted into an aqueduct-cum-fountain for supplying Moscow with water piped in from ten miles away, demolished during the widening of the Garden Ring in the 1930s. A small replica of the tower rises above one of the buildings on the northern side of Sukharevskaya ploshchad; before the Revolution the square was known for its flea market dealing in stolen goods.

Far easier to spot is the former **Sheremetev Hospital**, a huge curved building painted sea-green and turquoise. Founded by Count Nikolai Sheremetev, the hospital was built (1794–1807) by the serf-architect Elizvoi Nazarov, and had a poorhouse in its left wing. After the death of his beloved serf-actress wife, the Count commissioned Catherine the Great's court architect Quarenghi to change the hospital's church into a memorial chapel, which he enhanced by adding a semicircular portico. Since Soviet times, the building has housed the Sklifosovskiy Institute, named after a pioneering surgeon of the late nineteenth century.

The next stretch of the Ring – **Sadovaya-Spasskaya ulitsa** – bears no resemblance to the gracious avenue that it was in Tsarist times, and nowadays business and administration are the keynotes, with the triple bronzed-glass towers of the **International Banking Centre** visible off to the right, just before you sight the rust-red **Ministry of Agriculture**. One of the last Constructivist edifices built (1928–33) in Moscow, the ministry was designed by Shchusev, the architect of Lenin's Mausoleum.

This thoroughfare is named after Dr Andrei Sakharov (1921–90), the nuclear physicist and human rights campaigner who lived at no. 47 after he and his dissident wife, Yelena Bonner, were allowed to return from exile by Gorbachev. The 1980s Banking Centre opposite their flat is a logical outgrowth of the older economic administration blocks that flank the section of the prospekt nearer the Boulevard Ring, where fans of Brutalist architecture will go for the **Tsentrosoyuz building** designed by Le Corbusier. Built in 1929–36 for the Union of Consumer Societies, this hideous clinker-block structure is now occupied by the State Statistical Commission, which produced 30,000 million forms a year during Soviet times.

The building also overlooks ulitsa Myatninskaya, where the former **Baryshnikov Mansion** at no. 42 houses the editorial staff of the magazine *Argumenty i Fakti* ("Arguments and Facts"), a torch-bearer of *glasnost* in the mid-1980s.

## Krasnye vorota

The junction known as **Krasnye vorota** (Beautiful Gate) takes its name from a Baroque triumphal arch erected in honour of Empress Elizabeth in 1742. For the coronation of Tsar Paul in 1796, the streets were lined with tables spread with food and drink for the populace, all the way from here to the Kremlin. Although the arch was demolished in 1928, the locality is still popularly called Krasnye vorota – which means "Red Gate" in modern Russian and seems an apt name for a square dominated by a **Stalin skyscraper** faced in reddish-brown granite. Erected in 1947–53, its 24-storey central block is shared by the Transport Construction Ministry and the Directorate for the Exploitation of Tall Buildings, while the wings contain communal flats. Typically, the main portal is flanked by propylae and urns, while once again nets are hung from the facade to catch falling pieces of statue.

A plaque on the wall around the southeast corner attests that the Romantic poet Mikhail Lermontov was born on this spot in 1814, which accounts for the triangular-shaped square being named **Lermontovskaya ploshchad**, and its **monument to Lermontov**. Behind his frock-coated statue is a concrete frieze of a man wrestling a lion, inscribed with Lermontov's words:

*Moscow, my home – I love you as a son,*
*Love like a Russian, strong and fierce and gentle!*

# Around the backstreets – and Kursk Station

The **backstreets** between the Garden and Boulevard Rings represent an older Moscow that turns its back on Stalinist giganticism, preserving an intimate, residential character. Once elegant mansions turned into institutes or communal flats are juxtaposed with post-war low-rises, schools and clinics. Though specific sights are limited, it's a nice area to wander around. Sticking to the Garden Ring, instead, inevitably leads to Kursk Station, the largest train terminal in Moscow.

## The Yusupov Mansion

By heading 500m south from Krasnye Vorota metro and turning off onto Bolshoy Kharitonevskiy pereulok, you'll find the **Yusupov Mansion** behind a swirly iron fence and a grove of trees. Painted a deep red, with its pilasters and *nalichniki* picked out in white, the mansion's melange of undercrofts, wings and annexes typifies the multi-cellular architecture of the late seventeenth century, unified by a checkerboard roof. The mansion is entered via an enclosed porch around the back, added in the 1890s, like the ceremonial gateway that bears the Yusupov crest. An immensely rich family descended from the Nogai Tatar Khans – now chiefly remembered for the last of the dynasty, Prince Felix, who murdered Rasputin – the Yusupovs acquired the mansion in 1727, but preferred to live in St Petersburg and rent it out; Pushkin lived here as a child. After the Revolution it became the Academy of Agriculture, where the eminent geneticist Vavilov worked from 1929 to 1935. Though it's not open to the public, you could try begging a peep at its romantic **interior**, a warren of pseudo-medieval chambers furnished with tiled stoves.

## The Vasnetsov Flat-Museum

More accessible but less enticing is the **Apollinarius Vasnetsov Flat-Museum** at Furmanniy pereulok 10 (Thurs, Sat & Sun 11am–5pm, Wed & Fri 1–7pm), a few minutes' walk from the Yusupov mansion. The historical artist Apollinarius Vasnetsov (1856–1933) lived here from 1903 until his death, an "internal exile" from Soviet life and Socialist art. Flat no. 22 displays his carefully researched drawings of Old Muscovy and the Simonov Monastery, plus a portrait of Apollinarius by his artist brother, Viktor. His living quarters are preserved across the landing, where the drawing room is festooned with pictures given as gifts by Sarasov, Polonev and other artist friends, while the study contains an ingenious chair that "changes sides" (demonstrated by the curator). The tour ends in Vasnetsov's studio, hung with cloud and light studies; notice his travelling painting kit, and the preparatory drawing for his last work, on the easel.

*Viktor Vasnetsov's house has also been preserved as a museum, which shouldn't be missed. See p.256 for details.*

# Other sights

Starting from the vicinity of Chistye prudy, there are a couple of sights up the road from the Apraksin mansion (p.138). The former **Church of the Resurrection in Barashi** is where Empress Elizabeth is said to have secretly married her lover Alexei Razumovskiy in 1742. Much altered since then and now a fire station, the shocking-pink edifice will set you in the direction of the **Church of the Presentation in Barashi** (*tserkov Vvedeniya v Barashakh*), down a lane to the right. Built in 1701, its strawberry facade is decorated with cable-mouldings, crested and scalloped *nalichniki*, while ventilation flues and builders' rubble attest to the church's use as a factory in Soviet times, and recent efforts to restore it. The Tsar's tent-makers (*Barashi*) lived here in the fifteenth century – hence the name of the local churches.

# Kursk Station

Modernized in 1972, the vast steel-and-glass shed of **Kursk Station** (*Kurskiy vokzal*) could have been even larger, given a 1930s plan to combine all of Moscow's mainline stations into a single mega-terminal serving every point in the USSR. Fortunately this never happened; the existing station (for Crimea, the Caucasus and eastern Ukraine) is bad enough, with a dank labyrinth of underpasses where travellers slump amidst their baggage. It was from the Tsarist forerunner of Kursk Station that Lenin departed for his Siberian exile in 1897. Beneath lies **Kurskaya metro**, featuring a splendid vestibule upheld by massive ornamental pillars, like a medieval hall in the Kremlin – which almost justifies a visit using the Circle line.

Chapter 6

# Krasnaya Presnya, Fili and the southwest

Beyond the Garden Ring, Moscow seems an undifferentiated sprawl of blocks and avenues, attesting to its phenomenal growth in Soviet times. Yet on closer inspection, each arc of the city contains a scattering of monuments and institutions that command attention. This is particularly true of **KRASNAYA PRESNYA, FILI AND THE SOUTHWEST** – a swathe of the city defined by the loops of the Moskva River and the approaches to the Sparrow Hills.

Krasnaya Presnya is chiefly notable for the ex-parliament building known as the **White House** – whose role in the crises of the 1990s has invested it with symbolic potency – but also harbours the lovely **Vagankov Cemetery**. Over the river, a showpiece avenue that epitomizes Stalinist planning forges out past the **Borodino Panorama Museum** and the newly opened **Victory Park**. Here, the beautiful **Church of the Intercession at Fili** is a sole reminder of the estates and villages that once flanked Moscow's western approaches, where Napoleon marched into the city in 1812, and the Red Army confronted the Nazis in 1941.

Closer to the centre, a peninsula defined by the Moskva River boasts **Tolstoy's house** and the fairytale **Church of St Nicholas of the Weavers** in the Khamovniki district, while further out lies the **Novodevichiy Convent and Cemetery**, the grandest of Moscow's monastic complexes. Across the river from the Lenin Stadium, further south, a magnificent view of the city is afforded by the **Sparrow Hills**, dominated by the titanic Stalin skyscraper of **Moscow State University (MGU)**.

This chapter is largely structured with **transport** in mind, each major section corresponding to a metro line used to reach the sights. All of them connect with the Circle line, enabling you to switch from one itinerary to another with relative ease. As the distances between stations increase further out, so the return journey takes longer (up to 25min).

# Krasnaya Presnya

The **Krasnaya Presnya** district just beyond ploshchad Vosstaniya (p.153) is an old working-class quarter that was once Moscow's most radical and has now become one of Moscow's "better" neighbourhoods, with clinics, shops and restaurants catering to wealthy Muscovites and foreigners. Besides amenities, the district has political and financial clout, harbouring the Russian White House, the new US Embassy annexe and the World Trade Centre. These all seem a far cry from the proletarian militancy evoked by huge sculptures, faded murals and names bestowed on streets and metro stations in honour of the 1905 uprising, until one remembers how Russia's fate has twice been decided here in the 1990s. If seeing where it all happened doesn't grab you, there's the Tishkin flea market for browsing and the lovely Vagankov Cemetery to explore, while scraping the bottom of the barrel one finds the Zoopark and a couple of obscure museums.

The district's early history reads like a Marxist tract, as the local textiles industry boomed and slum landlords made fortunes by exploiting rural migrants, creating an urban proletariat receptive to revolutionary agitation. Originally called simply Presnya after a tributary of the Moskva River running through the district, it earned the name "Red" (*Krasnaya*) during the December uprising of 1905, when local workers heeded the Moscow Soviet's rash call to overthrow the Tsarist government, which had just suppressed the Soviet in St Petersburg. The poorly armed insurgents failed to break through into central Moscow and withdrew behind barricades in Presnya, only surrendering after days of bombardment and close-quarter fighting, whereupon hundreds more fell to army firing squads. During the Brezhnev era, Presnya's profile was transformed by new housing and amenities, as bureaucrats awoke to the potential of a waterfront site only fifteen minutes' drive from the Kremlin.

## Around Presnya

Most of Presnya is a jumble of post-war architecture whose few landmarks are only worth noting should you happen to pass by. Exiting from **Barrikadnaya** or **Krasnopresnenskaya metro**, you'll spot Moscow's **Zoopark** (daily May–Sept 9am–7pm; Oct–April 9am–5pm) on the corner of Bolshaya Gruzinskaya ulitsa. Founded in 1864 and nationalized in 1919, the zoo is now badly antiquated and in need of relocation to a better site, but can only just afford to struggle on under deeply depressing conditions. The large pond just inside the entrance is the only part of the Presnya River that's visible, since the rest was channelled underground in 1908.

**Krasnaya Presnya ulitsa**, between Barrikadnaya and Ulitsa 1905 Goda metros, features the *Dehli* restaurant and the *Olimp* supermarket, which serve as pointers for anyone determined to

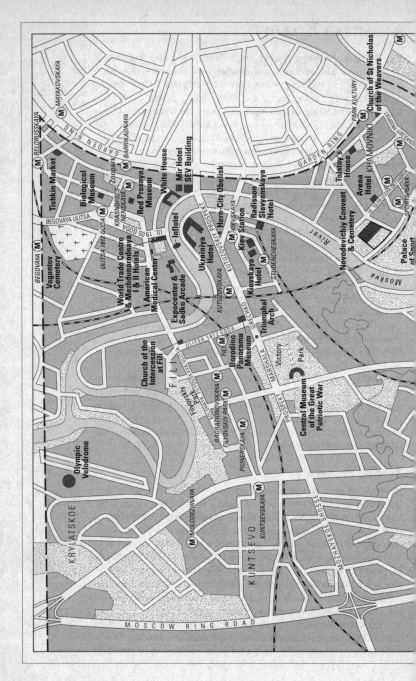

**KRASNAYA PRESNYA,
FILI & THE SOUTHWEST**

Central Stadium

Sparrow Hills

Friendship Sporting Hall

Pioneers' Palace

Orlyonok Hotel

Sputnik Hotel

Children's Musical Theatre

New Circus

Moscow State University (MGU)

Universitetskaya Hotel

Troekurovo Cemetery

MOSCOW RING ROAD

ULITSA PEISHE

Spros Hotel

PROSPEKT VERNADSKOVO

UNIVERSITET

Tsentralniy Dom Turista

LENINSKIY PROSPEKT

YUGO-ZAPADNAYA

PROSPEKT VERNADSKOVO

Pallada Hotel

Prakesh Guest House

AKADEMICHESKAYA

NOVYE CHEREMUSHKI

KALUZHSKAYA

BELYAEVO

KONKOVO

ULITSA OSTROVITYANOVA

LENINSKIY PROSPEKT

PLOSHCHAD GAGARINA

LENINSKIY PROSPEKT

ULITSA KOSYGINA

MICHURINSKIY PROSPEKT

N

0    2 km

track down two museums in the backstreets to the north and south. The nearest is the **Biological Museum** at Malaya Gruzinskaya 15 (Tues–Sun 10am–6pm), where school kids gawp at the deformed foetuses in room six. Named after the biologist Timiryazev, the museum also celebrates the work of Pavlov and the plant-breeder Michurin. Several city blocks in the other direction, at Predtechenskiy pereulok 4, a neglected **Red Presnya Museum** (Wed–Sun 10am–6pm) relates the revolutionary history of the district. This single-storey wooden house served as the local Bolshevik headquarters in 1917.

Anyone arriving at **ulitsa 1905 Goda** (1905 Street) metro should beware of the multiple exits around this major intersection. The main one brings you out on Krasnopresnenskiy Zastavy ploshchad, where shoppers ignore a huge Brezhnev-era **Monument to the 1905 Revolution**, featuring a woman unhorsing a Gendarme and men in ragged shirts waving rifles. Another surfaces on Bolshaya Dekabrskaya ulitsa (see "Vagankov Cemetery"), while a third emerges on a verge to the south of the intersection – the one to take if you're trying to reach the **American Medical Center** (AMC), further downhill.

**Tishkinskaya ploshchad**, further north, is easier to walk to from Mayakovskaya metro (10min). Though recognizable from afar by its revolutionary monument – a lofty column composed of chains, flames, hammers and rifles – the main attraction here is the **Tishkin flea market** (*Tishkinskiy rynok*; daily 8am–4pm), a now gangster-controlled affair, which supplants the weekday fruit and veg market at weekends. Young trendies come to hunt for 1960s clothing and you can find the odd *samovar*, but mostly it's just junk, given value by the crazy logic of Russian poverty: lightbulbs sold to substitute for the good ones stolen from work and empty *Heineken* cans to create an impression that you regularly drink the stuff.

## Down towards the river

Heading for the White House, you're likely to make straight for the river from Krasnopresnenskaya or Barrikadnaya metro. Bear off to the right towards the distant Stalin-Gothic skyscraper of the *Ukrainiya Hotel* (not to be confused with the block on Vosstaniya, nearby). Catch any bus or trolleybus heading south along Konyushovskaya ulitsa.

En route you'll pass the **Metostroy Stadium** and the red-brick blocks of the **new US Embassy**, across the road. In the mid-1980s, this caused grave embarrassment when it was found to be riddled with KGB bugs, implanted during construction. The US reckoned that it would be cheaper to tear the whole place down and start afresh rather than de-bug it, until the Soviets agreed to tell them where to look. Naturally, the Americans never believed that *all* the bugs had been exposed, so the building remains empty, and most embassy business is still conducted at the old embassy block on the Garden Ring (p.157).

## The SEV building

Approaching the White House and Moskva River, glance to the left, where the *Mir Hotel* is dwarfed by the former SEV building, whose 31 floors extrude from a central core. SEV (pronounced "sef") is the Russian acronym for the Socialist trading bloc known in the West as "Comecon", founded in 1949. Until SEV's dissolution in 1991, Soviet guidebooks waxed lyrical about how the building symbolized the co-operation shown between the bloc's member countries, having Czechoslovak-made elevators, doors crafted in Bulgaria, ceiling tiles from Hungary, East German parquet, Polish glass and Soviet lamps. Russians mocked this litany with jokes about a sheep that is raised in Romania, shorn in Bulgaria, has its wool processed in Hungary and spun into cloth in Czechoslovakia, to be made into a coat in Poland, given buttons in the GDR and then sent to the USSR for export to Romania.

SEV's demise flushed out a KGB listening post on the thirtieth floor that monitored the US Embassy, and left a vacant block that was snapped up by Moscow's Mayoralty. During the "October events" of 1993, a mob stormed the building and set the lower floors alight, before heading off to attack the TV centre. After the crisis was over and the SEV building had been repaired, it was designated as the seat of the lower house of the new Russian parliament, but the deputies complained that the walls were so thin they couldn't discuss secrets without being overheard, and the government let them have the Gosplan building (p.107) instead. Many deputies still have their offices here, however, and militiamen ring the perimeter, which bristles with satellite dishes.

## Encounters on the Hunchback Bridge

Across the road, a gap in the fence around the White House reveals the Gorbaty most (Hunchback Bridge), a small cobbled structure that's used to trouble. In December 1905, workers barricaded it to bar the Cossacks from Presnya, until artillery blew them away. Later, the bridge was covered over and forgotten till it was unearthed and restored in 1979, when a monument showing three generations of workers fighting side by side was erected nearby. This proved apposite when the barricades went up again in recent years, as people gathered to defend the White House. In 1991, bikers mingled with ruble millionaires and professors, while over the weeks leading up to the bloodshed of 1993 one saw Cossacks with Tsarist banners, Nazi paramilitaries, and "Red *babushkas*" with photo-collages illustrating the depravity of Yeltsin's Russia. Nowadays the bridge is a site for demonstrations by the "Red-Brown" alliance, or workers protesting against falling living standards – so you may see busloads of militia parked nearby.

# The White House

The White House or Beliy dom is a marble-clad hulk crowned by a gilded clock and the Russian tricolour, and is known around the world for its starring role in two confrontations telecast by CNN. When the building was completed in 1981 to provide spacious offices for the Council of Ministers of the Russian Federation, nobody dreamed that its windowless Hall of Nationalities would serve as a bunker ten years later, despite the paranoid foresight that specified the construction of a network of escape tunnels from the building. All this changed after the Russian parliament took up residence and Yeltsin was elected president with a mandate to take on the *apparat*. When the old guard staged a *putsch* against Gorbachev on August 19, 1991, the democratic opposition made the White House their rallying point.

The August putsch was an epic moment of self-discovery, as a hundred thousand Russians from all walks of life found the courage to form human barricades fifty layers deep around the building, where Yeltsin, Rutskoy and Khasbulatov were holed up on the third floor, phoning around the garrisons and broadcasting defiance. The expected assault on August 20 never materialized, as the KGB unit assigned to storm the White House baulked, and the *putschists* lost their nerve. This brought the whole edifice of Soviet power crashing down, as symbolized by the toppling of Dzerzhinsky's statue outside the Lubyanka. At the time, it was easy to agree with poet Yevtushenko's declamation that "the Russian Parliament, like a wounded marble swan of freedom/ defended by the people, swims into immortality".

Two years later the myth was turned inside out, as the White House became the crucible of conflict between parliament and the president, culminating in what Russians call the October events, a neutral tag for something tragic and divisive. The dubious legality of Yeltsin's dissolution of parliament and his sanctions against the deputies who occupied the White House enabled Khasbulatov and Rutskoy to claim that they were only defending the constitution when they urged a mob of supporters to seize the Ostankino TV centre on October 3. Next day, the army bowed to Yeltsin's orders and shelled the White House into submission. Yet, having smashed a hostile parliament to create a favourable one, Yeltsin found that the elections resulted in a majority of deputies who sympathized with the rebels, and voted an amnesty for all those arrested in October and the plotters of the August *putsch*, too.

Since then the building has been renamed the House of Government (*Dom Praiteltsvo*). There was also talk about the belated fire-fighting after the battle: rumour had it the government wanted to ensure that the eighth floor was consumed by fire, as one of the offices contained a top-secret report exposing corruption in the Cabinet. Whatever the truth, its present occupants have taken precautions against future trouble by erecting a concrete-slab fence

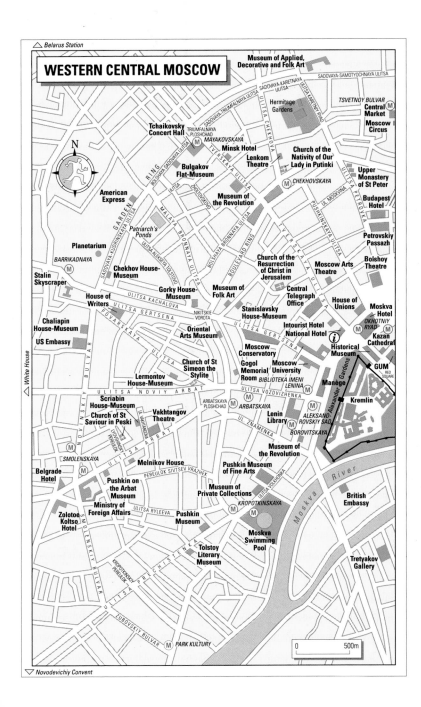

△ Belarus Station

# WESTERN CENTRAL MOSCOW

N

Museum of Applied, Decorative and Folk Art

SADOVAYA-SAMOTYOCHNAYA ULITSA

SADOVAYA-TRIUMFALNAYA ULITSA

SADOVAYA-KARETNAYA ULITSA

ULITSA KARETNIY RYAD

ULITSA CHEKHOVA

Hermitage Gardens

TSVETNOY BULVAR

Central Market Ⓜ

Moscow Circus

TRIUMFALNAYA PLOSHCHAD

Tchaikovsky Concert Hall

MAYAKOVSKAYA

Minsk Hotel

Church of the Nativity of Our Lady in Putinki

BOLSHAYA SADOVAYA ULITSA

RING

GARDEN

TVERSKAYA ULITSA

Lenkom Theatre

Bulgakov Flat-Museum

ZEMLEDSKOGO

Upper Monastery of St Peter

CHEKHOVSKAYA Ⓜ

ULITSA PETROVKA

PUSHKINSKAYA ULITSA

Budapest Hotel

American Express

MALAYA BRONNAYA ULITSA

Museum of the Revolution

Petrovskiy Passazh

Patriarch's Ponds

SADOVAYA-KUDRINSKAYA ULITSA

ULITSA ALEKSEYA TOLSTOGO

BOLSHAYA BRONNAYA ULITSA

BOULEVARD RING

TVERSKAYA

Planetarium

BARRIKADNAYA

Ⓜ

Chekhov House-Museum

Church of the Resurrection of Christ in Jerusalem

Moscow Arts Theatre

Bolshoy Theatre

Stalin Skyscraper

Gorky House-Museum

Museum of Folk Art

Central Telegraph Office

House of Unions

House of Writers

ULITSA KACHALOVA

POVARSKAYA ULITSA

ULITSA GERTSENA

NIKITSKIE VOROTA

Stanislavsky House-Museum

ULITSA GERTSENA

Moskva Hotel

OKHOTNIY RYAD Ⓜ

Chaliapin House-Museum

Oriental Arts Museum

Intourist Hotel

National Hotel

ⓘ

Kazan Cathedral

US Embassy

ULITSA

Moscow Conservatory

Church of St Simeon the Stylite

Gogol Memorial Room

Moscow University

BIBLIOTEKA IMENI LENINA

Historical Museum

Alexander Gardens

GUM

RED SQUARE

Lermontov House-Museum

ULITSA NOVIY ARBAT

Scriabin House-Museum

ARBATSKAYA PLOSHCHAD

ARBATSKAYA Ⓜ

ULITSA VOZDVIZHENKA

Manège

Kremlin

Church of St Saviour in Peski

Vakhtangov Theatre

UL ZNAMENKA

Lenin Library

ALEKSAND ROVSKIY SAD Ⓜ

BOROVITSKAYA Ⓜ

△ White House

SMOLENSKAYA Ⓜ

Melnikov House

PEREULOK SIVTSEV VRAZHEK

Museum of the Revolution

Moskva River

Belgrade Hotel

Pushkin on the Arbat Museum

Pushkin Museum of Fine Arts

Ministry of Foreign Affairs

ULITSA RYLEEVA

Museum of Private Collections

Pushkin Museum

KROPOTKINSKAYA

British Embassy

Zolotoe Koltso Hotel

SMOLENSKIY BULVAR

KROPOTKINSKIY PEREULOK

Tolstoy Literary Museum

KROPOTKINSKAYA Ⓜ

Moskva Swimming Pool

ULITSA PRECHISTENKA

Tretyakov Gallery

ZUBOVSKIY BULVAR

PARK KULTURY Ⓜ

0      500m

▽ Novodevichiy Convent

METRO

**Planernaya** Планерная
**Rechnoy Vokzal** Речной Вокзал
**Altufevskaya** Алтуфьевская
**Medvedkovo** Медведково
**Ulitsa Podbelskovo** Улица Подбельского
**Shchelkovskaya** Щёлковская
**Novogireevo** Новогиреево

Skhodnenskaya Сходненская
Tushinskaya Тушинская
Shchukinskaya Щукинская
Oktyabrskoye Pole Октябрьское Поле
Polezhavskaya Полежаевская
Begovaya Беговая
Ulitsa 1905 Goda Улица 1905 Года
Belorusskaya Белорусская
Krasnopresnenskaya Краснопресненская
Barrikadnaya Баррикадная
Mayakovskaya Маяковская
Chekhovskaya Чеховская
Okhotny Ryad Охотный Ряд
Tverskaya Тверская
Pushkinskaya Пушкинская

Vodniy Stadion Водный Стадион
Voykovskaya Войковская
Sokol Сокол
Aeroport Аэропорт
Dinamo Динамо

Bibirevo Бибирево
Otradnoe Отрадное
Vladykino Владыкино
Petrovsko-Razumovskaya Петровско-Разумовская
Timiryazevskaya Тимирязевская
Dmitrovskaya Дмитровская
Savelovskaya Савёловская
Mendeleevskaya Менделеевская
Novoslobodskaya Новослободская
Tsvetnoy Bulvar Цветной Бульвар
Sukharevskaya Сухаревская
Turgenevskaya Тургеневская
Chistye Prudy Чистые Пруды
Lubyanka Лубянка
Kuznetskiy Most Кузнецкий Мост
Teatralnaya Театральная

Babushkinskaya Бабушкинская
Sviblovo Свиблово
Botanicheskiy Sad Ботанический Сад
VDNKh ВДНХ
Alekseevskaya Алексеевская
Rizhskaya Рижская
Prospect Mira Проспект Мира
Komsomolskaya Комсомольская
Krasnye Vorota Красные Ворота
Kitay-Gorod Китай-Город

Cherkizovskaya Черкизовская
Sokolniki Сокольники
Krasnoselskaya Красносельская
Preobrazhenskaya Ploshchad Преображенская Площадь

Pervomayskaya Первомайская
Izmaylovski Park Измайловский Парк
Semyonovskaya Семёновская
Baumanskaya Бауманская
Kurskaya Курская
Chkalovskaya Чкаловская
Ploshchad Ilicha Площадь Ильича

Izmaylovskaya Измайловская
Elektrozavodskaya Электрозаводская

Shosse Entuziastov Шоссе Энтузиастов

Perovo Перово
Aviamotornaya Авиамоторная

Krylatskoe Крылатское
Molodezhnaya Молодёжная
Kuntsevskaya Кунцевская
Pionerskaya Пионерская
Filyovskiy Park Филёвский Парк
Fili Фили
Bagrationovskaya Багратионовская
Kutuzovskaya Кутузовская
Studencheskaya Студенческая
Kievskaya Киевская
Smolenskaya Смоленская
Arbatskaya Арбатская
Smolenskaya Смоленская

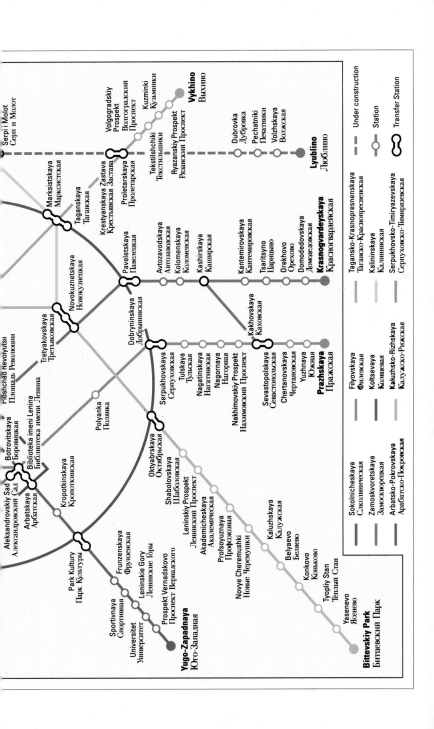

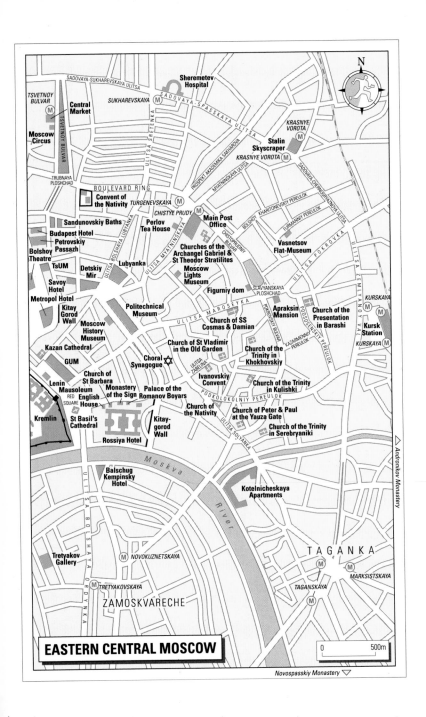

N

Sheremetev Hospital

TSVETNOY BULVAR

SADOVAYA-SUKHAREVSKAYA ULITSA

Central Market

SUKHAREVSKAYA

SADOVAYA-SPASSKAYA ULITSA

Moscow Circus

KRASNYE VOROTA

Stalin Skyscraper

ULITSA SRETENKA

KRASNYE VOROTA

TRUBNAYA PLOSHCHAD

PROSPEKT AKADEMIKA SAKHAROVA

SADOVAYA-CHERNOGRYAZSKAYA ULITSA

BOULEVARD RING

Convent of the Nativity

TURGENEVSKAYA

KHARITONEVSKIY PEREULOK

Sandunovskiy Baths

CHISTYE PRUDY

Perlov Tea House

Main Post Office

FURMANNIY PEREULOK

Budapest Hotel

BOLSHAYA LUBYANKA

BOLSHOY

Vasnetsov Flat-Museum

ULITSA POKROVKA

Petrovskiy Passazh

CHISTOPRUDNIY BULVAR

Bolshoy Theatre

Churches of the Archangel Gabriel & St Theodor Stratilites

TsUM

Lubyanka

ULITSA MYATNITSKAYA

Moscow Lights Museum

Detskiy Mir

Figurniy dom

SLAVYANSKAYA PLOSHCHAD

Savoy Hotel

ULITSA ZEMLYANOY VAL

Metropol Hotel

Politechnical Museum

KURSKAYA

Kitay Gorod Wall

ULITSA MAROSEYKA

Apraksin Mansion

Church of the Presentation in Barashi

Kursk Station

Moscow History Museum

Church of SS Cosmas & Damian

POKROVSKIY BULVAR

KURSKAYA

Kazan Cathedral

Church of St Vladimir in the Old Garden

LAZARMENNIY PEREULOK

PODSOSENSKIY PEREULOK

GUM

Choral Synagogue

ULITSA ZABELINA

Church of the Trinity in Khokhovskiy

Lenin Mausoleum

Church of St Barbara

Monastery of the Sign

Ivanovskiy Convent

Church of the Trinity in Kulishki

English House

RED SQUARE

Palace of the Romanov Boyars

PODKOLOKOLNIY PEREULOK

Kremlin

St Basil's Cathedral

Kitay-gorod Wall

Church of the Nativity

Church of Peter & Paul at the Yauza Gate

Church of the Trinity in Serebryaniki

Rossiya Hotel

ULITSA SOLYANKA

Moskva

Balschug Kempinsky Hotel

Kotelnicheskaya Apartments

River

ULITSA BOLSHAYA ORDYNKA

TAGANKA

Tretyakov Gallery

NOVOKUZNETSKAYA

MARKSISTSKAYA

TRETYAKOVSKAYA

TAGANSKAYA

ZAMOSKVARECHE

△ Andronikov Monastery

## EASTERN CENTRAL MOSCOW

0        500m

Novospasskiy Monastery ▽

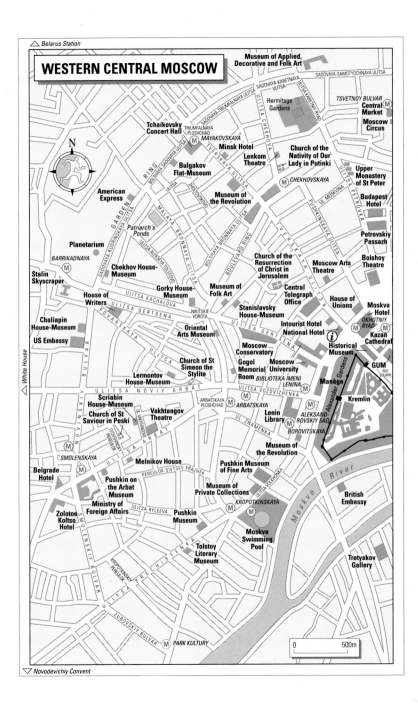

△ Belarus Station

# WESTERN CENTRAL MOSCOW

Museum of Applied,
Decorative and Folk Art

SADOVAYA-SAMOTYOCHNAYA ULITSA

SADOVAYA-KARETNAYA
ULITSA

SADOVAYA-TRIUMFALNAYA ULITSA

ULITSA CHEKHOVA

ULITSA KARETNIY RYAD

Hermitage
Gardens

TSVETNOY BULVAR

Central
Market Ⓜ

Moscow
Circus

Tchaikovsky
Concert Hall

TRIUMFALNAYA
PLOSHCHAD

Ⓜ MAYAKOVSKAYA

Minsk Hotel

BOLSHAYA SADOVAYA ULITSA

R I N G

TVERSKAYA ULITSA

Lenkom
Theatre

Church of the
Nativity of Our
Lady in Putinki

ULITSA CHEKHOVA

Upper
Monastery
of St Peter

Bulgakov
Flat-Museum

ULITSA DROGODOVO

Ⓜ CHEKHOVSKAYA

ULITSA PETROVKA

American
Express

G A R D E N

SADOVAYA-KUDRINSKAYA ULITSA

Museum of
the Revolution

PUSHKINSKAYA ULITSA

Budapest
Hotel

Patriarch's
Ponds

MALAYA BRONNAYA ULITSA

ULITSA ALEKSEYA TOLSTOGO

Petrovskiy
Passazh

Planetarium

BARRIKADNAYA

BOLSHAYA BRONNAYA ULITSA

BOULEVARD RING

TVERSKAYA ULITSA

Church of the
Resurrection
of Christ in
Jerusalem

Moscow Arts
Theatre

Bolshoy
Theatre

Stalin
Skyscraper

Ⓜ

Chekhov House-
Museum

Gorky House-
Museum

Museum of
Folk Art

Central
Telegraph
Office

House of
Unions

Moskva
Hotel

House of
Writers

ULITSA KACHALOVA

ULITSA GERTSENA

NIKITSKIE
VOROTA

Stanislavsky
House-Museum

ULITSA GERTSENA

House of
Unions

OKHOTNIY
RYAD Ⓜ

Chaliapin
House-Museum

POVARSKAYA

Oriental
Arts Museum

Intourist Hotel
National Hotel ⓘ

Historical
Museum

Kazan
Cathedral

US Embassy

B U L V A R

ULITSA

Church of St
Simeon the
Stylite

Moscow
Conservatory

Moscow
University

GUM
RED
SQUARE

Lermontov
House-Museum

Gogol
Memorial
Room

BIBLIOTEKA IMENI
LENINA

Manège

△ White House

Scriabin
House-Museum

ULITSA NOVIY ARBAT

ARBATSKAYA
PLOSHCHAD

ULITSA VOZDVIZHENKA

Ⓜ

Kremlin

Ⓜ

Church of St
Saviour in Peski

Vakhtangov
Theatre

ULITSA ARBAT

Ⓜ ARBATSKAYA

Lenin
Library

ALEKSAND-
ROVSKIY SAD

Alexander Gardens

BOROVITSKAYA

NOVINSKIY BULVAR

UL ZNAMENKA

Belgrade
Hotel

Ⓜ

UDYANSKIY
PEREULOK

Melnikov House

PEREULOK SIVTSEV VRAZHEK

Museum of
the Revolution

Pushkin
on the Arbat
Museum

SMOLENSKAYA

ULITSA RYLEEVA

Pushkin Museum
of Fine Arts

Moskva
River

Ⓜ SMOLENSKAYA

Ministry of
Foreign Affairs

Pushkin
Museum

Museum of
Private Collections

Ⓜ KROPOTKINSKAYA

British
Embassy

Zolotoe
Koltso
Hotel

SMOLENSKIY BULVAR

KROPOTINSKIY
PEREULOK

P R E C H I S T E N K A

Tolstoy
Literary
Museum

Moskva
Swimming
Pool

Moskva River

Tretyakov
Gallery

ZUBOVSKIY BULVAR

ULITSA

Ⓜ PARK KULTURY

0        500m

▽ Novodevichiy Convent

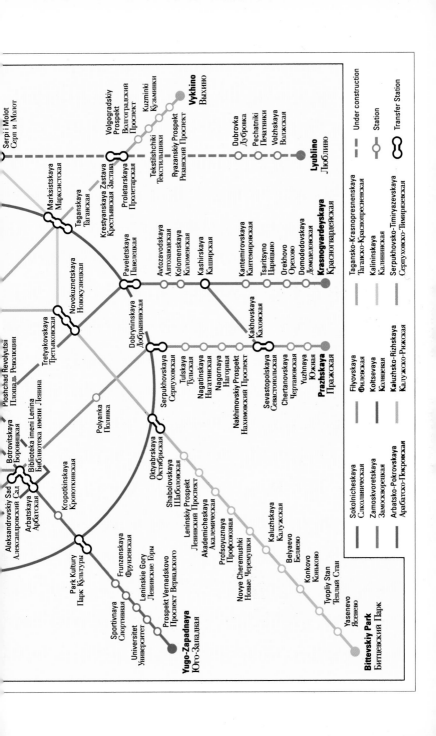

Serp i Molot
Серп и Молот

Vykhino
Выхино

Marksistskaya
Марксистская

Taganskaya
Таганская

Krestyanskaya Zastava
Крестьянская Застава

Proletarskaya
Пролетарская

Volgogradskiy
Prospekt
Волгоградский
Проспект

Kuzminki
Кузьминки

Tekstilshchiki
Текстильщики

Ryazanskiy Prospekt
Рязанский Проспект

Lyublino
Люблино

Dubrovka
Дубровка

Pechatniki
Печатники

Volzhskaya
Волжская

Pavaletskaya
Павелецкая

Avtozavodskaya
Автозаводская

Kolomenskaya
Коломенская

Kashirskaya
Каширская

Kantemirovskaya
Кантемировская

Tsaritsyno
Царицыно

Orekhovo
Орехово

Domodedovskaya
Домодедовская

Krasnogvardeyskaya
Красногвардейская

Novokuznetskaya
Новокузнецкая

Dobryninskaya
Добрынинская

Kakhovskaya
Каховская

Tretyakovskaya
Третьяковская

Serpukhovskaya
Серпуховская

Tulskaya
Тульская

Nagatinskaya
Нагатинская

Nagornaya
Нагорная

Nakhimovskiy Prospekt
Нахимовский Проспект

Sevastopolskaya
Севастопольская

Chertanovskaya
Чертановская

Yuzhnaya
Южная

Prazhskaya
Пражская

Ploschad Revolyutsii
Площадь Революции

Polyanka
Полянка

Aleksandrovskiy Sad
Александровский Сад

Botrovitskaya
Боровицкая

Biblioteka imeni Lenina
Библиотека имени Ленина

Arbatskaya
Арбатская

Kropotkinskaya
Кропоткинская

Oktyabrskaya
Октябрьская

Shabolovskaya
Шаболовская

Leninskiy Prospekt
Ленинский Проспект

Akademicheskaya
Академическая

Profsoyuznaya
Профсоюзная

Novye Cheremushki
Новые Черёмушки

Kaluzhskaya
Калужская

Belyaevo
Беляево

Konkovo
Коньково

Tyopliy Stan
Тёплый Стан

Yasenevo
Ясенево

Bittevskiy Park
Битцевский Парк

Park Kultury
Парк Культуры

Frunzenskaya
Фрунзенская

Leninskie Gory
Ленинские Горы

Sportivnaya
Спортивная

Universitet
Университет

Prospekt Vernadskovo
Проспект Вернадского

Yugo-Zapadnaya
Юго-Западная

## Legend

| | | | |
|---|---|---|---|
| Sokolnicheskaya<br>Сокольническая | Filyovskaya<br>Филёвская | Taganско-Krasnopresnenskaya<br>Таганско-Краснопресненская | --- Under construction |
| Zamoskvoretskaya<br>Замоскворецкая | Koltsevaya<br>Кольцевая | Kalininskaya<br>Калининская | ○ Station |
| Arbatsko-Pokrovskaya<br>Арбатско-Покровская | Kaluzhsko-Rizhskaya<br>Калужско-Рижская | Serpukhovsko-Timiryazevskaya<br>Серпуховско-Тимирязевская | Transfer Station |

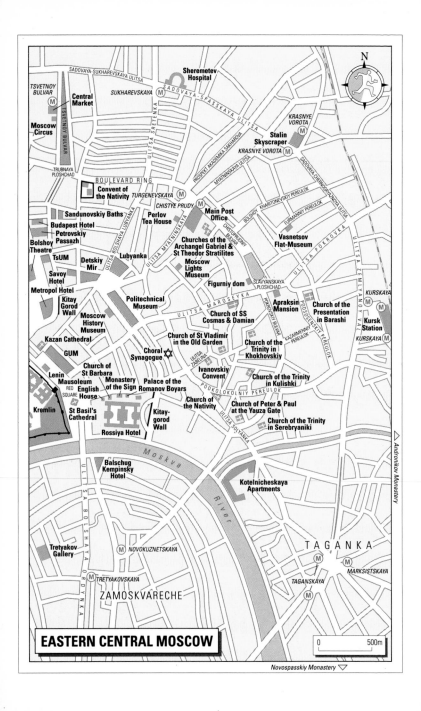

SADOVAYA-SUKHAREVSKAYA ULITSA

TSVETNOY BULVAR

**Central Market**

SUKHAREVSKAYA

**Sheremetev Hospital**

SADOVAYA-SPASSKAYA ULITSA

**Moscow Circus**

TSVETNOY BULVAR

ULITSA SRETENKA

**KRASNYE VOROTA**

**Stalin Skyscraper**

KRASNYE VOROTA

SADOVAYA-CHERNOGRYAZSKAYA ULITSA

TRUBNAYA PLOSHCHAD

BOULEVARD RING

**Convent of the Nativity**

TURGENEVSKAYA

CHISTYE PRUDY

**Main Post Office**

PROSPEKT AKADEMIKA SAKHAROVA

MYASNITSKAYA ULITSA

BOLSHOY KHARITONEVSKIY PEREULOK

FURMANNY PEREULOK

**Sandunovskiy Baths**

**Perlov Tea House**

**Budapest Hotel**

**Petrovskiy Passazh**

**Bolshoy Theatre**

**TsUM**

**Detskiy Mir**

**Lubyanka**

ULITSA MYASNITSKAYA

**Churches of the Archangel Gabriel & St Theodor Stratilites**

**Moscow Lights Museum**

CHISTOPRUDNY BULVAR

**Vasnetsov Flat-Museum**

ULITSA POKROVKA

ULITSA ZEMLYANOY

**KURSKAYA**

**Savoy Hotel**

**Metropol Hotel**

**Kitay Gorod Wall**

**Moscow History Museum**

**Politechnical Museum**

**Figurniy dom**

SLAVYANSKAYA PLOSHCHAD

ULITSA MAROSEYKA

**Church of SS Cosmas & Damian**

**Apraksin Mansion**

**Church of the Presentation in Barashi**

PODSOSENSKIY PEREULOK

**Kazan Cathedral**

**GUM**

**Church of St Barbara**

**Lenin Mausoleum**

RED SQUARE

**Monastery of the Sign**

**English House**

**Church of St Vladimir in the Old Garden**

**Choral Synagogue**

ULITSA ZABELINA

**Palace of the Romanov Boyars**

**Ivanovskiy Convent**

**Church of the Trinity in Khokhovskiy**

KAZARMENNIY PEREULOK

**Church of the Trinity in Kulishki**

KURSKAYA

**Kremlin**

**St Basil's Cathedral**

**Rossiya Hotel**

**Kitay-gorod Wall**

PODKOLOKOLNIY PEREULOK

**Church of the Nativity**

ULITSA SOLYANKA

**Church of Peter & Paul at the Yauza Gate**

**Church of the Trinity in Serebryaniki**

M o s k v a

**Balschug Kempinsky Hotel**

ULITSA BOLSHAYA ORDYNKA

River

**Kotelnicheskaya Apartments**

△ Andronikov Monastery

**Tretyakov Gallery**

NOVOKUZNETSKAYA

T A G A N K A

TRETYAKOVSKAYA

TAGANSKAYA

MARKSISTSKAYA

ZAMOSKVARECHE

## EASTERN CENTRAL MOSCOW

0          500m

*Novospasskiy Monastery* ▽

around the perimeter. The White House is best seen from the embankment side, where an outpost flying the Iraqi flag added a bizarre touch to the defences in 1993. From here you also have a striking **view** of the Stalin-Gothic *Ukrainiya Hotel* (p.181) across the river, and the World Trade Centre, 700m west along the embankment.

## The World Trade Centre and the Mezh

Moscow's **World Trade Centre** (*Tsentr Mezhdunarodnoy Torgovli*) was initiated by the late Armand Hammer of Occidental Petroleum, who began doing business with the USSR in the 1920s and personally knew every Soviet leader since Lenin. Inaugurated in 1980, the glass and concrete complex was an early beach head of Western business culture, in tandem with the adjacent *Mezhdunarodnaya* (International) hotel, whose expatriate clientele dubbed it "the Mezh". Further east across a park stands the newer **Expocenter**, and the **Sadko Arcade**, one of the swankiest malls in Moscow – though usually fairly empty owing to its remote location.

## Vagankov Cemetery

Cut off from the rest of Presnya by main roads and freight yards, the **Vagankov Cemetery** (*Vagankovskoe kladbishche*) is an oasis of mournful beauty, redolent of another age. Russians are familiar with their dead, coming to commune with friends or family, or pay homage to cultural idols. In Moscow's hierarchy of prestigious burial grounds, the Vagankov runs a close second to the Novodevichiy cemetery, which takes people who never quite made it into the Kremlin Wall. Though it doesn't have such a profusion of sculptural monuments, there are enough surprises to make wandering around a pleasure. The cemetery itself dates from 1771, when an outbreak of plague impelled the authorities to dig up all the graveyards in central Moscow and establish new ones beyond the city limits. It takes its name from the parish cemetery that belonged to the Church of St Nicholas in Old Vagankov, near the Borovitskiy Gate of the Kremlin.

To **get there**, take the metro to Ulitsa 1905 Goda, surface by the Bolshaya Dekabrskaya ulitsa exit, turn right and head on to the end of the road, where you can't miss the pair of churches just inside the entrance to the cemetery (Wed–Sun 10am–6pm).

### Some notable graves

Located off to the right between the churches is the much-visited grave of **Vladimir Vysotskiy**, the maverick actor-balladeer of the Brezhnev era. Though hundreds of fans braved militia cordons to attend his hushed-up funeral in 1980, no monument was permitted until the advent of *perestroika*, five years later. It portrays Vysotskiy garbed in a shroud like a martyr, his guitar forming a halo

*See p.236 about
Vysotskiy, or
"The Tretyakov
Gallery"
(pp.206–214)
regarding the
painters buried
here.*

behind his head. Further west, beyond the **Church of the Resurrection**, is the last resting place of the impresario **Alexei Bakhrushin**, who founded Moscow's Theatre Museum.

Heading south from here along Timiryazevskaya alleya, you'll pass the tombs of the biologist **Nikolai Timiryazev** and the lexicographer Vladimir Dal, whose works are known to every Russian student. Off to the left at the far end, a tender bas-relief marks the grave of the heart-throb poet **Sergei Yesenin** (1895–1925), who cut his wrists and hanged himself, leaving a final poem written in his own blood: *To die is not new – but neither is it new to be alive*. An admirer, **Galina Benislavskaya**, shot herself on his grave exactly a year later and is buried nearby in plot #20. In the same neck of the woods are the grave of the historical painter **Vasily Surikov** – marked by a palette and brushes – and a simple wartime headstone to the Cubist **Aristakh Lentulov**. Buried near the eastern wall are the landscape painter **Alexei Sarasov** and the Style Moderne architect **Fyodor Shekhtel**.

More recently, the cemetery witnessed the funerals of seventeen **policemen** killed during the October events – who received state honours – and the Mafia boss **Otari Kvantrishvili**, shot by a contract sniper as he left a local bathhouse in 1994. His gang secured him a plot near Vysotskiy's grave, and his funeral was shown on TV accompanied by the theme tune from *The Godfather*, a movie that Russian mobsters cherish as a role model.

# To Fili and Victory Park

Across the river from Presnya, the hand of Stalinist planning is writ large in gigantic avenues and residential blocks whose pomposity is underscored by the vibrant **Church of the Assumption** in Fili and a string of Napoleonic and World War II memorials culminating in a grandiose Victory Park. Though relatively low on Moscow's list of tourist attractions, they say much about Soviet aesthetics and Russian patriotism. Almost everywhere is within walking range of a metro station on the (light blue) Filyovskaya line, but so far apart that you're obliged to retrace your steps before riding on to the next place. Further out towards the Moscow Ring Road are the suburb of Kuntsevo, where Stalin had his dacha, and the stunning Olympic Velodrome at Krylatskoe.

## Around Kiev Station

Kievskaya metro is the obvious starting point, being close to a few places worth noting, and an interchange onto the metro line that serves everywhere else. Its name comes from the **Kiev Station** (*Kievskiy vokzal*) that handles trains from Ukraine and Moldova, built by Ivan Rerberg in 1913–17 and modernized in the 1980s; its tall clocktower overlooks a monument commemorating the unification of Ukraine and Russia in the seventeenth century. A short distance away on the embankment is a **boat pier** for river cruises – an enjoyable way to see Moscow in the summer. The locality had a few days of stardom during the Clinton–Yeltsin Summit of 1994, when the US presidential party stayed at the Radisson Slavyanskaya hotel, off to the right of the station.

**To Fili and Victory Park**

*Cruises on the Moskva River are detailed on p.330.*

## Kutuzovskiy prospekt

**Kutuzovskiy prospekt** was laid out in the mid-1950s as a prestigious residential area for diplomats, top scientists, and even the Soviet leadership, whose town apartments were conveniently located midway between the Kremlin and their suburban *dachas* to the west of Moscow – all rapidly accessible by the Chaika Lane (see box below). The avenue is named after Field Marshal Kutuzov, whose troops marched this way to confront Napoleon's *Grande Armée* at Borodino and retreated back along the road after Kutuzov's fateful decision to abandon Moscow. In 1941, Stalin evoked the shades of 1812 as Soviet regiments streamed towards the advancing *Wehrmacht*; the sacrifices and victories of both wars are commemorated by a series of monuments along several miles of the avenue.

Kutuzovskiy's initial stretch is notable for the **Ukrainiya Hotel**, a tawny coloured Stalin-Gothic leviathan that boasts one thousand rooms. Completed in 1956, its 36-storey central tower is flanked by turreted wings and culminates in a 72-metre-high spire crowned with a Soviet star. During the crises of 1991 and 1993, the hotel's guests had a ringside view of events at the White House, across the river.

If you want to see more of the prospekt, trolleybus #39 or any bus going west will take you past the **Moscow-Hero-City Obelisk** erected at the junction of Bolshaya Dorogomilovskaya ulitsa in 1977. The Stalinist blocks on either side of the prospekt contain high-ceilinged apartments of up to a dozen rooms that are each the

---

**The Chaika Lane**

The **Chaika Lane** is the nickname given to the central lane of Moscow's main avenues, reserved for the cars of the elite to travel at high speed as the GAI wave other traffic aside. In Soviet times, cars were allotted to the Party *nomenklatura* according to a strict protocol. Politburo members rated armoured ZiLs – a kind of stretch limo – and often travelled together in convoys. Stalin used six cars, riding a different vehicle each time as a precaution (but sometimes offered lifts to pensioners), while Khrushchev reduced the motorcade to four vehicles. Far commoner were the chauffeur-driven **Chaikas** of the second echelon cadres – hence the Chaika Lane – and the vast fleet of black **Volgas** used by lower ranking bureaucrats. Nowadays, only top officials have retained the privilege of using the Chaika Lane and they're more likely to be driving Volvos or BMWs.

---

size of an entire flat for the average Muscovite family. Notice no. 26, which used to be known as the **Politburo block**. Here, Brezhnev had an opulent two-floor apartment (now used by Ruslan Khasbulatov) and his Interior Minister, Shchelokov, an entire floor – in contrast to the ascetic KGB chief, Andropov, with his one-bedroom flat.

## The Borodino Panorama

The *War and Peace* trail begins beyond Kutuzovskaya metro station; take the exit near the front of the train, turn right outside and head towards the Triumphal Arch 500m away. Shortly before this is the circular blue pavilion of the **Borodino Panorama Museum** (*muzey Panorama Borodinskaya Bitva*), which should reopen soon (probably Mon–Fri 10am–5pm). Inaugurated in 1962 on the 150th anniversary of Borodino, its 115-metre-long circular painting by Franz Roubaud depicts a critical moment in the battle of Borodino, which occurred 129km west of Moscow on August 26, 1812. Casualties were unprecedented in world history, with forty thousand Russians and thirty thousand French killed in fifteen hours – but neither side emerged the winner. Visitors admiring the painting can survey the battle raging all around from the standpoint of Russian troops holding the village of Semyonovskaya. Napoleon can be identified in the distance by his white horse.

Outside the pavilion, an equestrian **statue of Kutuzov** bestrides a pedestal flanked by bronzes of Russian soldiers and peasant guerillas. Mikhail Kutuzov (1745–1813) was a one-eyed giant who used to close his good eye and pretend to be asleep so that his aides could express their opinions freely. Five days after Borodino, with the French still advancing, a council of war was held in the *izba* (hut) of a peasant named Frolov, at which Kutuzov resolved to withdraw from Moscow to avoid being outflanked. His decision aroused anger but was soon vindicated by events: the burning of Moscow left Napoleon's *Grande Armée* bereft of shelter as winter approached, and obliged to retreat under the constant threat of Russian attacks.

In 1887, a supposedly exact copy of the historic *izba* was opened as a museum. Located in a park behind the pavilion, the **Kutuzov Hut** (Tues–Thurs 10am–6pm, Sat & Sun 10.30am–5.30pm; closed every Mon & Fri & the last Thurs of each month) musters an array of weapons, banners and oil paintings of the battle. Tickets are sold at the brick hut next door.

## The Triumphal Arch

Russia's victory over Napoleon is commemorated on a grander scale by a **Triumphal Arch** designed by Osip Bove, originally erected (1829–34) where the St Petersburg road entered Moscow, near what is now Belarus Station; imperial processions passed beneath it and along Tverskaya ulitsa, towards the Kremlin. Like the Triumphal Arch in Leningrad, this was deemed an impediment to traffic and demolished in the 1930s, but Vitali's sculptures were preserved at the Donskoy Monastery until it was decided to reconstruct the arch in the patriotic upsurge that followed World War II. Completed in 1968, the weathered stone arch is bracketed by Corninthian columns flanking Classical warriors, decorated with the coats-of-arms of 48 Russian provinces and surmounted by the winged figure of Glory urging his chariot westwards. To inspect it at closer quarters, follow the underpass that surfaces near the arch in the middle of the avenue.

## Victory Park

Patriotic ardour reaches a climax at the sprawling **Victory Park** (*Park Pobedy*) on the far side of the highway, 500m past the arch. The idea for this memorial complex to the Soviet victory in World War II goes back to the Era of Stagnation, when the Party erected ever larger war memorials in an effort to overcome ideological apathy among the masses.

In 1983, the Politburo gave its approval to a design by Nikolai Tomskiy that involved levelling the **Poklonnaya gora** (Hill of Greetings), where generations of travellers had exclaimed with joy as they reached its summit to suddenly behold Moscow ahead of them, and where Napoleon had waited in vain for *boyars* to present him with the keys to the city. The intention was to erect a 250-foot-high monument to Mother Russia, supported by a host of allegorical figures. With the advent of *glasnost*, the project aroused a public outcry and was cancelled, only to be revived in a toned-down form by Yeltsin's government. Billions of rubles and battalions of conscripts were committed to "storm" the final stage, so that the park could be ready for the 49th anniversary of Victory Day, in 1994.

Indeed, it's best to come here on **Victory Day** (May 9) – the only anniversary in Soviet times that was genuinely heartfelt – when crowds stream towards the park carrying bouquets. Bemedalled old women and bowlegged ex-cavalrymen in archaic uniforms reminisce, weep, sing and dance to accordion music, while younger Russians queue up at field-kitchens to try bowls of wartime-style *kasha* (buckwheat porridge). The mood is deeply sentimental, dwelling less on the triumphs of Stalingrad and Berlin than on the terrible autumn of 1941, when the Red Army was repeatedly savaged and forced back towards Moscow – as in a poem by Konstantin Simonov, whose opening lines are known to every Russian:

> *Do you remember, Alyosha*
> *The Smolensk roads*
> *Where the dank rains fell unending.*

The park itself is laid out around a grand fountain-lined axis culminating in the **Central Museum of the Great Patriotic War** (Wed–Sun 10am–6pm). This vast concave structure, raised on stilts and surmounted by a spiked bronze dome, contains the ultimate exposition of World War II from the Soviet perspective, with hall after hall of maps, weaponry, models and photos. What Russians call the Great Patriotic War (*viz* the Patriotic War of 1812) is only deemed to have begun in 1941 with Hitler's invasion of the USSR, and ended with the liberation of Prague two days *after* the formal German surrender that's taken in the West as VE Day. This ethnocentric bias is perhaps more excusable than most, since Soviet losses were greater than any other country's, and even Churchill acknowledged that it was the Red Army that "tore the guts from the Nazi war-machine".

In a section of the park to the left of the **Eternal Flame**, replica **anti-tank traps** and **trenches** of the kind that once defended Moscow are a big hit with kids, while on Victory Day elders nod sagely as loudspeakers play wartime radio **broadcasts**, such as the famous call to arms by Stalin that opened with the Orthodox salutation "Brothers and Sisters", and went on to invoke the warrior-saints of Holy Russia.

## Fili

While the estates and villages that once flourished to the west of Moscow vanished long ago, an outstanding church of the pre-Petrine era survives in the 1950s suburb of Fili. It can be reached on foot from the Borodino Panorama via ulitsa 1812 goda (1.5km), though it's easier to catch the metro to Fili station instead. Leaving by the exit nearest the front of the train and turning left outside, you'll be lured by a golden dome above the treetops just 350m down an avenue towards the junction with Bolshaya Filyovskaya ulitsa.

The **Church of the Intercession at Fili** (*tserkov Pokrova v Filyakh*) is the first real masterpiece of Naryshkin Baroque. Delightfully exuberant yet firmly controlled, it seems a world apart from the gloomy, rambling Upper Monastery of St Peter that the Naryshkins endowed a few years earlier. Nobody knows the identity of the architect who was commissioned by Prince Lev Naryshkin, but his design was inspired. Constructed (1690–93) in the form of a Greek cross with short rounded arms, the church rises in wedding-cake tiers of orange stucco ornamented with engaged columns and "cockscomb" cornices, offset by gilded rhomboids above the second level and a larger dome crowning the belltower. The locked summer church is reached by three stairways incorporating sharp turns that were intended to heighten the drama of processions. In 1812, the French turned it into a tailors' workshop and stabled their horses in the lower winter church, which now contains some fragmentary murals and an **exhibition of modern icons** (Mon, Tues & Thurs–Sun 11am–5.30pm; closed the last Fri of each month; $2).

You may feel it's not worth buying a ticket from the hut nearby, as the church's exterior can be admired for free. Occasional concerts in the summer are advertised on the spot.

To Fili and Victory Park

## Filyovskiy Park

While in this neck of the woods, it would be a shame not to visit **Filyovskiy Park**, which hugs a bend in the Moskva River further along Bolshaya Filyovskaya ulitsa. Besides the obvious attraction of greenery and breezes, there is the weekly **Gorbunov collectors' fair**, where music lovers trade vintage albums, CDs, hi-fis, videos and TVs at a clubhouse near the northern edge of the park. Known to regulars as the *tolkuchka* (crowd), this is better natured than most of Moscow's other flea markets and offers some real bargains; it is held every Saturday and Sunday from 11am to 2pm. You can reach the park from the church by riding trolleybus #54 along Bolshaya Filyovskaya, or by catching the metro to Bagrationovskaya station and walking from there. During summer, the park is also a stop for **boats** cruising upriver from Kiev Station.

# Further out: Kuntsevo and Krylatskoe

West of Fili, the former village of **KUNTSEVO** rates a mention for having once been the site of **Stalin's dacha**, *Blizhnoe*, where he largely spent his final years and died of a brain haemorrhage in 1953. Stalin, who hated being alone, obliged his cronies to watch films until the small hours, or drink endless alcoholic toasts while he consumed mineral water and jovially accused them of being British agents, or snarled: "Why are your eyes so shifty?". Yet only belatedly did Stalin realize that he was surrounded by Georgian staff chosen by Beria, a skilled dissembler who later danced beside his corpse. As they feared to disturb him, hours passed before Stalin was found unconscious in his bedroom, and a further ten elapsed before any treatment (with leeches) was authorized, which kept him barely alive until March 5. At 4am the next day, Moscow Radio announced that "the heart of the comrade-in-arms and continuer of the genius of Lenin's cause, of the wise leader and teacher of the Communist Party and the Soviet Union, has ceased to beat". Within a few years, the Party elite had abandoned Kuntsevo for Zhukovka – a new *dacha* colony beyond the Ring Road – leaving Kuntsevo to be swallowed up by the city.

Further upriver lies the leafy suburb of **KRYLATSKOE**, where apartment blocks have sprouted around a 130-hectare sports complex that was beefed up for the 1980 Olympics. Spread across the Tartarovo Flats are a 2300-metre-long artificial **rowing canal**, archery facilities, a thirteen-kilometre outdoor **cycling track** and the high-tech indoor **velodrome**. Designed by a team under Natalya Voronina, the velodrome resembles a giant silvery-white butterfly, enclosing a steeply banked cycling track of Siberian larch, flanked

by seating for six thousand spectators. The track's sweeping lines
are mirrored by the plunging and soaring roof, held taut by steel
filaments stretched between pairs of arches, supported by a truss-
frame system. In 1992, the velodrome hosted one of Moscow's first
raves, whose theme – sport, energy and strength – was expressed by
cyclists racing around the track as people danced in the middle until
dawn. To get there, ride the metro to Molodezhnaya and then bus
#286 to the end of the line, or travel to Krylatskoe station and walk
(10min).

Lastly, amid a high-rise district to the south of the Mozhaysk
highway, the **Troekurovo Cemetery** contains the **grave of Kim
Philby**, the KGB mole within British Intelligence who was dubbed
"The Third Man" in the 1960s. Buried alongside a row of Soviet
generals, his headstone is simply marked in Russian: *Kim Philby
11.1.1912–11.5.1988*.

# Khamovniki and Luzhniki

The **Khamovniki** and **Luzhniki** districts are somewhat removed
from the rest of the city, covering a peninsula bounded by the
Moskva River and the Garden Ring, and best approached by metro.
From Park Kultury station, it's a short walk to the lovely Church of
St Nicholas of the Weavers and thence to Tolstoy's House. But the
star attraction has to be the Novodevichiy Convent and Cemetery, a
magnificent fortified complex with a history of intrigues, next to a
necropolis that numbers Gogol and Shostakovich among its dead.
This lies a bit further from Sportivnaya metro, which also serves for
reaching the Luzhniki sports complex and flea market at the far end
of the peninsula. When deciding what to see, it's worth considering
how you can tie the sights in with **other itineraries**. Park Kultury
station lies across the river from Gorky Park and the Krymskiy val
centre (see p.214), while the red metro line runs southwest to
Moscow University in the scenic Sparrow Hills (covered later in this
chapter).

## The Church of St Nicholas of the Weavers

Emerging from Park Kultury station, the 200m of roadworks and
kiosks along Komsomolskiy prospekt make the **Church of St
Nicholas of the Weavers** (*tserkov Nikolay v Khamovnikakh*)
appear even more striking by contrast. A fine example of the colourful parish churches of the mid-seventeenth century, its long refectory and elaborate tent-roofed belltower are painted a snowy white,
while all the *nalichniki*, gables, drums, pendentives and columns
are outlined in dark green or dayglo-red, like a chromatic negative
of a Russian church in winter. The exterior is rounded off with
wrought-iron porches and strategically placed images of St Nicholas
the Wonderworker. A protector of those in peril (and the saint from

whom Father Christmas originated), St Nicholas is regarded in Russia as the patron of weavers, farmers and sailors. His name day (December 19) and the day on which his relics were removed to Bari in Italy (May 22) are both celebrated here.

The church was founded by a weavers' (*khamovniki*) settlement that was established in the 1620s. One of many settlements (*slobody*) in Moscow based on crafts guilds, it forbade non-weavers from living there and marriages outside the community, whose prized looms occupied the **Palace of Weavers**, up a side road from the church. This whitewashed brick edifice with a wooden roof counted as a palatial workplace by the standards of seventeenth-century Moscow. On the way, you'll pass two **wooden houses** from the last century, when such dwellings were still the norm in Moscow's suburbs.

## Tolstoy's House

Slightly further north, on the left-hand side of ulitsa Lva Tolstovo, a tall brown fence with a plaque announces **Tolstoy's House** (Tues–Sun 10am–6pm; closed the last Fri of each month). Count Lev Tolstoy purchased the wooden house in October 1882 to placate his wife, Sofia Andreevna, who was tired of provincial life at Yasnaya Polyana and feared that their children's education was suffering. By this time, Tolstoy had already written *War and Peace* and *Anna Karenina*, and seemed bent on renouncing his wealth and adopting the life of a peasant – to the fury of Sofia. The children generally sided with her but felt torn by love for their father, who found it hard to reconcile his own paternal feelings with the dictates of his conscience. To strain family relations further, Tolstoy alternated between anguished celibacy ("I know for certain that copulation is an abomination") and boundless lust for his wife, who bore thirteen children (eight of whom lived) and wrote: "I am to gratify his pleasure and nurse his child, I am a piece of household furniture, a *woman*!".

### Around the house

Although this psychodrama was played out over the twenty winters that the Tolstoys lived in Khamovniki, the house-museum enshrines the notion of one big happy family. Its cheery ground-floor **dining room** has a table laid with English china, oilcloth wallpaper and a painting of their daughter Maria by her sister, Tatyana. Tatyana's own portrait (by Repin) hangs in the **corner room** that belonged to the older sons, Sergei, Ilya and Lev, where Tolstoy once wept with relief upon learning that Ilya was still a virgin at the age of twenty.

The **Tolstoys' bedroom** doubled as Sofia's salon and study, with a sofa for guests and a mahogany bureau where she made fair copies of his draft manuscripts; their walnut bed is hidden behind a screen. Down the corridor, their youngest, Vanichka, slept in a truckle-bed with his rocking horse at hand, within earshot of his foreign governess and the scullery where the maids took tea. While Andrei and Mikhail leave little impression, **Tatyana's room** bespeaks a bright, artistic young woman who often chafed at Tolstoy's strictures. Hung with her paintings and sketches, it contains a table covered with black cloth that she got family and friends to sign, and embroidered their signatures in coloured thread. Everyone drank tea constantly, so the **buffet's** *samovar* was rarely cold.

**Upstairs** in the **salon** Scriabin, Rachmaninov and Rimsky-Korsakov played on the piano and Tolstoy read his latest works to Chekhov and Gorky (an early recording can be heard). The carpeted **drawing room** full of knick-knacks was favoured by Sofia Andreevna, who read Tolstoy's proofs by the window; her portrait (by Serov) hangs on the opposite wall. Conversely, **Maria's room** is low and spartan, in keeping with her Tolstoyan ideals; she taught at the Yasnaya Polyana peasants' school every summer. Further down the passage are the tiny housekeeper's room (she was with them for thirty years), and the room of Tolstoy's valet, who cared devotedly for his ailing master but avoided other work as demeaning.

**Tolstoy's study** with its heavy desk and dark leather furniture fits his gloomy literary output in the 1880s. Here he penned *The Death of Ivan Ilyich* and *The Power of Darkness*; the moral treatises *On Life* and *What Then Are We to Do?*; and began his famous polemic against sex and marriage, *The Kreutzer Sonata* (which Sofia read aloud to the family without a blush). Next door is a small room devoted to Tolstoy's enthusiasms: weightlifting, bootmaking and bicycling (which he took up at the age of 67). Tolstoy usually reached his study by the back stairs near the pickling-room. Sadly, the house's large back **garden** is only accessible to groups; off to one side of the former yard are the **stables**.

At the far end of the street lies a triangular wooded park known as the **Maidens' Field** (*Skver Devichovo pole*), where teenage girls were once left as tribute to the Tatars. Nearby, Tolstoy set the scene in *War and Peace* where Pierre Bezhukov witnesses the execution of prisoners by the French. A seated **statue of Tolstoy** broods beside the entrance to the park.

## Novodevichiy Convent

Where the Moskva River begins its loop around the marshy tongue of Luzhniki, a cluster of shining domes above a fortified rampart proclaims the presence of the **Novodevichiy Convent** (*Novodevichiy monastyr*) – one of the loveliest monasteries in Moscow, and a perennial favourite with tour groups. Though purists might prefer the Donskoy Monastery for its tourist-free ambience, Novodevichiy is undeniably richer in historical associations and a more coherent architectural ensemble, with the added attraction of being right next to Moscow's most venerable cemetery.

The Novodevichiy or New Maidens' Convent was founded in 1524 to commemorate Vasily III's capture of Smolensk from the Poles a decade earlier. It had many highborn nuns and often played a role in politics – one of its own nuns prevented the convent from being blown up by the French in 1812, by snuffing out the fuses. Here, Irina Godunova retired after the death of her imbecilic husband, Fyodor I, and her brother Boris Godunov was proclaimed Tsar. Ravaged during the Time of Troubles, the convent was rebuilt in the 1680s by the Regent Sofia, who was later confined here by Peter the Great, along with his unwanted first wife. Bequests made Novodevichiy a major landowner with fifteen thousand serfs, but after the Revolution its churches were shut and the convent was turned into a museum, which spared it from a worse fate until the cathedral was returned to the Church in 1945 as a reward for supporting the war effort, and an episcopal see was established in

Khamovniki
and
Luzhniki

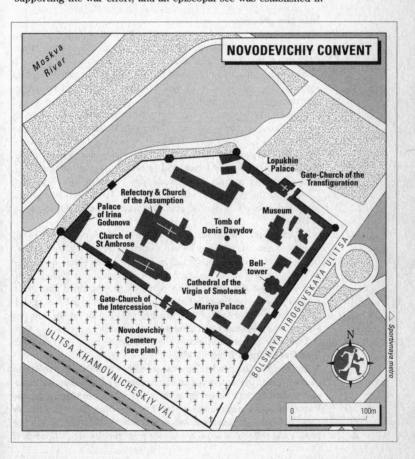

1988. Though once again a convent, its nuns keep a low profile and bus-loads of tourists continue to arrive, especially on Sundays.

## Practicalities

**Getting there** entails riding the metro out to Sportivnaya, taking the ulitsa 10-ya Letiya Oktyabrya exit and turning right outside; a ten-minute walk past the *Arena Hotel* to the end of the road brings you within sight of the convent's towers and ramparts. As a place where people come to worship, Novodevichiy is usually **open** every day from 8am to 7pm. While tour groups are liable to be charged the equivalent of $2 a head, individual visitors don't require **tickets** to look around, except to enter the museum (which isn't the main attraction). Aside from Easter, the convent is busiest on the **feast days** of the icons of the Virgin of Smolensk (August 10) and the Tikhvin Virgin (July 9).

## Into the grounds

Surrounded by a massive brick wall with swallow-tailed crenellations and twelve bastions, the convent is entered via the **Gate-Church of the Transfiguration** (*Preobrazhenskaya tserkov*), a Moscow Baroque tower crowned by five gilded coronet-domes. Its shell-scallop gables and carved pilasters are of white stone, contrasting with the russet-hued stucco – a colour scheme repeated throughout the convent, enhanced by green roofs and gilded domes and softened by trees and ivy. The Gate-Church was built at the behest of the Regent Sofia in 1687–89, as was the **Lopukhin Palace** (*Lopukhinskiy korpus*) just inside the entrance, which now houses the Metropolitan of Moscow and sports a painted sundial. The palace's name recalls the involuntary sojourn of Yevdokiya Lopukhina, the pious first wife of Peter the Great, who was forced to enter a convent in Suzdal, and later transferred to Novodevichiy (1727–31).

Further into the grounds, a **museum** (Wed–Mon 10am–6pm) of icons and manuscripts may be supplemented by exhibitions in other outbuildings. If not, feast your eyes on the 72-metre-high **belltower** (*Kokolnya*), whose six decorative tiers culminate in a gilded onion dome on a slender drum, all so perfectly proportioned that many reckon it to be the finest belltower in Moscow. Unusually, it is situated near the east wall of the convent, rather than on the western side, as was customary with Russian monasteries.

## The Cathedral of the Virgin

At the heart of the convent stands the white **Cathedral of the Virgin of Smolensk** (*sobor Smolenskoy Bogomateri*), whose tall *zako-mary* gables and apses give it a strong resemblance to the Cathedral of the Assumption in the Kremlin, built fifty years earlier though Smolensk Cathedral was constructed (1524–25) in half the time. Its architects borrowed a device from the Kremlin's Church of the Deposition of the Robe, by sitting the cathedral on top of a high *podklet* or undercroft, to enhance its majesty. But what really makes it are the massed onion domes, added in the seventeenth century: the central one gilded and the others green with gold frills, supporting tall crosses that glitter in the sunlight.

The interior is often closed, but worth seeing if you get the chance. Its **frescoes** weren't painted until 1684 (reflecting the troubled century after the completion of the cathedral), executed in only three months by a team of 35 painters under Dmitry Grigorev of Yaroslavl. The enormous five-tiered **iconostasis** also dates from Petrine times, but was salvaged from the Church of the Assumption in Pokrovka, demolished in the Soviet era. Flowers and ribbons garland the icons of the Smolensk and Tikhvin Virgins on feast days. Notice the large copper font and wooden ciborium, dating from the latter half of the seventeenth century. Regent Sofia and the two other sisters of Peter the Great are buried in the (inaccessible) vaults underfoot.

Graves and monuments cluster around the cathedral. To the left, a bronze mustachioed bust marks the **tomb of Denis Davydov**, a poet and Hussar who was slain battling the French in 1812, immortalized in verse by his friend Pushkin, and now lends his name to a society that re-enacts the Battle of Borodino. Nearby you'll see a weird Pseudo-Russian **mausoleum** whose stone base, carved with birds and flowers, rises in tiers of gilded wings.

## Other sights within the grounds

The single-domed **Church of the Assumption** (*Uspenskaya tserkov*) and its adjacent **Refectory** were constructed at Sofia's behest in the 1680s. Access to the church is by the far stairway; between services (8am & 5pm) you can only peer through the doors at its rows of vaulted windows interspersed by icons, and the gilded iconostasis fronted by tall candle-holders. Lurking in a dell around the back is the lower, all-white **Church of St Ambrose**, which has yet to be reopened.

Further west you'll see the modest two-storey **Palace of Irina Godunova**, where the widow of the last of the Rurik monarchs retired in 1598. State business continued to be transacted in her monastic name of Alexandra until Patriarch Job and the clergy came *en masse* to the convent, to implore her brother, Boris Godunov, to assume the vacant throne – a show of popular support that he had orchestrated himself.

The southern wall of the convent is breached by the triple-domed **Gate-Church of the Intercession** (*Pokrovskaya tserkov*), whose red-and-white facade surmounts a gateway wide enough to drive a hearse into the adjacent Novodevichiy Cemetery. Alongside stands the three-storey **Mariya Palace** (*Mariinskiy korpus*) where Peter the Great confined his half-sister, Sofia, after deposing her as Regent (see box). Sofia was allowed no visitors except her aunts

**The Regent Sofia**

Tsarevna Sofia (1657–1704) was remarkable for ruling Russia at a time when noblewomen were restricted to the stultifying world of the *terem*. As a child, she persuaded her father, Tsar Alexei, to let her share lessons with her brother, the future Fyodor III, and from the age of nineteen attended the *boyars'* council. After Fyodor's death she feared being relegated by the Naryshkin relatives of the new heir, Peter, and manipulated the *Streltsy* revolt of 1682 in order to get another sibling, Ivan, recognized as co-Tsar, and make herself **Regent**. As Ivan was half-witted and Peter only ten years old, she prompted them by whispering from a grille behind their specially made double throne, and privately received ambassadors in person, seated on the Diamond Throne. The diplomat De Neuville noted that "though she has never read Machiavelli, nor learned anything about him, all his maxims come naturally to her".

Nonetheless, Sofia's regency was inevitably threatened as Peter came of age. In August 1689, rumours that she was about to depose him and crown herself Empress impelled the 17-year-old Tsar to flee to a monastery outside Moscow and rally supporters. By October, Sofia's allies had deserted her and she was ceremonially escorted to the convent. When the *Streltsy* rebelled again, nine years later, Peter was sure of her involvement but refrained from executing her through admiration, confessing: "What a pity that she persecuted me in my minority, and that I cannot repose any confidence in her, otherwise, when I am employed abroad, she might govern at home." She died of natural causes as the nun Susanna.

and sisters, but wasn't obliged to forego any comforts until after the *Streltsy* revolt of 1698, when she was forced to take religious vows, making her "dead" to the world. More brutally, 195 rebels were hanged in full view of the palace, while three ringleaders who had petitioned Sofia to join them were strung up just outside her window and left hanging all winter.

## Novodevichiy Cemetery

Beyond the convent's south wall lies the fascinating **Novodevichiy Cemetery** (*Novodovicheskoe kladbische*; Wed–Sun 10am–6pm), where many famous writers, artists and politicians are buried. During Soviet times, only burial in the Kremlin Wall was more prestigious. During the Brezhnev era, the disgraced former leader, Khrushchev, was buried here, after which the cemetery was closed to prevent any demonstrations at his grave. Now that visiting restrictions have been lifted, Russians of all ages come to gravespot, laying flowers on the tombs of some, tutting or cursing over others.

Admission **tickets** are sold from a kiosk across the road from the main gate, 100m south of the convent. Once inside the cemetery, try to make sense of its division into three main sections, each composed of several large plots with at least a dozen double rows of graves. Though some of the tombs can be hard to find, you're sure

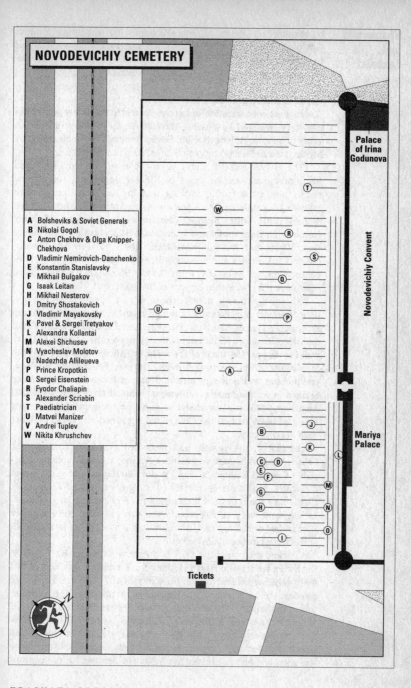

# NOVODEVICHIY CEMETERY

A   Bolsheviks & Soviet Generals
B   Nikolai Gogol
C   Anton Chekhov & Olga Knipper-Chekhova
D   Vladimir Nemirovich-Danchenko
E   Konstantin Stanislavsky
F   Mikhail Bulgakov
G   Isaak Leitan
H   Mikhail Nesterov
I   Dmitry Shostakovich
J   Vladimir Mayakovsky
K   Pavel & Sergei Tretyakov
L   Alexandra Kollantai
M   Alexei Shchusev
N   Vyacheslav Molotov
O   Nadezhda Allileueva
P   Prince Kropotkin
Q   Sergei Eisenstein
R   Fyodor Chaliapin
S   Alexander Scriabin
T   Paediatrician
U   Matvei Manizer
V   Andrei Tuplev
W   Nikita Khrushchev

Palace
of Irina
Godunova

Novodevichiy Convent

Mariya
Palace

**Tickets**

to stumble on plenty of interest simply by wandering around. Obviously, this isn't so easy in winter, when snow covers many of the graves and you can only endure the cold for so long – but the cemetery looks even more romantic than usual.

## Some notable graves

The highest concentration of famous dead is in the oldest part of the cemetery, reached by passing through a gap in the wall near an array of veteran **Bolsheviks** and **Soviet generals** commemorated by lifesize statues flourishing pistols or talking into telephones.

The artistic roll-call starts in plot 2 with a tragedy, for when historians examined the grave of **Nikolai Gogol** they found claw marks inside the coffin, proving that he had been buried alive following a cataleptic fit. A few rows on, **Anton Chekhov** and his actress wife **Olga Knipper-Chekhova** lie near to **Vladimir Nemirovich-Danchenko** and **Konstantin Stanislavsky**, a proximity that reflects their fruitful collaboration at the Moscow Arts Theatre (see p.110). Posies and messages litter the grave of the twentieth-century **Mikhail Bulgakov**, while **Dmitry Shostakovich** reaps more restrained tributes within earshot of the main road.

An equally diverse bunch repose in plot 1, where the Futurist poet **Vladimir Mayakovsky** is buried a few rows from the philanthropist **Tretyakov brothers**, Pavel and Sergei, while the Bolshevik feminist **Alexandra Kollantai** is interred nearer the convent wall. By walking on past the tomb of the architect **Alexei Shchusev** and the family plot of the wartime Foreign Minister **Vyacheslav Molotov**, you'll come to a poignant bust and pair of hands commemorating Stalin's wife, **Nadezhda Allileueva**, who shot herself in 1932. Amazingly, Molotov continued to serve Stalin even after his own wife had been sent to the Gulag, and remained an ardent Stalinist until his dying day.

In plot 4, the austere and neglected grave of the Anarchist **Prince Kropotkin** contrasts with the flamboyant, well-tended memorials to **Sergei Eisenstein** and **Fyodor Chaliapin**. The great movie director's headstone is carved to suggest a roll of film, while Chaliapin's tomb bears a lifesize statue reclining in a languid pose. In the same neck of the woods you can also find the composer **Alexander Scriabin**, and an amusing statue of a **pediatrician** smacking a newborn baby's bottom.

Tucked away near the back is the grave of **Nikita Khrushchev**, the Soviet leader who risked de-Stalinization and reform, was ousted by his colleagues and died in obscurity in 1971. (*Pravda* reported the death of "pensioner N.S. Khrushchev" in one line, 36 hours after the news broke.) The striking headstone was designed by Ernst Neizvestniy, whom Khrushchev had once lambasted, but posthumously requested to create his memorial – a bronze cannon-ball headlocked between jagged white and black monoliths, symbolizing the good and bad in Khrushchev's life. On October 14, the anniversary of his fall from power, men and women who were freed from the Gulag by his decree of 1955 come to pay tribute.

## Luzhniki Sports Complex

The busy Khamovnicheskiy val and an elevated railroad separate the cemetery from the 180-hectare **Luzhniki Sports Complex**, laid out in the 1950s and modernized for the Olympics. Its parking lot has since provided a setting for the funeral service of Andrei Sakharov – which drew fifty thousand mourners – and rallies by hardline Communists who take comfort from the statue of Lenin outside the stadium that still bears his name. En route there or back, you can visit a small **Metro Museum** (Wed–Sun 10am–6pm) attached to the southern exit of Sportivnaya metro station. Its photos and models give a good idea of the metro's development, despite a one-sided focus on the Komsomol volunteers who helped build the first lines – omitting any mention of the slave-labourers who toiled alongside.

The **Lenin Central Stadium** has seating for 103,000 spectators and all kinds of training facilities, but is nowadays better known for hosting pop concerts and one of Moscow's biggest markets. This **flea market** (Wed–Sun 6am–4pm) deals in goods imported by the Trans-Siberian Express rather than second-hand items. If you can't be bothered to queue up for an admission ticket at the box office, they can be purchased from touts at double the cost. Prices for everything are lowest before 9am, and haggling is the norm.

To the east of the stadium are the 13,000-seater **Palace of Sport** and a dull **Museum of Physical Culture and Sport** (Wed–Sun 10am–6pm). On the far side of Komsomolskiy prospekt can be seen one of the most successful buildings constructed for the Olympics, the multi-purpose **Friendship Sporting Hall** that Muscovites nicknamed the "Golden Tortoise" – though its gold-coloured epoxy roofing actually looks more like a giant sunflower that has wilted over the complex. From here you can see the enclosed bridge that carries the metro **across the river** towards the Sparrow Hills and Moscow University. Since the closure of Leninskie Gory station (which has exits on both sides of the river), the only feasible approach is to ride on to the next stop, Universitet.

# The Sparrow Hills

A wooded ridge overlooking the city, the ex-Lenin Hills (*Leninskie gory*) have now reverted to their Tsarist-era name, the **Sparrow Hills** (*Vorobyovie gory*), but still look quintessentially Soviet. The main reason is the Moscow State University, whose stupendous Stalin-Gothic skyscraper dominates the plateau, its formal gardens extending to the granite esplanade where newlyweds used to come to be photographed in Soviet times. Besides the university, the attraction is quite simply the **panoramic view of Moscow**, with

Luzhniki stadium and the Novodevichiy Convent (left) in the foreground, the White House and the Kremlin in the middle distance, and six Stalin skyscrapers ranged across the city. More dubiously, there are also many souvenir vendors and two perilous **ski jumps** reached by rickety stairways, plus a small, early nineteenth-century **Trinity Church**, just downhill on the left.

The most direct way of **getting there** is to travel to Universitet metro and exit near the back of the train; you'll see the University tower above the trees to the left, and the silvery dome of the New Circus off to the right. A less direct approach is to take the orange metro line to Leninskiy Prospekt station, and then a trolleybus #7 from ploshchad Gagarina out along ulitsa Kosygina, past Gorbachev's residence and the Pioneers' Palace.

## MGU

**Moscow State University** – known by its initials as **MGU** (pronounced "em-gay-oo") – occupies the largest of the city's skyscrapers. When the Supreme Soviet decreed in 1947 that Moscow's skyline should be embellished by eight such buildings (of which seven were raised), grouped around the colossal (but never built) Palace of Soviets, it affirmed faith in the Communist future at the cost of the more pressing tasks of post-war reconstruction. Sixty trains were required to transport the building's steel frame from Dneiprpetrovsk, and thousands of free and slave-workers toiled night and day from 1949 to 1953 – a construction period that almost matched the duration of the whole skyscraper programme, overseen by Beria from the half-built main hall of MGU. One wonders if he ever knew that Ivan the Terrible had forbade building on the site, deeming it "too windy".

The MGU **building** consists of a 36-storey teaching block flanked by four huge wings of student accommodation, said to have 33km of corridors. Wheatsheaf pinnacles cap the side towers, which bear giant clocks and temperature/humidity indicators, while the central tower is festooned with swags and statues, carved with the Soviet crest, and surmounted by a gilded **spire** that looks small and light but is actually 240m tall with a star that weighs twelve tons. The most impressive facade faces northeast towards the city, across a terrace with heroic statues of a male and female student gazing raptly not at each other, nor at the books in their laps, but apparently into the future.

Try to plead or bluff your way past the guard outside its massive columned portico, to see the green marbled, colonnaded **foyers** lined with medallions of world famous scientists, culminating in bronze figures of illustrious Soviet ones. On the wall is a quote from the plantbreeder Ivan Michurin: "We cannot await charity from Nature. To take it from Nature is our task." As yet, there is no statue of Mikhail Gorbachev, who graduated from MGU with a law degree in 1955.

MGU's thirty thousand-plus residents include many "illegals" who lack a Moscow *propiska* (residency permit), and African and Asian students who stand out more for robbers. In an attempt to control the situation, anyone entering or leaving the building is obliged to produce a pass. Yet the crumbling dormitories and class-rooms rented out to shady businesses point to a deeper crisis, reflected in the low morale all round. While students struggle to survive on grants of $8 a month, academics try to salvage what they can of departments that once enjoyed lavish funding, unrivalled prestige in their own country and a high regard abroad.

## Other sights

Ranged along prospekt Vernadskovo as it runs past the grounds of MGU are three buildings devoted to the amusement and education of children. If you have kids, a performance at the New Circus or the Children's Music Theatre could be just the ticket; see p.321 for details.

The New Circus is visible from Sportivnaya metro, but rates a closer look for its silvery, wavy-edged cupola, resembling a giant jelly-mould. The glass curtain walls allow a glimpse of the ring, which has four interchangeable floors that can be switched in five minutes (including a pool for aquatic events and a rink for ice shows), with seating for 3400 spectators. Its opening in 1971 coincided with the closure (for refurbishment) of the original Moscow State Circus on Tsvetnoy bulvar.

Further up the prospekt stands the Children's Musical Theatre created by Natalya Sats, who founded Moscow's Central Children's Theatre as a teenager, inspired Prokofiev to write *Peter and the Wolf* in 1936, and spent sixteen years in the Gulag after the execution of her husband, Marshal Tukhachevskiy. Initially set up in a tiny hall in 1965, the company now enjoys a purpose-built theatre with a giant filigree birdcage and a *Palekh Room* painted with fairytale scenes, where actors costumed as animals mingle with the children before each performance.

From here, trolleybus #28 trundles up the prospekt to the Pioneers' Palace on the corner of ulitsa Kosygina. Recognizable by its tall flagstaff, the complex's main block bears a mosaic of Pioneers blowing bugles and pursuing hobbies under the benign gaze of Lenin, as befits the variety of studios and workshops within – and the Lenin Hall, where children used to be sworn into the Young Pioneers. Founded in 1922 to socialize 9 to 14 year-olds, the organization eventually had over 25 million members; its watchword was *If the Party says jump, we ask: How high?*. Though few Russians mourn its demise on ideological grounds, its provision of cheap facilities is sorely missed; the Palace now charges premium rates.

Should you opt to reach MGU by trolleybus #7 from ploshchad Gagarina, this will take you past ulitsa Kosygina 10, a guarded yellow building that has been Gorbachev's residence in Moscow

since 1984. In the days when he was Party leader, the rumour was
that the house had five sublevels and was connected to the Kremlin
by an underground railway. Secret tunnels often feature in the
mythology of Russia's leaders. Ivan the Terrible supposedly had one
from the Kremlin to his palace 100 miles from Moscow, while the
Mayor of St Petersburg is said to *fly* to the capital through a tunnel
that's 400 miles long and hundreds of metres wide.

# Chapter 7

# Zamoskvareche and the south

Z AMOSKVARECHE AND THE SOUTH are clearly defined by geography and history. The Zamoskvareche district dates back to medieval times and preserves a host of colourful churches and the mansions of civic-minded merchants. The same merchants founded the **Tretyakov Gallery**, Moscow's pre-eminent gallery for Russian art, with a superlative collection of medieval icons. In pre-Petrine times, Moscow ended at its earthern ramparts (now the Krymskiy and Vatsepskiy val), beyond which the fortified **Donskoy and Danilov monasteries** overlooked fields and orchards.

By the mid-eighteenth century, Moscow had expanded as far as the Kamerkollezhskiy boundary, drawn by the Tsar's taxmen; over the next century, slums and factories surrounded what had been suburban estates. In the Soviet era, these were collectivized into **Gorky Park**, vast new thoroughfares were laid out, and the city spread out past the magical summer retreats of **Kolomenskoe** and **Tsaritysno**, to what is now the Moscow Ring Road.

## Zamoskvareche

**Zamoskvareche** simply means "Across the Moskva River", a blunt designation in keeping with the character of its original inhabitants. As the part of Moscow most exposed to Tatar raids, it was once guarded by twenty companies of *Streltsy*, settled here with their families, and separated from the other, civilian settlements by meadows and swamps. In the long term, these communities of skilled artisans and shrewd merchants did more for Zamoskvareche than the riotous *Streltsy*. The artisans erected the parish churches that are still its glory, while the merchants' lifestyle provided inspiration for the playwright Ostrovskiy and the artist Tropinin in the nineteenth century. By the 1900s, Zamoskvareche had become a major industrial district, with a fifth of Moscow's factories and a third of

ZAMOSKVARECHE
AND THE SOUTH

see Zamoskvareche
map for detail

Moskva River

Lenin Funerary Train

Southern
River Terminal

PROSPEKT ANDROPOVA

M TAGANSKAYA

M PROLETARSKAYA

Theatre
Museum

Pavelets
Station

M

PAVELETSKAYA

Danilov
Monastery

M

M TRETYAKOVSKAYA

Tretyakov
Gallery

NOVOKUZNETSKAYA

M

SERPUKHOVSKAYA

TULSKAYA

M

Danilov Cemetery

Danilov
Market

POLYANKA M

Church of St John
the Warrior

French Embassy

VALOVAYA ULITSA

DOBRYNINSKAYA

OKTYABRSKAYA

M

Donskoy
Monastery

Central House
of Artists

Gorky
Park

LENINSKY PROSPEKT

Patrice Lumumba
Friendship of
Peoples' University

Muslim Cemetery

AKADEMICHESKAYA

Academy
of Sciences

M

LENINSKY
PROSPEKT

Gagarin
Monument

PARK KULTURY M

NINSKIY PROSPEKT

▽ Moscow State University

Domodedovo airport & Leninskie Gorki ▷

Moskva River

Kolomenskoe
Estate

Tsaritsyno
Estate

KASHIRSKOE SHOSSE

PROSPEKT ANDROPOVA

KANTERMIROVSKAYA

Ⓜ KOLOMENSKAYA

Ⓜ OREKHOVO

Ⓜ DOMODEDOVSKAYA

Ⓜ TSARITSYNO

Ⓜ KASHIRSKAYA

VARSHAVSKAYA

Ⓜ NAGATINSKAYA

KASHIRSKOE SHOSSE

Ⓜ NAGORNAYA

Ⓜ VARSHAVSKAYA

VARSHAVSKOE SHOSSE

Ⓜ YUZHNAYA

Ⓜ PRAZHSKAYA

MOSCOW RING ROAD

Ⓜ NAKHIMOVSKIY PROSPEKT

NAKHIMOVSKIY PROSPEKT

KAKHOVSKAYA

Ⓜ SEVASTOPOLSKAYA

Ⓜ CHERTANOVSKAYA

BALAKISKIY PROSPEKT

UTSA

Ⓜ PROFSOYUZNAYA

Ⓜ NOVYE
CHEREMUSHKI

Ⓜ KALUZHSKAYA

PROFSOYUZNAYA

MOSCOW RING ROAD

N

0          2km

its workers. Today, it is still defined by three long, narrow thoroughfares, lined with modest stuccoed houses and grand churches.

## The island

Directly across the river from the Kremlin is an oddly nameless
island that came into being with the digging of the 4km-long
Drainage Canal in the 1780s; hitherto, it had formed part of
Zamoskvareche and been the Tsar's market garden. Stroll across the
Bolshoy Kamenniy most (Great Stone Bridge) and along the Sofia
Embankment for a glorious view of the Kremlin, with its yellow
palaces and thirty golden domes arrayed above the red battlements.

The embankment itself features an old foundry with statues of
workers above its gates, almost next door to the **British Embassy** at
Sofiyskaya naberezhnaya 14. British diplomats have long enjoyed
the best embassy in Moscow: a Neo-Gothic mansion designed by
Shekhtel for the Kharitonenko family, which they got for a song in
the 1920s. Though Stalin once attended a banquet there hosted by
Churchill, he was always irked that he could see the British flag
from his Kremlin office.

To the west of the Bolshoy Kamenniy bridge rises a vast grey
apartment block built (1928–31) for the Soviet elite and nicknamed
the **Government House** (*dom Praiteltsva*). Its front wall bears
plaques commemorating former residents such as Marshal
Tukhachevskiy, Nikolai Bukharin, the MiG aircraft designer Artyom
Mikoyan and the Comintern leader Georgi Dimitrov – half of whom
perished in Stalin's purges.

Behind the block lurks a rare example of a Muscovite town-
estate of the mid-seventeenth century. The owner, Averky Krillov,
was a member of Tsar Alexei's council and supervisor of his market
gardens. The nearby **Church of St Nicholas** was once his private
chapel, and, like his adjacent mansion, its exterior is festive with
coloured tiles and stone carvings. Both were built in the 1650s, but
the house was altered the following century by the addition of an
elaborate Dutch gable on the river-facing side, though the other side
retains a typically seventeenth-century Muscovite porch with fat-
bellied columns.

## Ulitsa Bolshaya Ordynka

Ulitsa Bolshaya Ordynka gets its name from the Mongol–Tatar
Golden Horde (*Zolotaya Orda*), the name of their kingdom on the
lower Volga. The Horde's ambassadors to the Kremlin lived near the
road that led to their homeland, which came to be called Ordynka
(pronounced "Ardynka"). This lies off to the left as you surface from
Tretyakovskaya metro, where orientation is facilitated by two
unmissable landmarks: the gilt-topped Church of the Consolation of
All Sorrows, to the north, and the maroon Church of St Clement,
east towards Pyatnitskaya ulitsa.

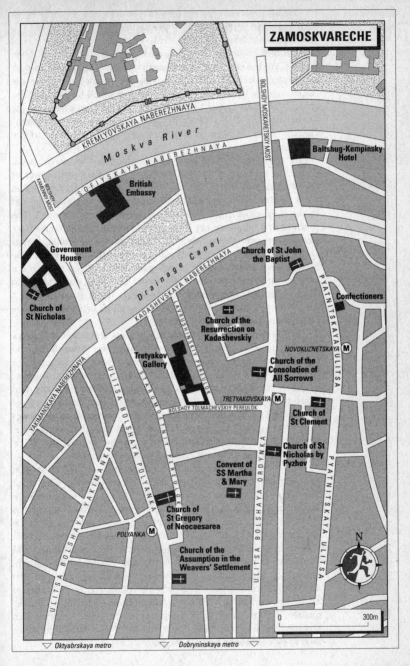

ZAMOSKVARECHE

Baltshug-Kempinsky Hotel

British Embassy

Church of St John the Baptist

Confectioners

Government House

Drainage Canal

Church of St Nicholas

Church of the Resurrection on Kadashevskiy

Tretyakov Gallery

Church of the Consolation of All Sorrows

NOVOKUZNETSKAYA Ⓜ

TRETYAKOVSKAYA Ⓜ

Church of St Clement

Church of St Nicholas by Pyzhov

Convent of SS Martha & Mary

Church of St Gregory of Neocaesarea

POLYANKA Ⓜ

Church of the Assumption in the Weavers' Settlement

N

0        300m

Moskva River

KREMLYOVSKAYA NABEREZHNAYA

SOFIYSKAYA NABEREZHNAYA

BOLSHOY MOSKARETSKIY MOST

BOLSHOY KAMENNY MOST

KADASHEVSKAYA NABEREZHNAYA

LAVRUSHINSKIY PEREULOK

STAROMONETNIY PEREULOK

BOLSHOY TOLMACHEVSKIY PEREULOK

YAKIMANSKAYA NABEREZHNAYA

ULITSA BOLSHAYA POLYANKA

ULITSA BOLSHAYA YAKIMANKA

ULITSA BOLSHAYA ORDYNKA

PYATNITSKAYA ULITSA

PYATNITSKAYA ULITSA

▽ Oktyabrskaya metro        ▽ Dobryninskaya metro ▽

ZAMOSKVARECHE AND THE SOUTH

Consider heading south first to the all-white **Church of St Nicholas by Pyzhov** (*Sv. Nikolay shto v Pyzhakh*), a seventeenth-century building that exemplifies the traditional Russian abhorrence of empty spaces, seething with ogees, blind arcades, fretted cornices, and a massive pendant drooping from its tent-roofed porch. The tiny crowns on top of the crosses on the domes indicate that it was built with funds donated by *Streltsy*. The church itself was looted by the French in 1812 and closed by the Communists in 1934, when its bell was given to the Bolshoy Theatre. After decades as a laboratory, it was returned to the Orthodox Church in 1991.

By crossing the road and walking 150m further south, you'll find a low archway at no. 36, leading to the secluded **Convent of SS. Martha and Mary** (*Marfo–Mariinskaya Obitel*), founded in 1908 by Grand Duchess Elizabeth Fyodorovna, who was captured by the Bolsheviks in 1917 and thrown alive down a mineshaft. The Convent was suppressed in 1926 and revived in 1993; its nuns have since taken over the running of a hospital whose shabby wings enclose the yard. Its pretty Pseudo-Russian **Church of the Intercession** is carved with Slavonic runes and mythical creatures, a curious early work by Alexei Shchusev, who later built the Lenin Mausoleum and much else for the Soviets. While you can view it from behind a fence, admission is restricted to believers, who are vetted at the lodge inside the archway.

Alternatively, head north along Ordynka towards the Moskva River, where a yellow belltower heralds the **Church of the Consolation of All Sorrows** (*tserkov Vsekh Skoryashchikh Radosti*). This embodies the skills of two leading architects working in different styles: Bazhenov's Classical porticoed refectory and pilastered belltower of the 1780s; and Bove's lusher Russian Empire-style rotunda (1828–33). The narthex contains more oil paintings than frescoes, while a ring of thick Ionic columns defines the pale-blue, white and gold sanctuary, partly obscuring its iconostasis. The feast day of the Madonna of Tenderness is on November 6.

Some 300m further north, an alley on the left called 2-ya Kadashevskiy pereulok leads to the awesome, derelict **Church of the Resurrection on Kadashevskiy** (*tserkov Voskresenie v Kadashakh*). Built in 1687, in the Naryshkin Baroque style, it is rich in limestone ornamentation, with a fancy parapet instead of the usual pyramid of *kokoshniki*, while the belltower, added in 1695, rises from a ponderous base through delicate tiers emblazoned with flame-shaped mouldings. Although its name alludes to the Kadeshi quarter of barrel-makers that existed here in the fifteenth and sixteenth centuries, the church's construction was actually funded by factory workers in what had by then become a textile-producing quarter. True to its industrial pedigree, the church now serves as a restorers' workshop within the grounds of the *MEKZ* furniture factory (accessible by holes in the fence).

# Pyatnitskaya ulitsa

Zamoskvareche's busiest thoroughfare and traditional marketplace, Pyatnitskaya ulitsa remains the heart of the neighbourhood, flushed with kiosks and shops in the vicinity of **Novokuznetskaya metro** – a palatial 1950s station smothered in bas-reliefs and murals of military heroes.

If you don't start there, the best approach is via the **Church of St Clement** (*tserkov Klimenta*), near Tretyakovskaya metro. This hulking edifice was Moscow's last great monument of Baroque relig-ious architecture, built sometime between 1740 and 1770. Corinthian pilasters and seraphim-topped windows rise from a lower level clad in fretted stucco to a parapet with flame-patterned rail-ings. Its five black domes rest on massive dark red drums of equal height; the four corner ones are spangled with gold stars. Unfortunately the church is locked and derelict, so there's no need to linger.

Up the road past Novokuznetskaya metro, keep an eye out for the **confectioners** (*Konditerskiy*) at no. 9, on the right. Its interior dates from the early 1900s and remains intact: pale blue and laven-der stucco overlaid by swags and urns, walnut counters with brass fittings, and faceted lights that wouldn't look amiss in a disco. From here you can see the urn-festooned green and white belltower of the **Church of St John the Baptist** (*tserkov Ioanna Predtechi*), on the corner of Chernigovskiy pereulok to the left. While this was raised in 1758, the church's belfry further along is exactly a century older, and less ambitious: a red and white refectory allied to a small sanc-tuary with intricate *nalichniki*. St John "the Forerunner" (as Russians call him) is honoured by two feast days, on August 7 and September 11.

## Ulitsa Bolshaya Polyanka

Though quite close to the Ordynka, ulitsa **Bolshaya Polyanka** is surprisingly awkward to actually get into. You must either venture into the intervening maze of cul-de-sacs, or change lines twice in order to get there by metro from Tretyakovskaya or Novokuznetskaya.

Emerging from Polyanka station, you can't miss the silvery domes of the **Church of St Gregory of Neocaesarea** (*tserkov Grigoriya Neokesariiskovo*), built in 1667–69 by Peter the Great's father, Alexei. This lovely church is unusual on two counts: the arched porch at the base of its belfry straddles the pavement out to the kerb, while the main building is girdled by a broad frieze of dark blue, turquoise, brown and yellow tiles, whose floral motifs so resemble plumage that Muscovites dubbed the church "the Peacock's Eye". Even without the tiles, its facade would be colourful enough: the ribbing and *nalichniki* are all painted blue and white. After decades of being occupied by the Soviet Department of Art

Exports – which bought valuable icons cheaply and sold them
abroad for hard currency – St Gregory's is now used by a group of
nuns that helps war refugees (services 9am & 5pm daily.)

# The Tretyakov Gallery

Located in the heart of Zamoskvareche, the **Tretyakov Gallery**
(*Tretyakovskaya galereya*) is to Russian art what the Pushkin
Museum of Fine Arts is to European masterpieces. Founded in 1892
by the financier Pavel Tretyakov – who donated 1200 paintings
collected over 36 years, and his own home for the premises – the
gallery was given a striking Pseudo-Russian facade, designed by the
Slav Romantic artist Viktor Vasnetsov. Having acquired a host of
expropriated icons and paintings after the Revolution, the Tretyakov
went on to purchase Socialist Realist art in Soviet times. By the
1970s, its collection far exceeded its gallery space, which needed
renovation anyway. The solution adopted was to build a new exhibition hall on the Krymskiy val, close the old gallery for renovation,
and erect a modern wing alongside. While the old gallery is still
under scaffolding, its new, French-built wing is up and running,
covering Russian art from medieval times until the Revolution; art
from the Soviet era appears at the new "Tretyakovka" annexe on
Krymskiy val (see p.214).

### Visiting the Tretyakov

The gallery is about five minutes' walk from Tretyakovskaya metro.
**Opening hours** are from Tuesday to Sunday 10am to 8pm, but the
ticket office shuts an hour before the museum. In the first-floor
foyer you'll be asked to shed your coat and get into *tapochki*.
Foreigners pay the ruble equivalent of about $4, card-carrying
students half that.

Guided tours can be arranged by *Intourist* and other agencies,
or you can simply tag along behind a group for a free commentary,
as **labelling** in English is fairly minimal in the icons section and
entirely absent elsewhere. Our **floor plans** should help you identify
what's what in the four rooms that are currently open, but you
should expect a few exhibits to have been moved around, or
replaced. In the Russian fashion, the ground-floor lobby is
numbered as the first floor; the exhibition begins upstairs.

## The second floor: Russian icons

The **second floor** consists of one large room and an antechamber
entirely devoted to **Russian icons**. Icons (from the Greek *eikon*,
"image") came to Russia from Byzantium, like Orthodox
Christianity. Painted on wooden panels varnished with linseed oil
and amber, their patina darkened by candle-smoke, these holy
images were mounted in tiers to form iconostases, and hung in the

*krasniy ugol* ("beautiful corner") of every Russian household. While generally venerated, those that failed to "perform" were sometimes beaten by their irate owners.

Russian icons were valued for their religious and spiritual content rather than artistic merit. One Russian critic argues that their visual flatness reflects a view of each human soul as the centre of the universe, unlike the spatial and moral distancing implied by Renaissance perspective. Anatomical realism was initially taboo as a reminder of mortal imperfections, but gradually became more accepted. Though distinguishing one school from another and deciphering their arcane language of gesture and colour isn't easy, it's worth remembering that icons weren't just venerated as holy, but (like church frescoes) constituted almost the only form of pictorial art in Russia for 600 years, other kinds being condemned by the Church as vanity.

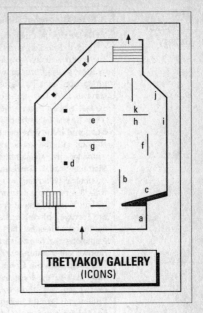

**TRETYAKOV GALLERY**
(ICONS)

## The anteroom

The anteroom focuses on the twelfth and thirteenth centuries and constitutes an introduction to Russian iconography. The Russians inherited from Byzantium two conventions for dealing with the Mother of God: the *Hodegetria*, who sits serenely unrelated to the miniature adult in her lap; and the *Eleousa*, or Madonna of Tenderness, who lovingly embraces the Christ child. Significantly, the Russians have always preferred the latter, and referred to Mary as the Mother of God (*Bogomateri* or *Bogroditsa*), not as the Virgin. This is Mother Russia, after all.

To the right as you enter, enthroned Mothers of God from Tolga and Sven lead you towards the most revered of all icons – the early twelfth-century *Virgin of Vladimir* [a], reputedly painted by St Luke himself. Brought from Constantinople to Kiev, then to Vladimir and in 1395 to the Kremlin's Cathedral of the Assumption, the icon became a symbol of national unity and was credited with saving Moscow from the army of Timerlane. Given to the Tretyakov in 1918, its ownership is now in dispute following Yeltsin's promise to return it to the Church.

Two more **politically significant icons** can be found just inside the main room. An obvious example is the fifteenth-century *Battle between the Men of Novgorod and Suzdal* [b], commemorating the siege of Novgorod (1169–70) and its deliverance by an icon of

> ### A Brief History of Russian Icons
>
> While it's true that much icon-painting was done by monks and priests as
> a spiritual devotion, workshops of decorators who specialized in churches
> and produced icons to order were equally active – if not more so.
>
> Kiev, where Christianity took root in 988, was the main centre of icon
> production until its devastation by the Mongols in 1240. What little
> survives from this era shows a taste for figures in dark, earth colours,
> against a plain backround, often of gold (representing the Holy Ghost).
> After Kiev's fall, other schools began to develop regional identities.
> Novgorod icons were painted in emerald green, vermilion and other bold
> colours, with figures defined by resolute, angular lines, their faces given
> character by highlighting and shading. The "Northern School" of
> Vladimir-Suzdal, Yaroslavl and Pskov combined bright colours and
> rhythmical patterning with simpler forms and more gestural symbolism,
> while Tver icon-painters preferred paler, more delicate hues.
>
> The Moscow school developed in the late fifteenth century after Ivan
> the Terrible ordered artists to reside and work in the Kremlin; only then
> did this style become the most prevalent. However, the Kremlin had been
> employing the finest artists ever since the dawn of the golden age of
> Russian icon-painters such as Rublev and Theophanes, in the 1370s.
>
> Theophanes the Greek made his mark in Novgorod sometime in the
> latter half of the fourteenth century, starting an illustrious career that
> overlapped with those of the earliest known native masters, Andrei
> Rublev and Daniil Cherniy. The torch was carried on by Dionysius, and
> handed down to Simon Ushakov in the seventeenth century, after which it
> spluttered out. So far as is known, there were no women icon-painters
> until the late nineteenth century.

the Virgin of the Sign, which, hit by an enemy arrow, recoiled, so
outraging the Novgorodians that they stormed out of the city and
routed the Suzdalians. Nearby hangs the icon of *St George and the
Dragon* [c] that Ivan III adopted as the coat-of-arms of Muscovy in
the mid-1400s, and which has featured on the city's eschutcheon
ever since.

### The main room

One of many craftsmen and scholars who fled to Russia before the
fall of Constantinople, Theophanes the Greek (c.1340–1405) has
been justly called the "Russian El Greco". Though he is said to have
decorated forty churches before coming to Moscow, all that survive
*in situ* are his murals in the Church of the Transfiguration in
Vladimir, and his icons in the Cathedral of the Annunciation in the
Kremlin. The Tretyakov owns his severe Byzantine *Don Virgin* [d],
and also attributes to Theophanes the early fifteenth-century
*Transfiguration* [e], an extraordinary proto-Cubist icon that shows
Christ atop a pyramid of energy and lesser mortals smitten by its
rays, like something from *Raiders of the Lost Ark*.

Pride of place is given to a series of icons by the monk Andrei
Rublev (c.1370–1430) and his fellow monk Daniil Cherniy, who in

1406–08 painted the iconostasis of Vladimir's Cathedral of the Dormition; the Tretyakov owns three panels from its festival row: *The Descent into Hell*, *The Annunciation* and *The Assumption* [f]. Rublev's *Old Testament Trinity* [g] is a later icon whose gold and blue angels seem "full of joy and brightness", as Rublev himself was said to be; he painted it at the request of the Trinity Monastery, where he had served his novitiate.

The
Tretyakov
Gallery

*For more about
Rublev, see
p.240.*

Rublev's most haunting work is a triptych for the Deesis tier of the iconostasis of Zvenigorod Cathedral [h]. To contemporaries, the huge faces of *Our Saviour*, the *Archangel Michael* and the *Apostle Paul* seemed "as though painted with smoke". Rublev's draughtsmanship is at once bold and gossamer-fine, the colours tender and contemplative.

Rublev's immediate successor, **Dionysius** (c.1440–1508), was the first famous lay-painter. His career coincided with a rising demand for icons, which spread from the noble and mercantile classes to the peasantry. A prolific artist whose sons pursued the same trade, his icons were more decorative and less searching than Rublev's. Their unreality is exemplified by the placid figures and swooning rhythms of *The Crucifixion*, which Dionysius painted for the Pavlovo-Obnorskiy Monastery in 1500 [i]. When buildings appear in his icons, they float in improbable hues of pink against a cerulean background.

Further along the same wall are a slew of **Pskov icons** from the fourteenth and fifteenth centuries. The sharp reds, deep greens and bold patterning associated with this school are typified by the icon of *St Paraskeva and the Three Hierarchs*, in white surplices emblazoned with black crosses [j].

The last great painter of old Russia was **Simon Ushakov** (1626–86), who headed the icon-painting studio in the Kremlin Armoury from 1644. Also a skilled engraver, art theorist and muralist, his finest frescoes grace the Church of the Trinity in Nikitinov Lane (p.102). Ushakov tried to bring art closer to life by rendering figures three-dimensionally and imparting spatial depth to the background by using landscape and architectural motifs from European art – but also knew how to please his patrons. *The Holy Virgin of Vladimir* (1668) is really a homage to Muscovy, casting Tsar Alexei and Tsaritsa Mariya against the background of the Kremlin and the Cathedral of the Assumption, beneath a family tree of saints [k].

The **eighteenth century** witnessed a simultaneous decline in the potency of the icon and the rise of the portrait as an art form. Icons became mannered and secular, as in the pair depicting Death entering a room where two well-dressed burghers contemplate a table laden with astrological devices [l].

Leaving the icons section and ascending to the third floor, you abandon the symbols of Holy Russia for the traditions of Western secular art.

# The third floor: Russian secular art

The **third floor** is divided into three sections corresponding to great watersheds in Russian art, which began to develop in the Western sense as the taboo on secular imagery began to weaken in the seventeenth century. The first sign was the emergence of the *parsuna*, a stylized form of **portraiture** that broke ground by depicting living persons. However, as no examples of the style are currently on display in the Tretyakov, it's more instructive to focus on what came after.

While Peter the Great was the first to collect foreign paintings and sent native artists to be trained in Europe, it was Elizabeth and Catherine the Great who established the **Academy system** that was to dominate Russian art until the second half of the nineteenth century. Its curriculum was modelled on the French Academy's and further circumscribed by Tsarist censorship: artists were told to stick to Classical themes, safe genre scenes or flattering portraits. Since state commissions accounted for much of their earnings, most obliged – or worked abroad.

## Portraiture and the Academy

The first room opens with a brace of aristocrats portrayed by **Alexei Antropov** (1716–95), a trained icon-painter who turned to portraiture under the tutelage of the Italian Pietro Rotari [a]. Rotari also influenced **Fyodor Rokotov** (1736–1808), whose later use of soft indirect lighting and silvery olive hues has been likened to

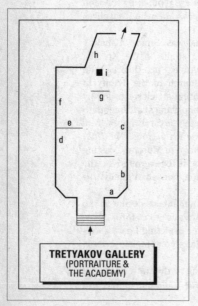

**TRETYAKOV GALLERY**
(PORTRAITURE &
THE ACADEMY)

Gainsborough [b]. The first familiar subject is Catherine the Great, an enthusiastic if undiscerning patron of the arts whom the Ukrainian-born **Dmitry Levitskiy** (1732–1822) depicted against a backdrop of drapery and smoke [c]. Typical of the state portraits that she gave as gifts to other monarchs, it's less revealing than the picture of the Empress walking her dog at Tsarskoe Selo in a dressing-gown and bonnet [d], by Levitskiy's pupil, **Vladimir Borovikovskiy** (1735–1825).

Beyond the partition are a Canaletto-like *View of the Winter Palace Quay* in St Petersburg, by **Fyodor Alekseev** (1753–1824) [e], and portraits by **Karl Bryullov** (1799–1852) [f], a fellow Academician and lover of Italy who is best known for his melodramatic *The Last Days of Pompeii*, in the Russian Museum. Another artist who spent much

# FLATTERY WILL GET YOU ROUND THE WORLD!

"The excellence of the TV series is only surpassed by the books. All who have had any involvement in Rough Guides deserve accolades heaped upon them and free beer for life."
**Diane Evans, Ontario, Canada**

"I've yet to find a presentation style that can match the Rough Guide's. I was very impressed with the amount of detail, ease of reference and the smooth way it swapped from giving sound advice to being entertaining."
**Ruth Higginbotham, Bedford, UK**

"What an excellent book the Rough Guide was, like having a local showing us round for our first few days."
**Andy Leadham, Stoke, UK**

"Thank you for putting together such an excellent guidebook. In terms of accuracy and historical/cultural information, it is head and shoulders above the other books."
**John Speyer, Yorba Linda, California**

"We were absolutely amazed at the mass of detail which the Rough Guide contains. I imagine the word Rough is a deliberate misnomer!"
**Rev. Peter McEachran, Aylesbury, UK**

"I have rarely, if ever, come across a travel guide quite so informative, practical and accurate! Bravo!"
**Alan Dempster, Dublin, Ireland**

"The Rough Guide proved to be a very popular and useful book and was often scanned by other travellers whose own guides were not quite so thorough."
**Helen Jones, Avon, UK**

"My husband and I enjoyed the Rough Guide very much. Not only was it informative, but very helpful and great fun!"
**Felice Pomeranz, Massachusetts, USA**

"I found the Rough Guide the most valuable thing I took with me – it was fun to read and completely honest about everywhere we visited."
**Matthew Rodda, Oxford, UK**

"Congratulations on your bible – well worth the money!"
**Jenny Angel, New South Wales, Australia**

"Our Rough Guide has been as indispensable as the other Rough Guides we have used on our previous journeys."
**Enric Torres, Barcelona, Spain**

We don't promise the earth, but if your letter is really useful (criticism is welcome as well as praise!), we'll certainly send you a free copy of a Rough Guide. Legibility is a big help and, if you're writing about more than one country, please keep the updates on separate pages. All letters are acknowledged and forwarded to the authors.

Please write, indicating which book you're updating, to:

Rough Guides, 1 Mercer St, London WC2H 9QJ, England,
or
Rough Guides, 3rd floor, 375 Hudson St, New York, NY 10014-3657, USA

# Travel the world
# HIV *Safe*

# Travel *Safe*

HIV, the virus that causes AIDS, is worldwide.

You're probably aware of the dangers of getting it from unprotected sex, but there are many other risks when travelling.

Wherever you're visiting it makes sense to take precautions. Try to avoid any medical or dental treatment, but if it's necessary, make sure the equipment is sterilised. Likewise, if you really need to have a blood transfusion, always ask for screened blood.

Make sure your travelling companions are aware of the risks and the necessary precautions. In fact, you should take your own sterile medical pack, available from larger high street pharmacies.

Remember, ear and body piercing, acupuncture and even tattoos could be risky, because they all involve puncturing the skin. And although you might not normally consider any of these things now, after a few drinks - you never know.

Of course, the things that are dangerous at home are just as dangerous when you travel. So don't inject drugs or share works.

Avoid casual sex and always use a good quality condom when having sex with a new partner (and each time you have sex with them).

And it's not just a 'gay disease' either. In fact, worldwide, it's most commonly transmitted through sex between men and women.

For information in the UK:

Ring for the TravelSafe leaflet on the Health Literature Line freephone 0800 555 777, or pick one up at a doctor's surgery or pharmacy.

Further advice on HIV and AIDS: National AIDS Helpline: 0800 567 123. (Cannot be reached from abroad).

The Terrence Higgins Trust Helpline (12 noon–10pm) provides advice and counselling on HIV/AIDS issues: 0171 242 1010.

MASTA Travellers Health Line: 0891 224 100.

**Travel** *Safe*

**Travel the world HIV** *Safe*

of his life in Italy was **Orest Kiprenskiy** (1782–1836), the illegitimate son of a nobleman and a serf, who became involved with the Decembrists while painting his *Portrait of Pushkin* [g], and died in exile from tuberculosis.

More successful was **Alexander Ivanov** (1806–58), whose Italian sojourn (recalled by *Apollo with Youths* and *Olive Trees at Albano*) was followed by a spate of religious works culminating in his enormously popular *Christ Among the People*. Various studies stand in for the actual painting, which is too large to display at present [h].

The final section consists mostly of sugary genre paintings by **Vasily Tropinin** (1776–1857), who trained as a confectioner before graduating from the Academy at the age of 48 [i]. More interesting – though not as bitingly satirical as some of his other works – are two pictures by **Pavel Fedotov** (1815–52), who was censored and finally expelled by the Academy, went mad and died in an asylum. *The Major's Courtship* depicts a merchant's daughter recoiling from the attentions of a preening soldier, while *A Poor Aristocrat's Breakfast* shows a dissolute youth surprised by visitors [j].

## The Wanderers

The mid-nineteenth century saw a revolt against the Academy that was the start of a wave of artistic movements that washed over Russia as the Revolution approached. It was the **Wanderers** (*peredvizhniki*) who broke away from the Academy, evaded its censorship by exhibiting in the provinces, and used their art to express social criticism.

Walking clockwise around the room, the first paintings you see are by the Wanderers: winter scenes and a *Portrait of Dostoyevsky* [a] by **Vasily Perov** (1834–82), whose notorious *Village Easter Procession* – with its drunken priest lurching from an inn – is also owned by the Tretyakov. Nearby hang *The Rooks Have Returned*, a famous work by **Alexei Sarasov** (1830–97), the "father of Russian landscape painting" [b], and lively portraits by **Ivan Kramskoy** (1837–87), including those of Tretyakov, Tolstoy [c] and a pert *Nameless Lady* who is thought to have been the model for Anna Karenina [d]. You might also encounter his Slavic *Christ in the Wilderness*, which Kramskoy painted because "The Italian Christ is handsome, one may say divine, but he is alien to me".

The historical painter **Vasily Surikov** (1846–1916) is well represented by a

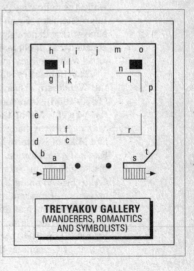

**TRETYAKOV GALLERY**
(WANDERERS, ROMANTICS
AND SYMBOLISTS)

huge picture of *Menshikov in Berezov*, showing the grizzled ex-Prince brooding in a hut on his days of fortune under Peter the Great [e], and studies for the *Boyarina Morozova* that portray the shrieking leader of the Old Believers being dragged away on a sledge [f].

Less justice is done to **Viktor Vasnetsov** (1846–1926), whose small pictures of warring Scythians [g] aren't a patch on the huge canvases inspired by fairy-tales that remain in his studio (see p.256).

In the far corner hangs a powerful *Golgotha* by **Nicholas Ge** (1831–94), who turned from landscapes to religious themes, in a style that prefigured Expressionism [h]. Meanwhile, **Isaak Levitan** (1860–1900) blossomed into the greatest Russian landscapist of the nineteenth century, revered for his limpid rivers and soft winter light, epitomized by *Eternal Peace* [i].

Both were eclipsed by **Ilya Repin** (1844–1930), whose Populist sympathies were expressed in the famous *Barge-Haulers on the Volga* (now in the Russian Museum) and narrative works like *They Did Not Expect Him*, depicting a dissident's return from exile [j]. Notice, too, Repin's frank portrait of the alcoholic composer Mussorgsky.

The Wanderers section is rounded off by a trio of Russian scenes by **Vasily Polonev** (1884–1927), which includes his popular favourites *Moscow Courtyard* and *Grandmother's Garden* [k], and informal portraits by **Valentin Serov** (1865–1911), whose *Girl with Peaches* depicts the daughter of Mamontov, the patron of the Abramtsevo artists' colony [l].

## Romantics and Symbolists

Many artists who began as Wanderers subsequently became Slav Romantics, in thrall to the Russian countryside or ancient legends, while the following generation tended towards Symbolism. Post-Impressionism, Symbolism and Expressionism reached Russia almost simultaneously, producing a heady brew whose ferment equalled that of contemporary Western European art, but also coincided with a political avalanche.

The Romantics start innocuously enough near the tail end of the Wanderers display, with small paintings by **Konstantin Yuon** (1875–1958), who specialized in joyous evocations of nature and the peaceful life of the monks of Solovetskiy Monastery – as in *Silence*. Nearby hang others by **Andrei Ryabushkin** (1861–1904) and **Mikhail Nesterov** (1862–1942), who looked to ancient Kievan Russia for inspiration. Though Ryabushkin's work can be hard to distinguish from Yuon's [m], you can't mistake Nesterov's *The Child Bartholomew's Vision*, with its innocent boy and cowled apparition, representing the moment when St Sergei of Radonezh first felt the touch of God (see p.273) [n].

The far wall is dominated by three large canvases by **Mikhail Vrubel** (1856–1940), whose impact on Russian art was comparable to that of Cézanne in the West [o]. *The Demon* is one of a series inspired by Lermontov's poem of the same name, which obsessed Vrubel to the point of madness. In 1902, on the night before the opening of the fourth World of Art exhibition, he locked himself in the gallery with a bottle of champagne and totally repainted *The Demon*; the next morning he was found gibbering incoherently and committed to an asylum.

Another tortured Symbolist was **Viktor Borissov-Mussatov** (1870–1905), who was crippled in childhood and secretly lusted after his sister. His *Sleep of the Gods* [p] typically juxtaposes young women and statues amid a country estate pervaded with foreboding, similar to the garden featured in *The Letter* [q] by **Konstantin Somov** (1869–1939).

By the early 1900s Russian and Western art were evolving in tandem and mutually indebted, with Kandinsky and Chagall teaching in Munich and Paris, and international Symbolist exhibitions held in Moscow. The leading lights of the Blue Rose Russian Symbolist movement were **Pavel Kuznetsov** (1878–1968) – represented here by a Fauvish view of Central Asia, *Mirage on the Steppe* – and the Armenian **Martiros Saryan** (1880–1972), whose mysterious, static landscapes influenced the German *Blaue Reiter* school [r]. As a foretaste of the artistic fireworks that erupted before World War I and climaxed with the Revolution, the room ends with a coruscatingly Cubist *St Basil's Cathedral* by **Aristakh Lentulov** (1882–1943) [s].

## Primitivism, Futurism and Constructivism

The final room presents a sample of the Tretyakov's vast collection of avant-garde art, which is regularly changed to compensate for the small number of works on display, but sure to feature the main exponents of what became known as **Primitivism**: principally **Natalya Goncharova** (1881–1962), who asserted that all art was dead or decadent, except in Russia, and **Mikhail Larionov** (1881–1964), who painted soldiers and whores and scrawled obscenities on his canvases. Larionov soon took to Italian Futurism, launching a new style called **Rayonism**, whose manifesto declared that the genius of the age consisted of "trousers, jackets, shoes, tramways, buses, aeroplanes . . .".

**Futurism** is a catch-all term for the explosion of artistic styles and theories between 1910 and 1920, embracing the prankish "happenings" of Mayakovsky and the Burlyuk brothers, and the more cerebral work of **Kazimir Malevich** (1878–1935), who derived his Cubo-Futurism from the bold lines and colours of icons and woodcuts, and developed both to a pitch of theory that he termed **Suprematism**, the "art of pure sensation". His main rival for ascendancy over the avant-garde movement was **Vladimir Tatlin** (1885–1953), who anticipated Dada with his junk collages before experimenting with theatre design and the "Culture of Materials". What came to be called **Constructivism** owed much to his collaboration

*Larger exhibitions of avant-garde and Socialist Realist art are held in the "Tretyakovka" gallery on Krymskiy val (p.215).*

with the director Meyerhold and the painter **Lyubov Popova** (1889–1924), whose dynamic *Constructions* and *Squares* are akin to Malevich's.

As they all welcomed the Revolution and strove to create art worthy of utopia, it was a bitter irony that the Communists soon turned hostile towards Futurism. The first artist to leave Russia in 1921 was **Vasily Kandinsky** (1866–1944), whose numinous abstracts were branded "empty formalism" – followed by Marc Chagall and Naum Gabo. Within a few years, those who remained had been restricted to design or sidelined altogether, as Socialist Realism became the only form of art permitted.

# Krymskiy val and Gorky Park

Named after the bygone "Crimean Rampart" of the Zemlyanoy Gorod, the Krymskiy val is the only part of the Garden Ring's southern arc that tourists are likely to be concerned with, running as it does past Gorky Park, the Central House of Artists and the Graveyard of Fallen Monuments. Though none of them is a must, their proximity and the river views encourage a visit.

Both ways of **getting there** involve a ten to fifteen minute walk from a metro station. It's better to start from Park Kultury (p.186) and cross over the bridge rather than begin at Oktyabryskaya (see below). That way, your appetite for Soviet leisure culture is whetted by the cute reliefs in Park Kultury station, and further aroused by the grand arch at the entrance to the park, as its planners intended. During summer, you can also get there by boat from Kiev Station (see p.180).

## Gorky Park

**Gorky Park** is famous abroad from Martin Cruz Smith's classic thriller of the same name, which opens with the discovery of three faceless corpses in the snow, setting Investigator Renko on the trail of a wealthy American. The reality is less sinister but still a bit creepy in another way, as Pepsi culture flourishes amid the decayed relics of a totalitarian regime's fun side. If you can, filter out the skateboarders and cast your imagination back to when the flower-beds were pristine, red flags rippled overhead, and citizens at rest and play were edified by speeches from the Kremlin, broadcast across the park.

Inaugurated in 1928, the Soviet Union's first "Park of Culture and Rest" was formed by uniting an exhibition zone near the Krymskiy val with the vast gardens of the Golitsyn Hospital and the Neskuchniy Palace. The park's 300 acres now include two funfairs, a large outdoor skating rink and lots of woodland (daily 9am–10pm; small admission fee). The highlights are an American **rollercoaster** (scary but safe) and a retired Soviet **space shuttle**, near the entrance. When the weather's fine, hip-hop fans gather with their blasters at the crossroads, while live rock music may occur at the outdoor "Green Theatre" or the *Hard Rock Café*, deeper into the park. Over winter, there is usually a festival of ice sculptures in February and an **ice-skating disco** most evenings, which you'd be unwise to join without medical insurance.

**Krymskiy val and Gorky Park**

## The Central House of Artists and Graveyard of Fallen Monuments

On the other side of the Krymskiy val, a tacky array of **pictures for sale** heralds Yevgeny Vuchetich's dramatic "Swords into Ploughshares" (a copy of the original sculpture presented to the UN in 1957) and the **Central House of Artists** (*Tsentralniy dom Khudozhnikov*; Tues–Sun 11am–8pm), an enormous boxy complex used for exhibitions of contemporary art. Entered from the side facing the Krymskiy val, it also contains a new branch of the Tretyakov Gallery, known as the "**Tretyakovka**" (Tues–Sun 10am–8pm; $4), which often mounts individual retrospectives or big thematic exhibitions from different periods of the Soviet era. The entrance to this is on the eastern side of the building.

*Current exhibitions are listed on Saturdays in the Moscow Times and Moscow Tribune.*

To round things off, a nearby field has been turned into a **Graveyard of Fallen Monuments** of Communism. Pride of place is given to the three-times-life-size statue of "Iron Felix" Dzerzhinsky that stood outside the Lubyanka until it was toppled in 1991; the pedestal alone is as high as a London double-decker bus.

# Oktyabrskaya, Leninskiy prospekt and Pavelets Station

For tourists, everywhere **beyond Gorky Park** is reducible to a few clusters of attractions miles apart, and the avenues and metro lines that connect them. **Oktyabrskaya ploshchad** (October Square) is an urban showpiece from the Era of Stagnation (*zastoy*): ugly blocks that count as prestigious accommodation, frowning over a major road junction and the last **statue of Lenin** to be erected in Moscow (in 1985). Bestriding a plinth flanked by peasants and workers fired by his vision, he is depicted as a giant of world history – and is now a focal point for **Communist demonstrations**.

There are two fine sights 150m north of here, on ulitsa Bolshaya Yakimanka. The **Igumnov House**, built for a rich merchant in 1893, is a Pseudo-Russian fantasy of peaked roofs and gables, pendant arches, coloured tiles and a blend of Gothic, Byzantine and Baroque decor. While tales that Igumnov buried his mistress in one of the walls and the architect hanged himself in the hallway are probably untrue, the mansion did later contain the so-

Okt-
yabrskaya,
Leninskiy
prospekt and
Pavelets
Station

called Institute of the Brain, where Lenin's brain was cut into three thousand sections and studied, with the aim of discovering the source of his genius – a procedure later applied to the brains of Stalin, Pavlov, Eisenstein, Mayakovsky and Sakharov. In 1938 the house became the **French Embassy**, a role better suited to its splendid decor, but you can't see inside the building except as a guest of the Ambassador.

Directly opposite stands the **Church of St John the Warrior** (*tserkov Ivana Voina*), one of the few buildings erected in Moscow under Peter the Great, who is said to have personally chosen its site and even sketched out a plan. Its construction (1709–13) was entrusted to Ivan Zarudniy, whose design married the configuration of a Moscow Baroque church with new European decorative forms, on a maroon facade. The interior is obviously European in its lavish use of sculptural mouldings, but holds such native treasures as the *Icon of Saviour* that once hung above the Saviour Gate of the Kremlin. St John's became the custodian of all kinds of relics, as it was one of the few churches in Moscow to escape closure in the 1920–30s. Its saint's feast day falls on August 12.

## Leninskiy prospekt

**Leninskiy prospekt** is Moscow's longest avenue, running for 14km from Oktyabrskaya ploshchad to the outer Ring Road. The initial 2.8km stretch as far as ploshchad Gagarina is flanked on one side by Stalinist blocks, and on the other by Gorky Park and two eighteenth-century palatial buildings, Moscow's massive **Golitsyn Hospital** and the **Neskuchniy Palace**, now respectively the headquarters of the Academy of Sciences, and a repository for four hundred antique vases, paintings and furniture.

However, as a visit to either involves a long trolleybus ride (#4, #7, #33 or #62) and maybe getting past doormen, you'll probably settle for **ploshchad Gagarina**. Here, Leninskiy Prospekt metro exits behind a Stalinist apartment block that forms one half of a gigantic crescent defining the northern edge of the plaza, which used to be called Kaluga Gate Square. These flats for the elite were built by German POWs and Russian convicts – including Alexander Solzhenitsyn.

Near the exit of the Leninskiy Prospekt metro, the giant titanium **Gagarin Monument** is a muscular superhero braced to blast off on a column of energy. The square was renamed after tens of thousands of Muscovites turned out to welcome Gagarin as he arrived from Vnukovo Airport, following his sensational orbit around Earth in April 1961.

## Pavelets Station

From Oktyabrskaya, the Circle line and trolleybus 6 run to **Pavelets Station** (*Paveletskiy vokzal*), designed in the nineteenth century to resemble a Loire Valley château and tastefully modernized in the 1980s. To visit the sights on either side of the traffic-choked square outside, use the long, gloomy **underpass** that connects Pavelets Station to the northern exit of Paveletskaya metro.

The main reason for coming out here is the **Lenin Funerary Train** (Mon–Fri 10am–6pm), in a small park behind some kiosks to the east of Pavelets Station. Beyond a gateway, you'll find its pavilion atop a terrace beside a marble wall whose inscription asserts: *The name of V.I. Lenin is immortal, like his ideas and his deeds.* Though now a luxury car showroom, its glory is still the gleaming orange and black steam engine and wagon that brought Lenin's body to Moscow on January 23, 1924, for his funeral on Red Square, and the giant bust of Lenin that gazes blindly from a flame-shaped aperture at the back of the hall.

Across the square on the corner of ulitsa Bakhrushina, a Neo-Gothic mansion contains a **Theatre Museum** (Mon, Thurs, Sat & Sun noon–7pm; Wed & Fri 1–8pm; closed the last Mon of each month) named after the house's owner, Alexei Bakhrushin, a rich tanner turned impresario. Downstairs are opera set designs for *Boris Godunov* and *Ivan the Terrible*, and costumes worn by Chaliapin in the title role of Boris. Upstairs there's a gorgeous puppet theatre; Nijinsky's dancing shoes; decadent gouache designs by Michael Fokine; and stage-models for Constructivist dramas like *Zori*, which involved architects and painters. Though poorly laid out and only captioned in Russian, the museum should appeal to aficionados of theatre history or design.

# The Donskoy and Danilov monasteries

Indisputably the main attractions in this part of Moscow, the Donskoy and Danilov monasteries originally stood a mile or so beyond the city walls, playing a vital role as defensive outposts and sanctuaries. After decades of misuse, believers can once again pray before their icons and relics, while tourists are enticed by their historical associations and architecture. While both are interesting, the Donskoy is more appealing for its decrepitude and lovely cemetery. The Danilov's own cemetery lies further south, near the city's Muslim burial ground.

The **cemeteries** are out here because of an Imperial edict following the last visitation of the Black Death in 1770–71. To combat its spread, a quarter of Moscow's houses were burnt when somebody died in them, and all the medieval cemeteries within the centre were dug up and removed. Seven large new Orthodox cemeteries were then prepared beyond the city limits, as the death toll soared. In Moscow province, a third of the population – over two hundred thousand people – died of plague that year.

Both monasteries are open daily and can easily be seen sequentially if you follow the right **itinerary**. Start with the Donskoy (taking in the Church of the Deposition of the Robe en route from Shabolovskaya metro) and then catch any bus along Serpukhovskiy val towards the Danilov Monastery. If you only want to visit the Danilov or Muslim cemeteries, bus #26 or #38 heading south along 1-y Roshchinskiy pereulok will take you most of the way.

## The Donskoy Monastery

The massive red-brick walls of the fortified **Donskoy Monastery** (*Donskoy monastyr*), with their height and thickness, reflect a historic fear of Mongols shooting catapults and fire-arrows rather than of European armies fielding massed cannons – as do the dozen towers spaced at regular intervals. The monastic enclosure covers 42,000 square metres, with plenty of room for an old graveyard that shouldn't be confused with a larger walled crematorium next door.

### Some history

The monastery dates back to 1591, when Boris Godunov routed the last Crimean Tatar raid on Moscow. His victory was attributed to the icon of the Don Virgin, which had accompanied Dmitry Donskoy to war against the Mongols and ensured his victory at Kulikovo in 1380. To hearten his own troops, Godunov paraded the icon around camp on the eve of the battle and, following a brief skirmish the next day, Khan Kazy-Gire's army fled. In thanksgiving, the Russians erected a church to house the icon and founded a monastery on the spot.

Robbed and abandoned in the Time of Troubles, the monastery was restored by Tsars Fyodor and Alexei, but remained small and poor until renewed warfare against the Tatars prompted the Regent Sofia and her lover Prince Golitsyn to strengthen its defences. Continued by Peter the Great, this building programme (1684–1733) resulted in the existing fortifications and Great Cathedral. By the late eighteenth century the Donskoy had become not only prosperous, but a fashionable burial ground for Georgian and Golitsyn princes and cultural figures.

Soon after the Revolution the monastery was closed down by the Bolsheviks, though its monks continued to live there until 1929, when they were evicted to make way for a **Museum of Atheism**. The monastery's hospital had by then been converted into Moscow's first crematorium, to promote secular funerals. During the mid-1930s it incinerated thousands of corpses – including Bukharin's, apparently – delivered at night from the Lubyanka or the Military Collegium, whose ashes were shovelled into pits and asphalted over. Meanwhile, the erstwhile monastery became a branch of the **Shchusev Architectural Museum**, collecting sculptures from demolished churches across Moscow.

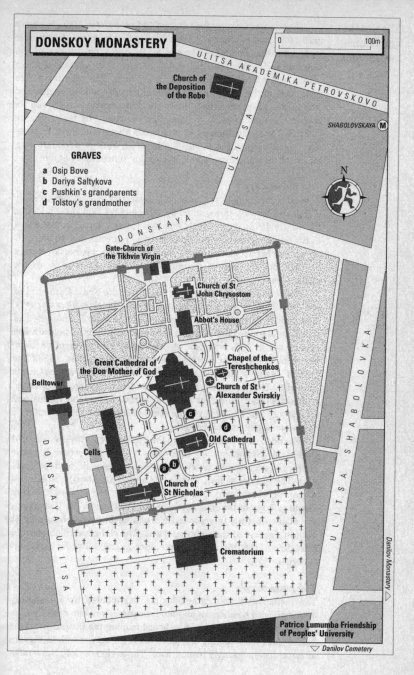

# DONSKOY MONASTERY

0      100m

ULITSA AKADEMIKA PETROVSKOVO

Church of
the Deposition
of the Robe

ULITSA

SHABOLOVSKAYA Ⓜ

N

### GRAVES

**a** Osip Bove
**b** Dariya Saltykova
**c** Pushkin's grandparents
**d** Tolstoy's grandmother

DONSKAYA

Gate-Church of
the Tikhvin Virgin

Church of St
John Chrysostom

Abbot's House

Great Cathedral of
the Don Mother of God

Chapel of the
Tereshchenkos

Church of St
Alexander Svirskiy

Belltower

Ⓒ

Ⓓ

Old Cathedral

DONSKAYA ULITSA

Cells

Ⓐ Ⓑ

Church of
St Nicholas

ULITSA SHABOLOVKA

Danilov Monastery ▷

Crematorium

**Patrice Lumumba Friendship
of Peoples' University**

▽ Danilov Cemetery

Though services resumed at the Old Cathedral in 1946, it wasn't until 1992 that **Patriarch Tikhon**'s sanctified body was laid to rest there with due honours. Invested as Patriarch on the eve of the Revolution, he had been jailed and buried in an unmarked grave within the monastery in 1925. Soon after his reburial a fire destroyed all the icons in the cathedral except the Don Virgin, and when restorers opened the tomb to check for damage they found his body to be uncorrupted. He was then canonized by the Orthodox Church. Today, the monastery still needs a vast amount of restoration, but already runs a publishing house, a workshop for restoring icons and an embroidery and icon-painting school for children.

## The monastery

You enter the monastery (daily 8am–6pm) from Donskaya ulitsa by a chunky **gateway**, surmounted by a three-tiered **belltower** added in the 1750s. Its medley of bells breaks a tranquil hush, as the noises of the city are muted by the monastery's high walls and drowned by crows cawing from the trees. Piles of rubble and mossy statues abound, but the monks are slowly restoring some order to the chaotic dereliction.

At the exact centre of the complex rises the **Great Cathedral of the Don Mother of God** (*Bolshoy sobor Donskoy Bogomateri*), also known as the "New Cathedral" (*Noviy sobor*). Composed of four rotund tower bays grouped around a central drum beneath five bronze domes, this was one of the largest structures of its time, begun in 1684 under Golitsyn and finally finished in 1698. The interior features Apocryphal frescoes and images of the saints framed by fruity wreaths, and is dominated by a huge seven-tiered **iconostasis** that took four years to carve. Notice the friezes and tombstones stacked beneath the steps, a legacy of the monastery's days as an architectural museum.

Founded in tandem with the monastery, the small **Old Cathedral** (*Stariy sobor*) resembles a simple Moscow Baroque church, painted a soft russet, with tiers of green and white *kokoshniki*. The interior is low, white and vaulted, its floor polished by a stream of worshippers. All light a candle to the **icon of the Don Virgin** (a copy of the fourteenth-century original in the Tretyakov), and many prostrate themselves before the gold casket containing **St Tikhon's relics**, by the right-hand wall. The cathedral celebrates the feast days of the Don Virgin (September 1) and St Fyodor Stratilites (February 21).

## The cemetery

The monastery's two cathedrals are surrounded by a **cemetery** crammed with headstones and monuments. If you can read Cyrillic, each plot is identified by a map-board naming the famous Russians buried there – though the only ones likely to register with foreigners all have disappointingly plain graves. The architect **Osip Bove** rates a black granite slab next to one shaped like a bomb, while the serf-murdering Countess **Dariya Saltykova** is recalled by an obelisk without any inscription. Still more nondescript are the graves of **Tolstoy's grandmother** and **Pushkin's grandparents**.

The dark red **Church of St Nicholas** was built in 1806–09 as the private chapel of the Golitsyns. Nearby stands the tent-roofed Pseudo-Russian **Chapel of the Tereshchenkos**, decorated with Orthodox crosses and raised in 1899. Best of all is the Neo-Byzantine **Church of St John Chrysostom** (*tserkov Ioanna Zlatousta*), built by the Pervushins in 1891, past the **Abbot's House**.

Beyond it rises the **Gate-Church of the Tikhvin Virgin** (*tserkov Tikhvinskoy Bogomateri*), an imposing structure that is one of the last examples of Moscow Baroque. It was completed in 1713, the year after Peter the Great moved the capital to St Petersburg and forbade building in stone anywhere else in Russia, to spur the creation of his city on the Neva.

### Other sights

Close by Shabolovskaya metro station, take time to seek out the **Church of the Deposition of the Robe** (*tserkov Ripolozheniya*), built in 1701 and combining the traditional forms of a Moscow parish church with the attenuated drums and domes of the early medieval Yaroslavl style. Its ornamentation is similar to the gate-churches of Novodevichiy, with white scalloped gables, double-crested *nalichniki* and engaged columns with acanthus-leaf capitals against a rose facade. The congregation are called to services (8am & 5pm) by an amazingly deep bell, and a peal of smaller ones. From here you can see the Donskoy Monastery, 400m along Donskaya ulitsa.

You can also check out the **Patrice Lumumba Friendship of Peoples University** on ulitsa Ordzhonikidze, en route to the Danilov Monastery, which impresses as a huge Stalin-style block with garish red and white pillars. Established in 1960 to train students from the Third World, the university was named after the murdered leader of the independence movement in the Belgian Congo, and was long seen by Western governments as a school for revolutionaries: Carlos "the Jackal" studied here.

At the end of the road past the university, you can either cross the junction and head off along Serpukhovskiy val towards the Danilov Monastery, or catch bus #26 or #38 down 1-y Roshchinskiy pereulok to a pair of picturesque cemeteries.

## The Danilov and Muslim cemeteries

Alighting at the 3-y Verkhniy Mikhailovskiy stop, before the bus turns off Roshchinskiy, a 200-metre walk will bring you to the **Danilov Cemetery** (*Danilovskoe kladbische*; Wed–Sun 10am–6pm).

Overgrown and archaic, its funerary monuments are as fine as those in the Donskoy's graveyard, owing to the numerous orthodox Metropolitans and nouveaux riches *Kuptsy* buried here.

The **Muslim Cemetery** (*Musalmanskoe kladbishche*; Wed–Sun 10am–6pm) lies 300m along a lane to the west. Established in 1771, its thousands of graves attest to a sizeable Muslim community in Moscow. Most of the headstones bear Tatar names, sometimes written in Arabic script. The most illustrious is that of **Imam Abdullah Shamsutdinov**, who was shot by the NKVD in the courtyard of his own mosque in 1937; his ashes were belatedly interred here in 1992. Normally frequented by a few amiable old Tatar ladies, the cemetery gets surprisingly busy on Islamic holidays.

### Serpukhovskiy val and the Danilov Market

There's little reason to walk 1km along **ulitsa Serpukhovskiy val** when you can ride a bus instead. The avenue has a couple of decent restaurants, but is otherwise notable only for its wooded strip culminating in a Stalinesque flourish of giant urns and ornamental lamps – and for its past. Like the Khamovnicheskiy val near Novodevichiy Convent, this once delineated the city's customs' boundary, where goods entering or leaving Moscow were taxed. Despite being termed a *val* (rampart), it had no defensive purpose.

At the far end you can orientate yourself by the rusty domed **Danilov Market** (*Danilovskiy rynok*; Mon–Sat 7am–7pm, Sun 7am–6pm) on the corner of Mytnaya ulitsa, near Tulskaya metro. Pungent and colourful, the market is unusual for being controlled by Cossacks, who drove out the Central Asian mobsters and drug dealers that formerly held sway. Though it's fine to look around and taste the produce, taking **photos** could result in you being shown the exit by several beefy fellows. The Danilov Monastery is five minutes' walk from here.

## The Danilov Monastery

As the official residence of the Russian Orthodox Patriarch, Alexei II, the **Danilov Monastery** (*Danilovskiy monastyr*) differs from Moscow's other monasteries in its modernity and businesslike air, the antithesis of their romantic desolation. While this might disappoint some visitors, it undeniably represents a comeback by the Orthodox Church, whose new self-assurance is undeniable and even extends to the political arena: the Patriarch tried to mediate between Yeltsin and parliament in the crisis of 1993, but failed.

Founded by **Prince Daniil** of Moscow in 1282, the Danilov claims to be the city's oldest monastery although its monks and icons were moved into the Kremlin in 1330 by Ivan I, and only came back when Ivan the Terrible revived the original site, 230 years later. In 1652, Daniil was canonized and the monastery was renamed in his honour; expanded over decades behind a crenellated wall with ten bastions, it ultimately included an almshouse and a hospital.

Though officially closed soon after the Revolution, it somehow survived as the last working monastery in Russia until 1930, when the monks were expelled and a **borstal** was established here. Most of the inmates were children whose parents had been arrested or shot in the purges; they had to chant: "We are all indebted to our Motherland – we are in debt for the air we breathe." As a condition of being allowed to reclaim the premises in 1983, the Church was obliged to finance another borstal, somewhere else.

Following the monastery's rededication ceremony, five years later it became the seat of the Patriarch and the Holy Synod, which had previously been at the Trinity Monastery of St Sergei, outside Moscow.

## The monastery

The best way of **getting there** is to catch the metro to Tulskaya station, exit near the front of the train, bear right across a waste-ground past some charred kiosks, and walk 200m along ulitsa Danilovskiy val.

Unless closed under unusual circumstances, the Danilov Monastery is open daily (8am–6pm), free of charge. Visitors enter by the **Gate-Church of St Simeon the Stylite** (*Nadvodyashiy tserkov*

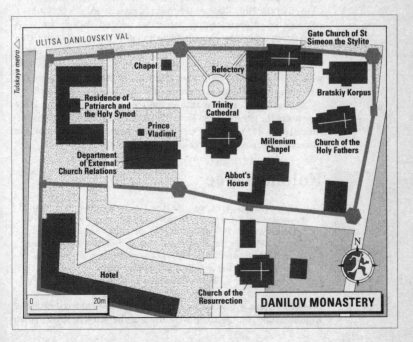

*Simeonia Stolpnika*) on Danilovskiy val, which had to be entirely rebuilt as the original gate-tower was torn down in the 1920s and its bells sold to Harvard University. Painted a soft pink, with its archway framed by fat-bellied columns and an elaborate cornice, the gate is surmounted by a triple-tiered belltower inset with pictures of the saints, ending in a gold finial.

Inside the compound, you'll see some of the monastery's 45 monks putting the finishing touches to the administrative blocks and garden, while old women genuflect before the holy images on the walls of the churches – maybe you'll even spot a spurred and booted Cossack with a sabre, strutting across the yard. Straight ahead stands the gold-domed **Millennium Chapel**, with a quadruple arch erected to mark the millennial anniversary in 1988.

A bronze **statue of Prince Vladimir** waves a crucifix near the turquoise building housing the **Department of External Church Relations**, while a huge gilded mosaic of the Saviour stares down from the modern **Residence of the Patriarch and the Holy Synod**, at the far end. The Patriarch is known to prefer living at the Trinity Monastery of Sergei or at his *dacha* in Peredelkino, outside Moscow, so is seldom in residence.

Osip Bove built the Classical **Trinity Cathedral** (*Troitskiy sobor*) in the 1830s. Aside from the porticoes on three sides and a votive lamp hanging on the fourth, its austerity is relieved only by a green cupola and a buttercup yellow exterior. By contrast, the **Church of the Holy Fathers** (*khram vo imya Svyatykh Ottsov*) is a complex seventeenth-century structure, painted entirely white. A deep porch topped by a green dome and gold finial leads through a refectory with arched windows to two chapels. The northern one is dedicated to St Daniil, the southern one to SS. Boris and Gleb, who were killed by their own brother (feast day on August 6). Notice the sixteenth-century **icons** of *St Daniil* and the *Virgin of Vladimir*.

By passing through a gate in the rear wall, you'll find a large new **hotel** for guests of the Patriarchate, harbouring a good **restaurant** (see p.311). Around the corner stands the **Church of the Resurrection**, a square towered Neo-Classical edifice.

# Kolomenskoe

*I have seen much in my life that I have admired and been astounded at, but the past, the ancient past of Russia which has left its imprint on this village, was for me something most miraculous . . . Here in the mysterious silence, amid the harmonious beauty of the finished form, I beheld an architecture of a new kind. I beheld man soaring on high. And I stood amazed.*

Hector Berlioz, recalling Kolomenskoe in 1847.

One of the most evocative sites in Moscow is the old royal estate of **Kolomenskoe**, on the steep west bank of the Moskva River, 10km

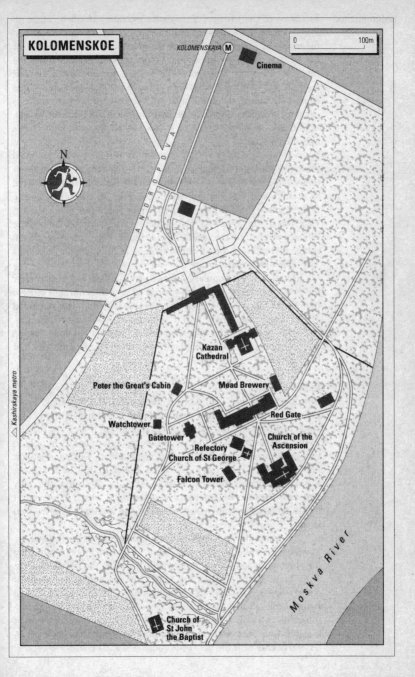

**KOLOMENSKOE**

*KOLOMENSKAYA* Ⓜ

Cinema

0          100m

N

Kazan
Cathedral

Peter the Great's Cabin      Mead Brewery

Watchtower        Red Gate

Gatetower

Refectory       Church of the
Church of St George      Ascension

Falcon Tower

*Moskva River*

Church of
St John
the Baptist

◁ *Kashirskaya metro*

*P R O S P E K T   A N D R O P O V A*

**Kolomenskoe** southeast of the Kremlin. Though its legendary wooden palace no longer exists, Kolomenskoe still has one of the finest churches in the whole of Russia, and vintage wooden structures such as Peter the Great's cabin, set amid hoary oaks above a great bend in the river. In summer, Muscovites flock here for the fresh air and sunbathing; in winter, the eerie Church of the Ascension rises against a void of snow and mist with nobody around except kids sledging down the slopes, as flocks of crows croak from the woods. If you make only one excursion to the edge of Moscow, it should be to Kolomenskoe.

It was originally a village founded by refugees from Kolomna during the Mongol invasions of the thirteenth century, which eventually became a royal summer retreat where Ivan the Terrible stayed as a child, and with his first wife, Anastasia. In 1667, despite the seven thousand slain here in the Copper Riots five years earlier, Tsar Alexei went ahead with a new palace that courtiers dubbed the "eighth wonder of the world". As a child, Peter the Great took refuge there during the *Streltsy* revolt of 1682, and later drilled his "toy" regiments on the estate.

Kolomenskoe's popularity waned, and its fate was sealed after the Revolution. The cemetery was razed and the churches closed; then the village was destroyed by collectivization and what remained of the estate was turned into a Museum of Wooden Architecture. Not until 1974 was the area declared a conservation zone, saving 400 hectares of ancient woodland from the factories and flats that have advanced on all sides.

## Practicalities

Despite its distance from the centre, **getting there** is easy. From Teatralnaya metro, located near the Bolshoy Theatre, it's only four stops to Kolomenskaya station, fifteen minutes' walk from the site itself. Take the exit near the back of the train; turn left, then right in the underpass to surface at the right point. During summer, another, less direct, approach is to travel to the next station, Kashirskaya; cross Kashirskoe shosse and cut down into the gully that runs between Kolomenskoe and Dyakovo, where the sound of traffic fades away until you emerge by the riverside in a magical silence.

The **grounds and museum** at Kolomenskoe are closed on Monday, but are otherwise open from 11am to 5pm, except during the summer, when on Wednesday and Thursday the hours are from 1 to 8pm. From October to April, the museum's management reserves the right to close if the temperature falls below –25°C, and Peter's cabin is shut all the time. **Tickets** to enter the museum and the cabin can only be purchased at the *kassa* on the inner side of the Red Gate, but no ticket is required to wander the grounds. A basement **café** near the gate sells vodka, tea and cookies.

Entering the grounds from the direction of prospekt Andropova, you are greeted at a distance by the **Kazan Cathedral** (*Kazanskiy sobor*), whose sky-blue domes spangled with gold stars glint alluringly. Its boxy refectory and covered stairway are typical of churches from the reign of Alexei, who had it built for the centenary of Ivan the Terrible's capture of Kazan in 1551. Initially enshrined in her other cathedral on Red Square, the revered icon *Our Lady of Kazan* was later transferred to St Petersburg's basilica, whence it vanished in 1904 – only to miraculously reappear in other places, the last reported sighting being at Kolomenskoe on the day of Nicholas II's abdication. As the cathedral was closed down in 1941 and only reopened a few years ago, the *babushkas* who look after it are rather possessive, and don't like tourists dropping in between services (8am & 6pm).

Originally, the cathedral was connected to the great palace by a covered walkway that sprawled to the east, until it was pulled down in the reign of Catherine the Great (see box). Today, you are drawn into the adjacent **oak woods**, where one of the trees is six hundred years old and others were planted by Peter when he was young. Sited in the vicinity is a trio of historic structures placed here in 1930–34, when the Museum of Wooden Architecture was created. The best is **Peter the Great's cabin**, originally erected in 1702 on an island off Arkhangelsk, so that he could observe the construction of the Novodvinskaya fortress. Its four rooms have tiled stoves, log walls and mica windows; notice the huge wooden beer-scoop in the

---

**The Wooden Palace and the death of Anastasia**

Tsar Alexei's **Wooden Palace** was renowned as a marvel of Russian carpentry. Constructed without using saws, nails or hooks, it boasted 250 rooms and 3000 mica windows distributed around a maze of wings interspersed by bulbous domes and tent-roofed towers. "Its carved wooden ornamentation frothed like lace and its roofs were covered with multicoloured wooden tiles painted in delicate colours and gilded with gold" (Princess Shakhovskoe). Each member of the royal family had their own separate *terem*, or quarters, and the entire population of five villages and nine hamlets was enserfed to the estate. However, during Peter's reign the palace came to be regarded as an archaic liability, and fell into such disrepair that it had to be demolished later that century.

In an earlier age on the same spot, Ivan the Terrible mourned the **death of Anastasia Romanova**, his first – and only beloved – wife, in 1560. As her demise occurred suddenly at a time when the *boyars* were trying to isolate him, Ivan decided that she had been poisoned. This revived his deep-rooted paranoia and liberated his darkest impulses, which Anastasia had restrained. Having buried her, he embarked on a debauch and a purge on his enemies with equal zeal. None of his other wives ever lasted for more than a few years – indeed, their life expectancy diminished as he grew older and crazier.

dining room, and the low ceilings that the six-foot four-inch-tall Tsar accepted without a qualm. Further south you'll come upon a log **watchtower** from the Bratskiy *ostrog*, a Cossack fort founded in 1652 on the Angara River in Siberia, which also served as a prison. Nearby stands an equally rough-hewn **gate-tower** from the St Nicholas Monastery in Karelia, whose hexagonal tower with its witch's hat brim straddles an archway big enough to admit a wagon – all crafted to interlock without using any nails. Lastly – and off in the other direction – there's a **mead brewery** (*medovarnya*) from the village of Preobrazhenskoe, outside Moscow, where Peter spent much of his youth.

## The Red Gate and around

Near the brewery, the museum zone gives way to the old core of the estate, beyond the **Red Gate** (*Krasniy vorota*). Surmounting the twin-arched gate is a tent-roofed clocktower whose **clock** was salvaged from the Sukharev Tower in central Moscow, which was demolished in the 1930s. It strikes the hour with a tinkling of small bells, followed by a deep, brazen one.

The section to the left beyond the gate contains a lovely 1:40 scale **model of Alexei's palace**, executed in 1868 from sketches; a recreation of the seventeenth-century **Prikaz Chamber**, where royal scribes worked at a long table covered in red cloth; and **metalwork**, including a bell made by Dmitry Motorin, whose descendants cast the Tsar Bell in the Kremlin. The exhibition continues on the front side of the gate with an impressive display of peasant **woodcarving** – panels and window frames swarming with mermaids, lions and birds, mostly from the Volga villages where this art reached its height in the mid-nineteenth century.

Lastly, you can visit a separate block that was once the Tsar's pantry – or **Service House** – whose ground floor is crammed with **icons**, and upstairs with decorative **stove-tiles**. Look out on the way in for the panels made by Vrubel and medieval tiles from the palace of the Romanov *boyars*. Hidden in the far left-hand corner are some risqué eighteenth-century ones. A fat guy seated backwards on a ram is captioned "Rich but stupid", while another shows his wife wagging her finger and promising a youth: "I will teach you how to f\*\*k".

## The Church of the Ascension

Soaring upwards as the ground falls away towards the river, the **Church of the Ascension** (*tserkov Vozneseniya*) has a stark primeval grandeur that rivals St Basil's Cathedral on Red Square. Though the two buildings look very different, they are related insofar as this church was commissioned by Vasily III in 1529 as a votive offering to be granted an heir, who as Ivan the Terrible would later decree the creation of St Basil's; this feeling of ancestoral kinship is almost palpable.

Aside from this, what makes the Ascension Church (which used to serve as one of Moscow's watchtowers) so remarkable is its stupendous **tent-roof**. Rising from an octagonal base culminating in tiers of *kokoshniki* resembling giant artichoke leaves, its facets are enhanced by limestone ribbing and rhomboid patterns, while a lantern, cupola and cross bring the total height to 70m. This was such a radical departure from the domed stone churches that then prevailed that architectural historians decided it must have sprung from the separate tradition of wooden tower churches, until new evidence that the Italian Petrok Maliy had supervised its design led some to argue that it represented a late development of the Romanesque pyramid-roofed tower.

Like a rocket clamped to its launch-pad by gantries, the church is girdled at its base by an elevated **terrace** reached by three stair-cases, incorporating sharp turns that would have heightened the drama of ritual processions in olden days. When filming *Ivan the Terrible*, Eisenstein used this to frame the unforgettable scene in which Ivan watches a long column of people snaking over the snow-clad hills to beg him to return to rule them. Sadly, the **interior** of the church is closed for repairs.

## Across the ravine to Dyakovo

In the vicinity of the Ascension Church stand two slender towers whose dereliction renders them faintly sinister. The cylindrical **Church of St George** was designed to serve as Kolomenskoe's main belltower and dates from the sixteenth century. In those days the courtyard was surrounded by huts and stables, while wagons rattled in through the gateway beneath the **Falcon Tower** (*Sokolnaya bashnya*) and its lofty eyrie, where the Tsar's hunting birds were kept. Unfortunately neither can be entered now, so there's no cause to linger.

If the ground isn't too icy or muddy, try negotiating the steep gully 150m to the south of the Church of St George, which divides Kolomenskoe from what was once the village of **Dyakovo**. Although this area was inhabited as early as the first century BC, its only tangible relic is a **Church of St John the Baptist** (*tserkov Ioanna Predtechi*) that Ivan the Terrible erected to celebrate his coronation in 1547, and to importune God to grant him an heir. Squatter and rounder than the Church of the Ascension, it has five chapels clus-tered around an octagonal core with a lofty onion dome.

# Tsaritsyno

The ruined palace of **Tsaritsyno** is an Imperial summer retreat that never was: a grandiose project that consumed resources for decades, only to be aborted as it neared fruition. The result is a haunting ruin whose enigma is encoded in stone, though it must be said that some visitors have been left cold. One Oxford Fellow "grudged the labour and particularly the fine stone which has been thrown away in this motley and tasteless undertaking".

Its history goes back to the sixteenth century, when Irina, the wife of Tsar Fyodor, had an estate here, which passed eventually from Peter the Great to the Moldavian Prince Dimitrie Cantemir, whose writer son sold it back to Catherine the Great for 25,000 rubles in 1775. She changed its dismal name, "Black Mud" (*Chyornaya Gryaz*), to "Empress's Village", and envisaged an estate to match her glorious summer palaces outside St Petersburg.

Catherine entrusted the building task to Vasily Bazhenov, perhaps as recompense for cancelling a scheme to rebuild the Kremlin, on which he had worked for years. His brief specified a park with pavilions in the Moorish-Gothic style that was fashionable in Europe, and adjoining palaces for the Empress and her son Paul. Ten years later she returned to inspect the nearly completed buildings – only to order that the main palace be torn down and built anew by Bazhenov's young colleague, Matvei Kazakov.

Some believe this was because Catherine objected to the **Masonic symbols** used as ornamentation; others that she could no longer bear the idea of living with Paul, who had grown to loathe her. In the event, Kazakov devoted over a decade to the project until its abrupt termination in 1797, owing to the drain on the treasury caused by a war with Turkey, and the aging Empress's waning desire for an estate outside Moscow.

Thereafter Tsaritsyno was abandoned to the elements, barring a brief interlude as a museum under Stalin, and there have been various plans to turn it into a barracks, a champagne factory or a diplomatic residential colony. Although a museum was established here in 1984, its collection remains stored in the cellars beneath the ruins, occasionally surfacing for exhibitions abroad. The latest scheme is to convert the shell of the palace into a luxury hotel, but this seems likely to prove as chimerical as the previous plans. To cap it all, Tsaritsyno has gained a reputation for **supernatural occurrences**: one of its bridges is reported to have moved several metres, and there have been sightings of "humanoid aliens" in the area.

## Practicalities

To **reach** the site – 3km south of Kolomenskoe – you need to board a Krasnogvardeyskaya-bound metro train, alight after two stops at Tsaritsyno station and surface by the Kaspiyskaya ulitsa exit. Head under the railway bridge and right around a building site and a fire station – Tsaritsyno's ruins loom on the hilltop beyond the ponds, straight ahead. As the **grounds** are open day and night all year round, no tickets are required to clamber around – just beware of slippery slopes and frozen ponds in winter, and thick mud in spring. Russians come here to picnic, fish, hunt for mushrooms or go sledging, depending on the season.

The map shows the following labels: Usadba Restaurant and Stables, Large Bridge, Third Kavalerskiy Building, Church of St Nicholas, Octahedron, Palace Administration, Patterned Bridge, Bread House, Bread Gate, Small Palace, Great Palace, Opera House, Patterned Gate, Belvedere, Ruin, Nerastankino, Temple of Ceres, Tsaritsyno Ponds, TSARITSYNO, 0 — 200m

For those able to afford it, there are **troyka rides** in winter ($60 per hour; a *troyka* seats six) and **horse-riding** all year round ($25 per hour). The stables are attached to the *Usadba* **restaurant** (daily noon–11pm), a posh establishment with a less expensive **bar** – the only place to eat or drink in the vicinity.

## The ruins

You approach by a causeway across the **Tsaritsyno Ponds** to pass beneath the **Patterned Bridge** (*Figurniy most*), which spans a cleft in the hillside. Built of pinkish brick, it bristles with white stone pinnacles and Gothic arches, Rosicrucian blooms and Maltese Crosses – a spookily kitsch combination that typifies the buildings at Tsaritsyno.

Predictably, the most imposing is the **Great Palace** (*Bolshoy dvorets*), whose twin wings stretch for 130 metres, replete with pilastered corner turrets and rows of pointed arches. In the nineteenth century its roof tiles and beams were purloined by a local factory, leaving a two-storey shell, crumbling and weed-choked. By following the palace back into the woods you'll reach the ornamental **Bread Gate** (*Khlebniy vorota*), leading into what was to have been the palace courtyard. Its name comes from the adjacent **Bread House** (*Khlebniy dom*) or kitchens, a "very large and ugly pile".

To the north lie the **Palace Administration** (now a music school); the ruinous **Octahedron** or servants' quarters; the newly restored nineteenth-century **Church of St Nicholas**; and a derelict guardhouse called the **Third Kavalerskiy Building**. Except for the church, they are all Bazhenov's work, like the **Large Bridge** across the ravine beyond.

Better still, head along the path running parallel to the pond, away from the semicircular **Small Palace** built for Gentlemen-in-Waiting, to a fantastically carved **Opera House** (*Operniy dom*) near the **Patterned Gate** (*Figurniy vorota*), a turreted Gothic arch that once formed the entrance to the park. Continuing southwards, you'll encounter a Classical **Belvedere** overlooking the pond, followed by an artificial **Ruin** such as was *de rigueur* for landscaped grounds in the late eighteenth century.

Here, the path turns east to slip by two more follies in the woods on the right, cryptically named **Nerastankino** and the **Temple of Ceres**. Like the Belvedere, these were both added to the park by Yegotov in 1803, when there was a brief revival of interest in Tsaritsyno.

# Chapter 8

# Taganka and Zayauze

T AGANKA AND ZAYAUZE are the beach heads of Moscow's eastern expansion far beyond the Moskva and Yauza rivers, originally spearheaded by Tsars and nobles who hunted in the forests and built country palaces that now stand marooned amid a tide of concrete. Eastern Moscow may be drab overall, but this area has enough sights and historical associations to justify a dozen forays into the hinterland.

Taganka, just east of the Yauza River, is the obvious starting point, with picturesque churches in the vicinity and a trio of monasteries further afield. The **Andronikov Monastery** is already known for its museum of icons, but the **Novospasskiy Monastery** has yet to be discovered by aficionados of Gothic gloom and decay, who would also enjoy what's left of the **Simonov Monastery** after half of it was bulldozed to make room for a Constructivist Palace of Culture. The ecclesiastical roll-call ends with the picturesque **Old Believers' Commune**, beyond the **Pet Market** a few miles east of Taganka. Further out lie the palatial **Kuskovo** estate of the Sheremetevs, and the neglected grounds of the **Kuzminki** mansion.

Zayauze's sights, further north, are more modest, and are only really worth a visit as part of a trip to somewhere else. The **Izmaylovo Art Market** attracts droves of tourists with a colourful glut of icons, handicrafts and Soviet kitsch, while in the vicinity is the **royal estate** where Peter the Great spent his childhood. Admirers of the Tsar may also be interested in the ex-stamping grounds of his "toy" regiments, and the **Lefort Palace** where he roistered with the Drunken Synod – even the house of his first mistress still remains.

## Taganka

The history of **Taganka** is as colourful as its main square and avenues are drab. Originally a quarter inhabited by smiths who made cauldrons (*tagany*) for the Muscovite army, it later became a shelter area for thieves and various undesirables who were obliged to live beyond the city walls. It was well known for its prison, which

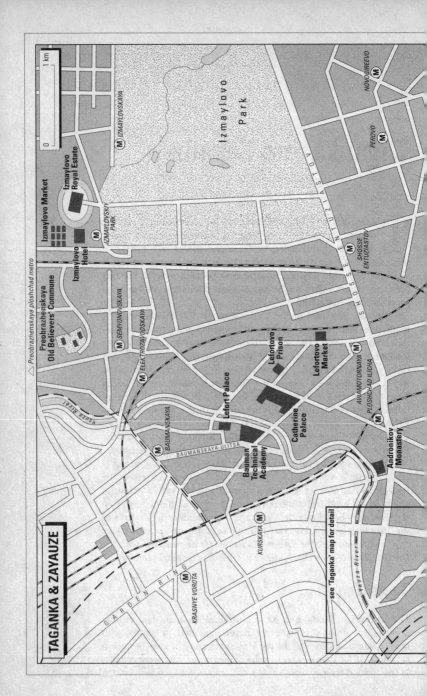

△ Preobrazhenskaya ploshchad metro

## TAGANKA & ZAYAUZE

0 ____ 1 km

**Izmaylovo Market**

**Izmaylovo Royal Estate**

**Izmaylovo Hotel**

IZMAYLOVSKY PARK

*Izmaylovo Park*

**Preobrazhenskaya Old Believers' Commune**

Ⓜ IZMAYLOVSKAYA

Ⓜ SEMYONOVSKAYA

Ⓜ ELEKTROZAVODSKAYA

Ⓜ NOVOGREEVO

PERDVO Ⓜ

Ⓜ SHOSSE ENTUZIASTOV

S H O S S E   E N T U Z I A S T O V

**Lefortovo Prison**

**Lefortovo Market** Ⓜ

**Lefort Palace**

AVIAMOTORNAYA Ⓜ

Ⓜ BAUMANSKAYA

BAUMANSKAYA ULITSA

**Bauman Technical Academy**

**Catherine Palace**

PLOSHCHAD ILICHA Ⓜ

**Andronikov Monastery**

YAUZA RIVER

Ⓜ KURSKAYA

G A R D E N   R I N G

KRASNYE VOROTA

see Taganka map for detail

Yauza River

### The Taganka Theatre and Vysotskiy

The **Taganka Theatre** was founded in 1964 by **Yuri Lyubimov**, one of the generation of *Shestidesyatniki* (literally "Sixties people") whose hopes of freedom raised by Khrushchev's "Thaw" were dashed by the return to orthodoxy under Brezhnev. During those years, Lyubimov managed to skirt the limits of censorship with dynamic plays that were understood as allegories of Soviet life. Eventually, with the indulgence of KGB boss Andropov, he was able to present such explicitly political drama as *The House on the Embankment* and stage Bulgakov's *The Master and Margarita*. In 1983 Lyubimov was exiled for openly criticizing the authorities; since being allowed back in 1988, his relationship with the theatre has gradually soured.

The theatre is also synonymous with **Vladimir Vysotskiy** (1938–80), whose black-jeaned, guitar-playing Hamlet electrified audiences in the 1970s. Actor, poet, balladeer and drunk, his songs of prison, low-life and disillusionment were spread by bootleg tape-recordings throughout the USSR and known to everyone from truck-drivers to intellectuals – even the KGB enjoyed them. Vysotskiy's death during the Olympic Games went unannounced in the media, but tens of thousands turned out to line the route to the Vagankov Cemetery, where Lyubimov spoke for millions when he called him "Our bard, the keeper of the nation's spirit, of our pain and all our joys". A small **Vysotskiy Museum** (no set hours) has been established on Nizhniy Taganskiy lane, near the theatre's modern, red-brick annexe.

was the inspiration for many ballads of the Thieves' World: "Taganka I am yours forever. My power and my talent perished inside your walls." This subculture profoundly influenced Vysotskiy's performances at the famous Taganka Theatre.

## Taganskaya ploshchad to the Kotelnicheskaya Apartments

Basically just a traffic junction, **Taganskaya ploshchad** is only traversable by the pedestrian subways that link its three metro stations. The Circle line station with its bas-reliefs of Soviet warriors will bring you out opposite the **Taganka Theatre**.

Across the street from the theatre, the **Church of St Nicholas by the Taganka Gate** (*tserkov Nikloy u Taganskikh vorot*) was originally hemmed in by the city walls. Its tall, narrow, dark red facade displays a panoply of engaged columns and *nalichniki*, crowned by slender domes and a tent-roofed belfry. Built in 1712, it has long been derelict but is now under repair, serving as a pointer towards the delightful **Church of the Assumption of the Potters** (*tserkov Uspeniya v Goncharakh*). This is painted maroon and white, offset by a tiled floral frieze and a golden dome surrounded by four blue, star-spangled ones. As the church's name suggests, it was founded by the local community of potters, in 1654; the bell tower on the corner was added in the mid-eighteenth century.

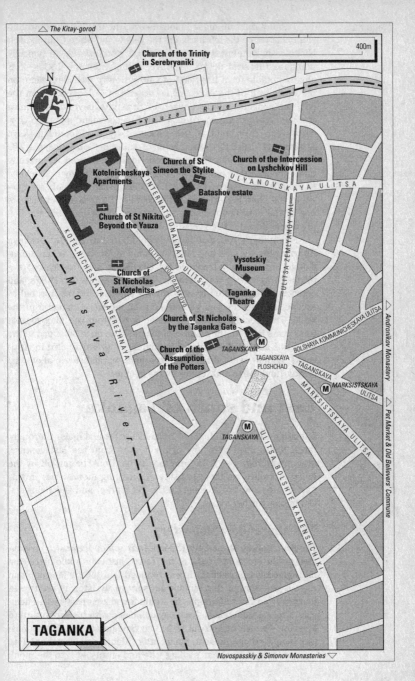

△ The Kitay-gorod

Church of the Trinity
in Serebryaniki

0       400m

N

Y a u z e   R i v e r

Church of St
Simeon the Stylite

Church of the Intercession
on Lyshchkov Hill

Kotelnicheskaya
Apartments

U L Y A N O V S K A Y A   U L I T S A

INTERNATSIONALNAYA ULITSA

Batashov estate

Church of St Nikita
Beyond the Yauza

K O T E L N I C H E S K A Y A   N A B E R E Z H N A Y A

ULITSA VOLODARSKOVO

ULITSA ZEMLYANOY VAL

Vysotskiy
Museum

Church of
St Nicholas
in Kotelnitsa

M o s k v a   R i v e r

Taganka
Theatre

Church of St Nicholas
by the Taganka Gate

△ Andronikov Monastery

BOLSHAYA KOMMUNICHESKAYA ULITSA

Church of the
Assumption
of the Potters

M
*TAGANSKAYA*

TAGANSKAYA
PLOSHCHAD

TAGANSKAYA

△ Pet Market & Old Believers' Commune

MARKSISTSKAYA

M
MARKSISTSKAYA
ULITSA

M
*TAGANSKAYA*

ULITSA BOLSHIE KAMENSHCHIKI

MARKSISTSKAYA ULITSA

**TAGANKA**

Novospasskiy & Simonov Monasteries ▽

Turning right up ulitsa Volodarskovo, the third of the downhill-sloping lanes on the left harbours the yellow and white **Church of St Nicholas in Kotelnitsa** (*tserkov Nikoly v Kotelnikakh*). A typically pompous Classical design by Bove, dating from the 1820s, it is chiefly notable for a bas-relief of Christ's entry into Jerusalem, on the outer wall of the nave. At the far end of Volodarskovo on the left, the peaceful hilltop **Church of St Nikita beyond the Yauza** (*tserkov Nikity shto za Yauzoy*) used to command a superb view across the river until it was obscured by the Kotelnicheskaya Apartments. Described as a heap of ruins in Solzhenitsyn's *The First Circle*, the church was rebuilt in 1958–60 and is currently undergoing further restoration, but its setting is in any case lovely. Its rounded *zakomary* gables and small cap-shaped cupola are typical of the churches erected in the reign of Boris Godunov. This is one of the very few remaining in Moscow, built in 1595; the bell tower was added in the 1680s.

From there you can head downhill to the **Kotelnicheskaya Apartments**, the first and most awesome of Moscow's seven Stalin-Gothic skyscrapers. Designed by Chechulin and Rostovskiy, the thirty-storey tower was built in the early 1950s by POWs and convicts, one of whom is said to have emulated Icarus in a bid to escape, as workers who perished on the job were immured in the walls. This could explain why water oozes from the plug-sockets forty years later, to the chagrin of tenants who once belonged to the elite. For all that, the exterior is mightily impressive, clad in rusticated granite with furled banners and wheatsheaves above its portals, and spires and statues on the heights.

# East and south of Taganka

Radiating east and south from Taganka are several major thoroughfares, some lined with low ochre houses from the last century, others with high-rise flats from the 1970s. Don't be put off by the initial stretches, as there are three interesting monasteries in this part of Moscow, not to mention the Pet Market and Old Believers' Commune, further out.

## The Andronikov Monastery

The **Andronikov Monastery** (*Spaso-Andronikov monastyr*) is situated on the steep east bank of the Yauza, just over a kilometre east of Taganskaya ploshchad. It was founded in 1360 by Metropolitan Alexei, who vowed that, should he survive the stormy return sea journey from Constantinople, he would found a monastery and dedicate it to the saint whose feast day coincided with his safe return to Moscow – which turned out to be Our Saviour (*Spas*). The monastery acquired its present name after Alexei was summoned to Crimea to treat the Khan's ailing wife and entrusted it to the monk

Andronik, who became its first abbot. Its most famous monk was the great icon painter, Andrei Rublev (see p.240).

East and
south of
Taganka

After the Revolution the monastery was turned into a prison camp, then into housing for workers at the nearby Hammer and Sickle Factory, and finally scheduled for demolition – but reprieved by the post-war upsurge of patriotism. In 1960 it was formally reopened as the **Andrei Rublev Museum of Early Russian Art**, in honour of the 600th anniversary of his birth. Though once again inhabited by monks, it still keeps museum **hours** (Mon, Tues & Thurs–Sun 11am–5pm; closed the last Fri of each month; $2 to visit the art collection, but not for the grounds). Bear in mind, though, that the museum doesn't actually contain any work by the master himself.

To get to the monastery, catch trolleybus #47 or #53 along Ulyanovskaya ulitsa to Andronevskaya ploshchad. Another method is to travel by metro to Ploshchad Ilicha station, and then ride the same trolleybus in the other direction, to approach the monastery from the east. Alternatively, walk along Bolshaya Kommunisticheskaya ulitsa, lined with two-storey dwellings from the last century, where the prosperous Old Believers lived.

## The monastery

The monastery is impressive from the outside but, except for the Refectory and the Archangel Michael church, is not nearly as romantic as the Donskoy or Novodevichiy monasteries. Enclosed by white stone ramparts with rounded crenellations and chunky towers at three corners, the complex is entered by a **Holy Gate** (*Svyatye vorota*). Flanked by turrets with conical wooden roofs, the gate was dominated by a Classical belltower until it was demolished in the 1930s. To the left of the gate stands the seventeenth-century **Abbot's Residence** (*Nastoyatelskie Pokoi*), decorated with ceramic insets; the ticket office and an early nineteenth-century **Seminary** (*Dukhovnoe Uchilishche*) lie off to the right.

The elaborate structure near the west wall was created over several centuries, starting with the two-storey tent-roofed **Refectory** (*Trapeznaya palata*) in 1504–06. A sawtoothed cornice integrates this with the Moscow Baroque **Church of the Archangel Michael** (*tserkov Arkhangela Mikhaila*) that rises alongside in variegated tiers. The church was commissioned in 1694 as a private chapel and burial vault for the family of Yevdokiya Lopukhina, Peter the Great's first wife. Four years later he forced her into a convent and exiled the Lopukhins to Siberia, whereupon the pace of construction slackened so much that the church wasn't finished until 1731.

The smaller **Cathedral of the Saviour** (*Spasskiy sobor*), in the centre of the grounds, was built in 1425–27 and decorated by Rublev. Although traces of his frescoes remain, the cathedral is closed for restoration, so you can only see its weathered stone facade, whose perspective-arch is surmounted by a relief of the

### Andrei Rublev

The monk **Andrei Rublev** (pronounced "Rubl*yov*") is revered as the greatest painter of medieval Russia, whose work remained a beacon throughout the dark centuries of the Tatar invasions and the Time of Troubles. His birthplace is unknown and the date uncertain (possibly 1360), but he probably served his apprenticeship in the icon workshop of the Trinity Monastery of St Sergei, outside Moscow. Having painted the icons for Zvenigorod Cathedral, 40km northwest of Moscow, in 1400, Rublev worked on the Cathedral of the Assumption in the Kremlin, and its namesake in Vladimir (with Daniil Cherniy). He painted his masterpiece, the *Old Testament Trinity*, in about 1411 or 1422, for the monastery where he had served his novitiate, before retiring to the Andronikov Monastery, where he is said to have died in 1430.

The Soviets honoured him as an artist, but delayed the release of Tarkovskiy's superb film, *Andrei Rublev*, with its scenes of Christian faith and pagan nudity, until the early 1980s. In 1989, he was canonized by the Russian Orthodox Church and a **statue of Rublev** was erected in the park outside the monastery, which hosts an annual **celebration** in his honour on July 17.

Saviour. The helmet-shaped dome and triple apses reflect the influence of early medieval Vladimir architecture, while the pyramid of *zakomary* and *kokoshniki* are characteristic of the early Moscow style. Much altered over the centuries, it was restored to its original appearance during the 1950s. The feast day of Our Saviour falls on August 16.

### The museum

The Rublev Museum's **collection of icons** is distributed around several buildings, some of which may be closed; your likeliest bets are the ground floor of the Refectory and the service block near the ticket office. Highlights include fifteenth-century icons by the school of Rublev (but none by the master himself), seventeenth-century icons from Novgorod, and an eighteenth-century *Tikhvin Virgin* from the Donskoy Monastery: the collection, however, doesn't compare with that of the Tretyakov Gallery. As a centre of research into Russian Orthodox culture, it also runs a **choristers school** that specializes in medieval liturgies. The Sirin Ensemble gives wonderful **concerts** on Wednesday evenings in the summer.

## Novospasskiy Monastery and the Krutitskoe podvore

The high-rise sprawl to the south of Taganka harbours two unexpected treats near the river: the Novospasskiy Monastery and Krutitskoe podvore, the seventeenth-century complex. Getting there from Taganskaya ploshchad entails walking 1km down ulitsa Bolshie Kamenshchiki, or taking the metro to Proletarskaya station,

leaving by the Dinamovskaya ulitsa exit and walking in the direction
of the Moskva River, keeping an eye out for the tall yellow belltower
that will guide you towards the monastery. From there, it's less than
ten minutes' walk to the Krutitskoe podvore.

## The Novospasskiy Monastery

The Novospasskiy Monastery (*Novospasskiy monastyr*) claims to
be the oldest in Moscow, tracing its foundation back to the twelfth-
century reign of Yuri Dolgurukiy, who established a monastery dedicated to the Saviour on the site of the present-day Danilov
Monastery. In 1300, Ivan I transferred this to the Kremlin, whence
Ivan III relocated it to its present site in 1490 – hence the appella-
tion, "New Monastery of the Saviour". Subsequently razed by the
Tatars, most of the existing complex dates from the seventeenth
century, when the monastery was surrounded by a thick wall with
seven bastions, which preserved it through the Time of Troubles
and determined its grim role in modern times, when it was used as a
concentration camp by the Bolsheviks, who imprisoned and shot
their victims in the almshouse and hospital alongside the northern
wall. It then became an orphanage, an NKVD archive, a furniture
factory, and finally a drunk-tank. Returned to the Church in 1991,
the buildings are slowly being restored, but the ravages of its recent
past are still evident.

Usually open daily from 9am to 5pm (if not later), the entrance
to the monastery is through an archway in its gigantic four-tiered
belltower, whose gold finial was once visible for miles around.
Above the archway is a small church dedicated to St Sergei of
Radonezh, the founder of the Trinity Monastery, outside Moscow,
where Rublev did his apprenticeship; beyond lies a muddle of sheds
and chapels.

The main Cathedral of the Saviour (*sobor Spasa
Preobrazheniya*) is a medieval-style edifice with huge arched
gables and helmet-shaped domes, erected on the site of the original
cathedral in 1645. An image of the Saviour watches over the portal
to the (locked) crypt that served as the family vault of the Romanov
*boyars* until Mikhail Romanov's ascension to the throne in 1613.
The cathedral's nave is dominated by a massive gilt-framed iconostasis that includes the icons of the *Image of Christ* and the *Virgin
of Smolensk*, a gift from the mother of Tsar Mikhail, who became a
nun in later life. Its walls are covered in frescoes representing the
genealogy of the sovereigns of Russia from St Olga to Tsar Alexei,
and the descent of the kings of Israel, while the refectory stairway is
flanked by images of ancient Greek philosophers.

The orange Baroque Church of the Sign, around the back of the
cathedral, contains the tomb of Parasha Kovalyova, whose marriage
to Count Sheremetev amazed Moscow society (see p.266). But the
most curious story relates to the derelict tent-roofed chapel that
stands in the yard to the north of the cathedral (see box overleaf).

**The legend of Princess Trakanova**

The chapel contains the remains of Sister Inokinya Dosieeya, better
known to Russians as **Princess Trakanova**. As the illegitimate child of
Empress Elizabeth and Count Razumovskiy, she was sent abroad to be
educated, enabling a Polish adventuress to claim her identity and the right
to inherit the throne of Russia. Though this imposter was swiftly incarcerated (and died in prison), Catherine the Great decided to lure Trakanova
back home and confine her to a nunnery "for the good of Russia". **Legend**
has it that the task was entrusted to Catherine's lover, Count Orlov, who
seduced Trakanova aboard a ship before locking her in their nuptial cabin
as they approached St Petersburg. The princess was then placed under
strict isolation in the Ivanovskiy Convent, where she remained for 25
years until Catherine's death, by which time Trakanova had come to
accept her fate and chose to remain a nun.

Beyond the west wall lies a large **pond** that once supplied the monks
with fish. During the mid-1930s, the NKVD used its steep bank as a
burial ground for the bodies of foreign Communists secretly shot in
the purges.

### Krutitskoe podvore

From the monastery, Krutitskaya ulitsa leads directly to the
**Krutitskoe podvore** (Wed–Mon 9am–6pm; closed the first Mon of
each month), a small complex or "yard" (*podvore*) of seventeenth-
century buildings that gets its name from the steep (*krutoy*) bank of
the nearby Moskva River. It served as the residence of the senior
Metropolitan of the Russian Church until Catherine the Great turned
it into a barracks – there's still a military camp around the back.

Its centrepiece is a **Cathedral of the Assumption** (*Uspenskiy
sobor*) constructed entirely of brick – onion domes included –
connected by an overhead **arcade** to the **Metropolitan's Palace** in
the far corner of the yard. The arcade passes through an impressive
arched structure called the **Teremok**, one wall of which is decorated
with turquoise tiles in colourful floral designs and has beautiful
window frames carved like grapevines. Incongruously juxtaposed
against the venerable buildings are several wooden huts dating from
the 1920s, when the Krutitskoe podvore was turned into a workers'
hostel.

## The Simonov Monastery and around

Founded in 1370 by the monk Fyodor, a nephew of Sergei of
Radonezh, the **Simonov Monastery** (*Simonovskiy monastyr*)
resisted many sieges until it was sacked by the Poles during the
Time of Troubles, but was rebuilt with even thicker walls in the
1640s, and remained one of Moscow's mightiest defensive outposts
– known as "Moscow's Sentinel" – for several hundred years.
However, its isolated spot by the river was considered a prime site

for a football stadium and palace of culture and it was bulldozed to make way. The stadium and palace now stand just to the north, and together with the monastery's ruins attest to both its former strength and to the Soviet ravages that surpassed anything inflicted by foreign invaders.

**Getting there** involves catching the (green) Zamoskvoretskaya line to **Avtozavodskaya metro station**. Outside the station, look out for ulitsa Vostochnaya, which slants off between a war memorial and a tall grey block; one of the monastery's towers is visible 500m up the road. Trolleybuses (#26 & #67) and buses (#9 & #670) run there from the metro station.

## The ruins

The most impressive feature of the ruins is a 250-metre-long section of **fortified wall** (which once totalled 655m in length), guarded by three massive stone towers that have recently been restored. Fyodor Kon, who designed the walls of the Beliy Gorod, is thought to have created the **Dulo Tower** on the corner by the river, with its tiers of windows at staggered intervals; the archers' gallery and tent-roofed spire were added in the seventeenth century, when the towers of the Kremlin received similar additions. Nearer the road, the **Solevaya and Kuznechnaya towers** resemble giant mushrooms, their white stalks capped by brown spires.

You enter the grounds (open during daylight) by a gate in the fence beyond the roadside tower, to find abandoned cars and heaps of rubble where nineteenth-century visitors were delighted by "gardens of marigolds and dahlias, and bees humming in hedges of spiraea". Ahead looms a huge derelict **church** containing a workshop that previously turned out busts of Lenin, and now makes theatrical props. Its exterior was once painted to resemble multi-coloured facets, traces of which remain. There used to be six churches (the oldest built in 1405), but in 1934 five of them were blown up in a single day.

Since regaining ownership of the Simonov in 1994, the Church has struck a deal with the firms on the premises: they are allowed to remain for a while but must contribute funds to its restoration. Depending on the pace of work, the church may still serve as a factory and the four-storey **refectory** as a warehouse, but the **monks' block** by the rear wall has already reverted to its proper function.

## Other sights in the vicinity

In its medieval heyday the monastery owned twelve thousand "souls" and a score of villages, while its walls encompassed three times the present area – a measure of how much was destroyed to create the **Torpedo Football Stadium** and the **ZiL Palace of Culture**, which was the largest and most lavishly appointed of the workers' clubs built in the 1930s. Designed by the Vsenin brothers, the foremost Constructivist architects of their day, the ZiL Palace, north of the monastery, is best viewed from the river-facing side, where an expansive curved gallery floods the interior with light. Otherwise, it has not aged well; like other Constructivist buildings of the time, its design required better materials than were available.

The Palace belongs to the **ZiL Motor Works** (*Avtozavod imeni Likhachova*), Russia's oldest car factory (founded in 1916), which although trucks form the bulk of its output, is best known for the ZiL limousine, used by Party leaders. Today, the factory, on the far side of the park outside the monastery, has fallen on hard times and will soon be as decrepit as the monastery; it is an odd setting for the resurrected **Church of the Nativity of the Virgin in Old Simonov**, built in 1509. Previously used as a compressor-shed, it now boasts a new iconostasis and a charming garden (services at 8am & 5pm). To have a look, enter the factory by the park gate and simply follow the walkway – you can't go astray.

# The Pet Market and the Old Believers' Commune

There are only two reasons for tourists to venture into the suburban hinterland 2–3km east of Taganskaya ploshchad: the Pet Market and the Old Believers' Commune. **Getting there** is easy. From the stand near the Taganskaya supermarket, catch trolleybus #16, #23 or #63 out along Taganskaya ulitsa, counting each stop. To reach the market, alight at the fifth stop and cut through onto Bolshaya Kalitnikovskaya ulitsa, where it should lie straight ahead. For the commune, ride on to the next stop and look out for its belltower on the far side of Nizhergorodskaya ulitsa. A path skirting a car park and crossing the tracks should bring you to the site in under ten minutes.

### The Pet Market

The outdoor **Pet Market** (*Ptichniy rynok*) off Bolshaya Kalitnikovskaya ulitsa – running parallel to Nizhergorodskaya – has no sign as such, but you can't miss the people clutching pets. A few sellers can be found any day, but on Sunday (9am–5pm) the place is jam-packed with folk selling puppies or kittens, standing three deep; rickety stalls stocking everything from birdfood to hunting gear; and sections for talking birds (their vocabulary is noted on labels) and guard dogs. When President Reagan asked to see the market during his visit to Moscow, it was spruced up for the occasion.

A grisly tale is attached to the **Kaltinovskie Cemetery** (*Kaltinovskoe Kladbische*), off behind the market, which was used to dispose of victims during the Terror. So many were tipped into pits at night that dogs gathered from all over town to scavenge, leaving limbs strewn about – but residents were too frightened to complain.

## The Old Believers' Commune

The **Old Believers' Commune** (*Staroobryadcheskaya Obshchina*)
is a relic of an Orthodox sect that once loomed large in Tsarist
Russia – especially in Moscow, where many of the merchants and
coachmen were so-called Old Believers (see box). Their commune
was founded in the 1770s after Catherine the Great granted them
limited rights and many returned from hiding in Siberia. Though
Nicholas I re-imposed discriminatory laws, the sect had become
established enough to weather official disapproval until the onset of
liberalization in 1905. After the Revolution, however, they were
doubly suspect for their piety and wealth, and suffered even more
severe repression, which forced the sect underground for decades.
Today, the commune is coming back to life, but their strict ethics
effectively disbar them from the cut-throat business world that is
the New Russia.

The commune's main landmark is its **belltower**, a soaring
Neo-Byzantine structure with elaborate blind arcades and Moorish
arches, which was built to celebrate the reopening of their churches
in 1905. Soon after the Revolution, the Bolsheviks closed them
down again and turned the **Cathedral of the Intercession**
(*Pokrovskiy sobor*) into a cobblers' workshop. Built in 1792 by
Kazakov, its Classical facade doesn't prepare you for the vastness
and magnificence of the interior, whose arches and pillars are
outlined in gold and covered with frescoes of saints and biblical
events. *Murray's Handbook* (1875) warned visitors that "the
singing will be found very peculiar . . . especially that of the women,

---

### The Old Believers

During the 1650s, Patriarch Nikon's reforms of Orthodox ritual were
rejected by thousands of Russians who felt that only their traditional rites
offered salvation. Calling themselves **Old Believers** (*Staroobryadtsy*) –
others termed them *Raskolniki* (Dissenters) – they held that crossing
oneself with three fingers instead of two was an infamy, and shaving a
beard "a sin that even the blood of martyrs could not expiate". Opposition
intensified under Peter the Great, whom they saw as the Antichrist for his
promoting tobacco; ordering men to cut their beards (which believers
kept to be buried with them, lest they be barred from paradise); and
imposing the Julian Calendar and a chronology dating from the birth of
Christ, rather than Creation – thus perverting time itself.

To escape forced conversions, the Old Believers fled into the wilds; if
cornered, they burned themselves to death, singing hymns. During generations in exile, they became divided into the less stringent *Popovtsy*, who
dealt with Orthodox priests and were willing to drink to the Tsar's health;
and the *Bezpopovtsy* (Priestless), who totally rejected both Church and
State. The latter included wilder **subsects** like the *Skoptsy* or "Mutilated
Ones", who castrated themselves, and the *Khlisty* (Flagellants), whose
orgies and lashings expressed their belief in salvation through sin
(Rasputin was said to have been one).

---

who perform Divine service in a chapel apart from the men". By turning up at 5pm, you can hear the liturgy and judge for yourself. Further north stands the attractive Pseudo-Russian **Church of St Nicholas** (*tserkov Nilolay*), whose white walls are jazzed up by red, white and blue *kokoshniki*, sage-green pendentives and turquoise shingled onion domes.

By passing through the church's tent-roofed archway – originally the entrance to the commune – you'll find the **Rogozhskoe Cemetery** (Tues–Sun 9am–6pm), established in the plague year of 1771. Although less exotic than the Novodevichiy Cemetery, it does contain an odd mixture of Old Believers and Soviet functionaries. The main path leads uphill past the modest headstone of **Admiral Gorshkov** (who headed the Soviet Navy under Brezhnev) to the **Morozov family** plot, beneath a wrought-iron canopy. A thrifty serf couple who sold their homespun cloth on the streets of Moscow after the great fire, the Morozovs bought their freedom and within thirty years owned a cotton mill which their son **Timofey** developed into a textiles empire. Alongside are buried Timofey's widow **Maria**, a fervent Old Believer who henceforth ran the show; their sons **Savva**, who sponsored the arts and left-wing causes before killing himself, and **Aseny**, who died of a stupid prank.

# Kuskovo and Kuzminki

It's a measure of Moscow's growth that the southeastern suburbs now incorporate what were country estates in the eighteenth and nineteenth centuries. Kuskovo and Kuzminki once embodied a way of life that amounted to a credo: the pursuit of pleasure and elegant refinement by an aristocracy that was no longer obliged to serve the state (as Peter the Great had insisted). The fate of Kuskovo and Kuzminki since the Revolution illustrates the Soviets' Janus-like view of Russia's aristocratic heritage, with one estate being preserved as a museum and the other being allowed to moulder away.

## Kuskovo

The industrial suburb of **KUSKOVO** takes its name from the former Sheremetev estate – Moscow's finest example of an eighteenth-century nobleman's country palace. The history of the estate dates back as far as 1715, when Peter the Great awarded the village of Kuskovo to one Boris Sheremetev, a general at the battle of Poltava, who built a summer residence there. Its present layout is owed to his son, Pyotr, who devoted himself to the management of the estate after inheriting some 200,000 serfs and marrying Varvara Cherkasskaya, whose dowry included the talented serf-architects

Fyodor Argunov and Alexei Mironov. After Pyotr's death the mansion gradually fell into disuse – his son Nikolai preferred his own palace at Ostankino – so, barring some repairs after Kuskovo was looted by French troops in 1812, its mid-eighteenth-century decor remained unchanged until the estate was nationalized by the Bolsheviks in 1919.

Kuskovo and Kuzminki

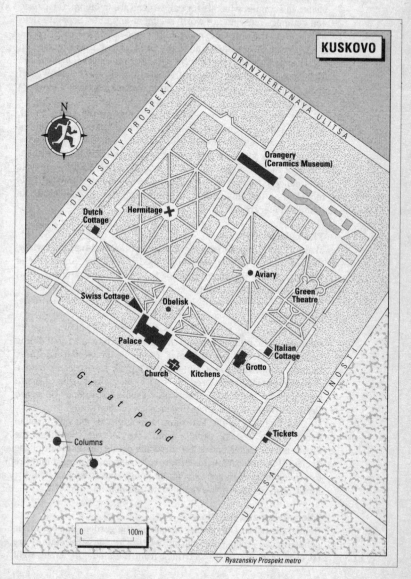

**KUSKOVO**

ORANZHEREYNAYA ULITSA

1-Y DVORTSOVIY PROSPEKT

N

Orangery
(Ceramics Museum)

Dutch Cottage

Hermitage

Aviary

Green Theatre

Swiss Cottage

Obelisk

Palace

Italian Cottage

Grotto

Church

Kitchens

Great Pond

YUNOSTI

Columns

Tickets

ULITSA

0      100m

▽ Ryazanskiy Prospekt metro

## Approaches

Getting to Kuskovo is easier than it sounds. Take the metro to Ryazanskiy Prospekt station and exit onto the street of the same name; then from the third bus stop on the right, ride bus #133 or #208 six stops to the main entrance, or alight one stop earlier to approach the palace through its extensive grounds. Though best visited in summer, when its formal gardens are in bloom, the palace and ceramics museum are worth seeing at any time. Separate **tickets** (sold by the entrance, and totalling about $2) are required for the park, the Palace, the Church, the Grotto, the Italian Cottage and the Orangery (which houses the ceramics museum) (all Wed–Sun May–Sept 10am–6pm; Oct–April 10am–4pm; closed the last Wed of each month). Finally, it's wise to bring a snack, as there's nowhere to eat in the vicinity.

The approach to the palace runs alongside the **Great Pond**, which is still used for boating in the summer. On the other side of the path you'll glimpse the Grotto pavilion (see below), and pass the ornate former **kitchens** and a grey and white **church** topped by a statue of the Archangel Michael, now once again used for services (and concerts, as advertised). The adjacent golden-yellow **belfry** is modelled on the Admiralty in St Petersburg, as a compliment to its founder, Peter the Great.

### The palace

Made of wood, plastered over and painted salmon-pink and white, the one-storey **palace** was built in 1769–77 by Argunov and Mironov, under the supervision of the professional architect Karl Blank. Ascending a ramp flanked by buxom sphinxes, visitors are obliged to put on *tapochki* before entering the **Grecian Vestibule**, replete with fake antique urns and marble.

The tour of the palace progresses through the silk-wallpapered **card room** and **billiard room** to the pink and white, mirrored **dining hall**, and thence to the "informal" rooms in the west wing. These include a **tapestry room** hung with Flemish tapestries; a **mauve drawing room** upholstered in cerise and silver silk; a **state bedchamber** with an allegorical fresco, *Innocence Choosing Between Wisdom and Love*; and an oak-panelled **study**.

The highlight is the **ballroom**, dripping with gilt and chandeliers, whose fresco, *Apollo and the Muses*, glorifies the Sheremetevs. Relief panels on the walls depict the exploits of the ancient Roman hero Mucius Scaevola, who thrust his hand into fire to prove his indifference to pain, an image that resonated with the Russians at the time of the Napoleonic invasion.

### The garden and pavilions

Behind the palace, an obelisk introduces the **garden**, laid out in the geometrical French style; during winter, its Classical statues are encased in boxes to protect them from the cold. Off to the right you'll find the **grotto** pavilion, with its prominent dome and ornate wrought-iron gates, by Argunov; the interior was decorated by the St Petersburg "Master of Grotto Work", Johannes Fokt, using shells, stones, textured stucco and porcelain. Nearby is the charming **Italian Cottage** (*Italyanskiy domik*), a miniature palace in its own right; if you're there on the hour, don't miss the melodious grand-father clock.

Further on, beyond the lattice-work **aviary** and the open-air **Green Theatre**, the old **Orangery** houses a **Ceramics Museum** displaying the former Savva Morozov collection of eighteenth- and nineteenth-century porcelain from the Gardner, Safronov and Popov factories. Notice the Egyptian service that belonged to Alexander I on the way in, and the figures of different ethnic groups of the Tsarist Empire in the central aisle. On the way back, cast an eye over Blank's Baroque **Hermitage** pavilion, topped by a statue of the goddess Flora; the steep-roofed brick **Dutch Cottage**, built in 1749; and the elaborately gabled **Swiss Cottage** created by the St Petersburg stage designer Nikolai Benois – all of which are closed for restoration at present.

## Kuzminki

A few miles to the south of Kuskovo lies another aristocratic estate of the same period, that of the Golitsyn family. KUZMINKI, however, has fared badly: its main house burned down in 1915, and during the Soviet era the other buildings were taken over or simply left to rot. While some are being repaired now, visitors shouldn't expect to find any palatial mansions or formal gardens; ruined follies and acres of birches, larch and spruce is what you'll get. In winter, especially, the isolation and solitude are Kuzminki's best features.

**Getting there** takes about an hour. Start by taking the metro to Kuzminki station. Cross the main road by an underpass and wait at the third stop on the right for bus #29, which eventually terminates near a **café** (daily 10am–10pm), 200m from the main entrance to the grounds.

### Exploring the park

At the end of the avenue through the woods, a domed **Mausoleum** and a ruined **Church of the Virgin** with a circular **belltower** presage what appears to be the mansion, but was in fact the estate's **Egyptian Pavilion**. Built by Voronikhin in 1811, the faded Classical edifice is hardly redolent of Egypt, but is handsomely set back behind a fence guarded by statues of fierce gryphons and dozy lions, augmented by a statue of Lenin up the drive. The pavilion now houses a biological research centre.

Crossing the bridge over a weir between the **Upper and Lower Ponds**, you'll see the crumbling brick mass of the **Konniy dvor**

**Kuskovo and Kuzminki**

(Stables) on the far bank. Actually a grandiose music pavilion built in 1793 by Rodion Kazakov, its name comes from the huge sculpted horses that rear beside the stairs to its entrance, which, though boarded up, are still visible through chinks in the planks.

# Zayauze

Strictly speaking, ZAYAUZE refers to the whole east bank of the Yauza as far downstream as Taganka, but here it only signifies the upper reaches of the river, plus a slice of the Baumanskiy district on the west bank, whose metro station is the jumping-off point for most of the sights. Despite the attractive riverside setting of Zayauze's palaces and their intimate associations with Peter the Great, their appeal is diminished by the fact that you can't get inside – so think twice before embarking on the trip. But if you really like exploring odd backwaters, the itinerary can be extended to include Lefortovo Prison, further out.

In the second half of the seventeenth century, Zayauze was the site of the so-called **German Suburb\*** (*Nemetskaya sloboda*), where foreigners were obliged to live by the edict of Tsar Alexei, so that their "heathen" churches and customs wouldn't outrage the xenophobic Muscovites. Ironically, what began as a form of quarantine ended up infecting Alexei's successor with the very ideas and habits that traditionalists deplored. The Suburb was a European oasis of brick houses and formal gardens, whose three thousand residents enjoyed mixed *soirées*, ballroom dancing and tobacco. In a society that mingled Dutch merchants, German architects and Scottish mercenaries, Peter not only enlarged his view of the world, but even took a foreign mistress, Anna Mons.

## From Baumanskaya to Lefortovo

Starting from Baumanskaya metro station on the (dark blue) Arbatsko-Pokrovskaya line, head south along Baumanskaya ulitsa until you reach the circular **Baumanskiy Market** (Mon–Sat 7am– 7pm, Sun 7am–6pm), and turn right along Starokirochniy pereulok, where the small house at no. 6 is where Peter visited **Anna Mons** at the start of their affair. The flaxen-haired daughter of a Westphalian wine merchant, Anna was encouraged to hope that she might become Empress because of Peter's lavish gifts and obvious disenchantment with his wife, Yevdokiya. Although their relationship lasted for twelve years, her ambition was ultimately fulfilled by her successor, Catherine, whose origins were even humbler than Anna's.

---

\* The Russian word for German, *Nemets* (meaning "dumb", because they couldn't speak Russian), was originally applied to all foreigners, whose diverse tongues were equally unintelligible to most Russians.

The lane emerges onto 2-ya Baumanskaya ulitsa opposite the **Lefort Palace** (*Lefortovskiy dvorets*) that Peter built in 1697 to host parties for his "Jolly Company". From this evolved the famous "**Drunken Synod**", dedicated to mockery of Church rituals, whose rulebook stated that members were to "get drunk every day and never go to bed sober". The palace's nominal owner was the Swiss adventurer Franz Lefort, who had introduced Peter to Anna in 1690. It was in the Lefort Palace that the Tsar's heir, Peter II, died of small-pox at the age of fourteen, on his wedding day. The palace's full size can only be appreciated by peering through the gateway; it now houses photographic and military archives.

Further along stands the former **Suburban Palace** (*Slobodskiy dvorets*) of "Mad" Tsar Paul. A pale ochre pile remodelled by various architects over the decades, it later became the Imperial Technical Academy, a hotbed of revolutionary activity where the Bolshevik Moscow Committee met in 1905; their local organizer, Nikolai Bauman, was beaten to death by ultra-rightists outside the building. It now contains the **Bauman Technical Academy**, which until a few years ago was a training school for technocrats destined for the Party elite.

Carry on to the end of the road, turn left into ulitsa Radio, and you'll be on the right track to a grander Imperial summer palace, visible across the Yauza. Backed by gardens descending to the river, the **Catherine Palace** (*Yekaterininskiy dvorets*) boasts the longest colonnade in Moscow, with sixteen columns set in a loggia facing the main road. Built in the second half of the eighteenth century by three leading architects – Quarenghi, Rinaldi and Camporesi – the palace was inherited by the Empress's soldier-mad son, Paul, who turned it into a palatial officers' school. Owned by the military ever since, it currently houses the Malinovskiy Tank Academy.

Alternatively, head 300m east along Energeticheskaya ulitsa to catch a glimpse of the notorious **Lefortovo Prison**, behind a row of houses on the left-hand side. During the 1930s, "enemies of the people" like Yevgenia Ginzburg waited here to be transferred to camps in Siberia, as did Brezhnev-era dissidents such as Father Gleb Yakunin. More recently, Khasbulatov, Rutskoi and their followers were bundled into Lefortovo after the storming of the White House, but were amnestied by parliament a few months later.

## Izmaylovo and Preobrazhenskoe

Further east lies the 300-hectare **Izmaylovo Park** named after the royal estate where Peter the Great grew up, and nowadays known for its weekend art market. The best way of getting there is to take the metro to Izmaylovskiy Park station. The **Izmaylovo Market** (*Izmaylovskiy rynok*; Sat & Sun 9am–6pm; small entry fee) is one of Moscow's major tourist attractions, offering a vast range of souvenirs. Besides the inevitable *matryoshka* dolls and KGB sweatshirts, you can find pre-war cameras, busts of Lenin, and all kinds of "folk" handicrafts. Prospective buyers should bear in mind that items predating 1960 are officially designated as antiques and need an export licence, while probably half of the icons on sale have been stolen from churches or private collections.

When the market palls, it's time to check out the **Izmaylovo Royal Estate**, on an island ten minutes' walk to the east. Owned by the Romanov *boyars* since the sixteenth century, Izmaylovo was the favourite country retreat of Tsar Alexei, whose son Peter spent much of his childhood here. In 1688, he discovered a small abandoned boat of Western design, and insisted on being taught how to sail by a Dutchman – the birth of his passion for the sea, which led to the creation of the Russian Navy and vistas of maritime power for what had previously been a landlocked nation.

Beyond a sports ground lies an enclosure of low whitewashed buildings; in the seventeenth century, a wooden palace occupied the centre. Ahead stands the **Ceremonial Gate**, an impressive triple-arched structure with a tent-roof that brings you out opposite the **Cathedral of the Intercession** (*Pokrovskiy sobor*), overhung by five massive domes clustered so closely that they almost touch. Behind this stands the **Bridge Tower** that once guarded the approaches to the estate.

## Preobrazhenskoe

Another stop on the Peter the Great trail is the old village of **Preobrazhenskoe**, immediately west of Izmaylovo market, where his childhood wargames gradually evolved into serious manoeuvres using real weapons from the Kremlin Armoury. Playmates and servants were drilled by experts from the German Suburb; Peter insisted on being treated like a common soldier and on mastering every skill himself. Eventually, there were two companies, each 300-strong, which formed the nucleus of the first units of the Imperial Guard – the Preobrazhenskiy and Semyonovskiy regiments. Russians who mocked **Peter's "toy" regiments** were obliged to revise their opinion after the Guards crushed the *Streltsy* revolt of 1689, and subsequently won honours at Poltava and other battles.

Though nothing remains of their former stamping grounds, you might care to visit the **Preobrazhenskaya Old Believers' Commune**, founded in the late eighteenth century by *Bezpopovtsy* (Priestless) sectarians. Several of their churches and dormitories remain at no. 17 ulitsa Preobrazhenskiy val, which runs past the local cemetery, midway between Preobrazhenskaya Ploshchad and Semyonovskaya metro stations.

# Chapter 9

# The Northern Suburbs

**M** oscow's **NORTHERN SUBURBS** lack the eclectic charm of the inner city, and even if you wanted to wander about, the distances are too vast. Instead, it has a scattering of interesting museums and sights that call for a targeted approach, relying on the metro to get you within striking distance of each attraction.

Foremost among them is the **VDNKh**, a huge exhibition park that has been likened to a Stalinist Disney World, juxtaposing extravagant pavilions and mothballed spaceships with foreign-made luxury goods and all the trappings of what Russians call "Wild Capitalism" (*dikiy kapitalism*). Moscow's **Botanical Gardens** and the **Ostankino Palace** and **TV Tower** are also in the vicinity.

Nearer to the centre of Moscow, an odd assortment of museums and theatres merits a few sorties beyond the Garden Ring. You'll find a superb collection of musical instruments at the **Museum of Musical Culture**; a weird **Animal Theatre**; the **Police and Army museums**; the fairytale **Vasnetsov House**; and a memorial museum in **Dostoyevsky's birthplace**. Travelling between these sights, you're likely to spot such Moscow landmarks as the **Olympic Sports Complex**.

## Near the Garden Ring

There are two fascinating museums a few blocks beyond the Garden Ring: one within ten minutes' walk of Triumfalnaya square (p.150); the other further away from Tsvetnoy Bulvar metro (p.167). To visit them, it's best to start with the Museum of Musical Culture, and then catch a trolleybus #6 further round the Ring to Sadovaya-Samotyochnaya ploshchad, for the Vasnetsov House.

### The Museum of Musical Culture

Two blocks north of Sadovaya-Triumfalnaya ulitsa, at ulitsa Fadeeva 4, the **Museum of Musical Culture** (Tues–Sun 11am–7pm; free admission Sun) exhibits all kinds of beautifully crafted instruments from around the world. By taking the trouble to book a **tour** (maximum 20 people; $10 flat rate) beforehand, you can even hear some

MOSCOW RING ROAD

Moscow Canal

PLANERNAYA Ⓜ

Ⓜ RECHNOY VOKZAL

Northern
River
Terminal ⚓

SKHODNENSKAYA Ⓜ

VODNIY
STADION

Ⓜ

TUSHINO

VOLOKOLAMSKOE SHOSSE

Ⓜ TUSHINSKAYA

Moskva River

Ⓜ VOYKOVSKAYA

LENINGRADSKOE SHOSSE

Ⓜ SHCHUKINSKAYA

Ⓜ SOKOL

AEROPORT

Ⓜ

Central Army
Sports Club
(TsKA)

Petrovskiy
Palace

Dinamo
Stadium

OKTYABRSKOE POLE Ⓜ

Air Terminal
Aerostar Hotel
CENTRAL AIRFIELD

Ⓜ DINAMO

Romen
Gypsy
Theatre

Serebryaniy
Bor

POLEZHAEVSKAYA

Hippodrome

LENINGRADSKIY PROSPEKT

BELORUSSKAYA

BEGOVAYA

Ⓜ

ULITSA

Belarus
Station

Ⓜ

Palace
Hotel

Moskva River

BEGOVAYA

MAYAKOVSKAYA Ⓜ

† † †
† † †
† †

Ⓜ ULITSA 1905 GODA

THE NORTHERN SUBURBS

MOSCOW RING ROAD

Ⓜ TIMIRYAZEVSKAYA

MEDVEDKOVO Ⓜ

Ⓜ DIMITROVSKAYA

BABUSHKINSKAYA Ⓜ

OTRADNOE

△ Sergiev Posad

YAROSLAVSKOE SHOSSE

Ⓜ SAVELOVSKAYA

SVIBLOVO

DIMITROVSKOE SHOSSE

Botanical
Gardens

Ⓜ
BOTANICHESKIY SAD

VDNKh

Ostankino
Palace

P
R
O
S
P
E
K
T

M
I
R
A

VDNKh
Ⓜ

see 'VDNKh' map for detail

Kosmos
Hotel

ALEKSEEVSKAYA
Ⓜ

Riga
Station

Rizhskiy
Market

ULITSA SUSHCHEVSKIY VAL

Sokolniki
Park

RIZHSKAYA

see 'North of the Garden Ring' map for detail

MENDELEEVSKAYA
Ⓜ Ⓜ NOVOSLOBODSKAYA

Travellers
Guest House

BOLSHAYA PEREYASLAVSKAYA ULITSA

SOKOLNIKI
Ⓜ

PROSPEKT MIRA Ⓜ

GARDEN RING

TSVETNOY BULVAR
Ⓜ

SUKHAREVSKAYA Ⓜ

Yaroslavl Station

KOMSOMOLSKAYA
Leningrad Station Ⓜ

Kazan Station

Leningradskaya
Hotel

0        2 km

N

of them being played. The museum also hosts **concerts**, lectures and temporary exhibitions (☎972-3237 for details).

The **instruments** are grouped according to their origins in colour-coded rooms, starting with pianos, guitars and zither-lyre hybrids in the red Western European section. Dragon-embossed Buryat horns and Shamen's skin drums from Yakutia are found in the green hall, along with a nineteenth-century 22-piece horn band from western Russia. The yellow room brings together Moldovian hurdy-gurdys, gorgeously inlaid Caucasian stringed instruments and a huge bowl-shaped contra-bass from Khirgizia. Casting its net still wider, the blue hall displays Eastern European and Oriental instruments, such as Polish bagpipes, Chinese drums and a horse-headed Korean *morinkhuur*. There is also a small **memorial room** devoted to the Russian conductor and violinist David Ostrakh.

### The Vasnetsov House

Amid the towerblocks that rise across the Ring from Tsvetnoy bulvar, a lovely relic of *fin-de-siècle* culture exudes the spirit of its former owner, **Viktor Vasnetsov** (1848–1926), a key figure in the Russian revival style that swept through the arts at the turn of the century. Vasnetsov believed that "a true work of art expresses everything about a people . . . It conveys the past, the present and, perhaps, the future of the nation", and sought to express this in his own work. An architect as well as a painter, he designed the facade of the Tretyakov Gallery, a church for the artists colony at Abramtsevo, and the wooden house in Moscow where he lived for the last 32 years of his life.

To reach the **Vasnetsov House** from Tsvetnoy bulvar (Wed–Sun 10am–5pm; closed the last Thurs of each month; $3), cross the Ring beneath the flyover and head up the grass slope into a housing estate, turning left 50m later; the house is at the far end of pereulok Vasnetsova. Entirely built of wood, its ground floor comprises five rooms, all cosily furnished with tiled stoves, chairs and cabinets, designed by Vasnetsov himself. The pieces are massive but so delicately carved as to be fit for a *boyar*'s palace. Echoes of medieval Russia abound, from pictures of processions to a chainmail tunic, fixed to the spiral staircase leading to his studio.

Although you now have to use the backstairs, the studio's impact is undiminished, its cathedral-like space filled by Vasnetsov's huge **paintings** of warriors confronting monsters, and various Russian fairy-tales. One wall is dominated by *The Sleeping Princess*, whose realm lies under an evil spell, awaiting revival – painted in the last year of Vasnetsov's life, at a time when Stalin was tightening his grip on Russia. In the corner, *Baba Yaga* flies through the woods on her broomstick, clasping a terrified stolen child: while you'll also recognize *Princess Nesmeyana*, whose glumness led to the classic offer of marriage and the kingdom to whoever made her laugh. The powerful *Golgotha* attests to

Vasnetsov's Christian faith and the cathedral frescoes that he painted before the Revolution.

# From Novoslobodskaya to Suvorovskaya

**Further out from the Garden Ring**, such diverse curiosities as Dostoyevsky's birthplace, the Durov Animal Theatre and the Ministry of the Interior and Army museums suggest an itinerary that offers something for everybody. Depending on what you omit or linger over, the route described below – from Novoslobodskaya metro to Suvorovskaya ploshchad – could take a little over an hour, or a whole afternoon.

### The MVD Museum

Anyone curious about crime and crime-fighting in Russia should try to visit the little-known **Museum of the Ministry of the Interior** (MVD) at Seleznevskaya ulitsa 11 (Tues–Sun 10am–4pm), although bear in mind that only group visits are permitted (☎258-0659).

Assuming you can get one, the **guided tour** is fascinating, repellent and funny by turns. One room is devoted to prisons and underworld subculture – with models of cells and pictures of criminals' tattoos – while another covers murder investigations, including horrific photos of the mutilated victims of the serial killer Andrei Chikatilo. Also displayed are drugs and weapons intercepted by border guards, and charmingly dated examples of "economic

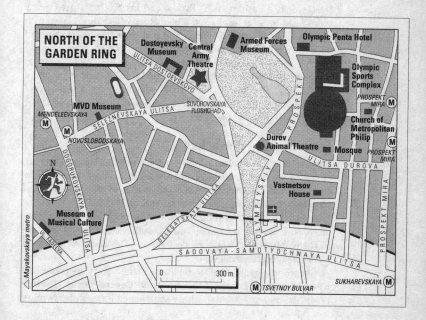

crimes" in the 1980s, like a counterfeit 25-ruble banknote and *matryoska* dolls portraying Soviet leaders. The latest exhibition is of memorabilia from the siege of the White House, such as Khasbulatov's business card, an array of homemade weapons, and a copy of the order imposing a curfew in Moscow.

When last visited, the building also contained a separate public **exhibition of paintings by Nikolai Roerich** (Tues–Thurs noon–8pm, Fri & Sat 10am–6pm). Roerich (1874–1947) was a Symbolist whose passion for Eastern mysticism led him to Central Asia, Tibet and India, where he died, leaving hundreds of pictures of mystics, steppes and mountains. As the ownership of much of his work in Russia is currently under dispute, the exhibition might go elsewhere in the future – but if it's still here, don't miss it.

### Dostoyevsky's birthplace

Five minutes' walk down a tramlined side street, the gloomy **Dostoyevsky Museum** (Thurs, Sat & Sun 11am–6pm, Wed & Fri 2–9pm; closed the last day of each month) is in the small house in the old Mariya Hospital that was granted to Dostoyevsky's physician father when he worked here. As his salary wasn't enough to maintain the standards expected of them, the family was dogged by financial worries, compounded by the doctor's alcoholism and violence (he was eventually murdered by his own serfs).

Unless you speak Russian, offers of a guided tour are best refused. The lobby exhibits the parish ledger recording Dostoyevsky's birth in 1821. Fyodor and his brother shared a tiny room filled by steel trunks and a tiled stove where they played with toy soldiers and a hobby horse, and had their lessons at the card table in the living room. A drawing room was so crucial to the family's social standing that their parents were prepared to sleep in a narrow bed behind a screen, jammed beside a washstand and a baby's crib. Beyond a lecture hall dominated by a portrait of Dostoyevsky, you'll find his quill pen and signature preserved under glass at the far end of the passage.

## Suvorovskaya ploshchad

**Suvorovskaya ploshchad**, to the southeast of the Mariya Hospital, is named after the Tsarist General Alexander Suvorov, honoured by Russians for his triumphs over the Turks in the Balkans and Napoleon in Italy and Switzerland, and reviled by the Poles for crushing their revolt in 1830. To avoid offending their Warsaw Pact allies, the Soviet leadership didn't authorize a monument to Suvorov until 1982, when the declaration of martial law in Poland made such niceties irrelevant.

Appropriately, most of the buildings in the square are connected with the Army. Foremost is the giant **Central Army Theatre** (*Tsentralniy teatr Armii*), whose star-shaped form is utterly unrelated to its function, and only apparent from the air. It's said that the design was the idea of the Moscow Party boss Lazar Kaganovich, doodling around his five-pointed inkpot. Completed in 1940, its facade combines aspects of the Colosseum and the Acropolis, while its Great Hall has a stage designed to allow battle scenes using real artillery and armoured cars, and a ceiling fresco of Olympian warriors and athletes.

## The Armed Forces Museum

A few minutes' walk from Suvorovskaya ploshchad, the **Armed Forces Museum** (Tues–Sun 10am–5pm; closed every Mon & the last week of each month; $2) is instantly recognizable by the T-34 tank and ballistic missile mounted out front, archetypal assertions of Soviet power that give no indication of how this bastion of ideological rectitude was shaken by *glasnost* and the fall of Communism. The first dozen halls, upstairs, are closed for a "reassessment" of the Civil War and Stalin's purges of the Red Army, and visitors are pitched straight into 1943 and the decisive tank battle at Kursk. The exhibition goes on to relate how the USSR's efforts turned the tide of war, liberated Eastern Europe and defeated Fascism. Hall 15 juxtaposes a replica partisan hideout with real human hair and tattooed skin from Maidenjak concentration camp, and a poster of a woman prisoner entitled *All hopes are on you, Red forces*. Victory is represented by a shattered bronze eagle from the Reichstag and the Nazi banners that were cast down before the Lenin Mausoleum in 1945 – as depicted in a huge painting.

The upbeat post-war section proudly displays the wreckage of an American U-2 spy-plane shot down over the Urals in 1960 (hall 20), and barely mentions the invasions of Hungary and Czechoslovakia. In the two rooms on Afghanistan, evidence of casualties and atrocities is confined to photo albums, easily overlooked beside the huge booster-stage of an SS-16 missile, which the Soviets agreed to scrap under SALT II. Don't miss the gleeful picture of the burning of Hitler's corpse, at the top of the stairs.

Parked around the sides and back of the museum is an array of hardware that includes an **armoured train** such as carried Trotsky into battle during the Civil War, and a **helicopter gunship** and a MiG-25 of the type used to slaughter Afghans in the name of Internationalism.

## The Durov Animal Theatre

For something completely different, head downhill from Suvorovskaya ploshchad to the bunker-like **Durov Animal Theatre** (*teatr Zvery imeni Durova*), a unique institution known to generations of Muscovites as "*Dedushka* (Grandpa) Durov". Its founder, **Vladimir Durov** (1863–1934), believed that circuses were cruel because they forced animals to perform tricks, rather than allowing their natural behaviour to be developed and shown on stage, accompanied by educational talks. His beliefs live on in this theatre, which still stages regular performances in which rabbits happily drum away and racoons wash their paws before meals, while monkeys appear to "read" a book by hiding seeds between the pages – Durov never used punishments, only rewards.

Durov once staged parodies of the Treaty of Versailles, and devised an act in which pigs and dogs boarded a train where a monkey punched their tickets, and a hen with a suitcase bustled up just as it departed "for Yalta". Sadly, this has now been relegated to the theatre's **museum** (Wed–Sun 10am–5pm; closed from May 27 to mid-Sept) and is now performed by mice – as demonstrated by Durov's granddaughter, Natalya Durova: a vivacious octagenarian who regards the animals as her family. Though hard-pressed to feed the elephant, pelicans and (retired) lion, she still takes in abandoned animals, housing them willy-nilly, so that the parrots caged above cats have learned to miaow. Visitors should try to attend a full-blown **show** (see p.321 for details).

# The Olympic Sports Complex and around

Across the highway from the animal theatre looms the **Olympic Sports Complex** (*Sportkompleks Olympiyskiy*), the largest of the facilities created for the 1980 Moscow Olympics. This prestige project was headed by Mikhail Posokhin, a fervent advocate of the international modern style, and the city's Chief Architect under Brezhnev. Its vast enclosed **stadium** seats up to thirty-five thousand, and is capable of being converted from a football ground into an athletics track or a skating rink. Dynamic murals of skaters and gymnasts decorate the adjacent training rink and gymnasium, while the smaller block to the north contains an Olympic-sized **pool**. Beyond this stands the *Olympic Penta Hotel*, built to accommodate spectators at the games.

### Prospekt Mira

Just east of the stadium, Moscow's main northbound thoroughfare, **prospekt Mira**, follows the medieval road to the Trinity Monastery and Yaroslavl, which from the sixteenth century also led to Russia's northern port at Arkhangelsk. Its present name – Peace Avenue – commemorates the 6th World Festival of Youth, in 1957, which had peace as one of its major themes. Ten kilometres long and groaning with traffic, prospekt Mira is really only of interest at two points – Rizhskiy Market and the fabulous VDNKh. Though both are best reached by the (orange) Kaluzhsko-Rizhskaya **metro** line, it's also possible to catch **bus** #85, from one block north of Sukharevskaya ploshchad (p.168), all the way to the VDNKh.

Two kilometres beyond the Ring, the first major intersection is named after **Riga Station** (*Rizhskiy vokzal*), the terminus for the Baltic states; as is **Rizhskiy Market** (Mon–Sat 7am–7pm, Sun 7am–

6pm), across the avenue. Moscow's largest food market offers a feast of sights, smells and free nibbles to tempt buyers, while vendors outside purvey everything from sex aids to sheepskins. Like most other markets here, the Rizhskiy is controlled by gangsters – two mobs, in this case: the Lyubertskiy, named after a grim Moscow satellite town whose illegal bodybuilding clubs spawned a generation of thugs in the 1980s, and the Chechen mob, whose fearsome reputation has only been enhanced by the recent bloodshed in Chechnya.

# The VDNKh and around

The main reason for venturing this far north is the **Exhibition of Economic Achievements** – known by its initials as the **VDNKh** ("Vay-den-ha") – a permanent trade fair-cum-shopping centre for Russian producers, which reflects the state of the national economy more faithfully than its founders intended. Grandiose architecture mocks the denuded halls where imported cars have ousted Soviet products, while crowds of shoppers ignore the gilded fountains and the sows that once attested to the fecundity of Soviet livestock, lured today by "Wild" capitalism rather than the Five Year Plan – a cameo of the New Russia. Add to this the amazing monuments at its entrance, and it's clear that the VDNKh is a must.

### Two great Soviet monuments

One of the best ever Soviet monuments, the **Space Obelisk**, near the metro exit, is another throwback to the old era, consisting of a rocket blasting nearly 100m into the sky on a stylized plume of energy clad in shining titanium. It was unveiled in 1964, three years after Gagarin orbited the earth, an unabashed expression of pride in this unique feat. Tableaux on either side of the obelisk's base show engineers and scientists striving to put a cosmonaut into his rocket, and Lenin leading the masses into space, as a woman offers her baby to the sun, while inside is a **Memorial Museum of Cosmonauts** (Tues–Thurs noon–8pm, Fri–Sun 11am–5.30pm), which now also embraces astrology. Outside, a **statue of Konstantin Tsiolkovskiy** (1837–1935), the "father of rocketry", gazes over the **Alley of Cosmonauts** that recedes towards prospekt Mira, flanked by bronze busts of intrepid cosmonauts.

Off in the other direction, past the main entrance to the VDNKh, stands an even more celebrated monument, the **Worker and Collective Farm Girl**. Designed by Vera Mukhina for the Soviet pavilion at the 1937 Paris Expo, its colossal twin figures stride forward in unison, raising the hammer and sickle. Weighing thirty tons apiece and fashioned from stainless steel blocks, they were hailed as the embodiment of Soviet industrial progress, though in fact each block had been hand-made on a wooden template, and the

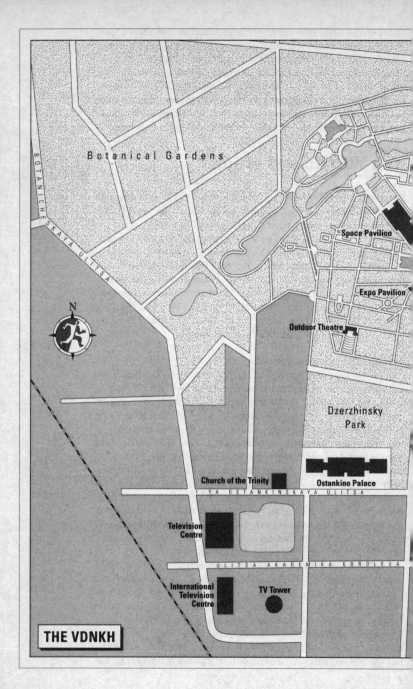

THE VDNKH

Botanical Gardens

Space Pavilion

Expo Pavilion

Outdoor Theatre

Dzerzhinsky Park

Church of the Trinity

Ostankino Palace

1-YA OSTANKINSKAYA ULITSA

Television Centre

ULITSA AKADEMIKA KOROLEVA

International Television Centre

TV Tower

BOTANICHESKAYA ULITSA

N

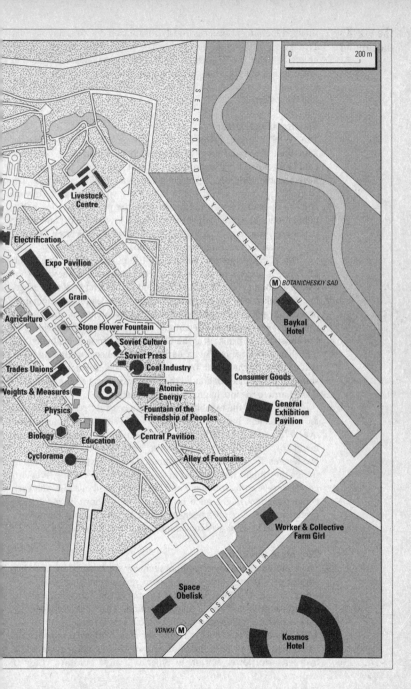

Livestock Centre

Electrification

Expo Pavilion

Grain

Agriculture

Stone Flower Fountain

Soviet Culture

Soviet Press

Coal Industry

Trades Unions

Weights & Measures

Physics

Biology

Education

Cyclorama

Atomic Energy

Fountain of the Friendship of Peoples

Central Pavilion

Alley of Fountains

Consumer Goods

General Exhibition Pavilion

(M) BOTANICHESKIY SAD

Baykal Hotel

SELSKOKHOZYAYSTVENNAYA

ULITSA

Worker & Collective Farm Girl

Space Obelisk

VDNKH (M)

PROSPEKT MIRA

Kosmos Hotel

0        200 m

finished monument was rigorously scrutinized due to a rumour that Trotsky's profile could be seen in the folds of the drapery. Once erected outside the VDNKh, Stalin was taken to view it at night, and loved it. Should you risk darting across the busy road for a closer look, notice the large service hatch visible beneath the Farm Girl's billowing skirts.

## Visiting the VDNKh

The VDNKh park (Mon–Fri 9am–8pm, Sat, Sun & holidays 9am–9pm; free) and its pavilions (which open and close one hour later and earlier) are open daily. Except for a few pavilions that have become "exclusive" showrooms, free admission is the rule. Try to avoid sale days (advertised in the press), when crowds of buyers jam the doorways and bring mayhem to the parking lots for half a mile around. In winter, when the fountains are turned off and its icy paths are hazardous, the VDNKh hosts a **Russian Winter Festival** (Dec 25–Jan 5) featuring *troyka* rides and folk dancing.

The **VDNKh's** genesis was the All-Union Agricultural Exhibition of 1939, a display of the fruits of Socialism and a showpiece of Stalinist monumental art that was intended to open two years earlier, but was delayed by the purging of many of its leading participants. Scores of pavilions trumpeted the achievements of the Soviet republics and the planned economy; there was even one devoted to the construction projects of the Gulag. While propaganda belied the fact that the USSR had been harrowed by collectivization and was still gripped by the Great Terror, paranoia was so rampant that the statue of Stalin that dominated the show was searched for bombs, as if any harm to the idol might endanger the state.

In the event, the exhibition was so successful that it was revived on a permanent basis in 1954, with some eighty pavilions spread over 578 acres. During Brezhnev's time, a tour of its pig farm was mandatory for every schoolchild and tourist, while canny Muscovites flocked to the Consumer Goods pavilion, previewing things they might hope to find in the future. By the 1980s, Western goods were starting to appear and the Soviet pavilions lost whatever conviction they might once have possessed. Shorn of ideological pretensions, it has now been renamed the **All Russia Exhibition Centre** (*VVTs*) – but everyone continues to call it the VDNKh.

## The main pavilions

The **main entrance** is a triumphal archway surmounted by towering statues of a tractor driver and a farm girl brandishing sheaves of wheat, which sets the scale for the avenue of fountains that leads to a **Lenin statue** and the **Central Pavilion**. This Stalinist wedding-cake structure culminates in a 35-metre spire, reminiscent of the Admiralty in St Petersburg; the interior once featured a huge illuminated map of the USSR, and dioramas of Lenin's home town and a hydroelectric power station in Siberia. It now boasts a "City of

Discovery and Creation", full of high-tech toys and holograms for kids of all ages to enjoy.

Beyond lies an octagonal square centred on the **Fountain of the Friendship of Peoples**, whose gilded statues of maidens in the national costumes of the sixteen Soviet republics demurely encircle a golden wheatsheaf. When operating, the basin erupts into 800 jets of water sprayed 24m into the air, illuminated at night by 525 spotlights.

Of the nine pavilions here, most are monuments to Soviet science, which have been denuded of their original exhibits and filled with goods for sale. The finest ones are on the right. **Atomic Energy** is sanctified by a Classical temple bearing a fresco of women and babes picking fruit, which promises Eden, not Chernobyl. It originally held a small working atomic pile, whose rods glowed underwater. The **Coal Industry**'s fruit-laden facade barely finds room beneath the pediment for two miners, while the **Soviet Press** flaunts a splendid wooden frieze of lumberjacks and truckers toiling in the wilderness, with not a journalist in sight. Best of all is **Soviet Culture**, fronted by a star-like pagoda and tiled arabesques derived from the mosques of Central Asia. Architects felt encouraged to draw on ethnic motifs by Stalin's pronouncement that art should be "national in form, socialist in content".

On the other side are ranged the **Education**, **Biology**, **Physics**, **Chemistry** and **Weights and Measures** pavilions, notably less decorative but not as dull as the post-Stalinist ones off the square. Unless you want to discover what's being sold inside, most of the other pavilions can be ignored, but the silvery clouds in the lobby of the **Trade Unions** building deserve a look.

The Soviet taste for mineral extravagance runs riot with the mosaic-encrusted **Stone Fountain**, flanked by spouting geese and fish, like a fountain at one of the Imperial palaces outside St Petersburg. Even wilder are the pavilions beyond, dedicated to **Agriculture** and **Grain**. The former is crowned by a florid rotunda and a gilded spire, and crenellated with ears of corn. When opened as the Ukrainian pavilion in 1939, it boasted of abundance when Ukraine was still depopulated and half-starved after collectivization. On either side of its fruit-heavy portal, statues of husky peasants enthuse over the harvest and Stalin's wisdom.

At the far end of the avenue, beyond Industry Square and its Vostok rocket, suspended from an enormous gantry, you'll find displays of luxury American cars and the occasional rave. Off to the right, past **Electrification** (which retains some model power stations and a stained-glass panel in the style of Léger), the **Livestock** centre, situated near a lake, still keeps a few stalls of prize-winning breeds on show, and displays of animal husbandry – good fun for kids. Around at the far side of the perimeter track, you'll also find reindeer and elks in pens attached to the **Hunting and Trapping** pavilion, fronted by a statue of grinning Yakut hunters.

In the opposite direction from the Space pavilion are the **Michurin Gardens**, planted with varieties of hard and soft fruits developed by Ivan Michurin (1855–1935), and a Neo-Gothic **outdoor theatre**, whence you can head off to the Botanical Gardens or cut through Dzerzhinsky Park to the Ostankino Palace. Alternatively, go in search of the **Cyclorama** off behind the VDNKh's Education pavilion, where a special action film show is projected onto a 360° screen at regular intervals.

## Ostankino, the TV Centre and the Botanical Gardens

To the west of the VDNKh, the former village of **Ostankino** is known for its **palace** – built as a love nest and later billed as a museum – and for its **television centre**, whose **tower** is the tallest structure in Moscow affording a great view on clear days. If neither appeals, the **botanical gardens** offer an exotic retreat to the northwest of the VDNKh. To reach Ostankino, you can either catch tram #7 or #11 from the vicinity of VDNKh metro to the final stop near the palace; or leave the VDNKh by the exit near the outdoor theatre, slip through a hole in the fence over the road, and walk through **Dzerzhinsky Park**. This takes you past some two-storey private houses, built for retired cosmonauts, who may sometimes be seen tending their allotments.

### Ostankino Palace

The **Ostankino Palace** has sadly been closed for years and seems unlikely to reopen soon, dashing hopes of revelling in its private theatre and *trompe l'oeil* decor. However, the exterior is as handsome as the story behind it is romantic. In 1789, the middle-aged Count Nikolai Sheremetev stunned his family by falling in love with Parasha Kovalyova, a serf girl on their Kuskovo estate whom he is said to have first set eyes on as she was leading a cow home from the woods. Tutored in the dramatic arts, she became a gifted opera singer with the stage name of "Zhemchugova" (from the Russian word for "pearl"), and the Count built them a sumptuous palace at Ostankino – although ten years passed before he found the courage to marry her. Three years later, Parasha died of tuberculosis soon after giving birth, whereupon the Count pined away, leaving their son an orphan.

Subsequently, the palace was occupied by Marshal Ney's staff and looted in the retreat of 1812. After the Revolution, the palace was opened as a **Museum of Serf Art**, in recognition of the fact that it had been built and decorated by serf-artisans. It's an ambitious Classical building, its grandeur best epitomized by a reception staged for Tsar Paul in 1795. As he rode through the woods, dozens of pre-sawn trees suddenly fell aside to reveal the palace in its glory.

### The TV Centre and Botanical Gardens

Close by the palace, the **Television Centre**, a boxy complex of 22 television studios and 70 radio stations, is still faintly scarred from

the night of October 3, 1993, when a mob of parliamentary supporters tried to capture the airwaves by assaulting the building with
rocket-launchers and machine-guns. Only the last-minute arrival of
an elite *Vympel* unit prevented it from falling into the hands of
Yeltsin's enemies. Eight people died in the battle, which was broadcast live around the world by journalists crouched outside;
Muscovites simply heard Ostankino warn: "They're breaking in",
followed by an ominous silence.

Across the pond looms the giant **TV Tower**, whose 35,000 tons
of ferro-concrete taper from 50m in diameter at the base, to a
needle-like shaft 540m tall. Constructed in 1967, it has an **observation deck** (9am–8pm) that provides a bird's-eye view of the VDNKh
and a distant panorama of Moscow from 337 metres up, above a
**revolving restaurant** called "Seventh Heaven" (*Sedmoe nebo*). To
buy a ticket ($2) for the observation deck, ask inside the main
entrance. The restaurant (Mon–Sun 11am–10.30pm; ☎282-2293)
advises reserving a table at weekends.

Founded in 1945, Moscow's lush **Botanical Gardens**
(*Botanicheskiy sad*) contain the finest collection of flora in Russia,
including such exotica as giant waterlilies in greenhouses, and a
Japanese rock garden. From nearer home, at the centre of the 860-
acre park, there are groves of birches and 200-year-old oaks to
delight the Russian soul, and rose gardens planted with sixteen
thousand varieties of blooms. The gardens are open Wednesday to
Sunday from 10am to 4pm (8pm in summer), except during April
and October.

# Komsomolskaya ploshchad and Sokolniki Park

Nearer the centre of town, the (red) Sokolnicheskaya metro line
provides rapid access to Komsomolskaya ploshchad and Sokolniki
Park, two disparate expanses that reflect Moscow's Janus-like
profile. Though hardly high on most visitors' list of priorities, anyone
with an hour or two to spare might consider checking them out.

## Komsomolskaya ploshchad

Notwithstanding its earnest name, **Komsomolskaya ploshchad**
(Young Communists Square) is one of Moscow's grungiest localities, dominated by three mainline stations swarming with provincial
visitors, homeless drunks and prostitutes. From being merely
disreputable in Soviet times, it has sunk to a level of squalor akin to
the notorious pre-Revolutionary Kalchanovka Market that used to
stand here, on what was then called "Three Stations Square". In an
effort to maintain order, access to the station waiting rooms is pres-
ently restricted to ticket-holders.

The two stations on the north side are separated by the
columned pavilion of Komsomolskaya metro. **Yaroslavl Station**
(*Yaroslavskiy vokzal*), built in 1902–04, is a bizarre Style Moderne
structure with Tatar echoes, whose hooded arch groans with reliefs

**The VDNKh and around**

of Arctic fishermen and Soviet crests. In July 1994, it was here that Alexander Solzhenitsyn arrived back in Moscow twenty years after his deportation from the USSR – promptly denouncing the post-Soviet Babylon outside. Further west is **Leningrad Station** (*Leningradskiy vokzal*), a yellow and white Classical edifice with a modern annexe around the back.

Directly opposite, the spectacular **Kazan Station** (*Kazanskiy vokzal*) was designed by Shchusev in 1912 but only completed in 1926. Its seventy-metre spired tower (based on the citadel in the old Tatar capital of Kazan), faceted facade and blue and gold astrological clock have led many a yokel stumbling off the train to ask if this was the Kremlin. At the end of the square nearest the Garden Ring looms the Gothic-spired **Leningrad Hotel**, a pocket-sized Stalin skyscraper that represents the functional nadir of Soviet architecture, utilizing only 22 percent of its space. After Stalin's death, architectural excess came in for criticism, and in 1955 the architects of the hotel were deprived of their Stalin Prizes.

### Sokolniki Park

After Komsomolskaya ploshchad, **Sokolniki Park**, several miles to the north, comes as light relief. Laid out in 1930–31, as Moscow's second "Park of Culture and Rest", it used to welcome citizens with martial music blaring from loudspeakers at the entrance. Nevertheless, it was cherished for its "emerald paths" through the old Sokolniki Woods, named after the royal falconers (*sokolniki*) who lived here in the seventeenth century. Nowadays the park swarms with Muscovites torn between the cash-and-carry warehouses at one end, and an **exhibition of mechanical dinosaurs** at the other (which may become a permanent fixture). More gruesomely, the ultra-nationalist **Zhirinovsky** sometimes comes here to rant from a soap box, surrounded by bodyguards.

Traditional pleasures are still enjoyed in Sokolniki Park. Off behind the cafes facing the *etoile*, pensioners meet in a glade for outdoor **ballroom dancing** on Sunday afternoons (weather permitting); while in the woods near the central pavilions is a special **chess** corner, where matches are played against the clock. The **Exhibition Pavilions** are used for international trade fairs; at the first US–Soviet exhibition in 1959, Khrushchev and the then Vice-President Nixon had a famous, impromptu "washing-machine debate" over the superiority of their respective systems.

# Leningradskiy prospekt and Serebryaniy Bor

**Leningradskiy prospekt** is the main artery of the northwestern suburbs, running from Belarus Station out to Sheremetevo Airport. Before the Revolution it was the road from Moscow to the Imperial capital of St Petersburg. After World War II, the avenue was transformed into an eight-lane motorway flanked by monumental apartment blocks, superseded by humbler *Khrushchoby* and newer, highrise estates further out. For all that, it does have several points of interest – notably the Hippodrome and the Petrovskiy Palace – and leads to Moscow's favourite summer bathing spot, **Serebryaniy Bor**.

While most are within walking distance of a **metro** station on the (green) Zamoskvoretskaya line, a few sights are better reached by trolleybus (#12, #70) or tram (#23) along the prospekt, which begins at ploshchad Belorusskovo Vokzala, named after seedy **Belarus Station** (*Belorusskiy vokzal*) on the western side of the square. However, the first sight is well over 1km from the station.

## The Hippodrome

Moscow's **Hippodrome** (*Ippodrom*) race course is a world unto itself, its fans hooked on *troyka* races that seem lame compared with Western flat racing. They are also indifferent to the crumbling premises, reconstructed in a monumental Classical style in the 1950s, and now containing a plush **casino** that cold-shoulders the plebeian **grandstand**, patrolled by gun-toting OMON. Everyone is drunk and into betting, often with illegal bookies who take wagers over the 1000-ruble limit in the betting office beneath the stands. You don't have to enjoy racing to find it interesting; for example, anyone studying Russian can vastly improve their knowledge of *mat* (obscenities) by spending an hour here. To get into the spirit, buy a cup of vodka before heading up the backstairs to the highest tier of the stands.

*See p.331 for more about visiting the races.*

The hippodrome is located 500m down Begovaya ulitsa (Running Street), which turns off the prospekt just after another side street, flanked by twin statues of horses. To avoid trudging 1km from Dinamo metro, ride overground to Begovaya and switch to any vehicle heading in the right direction. Some turn off shortly before the Hippodrome, near the Botkin Hospital.

## Between Dinamo and Aeroport metro

There are several places worth a visit along the 1500m stretch of the Leningradskiy prospekt between Dinamo and Aeroport metro stations. The **Dinamo Stadium** is Moscow's main venue for premier league football matches, and the heart of a 1930s sports complex whose architecture exudes "Strength through Joy".

A bit further from Dinamo metro stands the romantic **Petrovskiy Palace**. Founded as a rest house for travelling royalty by Catherine the Great, the palace served as a refuge for Napoleon at the height of the fire of 1812. An early work by Kazakov, the palace is sheltered by crenellated walls and outbuildings; its red brick and white masonry prefigure his design for Catherine's Gothic summer palace at Tsaritsyno. During the nineteenth century it was fashionable for the rich to show off their carriages or *troykas* here, while bourgeois families picnicked on the grass with *samovars*. In 1923 the palace became the Zhukovskiy Air Academy, with the designers Mikoyan and Ilyushin and the cosmonauts Gagarin and Tereshkova among its graduates.

Nicholas II was the last monarch to stay at the palace for his ill-fated coronation in May 1896, when disaster struck on the **Khodynka Field** across the road, which had been chosen as the site for the traditional distribution of gifts. The arrival of the beer wagons coincided with a rumour that the souvenir mugs were running out, causing a stampede in which more than 1500 people were trampled to death. In Soviet times, Khodynka Field became Moscow's first civilian airport, the **Central Airfield**, which is nowadays used by sports flyers.

*Airport buses
are detailed on
p.22.*

Closer to the highway, a pair of sea-green blocks identify the **Air Terminal** (*Aerovokzal*), from which buses depart for the five airports outside Moscow; while further on towards Aeroport metro, the grounds of the **Central Army Sports Club** – or **TsKA** – are packed with shoppers at weekends, when a big **market** (9am–5pm) for imported goods occurs in the main building.

### Further out: the Moscow Canal and Serebryaniy Bor

Further northwest, the prospekt runs past the Khimkinskoe Reservoir, where the **Northern River Terminal** (*Severniy rechnoy vokzal*) is the point of departure for ships to St Petersburg and the Volga cities. A grand, spired edifice near Rechnoy Vokzal metro, the terminal was inaugurated with great fanfare upon the completion of a 128-kilometre-long canal joining the Moskva and Okha rivers to the Volga. One of the "hero projects" of the Second Five Year Plan, the **Moscow Canal** was constructed (1932–37) by forced labour. Mostly peasants convicted of being *kulaks*, they toiled all winter in thin jackets, using only hand tools and wheelbarrows, with up to five hundred thousand perishing from cold and exhaustion. Needless to say, the two colossal **statues of workers** that ennoble the canal banks near Vodnoy Stadion metro look well-fed and pleased with themselves.

The final leg of the Moscow Canal descends through two locks to join the Moskva River just upstream of **Serebryaniy Bor**, a popular recreation area named after its **giant silver pines**, some of which are over two hundred years old. Aside from its trees, the resort is noted for its colonies of wooden *dachas* and a variety of bathing and fishing spots – there is even a semi-offical **nudist beach** and a more discreet one for **gays**. It's best not to visit on a weekend over the summer, when Serebryaniy Bor is inundated by three hundred thousand visitors a day. From May to October, **motorboats** ply the river between the Strogino and Serebraniy Bor-4 landing stages, calling at several points en route, including the Troitse-Lykovo stop near the Moscow Baroque **Church of the Trinity** (also accessible by bus #137 from Tushkinskaya metro).

The simplest way of **getting there** is to catch trolleybus #20 all the way from Okhotniy ryad in downtown Moscow, which terminates near Serebryaniy Bor-4. However, it's faster to travel to Polezhaevskaya metro (on the Filyovskaya line) and get trolleybus #21 to Serebryaniy Bor-2.

**Lenin-gradskiy prospekt and Serebryaniy Bor**

# Chapter 10

# Outside Moscow

The chief reason to venture **OUTSIDE MOSCOW** is the glorious **Trinity Monastery of St Sergei**, a Kremlin-like citadel. It is better known in the West as "Zagorsk", after the Soviet-era name of the town in which it is located, 75km northeast of Moscow. A bit closer to the capital is the former artists' colony of

Abramtsevo, a lovely estate, where most of the big names of late nineteenth-century Russian art painted the local landscape and created fairytale buildings that still stand. While both can be enjoyed by anyone, the appeal of the other sites is more particular. If stately homes and parks are your thing, there is the romantic, half-ruinous **Arkhangelskoe** estate, and Lenin's country retreat at **Leninskie Gorki**. Lovers of the arts will be drawn to Tchaikovsky's home in **Klin** or Pasternak's *dacha* in **Peredelkino**; while those into military history can tread the famous battlefield of **Borodino**, and even see the battle re-enacted in September.

## Practicalities

Almost all these places can be visited as day trips, and reached by public transport or an organized tour. **Getting there** yourself costs very little, but requires patience and some knowledge of the language. Many of the sites are accessible by a suburban line (*prigorodnye poezda* or *elektrichka*) train from one of the big mainline stations in Moscow, some of which have separate ticket offices and platforms for these services. Their frequency varies from every forty minutes to two hours, with longer intervals in the afternoon, so it's easy to waste time hanging around. This is also a problem with sites that are accessible by bus from an outlying district of the city. If you don't speak Russian, get somebody to write your destination in Cyrillic to show to ticket-sellers and fellow passengers. Foreigners with a car will find that the highway junctions on the Moscow Ring Road (MKhAD) are clearly numbered, but side turnings off the main roads can be hard to identify.

To avoid such hassles, sign up for **excursions** with companies such as the US–Russian joint-venture *Patriarchi Dom*, which runs a monthly programme of tours covering all the main sites outside Moscow. Current schedules are advertised in leaflets distributed around the foreign supermarkets (see p.325); it's best to book by phone (☎255-4515), although you can usually join a tour by simply turning up at the designated point of departure (usually Bolshoy Devyatinskiy pereulok, on the south side of the US Embassy). The only problem is that most tours are so infrequent (once or twice a month) that the chances of you being around at the time are slim – although the highly popular excursion to the Trinity Monastery is scheduled every week or so. Also, the range of places to eat outside Moscow is severely limited – or nonexistent at some locations – so it's wise to bring a snack.

# The Trinity Monastery of St Sergei

The monastery is named after **St Sergei of Radonezh** (c.1321–91), who is said to have cried from his mother's womb while in church; refused to consume milk on Wednesdays or meat on Fridays as a

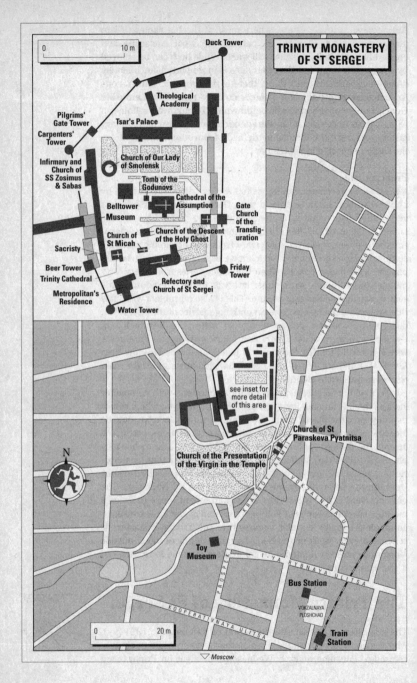

TRINITY MONASTERY
OF ST SERGEI

Duck Tower

0     10 m

Theological
Academy

Pilgrims'
Gate Tower

Tsar's Palace

Carpenters'
Tower

Church of Our Lady
of Smolensk

Infirmary and
Church of
SS Zosimus
& Sabas

Tomb of the
Godunovs

Cathedral of the
Assumption

Gate
Church
of the
Transfig-
uration

Belltower
Museum

Church of the Descent
of the Holy Ghost

Church of
St Micah

Sacristy

Beer Tower

Friday
Tower

Trinity Cathedral

Metropolitan's
Residence

Refectory and
Church of St Sergei

Water Tower

see inset for
more detail
of this area

Church of St
Paraskeva Pyatnitsa

Church of the Presentation
of the Virgin in the Temple

N

Toy
Museum

Bus Station

VOKZALNAYA
PLOSHCHAD

Train
Station

0     20 m

▽ Moscow

baby; and had a vision of a hooded figure who explained the Bible to him as a child. Forsaking a diplomatic career to become a hermit in the forest with his brother, he later urged Prince Dmitry Donskoy to fight the Tatars at Kulikovo, blessing his army as it left Moscow. After Sergei's death the Tatars sacked the monastery, but his body miraculously survived to become the focus of a cult, resulting in his canonization in 1422 and the reconstruction of the monastery.

In 1552, Abbot Bassyan persuaded Ivan the Terrible to mount a last assault on the Tatar stronghold of Kazan, succeeding where seven attempts had failed. In the **Time of Troubles**, the monastery was besieged for sixteen months by thirty thousand Poles, whose cannonballs bounced off its walls. Later, it was here that young Tsars Peter and Ivan hid from the *Streltsy* in 1685; and the seventeen-year-old Peter again sought refuge during his struggle with the Regent Sofia.

*This inspired Nesterov's famous painting, The Child Bartholomew's Vision (the original can be seen at the Tretyakov Gallery). Sergei's baptismal name was Bartholomew.*

In recognition of his debt, Peter the Great showered the monastery with gifts, while Catherine the Great, who was also keen on pilgrimages to the Trinity Monastery, had no qualms about confiscating its huge estates in 1763, reproving the clergy, "You are the successors of the Apostles, who were very poor men". Nevertheless, it was the centre of Holy Russia until 1920, when the Bolsheviks closed it down and sent the monks to the Gulag. To add insult to injury, the surrounding town of Sergeiovo was renamed **Zagorsk** in 1930, after the Bolshevik "martyr" Vladimir Zagorskiy – the name it bore until September 1991, when it was changed to **Sergiev Posad** (Sergei's Settlement). Despite having grown into an industrial town of over one hundred thousand people, the centre is still dominated by the *lavra*, whose panoply of towers and domes rivals the Kremlin's.

## Visiting the monastery

Traditionally, rulers on **pilgrimages** took six or seven days to get to the monastery, resting at palaces and hunting on the way. Tsar Alexei's party was preceded by two hundred messengers, with a dozen horses pulling the Tsaritsa's carriage, followed by a smaller gold one containing the infant Peter – while the pious Alexei chose to emulate ordinary pilgrims by walking to the monastery, which was believed to purify one's spirit. Though few Russians go to such lengths today, many old folk arrive with nothing to sustain them but a hunk of bread, and even day-trippers often fast or abstain from sex beforehand.

Without a car, the easiest way of **getting there** is a *Patriarchi Dom* tour ($15, excluding admission charges), which spends about three hours at the monastery. To stay longer or pay less, catch one of the regular trains from Moscow's Yaroslavl Station (every 40min; 1hr 30min). On leaving the Sergiev Posad station, head right across the square and along Vokzalnaya ulitsa to reach the *lavra*.

The monastery is **open** daily from 8am to 6pm, though its churches are closed to the public at weekends, and the museum and sacristy are closed on Monday. Inside the gate is a kiosk selling photo permits, where tourists **with a guide** are charged the ruble equivalent of $3; other visitors enter free of charge. You'll need separate **tickets** to visit the museum and sacristy, which are sold on the spot; however, don't feel obliged, as neither compares with the monastery itself. Visitors must **dress** decorously (no shorts), and are forbidden to take photos inside the museums and churches, or smoke in the grounds.

## The monastery complex

The monastery is enclosed by brick **walls** a mile in circumference, which replaced the original wooden ramparts in 1540–50 and were doubled in height a century later, when tent-roofed spires were added to six of the twelve towers (as happened to the Kremlin around the same time). A gate in the bronze-mantled **Beautiful Tower** and a tunnel painted with scenes of Sergei creating his hermitage in the wilderness bring you out below the **Gate-Church of St John the Baptist**. Built by the Stroganov *boyars* in 1693, its terracotta walls, Venetian scallops and gilded domes pale before the glorious buildings ahead, whose harmony belies their "picturesque carelessness of arrangement".

The **Refectory** (*Trapeznaya*), just inside the gates, resembles a gaudy version of the Faceted Palace in the Kremlin, with painted red, yellow and grey facets, and slender columns entwined in carved vines. Late last century, Augustus Hare found four hundred monks dining in its vaulted hall, glittering with gold and "smelling terribly of the cabbage they adore". These days, the hall is only used for ceremonies and is often locked.

### The cathedrals

Across from the Refectory looms the **Cathedral of the Assumption** (*Uspenskiy sobor*), similar in shape to its namesake in the Kremlin, but with four azure onion domes clustered around a huge gilded one. Begun by Ivan the Terrible to honour the fall of Kazan, it was completed in 1585 by his imbecile son, Fyodor – a cat's-paw of the Regent, Boris Godunov, who succeeded him as Tsar. It's indicative of their bad name that the **tomb of the Godunovs** is half-sunk into the ground outside the church, while dozens of Golitsyns, Trubetskoys and other nobles are entombed inside.

*Boris
Godunov's
story is related
on p.340.*

In the nave, a Tsarist eagle commemorates the moment in 1685 when the *Streltsy* found Peter's mother and her two sons hiding behind the iconostasis, and were about to kill them when a mutineer shouted "Comrades, not before the altar!", and loyal cavalry arrived to rescue them. Visitors should enter by a door facing the Refectory.

Downhill stands the **Church of the Descent of the Holy Ghost** (*Dykhovskaya tserkov*), whose rounded apses and silvered *kokoshniki* taper into a belltower with a blue and gold, star-spangled dome.

Built by craftsmen from Pskov in 1476–77, it is unusual for having its bells in the base of the tower, which was used as a lookout post in the days when the monastery walls were much lower.

Before the walls were raised in the sixteenth century, the white stone **Trinity Cathedral** (*Troitskiy sobor*), near the southwest corner, was the tallest structure in the monastery. Erected in 1422–23, it pioneered the use of *kokoshniki* – the leitmotif of Muscovite church architecture – and inspired the "gold-topped" Cathedral of the Assumption in the Kremlin. The nave is astir with believers queuing up to kiss a silver shrine containing the **relics of St Sergei**, and tourists jostling to see the **iconostasis**, by Andrei Rublev and Daniil Cherniy, and the copy of Rublev's *Old Testament Trinity*. Also notice the Chapel of St Nikon in the southeast corner, which was built over the tomb of Sergei's successor, Nikon of Radonezh.

Behind the cathedral is an eighteenth-century **Metropolitan's Residence** that served as the home of the Patriarch of All Russia from 1946 until 1988, when the Danilov Monastery (p.222) became the Patriarchal seat.

## Chapels, towers and museums

Between the cathedrals, you can't miss the small octagonal **Chapel over the Well** (*Nakladeznaya chasovnya*), whose pillars and *nalichniki* are carved with flowers and vines, offset by blue arabesques and lozenges. The chapel was built over a spring discovered by the monks in 1644, and today its interior (daily 8.30am–5pm) is packed with people filling bottles with holy water, and with photos of miraculous cures.

Building continued into the late eighteenth century, when Prince Ukhtomskiy erected an 88-metre **Belltower** (*Kolokolnitsa*), whose five royal-blue and white tiers are equal in height to the surrounding churches, and which once boasted fifty bells. Ukhtomskiy also built the rounded Baroque **Church of Our Lady of Smolensk**, with its pilastered facade and gold finial, to house an icon of the same name. Off to the left stand the former **Infirmary** and **Church of SS Zosimus and Sabas**, dating from the 1630s; this church is the only one in the monastery with a tent-roofed spire.

Further south you'll find a hatch selling tickets for the **museum** ($3) and **sacristy** ($5) (Tues–Sun 10am–5pm). Unless you're besotted with icons, head for the final room on the ground floor of the museum, which exhibits Simon Ushakov's *Virgin of Vladimir* and *Venerable Nikon of Radonezh*, painted in the 1670s. Upstairs is more interesting, with two English coaches belonging to former Metropolitans; some arresting royal portraits (notice Peter's first wife, Yevdokiya, to the right as you enter); and a surfeit of gold plate, pearl-encrusted mitres and robes that leave you cold for more of the same in the sacristy (*riznitsa*).

From here, aim for the ramparts between the **Beer Tower** and the **Carpenters' Tower**, or bear right at the green-spired **Pilgrims'**

Gate Tower to reach the **Tsar's Palace** (*Tsarskie Chertogi*). Constructed in the late seventeenth century for Tsar Alexei and his entourage of 500, its elongated facade is patterned with red and mauve facets and crested *nalichniki*. As it now houses the main wing of a **Theological Academy**, only its students can feast their eyes on the ceiling fresco of the triumphs of Peter the Great, added the following century. While sheltering here in 1685, Peter relaxed by shooting fowl from what was henceforth called the **Duck Tower**.

## Other sights

The square outside the monastery hosts a lively **market** in religious kitsch and handicrafts. Off to the right stand the gold-domed **Church of St Paraskeva Pyatnitsa** – dedicated to the "Friday Saint" revered in Orthodox countries – and the **Church of the Presentation of the Virgin in the Temple**, likewise built in 1547. Further downhill, the **Kelarskiy Pond** is rimmed by garden walls, offering splendid views of the monastery, and frequented by artists in summer. Uphill on the far side of the pond, the **Toy Museum** (Tues–Sun 10am–5pm) boasts a fine collection of historic toys. Sergiev Posad has long been known for its woodcarving (the *matryoshka* doll has it origins here) and still specializes in handmade wooden toys. You can buy all kinds in the market or the souvenir section of the museum.

# Abramtsevo

If the Trinity Monastery redeemed Russia's soul in medieval times, the **ABRAMTSEVO** estate helped define it during the nineteenth century, when disputes between Slavophiles and Westernizers dominated cultural life. Indeed, Abramtsevo was acquired by the devout Slavophile writer Aksakov because of its proximity to the *lavra*, which made it an apt meeting place for like-minded, devoutly Orthodox intellectuals. The estate's next owner, the millionaire Mamontov, was equally passionate about Russian culture, supporting an **artists colony** that gave rise to Russia's modern art movement. Many of the works in the Tretyakov Gallery – by Repin, Serov, Vrubel and the Vasnetsov brothers – reflect their shared interest in medieval architecture, folk art and mythology – as do the fairytale buildings on the Abramtsevo estate, whose rolling woodlands have been depicted on canvas more than any other landscape in Russia.

### Practicalities

Abramtsevo lies about 6km south of Sergiev Posad; the turnoff is clearly signposted. By car, follow the road left to **Khotkovo** and bear left again before a half-derelict convent. En route to the estate, you'll pass a big pond; the entrance to the grounds is further uphill. Trains should stop at Abramtsevo on the way to Sergiev Posad; unfortunately, the station is almost 2km from the site.

The estate (☎(8)253-2470) is **closed** during April and October, on Monday and Tuesday, and the last Thursday of each month; **opening hours** are 10am to 5pm. Tickets ($2) and Russian-language brochures are sold at the entrance; the **café** on the far side of the car park is seldom open. Summer or autumn are the best times to visit.

The charm of the estate is best appreciated by wandering around the outbuildings constructed by the artists, which lead you away from the main house. As you don't have to understand their cultural significance to enjoy them, it's quite in order to visit the house-museum later.

## The main house

Knowing that Chekhov used the house as a model for the manor in his play *The Cherry Orchard* raises your expectations of the plain, grey-and-white clapboard building. The interior of the **main house** is a vivid reflection of its former flamboyant owners: **Sergei Aksakov** (1791–1859) was a foe of Westernizers such as Herzen, and was mocked for wearing "a dress so national that people in the street took him for a Persian". In 1870, the house was bought by the railroad tycoon **Savva Mamontov** (1841–1918) and his wife Elizabeth, who vowed to continue its traditions and preserved half of the house as Aksakov had left it – hence the different decors in each wing. While the Slavophile Aksakov shared the mid-nineteenth-century gentry's taste for French Empire, the worldlier Mamontovs preferred Pseudo-Russian and Style Moderne.

Across the way is a larger white building housing an **exhibition** of modernist paintings by Aristakh Lentulov, Robert Falk and other artists of the Soviet era who also worked at Abramtsevo, with graphics such as Alimov's illustrations for *Dead Souls* and *The Master and Margarita* upstairs.

## The outbuildings

More alluring is the tiny wooden **studio**, with its picturesque fretwork roof, where the painters Serov and Vrubel tried their hands at ceramics. The small Egyptian and Russian figures on display here presage Vrubel's bas-relief for the *Metropol Hotel* in Moscow, while the tiled stove epitomizes the colony's interest in old Russian applied arts. Peasant crafts were a major source of inspiration: the **kitchen** now displays part of their collection of artefacts (including cake moulds and ironing boards) as a **Museum of Folk Art**.

Their vision of an ideal cottage was realized in the **Teremok**, or guest house, whose steep roof and gable call to mind the *podvore* of medieval Muscovy. Its interior is furnished with heavy, carved furniture, like the Mamontovs' section of the main house. Further into the woods you'll come upon the **House on Chicken Legs**, built by the Vasnetsov brothers for the estate's children to play in. A tiny hut on chunky stilts, the house is based on the fairytale cottage of Baba

Yaga, which shuffled around to face trespassing kids who uttered the words "*Izbushka, izbushka, povernis k mne peredom, a k lesy zadom*" (literally, "Little House, Little House, turn around to face me with your back to the woods") – just before she flew out and threatened to eat them.

The whole colony collaborated on the **Church of the Saviour Not Made by Human Hand**, a diminutive structure based on medieval churches at Novgorod, whose strong lines and whitewashed walls were softened by curvaceous ogees and tiled friezes. The icons were painted by Repin, Polonev, Nesterov and Apollinarius Vasnetsov, whose brother Viktor designed and laid the mosaic floor in the form of a spreading flower, while Vrubel made the tiled stove, and the pulpit was painted by Andrei Mamontov, who died as a child and was buried in a vault to the left of the nave.

The **woods** beyond are a quintessentially Russian mixture of birch, fir, oak, larch, elder and hazel, with sedge creeks and ponds marking the course of the Vorya River.

# Arkhangelskoe

During the heyday of the Russian aristocracy in the late eighteenth and early nineteenth centuries, the epicurean ideal of enjoying life to the hilt reached its apotheosis at **ARKHANGELSKOE**, the suburban estate of **Prince Nikolai Yusupov** (1751–1831), west of Moscow. So rich that he was apparently unable to count all his properties without the aid of a notebook, Yusupov collected art, dabbled in science, discussed philosophy with Voltaire and poetry with Pushkin, and kept a harem at Arkhangelsoe. The estate was described by the historian Shamurin as a "corner of paradise" remote from the "cold, grey and disorderly" Russia beyond its boundaries.

Arkhangelskoe's allure for visitors has waned since the palace was closed for repairs in 1989, and its appeal now lies mainly in the mournful beauty of the park, dotted with crumbling pavilions and statues – best seen in summer, when its roses are blooming; in winter, the statues are encased in boxes to prevent them from cracking in the cold.

### Practicalities

There are no organized excursions to Arkhangelskoe, so you'll need to take the metro to Tushkinskaya station, then find the stop for #549 buses (at roughly five past, half-past and a quarter to each hour), which take thirty minutes. Alternatively, catch bus #520 or #541 from Pobshino, a township that's accessible by suburban train from the vicinity of Voykovskaya metro, on a different line. To get there by car, drive out along the Volokolamskoe shosse (M9) and turn left onto the Ilyinskoe shosse, a few miles past the Moscow Ring Road.

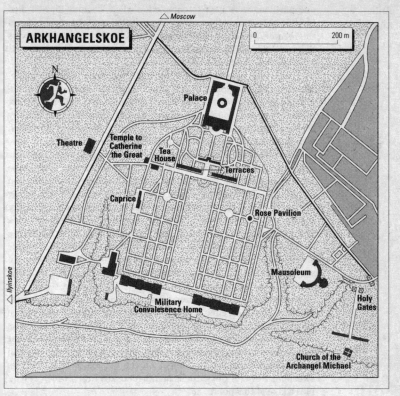

Map labels (within image):

△ Moscow

**ARKHANGELSKOE**

0 | 200 m

N

Palace

Theatre

Temple to Catherine the Great

Tea House

Terraces

Caprice

Rose Pavilion

Mausoleum

△ Ilyinskoe

Military Convalesence Home

Holy Gates

Church of the Archangel Michael

Official **opening hours** (Wed–Sun 11am–6pm; closed every Mon & Tues & the last Fri of each month) seem to be honoured more in the breach than the observance – but in practice you can slip through a hole in the fence and wander around any day of the week.

If hunger strikes, there is the *Grill Bar* (daily 11am–9pm) across the road from the entrance gates of the convalescence home. Classier **meals** can be enjoyed at the *Russkaya Izba* (☎561-4244; ⑤; call ahead to reserve) in **Ilyinskoe**, 7km away, whose menu features bear and venison and traditional Russian drinks such as *kvas* and mead.

## Around the estate

Although the **estate** dates back to the 1670s, its features recall the era of Catherine the Great, who put Prince Nikolai Golitsyn in charge of the building project. When Golitsyn died in 1809, his heirs sold the estate to Yusupov, who continued with the project undaunted by a serf riot in 1812 and a fire in 1820. Embodying five decades of Neo-Classical architecture and interior design, the palace and pavilions were near to completion when Yusupov himself died in 1831, whereupon the estate was neglected until the early years of this century, when it had a brief revival. In 1919, the Bolsheviks decreed Arkhangelsoe a public museum; a convalescence home was built in the grounds after World War II.

Today, the **palace** is fenced off while restoration work drags on, allowing only glimpses of its inner courtyard, flanked by Ionic-pillared arcades, while shutters prevent even a peek into the rooms, which were fabulously decorated and hung with paintings by Tiepolo, van Dyck and Boucher; reportedly, there was one filled with portraits of Yusupov's mistresses and lovers.

Two dilapidated **terraces** topped with Classical busts and urns descend to a formal garden stretching towards the river, with grape arbours running the length of its parterre and derelict pavilions on either side. Whereas the **Rose Pavilion** was meant to be purely decorative, the two-storey **Caprice** was furnished like a miniature palace for garden *soirées*, and the **Tea House** started out as a library pavilion. Further north stands a small **Temple to Catherine the Great** – who is sculpted in bronze as Themis, goddess of justice – while across the road that has been cut through the estate you'll see the **theatre** built for Yusupov's troupe of serf-actors. Sadly, none of these buildings is open.

At the far end of the parterre looms an enormous Palladian-style **Military Convalescence Home** that's easily mistaken for the palace at first sight. Fans of Stalinist decor will absolutely adore its marbled foyers, carpeted in red and hung with inspirational war paintings, but keep a lookout for the *babushka* on duty. No one will mind, however, if you just linger on the terrace outside, with its sweeping **views** of the gardens and the Moskva River, which resembles a lake at this point.

The rest of the park is landscaped in true Italian fashion, with romantic follies. To honour their ancestor, the later Yusupovs had the architect Roman Klein build an imposing rose granite and limestone temple with curved wings, intended to be the family **mausoleum** but never used as such due to the Revolution. Further along, the older, Gothic-style **Bridge over the Ravine** is followed by the Corinthian-columned **Holy Gates**, framing the path to the **Church of the Archangel Michael**. A tiny whitewashed edifice with a shingled dome atop a pyramid of *kokoshniki*, the church was built as early as 1667, and subsequently gave its name to the estate.

# Klin

By the mid-fourteenth century, the Grand Duchy of Muscovy encompassed a ring of towns straddling the rivers that were Russia's chief lines of communication. **KLIN** was founded on the banks of the Sestra (a tributary of the Volga) in 1318, with a Kremlin as its nucleus. As an overland route to Novgorod (and, later, St

Petersburg) grew, Klin became more of a stopover than an *entrepôt*, and eventually found favour with **Tchaikovsky**, who had spent his summers in the region since 1885, avowing: "I can't imagine myself living anywhere else. I find no words to express how much I feel the charm of the Russian countryside, the Russian landscape and the quiet that I need more than anything else."

There isn't much to see in Klin, but Tchaikovsky-lovers can visit his former residence on a *Patriarchi Dom* excursion ($15) if **getting there** by train from Leningrad Station (1hr 15min), and then the short bus ride within Klin, sounds problematic. Travelling by car, Klin is about 80km from Moscow on the Leningradskoe shosse (M10); both the town and the museum are well signposted.

## Tchaikovsky's house

A few years before his death in 1893, Tchaikovsky rented a house in the woods below town, telling his brother Modeste, "What a blessing it is to know that no one will come, no one will interrupt neither work, reading nor strolling" – before writing *The Sleeping Beauty*, *The Nutcracker* and his Fifth and Sixth symphonies. At his death, Modeste inherited the house and converted it into a **Tchaikovsky Museum** (Fri–Tues 10am–6pm; closed the last Mon of each month), which has been preserved ever since.

Painted a soft blue with a white trim, the house has a verandah opening onto the back garden, where Tchaikovsky strolled with his dogs. The interior is warm and cosy, with flesh-toned stucco or wood-panelled walls hung with portraits of composers and relatives. On the composer's birthday, May 7, the winners of the international Tchaikovsky Competition have the honour of playing his **grand piano** in the sitting room where he wrote his Sixth Symphony. While the **library**, with its jigsaw ceiling, verges on baronial grandeur, the bedroom is simple and homely, with his slippers placed beside the bed. In 1964, a concert hall was built in the grounds, where visitors can hear recordings and watch **films** about the composer.

# Peredelkino

Southwest of Moscow, the forested countryside harbours numerous *dacha* colonies, including the famous writers' village of **PEREDELKINO**, where **Boris Pasternak** is buried. In the Brezhnev era, a visit to Pasternak's grave was a kind of rite of passage for the Muscovite intelligentsia, while foreign journalists found weekend house-parties at Peredelkino the best source of gossip about the Kremlin and Moscow's cultural life. Today, Peredelkino signifies less, if only because its best-known living residents have either left or are now regarded as has-beens – except for the orthodox Patriarch, Alexei II, who has a villa here. In 1991, after decades of official hostility towards the writer and his memory, Pasternak's *dacha* was opened as a museum, assuring his place in the literary firmament.

As with other sites, a *Patriarchi Dom* excursion ($15) will save you the trouble of getting there by train from Kiev Station (30min), or driving out along the Minskoe shosse (M1) and turning left at the 21km marker. As a sign of how fashionable Peredelkino has become in the last five years or so, there is now an Italian restaurant (⑥) and an Irish-managed hotel (⑨) called the *Villa Peredelkino* (☎435-1211) on Chobotovskaya alleya. The surrounding woods are great for nature rambles or cross-country skiing – skis can be rented from the hotel.

## Pasternak's dacha

Pasternak's dacha (Thurs–Sun 10am–4pm; $2) stands on a nondescript side road that's impossible to locate without asking locals for directions (*Izviníte, pozhálsta, kak praíti k dómu Pasternáka?*). The house itself can be identified by its wooden fence, the only one on the street. Painted dark brown with a white trim, its main feature is an oblong verandah wing covered by windows that juts into the garden. Built by his artist father, Leonid, in 1937, the house became Pasternak's refuge after he was forced to decline the Nobel Prize for Literature that he was due to receive for his novel *Doctor Zhivago* in 1953. Vilified by the Soviet media and the Writers' Union, Pasternak spent his final years gardening, writing poetry and entertaining friends at the *dacha*, where he died of lung cancer in 1960 at the age of seventy.

The dining room is filled with sketches and portraits by his father, including a large oil painting of Tolstoy, a family friend. It also contains Pasternak's collection of Georgian ceramics and a huge television set that he never watched, preferring to hear news only from visitors. His favourite place was the glassed-in verandah, with its wicker furniture and antique *samovar*. Notice the bucket filled with glass clubs, a "winter bouquet" given as a gift by a crystal factory. Visitors are led upstairs to his study-bedroom, covering most of the top floor. His coat and boots are where he last placed them, next to a bookshelf lined with Russian encyclopedias and novels by Virginia Woolf in English. Pasternak knew the language well, having translated Shakespeare into Russian during the Terror years, when translations were a safer way of earning a living than writing poetry or novels.

The village cemetery (*kladbische*) where Pasternak is buried can be found by walking up the road from the train station to the church at the top of the hill, and then following the path to the left. Pasternak's grave lies beside those of four other members of the family, in a pine grove. His headstone – bearing his signature and a faint portrait – is always laid with flowers by admirers. The bells of the nearby Church of the Transfiguration toll at 6pm.

# Gorki Leninskie

South of Moscow, the country estate of **GORKI LENINSKIE**, where Lenin died, used to be a place of pilgrimage for the faithful, employing two hundred tour guides to handle the busloads of visitors. Today there are few visitors, and the estate-museum's future has been in doubt since 1991, as proposals to revitalize it or auction it off have been debated. Nevertheless, the museum has a morbid fascination, and would make an ideal home for the Leninalia formerly displayed in Moscow's Lenin Museum (p.96). Assuming it remains open to the public, Gorki Leninskie will appeal to anyone with an interest in Lenin or the kind of idolatry that was ubiquitous in Soviet times but is all but extinct in Russia today.

### Practicalities

As the estate is 32km south of the Kremlin, it's worth taking a *Patriarchi Dom* excursion ($15) to avoid the hassle of **getting there** by public transport. This involves taking the metro to Domodedovskaya, and then a bus from the depot 200m down the road. It's unclear whether the service will be numbered #513 or #313 in the future; at the time of writing, buses ran every ninety minutes and dropped passengers on the highway near the main entrance.

To reach Gorki Leninskie by car, take the Kashirskoe shosse (M4); 15km beyond the Moscow Ring Road, the turnoff is indicated by a small sign 200m *before* the bronze statue of Lenin that strides away from the gates of another (locked) entrance to the grounds. Although it's wise to phone (☎ 136-2334) to check, the estate should be **open** from 10am to 4pm, except on Tuesday. Admission is free.

## The Lenin Museum

In sight of the gates is a monstrously ugly block with a quasi-pharaonic portico, containing the last **Lenin Museum** opened in the USSR (in 1987). Built of black and white marble and furnished with bronze fittings and ruched curtains, its opulence would have appalled Lenin. Visitors are greeted at the top of the stairs by a giant effigy of the leader, seated against a billowing scarlet backdrop in an enclosure paved with cobblestones taken from Moscow's "Red" Presnya district, hallowed for its part in the 1905 and 1917 revolutions.

With its auto-controlled tedious video-montages accompanied by portentous music, the exhibition manages to be dull despite its technical wizardry. As the guide's spiel (in Russian) is of post-*glasnost* vintage, visitors who ask probing questions are rewarded with the sight of some pages from Lenin's Testament (see below), and told that the attempt to assassinate him in August 1918 may not have been carried out by Fanya Kaplan, the Left SR who was executed for the deed. The attack left Lenin with a bullet lodged in his body and led to his first period of convalescence at Gorki (as it was then called), where he later suffered a series of incapacitating strokes.

# The mansion

The real attraction is the elegant yellow and white stucco **mansion**, ten minutes' walk through the forest of blue firs. Previously owned by the Borodino hero General Pisarov and Zinaidia Morozova, the widow of Savva Morozov (p.154), the estate was expropriated in 1918 to become a sanatorium for Party leaders. Lenin only agreed to convalesce there because it had a phone line to Moscow – a vital consideration during the Civil War.

Initially, Lenin resided with his wife, Krupskaya, in the small, detached **northern wing**, above his doctors and bodyguards on the floor below. They shared their meals in a dining room with walnut furniture in striped dustcovers, where his sister Maria (a *Pravda* journalist) often slept. Their austere separate bedrooms were softened only by wolfskin rugs; the largest room, with a tiled stove, was reserved for guests such as Lenin's other siblings, Dmitry and Anna, who lived here after his death. Lenin himself was moved into the main house in December 1922, following a stroke.

Entering the **main house** via its glassed-in verandah, you'll see a telephone room with three direct lines to the Kremlin, off a hallway where the clock has been stopped at the moment of Lenin's death, and his jacket, boots and hunting gear are preserved in glass cases. The **library** contains four thousand books (Lenin had a working knowledge of nine foreign languages) and a desk set carved with worker and peasant figures, made for the first VDNKh. Next door is a sunny, palmy **conservatory** with a projector for showing silent films and a piano for sing-songs in the evening. Notice the flies embroidered on the curtains, and the special mechanized **wheelchair** at the foot of the stairs. A gift from factory workers, they never knew that he was paralyzed on his right side and made the wheelchair's controls right-handed, so it was never used.

Upstairs, the dining room displays a large map of Germany, in expectation of the next outbreak of revolution in Europe. Lenin worked in a pretty **study-bedroom**, where he dictated his last Testament, with a postscript proposing Stalin's dismissal from the post of General Secretary. After Lenin's death, Stalin brushed it aside as the delusion of "a sick man surrounded by womenfolk", and the postscript was suppressed.

*Lenin's funerary train can be seen near Pavelets Station in Moscow (p.217).*

Lenin's final hours on January 21, 1924, were spent in a small, gilded room, where he went into a coma at 5.30 in the evening and expired over an hour later. His body was laid out in the **salon**, whose mirrors and chandeliers were draped in black according to Russian custom, while the sculptor Merkurov made a death mask and casts of Lenin's hands (the right one clenched into a fist). Next day, his coffin was taken to Moscow by train. Visitors can peer into a shrouded aperture to see a lifesize photo of the body, surrounded by wreaths. In contrast, the last room you enter is richly decorated and crammed with porcelain objects, as it was when inhabited by Morozova.

For the *pièce de resistance*, you're taken to the garage to view Lenin's **Rolls Royce**. One of two expropriated Rolls Royces used by the Soviet leader, this vehicle was fitted with caterpillar tracks and skis for travelling across country in winter, and converted to run on pure alcohol, which was easier to obtain than petrol during the Civil War. Large enough to seat six bodyguards, it had a top speed of forty kilometres an hour.

Gorki Leninskie

# Borodino

The furthest place of interest within day-trip range of Moscow is **BORODINO**, the site of the bloodiest **battle** of the Patriotic War. On August 26 (September 7 by today's calendar), 1812, Napoleon's *Grande Armée* of 135,000 men and 600 cannons fought a 121,000-strong Russian host led by Mikhail Kutuzov. In fifteen hours the Russians lost 40,000 men and the French 30,000; Napoleon considered it the "most terrible" of all his battles. Though the Russians withdrew the next day – allowing the French to claim victory and continue advancing – Kutuzov's decision to sacrifice Moscow to preserve his army, and to burn the city to deny the French shelter, was vindicated by events – so Russians see Borodino as a defeat for the French.

The entire **battlefield** covers 130 square kilometres, but its salient features are all within a few miles of Borodino village. Less than 1km to the south is a **museum** (Tues–Sun 10am-6pm; closed the last Fri of each month) detailing each phase of the battle. To mark its centenary, 34 monuments were erected across the battlefield, including obelisks signifying Kutuzov's headquarters. There stands the **Convent of the Saviour of Borodino**, built in the 1830s, which saw service as a field-hospital in 1941, when the Russians halted the Nazi advance just in time for "General Winter" to come to their aid yet again. Nearby is the **inn** where Tolstoy stayed in 1867, while researching *War and Peace* – now a museum devoted to his sojourn.

A scaled-down **re-enaction of the battle** occurs every year on the first Sunday of September, when hundreds of military enthusiasts in period costume mount cavalry charges, skirmish with muskets and fire cannons. After two hours the field is obscured by smoke, and solemn music rises from the loudspeakers as a voice intones the names of the Russian regiments, to a chorus of *Vechnaya Slava!* (Immortal Glory!). If you enjoy such spectacles, this is definitely the occasion to visit Borodino. The event kicks off with a religious service by the gilt-topped monument on the Ravetskiy Battery, a high point at the centre of the battlefield.

Borodino is 129km west of Moscow, on the main road (M1) to Minsk; trains from Kiev Station in Moscow take about two and a half hours to **get there**.

# Moscow: Listings

# Chapter 11

# Accommodation

Anyone travelling on a tourist visa to Russia must have **accommodation** arranged before arriving in Moscow (see p.16 for details). However, now that it is easier to obtain business visas – which don't oblige you to prebook lodgings – independent travellers may be faced with the challenge of finding somewhere to stay on arrival. Having been spoon-fed with guests for years by *Intourist*, most hotels are still unused to coping with people just turning up. That's not to say that they won't have a room for you, but the price will in all likelihood be far above the rate charged to package tourists.

As **hotels** in Moscow are expensive, anyone on a tight budget will be limited to the dingiest, dodgiest ones, and will almost certainly do better by opting for a **hostel** or **private accommodation** instead. Forget about **campsites**, which are miles outside the city, have poor facilities and security, and only function over the summer (if at all).

## Hostels

Moscow's two foreign-run **hostels** are the best-value accommodation in town. Both are much safer than the small number of hotels that charge similar rates, and can help out with many of the problems that face low-budget travellers in Russia. Over summer, it's wise to reserve in advance at the *Travellers Guest House*.

**Prakash Guest House**, Profsoyuznaya ul. 83, korpus 1, entrance 2 (to the right of the main entrance); ☎334-2598 or 333-8263; 5min from Belyaevo metro (20min ride from the centre). Cosy, Indian-run guest house on the 3rd floor; exit near the rear of the train, and go left at the far end of the underpass. The building itself is largely inhabited by African and Asian students. Has a small restaurant serving real Indian food. Rooms $25–80, depending on facilities.

**Travellers Guest House**, Bolshaya Pereslavskaya ul. 50; ☎971-4059; fax: 2807686; e-mail: tgh@glas.apc.org; 10min from Prospekt Mira metro. Hidden away on the 10th floor, this American-run hostel is pleasant, clean and fairly central, with a laundry, café and bar. Can provide visa support, obtain tickets for the Trans-Siberian Express and overnight trains to St Petersburg, and book hostel beds in St Petersburg. Has singles ($30), doubles ($35) and dormitories with four beds ($15 each).

## Private accommodation – and renting a flat

**Private accommodation** for tourists is slowly catching on in Moscow, but there is still no booking office where you can just turn up and find a room: it has to be arranged in advance, from abroad. Some agencies provide self-contained flats, but most offer **bed and breakfast** in Moscow households. Your hosts may volunteer to act as guides or drivers, and are often keen to offer insights into Russian life. Most people in the habit of renting rooms to foreigners speak some English or

**Accommodation**

another foreign language. Your room should be clean and comfortable, though it can be disconcerting to discover that it belongs to one of the family, who will sleep elsewhere for the duration of your stay – as happens in smaller apartments.

The **cost** varies from $25 to $70 per person per night, depending on factors such as the location of the flat and whether you opt for B&B or full board, so it definitely pays to shop around. If possible, you should try to get the address of the flat and check how far it is from the centre, and the nearest metro station.

Since **visas and accommodation** are interrelated (see p.16), you'll need to obtain a business visa before leaving home. Most foreign agencies that supply private rooms in Moscow can also provide visa support; there's no point in doing business with them if they can't. See the box opposite for addresses.

## Renting a flat

If you're planning to stay over a month in Moscow, **renting a flat** will probably prove the most economical option. That said, rents are rising constantly and real bargains are few. A nice two- or three-bedroom flat within the Garden Ring is likely to cost over $1000 per month, and even a spartan one-room flat within walking distance of a metro station beyond the Circle line will probably cost upwards of $300. If you don't speak Russian or have Russian friends to make enquiries on your behalf, the obvious place to start looking are the classified ads in the back of the *Moscow Times* and *Moscow Tribune*. Going through an agency, expect to pay commission, which can go as high as fifty percent of the first month's rent.

Without going too deeply into the intricacies of **living in Moscow**, a few points should be kept in mind. Proximity to a metro station is crucial, as are decent shops or a market in the vicinity. Security is also vital: look for a flat with a steel door; keep as low a profile as possible, and don't let strangers or casual acquaintances know where you live. Check that the hot water works and the phone bill has been paid before committing yourself.

Flats with their own boiler are rare, but preferable to those reliant on district heating systems, which may be deprived of hot water for a week over the summer, when the system is shut down for cleaning and maintenance.

## Hotels

Moscow's **hotels** run the gamut from opulent citadels run as joint ventures with foreign firms – which can be relied upon to deliver the goods at a price that warps your credit card – to seedy pits inhabited by mobsters, where strangers risk more than their property. In between fall numerous hotels that are far from perfect but might be tolerable. The buildings themselves range from Art Nouveau edifices to stupendous Stalin skyscrapers or spartan, low-rise blocks. Some are in prime locations but most are in dreary suburbs. Given all this, it definitely pays to shop around (or, in the case of package tourists, check in advance where you'll be accommodated).

While joint-venture hotels are comparable to their Western four- and five-star counterparts, wholly Russian places tend to have lower **standards** than suggested by the *Intourist* system of two to four stars, which should be taken with a pinch of salt. Two-star hotels mostly consist of 1950s low-rises with matchbox-sized rooms, while three-star hotels are typical 1960s and 1970s tower blocks, equipped with several restaurants, bars and night-clubs. Four-star hotels tend to date from the 1980s and come closest to matching the standards (and prices) of their Western counterparts. Conversely, the older, low-rate places are generally shabby, with erratic water supplies and surly staff.

Absurdly, some hotels still insist that guests show a **letter of invitation** from a firm or institution in Moscow. If you haven't got one, they might be open to persuasion on the spot, but enquiries by phone are unlikely to get far. Wherever you're hoping to stay, it's obviously safer to book a room before you arrive; **reservations** from abroad are best made by fax, through a travel agent or booking system (see box). In Moscow, you can

## Accommodation Agencies

**American International Homestays**, Route 1, Box 68, Iowa City, IA 52240, USA; ☎319/626-2125; fax: 319/626-2199. Can also book rooms in St Petersburg and other major cities.

**B&B**, in Moscow; ☎095/252-4451 or 095/252-5302; fax: 095/2057683 (mark "Attention Bed & Breakfast"). Small Russian agency with a dozen flats in the vicinity of Belarus Station.

**East-West Ventures**, PO Box 14391, Tucson, AZ 85732, USA; ☎800/833-4398. Also has rooms in St Petersburg and Kiev.

**Goodwill Holidays**, Manor Chambers, The Green, School Lane, Welwyn, Herts, AL6 9EB, England; ☎0438/716421; fax: 0438/840228.

**IBV Bed and Breakfast Systems**, 13113 Ideal Drive, Silver Spring, MD 20906, USA; ☎301/942-3770; fax: 301/933-0024. Okay for rooms, but be wary of paying in advance for any other services.

**Moscow Bed & Breakfast**, in Moscow; ☎095/193-2514 or 095/457-3508; fax: 095/152-7493. Big choice of flats, also bookable through the *Russian Travel Service* (see below). Director Alla Kashtanova only speaks Russian.

**Pioneer East/West Initiatives**, 88 Brooks Ave, Arlington, MA 02174, USA; ☎617/648-2020; fax: 617/648-7304.

**Progressive Tours**, 12 Porchester Place, London W2 2B5, England; ☎0171/262-1676. Can book rooms for people on its package holidays.

**Red Bear Tours**, 320B Glenferrie Rd, Melbourne, Victoria 3144, Australia; ☎3/824-7138; fax: 3/822-3956. Also rooms in St Petersburg.

**Russian Travel Service**, PO Box 311, Fitzwilliam, NH 03447, USA; ☎ & fax: 603/585-6534 (mark "Attention Helen Gates"). The US end of *Moscow Bed & Breakfast* (see above).

---

reserve a room and pay for it on the spot at the *Intourist* office on Manezhnaya pl., or the hotel reservations desk at Sheremetevo-2 airport. It's best to pay for one night only, in case you decide to move somewhere else the next day.

Without being alarmist, there's a real risk of break-ins or muggings at hotels frequented by Westerners that don't maintain adequate **security**; or in places where all the other guests are from the former Soviet republics, so that you stick out a mile (staying there is only advisable if you speak Russian and know the score). Don't leave valuables in your room (or put *all* your money in the hotel safe); stash most other items in a locked suitcase under the bed; and lock the door before going to sleep. Hotels geared towards businessmen tend to have lots of **prostitutes** whose late-night phone calls (or surprise visits with the use of a pass-key) are disturbing, to say the least.

When checking in, you should receive a *propusk* or **guest card** that enables you to get past the doorman and claim your room key – don't lose it. Most hotels have a **service bureau**, which can obtain theatre tickets, arrange tours, rental cars and the like. Each floor is monitored by a *dezhurnaya* or concierge, who will keep your key while you are away and can arrange to have your laundry done. A small gift to her upon arrival should help any ensuing problems to be resolved, but her presence is no guarantee of security. Though relatively few hotels still include **breakfast** in the price, it does no harm to ask; indeed, in low-rated places it's wise to check if there's anywhere to eat at all.

## Central Moscow

We've taken this to mean anywhere within fifteen minutes' walk of Red Square, Pushkinskaya pl. or the Arbat, thus including the whole area within the Garden Ring, plus a few places just outside it or across the river from the Kremlin. High prices are the rule for everywhere with excellent facilities and security, but if

## Accommodation

### Hotel Prices

All the hotels below are listed in alphabetical order under area headings, according to their location in the city. After each entry you'll find a symbol that corresponds to one of eight **price categories**:

① under $20   ⑤ $100–150
② $20–40   ⑥ $150–200
③ $40–70   ⑦ $200–300
④ $70–100   ⑧ over $300

All prices are for the lowest priced **double room** available, which may mean without a private bathroom or shower in the cheapest places. For a **single room**, expect to pay around two-thirds the price of a double. Some hotels also offer "lux" or "half-lux" rooms with a lounge and/or kitchen, suited to several people self-catering.

Note that these **prices** can only be a guideline, for two reasons. Although we've reckoned them in US dollars, you may well be obliged to pay in rubles, and should beware of hotels setting a rate of exchange that inflates the cost (this can be avoided by paying by credit card). Secondly, there's no way of knowing whether the level of **VAT** will rise above 23 percent, where it stood when this was written (and has been included in the prices), so be sure to verify that the rate includes taxes.

you're not bothered, it's worth investigating cheaper hotels in prime locations, such as the *Moskva* or the *Rossiya*.

**Baltschug-Kempinski Hotel**, ul. Balchug 1; ☎230-6500; fax: 230-6502; 15min from Kitay-Gorod or Novokuznetskaya metro. Across the river from Red Square, with an amazing view from its deluxe corner rooms, this tastefully modernized establishment has all the amenities you'd expect from a top-class hotel under German management. ⑧.

**Belgrad Hotel**, Smolenskaya pl. 5; ☎248-1643; fax: 230-2129; near Smolenskaya metro. One of two 1970s blocks that used to be under the same management, just beyond the Arbat. Reasonably clean, safe and reliable, with a decent Greek restaurant. Breakfast included. ④.

**Budapest Hotel**, Petrovskie Linii 2/18; ☎921-1060; fax: 921-1266; 10min from Teatralnaya or Kuznetskiy Most metro. Just off ul. Petrovka, between the Bolshoy Theatre and the Sandunovskiy Baths. Quiet, old-fashioned and Mafia-free. Letter required. ④.

**Intourist Hotel**, Tverskaya ul. 3/5; ☎203-4008; near Okhotniy Ryad metro. Located just off Manezhnaya pl., within sight of

Red Square, this archetypal three-star hotel is jazzed up by a Mexican restaurant and the *Casino Gabriella* next door. ⑤.

**Marco Polo Presnya Hotel**, Spiridonovskiy per. 9; ☎202-4834 or 202-0381; fax: 230-2704; 10min from Mayakovskaya or Pushkinskaya metro. Small, cosy Austrian-run hotel with good facilities, in a side street near the Patriarch's Ponds. ⑦.

**Metropol Hotel**, Teatralniy proezd 1/4; ☎927-6000 or 927-6096; fax: 927-6061; near Teatralnaya, Ploshchad Revolyutsii and Okhotniy Ryad metros. Luxuriantly Art Nouveau building, and generally acknowledged to be the finest hotel in Moscow. ⑧.

**Minsk Hotel**, Tverskaya ul. 22; ☎229-1213; 5min from Mayakovskaya or Pushkinskaya metro. Anonymous 1960s block near the *Baku* restaurant, which makes it popular with Azeris. ③.

**Moskva Hotel**, Okhotniy ryad 7; ☎292-1000; fax: 925-0155; near Okhotniy Ryad and Teatralnaya metros. Sombre Stalinist warren whose west-facing rooms overlook the Kremlin, nearby. The best-furnished ones are on the 15th, 16th and 17th floors. Reservations cost 50 percent of one night's stay. ③.

**National Hotel**, Okhotniy ryad 14/1; ☎203-6539; near Okhotniy Ryad and Teatralnaya metros. Another Art Nouveau pile that once rivalled the *Metropol* for grandeur, and hopes to make a comeback after total refurbishment. Should reopen in 1995. ⑧.

**Pekin Hotel**, ul. Bolshaya-Sadovaya 5/1; ☎209-3400; fax: 200-1420; near Mayakovskaya metro. Built in the era of Sino-Soviet friendship, this antiquated wedding-cake edifice has a certain period charm and a real Chinese restaurant. ⑤.

**Rossiya Hotel**, ul. Varvarka 6; ☎298-1567; fax: 298-1567; 5min from Kitay-Gorod or Ploshchad Revolyutsii metro. Gigantic mice-infested labyrinth with 3070 rooms and poor security, redeemed only by its lowish prices and great location, just off Red Square. It also boasts the *Manhattan Express* nightclub. May close for a refit in the future. ③.

**Savoy Hotel**, ul. Rozhdestvenka 3; ☎929-8555; fax: 230-2186; near Kuznetskiy Most metro. Small deluxe hotel with magnificent Art Nouveau decor, impeccably jointly managed by *Finnair* and *Intourist*. Breakfast included. ⑧.

**Tsentralnaya Hotel**, Tverskaya ul. 10; ☎229-0848 or 229-8957; near Tverskaya, Pushkinskaya and Chekhovskaya metros. Gloomy place occupied by shady characters, without private bathrooms and toilets. ③.

**Zolotoe Koltso Hotel**, Smolenskaya pl. 5; ☎248-7395; fax: 248-7395; near Smolenskaya metro. The former twin of the *Belgrad Hotel* (see above), now renamed and gone downhill. ④.

## Zamoskvareche and the South

This corresponds to the area covered by Chapter 7, minus the island opposite the Kremlin. Most of its hotels are around Oktyabrskaya pl. – not an attractive area, but handy for reaching many sights by metro.

**Akademicheskaya Hotel**, Leninskiy pr. 1, korpus 1; ☎238-2114 or 238-0902; near Oktyabrskaya metro. A kind of hostel block once reserved for guests of the Academy of Sciences which now takes anyone with a letter (and maybe without). Singles only, some with kitchens. ②.

**Danilovskiy Hotel**, Bolshoy Stariy Danilovskiy per.; ☎954-0750; fax: 954-0750; 10min from Tulskaya metro. Built alongside the Danilov Monastery to lodge Patriarchal guests, but open to anyone associated with a reputable organization if they book in advance. The facilities aren't first class, but the restaurant is great. ⑦.

**Rossiyanka Hotel**, Donskaya ul. 1; ☎236-8260; near Oktyabrskaya metro. A former branch of the *Akademicheskaya* (see above) that's gone its own way, and has doubles. ⑦.

**Tsaritsyno Hotel**, Shipilovskiy proezd 47, korpus 1; ☎343-4343; fax: 343-4363; 10min from Orekhovo metro (30min ride from the centre). Located in a fresh-air zone near Tsaritsyno, this residential hotel has "Western standard" one-room flats with TV, phone, kitchen and washing machine, plus breakfast (⑤), and "Russian standard" ones with just a kitchen (②). Renting either by the month, there's a fifty percent reduction.

**Varshava Hotel**, Leninskiy pr. 2; ☎238-8908; near Oktyabrskaya metro. A rather dingy building opposite the *Akademicheskaya*. Letter required. ③.

## Krasnaya Presnya, Fili and the Southwest

Muscovites and expats rate Krasnaya Presnya and Fili as good areas to live, owing to their superior amenities. However, less expensive accommodation is generally located miles out along Leninskiy pr. or in the Sparrow Hills, so the number of metro stops from the centre and the walking distance to the hotel are crucial.

**Arena Hotel**, ul. 10-letiya Oktyabrya 11; ☎245-2802; 5min from Sportivnaya metro. Standard three-star hotel, chiefly notable for being located near the Novodevichiy Convent. ③.

**Kievskaya Hotel**, Kievskaya ul. 2; ☎240-1234 or 240-1444; near Kievskaya metro. Extremely unsavoury hotel used by traders passing through Kiev Station. ②.

**Accommodation**

**Accommodation**

**Mezhdunarodnaya Hotel I & II**, Krasnopresnenskaya nab. 12; ☎253-2382; fax: 253-2051; 20min from Krasnopresnenskaya metro. Known as the "Mezh", this complex of corporate offices and flats incorporates an indoor pool and the *Sadko* arcade. The Mezh II annexe (☎253-2378; fax: 253-2051) charges slightly less for doubles. ⑦.

**Mir Hotel**, Bolshoy Devyatinskiy per. 9; ☎290-9150; fax: 252-0140; 10min from Krasnopresnenskaya or Barrikadnaya metro. 1970s hotel beside the old SEV building, near the White House. ⑤.

**Orlyonok Hotel**, ul. Kosygina 15; ☎939-8884 or 939-8845; Leninskiy Prospekt metro and then trolleybus #7. On the edge of the Sparrow Hills, with fine views of Moscow from its upper floors, and fronted by the *Russkaya Troyka* nightclub. Letter required. ②.

**Pallada Hotel**, ul. Ostrovityanova 14; ☎335-9566; fax: 336-9602; near Konkovo metro (20min from the centre). Small new private hotel, with deluxe and ordinary doubles; all have fridges and TV. ③.

**Radisson Slavyanskaya Hotel**, Berezhovskaya nab. 2; ☎941-8020; fax: 240-6915; near Kievskaya metro. Moscow's only US-managed chain hotel contains a pool, the *Americom House of Cinema* and several TV news agencies. ⑦.

**Sport Hotel**, Leninskiy pr. 90/2; ☎131-3515; 15min from Prospekt Vernadskovo metro. Typical of the grotty, Soviet-style hotels in this part of Moscow; low prices are its only redeeming feature. Letter required. ②.

**Spros Hotel**, Leninskiy pr. 95/15; ☎133-4394; fax: 938-2100; 15min walk from Prospekt Vernadskovo or Novye Cheremushki metro. Russo-Swiss corporate ghetto with all mod cons and high security. ⑦.

**Sputnik Hotel**, Leninskiy pr. 38; ☎938-8818; 5min from Leninskiy Prospekt metro. Pebble dashed block with fairly basic rooms but not bad security. Letter probably required. ③.

**Tsentralniy Dom Turista**, Leninskiy pr. 146; ☎438-5510; fax: 438-7756; near Yugo-Zapadnaya metro (30min from the centre). Despite its way-out location, this 22-storey building is one of the best budget hotels in Moscow, priced at the lower end of band. ③.

**Ukrainiya Hotel**, Kutuzovskiy pr. 2/1; ☎243-3030 or 243-2596; fax: 243-3092; 10min from Kievskaya metro. Stalinesque behemoth across the river from the White House, noted for its spacious rooms. Probably the best of the old Soviet-style hotels. ④.

**Universitetskaya Hotel**, Michurinskiy pr. 8/29; ☎939-9451; Universitet metro. Formerly used for guests of MGU; the ambience is deeply Soviet. ③.

## Northern Suburbs

This refers to the area covered by Chapter 9, plus Izmaylovo (see p.25). Except for Izmaylovo, the locations are generally unpleasant, if not awful. Unless your hotel provides a bus into the centre, proximity to a metro station is as vital as good security.

**Aerostar Hotel**, Leningradskiy pr. 37; ☎213-900; fax: 213-9001; 15min from Dinamo or Aeroport metro. Canadian-managed hotel off the airport road, which often hosts social events. ⑦.

**Altay Hotel**, Botanicheskaya ul. 41; ☎482-5703; fax: 488-6829; 5min from Vladykino metro, near the northwestern edge of the Botanical Gardens. Pretty dodgy and basic; they advise reserving ahead. ②.

**Baykal Hotel**, Selskokhozyaystvennaya ul. 15/1; ☎189-8802; fax: 189-7553; 5min from Botanicheskiy Sad metro. Only slightly better than the *Altay*, and requiring a letter of invitation. ③.

**Izmaylovo Hotel**, Izmaylovskie shosse 71; ☎166-3627 or 166-0145; near Izmaylovskiy Park metro (20min from the centre). Well-equipped high-rise complex near the Izmaylovo Art Market. By pleading with the administration in korpus A, you might get a room without a letter. ②.

**Kosmos Hotel**, pr. Mira 150; ☎217-0786 or 217-0785; fax: 215-8880; 5min from VDNKh metro. Sited opposite the Space Obelisk and the Worker and Collective Farm-Girl monument, this vast four-star hotel teems with prostitutes who won't take no for an answer. ⑤.

**Leningradskaya Hotel**, Kalanchovskaya ul. 25; ☎975-3032; near Komsomolskaya metro. Dowdy pint-sized Stalin skyscraper at the end of the teeming, low-life Komsomolskaya pl. (see p.267). ④.

**Novotel Hotel**, near Sheremetevo-2 airport; ☎578-9401 or 578-9408; fax: 578-2794 or 220-6604. Comfortable though soulless hotel miles outside the city, connected by a shuttle-bus to the centre. ⑦.

**Olympic Penta Hotel**, Olympiyskiy pr. 18/1; ☎971-6101; fax: 975-2401; 15min from Prospekt Mira metro. Run by a subsidiary of *Lufthansa*, this four-star block near the Olympic Sports Complex has its own pool, and a "Mediterranean Village" attached. ⑧.

**Palace Hotel**, 1-ya Tverskaya-Yamskaya ul. 19; ☎956-3152; fax: 956-3151; near Belorusskaya metro. Well-equipped, and only 500m beyond the Garden Ring, it contains the best seafood restaurant in Moscow. ⑨.

**Pullman-Iris Hotel**, Korovinskoe shosse 10; ☎488-8000; fax: 096-0105. French-run hotel in a park with sports grounds, not near any metro station, but connected by shuttle-bus to the centre. ⑦.

**Zolotoe Kolos Hotel**, Yaroslavskaya ul. 15, korpus 3; ☎286-2703; 5min from VDNKh metro. Not to be confused with the similarly named hotel on Smolenskaya pl. – nor recommended unless you're into low-life. ②.

**Accommodation**

# Chapter 12

# Eating and Drinking

*When I eat pork at a meal, give me
the whole pig; when mutton, give the
whole sheep; when goose, the whole
bird. Two dishes are better than a
thousand provided a fellow can
devour as much of them as he
wants.*

*Dead Souls*, Gogol.

As the above quotation suggests, quantity
rather than variety has long characterized
the Russian appetite – especially under
Communism, when citizens made a virtue
of the slow service that was the norm in
Soviet restaurants, by drinking, talking and
dancing for hours. The modern Western
notion of a quick meal was unthinkable.

These days much has changed, as
many Russians can no longer afford to eat
out, while those who can enjoy a far
wider choice. Moscow now abounds in
**private cafés and restaurants** offering
everything from pizza to Indian, French
and Chinese food. The downside is that
most cater to the new rich or foreign businessmen on expense accounts, so prices
are frequently astronomical and the clientele obnoxious.

Partly for reasons of security, many
cafés and restaurants are difficult to spot,
located in basements with covered
windows and only the most discreet of
signs above the door. Those run jointly by
Russian and foreign partners tend to be
more obvious from the street. The old
distinction between **ruble** and **hard-
currency** places has effectively disappeared since hard-currency transactions in
cash were banned and prices rose to
Western levels across the board. Though

many places still display their prices in
dollars, you will have to pay in rubles at
an exchange rate that is marked up daily.
If this seems way out of line with the rates
elsewhere, you'll probably save money by
paying with a **credit card**. However, it's
unwise to assume that you can use one
in any restaurant.

## Breakfast, bakeries and snacks

At home, most Russians take **breakfast**
(*zaftrak*) seriously, tucking into calorific
dishes like buckwheat pancakes (*bliny*) or
porridge (*kasha*), with curd cheese (*tvorog*)
and sour cream (*smetana*) – though some
simply settle for a cup of tea and a slice of
bread. Hotels usually serve an approximation of the "Continental" breakfast, probably just fried egg, bread, butter and jam;
however, ritzier hotels may provide a
*buffet* (sometimes a *Shvedskiy stol* or
"Swedish table" – smörgasbord), and offer
a Western-style **brunch** on Sundays.

**Pastries** (*pirozhnoe*) are available from
cake shops (*konditerskaya*) and some
grocers (*gastronom*). Savoury pies
(*pirozhki*) are often sold on the streets
from late morning – the best are filled with
cabbage, curd cheese or rice; steer clear of
the meat ones.

**Bread** (*khleb*), available from bakeries
(*bulochnaya*), is one of the country's culinary strong points. "Black" bread (known
as *chorniy* or *rzhanoy*) is the traditional
variety: a dense, rye bread with a distinctive sourdough flavour and amazing

longevity. *Karelskiy* is similar but with fruit; *surozhniy* is a lighter version, made with a mixture of wheat and rye. French-style baguettes (*baton*) – white, mixed-grain or plaited with poppy seeds – are also popular. Unfortunately the old custom whereby shoppers could test a loaf's freshness with long forks has gone (people started stealing the forks), but the system of queuing at the *kassa* before queuing for the bread remains.

As in most of eastern Europe, the Russians are very fond of **cakes** (*tort*). There are over sixty varieties, but the main ingredients are fairly standard: a sponge dough, a good deal of honey and a distinctive spice like cinnamon or ginger or lots of buttery cream and jam. Whatever the season, Russians are always happy to have an **ice cream** (*morozhenoe*), cheaply available from kiosks all over town. Much of the locally produced ice cream is cheaper and of better quality than the imported brands; try the popular crème-brulée flavour or eskimo, a sort of choc-ice. Alternatively, there are a few *Baskin-Robbins* outlets dotted around town.

Western-style **fast-food** is now common in Moscow, with several branches of *Pizza Hut* and *McDonald's*, not to mention a host of kiosks dispensing dubious pizzas, burgers and hot dogs. Alternatively, most department stores feature a stand-up **buffet**, offering open **sandwiches** with salami, caviar or boiled egg, as well as other nibbles. Less appealing buffets can be found in train and bus stations, and around metro stations and markets.

## Zakuski

Despite the increasing popularity of fast-food and foreign cuisine, most Russians remain loyal to their culinary heritage – above all, to **zakuski**. These small dishes are the Russian equivalent of Spanish *tapas*, consumed before a big meal, to accompany vodka, or as a light snack at any time of the day. They can also constitute a meal in themselves.

*Zakuski* form the basis of the famous *Russkiy stol*, or "Russian table", a feast of awesome proportions, in which the table groans under numerous dishes while the *samovar* steams away. Among the upper classes in Tsarist times, this was merely the prelude to the main meal, as foreign guests would discover after gorging themselves on *zakuski*. Salted fish, like sprats or herrings, are a firm favourite, as are gherkins, assorted cold meats and salads. Hard-boiled eggs or *bliny*, both served with **caviar** (*ikra*), are also available. Caviar is no longer as cheap as during the Brezhnev era, when people tired of eating so much of it, but it's still cheaper than in the West. It comes in two basic varieties: red (*krasnaya*) or black (*chornaya*); the latter consists of smaller eggs and is more sought after.

**Eating and Drinking**

## Meals

For a **full meal**, you can go anywhere from an old-style workers' self-service **canteen** (*stolovaya*) to a proper **restaurant** (*restoran*). Most Russians eat their main meal of the day at lunchtime (*obed*), between 1 and 4pm, and traditionally only have *zakuski* and tea for supper (*uzhin*). Restaurants, on the other hand, make much more of the evening and may often close for a couple of hours in the afternoon.

If your main concern is price, the cheapest option is a *stolovaya*, but since most are grotty and frequented by beggars, you'll do much better in one of the growing number of privately run **cafés**, where you can order as few or as many dishes as you like.

**Menus** are usually written in Russian only, though some places offer a shorter version in English; the Russian menu is typed up every day, whereas the English version may give only a general idea of what's actually available. In such cases, you're probably better off asking what they recommend (*shto-by vy po rekomendovali?*), which can elicit some surprisingly frank replies.

### Russian cuisine

**Russian cuisine** owes many debts to Jewish, Caucasian and Ukrainian cooking, but remains firmly rooted to its peasant origins. In former times, the staple diet of

## Eating and Drinking

black bread, potatoes, cabbages, cucumber and onions made for bland eating – *Shchi da kasha, pishcha nasha* ("cabbage soup and porridge are our food"), as one saying goes – with flavourings limited to sour cream, garlic, vinegar, dill and a few other fresh herbs. These strong tastes and textures – salty, sweet, sour, pickled – remained the norm, even among the aristocracy, until Peter the Great introduced French chefs to his court in the early eighteenth century.

Most menus start with a choice of soup or *zakuski* (see above). **Soup** (*sup*) has long played an important role in Russian cuisine (the spoon appeared on the Russian table over 400 years before the fork). Cabbage soup, or *shchi*, has been the principal Russian dish for the last thousand years, served with a generous dollop of sour cream. Beetroot soup, or *borshch*, originally from Ukraine, is equally ubiquitous. Soups, however, are often only available at lunchtime and Russians do not consider even the large meaty soups to be a main meal; they will expect you to have a main course afterwards. Chilled soups (*okroshki*) are popular during the summer, made from whatever's available.

Main courses are overwhelmingly based on **meat** (*myaso*), usually beef, mutton or pork, and sometimes accompanied by a simple sauce (mushroom, sour cream or cheese). Meat may also make its way into *pelmeny*, a Russian version of ravioli, often served in a broth.

A wide variety of **fish and seafood** is available in Moscow, though it doesn't always find its way on to the menu. Pickled fish is a popular starter (try *selyotka pod shuboy*, herring "in a fur coat" of beetroot, carrot, egg and mayonnaise), while fresh fish occasionally appears as a main course – usually salmon, sturgeon or cod. Lobster and prawns only feature in a few deluxe restaurants, which boast of flying them in from America. However, if you're cooking for yourself, a vast range of fresh and frozen seafood can be found in fish shops, identifiable by the sign *Ryba* or *Okean*, or by their smell alone.

In cafés most main courses are served with boiled potatoes and/or sliced fresh tomatoes, but more expensive restaurants will serve a selection of accompanying **vegetables**. These are called *garnir* and occasionally have to be ordered and paid for separately. In ethnic restaurants, meat is almost always served on its own. Other vegetables are generally served boiled or pickled, but seldom appear separately on the menu.

**Desserts** (*sladkoe*) are not a strong feature of Russian cuisine. Ice cream, fruit, apple pie (*yablochniy pirog*) and jam pancakes (*blinchikiy s varenem*) are restaurant perennials, while in Caucasian restaurants you may get the flaky pastry and honey dessert, *pakhlava*.

### Caucasian, Central Asian and Korean food

After Russian food, the most common **ethnic cuisine** in Moscow is **Georgian**, which is lighter and spicier, using more fresh vegetables and herbs, as well as pulses, nuts and fruit. Starters include aubergine with pomegranate seeds; *lobio*, made from red or green beans; and chicken in walnut sauce (*satsivi*), which is eaten cold. Barbecued kebabs (*shashlyk*) are a standard main course, even in Russian restaurants. **Armenian** and **Azeri** cuisine is closer to Middle Eastern cooking (with the addition of dried fruits, saffron and ginger), while **Uzbek** features pilafs (*plov*) and *khinkali* (a spicier kind of *pelmeny*). Perhaps the best treat in store is **Korean** food, originally introduced by Koreans exiled to Kazakhstan in the 1930s. Marinated beef dishes like *bulkogi* are fried at your table, accompanied by raw vegetables and hot pickled garlic relish (*kimichi*).

Many **other cuisines** are represented by at least one restaurant in Moscow: Jewish, Hungarian, Greek, Italian, French, German, Spanish, Mexican, American, Chinese, Japanese, Indian, Vietnamese and Filipino.

### Vegetarians

Russia is no place for **vegetarians**; meat takes pride of place in the country's

## Eating and Drinking

### Vegetarian phrases

The concept of vegetarianism is a hazy one for most Russians, so simply saying you're a vegetarian may instil panic and/or confusion in the waiter – it's often better to ask what's in a particular dish you think looks promising.

The phrases to remember are *ya vegetarianets/vegetarianka* (masculine/feminine). *Kakiye u vas yest blyuda bez myasa ili ryby?*("I'm a vegetarian. Is there anything without meat or fish?"). For emphasis you could add *ya ne yem myasnovo ili rybnovo* ("I don't eat meat or fish").

cuisine, and the idea of forgoing it voluntarily strikes Russians as absurd. The various non-Russian dishes that find their way on to the menu offer some solace, and if you eat fish you will usually find something. *Bliny* are sometimes a good fall back; ask for them with sour cream, or fish if you eat it. If you're not too fussy about picking out fragments of meat, *plov* is a possibility, as are *borshch* and *shchi*, but the best dishes to look out for are mushrooms cooked with onions and sour cream, and *okroshka*, the cold summer soup.

*Lobio*, a widely available Georgian bean dish, is also recommended (served hot or cold). In general the ethnic restaurants (Georgian, Armenian, Indian or Chinese) are better for vegetarians.

## Drinks

The story goes that the tenth-century Russian prince Vladimir pondered which religion to adopt for his state. He rejected Judaism because its adherents were seen as weak and scattered; Catholicism because the pope claimed precedence over sovereigns; and Islam because his subjects would never tolerate renouncing alcohol, due to the fact that "Drinking is the joy of the Russians. We cannot live without it."

A thousand years on, **alcohol** remains a central part of Russian life, and

consumption is on the increase. The average citizen drinks over a litre of vodka a week, which means that many are putting away a lot more than that. In Moscow, drunks are everywhere – especially in train stations, markets and the metro – and dozens freeze to death in the snow every winter.

Gorbachev's ill-judged attempts to limit alcohol consumption merely succeeded in driving it underground, from where it emerged with a vengeance on to the streets as soon as restrictions were lifted. Nowadays, you can **buy alcohol** almost anywhere, from cafés, restaurants and theatres to street kiosks.

The last sell vodka, *spirt*, trashy brands of imported liquor and, increasingly, Moldavian, Crimean or Bulgarian wines. More basically, you'll just find someone dispensing beer bottles from a pile of crates: it costs a little more to take the stuff away (*s soboy*) than to drink it on the spot (*na meste*). Many kiosks are open 24 hours.

Moving indoors, there are the old Soviet-style **beer halls** (*pivnoy bar*), known as *pivnushka* – grim subterranean dives with a stand-up, spit-and-sawdust ambience and watered-down, warm beer. Although you can find bottled or canned imported beer in cafés now, to drink a decent pint in nice surroundings you really need to go to a **Western-run bar**. Few cafés serve Russian beer, but you can be certain of getting vodka and cognac, which are usually served in large measures of 100 grammes (*sto grama*).

### Vodka, samogon and spirit

**Vodka** (*vódka*) is the national drink – its name means something like "a little drop of water". Russians have a wealth of phrases and gestures to signify its consumption, the simplest and most common one being to tap the side of your chin or windpipe. Normally served chilled, vodka is drunk neat in one gulp, followed by a mouthful of food, traditionally pickled herring, cucumber or mushrooms; many people inhale deeply before tossing the liquor down their throats. Drinking small amounts at a time, and

# A FOOD GLOSSARY
## Useful Words

| | | |
|---|---|---|
| завтрак | *zavtrak* | breakfast |
| обед | *obéd* | main meal/lunch |
| ужин | *úzhin* | supper |
| нож | *nozh* | knife |
| вилка | *vílka* | fork |
| ложка | *lózhka* | spoon |
| тарелка | *tarélka* | plate |
| чашка | *cháshka* | cup |
| стакан | *stakán* | glass |
| десерт | *desért* | dessert |

## Basics

| | | |
|---|---|---|
| хлеб | *khleb* | bread |
| масло | *máslo* | butter/oil |
| мёд | *myod* | honey |
| молоко | *molokó* | milk |
| сметана | *smetána* | sour cream |
| яйца | *yáytsa* | eggs |
| яичница | *yaíchnitsa* | fried egg |
| мясо | *myáso* | meat (beef) |
| рыба | *ryba* | fish |
| фрукты | *frúkty* | fruit |
| овощи | *ovoshhi* | vegetables |
| зелень | *zélen* | green herbs |
| сахар | *sákhar* | sugar |
| соль | *sol* | salt |
| перец | *pérets* | pepper |
| горчица | *gorchítsa* | mustard |
| рис | *ris* | rice |
| плов | *plov* | rice dish |
| пирог | *piróg* | pie |
| хачапури | *khachapuri* | nan-style bread, stuffed with meat or cheese. |

## Soups – счпы

| | | |
|---|---|---|
| борщ | *borshch* | beetroot soup |
| бульон | *bulón* | consommé |
| рассольник | *rassólnik* | brine and cucumber soup |
| окрошка | *okróshka* | cold vegetable soup |
| щи | *shchi* | cabbage soup |
| солянка | *solyánka* | spicy, meaty soup |
| уха | *ukhá* | fish soup |

## Vegetables – овощи

| | | |
|---|---|---|
| лук | *luk* | onions |
| редиска | *redíska* | radishes |
| картофель | *kartófel* | potatoes |
| огурцы | *ogurtsy* | cucumbers |
| горох | *gorókh* | peas |
| помидоры | *pomidóry* | tomatoes |
| морковь | *morkóv* | carrots |
| салат | *salát* | lettuce |
| капуста | *kapústa* | cabbage |
| свёкла | *svyokla* | beetroot |

## Fruit – фрукты

| | | |
|---|---|---|
| яблоки | *yábloki* | apples |
| абрикосы | *abrikósy* | apricots |
| ягоды | *yágody* | berries |
| вишня | *víshnya* | cherries |
| финики | *fíniki* | dates |
| инжир | *inzhír* | figs |
| чернослив | *chernoslív* | prunes |
| груши | *grushi* | pears |
| сливы | *slivy* | plums |
| виноград | *vinográd* | grapes |
| лимон | *limón* | lemon |
| апельсины | *apelsíny* | oranges |
| арбуз | *arbúz* | watermelon |
| дыня | *dynya* | melon |

## Fish – рыба

| | | |
|---|---|---|
| карп | *karp* | carp |
| леш | *leshch* | bream |
| скумбрия | *skúmbriya* | mackerel |
| треска | *treská* | cod |
| щука | *shchúka* | pike |
| лососина /сёмга | *lososína/syomga* | salmon |

## Some terms

*Note: all adjectives appear in their plural form*

| | | |
|---|---|---|
| отварные | *otvarnye* | boiled |
| варёные | *varyonye* | boiled |
| на вертеле | *na vertele* | grilled on a skewer |
| жареные | *zhárenye* | roast/grilled/fried |
| тушёные | *tushonye* | stewed |
| печёные | *pechonye* | baked |
| паровые | *parovye* | steamed |
| копчёные | *kopchonye* | smoked |
| фри | *fri* | fried |
| со сметаной | *so smetánoy* | with sour cream |
| маринованные | *marinóvannye* | pickled |
| солёные | *solyonye* | salted |
| фаршированные | *farshiróvannye* | stuffed |

eating as you go, it's possible to consume an awful lot without passing out – though you soon reach a plateau of inebriated exhilaration.

Taste isn't a prime consideration; what counts is that the vodka is clean (*chistaya*), in other words free of suspect additives. Many of the well-known **brands** like *Stolichnaya*, *Pshenichnaya*, *Russkaya* and *Moskovskaya* are occasionally counterfeited by bootleggers, so unwary buyers can find themselves drinking diluted industrial alcohol.

Partly because of counterfeiting, foreign brands such as *Rasputin* and *Smirnoff* are highly popular. In shops and bars, you will also see **flavoured vodkas** such as *Pertsovka* (hot pepper vodka), *Limonaya* (lemon vodka), *Okhotnichaya* (hunter's vodka, with juniper berries,

## Eating and Drinking

---

### A FOOD GLOSSARY contd.

**Zakúski** – закуски

| | | |
|---|---|---|
| ассорти мясное | *assortí myasnóe* | assorted meats |
| ассорти рыбное | *assortí rybnoe* | assorted fish |
| ветчина | *vetchiná* | ham |
| винегрет | *vinegrét* | "Russian salad" |
| блины | *bliny* | pancakes |
| грибы | *griby* | mushrooms |
| икра баклажанная | *ikrá baklazhánnaya* | aubergine/eggplant purée |
| икра красная | *ikrá krásnaya* | red caviar |
| икра чёрная | *ikrá chornaya* | black caviar |
| шпроты | *shpróty* | sprats (like a herring) |
| колбаса копчёная | *kolbasá kopchonaya* | smoked sausage |
| маслины | *maslíny* | olives |
| огурцы | *ogurtsy* | gherkins |
| осетрина с майонезом | *osetrína s mayonézom* | sturgeon mayonnaise |
| салат из огурцов | *salat iz ogurtsóv* | cucumber salad |
| салат из помидоров | *salát iz pomidórov* | tomato salad |
| сардины с лимоном | *sardíny s limónom* | sardines with lemon |
| сельдь | *seld* | herring |
| столичный салат | *stolíchniy salát* | meat and vegetable salad |
| сыр | *syr* | cheese |
| язык с гарниром | *yazyk s garnírom* | tongue with garnish |

**Meat and poultry** – мясные блюда

| | | |
|---|---|---|
| азу из говядины | *azú iz govyádiny* | beef stew |
| антрекот | *antrekot* | entrecôte steak |
| бифстроганов | *bifstróganov* | beef stroganoff |
| биточки | *bitóchki* | meatballs |
| бифштекс | *bifshtéks* | beef steak |
| шашлык | *shashlyk* | kebab |
| свинина | *svinína* | pork |
| котлеты по-киевски | *kotléty po-kíevski* | chicken Kiev |
| кролик | *królik* | rabbit |
| курица | *kúritsa* | chicken |
| рагу | *ragú* | stew |
| телятина | *telyátina* | veal |
| сосиски | *sosíski* | sausages |
| баранина | *baránina* | mutton/lamb |
| котлета | *kotlet* | fried meatball |

---

## Eating and Drinking

ginger and cloves), *Starka* (apple and pear-leaf vodka) and *Zubrovka* (bison-grass vodka). Many Russians make these and other variants at home, by infusing the berries or herbs in regular vodka.

Ironically, the prime result of Gorbachev's anti-alcohol campaign was an extraordinary upsurge in home distilling. Now, however, with alcohol widely available, you are unlikely to be offered the Russian home-brewed spirit, *Samogon*. You may, however, come across **spirt**, 96 percent pure alcohol, which is diluted with five parts water and flavoured with a little cordial.

Other domestic liquors include **cognac** (*konyák*), which is pretty rough compared to the genuine article, but easy enough to acquire a taste for. The best stuff hails from Armenia (*Ararat*) and Moldova (*Beliy Aist*), but the Dagestani and Georgian versions are all right after you've downed the first round. Alternatively, you could indulge in the imported liquor that's now flooding the market, including *Bailey's Irish Cream* and the almond **liqueur** *Amaretto*, as well as numerous sickly fruit brandies from Austria. If you need your tot of **whisky**, avoid the dubious brands on sale in kiosks for a more recognizable

one, even if it means paying top prices in a hotel shop.

### Beer, wine and champagne

Russians drink **beer** (*pívo*) in the morning as a way of alleviating a vodka hangover, or as a mere thirst quencher. It can be good if fresh (it goes off after a few days) but few cafés sell it and it's sold and drunk mostly at street kiosks. The most common brands are *Kolos*, *Zhigulyovskoe* and *Moskovskie*, which could charitably be described as light ale; the various *Baltika* beers come in dark and pale and are increasingly popular, along with *Vena*, another good brand. The best regularly available dark beer is *Tverskoe*.

The **wine** (*vinó*) on sale in Moscow comes mostly from the vineyards of Moldavia, Georgia and the Crimea, though some of the Georgian wine has been subject to counterfeiting. The ones to look out for are the Georgian reds, *Mukuzani* and *Saperavi*, which are both dry and drinkable. Stalin preferred the sweeter *Kindzmarauli* and *Hvanchkara*, whose appearance may prompt a round of toasting to the dead dictator in conservative circles. Georgia also produces some of the best white wines, like the dry *Gurdzhani* and *Tsinandali* (traditionally

---

### A DRINK GLOSSARY

| | | |
|---|---|---|
| чай | *chay* | tea |
| кофе | *kófe* | coffee |
| без сахара | *bez sákhara* | without sugar |
| с молоком | *s molokóm* | with milk |
| сок | *sok* | fruit juice |
| пиво | *pívo* | beer |
| вино | *vinó* | wine |
| красное | *krásnoe* | red |
| белое | *béloe* | white |
| бутылка | *butylka* | bottle |
| лёд | *lyod* | ice |
| минеральная вода | *minerálnaya vodá* | mineral water |
| водка | *vódka* | vodka |
| вода | *vodá* | water |
| шампанское | *shampánskoe* | champagne |
| брют/сухое | *bryut/sukhoe* | extra dry/dry |
| полусухое/сладкое | *polsukhóe/sládkoe* | medium dry/sweet |
| коньяк | *konyák* | cognac |
| на здоровье | *na zdaróve* | cheers! |

---

served at room temperature), as well as the **fortified wines** *Portvini* (port) and *Masala*. Avoid what the Russians call *baramatukha* or "babbling juice", the equivalent of *Thunderbird* in the States. Since serious Russian drinkers prefer fortified wines, drier wines are often cheaper, but harder to find.

Last but not least there's Russian **champagne** (*shampánskoe*), some of which is pretty good if served chilled, and extremely cheap compared to the French variety. The two types to go for are *sukhoe* and *bryut*, which are both reasonably dry; *polusukhoe* or "medium dry" is actually very sweet, and *sladkoe* is the nearest you'll get to connecting yourself to a glucose drip. It's indicative of Russian taste that the last is the most popular of the lot.

### Tea, coffee and soft drinks

**Tea** (*chay*) is brewed and stewed for hours, and traditionally topped up with boiling water from an ornate tea urn, or *samovar*, but even the more run-of-the-mill cafés now tend to serve imported teabags. If you're offered tea in someone's home, it may well be *travyanoy*, a tisane made of herbs and leaves. Russians drink tea without milk; if you ask for milk it is likely to be condensed. **Milk** (*molokó*) itself is sold in shops and on the streets, along with *kefir*, a sour milk drink.

**Coffee** (*kófe*) is readily available and often of reasonable quality. Most places offer imported espresso brands like *Lavazza*, and occasionally you will be served an approximation of an espresso, or better still, a Turkish coffee – both served strong and black. Another favourite drink is weak, milky **cocoa**, known as *kakao*, poured ready-mixed from a boiling urn. Note that both tea and coffee are usually served with sugar already added, so you should make it clear when you order if you don't want sugar.

*Pepsi* and *Coca-Cola* predictably enough lead the market in **soft drinks**, although they are being challenged by cheaper brands imported from former eastern bloc countries. Russian lemonades have all but disappeared and even

*kvas*, an unusual but very Russian thirst quencher made from fermented rye bread and sold on the street from big vats, is getting harder to find. Native mineral water is all right, if a bit too salty and sulphurous for most Westerners; *Narzan* and *Borzhomi* from the Caucasus are the best-known brands. Imported mineral waters are also widely available. Lastly, if you're staying with Russians, you may be offered some *gryb*, a muddy-coloured, mildly flavoured infusion of a giant fungus known as a "tea mushroom".

## Breakfast places

Unless **breakfast** is included in the price of your accommodation, you might find it hard to know exactly what – and where – to eat. Only a few of the newer bakeries offer croissants, pastries and coffee under the same roof, so cafés (see "Cafés and Bars") offer more scope if you can wait until after 10am. If you're willing to splurge, however, all the major hotels offer buffet-style breakfasts (Mon–Sat 8–11am) and a sumptuous, all-you-can-eat **brunch** on Sundays.

**Café Taiga**, *Aerostar Hotel*, Leningradskiy pr. 37; 15min from Dinamo or Aeroport metro. Serves an expensive "Mediterranean Champagne Brunch" buffet, Sun 11.30am–2.30pm.

**Intourist Hotel**, Tverskaya ul. 3/5; near Okhotniy Ryad metro. Another good-value Russian buffet. Climb the stairs next to the elevators to the second floor. Daily 8–11am.

**Metropol Restaurant**, *Metropol Hotel*; Teatralniy proezd 1/4; near Teatralnaya, Ploshchad Revolyutsii and Okhotniy Ryad metros. Fabulous but costly buffet (children half-price) in a lovely hall, with a jazz or dixie band. Sun 11am–3pm.

**Moskovskiy Khleb**, Kutuzovskiy pr. 25; 15min from Kievskaya or Kutuzovskaya metro. Inexpensive bakery serving croissants, Danish pastries and espresso. Mon–Sat 8am–8pm, Sun 10am–5pm.

**Moskva Hotel**, Okhotniy ryad 7; near Okhotniy Ryad or Ploshchad Revolyutsii metro. Use the *Spanish Bar* entrance, and

## Eating and Drinking

head up to the second floor; the buffet on the left is one of the best deals in town. Daily 8–11am.

**Rosie O'Grady's**, ul. Znamenka 9/12; near Borovitskaya metro. Affordable Sunday brunch of pub grub, noon–3pm.

**Skandia Restaurant**, *Radisson Slavyanskaya Hotel*, Berezhovskaya nab. 2; near Kievskaya metro. Delicious Swedish *smörgasbord* buffet, with lots of smoked meats and marinaded fish – moderately priced.

**Vienna Café**, *Olympic Penta Hotel*, Olympiyskiy pr. 18/1; 15min from Prospekt Mira metro. Brunch includes pancakes and salads at high prices (children half-price). Sun 10.30am–3pm.

## Fast food and ice cream

Street kiosks all over town sell pizzas, burgers or hot dogs, but the quality is so bad that you'd do better in one of the inexpensive **fast-food** places listed below. *McDonald's* has the advantage of hygienic toilets, while *Kombi's* and the *Livan-Nasr* offer a change from burgers and fries.

Russians eat **ice cream** in all weathers, and will queue for ages to buy it. Assuming you're less patient, we've only listed outlets where queuing is minimal or nonexistent.

**Baskin Robbin's**, ul. Arbat 20 (10min from Arbatskaya metro), Tverskaya ul. 27/5 (5min from Tverskaya metro), and in the *Rossiya Hotel* off Red Square. Daily 10am–9pm.

**Burger Queen**, Suvorovskiy bulvar 25; 10min from Arbatskaya metro, near Nikitskie vorota. Good French fries, but otherwise inferior to *McDonald's*. Daily 10am–10pm.

**Italian Dream**, on the ground floor of GUM between the first and second lines. Busy stand-up outlet for pizzas, sandwiches and Italian ice cream. Mon–Sat 9am–8pm.

**Kombi's**, Sadovaya-Triumfalnaya ul. 2 (near Mayakovskaya metro) and pr. Mira 46/48 (near Prospekt Mira metro). Two squeaky clean sandwich bars popular

with Americans and Russian yuppies. No smoking. Daily 11am–10pm.

**Livan-Nasr**, Tverskaya ul. 24; 5min from Pushkinskaya or Mayakovskaya metro. Takeaway and stand-up joint serving chicken and beef doner-kebabs, *dolmas* (stuffed vineleaves), *plov* (pilaf) and other Middle Eastern snacks. Daily 10am–10pm.

**McDonald's**, ul. Ogareva 2 (5min from Okhotniy Ryad metro), Bolshaya Bronnaya ul. 29 (near Tverskaya metro) and ul. Arbat 50/52 (near Smolenskaya metro). The ul. Ogareva branch is the least crowded. Daily 10am–8pm.

**Pinguin Ice Cream**, Nikolskaya ul. 4/5 (near Ploshchad Revolyutsii metro) and Leninskiy pr. 37 (5min from Leninskiy Prospekt metro). The former is open Mon–Sat 8am–8pm, Sun 8am–7pm; the latter opens two hours later.

**Pizza Hut**, Tverskaya ul. 12 (5min from Tverskaya metro) and Kutuzovskiy pr. 17 (10min from Kievskaya metro). Not the best pizza in Moscow, but okay for a takeout. The Tverskaya branch is open daily 11am–11pm, while the one on Kutuzovskiy closes an hour earlier.

**Rostik's**, on the first floor of GUM at the Nikolskaya ul. end of the store. Fried chicken in a box and soft drinks. Access by the street behind GUM when the store is closed on Sun. Daily 9am–8pm.

## Cafés and bars

Despite the recent proliferation of **cafés**, Moscow has yet to become a city where you can easily find one wherever you happen to be – and the most obvious ones tend to be the dearest. That said, most cafés serve some sort of food, at much lower prices than full-blown restaurants, and seldom require bookings, making them a boon for budget travellers. Our list covers the spectrum, both in terms of cost and the range of food and drink available; simpler places may have only a few dishes on the menu.

Surprisingly for a city awash with alcohol, the outlook for **bars** is quite dismal. Russians usually buy from a kiosk and drink at home, since bar prices are prohibitive: most places charge at least $5–6 for a pint of beer. Unless you're willing to slum it in a *pivnushka*, the cheapest places to drink are the Western **embassy clubs**, where a beer costs under $3. Usually open only once a week, these clubs admit their own nationals, and sometimes citizens of other countries, too. It's wise to phone and check to avoid a wasted journey. Always bring your passport along.

The cafés and bars below are listed in alphabetical order under area headings that roughly correspond to the first four chapters in the guide section. Those that take **credit cards** are marked CC.

## Red Square and the Kitay-Gorod

**Armadillo Bar**, Khrustalniy per. 1; 10min from Ploshchad Revolyutsii or Kitay-Gorod metro. Snugly converted cellar in the Stariy Gostiniy dvor (p.99), offering reasonably priced Tex-Mex snacks, *Miller Lite*, cocktails, darts, and a live band most evenings. Full of Americans. Mon–Sat 5pm–5am.

**Copacabana**, on the first floor of GUM, at the ul. Ilinka end. Trendy and inexpensive café serving espresso, ice cream, pastries and toasted sandwiches. No smoking. Mon–Sat 9am–8pm.

**Don Sancho Bistro**, Vetoshniy per. 13, on the third floor across the road behind GUM. Popular with shoppers, *biznessmeni* and mobsters. Despite its name, serves moderately priced Russian food. Daily 11am–6pm.

**Feniks**, on the first floor of GUM at the Ilinka end of the first line. Small stand-up café offering Russian snacks at lower prices than most places in GUM. Mon–Sat 9am–8pm.

**Fiord**, Nikolskaya ul. 5; near Ploshchad Revolyutsii metro. Smart yet reasonably priced café-bar serving hot and cold meals and drinks. Daily 11am–11pm.

**Ogni Moskviy**, *Moskva Hotel*; near Okhotniy Ryad and Ploshchad Revolyutsii metros. Tucked away on the fifteenth floor, its grand view of the Kremlin is the real attraction of this Soviet-style café, which can only be reached by lift from the seventh floor. No smoking. Daily 11am–4pm & 6–10pm.

**Shalyapin Bar**, *Metropol Hotel*; near Okhotniy Ryad and Ploshchad Revolyutsii metro. Its soothing gilt, marble and brocade decor might allay your anxiety about the stonking bill. Cocktails, coffee and snacks. Daily 7am–1am.

**Smirnov Bar**, through a shop on the ground floor of GUM, facing Red Square. Has a great view and good ice cream and coffee, but seriously pricey. Mon–Sat 9am–8pm.

**Zolotoy Drakon**, on the first floor of the third line of GUM, at the ul. Ilinka end. A nice spot for an affordable coffee, fruit salad or a stiff drink. Mon–Sat 9am–8pm.

## Beliy Gorod

**Della Palma**, ul. Petrovka 10; 10min from Teatralnaya metro. Moderate Italian café at the far end of the Petrovskiy Passazh, serving lobster, chicken, sandwiches, espresso and booze. Mon–Sat 9am–8pm.

**La Kantina**, Tverskaya ul. 5; 5min from Okhotniy Ryad metro. Relaxed Tex-Mex bistro with a Mexican chef. Try the chicken *fajitas* and the *enchilada*. Also serves cocktails. Moderate prices. Daily noon–midnight.

**News Pub**, ul. Petrovka 18; 15min from Teatralnaya or Kuznetskiy Most metro. Often empty due to the absurdly overpriced drinks and its very dark interior. International newspapers to read by day (if you can), and live music some nights ($5 admission). Daily noon–5am.

**Rosie O'Grady's**, ul. Znamenka 9/12; 5min from Borovitskaya metro. The only real pub in town, with draught *Guinness*, darts and hot food. Packed with foreigners – apart from the high prices, you'd never guess you were in Moscow. Open Sun–Thurs noon–midnight, Fri & Sat noon–1am.

**Sverchok**, ul. Moskvina 10; 15min from Pushkinskaya metro. Informal, cheap and cheerful café with folksy decor and a fair

**Eating and Drinking**

## Eating and Drinking

choice of Russian starters and main courses. Not too crowded at peak times. Daily noon–4pm & 5–9pm.

**Uncle Gilly's**, Stoleshnikov per. 6; ☎229-2050; 10min from Okhotniy Ryad metro. Now in its latest mutation as a Russo-American bar, grill and restaurant, this was once the haunt of Gilyarovskiy (see p.112). Must reserve for supper. High prices. Daily noon–midnight.

### Zemlyanoy Gorod

**Aist** (The Stork), Malaya Bronnaya ul. 1/8; 15min from Arbatskaya or Mayakovskaya metro. Caucasaian mafia hang out near the Patriarch's Ponds, which is best avoided. Daily noon–10pm.

**Arbatskie vorota** (Arbat Gate), ul. Arbat 11; 5min from Arbatskaya metro. Dark café serving Russian soups, starters and light main dishes at moderate prices. Daily 11am–2pm & 4pm–midnight.

**Australian Embassy Down Under Club**, Kropotkinskiy per. 13; ☎956-6070; 10min from Park Kultury metro. Lively and inexpensive basement bar with draught *Fosters*, which may admit non-Aussies – phone to check. Fri 5.30–10pm.

**Bar Italia**, ul. Arbat 49; near Smolenskaya metro. Slick, cramped Italian bistro, offering three-course set meals with wine, and a range of imported drinks at moderate prices. Daily noon–midnight. CC.

**Café Margarita**, Malaya Bronnaya ul. 28; ☎299-6534; 10min from Tverskaya or Mayakovskaya metro. Named after the heroine of Bulgakov's novel, this once trendy café is fast becoming a tourist trap. Russian food, with a pianist in the evenings (when you need to book). Daily noon–2pm & 5–11pm.

**Café Rioni**, ul. Arbat 43; 10min from Arbatskaya or Smolenskaya metro. Simple Georgian meals and draught *Holsten*. Could become popular. Daily 11am–7pm.

**Café Rosa**, ul. Arbat 31; 10min from Smolenskaya or Arbatskaya metro. Small, dim and inexpensive espresso bar with open sandwiches and draught *Holsten*. Daily 10am–9pm.

**Canadian Embassy Club**, Starokonyushenniy per. 23; ☎241-5882; 10min from Kropotkinskaya metro. Guests may have to be signed in by a Canadian; phone to check. Good burgers. Fri 6.30–11pm.

**Elefant Bar**, ul. Noviy Arbat 14; 10min from Arbatskaya metro. Fairly smart, quiet place with snacks, steaks and imported booze. Daily 1pm–1am.

**Gosser Bar**, ul. Noviy Arbat 46; 15min from Arbatskaya metro. A pit-stop for shoppers at the back of the upper floor of a 24-hour supermarket. Serves affordable hot snacks. Daily 10am–11pm.

**New Zealand Embassy Kiwi Club**, Povarskaya ul. 44; ☎956-3579; 15min from Arbatskaya or Barrikadnaya metro. Usually admits non-Kiwis, but phone to check. Sun 7–10.30pm.

**Ogni Arbata** (Fires of the Arbat), ul. Arbat 12; 5min from Arbatskaya metro. Small budget café serving soups, stews and hot drinks, whose gloom belies its name. Daily noon–8pm.

**Shamrock Bar**, ul. Noviy Arbat 19; 5min from Arbatskaya metro. Popular foreigners' nightspot on the upper floor of the *Irish House*, with draught *Guinness*, and live music some evenings. Reasonable prices. Daily noon–midnight.

**TrenMos Bistro**, ul. Ostozhenka 1/9; near Kropotkinskaya metro. American-style bistro specializing in salads and pasta; the adjacent bar does cocktails and club sandwiches. Daily noon–5pm & 7–11pm. CC.

**Vareniki**, on the corner of Skaterniy per. and ul. Paliashvili; 15min from Arbatskaya metro. Humble café dishing up the Ukrainian versions of *pelmeny* (called *vareniki*), Chicken Kiev and *shchi* soup. Order at the counter before trying to find a seat. Mon–Sat 10am–8pm.

### Other parts of Moscow

**Baltschug Bar**, *Baltschug-Kempinski Hotel*, top floor, ul. Balchug 1; 15min from Kitay-Gorod or Novokuznetskaya metro. Plush, cosy bar with a library of novels in foreign languages. Good value. Daily noon–11pm.

**British Club**, Kutuzovskiy pr. 7/4; 10min from Kievskaya metro. Expats' club behind the police box opposite the *Ukrainiya Hotel*. Usually active one Saturday a month; phone the Embassy's Commercial Section (☎956-7480) to check. Either $15 entry and free drinks, or free admission and $2 a drink. 8am–11pm.

**Crazy Horse Bar**, Shmitovskiy proezd 3; 10min from Ulitsa 1905 Goda metro. Relaxed, inexpensive watering hole attached to the *Golden Ostap* restaurant (see p.311). Daily 5pm–2am.

**EKU**, Komsomolskiy pr. 26; near Frunzenskaya metro. Shiny new café with steak, prawns, pizzas, croissants and booze on the menu. Moderate prices. Daily 10am–midnight (may go on all night in the future).

**Gelateria**, pr. Mira 58; 5min from Prospekt Mira metro. Lively Italian café, full of groups of friends. Ices, pizzas, espresso and liquor at affordable prices. Handy if you're staying at the *Travellers Guest House*. Daily 10am–10pm. CC.

**German Embassy Bar**, ul. Mosfilmovskaya 56; ☎956-1080; 30min from Universitet metro. Usually open to non-Germans on Tues night, but phone to check. Cheap German beer is the main attraction.

**Holsten Bistro**, Taganskaya pl.; near Taganskaya metro. Small outlet for draught *Holsten* and good-value Italian sandwiches. Daily 9am–6pm.

## Restaurants

Moscow's **restaurants** vividly reflect the social revolution of the last decade, as ever more exotic places pander to the *novie bogatie* (new rich), while the old Soviet-style restaurants somehow manage to stagger on. At the top end of the scale, you'll probably feel uncomfortable if you're not dressed to the hilt – though few places impose a formal dress code. At most restaurants, it's customary to consign your coat to the *garderob* on arrival; if it helped to put it back on later, a small tip is warranted.

If you can afford to join the *novie bogatie*, Moscow is a feast; but if your

**Eating and Drinking**

spending power is merely average, you'll be hard pressed to find good alternatives. The wide gap between the top and bottom ends of the market and the relative shortage of places in between means that good, affordable restaurants are usually full in the evenings, so **reserving** in advance is strongly advised. We've given telephone numbers for all the restaurants listed below. Many have at least one member of staff with a rudimentary grasp of English. If not, try to get your tongue around *Ya khochu zakazat stol na . . . cheloveka, sevodnya na . . . chasov* (I want to reserve a table for . . . people, at . . . o'clock today).

Many restaurants offer some kind of **entertainment** in the evening – a dance band, Gypsy music or a glitzy floorshow, often with a striptease act – for which they may levy a surcharge on each guest. Venues where the show takes precedence over the meal have been assigned to "Nightclubs" (see p.313).

The restaurants below are listed in alphabetical order under area headings corresponding to the chapters in the guide section. Those that take **credit cards** are marked CC.

### Red Square and the Kitay-Gorod

**Boyarskiy Zal** (Boyar's Hall), *Metropol Hotel*, fourth floor; ☎927-6089; near Ploshchad Revolyutsii, Okhotniy Ryad and Teatralnaya metros. Princely Russian cuisine and folk music in a room decorated in the style of a sixteenth-century

**Eating and Drinking**

*boyar's* palace. Daily 7–11pm. CC. Very expensive.

**Lobster Grill**, *Metropol Hotel;* ☎927-6739. Delicious lobster, shrimp, tiger prawns and other imported seafood. The decor could be improved by junking the paintings. Daily 11am–2am. CC. Very expensive.

**Slavyanskiy bazaar** (Slav Bazaar), Nikolskaya ul. 17; ☎921-1872; 5min from Lubyanka metro. Currently under repair, but worth checking out once it reopens. More appealing for its past (see p.98) and music hall-style decor rather than for its Russian food or the band. Daily noon–5pm & 6–11pm. Inexpensive.

### Beliy Gorod

**Budapest**, *Budapest Hotel,* Petrovskie linii 2/18; ☎924-4283; 10min from Teatralnaya or Kuznetskiy Most metro. Elegant, fake marble columned Hungarian restaurant founded in 1856. Fine Magyar cuisine, with Gypsy music and a variety show ($10 surcharge). Moderate.

**Don Quijote**, Pokrovskiy bul. 4/17; ☎297-4757; 10min from Chistye Prudy metro. Cosy Spanish restaurant offering a three-course lunch until 5pm, and a wider range of dishes *à la carte*. Daily noon–11pm. Very expensive.

**Iberiya**, ul. Rozhdestvenka 5/7; ☎928-2672; near Kuznetskiy Most metro. Elegant Georgian place with Spanish music in the evenings. Good food, moderately priced, but drinks are costly. Daily noon–5pm & 7pm–11.30pm. CC. Moderate.

**Moscow–Bombay**, ul. Nemirovich-Danchenko 3; ☎292-9731; 5min from Pushkinskaya metro. Tasty Indian cuisine, with lots of options for vegetarians. Does 15 varieties of lunch at reduced rates (moderate), and take-outs. Daily noon–3.30pm & 6–11pm. CC. Moderate.

**Panda**, Tverskoy bul. 3/5; ☎298-6505; 5min from Tverskaya metro. Moscow's finest, most expensive Chinese restaurant. Daily noon–2pm & 4–11pm. CC. Very expensive.

**Patio Pizza**, ul. Volkhonka 13a; ☎201-5000; 5min from Kropotkinskaya metro.

Across the road from the Pushkin Museum of Fine Arts. Tasty pizzas and an excellent salad bar ($6 for all you can eat). Very busy evenings and Sun afternoons. Daily noon–midnight. CC. Moderate.

**Savoy**, *Savoy Hotel,* ul. Rozhdestvenka 3; ☎929-8600; near Kuznetskiy Most metro. One of the best restaurants in Moscow, with magnificent Rococo decor, superb French, Russian and Scandinavian cuisine, and top-class service. Daily noon–11pm. CC. Very expensive.

### Zemlyanoy Gorod

**American Bar & Grill**, Tverskaya-Yamskaya ul. 1; ☎251-2847; near Mayakovskaya metro. Located inside the moribund *Sofia Restaurant*, Moscow's latest purveyor of Mexican food tries hard to please, but some of the dishes need improving. Won't take reservations. Daily noon–2am. Inexpensive.

**Baku-Livan**, ul. Tverskaya 24; ☎299-8506; 5min from Pushkinskaya or Mayakovskaya metro. Tasty Azeri food – try the hummus and pine nuts, chicken *shashlyk* or beef *lyula-kebab*. Floorshow (surcharge). Daily 11am–5.30pm & 6–11pm. CC. Moderate.

**Dionyssos**, *Belgrade Hotel,* Smolenskaya pl. 5; ☎248-2063; near Smolenskaya metro. Bar, café, pizzeria and restaurant rolled into one. Big choice of Greek-Cypriot food and pizzas, both done well. Daily noon–5pm & 6–11pm. Inexpensive.

**Grand Imperial**, ul. Ryleeva 9/5; ☎291-6063; near Kropotkinskaya metro. Exclusive restaurant recreating the opulence and *haute cuisine* of the Russian nobility, with antique silver cutlery, vintage wines and cognacs, accompanied by soothing music. Reservations obligatory. Daily noon–11pm. Very expensive.

**Kropotkinskaya 36** ul. Prechistenka 36; ☎201-7500; 15min from Kropotkinskaya or Park Kultury metro. Moscow's first co-op café has moved upmarket since it opened in 1987. Fine Russian cuisine, 1920s decor and piano music. Daily noon–5pm & 6–11pm. CC. Expensive.

**Mziuri**, ul. Arbat 42; ☎241-0313; 5min from Smolenskaya metro. Cavernous, marble-clad room with a "tree" growing through the roof, beneath the Georgian Cultural Centre. Lots of tables, and music in the evenings. Better for starters than full meals. Daily noon–11pm. Moderate.

**Pekin**, *Pekin Hotel*, Bolshaya Sadovaya ul. 1/7; ☎209-1815; near Mayakovskaya metro. Moscow's oldest Chinese restaurant is still going strong, and better than most. Daily noon–4pm & 6–11pm. Expensive.

**Praga** (Prague), ul. Arbat 2; ☎290-6171; near Arbatskaya metro. Once the top restaurant in Moscow, now chiefly worth visiting for its decor; each hall is different, but Neo-Gothic prevails. Serves Russian cuisine, not Czech. Plenty of tables. Daily noon–11pm. Inexpensive.

**Rus**, ul. Arbat 12; no phone; 5min from Arbatskaya or Smolenskaya metro. Dark den that manages to squeeze in a violinist, pianist and a singer most evenings. Georgian–Russian menu. Daily 11am–11pm. Moderate.

**Trenmos Restaurant**, Komsomolskiy pr. 21; ☎245-1216; 10min from Park Kultury metro. American-style restaurant offering chilli con carne, sirloin steak and baked alaska. Daily noon–5pm & 7–11pm. CC. Expensive.

### Krasnaya Presnya, Fili and the Southwest

**Ariang Seoul**, Strelbichevskiy per. 5; ☎256-0892 or 256-0894; 15min from Ulitsa 1905 Goda metro, or the penultimate stop for the #18 trolleybus. Discreetly located on the ground floor of a block of flats. Delicious Korean food and relaxed ambience. Daily noon–10pm. Very expensive.

**Dehli**, ul. Krasnaya Presnya 23b; ☎252-1766; 5min from Ulitsa 1905 Goda metro. Indian food, subdued for Russian tastes. Steer clear of the dearer section just inside the door and head for the main room, which has a floorshow ($6 surcharge) – avoid seats near the front lest you be nauseated by the contortionist "foot artist". Daily noon–3pm & 6–11pm. CC. Inexpensive.

**Golden Ostap**, Shmitovskiy proezd 3; ☎259-4795; 10min from Ulitsa 1905 Goda metro. Very elegant, intimate restaurant with a private casino, owned by a famous Georgian actor. Fine European-Russian-cuisine and soothing music. Daily 1am–5pm & 7pm–2am. Very expensive.

**Guriya**, Komsomolskiy pr. 7/3; ☎246-0378; near Park Kultury metro. Hidden in a courtyard, and not long ago "discovered", the *Guriya* does superb Georgian food at low prices, with a dash of sleaze. Bring your own bottle. Daily noon–11pm. Inexpensive.

**Manila**, ul. Vavilova 81; ☎132-0055; 10min from Profsoyuznaya metro. Moscow's only Filipino restaurant. Exotic dishes, stylish decor and light music. Daily noon–4pm & 5pm–midnight. CC. Expensive.

**U Pirosmani** (At Pirosmani's), Novodevichiy proezd 4; ☎247-1926; 15min from Sportivnaya metro. One of the best Georgian restaurants in town, named after their national painter. Piano and violin music at night. Daily noon–11pm. CC. Expensive.

**Westphalia**, ul. Garibaldi 1; ☎134-3026; 15min from Novye Cheremushki or Prospekt Vernadskovo metro. German food and *Dab* beer, with a floorshow ($15 surcharge). Daily noon–2pm & 4–11pm. CC. Moderate.

**Zolotoy Drakon** (Golden Dragon), ul. Plyushchikha 64; ☎248-3602; 15min from Frunzenskaya metro. Okay Chinese restaurant in the basement of a derelict House of Culture; band from 8am to midnight. Daily noon-5pm & 6pm-4am. CC. Moderate.

### Zamoskvareche and the South

**Danilovskiy**, in the Danilov Monastery's hotel; ☎954-0566; 10min from Tulskaya metro. Excellent Russian food. Guests must book in advance and may be asked to prove that they're associated with a reputable organization. Daily noon–11pm. Moderate.

**Eating and Drinking**

## Eating and Drinking

**Seoul Plaza**, ul. Serpukhovskiy val 14; ☎952-8254; 10min from Tulskaya metro. Drab exterior, but the Korean food is great and the service good. Daily noon–4pm & 6–10.30pm. Expensive.

**U Babushki** (At Granny's), ul. Bolshaya Ordynka 42; ☎230-2797; 10min from Tretyakovskaya or Polyanka metro. Friendly ambience and fine Russian food. Tastefully decorated with theatrical memorabilia: the owner is a former actress. Daily 2pm–midnight. Moderate.

**Usadba** (The Estate), near the ruins of Tsaritsyno; ☎343-1510; 15min from Tsaritsyno metro. Russian cooking, Gypsy songs and antique decor. Can arrange horse-riding, *troyka* rides, and even fireworks should you wish to celebrate. Daily noon–11pm. Expensive.

**Yakimanka**, ul. Bolshaya Polyanka 2/10; ☎238-8888; 10min from Polyanka metro, on the Drainage Canal embankment. Shabby Uzbek joint, best by day when there isn't a band. Try the meaty *shurpa* soup, or *khinkali*, a kind of *pelmeny*. Mon–Sat 2–11pm, Sun 4–11pm. Inexpensive.

### Taganka and Zayauze

**Nemetskaya Sloboda** (German Suburb), Baumanskaya ul. 23; ☎267-4476; near Baumanskaya metro. Cosy, tasteful Russian restaurant named after the foreign colony that existed in the locality during the eighteenth century. Daily noon–5pm & 6–11pm. CC. Inexpensive.

**Razgulyai** (Drunken Jollity), Spartakovskaya ul. 11; ☎267-7613; 5min from Baumanskaya metro. Three halls decorated in different folk styles, with Russian cuisine and a Gypsy orchestra. Lively ambience; very popular. Daily noon–midnight. CC. Inexpensive.

### Northern Suburbs

**Anchor**, *Palace Hotel*, 1-ya Tverskaya-Yamskaya ul; ☎56-3152; near Belorusskaya metro. Styled in the form of a frigate's deck, this is the finest seafood place in town, using products flown in from Maine. Daily noon–5pm & 9pm–midnight. CC. Very expensive.

**Mei-Hua**, Rusakovskaya ul. 2/1; ☎264-9574; 10min from Krasnoselskaya metro. Decent Chinese food, despite an offputting menu ("Hairy crab", "Meat with fish smell"). Handy for a meal before catching the overnight train to St Petersburg. Daily noon–11pm. Inexpensive.

**Sedmoe Nebo** (Seventh Heaven), ul. Akademia Korolyova 15; ☎282-2293; 15min from VDNKh metro. Revolving Russian restaurant midway up the TV Tower whose chief attraction is the view. Daily 11am–10.30pm. Inexpensive.

# Chapter 13

# Nightlife

Moscow's **nightlife** has come a long way since *glasnost* brought the underground music scene into the open, and rave parties in the Space Pavilion caused outrage. Though new **nightclubs** and **discos** are still opening all the time, the club scene is increasingly mercenary and predictable. All too often, you'll find yourself wishing to leave only an hour after you paid mega-bucks to get in, and feeling ripped-off. Fortunately, the **live music** scene is a lot more promising, with regular gigs at half a dozen venues, plus occasional concerts at discos.

The chief deterrent to clubbing is the **cost**. Most nightclubs charge $20–30 admission and $6–10 a drink, while discos generally have a cover charge of $10–20 (sometimes less for women) and sell drinks for $4–6. (All the prices here are quoted in dollars, but actually payable in rubles.) The other factor to consider is **safety**, as many places are frequented by mobsters and can be dangerous for foreigners who don't know the score. We've warned of some troublespots, but there's no guarantee that once safe places won't turn risky. If you're going to visit such places, only take as much money as you want to spend, and be extremely wary of trouble (without appearing to be too nervous, of course).

To find out the latest on up-and-coming events, check the **listings** sections in the *Moscow Times* and *Moscow Tribune* (their Saturday editions have the fullest coverage). Gigs may also be advertised on the noticeboard of the *La Kantina* bistro, Tverskaya ul. 5; or fly-posted around the bottom end of the Arbat or Neglinnaya ulitsa.

## Nightclubs

Most of the **nightclubs** advertised in the foreign-language press are tacky homages to Las Vegas, with a restaurant and dance floor full of Mafiosi, *bizness-meni* and prostitutes – the only Russians who can afford them. Exclusivity is part of their appeal, so foreigners who don't look rich are treated with the same disdain as ordinary Russians. Being sized up by a uniformed thug acting as the arbiter of style and wealth can be a demeaning experience: women are expected to **dress** like hookers, and a jacket and tie are *de rigueur* for men. It's hard to know whether being scanned for guns is a good sign or a bad one. Some will also be deterred by the **floorshows**: topless (or raunchier) acts are often the main entertainment besides the disco. The following are the best and the worst Moscow has to offer.

**Alexander Blok Casino**, *Inflotel*, Krasnopresnenskaya nab. 12; ☎255-9284; 20min from Ulitsa 1905 Goda metro. High profile, Mafia-infested night-club aboard a hotel-ship, to be avoided at all costs.

**Arlecchino Night Show**, *Cinema Centre on Krasnaya Presnya*, Druzhnikovskaya ul. 15; ☎268-8500; near Barrikadnaya metro. Disco, dance show and Italian restaurant. Also hosts live concerts of

Nightlife

gangsta pop or traditional bands like *Bravo*. Tickets ($30–40) at the door; Fri, Sat & Sun 11pm–5am.

**Cynderella** (or *Cenerentola*), Novosyshchyovskaya ul. 26a; ☎972-1450; Rizhskaya metro, then bus #84 or trolleybus #18 or #42 to the *Minaevskiy rynok* stop. Italian restaurant, barmen and DJs. Chart music. $20 cover charge. Open Tues–Sun 10pm–5am.

**Golden Horseshoe Club**, *Romen Gypsy Theatre*, Leningradskiy pr. 32/2; ☎270-7334; 5min from Dinamo metro. An affordable and enjoyable night out if you like Gypsy music and dancing (after midnight); the food is Russian and good. Costs about $25 each with drinks, plus $8 admission. Reservations only. Daily 10.30pm–6am.

**Karo**, *Rossiya Cinema*, Pushkinskaya pl. 2; ☎229-0003; near Pushkinskaya metro. Steak and seafood restaurant with a cabaret (Thurs–Sun) and disco (mostly Latin music; oldies Tues). $30 entry charge includes free snacks and first drink. Daily 9pm–5am.

**Manhattan Express**, on the Red Square side of the *Rossiya Hotel*, ul. Varvarka 6; ☎298-5354 or 298-5355; 10min from Kitay-Gorod metro. Billed as "Moscow's only New York supper club", and modelled on *Studio 54*, it hosts weekly fashion shows and themed extravaganzas. Fine restaurant 7pm–1am; disco 11.30pm–4am. $20–25 cover charge except on Thurs, when Americans get in free (bring your passport), or if you reserve a table to eat on any night. Daily.

**Metelitsa** (Snowstorm), ul. Noviy Arbat 21; ☎291-1130 or 291-1301. Disco for the brash new rich and their hangers-on, above the *Cherry Casino*. Live entertainment and dance floor 9pm–5am; Western-style kitchen 1pm–2am. Admission $20 till 9pm, $30 thereafter. Daily 9pm–5am.

**Moskovskiy Club**, Tverskaya ul. 6; ☎292-3688 or 292-0331; 5min from Okhotniy Ryad metro. Casino, disco and bar that hosts fashion shows ($50) on Sat; admission otherwise $20. Daily 10pm–6am.

**Night Flight**, Tverskaya ul. 17; ☎229-4165; 5min from Tverskaya metro. Split-level bar with a dance floor full of hookers and sleazy foreign businessmen. Cover charge ($25) includes one drink. Daily 9pm–5am; restaurant noon–4am.

**Russkaya Troyka Club**, *Orlyonok Hotel*, ul. Kosygina 15; ☎939-8609 or 939-8683; Leninskiy Prospekt metro, then five stops on trolleybus #7. Variety show, topless revue and disco. Cover charge ($20) includes one drink. Thurs–Sun 11.30pm–5am.

## Discos

Moscow's other clubs are essentially **discos**, some of which double up as venues for live music. They tend to come and go quite rapidly, as most seem intent on making a fast buck and getting out before the Mafia becomes too involved, while the honourable exceptions are prone to close for other reasons. Most specialize in chart music, techno, rap or house. There are no formal dress codes, but style counts: smart casual or black are okay almost anywhere. Note that some places go under slightly different names according to the language they're advertised in.

**Carousel** (*Karusel*), 1-ya Yamskaya ul. 11; ☎251-6444 or 250-5670; 10min from Mayakovskaya metro. Amazingly overpriced disco-cum-casino, with live music Fri, Sat & Sun ($30–50 admission). Daily 10pm–6am.

**Hermitage Club** (*Ermitzah*), Karetniy ryad 3; ☎299-1160; 10min from Chekhovskaya or Tsvetnoy Bulvar metro. Fashionable, arty den with distressed decor. Bar only Tues & Wed 11pm–6am (free admission); largely techno disco Thurs–Sun 10pm–6am ($5 till 11pm, then $10).

**Jump**, Luzhniki Sports Complex, Friendship Hall; ☎247-0343; 20min from Sportivnaya metro. Huge hall with a giant video screen; chart music and industrial house, with occasional live acts. Entrance $5 till midnight, $10 thereafter. Wed–Sun 11pm–5.30am.

**Lis's** (*u Lisa*), Olympic Sports Complex, Olympiyskiy pr.; 10min from Prospekt Mira metro. Tacky disco with strip shows and a casino. Lots of Mafiosi with their girlfriends, so a high risk of violence.

**Master Disco**, ul. Pavlovskaya 6; ☎ 237-1742; 10min from Dobrininskaya or Serpukovskaya metro. In-your-face dance floor and strip shows. Cover charge $10–20 for men, $5–15 for women. Live music Sat 1–2.30am. Fri & Sat 11pm–6am.

**Pilot**, Tryohgorniy val 6; ☎ 252-2764; 5min from Ulitsa 1905 Goda metro. Mainly Techno disco with a helicopter on the dance floor and a young trendy crowd, which also hosts gigs by reggae or dance bands. Admission $10 (men) or $5 (women). Thurs–Sun 11am–6pm.

**Red Zone**, TsKA Ice Palace, Leningradskiy pr. 39; ☎ 212-1676; 15min from Dinamo or Aeroport metro. Huge dance floor with caged, naked women in the centre. Can be dangerous. Entrance $10–15 for men, free for women. Daily 10pm–5am.

**Sports Bar**, ul. Noviy Arbat 10; ☎ 290-4311; 10min from Arbatskaya

metro. This is a hangout for Eurosports lovers, with dozens of TVs and a giant screen upstairs. There's also a disco some nights. This operates a genre rota: Thurs – a variety of dance music; Fri & Sat – hip-hop, techno and acid jazz; Sun – rock'n'roll. No cover charge Mon–Wed, and until 10pm Thurs–Sun. Daily 9.30am–5am.

**Tropicana**, ul. Noviy Arbat 21; ☎ 291-1134; 15min from Smolenskaya metro. Glitzy dance club on the second floor, beneath the *Aeroflot* globe. Entertainment by *Varadero*, a Cuban salsa band. $20 admission. Daily 8.30pm–3am.

## The music scene

Soviet **rock music** began in the 1960s, gained grudging official recognition in the late 1970s, and came of age with *perestroika*. Although the authorities in Leningrad permitted the first rock club to open in the early 1980s, Moscow bands like *Mashina Vremeni* (Time Machine) and *Bravo* were still being hassled by the KGB until the pop singer Alla Pugachova did a benefit concert for Chernobyl, which made rock unassailable. Alla still commands the pop scene, and in 1994 thrilled fans by marrying the Bulgarian crooner Filip Kirkorov, two decades her junior. Another veteran group that's still around is *Brigada S*, whose big-band funk-jazz fusion fits the current retro mood, epitomized by the reformed *Bravo*, playing songs that hark back to the Mods of 1960s Moscow.

The contemporary music scene runs the gamut from techno to reggae, by way of blues and rap. Hard rock and heavy metal **bands** like *Voyage* and *Cruise* enjoy a big following among teenagers. Less mainstream, but still in with the in-crowd, are the English-language rapper *MC Pavlov* and ambient techno bands like *Nochnoy Prospekt* and *MD Mengele*. Besides being the home of Russia's oldest reggae band, *Komitet Okhrany Tepla* (The Warmth Preservation Committee), Moscow is also the nation's blues capital, with *Crossroads, Liga Blusa, White Spirit, Bluesmobile* and other

**Nightlife**

**Nightlife**

groups playing regularly at the *Arbat Blues Club*. Also look out for visiting talent, such as the amazing Siberian rock group, *Kalinov Most*.

## Live music

The **live music** scene is generally more rewarding than discos. Most of the bands hail from Moscow, St Petersburg or the former Soviet republics, giving rise to all kinds of crossovers of ethnic music with rock, thrash, rap or reggae. As the audience is usually more intent on the music – or getting wasted – than macho posturing and fighting, gigs also tend to be safer than discos.

Besides the venues listed below, some of the aforementioned discos also host gigs, while famous Russian bands occasionally play at the *Rossiya Concert Hall*, or football stadiums – these are really the only events where you need to buy **tickets** in advance, rather than pay at the door.

Major Western bands only rarely include Moscow in their European tours, as tickets here have to be sold at a fraction of their price in the West (when Michael Jackson's promoters did otherwise, sales bombed). However, little-known **foreign bands** appear quite often at the *Sexton* and *Bunker* clubs and the *Armadillo Bar*, and for the past four years an **Independent Music Festival** with the odd name of *Indyuki* (Turkeys) has been Moscow's answer to *WOMAD*. Providing sponsorship is found, the festival is likely to happen in April. Concerts can occur at any of the venues below, and some of the discos above; the full programme is covered in the *Moscow Times* and *Moscow Tribune*.

**"A" Cultural Centre**, Berezhkovskaya nab. 28; ☎954-9193; Kievskaya metro, then bus (#91, #119, #505) or trolleybus (#7, #17, #34) to the *Biblioteka* stop. Mad concerts of indie music; the crowd is young and wild; booze prices are low. Fri & Sat.

**Arbat Blues Club** (*ABC*), per. Aksakova 11; ☎291-1546; 10min from Arbatskaya metro. Friendly, relaxed club for blues

aficinados. One room for dancing, the other for sitting, with artworks on the wall. $5–10 entry; moderately priced drinks. Daily 7.30pm–midnight.

**Armadillo Bar**, Khrustalniy per. 1; ☎298-5258; 10min from Ploshchad Revolyutsii or Kitay-Gorod metro. Tex-Mex bar in the Stariy Gostiniy dvor, with country or rockabilly bands some nights ($10–15). Expensive snacks and drinks. Mon-Sat 5pm–5am.

**Bunker Club**, ul. Trifonovskaya 56; ☎278-7043; near Rizhskaya metro. Consistently the best rock club in town, this dark, stylishly decorated basement has one room for live music and two for chilling out. $5 admission. Wed, Fri & Sat 8pm–midnight. Concerts at 8pm.

**Calypso Club**, *Dom Kultury "Ilyich"*, Krasnobogatyrskaya ul. 10; no phone; Preobrazhenskaya metro, then five stops on tram #7 or #11. Lesser known venue for indie and heavy metal bands ($2–5 admission). Fri & Sat 7pm–midnight.

**Jerry Rubin Club**, Profsoyuznaya ul. 32/2; ☎120-7006; 5min from Novye Cheremushki metro. Idiosyncratic basement club for indie gigs, art exhibitions and "happenings". Check listings for details of what's on. Around $10 admission.

**Sexton FOZD**, 1-y Baltiyskiy proezd 6/21, korpus 2; ☎151-1211 or 151-3682; 15min from Sokol metro. Punky, smoky, noisy basement, with Russian or foreign bands most nights, and daytime concerts on Sat. Free admission before 7pm; then $8–15, depending on the band; daytime concerts $3. Cheap drinks. Daily 24 hours.

**Ulitsa Radio Club**, Brodnikov per. 3; ☎370-8276; next to Polyanka metro. Still named after its original location in the Baumanskiy district, but these days situated in Zamoskvareche, this is a club frequented by fans of hardcore grunge and indie music. Gigs start at 7pm. $2–5 admission.

**Voyage Club**, Altufevskoe shosse 13/2; ☎401-9501 or 903-3665; 15min from Vladykino metro. Owned by the rock group *Voyage*, the club features hard rock on Fri and dance music on Sat; concerts start at 11pm. Admission $5 10–11pm; then $10 (half-price for women).

Nightlife

# Chapter 14

# The Arts

Alongside the city's restaurants and clubs, there's a rich cultural life in Moscow. **Classical music**, **opera** and **ballet** are strongly represented with a busy schedule of concerts and performances throughout the year, sometimes held in the city's palaces, churches or – in summer – parks and gardens. Rock, pop and jazz gigs have been covered in the "Nightlife" section. Russian **theatre** has done better than **film** in coming to terms with diminished audiences and the loss of state subsidies – if only because it doesn't face competition from Hollywood. Even if you don't speak Russian, **puppetry** and the **circus** transcend language barriers, while several cinemas show films in their original language. At any one time, there are dozens of **exhibitions** in Moscow's galleries.

## Tickets and information

For most concert and theatrical performances, you can buy **tickets** from the venue box office (*kassa*), or one of the many theatre ticket kiosks (*Teatralnaya kassa*) in the city, at low prices. The chief exceptions to this rule are gala concerts and the Bolshoy Theatre, tickets for which are seldom available except from touts outside the venue, hotel service bureaux or private **booking agencies**. Like the *Intourist* office on Manezhnaya pl., most hotels have a special desk for booking tickets; the most reliable private agency is *IPS*, in the *Metropol Hotel* (☎927-6728; Mon–Fri 10am–6pm, Sat & Sun 10am–3pm). As you'd expect, their **prices** are

higher, and the agencies also charge a booking fee.

The *Moscow Times* and *Moscow Tribune* carry extensive arts **listings** in their Saturday editions, with more limited coverage during the week. Alternatively, look out for posters around town, or ask about current events at *IPS* or a hotel service bureau. Lastly, bear in mind that some (though by no means all) theatres and concert halls are **closed in July and August**.

## Classical and folk music, opera and ballet

Russians are justifiably proud of their **classical music** tradition as Moscow has produced some of the world's best-known composers: Tchaikovksy, Rimsky-Korsakov, Prokofiev, Mussorgsky, Glinka and Shostakovich.

Moscow also has a long tradition of folk music. In metro underpasses and along the Arbat, buskers perform all kinds of **folk music**, from the balalaika and accordion variety beloved of Soviet cultural attachés to the Thieves' songs (*blatnye pesny*) that inspired the legendary Vladimir Vysotskiy (see p.236), whose songs are a perennial favourite. Also evocative of a certain mood and time are the lovesick ballads of Bulat Okhudzhava and the satirical ditties of Alexander Gallich, who, together with Vysotskiy, were the key figures of the semi-underground Bards' Movement of the 1950s and 60s.

Classical concerts take place throughout the year, but especially during two **festivals**. Over the Russian Winter or *Russkaya Zima* festival (Dec 25–Jan 5), the main venues are the Conservatory, the Tchaikovsky Concert Hall, and sometimes the Bolshoy; the Tchaikovsky Concert Hall is the focus of the *Moskovskiy Zvyodiy* (Moscow Stars) festival in May (aka the "May Stars" or *Mayskiy Zvyodiy*). Additionally, there may be an Alternative Music Festival of modern composers, video art and other things in April – although its future survival is uncertain.

Aside from the Bolshoy, tickets for performances should be available from the venue box office, or ticket kiosks. Besides the main permanent venues listed below, also keep an eye out for concerts in the city's museums, parks and churches (listed separately).

### The Bolshoy

**Bolshoy Theatre**, Teatralnaya pl. 1; ☎ 292-8661 or 292-0050; near Teatralnaya metro. Despite its problems (p.130), the Bolshoy still has the largest repertoire of any company in the world (22 ballets and 3 operas with balletic scenes). As interpretation is crucial, it's worth noting who's dancing in what ballet. Nina Aniashevilli, Alexei Fadeechev, Ina Petrova and Nina Semizorova are great in almost anything; Nadya Gracheva and Galya Stepanenko shine in *La Bayadère*, while Masha Bylova is best in the Grigorovich ballets: *Spartacus*, *The Stone Flower* and *Ivan the Terrible*. During the summer the company is usually abroad, leaving the junior *corps de ballets* to entertain visitors. In season, there are performances at 7pm, and sometimes a noon matinee on Sunday. The Bolshoy is closed on Monday.

Forget about getting **tickets** from the Bolshoy *kassa* or paying in rubles, whatever the ticket's face value. Whether you book through an agency (see above) or buy from a tout outside the theatre an hour before the performance, tickets sell for hard currency only, at much the same prices (though touts overcharge if they can): $15–20 for a seat in the fourth or

third tier balcony (poor views); $20–50 for the second or first tier (*beletazh*) balcony; $50–80 for the stalls (*parter*), depending on the row (*ryad*); and $200–300 for a seat in the Imperial Box (the best view in the house). Buying from a tout, you'll seldom get two seats together, and should check that the date of each ticket is correct.

### Other permanent venues

**Moscow Conservatory**, ul. Gertsena 13; ☎ 299-0658; 10min from Arbatskaya metro. Varied programmes of concerts in the Great, Small and Rachmaninov halls. The elegant Great Hall hosts the Tchaikovsky Competition (see p.116).

**Palace of Congresses**, in the Kremlin; ☎ 291-4849; near Biblioteka Imeni Lenina and Aleksandrovskiy Sad metros. The Kremlin Ballet Company performs *The Nutcracker* and *Swan Lake* in a 676-seat hall (p.76), which is also used for concerts of folk music and dancing.

**Rossiya Concert Hall**, Moskvaretskaya nab. 1; ☎ 298-1124; 10min from Kitay-Gorod metro, on the embankment side of the *Rossiya Hotel*. No regular programme, but often used for gala concerts (rock and pop as well as classical music).

**Russian Academy of Music**, ul. Paliashvili 1; ☎ 290-6737; 10min from Arbatskaya metro. The concert hall is behind the Academy building on Povarskaya ulitsa, which is next to another auditorium, the Gnesin Institute Opera Studio.

**Stanislavsky & Nemirovich-Danchenko Theatre**, Pushkinskaya ul. 17; ☎ 229-8388; 5min from Chekhovskaya metro. Regular programme of ballet, opera and musicals.

**Tchaikovsky Concert Hall**, Triumfalnaya pl. 4/31; ☎ 299-3681; near Mayakovskaya metro. Frequent performances by the Moscow Symphony Orchestra, and choral and instrumental ensembles.

### Semi-permanent venues

The following is a selection of churches, museums and mansions that regularly

**The Arts**

## The Arts

**Summer Concerts**

Summer concerts are held in the Gorky, Izmaylovo and Sokolniki **parks**, as advertised. The nearest metros are Park Kultury, Izmaylovskaya and Sokolniki.

hold concerts. Phone to enquire about concerts, and when you can buy tickets; these may also be available from kiosks.

**Andronikov Monastery**, pl. Pryamikova 10; ☎ 278-1489; 15min from Taganskaya metro. The monastery (p.238) is an ideal setting for stirring performances of ancient Russian spiritual music by the Sirin Ensemble, on Wed evenings over summer.

**Chaliapin House-Museum**, Novinskiy bul. 25; ☎ 205-6236; 5min from Barrikadnaya metro. Solo operatic renditions in the White Hall of the maestro's mansion (p.157).

**Church of the Intercession in Fili**, Novozavodskaya ul. 6; ☎ 148-4552; 10min from Fili metro. Choral and chamber music in one of Moscow's finest Naryshkin Baroque monuments (see p.184).

**Hall of Columns**, in the House of Unions, Pushkinskaya ul. 1; ☎ 292-4864; near Teatralnaya metro. Splendid, historic hall (p.110) sometimes used for concerts or political meetings.

**Museum of Musical Culture**, ul. Fadeeva 4; ☎ 972-3237; 10min from Mayakovskaya metro. Interesting programmes of classical, avant-garde and ethnic music. For details of the museum, see p.253.

**Pushkin Museum of Fine Arts**, ul. Volkhonka 12; ☎ 203-7998; near Kropotkinskaya metro. Hosts concerts during the "December Evenings". Mostly classics, but sometimes also modern composers. See p.121

## Theatre

Traditionally, **theatre** (*teatr*) has had a special place in Russian culture as an outlet for veiled criticism under autocratic regimes. In Soviet times, Muscovites came to expect top-class acting and dull plays; only a few theatres dared to stage bold drama. Nowadays there are no taboos, but audiences evidently prefer entertainment to soul-searching.

Sadly, theatre, which once relied on state subsidies, is finding it hard to come to terms with the post-Soviet era, especially long-hallowed institutions like the Moscow Arts Theatre (MKhAT). However, there is plenty of life in the smaller, more independent companies, and the high traditions of Soviet drama training (based on Stanislavsky's "Method") ensure that the acting is good, even when the production stinks. If you understand some Russian, Moscow has as much to offer drama-lovers as London does, and tickets still cost far less, though prices are rising.

**Lenkom Theatre**, ul. Chekhova 6; ☎ 299-0708; near Chekhovskaya metro. Colourful drama and musicals directed by Mark Zakharov, who introduced lasers and rock to the Soviet stage. Regularly performs *Fiddler on the Roof* – a homegrown adaptation of Sholem Aleichem's Yiddish tales.

**Malaya Bronnaya Theatre**, Malaya Bronnaya ul. 4; ☎ 290-4093; 15min from Tverskaya or Arbatskaya metro. Good actors and a fine reputation, but a bit quiet at present.

**Maly Theatre**, Teatralnaya pl. 1/6; ☎ 924-4083; near Teatralnaya metro. Productions of nineteenth-century Russian drama; many of the plays had their premiere at the Maly last century.

**Moscow Arts Theatre** (*MKhAT*), Kamergerskiy per. 3; ☎ 229-0443; 5min from Okhotniy Ryad or Teatralnaya metro. The birthplace of modern drama and the Method, and later home to a generation of great Soviet actors that is dying out (see p.110).

**Mossovet Theatre**, Bolshaya Sadovaya ul. 16; ☎ 299-2035; near Mayakovskaya metro. Farces, popular classics and musicals; performs Molière, Bulgakov's *The White Guard* and a Russian interpretation of *Jesus Christ Superstar*.

**Romen Gypsy Theatre**, Leningradskiy pr. 32/2; ☎ 250-7353; 5min from Dinamo metro. The all-singing-and-dancing plays in their repertoire are fun, but the "serious" ones are dire.

**Sovremennik Theatre**, Chistoprudniy bul. 19a; ☎ 921-1790; near Chistye Prudy metro. Famous 1960s theatre, enjoying a new lease of life and scandal under director Roman Viktyuk.

**Studio Theatre on Yugo-Zapade**, pr. Vernadskovo 125; ☎ 434-7483; 5min from Yugo-Zapadnaya metro. Intense amateurs (its star, Avilov, used to be a truck driver) in a tiny theatre beneath an apartment building. Repertoire includes Chekhov, Gogol, *Hamlet* and a five-hour-long adaptation of *The Master and Margarita*.

**Taganka Theatre**, ul. Zemlyanoy val 76; ☎ 272-6300; near Taganskaya metro. A breath of fresh air during the Era of Stagnation (see p.236), this famous theatre now finds itself in the doldrums.

**U Nikitskikh Vorot Theatre**, ul. Gertsena 23/9; ☎ 202-8219; 10min from Arbatskaya metro. A vehicle for the talents and ego of director, playwright, actor and designer Mark Rozovskiy. Repertoire includes Chekhov's *Uncle Vanya*.

**Vakhtangov Theatre**, ul. Arbat 26; ☎ 241-0728; 5min from Smolenskaya metro. One of the old heavyweights of Soviet drama, now rather confused about its role.

## Puppetry and the Circus

**Puppet theatre** (*Kukolniy teatr*) has a long tradition in Russia, and there are a handful of theatres devoted to the arts in Moscow. Other performing arts for which a knowledge of Russian isn't necessary may deter some visitors by their political incorrectness, namely the **Circus** – acclaimed as one of the best in the world – and animal dramas, at the Durov Animal Theatre.

**Central Puppet Theatre**, Sadovaya-Samotyochnaya ul. 3; ☎ 299-3310; 10min from Tsvetnoy Bulvar metro. The matinees are funny for

children of all ages; evening performances are often silent or mimed.

**Durov Animal Theatre**, ul. Durova 4; ☎ 971-3047; 15min from Novoslobodskaya or Tsvetnoy Bulvar metro. A unique institution loved by generations of kids (see p.259). Performances Wed–Fri at 5pm, Sat & Sun at noon, 3 & 5.30pm; closed from May 27 to mid-Sept.

**Moscow Puppet Theatre**, ul. Spartakovskaya 26; ☎ 261-2197; 10min from Baumanskya metro. Like the Central Puppet Theatre, its matinee and evening shows are usually pitched at different audiences.

**New Circus**, pr. Vernadskovo 7; ☎ 930-2815; near Universitet metro. Moscow's Circus is one of the finest in the world. Animal acts and clowns are its forte. Of the two branches, the New Circus is marginally superior. Performances at 7pm daily (except Thurs), also at 3pm on Sat and at 11.30am & 3pm on Sun.

**Old Circus**, Tsvetnoy bul. 13; ☎ 200-0668; near Tsvetnoy Bulvar metro. Performance times are the same.

**Shadow Theatre**, Izmaylovskiy bul. 60/10; ☎ 465-5070; near Pervomayskaya metro. Russian fairytales enacted with shadow puppets. Sat & Sun 10.30am & 1pm.

## Cinemas

In some ways the ending of censorship has been a disaster for Russian **cinema** (*kino*). **Film**, which once flourished through the local studio *Mosfilm*, has all but disappeared as a home grown art form, with most cinemas in Moscow now showing little more than Hollywood action movies, comedies and soft porn. Dubbing has almost ceased as funds have dried up, superseded by simultaneous voice-over translations, often with just one person doing all the speaking parts.

To find something better, check the *Moscow Times* or *Moscow Tribune* for current performances at the venues listed below. There's a much wider choice of Russian and (subtitled) foreign films

**The Arts**

The Arts

during the **Moscow International Film Festival**, running over two weeks in July every odd-numbered year, when two films a night are shown in the Rossiya Concert Hall, and others are screened elsewhere. Details appear in *Sputnik Kino Festival*, a Russian-language magazine published for the duration of the festival.

**Americom House of Cinema**, in the *Radisson Slavyanskaya Hotel*, Berezhkovskaya nab. 2; ☎941-8890; near Kievskaya metro. A regular programme of (mostly American) movies in English.

**Cinema Centre on Krasnaya Presnyna** (*Kino tsentr*), Druzhinnikovskaya ul. 15; ☎205-7306; near Barrikadnaya metro. The Muscovite film-buff's mecca, with various halls screening classic and new Russian and (dubbed) foreign films; also holds lectures.

**French Embassy**, Bolshaya Yakimanka ul. 45; ☎236-0003 or 236-1223; near Oktyabryskaya metro. French films on Mon & Wed at 7pm; phone for details, and bring your passport.

**Ilyuzion Cinema**, Kotelnicheskaya nab. 1/15; ☎227-4339; in a wing of the Kotelnicheskaya Apartments, 15min from Kitay-Gorod or Tanganskaya metro. Frequently shows art films or Soviet and foreign classics, sometimes in the original language.

**Mir Cinema**, Tsvetnoy bul. 11; ☎200-1695; near Tsvetnoy Bulvar metro. Wide-screen cinema that sometimes shows foreign art movies.

**Tsentralniy Detskiy Kinoteatr**, ul. Bakrushina 25; ☎233-4206; 10min from Pavletskaya metro. Screens films in foreign languages once a month.

# The visual arts

Moscow has dozens of **art galleries and exhibition halls**, in addition to the temporary displays on show in its museums and major galleries. Listed below are some of the best-known galleries, where you can be fairly sure of finding something interesting at most times of the year.

**Art Moderne**, ul. Bolshaya Ordynka 39; ☎233-1551; 10min from Tretyakovskaya metro. Situated in an old church, with some lovely frescoes on the top floor. Tues–Fri 11am–7pm, Sat & Sun 11am–6pm.

**Central Exhibition Hall** (Manège), Manezhnaya pl. 1; ☎202-9304; near Okhotniy Ryad, Biblioteka Imeni Lenina and Aleksandrovskiy Sad metros. Sometimes hosts large art exhibitions.

**Central House of Artists**, ul. Krymskiy val 10; ☎230-0091 or 238-0457; 10min from Park Kultury metro. Huge exhibition complex with over a dozen halls; some items for sale, others not (paintings are also sold outside). Tues–Sun 11am–8pm.

**Contemporary Art Centre**, ul. Bolshaya Yakimanka 6; ☎238-2454; 10min from Polyanka metro. Five galleries under one roof, so a good place to start if you're serious about buying. Mon–Fri noon–7pm.

**M'ARS**, Malaya Filyovskaya ul. 32; ☎146-2029; 5min from Pionerskaya metro. The city's first private art gallery, organized by previously underground artists. Wed–Sun noon–7.30pm.

**Moscow Palette**, Povarskaya ul. 35/28; ☎928-3352; 15min from Barrikadnaya metro. Good for contemporary paintings and graphics, and lesser-known artists of the 1920s and 1930s. Wheelchair access. Daily 1pm–7pm.

Chapter 15

# Shops and Markets

**Shopping in Moscow** brings home all you've ever heard about the failings of the Soviet economy and the wild capitalism of New Russia. The old, state-run stores stock a limited range of one category of goods, with queues for everything and no attempt to woo customers. At the other extreme are boutiques and supermarkets catering to the *novie bogatiy*, where everything is imported and even foreigners reel at the prices (up to six times what you'd pay back home). In between are the countless private shops and street kiosks, given to cut-throat trading and selling goods past their sell-by dates – that are indispensable as hit-and-miss convenience stores. Moscow is a jungle for consumers, rather than a playground.

**Opening hours** vary widely, but all but the largest department stores tend to take an afternoon break, usually 1–2pm for food stores, and 2–3pm for the others. Most shops are open six days a week, and many food stores and bread shops are also open on Sundays. Many kiosks function 24 hours a day.

Most state-owned shops still use the *kassa* **system**, where you order and get the price at the counter before paying at the cash desk (*kassa*) and taking the receipt back to claim your goods – a system that entails **queuing** at least twice. Some stores have a separate *kassa* for each counter, or require you to specify which one the receipt is for. If you don't speak Russian well, it's easy to make a mistake and be sent back to try again, which is infuriating.

Fortunately, shopping in the private sector is much easier, as most places operate on a self-service, pay-as-you-leave basis. Here, however, the pitfall is **pricing**. Items are often priced in US dollars or Deutschmarks, which the cashier converts into rubles at a rate (*kurs*) set by the store (which should be posted). If this is way out of line with the bank rate, you'll end up paying five to ten percent more in real terms, unless you pay by **credit card**. Credit cards are fairly widely accepted in private shops, but haven't yet penetrated the state sector.

## Antiques and souvenirs

As the new rich invest in **antiques**, prices are catching up with or surpassing those in the West. Export regulations used to be clear and strictly enforced; nowadays even customs officials admit confusion. On paper, anything made before 1945 counts as an antique and may not be taken out of Russia without a **permit** from the Cultural Assessment Committee, ul. Neglinnaya 8 (☎921-3258; Mon & Tues 10am–2pm). In practice, much is smuggled out via Belarus or Ukraine, where customs are more lax; at Moscow's airports, *samovars* and icons show up on the X-ray scanners. Antiques sellers seldom enquire about buyers' intentions or bother to mention the law.

**Souvenirs** are safer buys and widely available. Favourites include the *matryoshka* doll, which also comes in versions depicting Yeltsin, Gorby *et al*; *Palekh* boxes painted with fairy-tale

## Shops and Markets

scenes; colourful wooden spoons and bowls from Khokloma; banners, fur hats, army gear and KGB sweatshirts. While any of these can be taken abroad without difficulty, **icons** are sure to cause problems at customs, and even such mundane items as tea-glass holders can theoretically be confiscated for being made of "strategic metals". Whether the law is applied is another matter entirely.

### Antiques

**Aktrisa**, ul. Arbat 43; ☎ 241-3191; 5min from Smolenskaya metro. Chaotic jumble of pre-Revolutionary *objets* and Soviet kitsch. Fun to browse. Mon–Sat 10am–6pm.

**Antikvar**, ul. Butyurskiy val 2; ☎ 251-6873; 5min from Belorusskaya metro. Mainly timepieces, but also silver and porcelain, plus less valuable coins, icons and *samovars*. Mon–Sat 10am–2pm & 3–8pm.

**Antikvariat**, ul. Arbat 2; ☎ 291-7480; 5min from Arbatskya metro. The best of the many antique shops on the Arbat, particularly for porcelain – but don't expect any bargains. Mon–Sat 9am–7pm.

**Lavka Knigolyuba**, Tverskaya-Yamskaya ul. 22; ☎ 251-0921; midway between Mayakovskaya and Belorusskaya metros. Icons, silver trays and tea-glass holders galore. Mon–Sat 9am–6pm.

**Salon na Begovoy**, 1-y Botinskiy proezd 2/6; ☎ 946-0977; opposite the Botkin Hospital, 15min from Dinamo metro. Silver, crystal, porcelain and furniture. Auctions every Friday at 4pm. Daily 10am–7pm.

### Souvenirs

**Church of St George**, ul. Varvarka; 5min from Kitay-Gorod metro. The best of the souvenir shops in the Zaryade churches, with charming gifts and toys by local craftspeople. Mon–Sat 9am–6pm.

**Gorbunov Collectors' Fair**, Filyovskiy Park; 10min from Bagrationovskaya metro. All kinds of new and secondhand records, CDs, tapes, videos, cameras and audio equipment. Sat & Sun 11am–2pm.

**GUM** (see "Department Stores") has several souvenir shops on the second line of the ground floor. You might also find people selling embroidered cushion covers and tea cosies, made by schoolchildren.

**Izmaylovo Art Market** (aka the *Vernisazh*); 5min from Izmaylovskiy Park metro. Dozens of stalls selling handicrafts, icons, Soviet kitsch, vintage cameras and watches. The biggest choice of souvenirs, if not the lowest prices. Sat & Sun 8am–6pm.

**Tishkin flea market**, Tishkinskaya pl.; 10min from Mayakovskaya or Belorusskaya metro. Mostly junk, but known to retro dressers for its 1970s clothing and footwear. Sat & Sun 8am–5pm.

## Department stores and "things markets"

Owing to the recent influx of foreign retailers and imported products, Moscow's **department stores** are undergoing something of a renaissance, and the notion of shopping (or at least window-shopping) for pleasure is taking hold. On a humbler level, there are several large markets for clothing, appliances and cosmetics, held inside sports stadiums and known as "**Things markets**" (*Veshchevoy rynok*). As the goods are generally poor-quality imitations of international brand-products, made in China, Turkey or Poland, the scene is closer to a warehouse sale than a flea market. There's a small admission charge. Prices are lowest before 9am.

## Department stores

**GUM**, Krasnaya pl. 3; near Ploshchad Revolyutsii metro. Although *Benetton* and their ilk have colonized most of the ground floor, cheaper Soviet-style shops can still be found upstairs. Mon–Sat 8am–8pm.

**Detskiy Mir**, Teatralniy proezd 5; near Lubyanka metro. No longer the best toy shop in Moscow, but still worth a visit. Daily 8.40am–8pm.

**Dom Igrushki**, ul. Bolshaya Yakimanka 26; 10min from Polyanka metro. Stocks a big range of Russian and imported toys for kids of all ages. Mon–Sat 8am–8pm.

**Irish House**, ul. Noviy Arbat 19; 5min from Arbatskaya metro. Good selection of imported appliances, food and clothing, with a popular bar upstairs. Daily 10am–11pm.

**Petrovskiy Passazh**, ul. Petrovka 10; 5min from Okhotniy Ryad metro. Chic arcade popular with nouveaux riches; mostly French and German products priced in francs or DM. Mon–Sat 9am–8pm.

**Sadko Arcade**, Krasnogvardeyskiy pr. 1; in the Expocentre, 2km from Ulitsa 1905 Goda metro. Huge, half-empty mall of boutiques, foodstores, cafés and restaurants. Daily 9am–11pm.

**TsUM**, ul. Petrovka 2; near Teatralnaya metro. Soviet-style department store stocking Russian and imported clothing, household goods and toys. Mon–Sat 8am–8pm.

### "Things markets"

**Lenin Central Stadium**, Luzhniki; 15min from Sportivnaya metro. Wed–Sun 6am–4pm.

**TsKA Stadium**, Leningradskiy pr. 39; 15min from Dinamo or Aeroport metro. Daily 8am–6pm.

## Food stores and markets

**Buying food** is much easier now that all kinds of products are available from supermarkets and street kiosks, but the often dodgy quality of imported foodstuffs is cause for concern. Be especially cautious about meat or dairy products

sold on the streets: the frozen chicken legs nicknamed *Noshki Busha* ("Bush's Legs") are high on the list of dangerous goods. Since prices are sky high in private shops and markets, most Russians stick to the (generally) lower-priced state shops, where the *kassa* system prevails. All the stores listed below are pay-as-you-leave, unless stated otherwise.

### Food stores

**Colognia Supermarket**, Sadovaya Bolshaya ul. 5/1; near Mayakovskaya metro. German foods, priced in DM. Mon–Fri & Sun 10am–8pm, Sat 10am–9pm.

**EML**, Smolenskaya nab. 2/10; 10min from Smolenskaya metro. Cheaper than other supermarkets for imported food, as many of the items are nearing their sell-by date. Daily 24 hours.

**Garden Ring Supermarket**, Sadovaya Bolshaya ul. 1; 5min from Mayakovskaya metro. Irish-managed chain with branches at Leninskiy pr. 146 and ul. Serafimovicha 2. Daily 9am–9pm.

**Noviy Arbat 46**, ul. Noviy Arbat 46; 10min from Arbatskaya or Smolenskaya metro. Well-stocked Russian supermarket, using the *kassa* system. Daily 24 hours.

**Olimp Supermarket**, ul. Krasnaya Presnya 23; 5min from Ulitsa 1905 Goda metro. Good selection of imported food and drink at fairly reasonable prices. Mon–Sat 10am–8pm.

**Tverskoy M & S**, Tverskaya ul. 6. Belgian store with inexpensive booze. Mon–Sat 9am–11pm.

**Yeliseyev's**, Tverskaya ul. 14; near Pushkinskaya metro. Better known for its fabulous decor than its foodstuffs (see p.113). Uses the *kassa* system. Mon–Sat 8am–9pm, Sun 8am–7pm.

### Food markets

Every district of Moscow has a farmers' **market** (*rynok*) selling all kinds of fresh produce, where shoppers can sample morsels with no obligation to buy. Prices are comparable to supermarkets; in winter, much of the fruit is imported from the West. Opening hours are usually

**Shops and Markets**

## Shops and Markets

Mon–Sat 7am–7pm, Sun 7am–6pm. The best markets are the following.

**Central Market Hall**, Tsvetnoy bul. 15; near Tsvetnoy Bulvar metro (currently closed for refurbishment).

**Cheremushinskiy**, Lomonosovskiy pr. 1; 10min from Universitet or Profsoyuznaya metro. The largest and most expensive in Moscow.

**Danilovskiy**, ul. Mytnaya 74; near Tulskaya metro.

**Leningradskiy**, Chasovaya ul. 11; 15min from Aeroport metro.

**Rizhskiy**, pr. Mira 94; near Rizhskaya metro.

## Newspapers, books and video rental

**Foreign newspapers** are sold in all the big hotels and most of the supermarkets used by foreigners, but prices are steep and the selection is often limited. The wall kiosk near the *Irish House* and the *Troika* kiosk outside the *Hotel Metropol* have the best choice and lowest prices.

**Books in foreign languages** also fetch a high price, whether they're pictorial guides, textbooks or secondhand thrillers. All the hottest items are snapped up by traders for resale on the streets, often right outside the bookstore. Serious bibliophiles should check out the weekend **book market** in the Olympic Sports Complex (Prospekt Mira metro). Beware, however, that the restrictions on exporting books are as strict as on antiques. In theory, you must submit a form listing all the details of every book; reference books are liable to be taxed, and nothing printed before 1960 can be exported.

Whereas pirated **videos** of Western films dubbed into Russian can be rented

from kiosks all over town, the only sources for recordings in English are *VideoForce* (Mon–Sat 11am–8pm, Sun 11am–6pm), on the first floor of the hard-to-reach *Mezhdunarodnaya Hotel*, and the *Garden Ring Supermarket* near Mayakovskaya metro (which has a much smaller range). Both require a hefty deposit.

### Bookshops

**Akademkniga**, Tverskaya ul. 19; near Tverskaya metro. The upper floor has a few art books and a fair range of second hand novels. Mon–Sat 10am–2pm & 3–7pm.

**Biblio-Globus**, ul. Myasnitskaya 6; near Lubyanka metro. Art books and pulp fiction, spread around several departments located beneath the secret service's computer centre. Mon–Fri 10am–2pm & 3–7pm, Sat 10am–6pm.

**Dom knigi**, ul. Noviy Arbat 26; 5min from Arbatskaya metro. A huge store with art books at the far end of the second floor. Mon–Sat 11am–2pm & 3–8pm.

**Innostrannaya Kniga**, ul. Kachalova 16; 15min from Arbatskaya or Barrikadnaya metro. Art books, dictionaries and novels. Also sells souvenirs and antiques. Mon–Sat 10am–2pm & 3–7pm.

**Knizhnaya lavka "19 Oktyabrya"**, 1-y Kazachiy per.; 10min from Polyanka metro. If you read Russian and are seriously into literature, this bookshop-cum-salon in a wooden hut is a goldmine – especially for poetry. Tues–Sat 11am–7pm.

**Zwemmer's Bookshop**, ul. Kuznetskiy most 18; near Kuznetskiy Most metro. The best foreign-language bookstore, with a big range of novels, art books and stuff about Russia, all at British prices (payable in rubles). Mon–Sat 10am–7pm.

# Chapter 16

# Children's Moscow

If you've tried the patience of your **children** with too many churches and museums, any of the suggestions below should head off a rebellion. Many have already been covered in the text, so you can get more information by turning to the relevant page. For sporting suggestions or a trip to the steam baths, see the next chapter.

**Children's Musical Theatre**, pr. Vernadskovo 5; ☎930-7021; 10min from Universitet metro. Enacts *Peter and the Wolf* (*Petya i Volk*) and Russian fairytales that can be enjoyed by young children without understanding the language.

**Circus** Outstanding performances with lots of clowns and animals, at the Old and New Circuses; see "The Arts" (p.321) for details.

**Cinemas** Places that screen films in foreign languages are listed under "The Arts". Many other cinemas show cartoons in the afternoons.

**Durov Animal Theatre** A uniquely Muscovite institution whose shows are sure to charm younger children, and adults too (assuming they're not into animal lib). Details appear under "The Arts".

**Elevator rides** The glass-sided elevators in the *Mezhdunarodnaya Hotel* offer a spectacular view of the hotel's lofty atrium, while the lift in the TV Tower leads to an observation deck overlooking the northern suburbs (see p.267).

**Gorky Park** Its funfair has a rollercoaster, ferris wheel and mothballed Space

Shuttle (p.214), while the park hosts a festival of ice sculptures in February.

**Kolomenskoe** Spooky buildings to capture your children's imagination, in a wooded park that's great for sledging in wintertime (see p.224).

**Moscow Marathon** Best viewed from Gorky Park, where the race starts and finishes, or the Sparrow Hills, overlooking the route (p.331).

**Museums** Some that might be of particular interest to children include the Kremlin Armoury (p.88); the Palace of the Romanov Boyars in Zaryade (p.101); the Vasnetsov House (p.256); and the Armed Forces Museum (p.259).

**Pet Markets** If you don't feel up to visiting the big Sunday Pet Market out beyond Taganka (p.224), children can stroke puppies and kittens on the steps of the Arbatskaya pl. underpass any day of the week (p.119).

**Planetarium**, Sadovaya-Kudrinskaya ul. 5; ☎254-1838; 5min from Barrikadnaya metro. Tours of the cosmos and footage from Soviet space missions, with commentary in Russian. Tues–Sun 10am–6pm.

**Police Relay-Race** Fun to watch if you pick the right vantage point on the Garden Ring; the most exciting stages are the motorcycle and patrol car races. Described on p.331.

**Puppet theatre** See "The Arts" section for details of where to find puppet theatre for children in Moscow.

## Children's Moscow

**St Patrick's Day parade** of floats and bands along the New Arbat, staged by Moscow's small but active Irish community, on March 17.

**Streetlife** The Arbat is always busy with buskers, performing artists and street photographers (whose props include giant cuddly toys). Kids can also get their picture taken on Red Square with people dressed in medieval costumes.

**Toy shops** *Barbie* is currently all the rage while Russian-made toys are disappearing from the shelves, but you can still find charming wooden toys at remarkably low prices in the *Dom Igrushki* and *Detskiy Mir* (see "Department Stores", p.325).

**Tsaritsyno** Romantic ruins to scramble over and woods to play in. The stables attached to the *Usadba* restaurant can arrange horse-riding all year round, and *troyka* rides in winter. See p.231 for details.

**VDNKh** Stalinesque Disney World with some attractions for kids: holograms, a 360° cinema screen, live reindeer, a real space rocket, and *troyka* rides over winter. Described on p.261.

**Zoo** So run-down these days that it's probably only enjoyable by the really young or totally insensitive, though there is the odd pony ride to enliven proceedings (p.173).

# Chapter 17

# Sports, Outdoor Activities and Bathhouses

In Soviet times, **sport** was accorded high status: a carefully nurtured elite of Olympic medal-winning sportsmen and women were heralded as proof of Communism's superiority, while ordinary citizens were exhorted to pursue sporting activities to make them "ready for labour and defence". Consequently, there's no shortage of sports facilities in Moscow, though most are for club members only; visitors can try striking some kind of deal with the staff, or settle for paying higher rates to use hotel facilities. Without being alarmist, it's unwise to do any sports without medical insurance, in case of accidents.

For the slothful majority of Muscovites, however, the most popular activity remains visiting the **bathhouse**, or *banya*. Russian bathhouses are a world unto themselves, and are the preferred cure for the complaint known locally as "feeling heavy" – which encompasses everything from having flu to feeling depressed. For a truly Russian experience, a visit to the *banya* is a must.

## Bathhouses

The Russian *banya* is as much a national institution as the sauna is in Scandinavia. Traditionally, peasants stoked up the village bathhouse and washed away the week's grime on Fridays – a "*banya* for the soul". Townspeople were equally devoted to the *banya*: the wealthy had private ones, while others visited public

bathhouses, favoured as much for their ambience as the quality of their hot room. Today, these bathhouses are classless institutions, where all ages and professions are united in sweaty conviviality.

Before you set off, it's as well to know the procedure when **visiting a *banya***. Some bathhouses have separate floors for men and women, while others operate on different days for each sex, but whatever the setup, there's no mixed bathing, except in special deluxe saunas (available for private rental). The only thing that the *banya* will provide is a towel in which to wrap yourself. You should bring a towel, shampoo, some plastic sandals and maybe a hat to protect your hair. At the entrance you can buy a *venik* – a leafy bunch of birch twigs – with which bathers flail themselves (and each other) in the steam room, to open up the skin's pores and enhance circulation. This isn't compulsory.

Hand your coat and valuables to the cloakroom attendant before going into the changing rooms. Beyond these lies a washroom with a cold plunge pool or bath; the metal basins are for soaking your *venik* to make it supple. Finally you enter the hot room (*parilka*), with its tiers of benches – it gets hotter the higher you go. It's a dry heat, although from time to time water is thrown onto the stove to produce steam. Five to seven minutes is as long as a novice should attempt in the

## Sports, Outdoor Activities and Bath- houses

*parilka*. After a dunk in the cold bath and a rest, you can return to the *parilka* for more heat torture, before cooling off again – a process repeated several times, with breaks for tea and conversation.

Many *banya*-goers cover their hair (the heat can make it go frizzy), while others go in for traditional health cures and beauty treatments: some rub salt over their bodies or coat themselves with honey, to make their skin softer. As *banya*-going is a dehydrating experience, it's inadvisable to go drunk, with a bad hangover or on a full stomach.

There are inconspicuous *banyas* in every district of Moscow; the two listed below are the best known. Both include private *banyas*, which can be rented by groups.

**Krasnopresnenskiy Baths**, Stolyarniy per. 7; ☎255-5306; 10min from Krasnopresnenskaya metro. Archetypal Soviet-style *banya*, but with above aver- age amenities, and open for lascivious private parties that are popular with gang- sters. Phone for schedules and bookings.

**Sandunovskiy Baths**, Neglinnaya ul. 14; ☎925-4631; 15min from Teatralnaya or Kuznetskiy Most metro. Atmospheric, decrepit grandeur; it's worth paying more to enjoy the ornate *lux* baths with their majolica-tiled pools ($20), on the top floor. The so-called first class ($10) area, downstairs, has a nice lounge but is otherwise dreary. On both floors you can get a massage (*not* advised), haircut or manicure, and order food and drinks. Open 8am–10pm (last tickets sold at 8pm); closed Tues.

## Boating and yachting

In fine weather, **riverboat cruises** are an enjoyable way to see Moscow while getting some sun and fresh air. Services run from the last week in April to the first week in September, daily noon–8pm, unless it's raining or snowing. The cruise leaves **from the embankment near Kiev Station** (Kievskaya metro), calling at piers up and down the river (see map, p.174). Downriver is the most scenic route, pass- ing the Kremlin, Novodevichiy Convent,

the Sparrow Hills, and Novospasskiy Monastery (1hr 20min). Alternatively, you can sail upriver past the White House and Fili to Krylatskoe (1hr). Tickets for either route cost about $2; call ☎277-3469 for information.

From April to August, motorboats ply the beaches of **Serebryaniy Bor**, upriver from Krylatskoe; you can reach one of the the piers by trolleybus #21 from Polezhaevskaya metro. By way of contrast, the lower reaches of the river are flanked by dockyards and factories, interrupted by the ex-royal estate of Kolomenskoe, which can be reached by boat from the **Southern River Terminal** (*Yuzhniy rechnoy vokzal*), prospekt Andropova 11 (☎118-7811) 15min from Kolomenskaya metro – also the point of departure for passenger boats to Nizhniy Novgorod, via the Oka route.

River cruises **beyond the city limits** start from the **Northern River Terminal** (*Severniy rechnoy vokzal*), Leningradskoe shosse 51 (☎459-7476); 15min from Rechnoy Vokzal metro. From May to August, *raketa* **hydrofoils** cruise the reser- voirs along the Moscow Canal, which are surrounded by woods with abundant birdlife and fishing. The River Terminal is also used by boats to St Petersburg and Nizhniy Novgorod, and yachts sailing the waterways.

**Chartering a yacht** is a relaxing way to spend a day, if not the most obvious way to squander your cash in Moscow; for details, contact the *Spartak Yacht Club*, c/o the *Savoy Hotel* (☎929-8569) or *Volga Yacht Charter*, ul. Maksimova 6, room 121 (☎254-7998).

You can rent **skiffs** in Gorky Park or **rowing boats** at Serebryaniy Bor for a fraction of the cost of chartering a yacht.

## Bowling

Moscow has two ten-pin bowling alleys, mostly used by foreigners: the **Bowling Bar** in the *Mezhdunarodnaya Hotel*, Krasnopresnenskaya nab. 12 (☎253-2382) 20min from Ulitsa 1905 Goda metro; and **Kegelbahn** in the basement of the *Kosmos Hotel*, prospekt Mira 150 (☎217-8680), 5min from VDNKh metro.

## Chess

Once the Soviet sport par excellence, **chess** (*shakhmaty*) no longer has such a high profile in Russia, and attempts to revive the game's lustre by hosting an international tournament in 1994 misfired when two grandmasters complained of being threatened by the Mafia. However, amateur chess still thrives, with games in every courtyard and park over summer (Sokolniki and Gorky parks have special "chess corners"), where a foreign challenger will always be welcomed. Serious players could also contact the *Central Chess Club*, Gogolevskiy bulvar 14 (☎291-0641) 10min from Arbatskaya metro.

## Flying

If you're seriously into thrills, the Russian Federation of Superlight Aviation (UFSLA) offers **microlight flights** from Tushino Airfield (☎491-4219 or 490-6003) 10min from Tushinskaya metro. You don't need to have any flying skills, since the 40–65 horsepower aircraft also seats an instructor. They can reach 85–100km per hour, and an altitude of 600m; it feels like you're flying in a motorcycle sidecar with wings. A 15–20min flight costs $10–15.

## Horse-riding and racing

There are several places where you can go **horse-riding** within the city. Over summer, horses can be rented in Sokolniki and Kuzminki parks and at Tsaritsyno, but the best location is the **Bittsa Forest Park** (*Bittsevskiy Lesopark*) south of Moscow. Book through Larisa Ivanova at the *Bittsa Horseback Riding Complex*, Balaklavskiy pereulok 33 (☎318-6518) 10min from Chertanovskaya metro. The complex has indoor and outdoor facilities, competent instructors and well-trained thoroughbreds. Individual lessons cost $10–15.

For a seedier equestrian encounter, attend **horse races** at the **Hippodrome**, Begovaya ul. 22 (☎945-4516) 15min from Dinamo or Begovaya metro. Though merely trotting races, the drunken crowd takes it as seriously as the Kentucky

Derby. The racetrack is a grand structure gone to pot, with a bar and betting office beneath the stands. Bets (*stavki*) are placed on pairs (*parniy*) or combinations (*kombinatsiya*) of winners in each race (*zaezd*). The official maximum bet is 1000 rubles. You buy the admission ticket and programme (costing next to nothing) from the hatches by the green fence outside. Races are held over winter Wed & Fri 6–9pm, Sun 1–6pm.

## Ice hockey

**Ice hockey** is Russia's second most popular sport, and matches take place throughout the year at the Ice Palace of the TsKA complex, Leningradskiy prospekt 39 (☎213-6590) 15min from Aeroport or Dinamo metro. Here, the Russian Penguins (formerly the Soviet Army TsKA team) draw big crowds with American-style razzmatazz, hoping to recover their former glory (they won 13 consecutive championships between 1977 and 1989), while their traditional rivals, *Dinamo* and *Spartak*, play to dwindling audiences.

The hockey season starts in September and culminates in the annual World Championships the following summer, when the Russians do their best to defeat Canada and the US. Since "friendly" matches occur at the Ice Palace even out of season, you can always be sure of catching a game there.

## Marathons and the Relay-Race

Moscow has two annual **Marathons**: an international race in September, and a mostly Muscovite event in April. Both races start and finish at Gorky Park, following the Moskva embankment around to the Sparrow Hills before doubling back; the full marathon entails two laps of this circuit. The hills afford the best view of the course, and soon separate the well-trained from the dilettantes. The nearest metro station is Park Kultury.

A more amusing event for spectators is the annual **Police Relay-Race**, on the Sunday nearest to Police Day (Oct 24), when Moscow's militia, GAI and Fire

**Sports, Outdoor Activities and Bath-houses**

## Sports, Outdoor Activities and Bathhouses

Brigade field teams race around the Garden Ring. Starting from Triumfalnaya ploshchad at noon, runners, skiers and dogs carry the baton as far as Krasnye vorota; bikers take over at Pavelets Station; firemen drag hoses over an obstacle course near Park Kultury; policewomen sprint up Zubovskiy bulvar; squad cars manoeuvre outside the US Embassy; and cops in parade uniforms race to the finishing line. In the event of ice on the Ring, expect to see plenty of falls and skids.

### Skating, sledging, skiing and troyka rides

During winter, Russians dig out their ice skates or skis and revel in the snow. If you can borrow a pair of skates or rent some on the spot, there are outdoor **ice-skating** rinks at Gorky, Izmaylovo and Sokolniki parks – the first even has an ice disco in the evenings.

The steepest hills for **sledging** are at Kolomonsoe (see p.224) and near the ski runs at Krylatskoe, but you needn't go further than the Alexander Gardens beside the Kremlin to find shorter slopes where young children can enjoy themselves.

Although Russia's terrain dictates that cross-country rather than downhill **skiing** is the norm, experts can risk their necks on two ski jumps in the Sparrow Hills (p.196). The best place for cross-country skiing is **Losiniy Ostrov**, in the northeast of Moscow, which is named after the elks (*los*) that roam its 110 square kilometres of deciduous and evergreen forest. You can get there from Shcholkovskaya metro, or the Yauza station on the suburban train line from Yaroslav Station.

When the snow is deep, riding in a horse-drawn sleigh or *troyka* is a romantic option. To experience the thrill of speeding across a snowy wilderness, lash out $60 for an hour's ride at Tsaritsyno (☎343-1510, see p.229) and bring a bottle. Young children should settle for the tamer, 35-minute *troyka* rides ($20) around the pavilions of the VDNKh park (p.264). If the price seems steep, remember that a *troyka* seats four to six adults and children.

## Soccer

Russia's poor performance in the last World Cup shouldn't deter you from attending a **soccer** match. Two Moscow clubs dominate the national league: the Central Army Club, TsKA, who are the current champions, and their traditional rivals Dinamo, formerly the sports club of the secret police. Their home grounds are located on either side of Leningradskiy prospekt. Other local teams include Spartak Moskva, based at the Lenin Central Stadium in Luzhniki (also used for international matches), and Torpedo, whose grounds are near the ZiL plant.

During the football season from March to October, matches usually occur on Saturday afternoons. Seating is always plentiful and tickets are extremely cheap; the only drawback is the risk of violence from drunken fans (TsKA vs Dinamo matches are the worst).

**Dinamo Sports Stadium**, Leningradskiy pr. 36; ☎217-7092; near Dinamo metro.

**Lenin Central Stadium**, Luzhniki; ☎201-0155; 10min from Sportivnaya metro.

**TsKA Stadium**, Leningradskiy pr. 39; ☎213-6590; 15min from Aeroport or Dinamo metro.

### Sunbathing, swimming and working out

After the long dark winter, Muscovites are keen to go **sunbathing** as soon as the weather allows, stripping down to their underwear on any available patch of grass. The most popular bathing spot is **Serebryaniy Bor**, a series of beaches (see p.270) on a bend in the upper reaches of the Moskva River, with the cleanest water within the city limits (which isn't saying too much). You can get there by taking the metro to Polezhaevskaya and then trolleybus #21 or any bus heading west.

To go **swimming** in really pure water entails travelling 35km outside Moscow to the **Pirogovskoe Reservoir**, amid a forest. The reservoir can be reached by suburban trains from Leningrad Station to the Pirogovskiy halt; by driving along the M8 and turning left at Mytishchi; or by hydrofoil from the Northern River Terminal (see "Boating") during summer. At other times of the year, **indoor pools** come into their own – particularly since the closure of the huge outdoor pool near the Moskva River, which was heated in winter during the Soviet era. All the ones listed below are coupled with **gyms**, either in a Soviet-built sports complex or a luxury hotel. The latter are usually pricier.

### Pools and gyms

**Dinamo Swimming Pool**, Leningradskiy pr. 36; ☎212-8483; near Dinamo metro. Inexpensive pool in the Dinamo Sports Complex; phone to ask if bathers still need a medical certificate.

**Metropol Health Club**, *Metropol Hotel*, Teatralniy proezd 1/4; ☎927-6148; near Ploshchad Revolyutsii metro. Sauna, pool ($17 per hr), gym ($5 per hr) and massage ($30).

**Mezhdunarodnaya Health Club**, *Mezhdunarodnaya Hotel* (entrance 1), Krasnopresnenskaya nab. 12; ☎255-6691. Pool ($9), sauna and gym on the ground floor. Daily noon–8pm.

**Olympic Sports Complex**, Olimpiyskiy pr. 16; ☎903-5303; 10min from Prospekt Mira metro. Access to an Olympic-sized pool and gym for $2 a day or $40 a month. Also a solarium ($15 per hr). Contact Sergei Klimov, who speaks English. Daily 7am–9pm.

**Radisson Slavyanskaya Pool**, *Radisson Slavyanskaya Hotel*, Berezhovskaya nab. 2; ☎941-8027; near Kievskaya metro.

## Tennis

**Tennis courts** can be rented at the following places during summer. The privately owned courts are more expensive than the ones in public sports complexes. You can't usually rent equipment.

**Chaika Tennis Courts**, Korobeynikov per. 1/2; ☎202-0474; 10min from Park Kultury metro. Indoor courts. Daily 7am–10pm.

**Dinamo Stadium**, near Dinamo metro. Hard to locate, but the biggest choice, with some 40 indoor and outdoor courts scattered over several acres. The earth courts (*zemlyanoy kort*) are the best-maintained.

**Druzhba Tennis Courts**, Luzhniki Sports Complex; ☎201-1780; 20min from Sportivnaya metro. Indoor and outdoor courts. Daily 7am–4pm.

**Sports, Outdoor Activities and Bathhouses**

# The Contexts

# A History of Moscow

Moscow's turbulent history can be divided into three distinct phases. The first saw it rise from a minor principality to the capital of a unified Russian state, and the birth of the Romanov dynasty. During the second – from the reign of Peter the Great onwards – Moscow was eclipsed by the new Imperial capital, St Petersburg, and played a secondary role in Russian history until the collapse of Tsarism in 1917. Then, after a year that saw the October Revolution in Petrograd (as St Petersburg was then called), the Bolsheviks returned the seat of government to the Kremlin, and Moscow's modern era began.

## Beginnings

Despite evidence of human settlement as early as 500 BC, the first recorded mention of the city was in 1147 AD, when Prince **Yuri Dolgorukiy** of Rostov and Suzdal invited Svyatoslav of Novgorod and his *boyars* (nobles) to feast at Dolgoruky's hunting lodge, on a hill above the Moskva and Neglina rivers. Enlarged over the years and fortified with wooden walls and towers in 1156, this *Kreml* or **Kremlin** was the seed of a township named "Moskva", after the river. Though some claim this is a corruption of the Finnish word for "bear", it is more likely to derive from the Russian *mozgliy*, meaning "marshy". In any event, the town was conveniently located on the Moskva River that linked the great waterways of the Volga and the Okha – a major factor in its eventual rise to power.

Moscow's infancy coincided with two momentous events in Russian history. Early in the twelfth century, the great medieval civilization of the **Kievan Rus collapsed** amid internecine strife and invasions from the east and west. Much of the population fled northwards to the *zalesskiy* (beyond the woods) area of the Okha basin and the upper Volga, where Prince Andrei Bogolyubskiy established the new capital, **Vladimir**, in 1169.

Barely fifty years later, the Mongols surged across the Russian steppes, laying waste to villages and towns – including Moscow. The **Mongol invasion** (1237–40) seemed like the end of the world foretold in the bible, but in fact heralded two centuries of submission to their **Tatar allies**, who demanded tribute in gold, furs and slaves. The princes of Vladimir and other towns were only allowed to rule with the Tatar Khan's *yarlyk* (authority), which was auctioned off to the highest bidder. Their chief concerns were to squeeze as much wealth as possible from their fiefdoms, and to remain in favour with the Khan.

The Moscow princes of the **Rurik dynasty** were no exception to this rule. The town was first recognized as a principality under **Daniil** (1263–1303), the youngest son of Grand Prince Alexander Nevsky of Novgorod, who defeated the Teutonic Knights in a famous battle on Lake Peipus. His grandson, **Ivan "Kalita"** (1325–41), earned his nickname "moneybags" for his skill at extracting taxes and expanding his influence over other principalities, proving so adept as "the Tatar's hangman, sycophant and slave in chief" (as Marx put it) that he got to marry the Khan's daughter and become Great Prince of Vladimir. In recognition of his power, the seat of the **Russian Orthodox Church** was moved from Vladimir to Moscow in 1326. That same year, work began on strengthening the Kremlin with higher oak ramparts, completed in time for the accession of **Simeon the Proud** (1341–53).

# The rise of Muscovy

The **rise of Muscovy** (as the principality* was named) owed to more than mere servility. An underlying factor was its location in the *mezhdu-reche* (between the rivers) area at the crossroads of Russia's trade routes, roughly equidistant from the Tatar Khanate on the lower Volga, the Lithuanian-Polish empire to the west, and the powerful city-state of Novgorod to the north. Another was its prestige as the seat of the Russian Orthodox Church, which would assume messianic significance after the fall of Constantinople in the fifteenth century. Moreover, during the 1350s, the Mongol-Tatar Golden Horde was weakened by power struggles within its vast empire, and would later be battered by another force of nomadic invaders, under Timurlane. Meanwhile, the Kremlin was strengthened by the building of limestone walls, from 1367 onwards.

In 1380, Simeon's grandson, Dmitry, dared to argue over the annual tribute to the Tatars and, when Khan Mamai responded with a punitive invasion, Dmitry led a Russian army to confront the Horde at Kulikovo near the River Don. The **battle of Kulikovo** was the Russians' first victory in nearly a century and a half: a historic event commemorated by the foundation of the Donskoy Monastery on the site where his departing army had prayed for victory, while Dmitry himself assumed the title **Dmitry Donskoy**.

However, the Horde remained a formidable threat, and his successors, Vasily I and Vasily the Dark, paid tribute as normal. It was during this period that Russian **icon painting** and frescoes reached their zenith at the hands of Theophanes the Greek, Andrei Rublev and Daniil Cherniy (all of whom worked in Moscow), and that the Byzantine capital, Constantinople, fell to the Turks, in 1453.

### Ivan the Great

The Tatar yoke was finally thrown off in the reign of Ivan III (1462–1505), known as **Ivan the Great** (*Ivan Veliki*). His boldness stemmed from a politically shrewd marriage to the obese **Sofia Paléologue** of Byzantium, and his claim to rule the Eastern and Western Roman Empires was symbolized by the double-headed eagle that he

adopted as his emblem. Having gained power over Yaroslavl, Rostov, Tver and Pskov before his marriage, Ivan waited eight years before tearing up the Khan's *yarlyk* in the Cathedral of the Assumption, in 1480. By the end of his reign, the Lithuanians had been pushed back to the headwaters of the Dniepr and Dvina, and even proudly independent Novgorod had submitted, giving Muscovy control of a huge area as far north as the White Sea. This fourfold **territorial expansion** earned Ivan the titles "Gatherer of the Russian Lands" and "Autocrat of all the Russias".

Moscow – and the Kremlin in particular – were aggrandized to reflect this. In Sofia's wake came **Italian architects** who supervised the construction of the Kremlin's brick walls and two of its finest stone cathedrals. They also began work on a belltower intended to be the tallest building in Russia, later named after Ivan. The building programme was completed by his successor, who extended it to the Beliy Gorod, where stone parish churches were erected. However, stone buildings were still rare, and Moscow would remain a predominantly wooden city for three centuries, making **fires** a greater threat than Tatar raids. Yet Moscow thrived, its population rising to 100,000 by the mid-sixteenth century, when it was one of the largest cities in Europe.

Ivan the Great's successor, **Vasily III** (1505–33), is mainly remembered for clearing what is now Red Square, and siring the future Ivan the Terrible in 1530 – the moment of birth apparently coincided with a clap of thunder and lightning striking the Kremlin, which was held to signify the child's future greatness. Of equal importance to Moscow's destiny was a **prophecy** by the monk Philotey of Pskov, who told Vasily that "two Romes have already fallen but the third remains standing and a fourth there will not be". This belief that Moscow was the "third Rome" and the heir of Byzantium's sovereignty over Orthodox Christendom would inspire Russia's rulers for generations.

## Ivan the Terrible

Despite his infamous deeds, Russians have always had a soft spot for **Ivan the Terrible** (*Ivan Grozniy*). In modern times this can partly be attributed to Eisenstein's superb film, which portrays the Tsar as a tortured soul driven to cruelty by the imperatives of power – a view that was personally dictated by Stalin, who felt that

---

\* Muscovy actually ranked as a Grand Duchy, and its rulers as Grand Dukes, but most historians use the term principality, which seems a more accurate reflection of its size and power.

his own life and Ivan's had much in common. Historians have also pointed out that the title *Gronziy* (usually translated as "Terrible", but really closer to "Awesome" or "Formidable") was first adopted by his grandfather, Ivan the Great. Nevertheless, his life richly deserves the epithet "Terrible".

Ivan's **childhood** was spent in fear of the *boyars*, whose struggles for power after Vasily's death (when Ivan was three) worsened after his mother was poisoned five years later. Ivan only survived as the heir to the throne because no one could agree on an alternative figurehead. His chief pleasure was killing birds and dogs; then hunting and reading the bible. In 1547, aged seventeen, Ivan assumed the Crown of Monomakh and insisted on being proclaimed **Tsar** (Caesar) instead of Grand Duke. However, he left affairs of state to the **Glinskiys** until a rival family of *boyars*, the **Shyuskiys**, succeeded in blaming them for a spate of fires in Moscow, inciting a riot. Ivan dismissed the Glinskiys and publicly confessed his failings on Red Square, vowing to God to rule better in the future.

Foreign invaders were a major concern – particularly the Tatars, who made frequent incursions into Russia from **Kazan** on the lower Volga. After many attempts, Ivan's army captured Kazan in October 1552, and to celebrate, St Basil's Cathedral was built. **Ashtrakan**, on the Caspian Sea, fell to the Russians two years later. With the Tatars at bay, Ivan then turned to raid the Grand Duchy of **Livonia**, to the west, ignoring protests from Poland and Sweden.

In 1560, his triumphs turned to ashes when his beloved wife **Anastasia** died shortly after a fire in Moscow. This seemed to Ivan a betrayal of his contract with God, and aroused all his latent suspicions of the *boyars*. As once-favoured courtiers were exiled or met worse fates, others fled abroad, confirming his fear of traitors – until in the winter of 1564, Ivan abruptly quit Moscow, leaving the populace agog. A month later, they received word that he had **abdicated** in protest at the *boyars'* lack of patriotism. Mobs besieged the Kremlin, demanding that the traitors be identified, until a delegation of clerics went to beg his forgiveness and implore him to rule them again.

### The Oprichniki

In return, Ivan demanded that Russia be divided into two spheres: the *oprichnina* – constituting his personal domain – and the *zemshchina*, comprising the rest. The power of the *boyars* was broken by exiling 12,000 families to distant, inhospitable regions of the *zemshchina*, an act of expropriation carried out by a new militia, hand-picked by Ivan and devoted to his orders: the **Oprichniki**. As a symbol of their mission to hunt down and sweep away his enemies, they bore a dog's head and a broom on their saddles. Enjoying total licence to kill, loot, burn and torture, they took their cue from **Malyuta-Skuratov**, the most depraved of Ivan's favourites.

Initially quartered in the Oprichniy dvor (on the site of old Moscow University), they later moved with Ivan to the **Alexandrovskaya Sloboda**, a moated palace north of Vladimir whose interior reflected the different aspects of the Tsar's personality. Some rooms were luxurious; others crammed with books, some with a monastic bareness; torture chambers lay beneath them. To demonstrate Ivan's piety, the palace was transformed into a "monastery" where the *Oprichniki* attended services from 3am until 8pm, when nightly orgies commenced.

Another bizarre story was his **wooing of Queen Elizabeth** of England, which preoccupied Ivan from 1567 to 1569. Besides the prospect of uniting their two nations, Ivan was excited by reports of this Virgin Queen, having tired of his fourth, Circassian, wife. Tactful evasions angered him into placing the English ambassador under house arrest in the Kitay-gorod, but he later forgave the offender. Not so those *boyars* whom Ivan suspected of treason, who were fed to dogs or raped to death. The atrocious climax was the **massacre of Novgorod** in 1569, when up to 60,000 citizens were tortured to death for supposedly plotting to side with Poland, and 200 more met a similar fate on Red Square.

### Ivan's final years

In 1571, the Tatars made a devastating raid on Moscow, burning the city and carrying off thousands of citizens as slaves. Ivan fled to Yaroslavl, only returning once they had left. The last decade of his reign was given over to scheming to gain the throne of **Poland**, which fell vacant in 1572, and again in 1575. To Polish envoys, he confided: "Many people in your country say that I am inhuman; it is true that I am cruel and irascible, but only to those who behave badly towards me. The good ones? Ah, I would not hesitate to give them my gold chain and the coat off my back!". After the Polish Diet had twice rebuffed his overtures, Ivan invaded Livonia, whereupon **Stephen Bathory** led a Polish army into Russia, in conjunction with a Swedish assault further north. Facing defeat, Ivan asked the Vatican to mediate and conceded Livonia to the Poles in 1582.

The previous year, the Tsar had killed his heir, **Tsarevich Ivan**, by striking him with an iron staff in a fit of rage. Deeply remorseful, he sank into gloom, which even debauchery and sadism could no longer dispel. His dynastic hopes now rested on his eldest son, **Fyodor** – an imbecile – and a sickly infant, **Dmitry**. In the last year of his life, Ivan compiled a register of all those he had killed, and paid monasteries to recite prayers for their souls. His guts putrified and his testicles swelled; his only solace was fondling the gems in his treasury. When astrologers foretold the **Tsar's death** on March 18, 1584, he swore to have them burned alive if they were wrong. On that day, he collapsed over a game of chess and expired on the spot. In accordance with Ivan's wishes, he was buried as a monk.

## Boris Godunov and the Time of Troubles

News of Ivan's death was released to the populace only after the details of the succession had been agreed by a Council of Regents. Fyodor reluctantly became Tsar, but the power behind the throne was **Boris Godunov**, the brother of Fyodor's wife, Irina. During his regency, stone walls were built around the Beliy Gorod and the Trinity Monastery of St Sergei. Despised by the other boyars for his Tatar origins, Godunov was later suspected of having arranged the mysterious **death of Dmitry**, at Uglich in 1591 – though all that is certain is that he rewarded one of the Tsarevich's servants afterwards. The official explanation was that Dmitry fatally stabbed himself during an epileptic fit.

Whatever the truth, Godunov deftly staged his own **accession to the throne** after Fyodor died in 1598, bringing the Rurik dynasty to an end. At the instigation of his agents, a crowd of clerics and commoners went to the Novodevichiy Convent to beg Fyodor's widow to bless her brother as the heir. Godunov was waiting there, and with a show of dismay emerged from her quarters to be acclaimed as Tsar – a verdict later endorsed by the Assembly of Notables.

However, his devious statecraft was no match for a run of **disasters** after 1601. Famine and plague beggared the towns and rural areas fell into brigandage, while Godunov was compelled to raise taxes to combat disorder. Under such conditions, it was relatively easy for him to be challenged by an imposter claiming descent from the Ruriks – even one who identified himself as Ivan the Terrible's son Dmitry, miraculously saved from his killers at Uglich.

### The False Dimitrys

The **first False Dmitry** was a minor official's son named Grigory Otrepiev, who fled to Poland and pressed his claim with the aid of the Jesuits. His small invasion force was helped by Cossacks and robber bands, but, above all, by Boris Godunov's timely death in April 1605. Though popularly acclaimed as Tsar, Dmitry soon alienated Muscovites with his Polish ways and advisors; the boyars by ordering them to fight bears with spears; and the Church by violating nuns. The final straw was his wedding to a Polish bride in May 1606, at which the Poles sat on holy relics and lounged against the iconostasis in the Cathedral of the Ascension.

A week later, the boyar **Vasily Shyuskiy** led a force of conspirators into the Kremlin while supporters roused the city with cries of "The Poles are killing the Tsar". Inside the citadel, Shyuskiy had a different war cry: "Death to the heretics! Death to the imposter!". As the mob ransacked his palace, Dmitry leapt from the walls to escape and broke his leg. Captured by the Streltsy, he protested his sincerity till he was torn to pieces; his remains were fired from a cannon in the direction of Poland. The Shyuskiy clan took power, but their writ barely extended beyond Moscow.

In 1607, a **second False Dmitry** entered Russia backed by a Polish-Lithuanian army, and ensconced himself at Tushino, outside Moscow, to await the fall of the Shyuskiys. However, the "Scoundrel of Tushino" dallied too long, and early in 1610 the Shyuskiys drove him out, later bribing his servants to murder him. Meanwhile, Russia was ravaged by feuding boyars, serf and Cossack revolts, Swedish and Polish invasions. This **Time of Troubles** (Smutnoe vreme) was burned into the national psyche for generations afterwards, with the added humiliation that, in 1610, even "Holy Mother" Moscow succumbed to the Poles.

Then, when all seemed lost, Russia demonstrated the astonishing powers of recovery that would save it at other critical moments in history.

Abbot Palitsyn of the Trinity Monastery of St Sergei declared a holy war and vowed to excommunicate anyone who failed to support it. The **liberation of Moscow** was accomplished by a volunteer army under **Prince Pozharskiy** of Suzdal and the butcher **Kosma Minin** of Nizhniy Novgorod, whose citizens financed the campaign. Having recaptured Moscow in 1612, they went on to expel the Poles from Russian soil by the year's end.

## The early Romanovs

In the aftermath of the war, dissension arose again among the *boyars* over who should be elected as Tsar. Disgruntled that his own candidacy had been rejected, Prince Trubetskoy proposed the four-year-old son of the second False Dmitry, confiding to a friend: "Those sons of bitches won't have me, a Russian Prince and a Cossack *hetman*, so I'll slip in their way the son of a thief and a Polish whore. Then let them get out of that mess!" To resolve the impasse, Abbot Palitsyn proposed **Mikhail Romanov**, the brother of Ivan the Terrible's first wife, whose accession in 1613 marked the end of the Time of Troubles and the beginning of the Romanov dynasty.

Moscow made a dramatic recovery, with a spate of new stone churches in the tent-roofed style symbolizing the close co-operation between church and state, which reached its zenith under Mikhail's successor, **Alexei II** (1645–76), known as "The Quiet" for his piety and love of books. It was during his reign that **Patriarch Nikon** precipitated a schism in the Orthodox Church by reforming its rituals, leading to the exile of such prominent "Old Believers" as Bishop Avvakum and the *Boyarina* Morozova. Another innovation was the establishment of the so-called **German Suburb**, to house foreign soldiers, doctors, engineers and others with professional skills that Russia lacked, due to its backwardness and conservatism.

In 1669, the Tsar's wife, Maria Miloslavskaya, died during childbirth, leaving two young sons to continue the dynasty: the frail Fyodor and his imbecilic younger brother, Ivan. Within a year, Tsar Alexei took another wife, Natalya Naryshkina, whose Naryshkin relatives promptly displaced his former wife's kinsfolk at court, and congratulated themselves on their future prospects following the birth of a healthy son named Peter – subsequently known to history as Peter the Great.

## Peter the Great

**Peter the Great** (*Pyotr Veliki*) ranks alongside Ivan the Terrible and Stalin in the pantheon of despots who coaxed Russia through a series of fundamental transformations. His greatest monument is St Petersburg, the capital city that he created from nothing – to replace Moscow, which represented all that he detested and reminded him of his traumatic youth. His energy was as extraordinary as his physique: Peter was six feet four inches tall, with a disproportionately small head.

When Peter was three, his father's demise made him an unwanted offspring. His sickly half-brother, **Fyodor**, became Tsar, and the Miloslavskiy *boyars* returned to court, banishing Peter's Naryshkin relatives. Peter continued to live uneventfully at Kolomenskoe until 1682, when the death of Fyodor left him the heir to the throne, at the age of ten. The Miloslavskiys retaliated by organizing a **Streltsy revolt**, during which several Naryshkins were butchered in front of Peter in the Kremlin. The upshot was that his retarded sibling, **Ivan**, was recognized as co-Tsar, and his scheming half-sister, **Sofia**, became **Regent**.

While Sofia ruled from the Kremlin, Peter pursued his boyish enthusiasms at Preobrazhenskoe, staging wargames with his "toy regiments" and learning how to sail. However, **conflict** was inevitable as he came of age and, in August 1689, Sofia ordered the *Streltsy* to mobilize, spurring Peter to flee to the Trinity Monastery of St Sergei. Safe within its walls, his party issued appeals for loyalty, and were heartened by the defection of the Patriarch from Sofia's camp. By October, her support had collapsed and she was confined to the Novodevichiy Convent.

Initially, Peter left affairs of state to his Naryshkin elders, preferring to dally in the German Suburb, imbibing foreign ways with cronies like Lefort and Menshikov. His first serious venture was an attempt to capture the Turkish fort of **Azov**, which failed in 1695, but was pursued the following year until the city fell. It was the first Russian victory since Alexei's reign, and served notice that Russia could no longer be trifled with. Soon afterwards, Peter announced plans to colonize Azov and construct a fleet, followed by the astounding news that he intended to make a **"Grand Tour"** of Europe in 1697.

Never before had a Tsar travelled abroad; even stranger, Peter chose to go "incognito", to be free to study shipbuilding in Holland and England, where he mastered the skills by working in the dockyards. He also met monarchs and conversed with Isaac Newton and other learned figures of the age. Peter was gripped by it all, and became determined to drag his nation into the modern world. During his homeward journey in 1698, the *Streltsy* rebelled again, but were crushed by his foreign-officered Guards regiments. Peter later participated in the mass execution of the rebels, on Red Square.

### Peter's reforms

The Tsar lost no time in assailing everything that Russians held dear. Aided by his court jester, he shaved off the beards of his courtiers, forced them to smoke tobacco and wear frock coats instead of caftans. The nation's name was changed from Muscovy to Russia, and the Orthodox calendar replaced by the "Popish" Julian version. Foreigners were invited to settle where they liked and worship as they wished. Peter forced the sons of landowners into the military or civil service, and conscripted serfs into the army for 25 years. The Church's power was broken by replacing the self-governing Patriarchate with a Holy Synod, subordinate to the Tsar. Even beards were taxed to raise revenue.

To enforce such changes, Peter relied on traditional methods of repression, and invented new ones. He introduced the internal passport system, later so beloved of the Communists, and organized forced labour gangs to build his grand projects. Faced with opposition, he was ruthless, overseeing the torture and death of his own son, Alexei, whom he suspected of conspiring against him. Many of his reforms were simply intended to improve Russia's strength during the long **Northern War** against **Sweden** (1700–21), which began with their youthful monarch, Charles XII, putting the Russians to flight at **Narva**. However, Charles failed to press his advantage by marching on Moscow, concentrating on subduing the rebellious Poles instead.

### St Petersburg

This lull in the war enabled Peter to strengthen Russia's hold on the Gulf of Finland, and fulfil the **quest for a seaport and a navy** that had long dominated his thinking. According to Pushkin's poetic account of its foundation in 1703, the Tsar cut two lengths of turf, laid them crossways, and declaimed: "By nature we are fated here to cut a window through to Europe". As a place to found a city, it was hardly ideal: a fetid marshland prone to flooding, with few natural or human resources nearby.

The **creation of St Petersburg** was accomplished by forced labour, under terrible conditions. Thousands died of starvation, cold, disease and exhaustion. Basic tools were so scarce that earth had to be carried in the workers' clothing. In the summer of 1706, with the city barely on the map, Charles XII invaded from Poland and again came within an ace of victory before making the fateful decision to concentrate his efforts on Ukraine, culminating in his defeat at Poltava in 1709. The Northern War dragged on for another twelve years, but, as Peter put it, "Now the final stone has been laid on the foundation of St Petersburg".

In 1710, the Imperial family moved there together with all government offices, and in 1712 St Petersburg was declared the **capital**. To populate the city, landowners and nobles were obliged to resettle there and finance the building of their own houses. The Tsar drafted in 40,000 workmen a year from the provinces, and overcame a shortage of stonemasons by prohibiting building in stone elsewhere in Russia. In Moscow, church building ceased, and wealthy citizens complained of having to establish new households far from home, at vast expense. Though they hated St Petersburg and returned to Moscow whenever possible, the lure of the court would eventually ensure that the old capital was eclipsed by its new rival. As Pushkin wrote in *The Bronze Horseman*:

> Old Moscow's paled before this other
> metropolis; it's just the same
> as when a widowed Dowager Empress
> bows to a young Tsaritsa's claim.

## Peter the Great's successors

Having killed his only son, Peter was obliged to issue a decree claiming the right to nominate his successor, but when he died in 1725, he was so ill that he was unable to speak. Initially his wife, **Catherine I**, was hailed as Tsaritsa and ruled in tandem with Menshikov (see p.137), but she died after less than two years. Peter's young grandson, **Peter II**, became Tsar, exiled Menshikov to Siberia and moved the capital back to Moscow in 1728. However, on the eve of his wedding day in 1730, he died of smallpox in the Lefort Palace, leaving the throne vacant and no obvious successor.

In desperation, the Supreme Privy Council turned to the widowed Anna Ivanovna, a German-born niece of Peter the Great. **Empress Anna** re-established St Petersburg as the capital and brought with her an entourage of unpopular German courtiers. Her reign (1730–40) was cruel and decadent. Affairs of state were carried out by her German favourite, Ernst-Johann Biron, whose rule of terror, known as the *Bironovshchina*, involved the execution of thousands of alleged opponents.

Anna died childless, leaving the crown to her great-nephew, **Ivan VI** (1740–41), who because of his youth was put under the regency of his mother, Anna Leopoldovna. However, real power remained in the hands of the hated Biron until a coup, backed by the Preobrazhenskiy Guards and financed with French money, elevated Peter the Great's daughter Elizabeth to the throne.

## Empress Elizabeth

Like her father, **Elizabeth** was stubborn, quick-tempered and devoted to Russia, but, unlike him, she detested serious occupations and "abandoned herself to every excess of intemperance and lubricity". Elizabeth was almost illiterate and her court favourite, Razumovskiy (a Cossack shepherd turned chorister whom she secretly married), couldn't write at all. She liked dancing and hunting, and lived in chaotic apartments, with wardrobes stacked with 15,000 dresses, and the floors littered with unpaid bills. Her continual moving from palace to palace and from hunting party to monastery resulted in a budget deficit of eight million rubles.

Although Elizabeth hated the sight of blood, she would order torture at the slightest offence. Yet she abolished the death penalty and was sensible enough to retain as one of her principal advisors the enlightened Count Shuvalov, who encouraged her in the foundation of **Moscow University**, under the direction of **Mikhail Lomonosov** (1711–65), a polymath known as the "Russian Leonardo". In fact, the cultural achievements of Catherine the Great were based more than she liked to admit on the foundations laid in Elizabeth's reign. In foreign affairs, Elizabeth displayed a determined hostility towards Prussia, participating in both the War of Austrian Succession (1740–48) and the Seven Years' War (1756–63), during which Russian troops occupied Berlin.

## Peter III

On Elizabeth's death in 1761, the new Tsar – her nephew, **Peter III** – adopted a strongly pro-Prussian policy, forcing the army into Prussian uniforms and offending the clergy by adhering to the Lutheran faith of his Holstein homeland. The one concession to the nobility during his six-month reign was the abolition of the compulsory 25-year state service. It was a decree of great consequence, for it created a large, privileged leisured class, hitherto unknown in Russia. Childish, moody and impotent, Peter was no match for his intelligent, sophisticated wife, Sophia of Anhalt-Zerbst, who ingratiated herself with her subjects by joining the Orthodox Church, changing her name to Catherine in the process. Their marriage was a sham, and in June 1762 she and her favourite, Grigory Orlov, orchestrated a coup d'état with the backing of the Guards regiments. Peter was imprisoned outside St Petersburg, and later murdered by Orlov.

# Catherine the Great

The reign of **Catherine the Great** spanned four decades (1762–96) and saw the emergence of Russia as a truly great European power. Catherine was a woman of considerable culture and learning and a great patron of the arts. Inevitably, however, she is best known for her private life; her most prominent courtier – and lover – Prince Potemkin, oversaw one of the greatest territorial gains of her reign, the annexation of the Crimea (1783), which secured the Black Sea coast for Russia.

After consolidating her position as an autocrat – after all, she had no legitimate claim to the throne – Catherine enjoyed a brief honeymoon as a liberal. French became the language of the court and with it came the ideas of the **Enlightenment**. Catherine herself conducted a lengthy correspondence with Voltaire, while Lomonosov was encouraged to standardize the Russian language. However, the lofty intentions of her reforms were watered down by her advisors to little more than a reassertion of "benevolent" despotism. When it came to the vital question of the emancipation of the serfs, the issue was swept under the carpet. And when writers like **Alexander Radishchev** began to take her at her word and publish critical works, she responded by exiling them to Siberia.

Catherine's liberal leanings were given a severe jolt by the **Pugachev Uprising**, which broke out east of the River Volga in 1773, under the leadership of a Don Cossack named Pugachev. It was the most serious peasant revolt in the entire 300-year rule of the Romanovs. Encouraged by the hope that, since the nobility had been freed from state service, the serfs would likewise be emancipated, thousands responded to Pugachev's call for freedom from the landowners and division of their estates. For two years, Pugachev's forces conducted a guerilla campaign from Perm in the Urals to Tsaritsyn on the Volga, before being crushed by the army. The French Revolution killed off what was left of Catherine's benevolence, and in her later years she relied ever more heavily on the powers of unbridled despotism.

## Paul and Alexander I

On Catherine's death in 1796, her son **Paul** became Tsar. Not without good reason, Paul detested his mother and everything associated with her, and immediately set about reversing most of her policies: his first act was to give his father, Peter III, a decent burial. Like his father, Paul was a moody and militarily obsessed man, who worshipped everything Prussian. He offended the army by forcing the Guards regiments back into Prussian uniforms, earned the enmity of the nobility by attempting to curtail some of the privileges they had enjoyed under Catherine, and reintroduced the idea of male hereditary succession abandoned by Peter the Great.

In March 1801, Paul was strangled to death in St Petersburg, in a palace coup that had the tacit approval of his son, **Alexander I**. Alexander shared Catherine's penchant for the ideas of the Enlightenment, but also exhibited a strong streak of religious conservatism. His reign (1801–25) was, in any case, dominated by foreign affairs – the Napoleonic Wars, above all. Initially, Alexander sought to contain France by an alliance with Austria and Prussia, but when this failed he signed the Treaty of Tilsit (1807) with Napoleon, in a hut moored on the River Niemen, which separated their domains. Like the pact between Stalin and Hitler 132 years later, this *volte face* was intended to buy time to prepare for war, which seemed inevitable.

## The Patriotic War and the burning of Moscow

In June 1812, **Napoleon** crossed the Niemen and invaded Russia with his *Grande Armée* of 600,000 – twice the size of any force the Russians could muster. The Russians employed "scorched earth" tactics and harassed the French flanks with partisans, but public opinion demanded a stand. Against his wishes, Marshal Kutuzov was obliged to fight a pitched battle, despite being outnumbered. The **Battle of Borodino** (September 7) killed 70,000 on both sides and left Kutuzov's forces so weak that defending Moscow seemed impossible. To save his troops, Kutuzov withdrew northwards, allowing Napoleon to advance on Moscow, starting a frenzied exodus of civilians.

Having waited in vain for a delegation of nobles to offer him the keys to the city, Napoleon entered Moscow on September 14 to find that over 100,000 inhabitants had fled. That same night, agents of the Tsarist Governor started fires in the Kitay-gorod, which a powerful wind the next day fanned into a conflagration. The following day, Napoleon was obliged to flee to a palace outside Moscow, as the Kremlin was engulfed in smoke and cinders, while his troops abandoned firefighting to loot. **Moscow burned** for six days, until three-quarters of its buildings were reduced to ashes.

Though the French lived off neighbouring estates and villages as best they could, staying for long was hardly feasible, and Tsar Alexander refused to surrender. With winter approaching and Russian forces mustering to the north, Napoleon had no choice but to begin the long **retreat** home. Harassed by Cossacks and partisans, and unprepared for the ferocity of the Russian winter, the *Grande Armée* had shrunk to a mere 30,000 men when it finally reached Poland. The Russians didn't stop there but pursued Napoleon all the way back to Paris, which they occupied in 1814. At the Congress of Vienna the following year, Russia was assured of its share in the carve-up of Europe.

## The reconstruction of Moscow and the Decembrist revolt

Within months of the fire, a commission for the **reconstruction of Moscow** was formed, and submitted its proposals to Tsar Alexander. The plan involved creating new squares where

Moscow's radial avenues met the Beliy and Zemlyanoy Gorod walls, which were levelled and turned into boulevards. Private houses were swiftly rebuilt, and within five years Moscow had almost replaced its residential quarters (chiefly with wooden dwellings, which still accounted for over half the buildings in the city forty years later). The architect Bove was alone responsible for about 500 buildings, many in the Russian Empire style that reflected the widespread mood of patriotic pride.

Another result of the war was that it exposed thousands of Russians to life in other countries. The aristocracy and gentry noted parliaments and constitutional monarchies, while peasant foot soldiers saw how much better their lot could be without serfdom. As the Tsar and his ministers were sure that any reforms would endanger autocracy, opposition festered underground. Guards officers and liberal aristocrats formed groups with innocuous names such as the "Southern Society" and the "Northern Society", which disseminated propaganda and even planned to assassinate the Tsar.

When Alexander died in November 1825, without leaving a male heir, the plotters sought to take advantage of the dynastic crisis that ensued. The Guards initially swore allegiance to Alexander's brother, Constantine, who was next in line for the throne, but who had secretly relinquished the succession. A coup was hurriedly devised, to be staged on the day that troops were to swear a new oath of allegiance to Alexander's younger brother, Nicholas. On December 14, in St Petersburg, rebels and loyalist troops faced each other across Senate Square for six hours, both unwilling to shoot, until Nicholas gave the order to attack. Two hours later, the revolt was crushed and hundreds of corpses were tipped into the River Neva.

Those of the **Decembrists** who survived were personally interrogated by Nicholas, who sentenced five of the ringleaders to death and exiled more than a hundred to Siberia. Though no mention of this "horrible and extraordinary plot" (as he called it) was allowed in public, the fate of so many aristocrats inevitably resulted in gossip – especially when Countess Volkonskaya followed her husband into exile, inspiring other wives to do likewise. Although the Decembrists themselves failed, their example would be upheld by future generations of Russian revolutionaries.

## Nicholas I

The reign of **Nicholas I** (1825–55) was epitomized by the slogan "Orthodoxy, Autocracy, Nationality", as coined by one of his ministers. The status quo was to be maintained at all costs: censorship increased, as did police surveillance, carried out by the infamous **Third Section** of the Tsar's personal Chancellory. A uniformed gendarmerie was created and organized along military lines, while an elaborate network of spies and informers kept a close watch on all potential subversives.

As ever, the most intractable problem was **serfdom** – "the powder-magazine under the state", as his police chief dubbed it – which affected eighty percent of the population and gave rise to several rebellions in the late 1820s, though none approached the scale of the Pugachev revolt. It also hampered industrialization in Russia, which was mostly confined to the textiles and sugar-beet industries.

During the 1840s, the greatest change occurred in the upper echelons of society, as deferential admiration for Tsarism was gradually replaced by scorn and dissent. The writer Dostoyevsky was among those drawn to the clandestine **Petrashevskiy Circle** of utopian socialists, based in St Petersburg. In 1849, over a hundred of them were arrested as Nicholas clamped down in the wake of revolutions in Poland and Hungary, which his armies put down, earning him the nickname the "Gendarme of Europe".

In early 1854, the **Crimean War** broke out and Russia found itself at war with Britain, France and Turkey. The war highlighted the flaws and inadequacies inherent in the Tsarist Empire: Russian troops defending Sevastopol faced rifles with muskets; Russian sailing ships had to do battle with enemy steamers; and the lack of railways meant that Russian soldiers were no better supplied than their Allied counterparts, who were thousands of miles from home. The Allied capture of Sevastopol in 1855 almost certainly helped to accelerate the death of the despondent Nicholas, whose last words of advice to his heir were "Hold on to everything!".

## The Tsar Liberator: Alexander II

In fact, the new Tsar, **Alexander II** (1855–81), had little choice but to sue for peace, and for those who hoped for change in Russia, the defeats of the Crimean War came as a blessing. The surviving Decembrists and Petrashevskiy exiles were released, police surveillance eased and many of the censorship restrictions were lifted.

In 1861, Alexander II signed the historic decree allowing for the **emancipation of the serfs**, earning himself the sobriquet "Tsar Liberator". In reality, the Emancipation Act was a fraud, replacing the landowner's legal ownership with a crushing economic dependence in the form of financial compensation, which the freed serfs were forced to pay their landlords over a period of forty-nine years. However, Alexander did push through other reforms that represented a break with the past, introducing trial by jury and a limited form of local self-government through appointed zemstva (assemblies); and reducing military service from twenty-five years to six.

### Populists and assassins

However, Alexander's reforms stopped short of a constitutional shift from autocracy, disappointing those who had hoped for a "revolution from above". The 1860s witnessed an upsurge in peasant unrest and a radicalization of the opposition movement among the educated elite. From their ranks came the amorphous **Populist** (Narodnik) movement, which gathered momentum throughout the late 1860s and early 1870s. The Populists' chief ideologue, Nikolai Chernyshevskiy, was committed to establishing a socialist society based around the peasant commune. There were, however, widely differing views on the best means of achieving this end. The clandestine organization "Hell" – or **"Nihilists"** as Turgenev dubbed them in his novel Fathers and Sons (1862) – led the charge with the first attempt on the Tsar's life.

Others believed in taking the Populist message to the people. This campaign reached a climax in the "crazy summer" of 1874, when thousands of students, dressed as simple folk, roamed the countryside, attempting to convert the peasantry to their cause. Most of these exhortations fell on deaf ears, for although the peasantry were fed up with their lot, they were suspicious of all townspeople and, for the most part, remained blindly loyal to the Tsar. The authorities were nevertheless sufficiently alarmed to make mass arrests, which culminated in the much publicized trials of "the 50" and "the 193", later held in St Petersburg.

The failure of the campaign led to a return to conspiratorial methods. In 1876, a new revolutionary organization called **Land and Liberty** was founded, which rapidly split into the "**Black Partition**", which agitated for seizures of property in the countryside, and the notorious **People's Will** (Narodnaya Volya), whose run of urban terrorist acts culminated in the assassination of Tsar Alexander II in 1881.

## Alexander III and industrialization

However, regicide failed to stir the masses to revolution, and the new Tsar, **Alexander III** (1881–94), shelved all constitutional reforms, increased police surveillance and cut back the powers of the zemstva. His ultra-reactionary advisor, Pobedonostov, blamed dissent on the Jews, so that the police stood by during a wave of **pogroms** in 1881–82, which were followed by harsh anti-Semitic laws, under which 20,000 Jews were expelled from Moscow to the "Pale of Settlement".

**Industrialization** had burgeoned since the Emancipation Act, and foreign investment had nearly doubled, giving Russia a rate of growth outstripping that of other major European powers. In Moscow, huge suburban factories and slums sprang up, drawing in thousands of peasants and creating an increasingly large urban working class, whose impact would be felt in the late 1890s. Meanwhile, the nouveaux-riche **Kuptsy** whose ancestors had toiled as serfs displayed their wealth by commissioning architects like Shekhtel to build them fabulous Style Moderne mansions, and sponsored endeavours such as the Tretyakov Gallery and the Moscow Arts Theatre.

## Nicholas II

When Alexander III died in 1894, the throne passed to his son, **Nicholas II** (1894–1917), who signalled his intention to continue his father's policies by denouncing the constitutional reforms proposed by the zemstvo of Tver as "senseless dreams". In the same year, he married the German-born Princess Alexandra of Hesse, whose autocratic spirit and extreme Orthodoxy exerted an unhealthy influence. Their coronation in Moscow in May 1896 was marred by the **Khodynka Field disaster** (see p.270), widely seen as a bad omen for what would prove to be a doomed reign.

## The new opposition

Although Populism had been discredited by the failure of terrorism to ignite a revolution, a new generation of radicals emerged in the late 1890s as the Socialist Revolutionary Party, or **SRs**, publicizing their cause through acts such as the assassination of the Tsar's chief minister, Plehve – but still failed to attract the peasantry to its cause.

Meanwhile, a section of the Russian intelligentsia had begun to shift its ideological stance towards **Marxism**, which pinned its hopes on the urban proletariat as the future agent of revolution. The first Marxist organization, "Emancipation of Labour", was founded in 1883 by a handful of ex-Populist exiles in Switzerland, including the "father of Russian Marxism", **Georgy Plekhanov**. The group was so small that, when out boating on Lake Geneva, Plekhanov once joked "Be careful: if this boat sinks, it's the end of Russian Marxism".

Plekhanov teamed up with Vladimir Ilyich Ulyanov – later known as **Lenin** – to form the **Russian Social Democratic Labour Party** (RSDLP), which was founded (and immediately suppressed) in 1898. Forced into exile, divisions quickly began to appear: Lenin arguing for a conspiratorial, disciplined party, while his chief rival, Martov, wanted a more open, mass membership. In the split that followed, Lenin managed to claim for his supporters the description **Bolsheviks** (meaning "majority" in Russian), while his opponents became known as **Mensheviks** ("minority", with all its connotations of weakness).

Meanwhile, the non-radical liberal bourgeoisie tended to back the Constitutional Democratic Party, or **Kadets**, whose modest demands for freedom of the press, assembly and association were also revolutionary in the context of Tsarist Russia.

## The 1905 Revolution

The economic boom of the late 1890s came to an abrupt end in 1900 and was followed by a slump that put many of the urban working class out of work. In January 1904, Russia blundered into a **war with Japan**, which soon exposed the total incompetence of its Naval and Army High Commands. But worse was to follow on the home front, as the Tsarist regime faced its most serious challenge since the Pugachev uprising in the eighteenth century.

In early January 1905, a strike broke out at the giant Putilov engineering works in St Petersburg, which quickly spread to other factories. On January 9, 150,000 strikers and their families set off to hand a petition to the Tsar, demanding basic civil rights and labour laws. They marched peacefully, singing hymns and carrying portraits of the Tsar – until they met the Imperial Guard, which opened fire to disperse the crowds, killing and wounding several thousand. **Bloody Sunday** marked a fatal breach in the social contract, and for the rest of his reign, the Tsar would never quite shake off his reputation as "Bloody Nicholas".

When the first wave of strikes petered out, Nicholas hoped that a quick victory in the war against the Japanese would ease his troubles at home, but instead, the Russian Fleet was decimated at Tsushima Bay, and a mutiny occurred on the battleship *Potemkin*. Reluctantly, the Tsar was obliged to make peace with Japan and forced to agree to the establishment of a consultative assembly – or **Duma** – at home, but this limited concession failed to avert further strikes in St Petersburg or the growing unrest within the army.

Soon, Nicholas had little choice but to issue the so-called **October Manifesto**, promising basic civil liberties and the right of the future Duma to veto laws. Meanwhile, the workers seized the initiative and created the **St Petersburg Soviet**, made up of 500-odd delegates, elected by over 200,000 workers. Under the co-chairmanship of **Trotsky** (who had yet to join the Bolsheviks), it pursued a moderate policy, criticizing the proposed Duma, but falling far short of calling for an armed uprising – as the middle classes feared would happen.

By December, the regime had recovered its nerve and, emboldened by divisions among the opposition, clamped down in St Petersburg, where the leaders of the Soviet were arrested. In Moscow, local Bolsheviks misjudged the situation and led radical workers in a vain attempt to seize power. Having failed to break through into the centre of town, they barricaded themselves into the **Krasnaya Presnya** district. The government used artillery to smash the barricades, and then sent in cavalry and machine-gun units to crush any remaining resistance. In the aftermath, hundreds were summarily executed by field tribunals or exiled to Siberia.

### The last decade of Tsarism

With the revolutionary tide ebbing (though sporadic unrest persisted until 1907), the main task facing the Tsar was how to confront the new Duma, following the first nationwide elections in Russian history. The franchise was broad-based, though a long way from universal suffrage, and the Kadets emerged as the largest grouping. In May 1906, the opening of the **First Duma** in St Petersburg's Tauride Palace was attended by diverse figures, from Grand Dukes to peasants' and workers' deputies in overalls and muddy boots. After ten weeks of debate, the issue of land distribution reared its ugly head, prompting the Tsar to surround the palace with troops and dissolve the Duma. The succeeding Second Duma suffered a similar fate.

The most positive post-revolutionary repercussions took place within the **arts**. From 1905 to 1914, Moscow and St Petersburg experienced an extraordinary outburst of artistic energy: Diaghilev's *Ballets Russes* dazzled Europe; Chekhov premiered his works at the Moscow Arts Theatre; poets and writers held Symbolist seances; while Mayakovsky and other self-proclaimed Futurists toured the country, shocking the general public with their statements on art.

Meanwhile, the Imperial family abandoned the capital for the security of their palaces outside St Petersburg, and fell further under the influence of the charlatan **Rasputin**, upon whom they pinned all their hopes for the survival of the haemophiliac heir, Tsarevich Alexei. The celebrations in honour of the **tercentenary of the Romanov dynasty** in 1913 (during which the Court wore bejewelled caftans in the style of their seventeenth-century forebears) were effectively their swansong.

In the nationalistic fervour that accompanied the outbreak of **World War I** in August 1914, the name of the capital was deemed too Germanic and changed to **Petrograd**. Yet serious deficiencies in the structure of the army and military production were barely acknowledged, let alone tackled. The first Russian offensive ended in defeat at Tannenberg, with 170,000 casualties. From then on, there was rarely any good news from the front; in the first year alone, some four million soldiers lost their lives. Hoping to improve matters, the Tsar assumed personal command of the armed forces – a post for which he was unqualified.

By the end of 1916, even monarchists were voicing reservations. The Tsar's German-born wife was openly accused of treason, while Rasputin was assassinated by a group of aristocrats desperate to force a change of policy. Firmly ensconced with his son in the Imperial headquarters at Mogilev, Nicholas refused to be moved. As inflation spiralled and food shortages worsened, strikes began to break out once more in Petrograd. By the beginning of 1917 everyone, from generals to peasants, talked of an imminent revolution.

## The February Revolution

On February 22, there was a lockout of workers at the Putilov works in Petrograd – the **February Revolution** had begun. The following day (International Women's Day), thousands of women and workers thronged the streets attacking bread shops, singing the *Marseillaise* and calling for the overthrow of the Tsar. On February 27, prisons were stormed and the Duma was surrounded by demonstrators and mutinous troops, while Trotsky and the Mensheviks re-established the Soviet. On March 2, en route to the capital, the Tsar was persuaded to **abdicate** in favour of his brother, who gave up his own claim the following day, bringing the Romanov dynasty to an end.

Out of the revolutionary ferment, a system of "dual power" arose. The **Provisional Government**, under the liberal Count Lvov, attempted to assert itself as the legitimate successor to autocracy by decreeing freedom of speech and an amnesty. There were to be elections for a Constituent Assembly, but no end to the war. This pacified the generals, who might otherwise have tried to suppress the revolution, but eroded the government's popularity. The other power base was the Menshevik-dominated **Petrograd Soviet**, which was prepared to give qualified support to the "bourgeois revolution" until the time was ripe for the establishment of socialism. Their "Order No. 1", calling for the formation of Soviets throughout the army, subverted military discipline.

After ditching some of its right-wing elements, the Provisional Government co-operated more closely with the Petrograd Soviet. **Alexander Kerensky** became the Minister of War and toured the front calling for a fresh offensive against the Germans. The attack began well but soon turned into a retreat, while discontent in

Petrograd peaked again in a wave of violent protests known as the **July Days**. Lenin, who had returned from exile, felt that the time was not right for a coup and, indeed, loyalist troops soon restored order. Trotsky and others were arrested, Lenin was accused of being a German spy and forced once more into exile, and the Bolsheviks as a whole were branded as traitors.

Kerensky used the opportunity to tighten his grip on the Provisional Government, taking over as leader from Prince Lvov. In late August, the army commander in chief, General Kornilov, attempted to march on Petrograd and crush Bolshevism once and for all. Whether he had been encouraged by Kerensky remains uncertain but, in the event, Kerensky decided to turn on Kornilov, denouncing the coup and calling on the Bolsheviks and workers' militia to defend the capital. Kerensky duly appointed himself commander in chief, but it was the Left who were now in the ascendant.

## The October Revolution

During September, Russia began to slide into chaos: soldiers deserted the front in ever greater numbers, and the countryside was in turmoil, while the "Bolshevization" of the Soviets continued apace. By October, Lenin had managed to persuade his colleagues that the time to seize power was nigh. Bolshevik Red Guards were trained and armed under the aegis of the **Military Revolutionary Committee**, based in the former Smolniy Institute for Ladies.

The **October Revolution** began in the early hours of the 25th (November 7 by today's calendar), with the occupation of key points in Petrograd. Posters announcing the overthrow of the Provisional Government appeared on the streets at 10am, though it wasn't until 2am the following morning that the Cabinet were arrested in the Winter Palace. In contrast to the almost bloodless coup in Petrograd, Moscow witnessed a week of fierce battles between Red Guards and loyalist troops holed up in the Kremlin and the *Metropol Hotel*.

The coup had been planned to coincide with the Second All-Russian Congress of Soviets, at which the Bolsheviks' majority was enhanced when the Mensheviks and right-wing SRs walked out in protest. Lenin delivered his famous decrees calling for an end to the war and approving the seizure of land by the peasants. An all-Bolshevik **Council of People's Commissars** was established and issued a spate of decrees nationalizing banks and financial organizations and instituting an eight-hour working day.

Conditions in Petrograd and Moscow worsened. Food was scarcer than ever, while rumours of anti-Bolshevik plots abounded. In December 1917, Lenin created the "All-Russian Extraordinary Commission for Struggle against Counter-Revolution, Speculation and Sabotage", or **Cheka** for short (meaning "linchpin" in Russian). Although the Bolsheviks had reluctantly agreed to abolish the death penalty in October, the *Cheka*, under "Iron" **Felix Dzerzhinsky**, reserved the right to "have recourse to a firing squad when it becomes obvious that there is no other way".

Following elections, the long-awaited **Constituent Assembly** met for the first and only time on January 5, 1918. As the first Russian parliament elected by universal suffrage, this was meant to be "the crowning jewel in Russian democratic life", but Lenin regarded it as "an old fairy tale which there is no reason to carry on further". Having received only a quarter of the vote, the Bolsheviks surrounded the premises the next day, preventing many delegates from entering; Red Guards eventually dismissed those inside with the words, "Push off. We want to go home."

## The Civil War 1918–20

More pressing than the internecine feuds of the socialist parties was the outcome of the peace negotiations with Germany. In mid-February of 1918, talks broke down and the Germans launched a fresh offensive in Russia, which met little effective resistance. Eventually, on March 3, Trotsky signed the **Treaty of Brest-Litovsk**, which handed over Poland, Finland, Belarus, the Baltics and – most painfully of all – Ukraine, Russia's bread basket. But German artillery remained within range of Petrograd, and renewed hostilities seemed likely, so in March 1918, the Bolshevik government moved to **Moscow**, and proclaimed it the **capital** of the fledgling Soviet state. Lenin stayed at the *National Hotel* before moving into the Kremlin, while the *Cheka* took over the Rossiya Insurance Company building on Lubyanka Square.

At the Seventh Party Congress, held in the Bolshoy Theatre, the RSDLP was renamed the **Communist Party**, and the Left-SRs quit in protest at the Brest-Litovsk treaty. On July 6–7, the assassination of the German ambassador heralded an abortive **Left-SR coup** in Moscow, during which Dzerzhinsky was held hostage at SR headquarters. In August they struck again, with the murder of the Petrograd *Cheka* chief, and an unsuccessful attempt on Lenin's life at a factory in Moscow. The Bolsheviks responded with a wave of repression known as the **Red Terror**. Thousands of hostages were imprisoned and shot. Dzerzhinsky's deputy pronounced that one look at a suspect's hands would suffice to determine his class allegiance.

By this time a **Civil War** was raging across Russia, fuelled by **foreign intervention**. In a vain attempt to force Russia back into the war against Germany, but also from fear of Bolshevism spreading, the Western powers sent troops to fight the Reds. A Czechoslovak Legion seized control of the Trans-Siberian Railway; British troops landed in Murmansk and Baku; US, Japanese, French and Italian forces seized Vladivostok; while the Germans controlled the vast tracts of land given to them under the Brest-Litovsk treaty. Fearing that they would be freed from captivity in Yekaterinburg, Lenin and Sverdlov ordered the **execution of the Imperial family**, which was carried out by local Bolsheviks on July 16–17.

The survival of the Soviet regime owed to the Bolsheviks' ideological fervour and discipline, and their control of the **railways** emanating from Moscow, which enabled them to switch resources from one battlefront to another. Ex-Tsarist officers were forced to contribute their experience to the new **Red Army**, under the vigilant eye of regimental commissars, while Trotsky ranged across the Russian heartland in his armoured train, shooting commanders who disobeyed orders to hold ground at all costs. By contrast, the disparate anti-Soviet forces – or **Whites** – represented every strand of politics from monarchists to SRs, and lacked a unified command or centralized lines of communication. However, both sides were evenly matched in numbers and rivalled each other in ferocity when it came to exacting revenge on collaborators.

Not only did the Civil War cost the lives of thousands, but it promoted the militarization of Soviet society, under the rubric of "**War Communism**". Workers' control in the factories and the nationalization of land had plunged the Soviet economy into chaos just as the Civil War broke out. In an attempt to cope, the Bolsheviks introduced labour discipline of a kind not seen since the pre-trade union days of Tsarism. With money almost worthless, peasants had no incentive to sell their scarce produce in the cities, so Red Guards were sent into the countryside to seize food, and "committees of the poor" set up to stimulate class war against the richer peasantry, or *kulaks*.

## The Kronstadt revolt and the NEP

By 1921, Soviet Russia was economically devastated, and the Bolsheviks found themselves confronted with worker unrest at the same time as serious divisions began to appear within the Party. The most outspoken faction was the **Workers' Opposition**, whose main demands were for independent trade unions and fewer wage differentials. In February 1921, sailors at the Kronstadt naval base – who had been among the Bolsheviks' staunchest supporters since 1905 – turned against the Party. The **Kronstadt sailors' revolt** precipitated a general strike in Petrograd when troops once more refused to fire on crowds. Rejecting calls for negotiations, the Bolsheviks accused the sailors of treason and crushed the revolt.

Meanwhile, Lenin was presiding over the **Tenth Party Congress**, at which he declared a virtual end to democratic debate within the Party and banned all factions. From now on, real power was in the hands of the newly emerging Party bureaucracy, or **Secretariat**, whose first General Secretary, appointed towards the end of 1922, was the Georgian Bolshevik **Joseph Stalin**.

At the Congress, Lenin unveiled his **New Economic Policy** (NEP), which marked a retreat from War Communism. The state maintained control of the "commanding heights" of the economy, while reintroducing a limited free market for agricultural produce, giving the peasants an incentive to increase productivity. It was a compromise formula that favoured the peasantry (still the majority of the population) over the urban working class, who dubbed NEP the "New Exploitation of the Proletariat".

## The rise of Stalin

Following **Lenin's death** on January 24, 1924, an all-out power struggle began. Trotsky, the hero of the Civil War, and Bukharin, the chief exponent of the NEP, were by far the most popular figures in the Party, but it was Stalin, as head of the Secretariat, who held the real power. Stalin organized Lenin's funeral on Red Square and was the chief architect of his deification, which began with the renaming of Petrograd as **Leningrad**. By employing classic divide-and-rule tactics, Stalin picked off his rivals one by one, beginning with the exile of Trotsky in 1925, followed by the neutralization of Bukharin in 1929.

Abandoning the NEP, Stalin embarked on the **forced collectivization** of agriculture and industrialization on an unprecedented scale, under the **First Five Year Plan** (1928–32). Declaring its aim to be "the elimination of the *kulak* as a class", the Party waged open war on a peasantry that was overwhelmingly hostile to collectivization. The social and economic upheaval wrought on the country has been dubbed the "Third Revolution" – indeed, it transformed society more than any of the previous revolutions. The peasants' passive resistance, the destruction of livestock and the ensuing chaos all contributed to the **famine** of 1932–33, which surpassed even that of 1921–22, resulting in the death of as many as five million people.

### The General Plan for Moscow

In Moscow, however, many took pride in the achievements of Soviet power. Workers' families who had lived in shacks before the Revolution were now housed in subdivided apartments once owned by their social superiors, or even brand new flats in the apartment blocks that were rising across town – as in the famous Socialist Realist painting *A New Home on Tomorrow's Street.*

Future developments were laid out in the **General Plan for the Reconstruction of Moscow**, produced by a committee under Stalin and Kaganovich. Its aim was to transform Moscow into the showcase capital of the world's first socialist state; a city of grand boulevards and public buildings, converging on a ring of skyscrapers and the Palace of Soviets (see p.128). Its most ambitious aspect was the **Metro** (an idea that had been rejected as blasphemous when it was mooted in 1902). The first shaft was sunk in 1931, and the first line (with thirteen stations) opened in May 1935. *Pravda* lauded the efforts of Komsomol volunteers and drew a veil over the forced-labourers who also built the metro.

### The purges and show trials

It was in this climate that the Seventeenth Party "**Congress of Victors**" met in 1934. Stalin declared that the Party had triumphed over all opposition, and the nation was on the march to a glorious future. "Life has become better, Comrades. Life has become gayer." Of the 2000-odd delegates who applauded, two-thirds would be arrested in the course of the next five years.

The initial pretext for the mass purges was the mysterious assassination of the Leningrad Party boss, **Sergei Kirov**, on December 1, 1934. In Leningrad, 30,000 to 40,000 citizens were arrested during the spring of 1935 alone, while the total number across the Soviet Union over the next three years ran into millions. The **Great Terror** had a profound effect on society, instilling fear and conformity for long afterwards. Many believe that Stalin himself had ordered the murder of Kirov, to remove a potential rival in the Politburo and break any lingering resistance to his dictatorship.

In the summer of 1936, the first of the great **show trials** were held in Moscow's House of Unions, during which the veteran Bolsheviks Bukharin, Kamenev and Zinoviev "confessed" to Kirov's murder and were sentenced to death. In early 1937, similar accusations of spying on behalf of foreign powers were levelled at Yagoda, the head of the secret police, whose dwarfish successor, **Nikolai Yezhov**, gave his name to the Great Terror, which Russians call the *Yezhovshchina*. In December 1938, Yezhov was himself replaced by **Lavrenty Beria**, which the long-suffering Soviet people took as a signal that the worst was over, for the moment at least.

Few realized that purges within the **Red Army** had left it gravely weakened. From the defence minister, **Marshal Tukhachevskiy**, downwards, the majority of senior officers had either been shot or sent to labour camps, and their hastily promoted successors were underqualified and afraid to display any initiative. This was known to Hitler (whose secret service fed Stalin's paranoia about spies within the High Command), and figured in his calculations about the European balance of power.

As Anglo-French appeasement allowed Nazi Germany to invade Austria and Czechoslovakia, and to set its sights on Poland, Stalin feared that the USSR would be next on its *drang nach Osten* (Drive to the East) and authorized Foreign Minister Molotov to negotiate with his Nazi counterpart. The **Molotov–Ribbentrop pact** of August 1939 bound both parties to non-aggression, and the Soviets to deliver food and raw materials to the Nazis. It also contained secret clauses relating to the division of Poland and the Soviet occupation of the Baltic States, which were put into practice in the first weeks of World War II.

## The Great Patriotic War

Despite advance warnings from his agents in Germany and Japan, Stalin refused to believe that Hitler would break the pact, and was stunned by the Nazi invasion on June 22, 1941, which began what Russians call the **Great Patriotic War**. He is thought to have had a nervous breakdown and withdrawn to his *dacha* outside Moscow, while his subordinates attempted to grapple with the crisis. When Stalin returned to the Kremlin, he reputedly told them, "Lenin left us a great inheritance, and we, his heirs, have fucked it all up". Not until July 3 did he address the nation by radio, in a speech that began: "Brothers and sisters! I turn to you, my friends . . ."

In the first weeks of the war, over 1000 Soviet aircraft were destroyed on the ground; whole armies were encircled and captured; and local officials fled from the advancing *Wehrmacht*. Stalin had four army commanders shot and put two incompetent "cavalry generals" – Voroshilov and Budyonny – in charge of the western front (they were dismissed two months later).

By mid-October the Nazis were almost on the outskirts of **Moscow**; an advance patrol reportedly reached a suburban metro station. Four hundred and fifty thousand Muscovites were mobilized to dig trenches. On October 16, a decree on the evacuation of the government caused **panic**: the streets were choked with refugees and soot from burning archives. But Marshal Zhukov promised that Moscow could be held, so Stalin opted to stay and ordered that the traditional November parade should go ahead. The troops proceeded directly from Red Square to the battlefront, which was reinforced by fresh divisions from Siberia, equipped for winter warfare – unlike the Germans, clad in summer uniforms, with guns that jammed when the temperature sank to below 30°C. The front held, and Moscow was saved.

During four years of war, western Russia, Ukraine and Belarus were devastated, and twenty-seven million Soviet citizens were killed. Their sacrifices broke the back of Hitler's forces and brought the Red Army into the heart of Europe, determining the fate of those nations that subsequently formed the Eastern Bloc. On May 9,

1945, cannons and fireworks exploded above the Kremlin, to mark the end of war in Europe, and delirious crowds thronged the streets. At the great **victory parade** on Red Square, on June 22, Nazi banners were cast down before the Lenin Mausoleum, and trampled by stallions ridden by Soviet Marshals in magnificent uniforms.

## The post-war years and Stalin's death

In the immediate post-war years, Moscow was transformed by **huge construction projects**, using POWs and Soviet convicts as slave labour. The widening of the Garden Ring, the Kaluga Gates and the initial stages of Leninskiy and Kutuzovskiy prospekts were all completed at this time, as were several of the famous **Stalin skyscrapers**. Moscow was the mecca of world Communism, whose domain stretched from Berlin to the newly proclaimed Peoples' Republic of China – at least for the years of Sino-Soviet co-operation, symbolized by the *Pekin Hotel*, built to house visiting delegations. In 1949, Stalin's seventieth birthday occasioned a deluge of tributes, and his image was projected onto the clouds above the Kremlin, like a demigod's.

After the enormous sacrifices of the war, Soviet citizens longed for a peaceful, freer life. However, Stalin's advanced years prompted an intensification of the power struggle, which brought with it a fresh wave of arrests and show trials. The most powerful figure among his putative successors was **Andrei Zhdanov**, who had been in charge of Leningrad during the wartime siege. When Zhdanov died of alcoholism (or poison) in 1948, his enemies fabricated the "Leningrad Affair", in which his closest allies were accused of trying to seize power, and executed. Stalin's final show trial was the **"Doctors' Plot"**, in which a group of (mostly Jewish) physicians "confessed" to the murder of Zhdanov. Thankfully, two months into the charade, Stalin died, and the charges were later dropped.

The **death of Stalin** on March 5, 1953 (see p.110), occasioned a nationwide outpouring of grief, which was largely genuine. Nobody knows how many mourners were crushed to death outside the House of Unions, where his body lay in state in the Columned Hall where the show trials had been held in the 1930s. After decades of submission to the "Wise Father of all the Peoples", many citizens couldn't imagine how they could continue without him.

## Khrushchev and the "Thaw"

Following Stalin's death, the power struggle within the Soviet leadership continued unabated. Beria, the odious secret police chief, was the first to be arrested and executed in July 1953; Malenkov lasted until 1955, before he was forced to resign; whereas Molotov hung on until 1957. The man who was to emerge as the next Soviet leader was **Nikita Khrushchev**, who, in 1956, when his position was by no means unassailable, gave a **"Secret Speech"** to the Twentieth Party Congress, in which Stalin's name was for the first time officially linked with Kirov's murder and the sufferings of millions during the Terror. So traumatic was the revelation, many delegates are said to have had heart attacks on the spot. That year, thousands were rehabilitated and returned from the camps. Yet for all its outspokenness, Khrushchev's de-Stalinization was limited in scope – after all, he himself had earned the nickname "Butcher of the Ukraine" during the *Yezhovshchina*.

The **cultural thaw** that came in the wake of Khrushchev's speech was equally selective, allowing the publication of Alexander Solzhenitsyn's account of the Gulag, *A Day in the Life of Ivan Denisovich*, but rejecting Pasternak's *Doctor Zhivago*. Khrushchev emptied the camps only to fill them again, and added a new twist to the repression, sending many dissidents to psychiatric hospitals. In foreign affairs too, he was not one to shy away from confrontation. Soviet tanks spilled blood on the streets of Budapest in 1956; Khrushchev oversaw the building of the Berlin Wall; and in October 1962, he took the world to the brink of nuclear war during the Cuban Missile Crisis. He also boasted that the Soviet Union would surpass the West in the production of consumer goods within twenty years, and pinned the nation's hopes on developing the "Virgin Lands" of Siberia and Kazakhstan.

By 1964, Khrushchev had managed to alienate all the main interest groups within the Soviet hierarchy. His emphasis on nuclear rather than conventional weapons lost him the support of the military; his de-Stalinization was unpopular with the KGB; while his administrative reforms struck at the heart of the Party apparatus. As the Virgin Lands turned into a dust bowl, his economic boasts rang hollow and the Soviet public was deeply embarrassed by Khrushchev's *nekulturniy* (uncultured) behaviour at the United Nations, where he interrupted a speech by banging on the table with his shoe. In October 1964, his enemies took advantage of his vacation at the Black Sea to mount a bloodless coup and, on his return to Moscow, Khrushchev was presented with his resignation "for reasons of health". It was a sign of the changes since Stalin's death that he was the first disgraced Soviet leader to be allowed to live in obscurity, rather than being shot.

## The Brezhnev era

Under Khrushchev's ultimate successor, **Leonid Brezhnev**, many of the more controversial policies were abandoned. Military expenditure was significantly increased, attacks on Stalin ceased and the whole era of the Great Terror was studiously ignored in the official media. The show trial of the writers Sinyavsky and Daniel, which took place in February 1966, marked the official end to the "thaw", and was followed by a clampdown in all the major urban centres. The crushing of the Prague Spring in August 1968 showed that the new Soviet leaders could be just as ruthless as their predecessors, while at home, a tiny protest demonstration on Red Square was stamped out within minutes by the KGB.

Thanks to public indifference and press censorship, most Russian citizens knew little of **Alexander Solzhenitsyn** when he was deported to the West in 1974, and even less of **Andrei Sakharov**, the nuclear physicist sentenced to internal exile for his human rights campaigns. Despite the activities of the KGB, the Brezhnev era is now generally remembered in Russia as a rare period of peace and stability. With goods heavily subsidized, ordinary members of the public could bask in the knowledge that basic foodstuffs like meat and bread cost the same as they had done in 1950 (even if you did have to queue for them), while those with money had recourse to the burgeoning black market. The new-found security of the Party cadres, who were subjected to fewer purges than at any time since the Soviet system began, resulted in unprecedented levels of corruption.

As sclerosis set in across the board, industrial and agricultural output declined. By 1970, the average age of the Politburo was over seventy – embodying the geriatric nature of Soviet politics in what would later be called the **Era of Stagnation** (*zastoy*).

# Gorbachev's reforms

Brezhnev died in November 1982 and was succeeded by **Yuri Andropov**, the former KGB boss, who had hardly begun his anti-corruption campaign when he too expired, in February 1984. The Brezhnevite clique took fright at the prospect of yet more change and elected the 73-year-old **Konstantin Chernenko** as General Secretary, but when he also died, in March 1985, it was clear that the post required some new blood.

**Mikhail Gorbachev** – at 53, the youngest member of the Politburo – was chosen as Chernenko's successor with a brief to "get things moving". The first of his policies to send shock waves through Soviet society – a campaign against alcohol – was probably the most unpopular and unsuccessful of his career. This was followed shortly afterwards by the coining of the two now-famous buzz words of the Gorbachev era: **glasnost** (openness) and **perestroika** (restructuring). The first of these took a battering when, in April 1986, the world's worst nuclear disaster – at **Chernobyl** – was hushed up for a full three days, before the Swedes forced an admission out of the Soviet authorities. Muscovites realized that something was amiss when train-loads of evacuated children began arriving at Kiev Station. Similarly, Gorbachev denied the existence of political prisoners right up until Sakharov's unexpected release from exile in the "closed" city of Gorky. Sakharov returned to Moscow to a hero's welcome, and vowed to fight for the freedom of all.

Equally novel were the investigations into numerous officials who had abused their positions in the Brezhnev years. One of the most energetic campaigners against corruption was the new Moscow Party chief, **Boris Yeltsin**, whose populist antics, such as exposing black market dealings within the *apparat*, infuriated the old guard. In October 1987, Yeltsin openly attacked Gorbachev and the hardline ideologist Yegor Ligachev, and then dramatically resigned from the Politburo; shortly afterwards, he was sacked as Moscow Party leader.

Yeltsin's fate was a foretaste of things to come, as Gorbachev abandoned his balancing act between left and right and realigned himself with the hardliners. In the summer of 1988, radicals within the Party formed the **Democratic Union**, the first organized opposition movement to emerge since 1921. Gorbachev promptly banned its meetings and created a new Special-Purpose Militia unit – the **OMON** – to deal with any disturbances. Meanwhile, in the Baltic republics, nationalist **Popular Fronts** emerged, instantly attracting a mass membership. Estonia was the first to make the break, declaring full sovereignty in November 1988 and raising the national flag in place of the hammer and sickle in February of the following year.

## 1989 and all that

In the **elections** for the Congress of People's Deputies of March 1989, Soviet voters were, for the first time in years, allowed to choose from more than one candidate, some of whom were even non-Party members. Despite the heavily rigged selection process, radicals, including Yeltsin and Sakharov, managed to get themselves elected. When Sakharov called for an end to one-Party rule, his microphone was switched off – a futile gesture, since the sessions were being broadcast live on Russian TV.

Gorbachev's next crisis came with the **miners' strike** in July, when thousands walked out in protest at shortages, safety standards and low wages. He managed to entice them back to work with promises, but the myth of the Soviet Union as a workers' state had been shattered for ever. The events that swept across Eastern Europe throughout 1989, culminating with the **fall of the Berlin Wall** and the Velvet Revolution in Czechoslovakia, were another blow to the old guard, but Gorbachev was more concerned about holding together the Soviet Union itself. That Communism now faced its greatest crisis at home was made humiliatingly plain by unprecedented counter-demonstrations on Red Square during the October Revolution celebrations: one of the banners read: "Workers of the World – we're sorry."

## The beginning of the end

1990 proved no better a year for Gorbachev or the Party. On January 19, Soviet tanks rolled into the Azerbaijani capital, Baku, to crush the independence movement there – more than a hundred people were killed that night. In February, Moscow witnessed the largest **demonstration** since the Revolution of 1917, with scores of thousands converging on Red Square, calling for an end to one-Party rule and protesting against rising anti-Semitic violence. Gorbachev attempted to seize the initiative by agreeing to end one-Party rule and simultaneously electing himself President, with increased powers to deal with the escalating crisis in the republics.

The voters registered their disgust with the Party at the March **local elections**. In the republics, nationalists swept the board and declarations of independence soon followed, while in Russia itself, the new radical alliance, Democratic Platform, gained majorities in the powerful city councils of Leningrad and Moscow. A university professor, **Gavril Popov**, became chairman of the Moscow council, while the equally reformist Anatoly Sobchak was elected to the post in Leningrad. May Day 1990 was another humiliation for Gorbachev, who was jeered by sections of the crowd in Red Square. By the end of the month Yeltsin had secured his election as chairman of the Russian parliament and, two weeks later, in imitation of the Baltic states, declared **Russian independence** from the Soviet Union (June 12).

In July 1990, the Soviet Communist Party held its last ever congress. Yeltsin tore up his Party card in full view of the cameras – two million had done the same by the end of the year. The economic crisis, spiralling crime and chronic food shortages put Gorbachev under renewed pressure from Party hardliners. The first ominous signs came as winter set in, when a series of leadership reshuffles gave the Interior Ministry and control of the media back to the conservatives. On December 20, the liberal Soviet Foreign Minister, Edvard Shevardnadze, resigned, warning that "dictatorship is coming".

# 1991: the Putsch and the collapse of the Soviet Union

The effects of Gorbachev's reshuffle became clear on January 13, 1991, when thirteen Lithuanians were killed by Soviet troops as they defended the national TV centre. Yeltsin immediately flew to the Baltics and signed a joint declaration condemning the violence. A week later in Latvia, the OMON stormed the Interior Ministry in Riga, killing five people. Hours before this attack, Moscow witnessed its largest ever demonstration – 250,000 people came out to protest against the killings. The Russian press had a field day, mocking Gorbachev and backing the Baltics. Gorbachev responded by threatening to suspend the liberal press laws, while adding more hardliners to the Politburo and giving wider powers to the security forces.

In June, the citizens of Leningrad narrowly voted in a referendum to rename the city **St Petersburg**, to the fury of Gorbachev. Popular disgust with Party rule was manifest in the overwhelming majority of votes cast for Boris Yeltsin in the **Russian Presidential election** of June 12, despite efforts to block his campaign. As Russia's first ever democratically elected leader, he could claim a mandate for bold moves and within a month had issued a decree calling for the removal of Party "cells" from factories. It was the most serious threat yet to the dominance of the Communist Party in Soviet life, and prompted hardliners to publish a lengthy appeal for action "to lead the country to a dignified and sovereign future".

## The August Putsch

On Monday August 19, 1991, the Soviet Union woke up to the soothing sounds of Chopin on the radio and *Swan Lake* on television. A **state of emergency** had been declared, Gorbachev had "resigned for health reasons" and the country was now ruled by the self-appointed "State Committee for the State of Emergency in the USSR". The main participants included many of Gorbachev's most recently appointed colleagues, under the nominal leadership of Gennady Yenayev. Gorbachev, then on holiday in the Crimea, had been asked to back the coup the previous night, but had refused (to the surprise of the conspirators) and was consequently under house arrest. So began what Russians call the *putsch*.

In **Moscow**, tanks appeared on the streets from mid-morning onwards, stationing themselves at key points, including the Russian Parliament building, known as the **White House**. Here, a small group of protesters gathered, including Yeltsin, who had narrowly escaped arrest that morning. When the first tank approached, he leapt aboard, shook hands with its commander and appealed to the crowd (and accompanying radio and TV crews): "You can erect a throne using bayonets, but you cannot sit on bayonets for long". The Afghan war hero Alexander Rutskoy turned up and started organizing the defence of the building, making it harder for regular troops to contemplate attacking it. Actually, the role of storming the White House had been allocated to the crack KGB Alpha Force, but, for reasons unknown, they never went into action. News of the standoff – and Yeltsin's appeal to soldiers not to "let yourselves be turned into blind weapons" – was broadcast around the world and beamed back to millions of Russians via the BBC and the Voice of America.

On Tuesday, the defenders of the White House were heartened by the news that one of the coup leaders, Pavlov, had resigned due to "high blood pressure" (he had been drinking continuously) and the crowd grew to 100,000 in defiance of a curfew order. Around midnight, three civilians were killed when an advancing armoured column was stopped by barricades on the Garden Ring and firebombed. Next morning it was announced that several tank units had decamped to Yeltsin's side, and on Wednesday afternoon the *putsch* collapsed as its leaders bolted. One group flew to the Crimea in the hope of obtaining Gorbachev's pardon and were arrested on arrival. Yenayev drank himself into a stupor and several others committed suicide.

### The aftermath

Gorbachev flew back to Moscow, not realizing that everything had changed. At his first press conference, he pledged continuing support for the Communist Party and Marxist-Leninism, and openly admitted that he had trusted the conspirators as men of "culture and dialogue". He was, by now, totally estranged from the mood of the country. The same day, jubilant crowds toppled the giant statue of Dzerzhinsky that stood outside the Lubyanka. On Friday, Gorbachev appeared before parliament and was publicly humiliated by Yeltsin in front of the television cameras. Yeltsin then decreed the Russian Communist Party an illegal organization, announced the suspension of pro-coup newspapers such as *Pravda* and had the Central Committee headquarters in Moscow sealed up.

The failure of the *putsch* spelt the end of Communist rule and the break-up of the Soviet Union. Any possibility of a Slav core remaining united was torpedoed by loose talk of redrawing the border between Russia and Ukraine, and the new-found goodwill between Russia and its former satellites quickly evaporated. In December, Ukraine voted overwhelmingly for independence; a week later the leaders of Russia, Belarus and Ukraine formerly replaced the USSR with a Commonwealth of Independent States (CIS), whose nominal capital would be Minsk; the Central Asian republics declared their intention of joining. On December 25, Gorbachev resigned as

President of a state that no longer existed; that evening the Soviet flag was lowered over the Kremlin and replaced by the Russian tricolour.

## The new Russia

On January 2, 1992, Russians faced their New Year hangovers and the harsh reality of massive price rises, following a decree by Yeltsin that lifted controls on a broad range of products. The cost of food rose by up to 500 percent and queues disappeared almost overnight. According to the Western advisors shaping Russia's new economic policy, this would stimulate domestic production and promote the growth of capitalism in the shortest possible time. Initially, inflation was limited by keeping a tight rein on state spending, in accordance with the monetarist strategy of Prime Minister **Yegor Gaidar**, but despite Yeltsin's defence of his painful and unpopular measures the policy soon came unstuck after the Central Bank began printing vast amounts of rubles to cover credits issued to state industries on the verge of bankruptcy. Inflation soared.

### Stalemate and crisis

By the autumn of 1992, Gaidar's economic policy was in dire straits and pressure grew for his removal. The **Russian parliament** or Congress of Deputies consisted of numerous factions and parties and a mass of floating delegates known as "the Swamp", but the voting arithmetic favoured the old managerial elite and their ultra-nationalist allies. To ensure his own political survival, Yeltsin was forced to replace Gaidar with the veteran technocrat **Viktor Chernomyrdin**, who surprised parliament by immediately reneging on earlier promises by increasing subsidies to industry and restoring them for vital foodstuffs (including vodka).

For much of 1993, politics was dominated by a **"War of Laws"** between the government and parliament, with each flouting or repealing the other's decrees and budgets, as the Constitutional Court played piggy in the middle. The parliamentary Speaker, **Ruslan Khasbulatov**, exercised such influence over the deputies that articles in the press suggested he had them under some form of hypnosis – although as a leader, Khasbulatov suffered the political handicap of being a non-Russian (born in Chechnya), and few believed that his defence of parliamentary privilege was anything but self-serving.

Another erstwhile Yeltsin ally who now found himself in opposition was Vice-President **Alexander Rutskoy**, who denounced Gaidar's team as "boys in pink pants", and railed against the government as "scum" and "faggots".

In March 1993, Congress reneged on its earlier promise to hold a referendum on a new Constitution, so Yeltsin appeared on TV to announce the introduction of a special rule suspending the power of Congress and called for new elections. In the meantime, there was a nationwide vote of confidence in the President, plus a referendum on the draft Constitution and new electoral laws were passed. In response, Congress attempted to impeach Yeltsin, but a constitutional crisis was narrowly avoided and a referendum was held. This seemed largely to vindicate Yeltsin and his economic policies but not his calls for early parliamentary elections.

## The October "events"

The stalemate lasted until September 21, when Yeltsin brought things to a head by dissolving Congress by a decree of dubious legality. In response, almost 200 **deputies occupied the White House**, voted to strip Yeltsin of his powers and swore in Rutskoy as president, who promptly authorized the execution of officials guilty of "illegal actions". A motley band of supporters erected flimsy barricades: pensioners carrying placards denouncing "Yeltsin the Drunk and his Yid Cabinet"; Cossacks and neo-Nazis. The police cordon thrown around the area was so porous that hundreds of firearms were brought into the White House. As the "siege" continued into its second week, Rutskoy appealed to the police to switch sides, while the government tried to break parliament's morale by cutting off its electricity, gas and phones, and playing a tape-loop of the song *Happy Nation*, day and night.

During the third week, 1000 parliamentary supporters rallied on Smolenskaya ploshchad and set cars ablaze as the police stood by. On October 3, 10,000 marched there and broke through the cordon around the White House, seizing trucks and riot-shields as the police fled. Guns were handed out, and Rutskoy exhorted them to storm the mayor's office and the Ostankino Television Centre. The Mayoralty, nearby, was soon captured, and a convoy of trucks headed for Ostankino. Though the **battle for the TV Centre** was televized abroad, Russian viewers simply heard Ostankino warn "We're

under attack", and assumed the worst when it went off the air. Actually, the TV Centre was held by a unit of commandos that arrived just before the rioters did, but at the time it seemed that Yeltsin had lost control of the streets.

The ex-Prime Minister, Gaidar, appealed over local radio for democrats to defend the City Council on Tverskaya ulitsa, which was assumed to be the next target. Hundreds turned up, barricaded Tverskaya with trucks and benches, and spent the night expecting attack. Gun battles flared across the city, as parliamentary supporters attacked the offices of pro-government newspapers. Meanwhile, Yeltsin was in the Kremlin, trying to persuade the defence and security ministries to obey him and crush the rebellion. Defence Minister Grachev only agreed in the small hours, while the Alpha Force refused until one of their own men was shot by a sniper.

The **assault on the White House** began at 7am on October 4. For ten hours tanks shelled the building, watched by crowds of spectators from nearby vantage points, some of whom were killed by stray bullets. Civilians were also slain on the New Arbat, by snipers whose identity has never been established. By nightfall, the White House's occupants had been bundled into prison and the rebellion was over. Isolated shoot-outs continued, however, and a curfew was imposed for a fortnight, during which many Caucasians were expelled from Moscow in a racially slanted crackdown on crime that Muscovites welcomed as long overdue.

With his parliamentary foes behind bars, Yeltsin turned on his other opponents, the local councils who had supported Congress out of sympathy for their approach or simply as elected representatives. Councils all over Russia were abolished and new elections declared, leaving power concentrated in the hands of local mayors and their bureaucrats. Moscow's mayor, **Yuri Luzhkov**, proved as skilful a populist as Yeltsin had two years earlier. Yeltsin foolishly distanced himself from the party created to represent his government in the forthcoming elections, which bore the presumptuous name of **Russia's Choice** and campaigned as if its triumph was a foregone conclusion.

## The Nationalist backlash

The result of the December **1993 elections** to the new parliament or Duma was a stunning rebuff for Russia's Choice, which won only 14 percent of the vote, compared to 23 percent for the so-called Liberal Democratic Party of **Vladimir Zhirinovsky**. An ultra-nationalist with a murky past, Zhirinovsky appalled foreign governments by threatening to bomb Germany and Japan and to dump radioactive waste in the Baltic States. His success owed much to a superbly run TV campaign, whose effects lasted just long enough to get the LDP into parliament, which was dominated by the "red-brown" alliance of Communist groupings and ultra-nationalists. Fortunately for Yeltsin and Chernomyrdin, the new Constitution gave the president greater power than before, but they could do nothing to prevent parliament from promulgating a humiliating **amnesty** for the participants in the October "events", and the organizers of the 1991 *putsch*, as well.

In the wake of the elections, the government backpedalled on further economic reforms and tried to improve its nationalist credentials by taking a sterner stand on the rights of Russians in the ex-republics, or "Near Abroad". Resurgent **nationalism** was evident across the board in foreign policy, from warnings against expanding NATO into Eastern Europe or the Baltics, to arguments with Ukraine over Crimea, and covert interventions in local civil wars in Caucasia and Central Asia. The Russian Army's new strategic doctrine identified regional wars as the chief threat to national security and defending the old borders of the USSR as a top priority.

At home, cynicism, **crime and corruption** reached new heights in 1994, when car-bombs became the favoured means of disposing of business rivals in Moscow, and the finance ministry estimated that $40 billion had been smuggled out of Russia since the fall of Communism. The funeral of the Mafia boss **Otari Kvantrishvili** underscored the extent to which organized crime had meshed with politics and culture, with deputies and pop stars among the mourners. Later that year, thousands of Muscovites were ruined by the collapse of the

**MMM** investment fund, whose boss then ran for parliament on a pledge to restore their losses, only to scornfully dismiss them once elected. In a further blow to public morale, the murder of a journalist for exposing corruption in the Army was followed early in 1995 by the assassination of the crusading TV presenter **Vladislav Listev**.

In the last weeks of 1994, the government embarked on a **war in the province of Chechnya** that proved to be deeply unpopular in Russia and devastating for the Chechens. The Chechens put up fierce resistance in their capital, Grozny, which Russia's defence minister had boasted could be taken by a regiment of paratroops in two hours. However, it fell only after weeks of bombardment, leaving the city in ruins. In Russia, the ruble plunged and the national budget went haywire; the media came under heavy pressure to purvey official propaganda; while demonstrations by the mothers of conscripts symbolized a widespread feeling that young Russian lives were being sacrificed by a bungling, corrupt government.

Journalists attributed the Chechen debacle to the so-called "**Party of War**", a shadowy alliance of figures within the military, security and economic ministries, and increasingly painted Yeltsin as a drunken fool in thrall to his own security chief, **Alexander Korzhakov**. With Yeltsin's popularity down to ten percent in the opinion polls and a **presidential election** due in 1996, the race to succeed him has already begun. Besides Zhirinovsky and other devalued politicians of recent years, Mikhail Gorbachev has hit the campaign trail (though few rate his chances of a comeback). Some, however, aver that Russia's crisis will become so acute that a military dicatorship is inevitable, and envisage **General Lebed**, the commander of the 14th Army, as a future strongman. Others believe that democracy and capitalism are now rooted firmly enough to outlive Yeltsin, and that their wilder manifestations will eventually fade away.

# Books

The number of books available about Russia and the old Soviet Union is vast. We have concentrated on works specifically related to Moscow, and on a general survey of Russian and Soviet history, politics and the arts. Where two publishers are given, they refer to the UK and US publishers respectively. Where books are published in one country only, UK or US follows the publisher's name; where the publisher is the same in the UK and US, only the publisher's name is given; o/p signifies that the book is out of print.

## General travel accounts and specific guides

**Baedeker's Handbooks** (o/p). The 1914 *Baedeker's Handbook to Russia* was a stupendous work that almost bankrupted the company, with dozens of maps and reams of information that were soon rendered irrelevant by the Revolution. A facsimile edition was produced in the 1970s, but nowadays this, too, is almost as rare as the original, copies of which sell for up to £500 in antiquarian bookshops.

**Kathleen Berton** *Moscow: an Architectural History* (I.B. Tauris). Enjoyably erudite study of Moscow's evolution, illuminating scores of buildings and centuries of history, with assured critical appreciations and dozens of photos. Berton is a long-time resident of Moscow and an expert on her subject.

**John Freeman & Kathleen Berton** *Moscow Revealed* (Doubleday). Gorgeous photos of Moscow's finest interiors – metro stations, palaces, churches and private homes – in every style from Baroque to Stalin-Gothic. Berton's text provides an essential context and exposes certain aspects of Muscovite life in the early years of *perestroika*.

**Vladimir Chernov** *Three Days in Moscow* (Planeta in Moscow). The last in a classic Soviet series of city guides, giving pride of place to Lenin memorial sites and the like; the 1989 edition barely pays lip service to *perestroika*. Sold by street vendors in Moscow's touristy areas.

**Marquis de Custine** *Empire of the Czar* (Doubleday). Classic account of Tsarist Russia by a waspish French diplomat, whose observations on Moscow often ring as true today as when de Custine penned them in the 1830s.

**Christopher Hope** *Moscow! Moscow!* (Minerva, UK). Rather lacklustre but occasionally penetrating view of Moscow in 1988, when *perestroika* was in full swing but the old system still hung heavy.

**Lawrence Kelly (ed.),** *Moscow: A Travellers' Companion* (Constable/Macmillan). Alternately dull and amusing descriptions of court life, eyewitness accounts of historic events and excerpts from books long out of print, which stop short of the Revolution.

**Robert Bruce Lockhart** *Memoirs of a British Agent* (o/p). Vivid eyewitness account of Lockhart's efforts to subvert the fledgling Soviet state, which brought him into contact with Trotsky and Dzerzhinsky and resulted in his imprisonment in the Kremlin.

**Colin Thubron** *Among the Russians* (Penguin). Includes a chapter on Moscow, a visit that formed part of Thubron's angst-ridden journey around the USSR in the early 1980s. Sensitively written, but hardly true of Moscow today.

**Where in Moscow** (Russian Information Services, Inc.). Now in its fourth edition, this annually updated directory of goods and services will prove useful to anyone staying a while in Moscow, but doesn't offer much help for tourists on a brief visit, aside from its excellent map of the city.

## History, politics and society

**John T. Alexander** *Catherine the Great: Life and Legend* (Oxford University Press). Just what the title says, with rather more credence given to some of the wilder stories than Vincent Cronin's book (see below).

**Robert Conquest** *Stalin: Breaker of Nations* (Weidenfeld, UK); *The Great Terror. A Reassessment* (Pimlico). The first is a short, withering biography; the second perhaps the best study of the Terror. In 1990, this was revised on the basis of new evidence suggesting that Conquest's initial tally of the number of victims had been underestimated.

**Vincent Cronin** *Catherine, Empress of all the Russias* (Collins Harvill/Morrow o/p). Salacious rumours are dispelled in this sympathetic biography of the shy German princess who made it big in Russia.

**Isaac Deutscher** *Stalin* (Penguin). This classic political biography has been criticized for being too sympathetic towards its subject.

**Marc Ferro** *Nicholas II – The Last of the Tsars* (Penguin/OUP). A new, concise biography of the last of the Tsars, by a French historian who argues that some of the Imperial family escaped execution at Yekaterinburg.

**Stephen Handleman** *Comrade Criminal: The Theft of the Second Russian Revolution* (Michael Joseph, UK). Fascinating study of how organized crime spread through every level of Russian society and how the Communist *apparatchiki* transformed themselves into "businessmen".

**Michel Heller & Aleksandr Nekrich** *Utopia in Power* (Hutchinson/Summit Books). A trenchant *tour de force* by two émigré historians, covering Soviet history from 1917 until the onset of Gorbachev. Highly recommended.

**Adam Hochschild** *The Unquiet Ghost: Russians Remember Stalin* (Viking Penguin, US). A searching enquiry into the nature of guilt and denial, ranging from the penal camps of Kolyma to the archives of the Lubyanka. Hochschild concludes that the road to hell is paved with good intentions, and most people would behave no better had they lived under the Terror themselves.

**John Kampfner** *Inside Yeltsin's Russia* (Cassell, UK). Racy account of Yeltsin's presidency, focusing on political crises, crime and corruption, with vignettes of the dramatic highlights and leading characters. Highly accessible and relevant.

**Dominic Lieven** *Nicholas II* (John Murray). Another new study of the last Tsar, which draws comparisons between both the monarchies of Russia and other states of that period, and the downfall of the Tsarist and Soviet regimes.

**Robert Massie** *Peter the Great* (Abacus/Ballantine); *Nicholas and Alexandra* (Gollancz/Atheneum). Both the boldest and the weakest of the Romanov Tsars are minutely scrutinized in these two heavyweight but extremely readable biographies – the one on Peter is especially good.

**John Reed** *Ten Days that Shook the World* (Penguin). The classic eyewitness account of the 1917 Bolshevik seizure of power that vividly captures the mood of the time and the hopes pinned on the Revolution.

**David Remnick** *Lenin's Tomb* (Viking). Weighty, vivid account of the collapse of the Soviet Union, packed with riveting interviews and exposés by the *Washington Post*'s man on the spot. Recommended reading, but not a book to pack for the trip.

**Henri Troyat** *Alexander of Russia; Ivan the Terrible* (both New English Library/Dutton). A sympathetic portrayal of the "Tsar Liberator", Alexander II, and a more salacious romp through the misdeeds of Ivan.

**Dimitri Volkogonov** *Stalin: Triumph and Tragedy* (Prima Publishing, US). Weighty study of the Soviet dictator, drawing on long-withheld archive material, by Russia's foremost military historian.

**Andrew Wilson & Nina Bachkatov** *Russia Revisited* (Andre Deutsch, UK). Accessible history of the former USSR, covering the events up until just after the *putsch*. Written in a user-friendly style by two journalists based in Moscow.

## The arts

**Alan Bird** *A History of Russian Painting* (Phaidon/Macmillan). A comprehensive survey of Russian painting from medieval times to the Brezhnev era, including numerous black-and-white illustrations and potted biographies.

**John E. Bowlt (ed.)** *Russian Art of the Avant-Garde* (Thames & Hudson). An illustrated volume of critical essays on this seminal movement, which anticipated many trends in Western art that have occurred since World War II.

**William Craft Brumfield** *A History of Russian Architecture* (Cambridge University Press). The most comprehensive study of the subject, ranging from early Novgorod churches to Olympic sports halls, by way of Naryshkin Baroque monasteries and Style Moderne mansions, illustrated by hundreds of photos and line drawings.

**Matthew Cullerne Brown** *Art Under Stalin* (Phaidon/Holmes & Meier); *Contemporary Russian Art* (Phaidon, UK). The former is a fascinating study of totalitarian aesthetics, ranging from ballet to sports stadiums and from films to sculpture; the latter covers art in the Brezhnev and Gorbachev eras.

**Leslie Chamberlain** *The Food and Cooking of Russia* (Penguin). Informative and amusing cook book, full of delicious recipes.

**Camilla Gray** *The Russian Experiment in Art 1863–1922* (Thames & Hudson). A concise guide to the multitude of movements that constituted the Russian avant-garde, prior to the dead hand of Socialist Realism being imposed.

**Richard Sheed** *Ballet Russes* (Apple Press o/p/ Princeton University Press). An exhaustive rundown of the major trends in painting, sculpture and architecture in Russia, from Kievan Rus to the turn of this century.

**Vladimir Tolstoy** *Street Art of the Revolution* (Thames & Hudson/Vendom o/p). Covering much the same ground as the books by Bowlt and Gray (see above), with numerous photographs of street monuments and agitprop theatre.

**Artemy Troitsky** *Back in the USSR – the True Story of Rock in Russia* (Faber & Faber). First-hand account of the last 25 years of rock music inside Russia, by the country's leading music journalist and critic.

**A.N. Wilson** *Tolstoy* (Penguin). Heavyweight but immensely readable biography of the great novelist and appalling family man.

## Russian literature

**Mikhail Bulgakov** *The Master and Margarita; The Heart of the Dog; The White Guard* (all Harvill/ Harper Collins). *The Master and Margarita* is a brilliant satire about Satanic deeds in Moscow, entwined with the story of Pontius Pilate. Unpublished in Bulgakov's lifetime, it became *the* cult novel of the Brezhnev era. *The Heart of the Dog* is an earlier, trenchant allegory on the folly of Bolshevism, while *The White Guard* is a sympathetic portrayal of a monarchist family in Kiev during the Civil War. Stalin so enjoyed the

play of the last that Bulgakov was spared during the purges.

**Fyodor Dostoyevsky** *Crime and Punishment; Notes from the Underground; Poor Folk and Other Stories; The Brothers Karamazov; The Gambler; The House of the Dead; The Idiot; The Possessed* (all Penguin/Bantam). Pessimistic, brooding tales, often semi-autobiographical (particularly *The Gambler* and *The House of the Dead*). Though few of them are set in Moscow, their atmosphere is evocative of life there in the past.

**Boris Pasternak** *Doctor Zhivago* (Penguin). A multi-layered story of love and destiny, war and revolution, for which Pasternak was awarded the Nobel Prize for Literature, but forced to decline it. Russians regard him as a poet first and a novelist second. His *dacha* and grave outside Moscow are revered (see p.283).

**Anatoli Rybakov** *Children of the Arbat* (Arrow, UK). The first volume of Rybakov's trilogy (the only one published abroad) traces the lives of a dozen Muscovites up until the time of Kirov's murder. Its portrait of Stalin is compelling.

**Alexander Solzhenitsyn** *August 1914* and *Cancer Ward* (Penguin); *First Circle* (Collins Harvill); *The Gulag Archipelago* (Collins Harvill); *One Day in the Life of Ivan Denisovich* (Penguin). The last two books listed here constitute a stunning indictment of the camps and the purges, for which Russia's most famous modern dissident was persecuted by the state in Brezhnev's time and feted in the West (before he lambasted Western decadence).

**Lev Tolstoy** *Anna Karenina* and *War and Peace* (Penguin). The latter is the ultimate epic novel, tracing the fortunes of dozens of characters over decades. Its depiction of the Patriotic War of 1812 cast common folk in a heroic mould, while the main, aristocratic characters are flawed – an idealization of the masses that made *War and Peace* politically acceptable in Soviet times.

## Literature by foreign writers

**Alan Brien** *Lenin – The Novel* (Paladin/Morrow o/p). Brilliant evocation of Lenin's life and character, in the form of a diary by the man himself, whose steely determination and sly irascibility exude from every page.

**Martin Cruz Smith** *Gorky Park; Polar Star; Red Square* (HarperCollins). A trio of atmospheric thrillers featuring the maverick homicide detective

Arkady Renko. The first was deservedly acclaimed for its evocation of Moscow in the Era of Stagnation; the second finds Renko in exile aboard an Arctic trawler; while the third returns him to Moscow in time for the *putsch* of 1991.

**John le Carré** *The Russia House* (Coronet). Well-intentioned but overlong attempt to exorcize the ghosts of the Cold War, by the world's best-known spy novelist. Its snapshots of Moscow and Leningrad in the early days of *perestroika* are less illuminating than the author's own perspective as a former spy.

**George Feifer** *Moscow Farewell; The Girl From Petrovka* (both Viking, US). Two bitter-sweet tales of involvement in Moscow lowlife, based on the American author's own experiences as an exchange student. Laced with sex in a very 1970s way.

**Robert Littell** *Mother Russia* (Faber). Piquant comedy centred on a manic black-marketeer who moves into a commune in "the last wooden house in central Moscow" and becomes a pawn of the KGB and CIA. An early work by America's foremost spy novelist.

**Emanuel Litvinov** *A Death Out of Season; Blood on the Snow; The Face of Terror* (Penguin). A moving epic trilogy that follows a disparate group of revolutionaries from Edwardian Whitechapel to the cellars of the Lubyanka. The second and third volumes are partly set in Moscow. Highly recommended.

**Stuart M. Kaminsky** *A Fine Red Rain; A Cold Red Sunrise; The Man Who Walked Like A Bear* (Mandarin, UK). Three Soviet police procedurals starring the weightlifting Inspector Rostnkiov. Self-consciously modelled on Ed McBain's *87th Precinct* series, and just as formulaic.

**Jonathan Treitel** *The Red Cabbage Café* (Paladin, UK). Amusing story of an English idealist working on the Moscow metro in the 1920s, which turns darkly surreal and ends with a savage twist. Good holiday reading.

# Language

Russian is a highly complex eastern Slav language and you're unlikely to become very familiar with it during a brief visit to Moscow. German and English are the most common second languages, though few Russians know more than a phrase or two and any attempt to speak Russian will be heartily appreciated. At the very least you should try and learn the Cyrillic alphabet, so that you can read the names of metro stations and the signs around the city.

## The Cyrillic alphabet

Contrary to appearances, the **Cyrillic alphabet** is the least of your problems when trying to learn Russian. There are several different ways of **transliterating** Cyrillic into Latin script (for example "Chajkovskogo" or "Chaykovskovo" for Чайковского). In this book, we've used the Revised English System, with a few minor modifications to help pronunciation (see box). All proper names appear as they are best known,

---

**Cyrillic Characters**

| | | | | |
|---|---|---|---|---|
| Аа | **a** | | Рр | **r** |
| Бб | **b** | | Сс | **s** |
| Вв | **v** | | Тт | **t** |
| Гг | **g\*** | | Уу | **u** |
| Дд | **d** | | Фф | **f** |
| Ее | **e\*** | | Хх | **kh** |
| Ёё | **e** | | Цц | **ts** |
| Жж | **zh** | | Чч | **ch** |
| Зз | **z** | | Шш | **sh** |
| Ии | **i** | | Щщ | **shch** |
| Йй | **y** | | Ыы | **y\*** |
| Кк | **k** | | Ээ | **e** |
| Лл | **l** | | Яя | **ya** |
| Мм | **m** | | Ьь | a silent "soft sign" that softens the preceding consonant |
| Нн | **n** | | | |
| Оо | **o** | | Ммъ | a silent "hard sign" that keeps the preceding consonant hard\* |
| Пп | **p** | | | |

\*To aid pronunciation and readability, we have also introduced a handful of exceptions to the above transliteration guide:

Гг (g) is written as **v** when pronounced as such, for example Горкого – Gorkovo.

Ее (e) is written as **Ye** when at the beginning of a word, for example Ельцин – Yeltsin.

Ыы (y) is written as **i**, when it appears immediately before й (y), for example Хлебный – Khlebniy.

**Note:** just to confuse matters further, hand-written Cyrillic is different again from the printed Cyrillic outlined above. The only place you're likely to encounter it is on menus. The most startling differences are:

б which looks similar to a "d"
г which looks similar to a backwards "s"

и which looks like a "u"
т which looks similar to an "m"

---

not as they would be transliterated: for example "Tchaikovsky" not "Chaykovskiy".

The list below gives the Cyrillic characters in upper and lower case form, followed simply by the Latin equivalent. In order to pronounce the words properly, you'll need to consult the pronunciation guide below.

## Vowels and word stress

English-speakers find it difficult to pronounce Russian accurately, partly because letters that appear at first to have English equivalents are subtly different. The most important rule to remember, however, is that Russian is a language which relies on **stress**.

The stress in a word can fall on any syllable and there's no way of knowing simply by looking at it – it's something you just have to learn, as you do in English. If a word has only one syllable, you can't get it wrong; where there are two or more, we've placed accents over the stressed syllable, though these do not appear in Russian itself. Once you've located the stressed syllable, you should give it more weight than all the others and far more than you would in English.

Whether a **vowel** is stressed or unstressed sometimes affects the way it's pronounced, most notably with the letter "o" (see below).

а – a – like the *a* in father

я – ya – like the *ya* in yarn, but like the *e* in evil when it appears before a stressed syllable

– e – always a short *e* as in get

е – e – like the *ye* in yes

и – i – like the *e* in evil

й – y – like the *y* in boy

о – o – like the *o* in port when stressed, but like the *a* in plan when unstressed

ё – e – like the *yo* in yonder. Note that in Russia, this letter is often printed without the dots.

у – u – like the *u* in June

ю – yu – like the *u* in universe

ы – y – like the *i* in ill, but with the tongue drawn back

## Consonants

In Russian, **consonants** can be either soft or hard and this difference is an important feature of a "good" accent, but if you're simply trying to get by in the language, you needn't worry. The consonants listed below are those which differ significantly from their English equivalents.

б – b – like the *b* in bad; at the end of a word like the *p* in dip

в – v – like the *v* in van but with the upper teeth behind the top of the lower lip; at the end of a word, and before certain consonants like *f* in leaf

г – g – like the *g* in goat; at the end of a word like the *k* in lark

д – d – like the *d* in dog but with the tongue pressed against the back of the upper teeth; at the end of a word like the *t* in salt

ж – zh – like the *s* in pleasure; at the end of a word like the *sh* in bush

з – z – like the *z* in zoo; at the end of a word like the *s* in loose

л – l – like the *l* in milk, but with the tongue kept low and touching the back of the upper teeth

н – n – like the *n* in no but with the tongue pressed against the upper teeth

р – r – trilled as the Scots speak it

с – s – always as in soft, never as in sure

т – t – like the *t* in tent, but with the tongue brought up against the upper teeth

х – kh – like the *ch* in the Scottish loch

ц – ts – like the *ts* in boats

ч – ch – like the *ch* in chicken

ш – sh – like the *sh* in shop

щ – shch – like the *sh-ch* in fresh cheese

There are of course exceptions to the above pronunciation rules, but if you remember even the ones mentioned, you'll be understood.

## A Russian Language Guide

### Basic words and phrases

| | | |
|---|---|---|
| Yes/No | *da/net* | да/нет |
| Excuse me/don't mention it | *pozháluysta* | пожалуйста |
| Sorry | *prostíte* | простите |
| Thank you | *spasíbo* | спасибо |
| That's OK/it doesn't matter | *nichevó* | ничего |
| Bon appetit | *priyátnovo appetíta* | приятного аппетита |
| Bon voyage | *schastlívovo putí* | счастливого пути |
| Hello/goodbye (formal) | *zdrávstvuyte/do svidániya* | здравствуйтею/до свидания |
| Hello (informal) | *pree-vyet* | привет |
| See you later (informal) | *poká* | пока |
| Good day | *dóbriy den* | добрый день |
| Good morning | *dóbroe útro* | доброе утро |
| Good evening | *dóbriy vécher* | добрый вечер |
| Good night | *dóbroy noch* | доброй ночи |
| How are you? | *kak delá?* | как дела |
| Fine/OK | *khoroshó* | хорошо |
| Today | *sevódnya* | сегодня |
| Yesterday | *vcherá* | вчера |
| Tomorrow | *závtra* | завтра |
| The day after tomorrow | *poslezávtra* | послезавтра |
| Now | *seychás* | сейчас |
| Later | *popózzhe* | попозже |
| Go away! | *ostvte menya!* | оствте меня |
| Help! | *na pómoshch!* | на помощь |
| This one | *éta* | это |
| A little | *nemnógo* | немного |
| Large/small | *bolshóy/málenkiy* | большойюмаленькийь |
| More/less | *yeshyo/ménshe* | ещёюменьше |
| Good/bad | *khoróshiy/plokhóy* | хорошийюплохой |
| Hot/cold | *goryáchiy/kholódniy* | горячийюхолодный |
| With/without | *s/bez* | сю/без |

### Getting around

| | | |
|---|---|---|
| Over there | *tam* | там |
| Around the corner | *za uglóm* | за углом |
| Left/right | *nalévo/naprávo* | налевоюнаправо |
| Straight on | *pryámo* | прямо |
| Where is...? | *gde...?* | где |
| Is it far? | *etó dalekó?* | это далеко |
| By bus | *avtóbusom* | автобусом |
| By train | *póezdom* | поездом |
| By car | *na mashine* | на машине |
| By foot | *peshkóm* | пешком |
| By taxi | *na taksi* | на такси |
| Ticket | *bilét* | билет |
| Return (ticket) | *tudá i obrátno* | тула и обратно |
| Train station | *vokzál* | вокзал |
| Bus station | *avtóbusniy vokzal* | автобусный вокздл |
| Bus stop | *ostanóvka* | остановка |
| Is this train going to Sergiev Posad? | *étot póezd idét v Sergiev Posad?* | этот поезд идёт в сериев Посад |
| Do I have to change? | *núzhno sdélat peresádku?* | нужно сделать пересадку? |
| Small change (money) | *meloch* | мелочь |

## Questions and requests

| | | |
|---|---|---|
| Do you speak English? | *Vy govoríte po-anglíyski?* | выговорите по-английски |
| I don't speak Russian | *ya ne govoryú po-russki* | я не говорю по-русски |
| I don't understand | *ya ne ponimáyu* | я не понимаю |
| I understand | *ya ponimáyu* | я понимаю |
| Speak slowly | *govoríte pomédlenee* | говорите помедленее |
| I don't know | *ya ne znáyu* | я не знаю |
| How do you say that in Russian? | *kak po-rússki?* | как по-русски |
| Could you write it down? | *zapishíte éto pozháluysta?* | запишите это пожалуйста |
| What | *chto* | что |
| Where | *gde* | где |
| When | *kogdá* | когда |
| Why | *pochemú* | почему |
| Who | *kto* | кто |
| How much is it? | *skólko stóit?* | сколько стоит |
| I would like a double room | *ya khochú nómer na dvoíkh* | я хочу номер на двоих |
| For one night | *tólko sútki* | только сутки |
| Shower | *dush* | душ |
| Are these seats free? | *svobódno?* | свободно |
| May I ...? | *mózhno* | можно |
| You can't/it is not allowed | *nelzyá* | нельзя |
| The bill please | *schet pozháluysta* | счёт пожалуйста |
| Do you have...? | *u vas yest...?* | у вас есть |
| That's all | *eto vsé* | это всё |

## Some signs

| | | |
|---|---|---|
| Entrance | *vkhod* | ВХОД |
| Exit | *výkhod* | ВЫХОД |
| Toilets | *tualét* | ТУАЛЕТ |
| Men's | *múzhskoy* | МУЖСКОЙ |
| Women's | *zhénskiy* | ЖЕНСКИЙ |
| Open | *otkrýto* | ОТКРЫТО |
| Closed (for repairs) | *zakrýto (na remont)* | ЗАКРЫТО НА РЕМОНТ |
| Out of order | *ne rabótaet* | НЕ РАБОТАЕТ |
| No entry | *vkhóda net* | ВХОДА НЕТ |
| No smoking | *ne kurít* | НЕ КУРИТЬ |
| Drinking water | *piteváya vodá* | ПИТЬЕВАЯ ВОДА |
| Information | *správka* | СПРАВКА |
| Ticket office | *kássa* | КАССА |

## Days of the week

| | | |
|---|---|---|
| Monday | *ponedélnik* | понедельник |
| Tuesday | *vtórnik* | вторник |
| Wednesday | *sredá* | среда |
| Thursday | *chetvérg* | четверг |
| Friday | *pyátnitsa* | пятница |
| Saturday | *subbóta* | суббота |
| Sunday | *voskreséne* | воскресенье |

## Months of the year

| | | |
|---|---|---|
| January | *yanvár* | январь |
| February | *fevrál* | февраль |
| March | *mart* | март |
| April | *aprél* | апрель |
| May | *may* | май |
| June | *iyún* | июнь |
| July | *iyúl* | июль |
| August | *ávgust* | август |
| September | *sentyábr* | сентябрь |
| October | *oktyábr* | октябрь |
| November | *noyábr* | ноябрь |
| December | *dekábr* | декабрь |

## Numbers

| | | | | | | |
|---|---|---|---|---|---|---|
| 1 | *odín* | один | 40 | *sórok* | сорок |
| 2 | *dva* | два | 50 | *pyatdesyát* | пятьдесят |
| 3 | *tri* | три | 60 | *shestdesyát* | шестьдесят |
| 4 | *chetýre* | четыре | 70 | *sémdesyat* | семьдесят |
| 5 | *pyat* | пять | 80 | *vósemdesyat* | восемьдесят |
| 6 | *shest* | шесть | 90 | *devyanósto* | девяносто |
| 7 | *sem* | семь | 100 | *sto* | сто |
| 8 | *vósem* | восемь | 200 | *dvésti* | двести |
| 9 | *dévyat* | девять | 300 | *trísta* | триста |
| 10 | *désyat* | десять | 400 | *chetýresta* | четыреста |
| 11 | *odínnadtsat* | одиннадцать | 500 | *pyatsót* | пятьсот |
| 12 | *dvenádtsat* | двенадцать | 600 | *shestsót* | шестьсот |
| 13 | *trinádtsat* | тринадцать | 700 | *semsót* | семьсот |
| 14 | *chetýrnadtsat* | четырнадцать | 800 | *vosemsót* | восемьсот |
| 15 | *pyatnádtsat* | пятнадцать | 900 | *devyatsót* | девятьсот |
| 16 | *shestnádtsat* | шестнадцать | 1000 | *týsyacha* | тысяча |
| 17 | *semnádtsat* | семнадцать | 2000 | *dve týsyachi* | две тысячи |
| 18 | *vosemnádtsat* | восемнадцать | 3000 | *tri týsyachi* | три тысячи |
| 19 | *devyatnádtsat* | девятнадцать | 4000 | *chetýre týsyachi* | четыре тысячи |
| 20 | *dvádtsat* | двадцать | 5000 | *pyat týsyach* | пять тысяч |
| 21 | *dvádtsat odín* | двадцать один | 10000 | *désyat týsyach* | десять тысяч |
| 30 | *trídtsat* | тридцать | 50000 | *pyatdesyát týsyach* | пятьдесят тысяч |

# Glossaries

*The accents on Russian words signify which syllable is stressed.*

## General Russian terms

**bánya** bathhouse

**báshnya** tower

**bulvár** boulevard

**dácha** country cottage

**dom kultúry** communal arts and social centre; literally "house of culture"

**dvoréts** palace

**górod** town

**kládbishche** cemetery

**krépost** fortress

**kréml** citadel that formed the nucleus of most Russian towns, including Moscow – from this foreigners coined the name "Kremlin".

**lavra** the highest rank of monastery in the Orthodox Church

**monastýr** monastery or convent; the distinction is made by specifying whether it is a *muzhskóy* (men's) or *zhenskiy* (women's) *monastyr*

**móst** bridge

**múzhik** before the Revolution it meant a peasant; nowadays it means masculine or macho

**náberezhnaya** embankment

**óstrov** island

**ózero** lake

**pámyatnik** monument

**pereúlok** lane

**plóshchad** square

**prospékt** avenue

**reká** river

**restorán** restaurant

**rússkiy/rússkaya** Russian

**rýnok** market

**sad** garden/park

**shossé** highway

**sobór** cathedral

**storoná** district

**teátr** theatre

**tsérkov** church

**úlitsa** street

**vokzál** train station

**výstavka** exhibition

**zal** room or hall

**zámok** castle

## Art and architectural terms

**Art Nouveau** French term for the sinuous and stylized form of architecture dating from the turn of the century to World War I; known as *Style Moderne* in Russia.

**Atlantes** Supports in the form of carved male figures, used instead of columns to support an entablature.

**Baroque** Exuberant architectural style of the seventeenth and early eighteenth centuries, which spread to Russia via Ukraine and Belarus. Characterized by ornate decoration, complex spatial arrangement and grand vistas. See "Moscow and Naryshkin Baroque", below.

**Caryatids** Sculpted female figures used as a column to support an entablature.

**Constructivism** Soviet version of modernism that pervaded all the arts during the 1920s. In architecture, functionalism and simplicity were the watchwords – though many Constructivist projects were utterly impractical and never got beyond the drawing board.

**Deesis row** The third tier of an iconostasis (see below), whose central icon depicts Christ in Majesty.

**Empire Style** Richly decorative version of the neo-Classical style, which prevailed in Russia from 1812 to the 1840s. The French and Russian Empire styles both derived inspiration from Imperial Rome.

**Entablature** The part of a building supported by a colonnade or column.

**Faux mabre** Any surface painted to resemble marble.

**Fresco** Mural painting applied to wet plaster, so that the colours bind chemically with it as they dry.

**Futurism** Avant-garde art movement glorifying machinery, war, speed and the modern world in general.

**Icon** Religious image, usually painted on wood and framed upon an iconostasis. See p.208 for more about Russian icons.

**Iconostasis** A screen that separates the sanctuary from the nave in Orthodox churches, typically consisting of tiers of icons in a gilded frame, with up to three doors that open during services. The central one is known as the Royal Door.

**Kokóshniki** A purely decorative form of gable that evolved from *zakomary* (see below). Semicircular or ogee-shaped, they are often massed in a kind of pyramid below the spire or cupola.

**Moscow Baroque** Distinctly Russian form of Baroque that prevailed from the 1630s to the 1690s. Churches in this style are often wildly colourful and asymmetrical, with a profusion of tent-roofed spires and onion domes, *kokoshniki* and *nalichniki*.

**Nalichniki** Mouldings framing a window with pilasters, a scrolled or triangular entablature, and a scalloped or fretted ledge. A leitmotif of Moscow Baroque architecture.

**Narthex** Vestibule(s) preceding the nave of a church, which are strictly categorized as an esonarthex (if inside the main walls) or an exonarthex (if outside) – many Russian churches had both, to retain warmth. Also see "Refectory", below.

**Naryshkin Baroque** Late style of Moscow Baroque promoted by the Naryshkin family, characterized by monumental red-brick structures decorated with white stone crenellations and *nalichniki*.

**Nave** The part of a church where the congregation stands (there are no pews in Orthodox churches). Usually preceded by a narthex.

**neo-Classical** Late-eighteenth and early nineteenth-century style of architecture and design returning to classical Greek and Roman models as a reaction against Baroque and Rococo excesses.

**Ogee** A shape like the cross-section of an onion, widely found in Russian architecture in the form of gables or arches.

**Okhlad** Chased metal covering for an icon that left uncovered only the figure of the saint (or sometimes just their face and hands). Usually of gold or silver and studded with gems.

**Pendant** (or Pendule) An elongated boss hanging down from the apex of an arch, often used for decorative effect.

**Pilaster** A half-column projecting only slightly from the wall; an engaged column stands almost free from the surface.

**Podvóre** An irregular ensemble of dwellings, stables and outbuildings, enclosing a yard. Medieval Moscow was an aglommeration of thousands of *podvore*, of which only a few – built of stone – have survived.

**Portico** Covered entrance to a building.

**Pseudo-Russian** (or Neo-Russian) Style of architecture and decorative arts that drew inspiration from Russia's medieval and ancient past, its folk arts and myths. This rejection of Western styles was part of a broader Slavophile movement during the late nineteenth century.

**Refectory** The narthex of a medieval Russian church was called a Refectory (*Trapeznaya*), as monks and pilgrims were fed there.

**Sanctuary** (or Naos) The area around the altar, which in Orthodox churches is always screened by an iconostasis.

**Stalinist** Declamatory style of architecture prevailing from the 1930s to the death of Stalin in 1953, which returned to neo-Classical and Gothic models as a reaction against Constructivism, and reached its "High Stalinist" apogee after World War II. Also dubbed "Stalin-Gothic" or "Soviet Rococo". Moscow's seven Stalin skyscrapers epitomize the genre.

**Stucco** Plaster used for decorative effects.

**Style Moderne** Linear, stylized form of architecture and decorative arts, influenced by French Art Nouveau, which took its own direction in Russia, where its greatest exponent was the architect Fyodor Shekhtel.

**Tent-roof** Form of spire shaped like a wigwam, associated with stone churches in Moscow and wooden ones in northern Russia during the sixteenth and seventeenth centuries. Also added to towers, notably those of the Kremlin. The Russian term is *shatyor* (literally, "tent").

**Terem** The upper, tower-chambers of the houses of the nobility and the merchant class in medieval Moscow, where womenfolk were secluded.

**Trompe l'oeil** Painting designed to fool the onlooker into believing that it is actually three-dimensional.

**Zakomary** Rounded gables that outwardly reflect the vaulting of a church's interior, supporting the cupola. Typical of early churches from Yaroslavl, Novgorod and Pskov, which influenced Muscovite church architecture in the twelfth and thirteenth centuries.

## Historical terms and acronyms

**Bolshevik** Literally "majority"; the name given to the faction that supported Lenin during the internal disputes within the RSDLP during the first decade of this century.

**Boyars** Medieval Russian nobility, whose feuds and intrigues provoked Ivan the Terrible's wrath and caused the Time of Troubles. To diminish their power, Peter the Great instituted a new "service" aristocracy of fourteen ranks, open to anyone who served the state.

**Cheka** (Extraordinary Commission for Struggle against Counter-Revolution, Speculation and Sabotage), Bolshevik Party secret police 1917–1921.

**CIS** Commonwealth of Independent States – loose grouping that was formed in December 1991 following the collapse of the USSR. Most of the former Soviet republics have since joined, with the exception of the Baltic States.

**Civil War 1918–21**. Took place between the Bolsheviks and an assortment of opposition forces including Mensheviks, SRs, Cossacks, Tsarists and foreign interventionist armies from the West and Japan (collectively known as the Whites).

**Decembrists** Those who participated in the abortive coup against the accession of Nicholas I in December 1825.

**Duma** Parliament.

**February Revolution** Overthrow of the Tsar which took place in February 1917.

**Five Year Plan** Centralized masterplan for every branch of the Soviet economy. The First Five Year Plan was promulgated in 1928.

**FSK** (Federal Counter-Intelligence Service). The name of Russia's secret police since 1993; before then it was called the KGB.

**Golden Horde** (*Zolotaya Orda*) Powerful Tatar state in southern Russia whose threat preoccupied the Tsars until the seventeenth century.

**Gósplan** Soviet State Planning Agency, responsible for devising and overseeing the Five Year Plan. Its goals were set by the Politburo.

**GPU** (State Political Directorate) Soviet secret police 1921–23.

**Gulag** (Chief Administration of Corrective Labour Camps) Official title for Siberian hard labour camps set up under Lenin and Stalin.

**Kadet Party** (Constitutional Democratic Party) Liberal political party 1905–1917.

**KGB** (Committe of State Security) Soviet secret police 1954–91.

**Kuptsy** Wealthy merchant class, often of serf ancestry, that rose to prominence in the late nineteenth century.

**Menshevik** Literally "minority"; the name given to the faction opposing Lenin during the internal disputes within the RSDLP during the first decade of this century.

**Metropolitan** Senior cleric, ranking between an Archbishop and the Patriarch of the Russian Orthodox Church.

**MVD** (Ministry of Internal Affairs) Soviet secret police 1946–54; now runs the regular police (Militia) and the *OMON* (see below).

**Naródnaya Vólya** (People's Will) Terrorist group that assassinated Alexander II in 1881.

**NKVD** (People's Commissariat of Internal Affairs) Soviet secret police 1934–46.

**October Revolution** Bolshevik coup d'état which overthrew the Provisional Government in October 1917.

**OGPU** (Unified State Political Directorate) Soviet secret police 1923–34.

**Okhrána** Tsarist secret police.

**Old Believers** Russian Orthodox schismatics (see p.245).

**OMON** Ministry of the Interior Special Forces set up by Gorbachev in 1988. Initially used against the Baltic independence movements, and now for riot control and fighting civil wars within the Russian Federation.

**Oprichniki** Mounted troops used by Ivan the Terrible to terrorize the population and destroy any real or imaginary threat to his rule.

**Patriarch** The head of the Russian Orthodox Church.

**Petrine** Anything dating from the lifetime (1672–1725) or reign (1682–1725) of Peter the Great; Pre-Petrine means before then.

**Populist** Amorphous political movement of the second half of the nineteenth century that advocated socialism based on the peasant commune.

**Purges** The name used for the mass arrests of the Stalin era, but also for any systematic removal of unwanted elements from positions of authority.

**RSDLP** (Russian Social Democratic Labour Party) First Marxist political party in Russia, which rapidly split into Bolshevik and Menshevik factions.

**SR** Socialist Revolutionary.

**Streltsy** Riotous musketeers who formed Moscow's army in Pre-Petrine times. Many were beheaded on Red Square in 1682.

**Time of Troubles** (*Smutnoe vreme*) Anarchic period (1605–12) of civil wars and foreign invasions, following the death of Boris Godunov.

**Tsar** Emperor. The title was first adopted by Ivan the Terrible.

**Tsarevich** Crown prince.

**Tsarevna** Daughter of a Tsar and Tsaritsa.

**Tsaritsa** Empress; the foreign misnomer *Tsarina* is better known.

**USSR** Union of Soviet Socialist Republics. Official name of the Soviet Union from 1923 to 1991.

**Whites** Generic term for Tsarist or Kadet forces during the Civil War, which the Bolsheviks applied to almost anyone who opposed them.

# Moscow Place-names

## CHAPTER TWO:
## RED SQUARE AND THE KREMLIN

## CHAPTER THREE:
## THE KITAY-GOROD

## CHAPTER FOUR:
## THE BELIY GOROD

| | |
|---|---|
| Mokhovaya ulitsa | Моховая улица |
| Neglinnaya ulitsa | Неглинная улица |
| Nikitskie vorota | Никитские ворота |
| ploshchad Petrovskiy vorota | площадь Петровские ворота |
| ploshchad Yauzkie vorota | площадь Яузкие ворота |
| Podkolokolniy pereulok | Подколокольный переулок |
| Pokrovskiy bulvar | Покровский бульвар |
| Pushkinskaya ploshchad | Пушкинская площадь |
| Pushkinskaya ulitsa | Пушкинская улица |
| Rozhdestvenskiy bulvar | Рождественский бульвар |
| Serebryanicheskiy pereulok | Серебрянический переулок |
| Sovetskaya ploshchad | Советская площадь |
| Starosadskiy pereulok | Старосадский переулок |
| Stoleshnikov pereulok | Столешников переулок |
| Suvorovskiy bulvar | Суворовский бульвар |
| Tverskaya ulitsa | Тверская улица |
| Tverskoy bulvar | Тверской бульвар |
| Teatralnaya ploshchad | Театральная площадь |
| ulitsa Arkhipova | улица Архипова |
| ulitsa Bolshaya Lubyanka | улица Большая Лубянка |
| ulitsa Malaya Lubyanka | улица Малая Лубянка |
| ulitsa Gertsena | улица Герцена |
| ulitsa Granovskovo | улица Грановского |
| ulitsa Kuznetskiy most | улица Кузнецкий мост |
| ulitsa Maroseyka | улица Маросейка |
| ulitsa Myasnitskaya | улица Мясницкая |
| ulitsa Nezhdanovoy | улица Неждановой |
| ulitsa Petrovka | улица Петровка |
| ulitsa Pokrovka | улица Покровка |
| ulitsa Rozhdestvenka | улица Рождественка |
| ulitsa Vozdvizhenka | улица Воздвиженка |
| ulitsa Zabelina | улица Забелина |
| ulitsa Znamenka | улица Знаменка |

**Metro Stations**

| | |
|---|---|
| Arbatskaya | Арбатская |
| Biblioteka Imeni Lenina | Библиотека имени Ленина |
| Borovitskaya | Боровицкая |
| Chekhovskaya | Чеховская |
| Chistye Prudy | Чистые пруды |
| Kropotkinskaya | Кропоткинская |
| Lubyanka | Лубянка |
| Okhotniy Ryad | Охотный ряд |
| Ploshchad Revolyutsii | Площадь Революции |
| Pushkinskaya | Пушкинская |
| Teatralnaya | Театральная |
| Turgenvskaya | Тургенеская |
| Tverskaya | Тверская |

**Museums**

| | |
|---|---|
| Konenkov Studio Museum | музей-мастерская С.Т. Конёнкова |
| Moscow Lights Museum | Московский музей свеа |
| Museum of Books | музей Книги |
| Museum of the Federal Counter-Intelligence Service | музей Федеральной службы контразведки |
| Museum of Folk Art | музей Народново искусства |
| Museum of Private Collections | музей Личных Коллекций |
| Museum of the Revolution | музей Революции |
| Museum of Wax Figures | музей Восковых Фигур |
| Nemirovich-Danchenko Museum | музей-квартира Немировичф-Данченка |
| Nikolai Ostrovskiy Museum | музей-квартира Николя Островского |
| Pushkin Museum of Fine Art | музей изобразительных искусств им. А.С. Пушкина |
| Stanislavsky House-Museum | дом-музей К.С. Станиславского |
| Yermolova House-Museum | дом-музей М.Н. Ермоловой |
| Zoological Museum | Зоологический музей |

# CHAPTER FIVE:
# THE ZEMLYANOY GOROD

**Streets and squares**

| | |
|---|---|
| Bolshaya Sadovaya ulitsa | Большая Садовая улица |
| Bolshoy Kharitonevskiy pereulok | Большой Харитоньевский переулок |

| | |
|---|---|
| Delegatskya ulitsa | Делегатская улица |
| Denezhniy pereulok | Денежный переулок |
| Karetniy ryad | Каретный ряд |
| Krivoarbatskiy pereulok | Кривоарбатский переулок |
| Kropotkinskiy pereulok | Кропоткинский переулок |
| Lermontovskaya ploshchad | Лермонтовская площадь |
| Novinskiy bulvar | Новинский бульвар |
| pereulok Sivtsev Vrazhek | переулок Сивцев Вражек |
| ploshchad Vosstaniya | площадь Восстания |
| Povarskaya ulitsa | Поварская улица |
| Pushkinskaya ulitsa | Пушкинская улица |
| Sadovaya-Karetnaya ulitsa | Садовая-Каретная улица |
| Sadovaya–Triumfalnaya ulitsa | Садовая-Триумфальная улица |
| Sadovaya-Samotyochnaya ulitsa | Садовая-Самотёчная улица |
| Sadovaya-Spasskaya ulitsa | Садовя-Спасская улица |
| Spasopeskovskiy pereulok | Спасопесковский переулок |
| Smolenskaya ploshchad | Смоленская площадь |
| Sukharevskaya ploshchad | Сухаревская площадь |
| Triumfalnaya ploshchad | Триумфальная площадь |
| Tsvetnoy bulvar | Цветной бульвар |
| Trubnaya ploshchad | Трубная площадь |
| Tverskaya ulitsa | Тверская улица |
| ulitsa Alekseya Tolstovo | улица Алексея Толстого |
| ulitsa Arbat | улица Арбат |
| ulitsa Chekhova | улица Чехова |
| ulitsa Malaya Molochnaya | улица Малая Молочная |
| ulitsa Kachalova | улица Качалова |
| ulitsa Noviy Arbat | улица Новый Арбат |
| ulitsa Prechistenka | улица Пречистенка |
| ulitsa Vakhtangova | улица Вахтангова |

**Metro stations**

| | |
|---|---|
| Arbatskaya | Арбатская |
| Krasnye Vorota | Красные ворота |
| Kurskaya | Курская |
| Mayakovskaya | Маяковская |
| Pushkinskaya | Пушкинская |
| Smolenskaya | Смоленская |
| Tsvetnoy Bulvar | Цветной бульвар |
| Tverskaya | Тверская |

**Museums**

| | |
|---|---|
| Apollinarius Vasnetsov Flat-Museum | музей-квартира А.М. Васнецова |
| Alexei Tolstoy Flat-Museum | музей-квартира А.Н. Толстого |
| Bulgakov Flat-Museum | музей-квартира М.А. Булгакофа |
| Chekhov House-Museum | дом-музей А.П. Чехофа |
| Gorky House-Museum | дом-музей А.М. Горького |
| Herzen House-Museum | дом-музей А.И. Герцена |
| Museum of Applied, Decorative and Folk Arts | музей декоратино-прикладного и народного искусства |
| Museum of the Revolution | музей Революции |
| Pushkin Museum | музея А.С. Пушкина |
| Pushkin on the Arbat Museum | музей-квартира А.С. Пушкиа |
| Scriabin House-Museum | дом-музей Скрябина |
| Tolstoy Literary Museum | музей Л.Н. Толстого |

# CHAPTER SIX:
# KRASNAYA PRESNYA, FILI AND THE SOUTHWEST

**Streets and squares**

| | |
|---|---|
| Bolshaya Dekabrskya ulitsa | Большая Декабрьская улица |
| Bolshaya Filyovskaya ulitsa | Большая Филёвская улица |
| Bolshaya Gruzinskaya ulitsa | Большая Грузинская улица |
| Komomolskiy prospekt | Комсомольский проспект |
| Konyushovskaya ulitsa | Конюшовская улица |
| Krasnopresnenskiy Zastavy pereulok | Краснопресненский Заставы переулок |
| Kutuzovskiy prospekt | Кутузовский проспект |
| Predtechenskiy pereulok | Предтеченский переулок |

| | |
|---|---|
| prospekt Vernadskovo | проспект Вернадского |
| Timiryazevskaya alleya | Тимирязевская аллея |
| Tishkinskaya ploshchad | Тишкинская площадь |
| ulitsa 1905 goda | улица 1905 года |
| ulitsa 10-letiya Oktyabrya | улица 10-летия Октября |
| ulitsa Khamovnicheskiy val | улица Хамовнический вал |
| ulitsa Kosygina | улица Косыгина |
| ulitsa Krasnaya Presnya | улица Красная Пресня |

**Metro stations**

| | |
|---|---|
| Barrikadnaya | Баррикадная |
| Fili | Фили |
| Kievskaya | Киевская |
| Kransnopresnenskaya | Краснопресненская |
| Krylatskoe | Крылацкое |
| Kutuzovskaya | Кутузовская |
| Molodezhnaya | Молодежная |
| Park Kultury | Парк Культуры |
| Sportivnaya | Спортивная |
| Ulitsa 1905 Goda | Улица 1905 года |
| Universitet | Университет |

**Museums**

| | |
|---|---|
| Biological Museum | Биологический музей |
| Borodino Panorama Museum | музей-панорама Бородинска Битфа |
| Central Museum of the Great Patriotic War | Центральный музей Великой Отечественной войны |
| Metro Museum | музей Московского Метрополитена |
| Museum of Physical Culture and Sport | музей физической культуры |
| Tolstoy House-Museum | музей-усальбф Л.Н. Толстого |

# CHAPTER SEVEN: ZAMOSKVARECHE AND THE SOUTH

**Streets and squares**

| | |
|---|---|
| Bolshoy Kamenniy most | Большой Каменный мост |
| Donskaya ulitsa | Донская улица |
| 2-oy Kadashevskiy pereulok | 2-ой Калашевский переулок |
| Krymskiy val | Крымский вал |
| Leninskiy prospekt | Ленинский проспект |

| | |
|---|---|
| Oktyabrskaya ploshchad | Октябрьская площадь |
| ploshchad Gagarina | площадь Гагарина |
| Pyatnitskaya ulitsa | Пятницкая улица |
| 1-y Roshchinskiy pereulok | 1-я Рощинский переулок |
| Sofiyskaya naberezhnaya | Софийская набережная |
| ulitsa Bakhrushina | улица Бакрушина |
| ulitsa Bolshaya Ordynka | улица Большая Ордынка |
| ulitsa Bolshaya Polyanka | улица Большая Полянка |
| ulitsa Bolshaya Yakimanka | улица Большая Якиманка |
| ulitsa Danilovskiy val | улица Даниловский вал |
| ulitsa Ordzhonikidze | улица Орджоникидзе |

**Metro stations**

| | |
|---|---|
| Kashirskaya | Каширская |
| Kolomenskaya | Коломенская |
| Novokuznetskaya | Новокузнецкая |
| Oktyabrskaya | Октябрьская |
| Park Kultury | Парк Культуры |
| Paveletskaya | Павелецкая |
| Polyanka | Полянка |
| Shabolovskaya | Шаболовская |
| Tretyakovskaya | Третьяковская |
| Tsaritsyno | Царицыно |
| Tulskaya | Тульская |

**Museums**

| | |
|---|---|
| Central House of Artists | Центральный дом художника |
| Tretyakov Gallery | Третьяковская галерея |

# CHAPTER EIGHT: TAGANKA AND ZAYAUZE

**Streets and squares**

| | |
|---|---|
| Baumanskaya ulitsa | Бауманская улица |
| Bolshaya Kalitnikovskaya ulitsa | Большая Калитиковская улица |
| Energeticheskaya ulitsa | Энергеическая улица |
| Krutitskaya ulitsa | Крутитская улица |
| Nizhergorodskaya ulitsa | Нижергородская улица |
| Taganskaya ploshchad | Таганская площадь |

| | |
|---|---|
| Taganskaya ulitsa | Таганская улица |
| ulitsa Bolshie Kamenshchiki | улица Большие Каменщики |
| ulitsa Radio | улица Радио |
| ulitsa Volodarskovo | улица Володарского |
| ulitsa Vostochnaya | улица Восточная |

**Metro stations**

| | |
|---|---|
| Avtozavodskaya | Автозаводская |
| Baumanskaya | Бауманская |
| Izmaylovskiy Park | Измайловский парк |
| Kuskovo | Кусково |
| Kuzminki | Кузьминки |
| Marksistskaya | Марксистская |
| Preobrazhenskaya Ploshchad | Преображенская площадь |
| Proletarskaya | Пролетарская |
| Ryazanskiy Prospekt | Ряазанский проспект |
| Semyonovskaya | Семёновская |
| Taganskaya | Таганская |

**Museums**

| | |
|---|---|
| Andrei Rublev Museum of Early Russian Art | музей древнерусской культуры им. Андрея Рублева |
| Ceramics Museum | музей керамики |

# CHAPTER NINE: THE NORTHERN SUBURBS

**Streets and squares**

| | |
|---|---|
| Begovaya ulitsa | Беговая улица |
| Komsomolskaya ploshchad | Комсомольская площадь |
| Leningradskiy prospekt | Ленинградский проспект |
| pereulok Vasnetsova | переулок Васнецова |
| prospket Mira | проспект Мира |
| Sadovaya–Triumfalnaya ulitsa | Садовая-Триумфльная улица |
| Seleznevskaya ulitsa | Селезневская улица |
| Suvorovskaya ploshchad | Суворовская площадь |

| | |
|---|---|
| ulitsa Fadeeva | улица Фадеева |

**Metro stations**

| | |
|---|---|
| Belorusskaya | Белорусская |
| Dinamo | Динамо |
| Komsomolskaya | Комсомольская |
| Novoslobodskaya | Новослободская |
| Polezhaevskaya | Полежаевская |
| Prospekt Mira | Проспект Мира |
| Rechnoy Vokzal | Речной вокзал |
| Rizhskaya | Рижская |
| Sokolniki | Сокольники |
| Tsvetnoy Bulvar | Цетной бульвар |
| Tushinskaya | Тушинская |
| VDNKh | ВДНХ |

**Museums**

| | |
|---|---|
| Armed Forces Museum | музей Вооруженных Сил |
| Dostoyevsky Museum | музей-квартира Ф.М. Достоевского |
| Memorial Museum of Cosmonauts | Мемориальный музей космонавтики |
| Museum of Serf Art | дворец-музей творчества крепостых |
| Museum of the Ministry of the Interior | музей МВД |
| Viktor Vasnetsov House | дом-музей В.М. Васнецова |

# CHAPTER TEN: OUTSIDE MOSCOW

**Places**

| | |
|---|---|
| Abramtsevo | Абрамцево |
| Arkhangelskoe | Архангельское |
| Borodino | Бородино |
| Gorki Leninskie | Горки Ленинскуе |
| Ilyinskoe | Ильинское |
| Khotovo | Хотово |
| Klin | Клин |
| Peredelkino | Переделкино |
| Sergiev Posad | Сергиев Посад |

# Index

For easy reference see under the sub-indices headed "Architects", "Cathedrals and Churches", "Cemeteries", "Kremlin", "Monasteries and Convents", "Museums and Galleries", "Painters and Sculptors", "Palaces and Mansions", "Parks and Gardens", "Theatres" and "Writers".

# DIRECT ORDERS IN THE UK

| Title | ISBN | Price |
|---|---|---|
| Amsterdam | 1858280869 | £7.99 |
| Andalucia | 185828094X | £8.99 |
| Australia | 1858280354 | £12.99 |
| Barcelona & Catalunya | 1858281067 | £8.99 |
| Berlin | 1858280338 | £8.99 |
| Brazil | 1858281024 | £9.99 |
| Brittany & Normandy | 1858281261 | £8.99 |
| Bulgaria | 1858280478 | £8.99 |
| California | 1858280907 | £9.99 |
| Canada | 185828130X | £10.99 |
| Classical Music on CD | 185828113X | £12.99 |
| Corsica | 1858280893 | £8.99 |
| Crete | 1858281326 | £8.99 |
| Cyprus | 185828032X | £8.99 |
| Czech & Slovak Republics | 185828029X | £8.99 |
| Egypt | 1858280753 | £10.99 |
| England | 1858280788 | £9.99 |
| Europe | 185828077X | £14.99 |
| Florida | 1858280109 | £8.99 |
| France | 1858280508 | £9.99 |
| Germany | 1858281288 | £11.99 |
| Greece | 1858281318 | £9.99 |
| Greek Islands | 1858281636 | £8.99 |
| Guatemala & Belize | 1858280451 | £9.99 |
| Holland, Belgium & Luxembourg | 1858280877 | £9.99 |
| Hong Kong & Macau | 1858280664 | £8.99 |
| Hungary | 1858281237 | £8.99 |
| India | 1858281040 | £13.99 |
| Ireland | 1858280958 | £9.99 |
| Italy | 1858280311 | £12.99 |
| Kenya | 1858280435 | £9.99 |
| London | 1858291172 | £8.99 |
| Mediterranean Wildlife | 0747100993 | £7.95 |
| Malaysia, Singapore & Brunei | 1858281032 | £9.99 |
| Morocco | 1858280400 | £9.99 |
| Nepal | 185828046X | £8.99 |
| New York | 1858280583 | £8.99 |
| Nothing Ventured | 0747102082 | £7.99 |
| Pacific Northwest | 1858280923 | £9.99 |
| Paris | 1858281253 | £7.99 |
| Poland | 1858280346 | £9.99 |
| Portugal | 1858280842 | £9.99 |
| Prague | 185828015X | £7.99 |
| Provence & the Côte d'Azur | 1858280230 | £8.99 |
| Pyrenees | 1858280931 | £8.99 |
| St Petersburg | 1858281334 | £8.99 |
| San Francisco | 1858280826 | £8.99 |
| Scandinavia | 1858280397 | £10.99 |
| Scotland | 1858280834 | £8.99 |
| Sicily | 1858280370 | £8.99 |
| Spain | 1858280818 | £9.99 |
| Thailand | 1858280168 | £8.99 |
| Tunisia | 1858280656 | £8.99 |
| Turkey | 1858280885 | £9.99 |
| Tuscany & Umbria | 1858280915 | £8.99 |
| USA | 185828080X | £12.99 |
| Venice | 1858280362 | £8.99 |
| Wales | 1858280966 | £8.99 |
| West Africa | 1858280141 | £12.99 |
| More Women Travel | 1858280982 | £9.99 |
| World Music | 1858280176 | £14.99 |
| Zimbabwe & Botswana | 1858280419 | £10.99 |

## Rough Guide Phrasebooks

| | | |
|---|---|---|
| Czech | 1858281482 | £3.50 |
| French | 185828144X | £3.50 |
| German | 1858281466 | £3.50 |
| Greek | 1858281458 | £3.50 |
| Italian | 1858281431 | £3.50 |
| Spanish | 1858281474 | £3.50 |

Rough Guides are available from all good bookstores, but can be obtained directly in the UK* from Penguin by contacting:

Penguin Direct, Penguin Books Ltd, Bath Road, Harmondsworth, West Drayton, Middlesex UB7 0DA; or telephone our credit line on 0181-899 4036 (9am–5pm) and a for Penguin Direct. Visa, Access and Amex accepted. Delivery will normally be within 14 working days. Penguin Direct ordering facilities are only available in the UK.

The availability and published prices quoted are correct at the time of going to press but are subject to alteration without prior notice.

* For USA and international orders, see separate price list

# DIRECT ORDERS IN THE USA

| | ISBN | Price |
|---|---|---|
| ...terdam | 1858280869 | $13.59 |
| ...alucia | 185828094X | $14.95 |
| ...ralia | 1858280354 | $18.95 |
| ...elona & Catalunya | 1858281067 | $17.99 |
| ...n | 1858280338 | $13.99 |
| ...il | 1858281024 | $15.95 |
| ...any & Normandy | 1858281261 | $14.95 |
| ...aria | 1858280478 | $14.99 |
| ...ornia | 1858280907 | $14.95 |
| ...ada | 185828130X | $14.95 |
| ...sical Music on CD | 185828113X | $19.95 |
| ...ica | 1858280893 | $14.95 |
| ...e | 1858281326 | $14.95 |
| ...us | 185828032X | $13.99 |
| ...h & Slovak | | |
| ...publics | 185828029X | $14.95 |
| ...t | 1858280753 | $17.95 |
| ...and | 1858280788 | $16.95 |
| ...pe | 185828077X | $18.95 |
| ...da | 1858280109 | $14.95 |
| ...ce | 1858281245 | $16.95 |
| ...many | 1858281288 | $17.95 |
| ...ce | 1858281318 | $16.95 |
| ...k Islands | 1858281636 | $14.95 |
| ...temala & Belize | 1858280451 | $14.95 |
| ...and, Belgium | | |
| ...uxembourg | 1858280877 | $15.95 |
| ...g Kong & Macau | 1858280664 | $13.95 |
| ...gary | 1858281237 | $14.95 |
| ...a | 1858281040 | $22.95 |
| ...nd | 1858280958 | $16.95 |
| ... | 1858280311 | $17.95 |
| ...ya | 1858280435 | $15.95 |
| ...don | 1858291172 | $12.95 |
| ...literranean Wildlife | 0747100993 | $15.95 |
| ...aysia, Singapore | | |
| ...Brunei | 1858281032 | $16.95 |

| | ISBN | Price |
|---|---|---|
| Morocco | 1858280400 | $16.95 |
| Nepal | 185828046X | $13.95 |
| New York | 1858280583 | $13.95 |
| Nothing Ventured | 0747102082 | $19.95 |
| Pacific Northwest | 1858280923 | $14.95 |
| Paris | 1858281253 | $12.95 |
| Poland | 1858280346 | $16.95 |
| Portugal | 1858280842 | $15.95 |
| Prague | 1858281229 | $14.95 |
| Provence & the Côte d'Azur | 1858280230 | $14.95 |
| Pyrenees | 1858280931 | $15.95 |
| St Petersburg | 1858281334 | $14.95 |
| San Francisco | 1858280826 | $13.95 |
| Scandinavia | 1858280397 | $16.99 |
| Scotland | 1858280834 | $14.95 |
| Sicily | 1858280370 | $14.99 |
| Spain | 1858280818 | $16.95 |
| Thailand | 1858280168 | $15.95 |
| Tunisia | 1858280656 | $15.95 |
| Turkey | 1858280885 | $16.95 |
| Tuscany & Umbria | 1858280915 | $15.95 |
| USA | 185828080X | $18.95 |
| Venice | 1858280362 | $13.99 |
| Wales | 1858280966 | $14.95 |
| West Africa | 1858280141 | $24.95 |
| More Women Travel | 1858280982 | $14.95 |
| World Music | 1858280176 | $19.95 |
| Zimbabwe & Botswana | 1858280419 | $16.95 |

**Rough Guide Phrasebooks**

| | ISBN | Price |
|---|---|---|
| Czech | 1858281482 | $5.00 |
| French | 185828144X | $5.00 |
| German | 1858281466 | $5.00 |
| Greek | 1858281458 | $5.00 |
| Italian | 1858281431 | $5.00 |
| Spanish | 1858281474 | $5.00 |

...gh Guides are available from all good bookstores, but can be obtained directly ...e USA and Worldwide (except the UK*) from Penguin:

...rge your order by Master Card or Visa (US$15.00 minimum order): call 1-800-253-6476; or ...orders, with complete name, address and zip code, and list price, plus $2.00 shipping and ...lling per order to: Consumer Sales, Penguin USA, PO Box 999 – Dept #17109, ...enfield, NJ 07621. No COD. Prepay foreign orders by international money order, a ...que drawn on a US bank, or US currency. No postage stamps are accepted. All orders are ...ect to stock availability at the time they are processed. Refunds will be made for books not ...able at that time. Please allow a minimum of four weeks for delivery.

...availability and published prices quoted are correct at the time ...ping to press but are subject to alteration without prior notice. ...s currently not available outside the UK will be available by ...1995. Call to check.

...r UK orders, see separate price list

# You are
A STUDENT

# You travel
THE WORLD

# You want
TO SAVE MONEY

# Here's
# how

The International
Student Identity Card

Available at Student Travel Offices Worldwide.

Entitles you to discounts and special services worldwide.